Kentucky
Government, Politics,
and Public Policy

A
THOMAS
D. CLARK
MEDALLION
BOOK

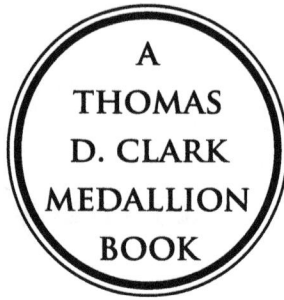

The Thomas D. Clark Medallion was established to honor the memory and contributions of Dr. Thomas Dionysius Clark (1903–2005). A beloved teacher, prolific author, resolute activist, and an enthusiastic advocate of publications about Kentucky and the region, Dr. Clark helped establish the University of Kentucky Press in 1943, which was reorganized in 1969 as the University Press of Kentucky, the state-mandated scholarly publisher for the Commonwealth. The Clark Medallion is awarded annually to one University Press of Kentucky publication that achieves Dr. Clark's high standards of excellence and addresses his wide breadth of interests about the state. Winners of the Thomas D. Clark Medallion are selected by the Board of Directors of the Thomas D. Clark Foundation Inc., a private nonprofit organization established in 1994 to provide financial support for the publication of vital books about Kentucky and the region.

KENTUCKY GOVERNMENT, POLITICS, AND PUBLIC POLICY

EDITED BY JAMES C. CLINGER
AND
MICHAEL W. HAIL

Forewords by Senator Mitch McConnell
and Trey Grayson

UNIVERSITY PRESS OF KENTUCKY

Scholarly publisher for the Commonwealth, serving Bellarmine University, Berea College, Centre College of Kentucky, Eastern Kentucky University, The Filson Historical Society, Georgetown College, Kentucky Historical Society, Kentucky State University, Morehead State University, Murray State University, Northern Kentucky University, Transylvania University, University of Kentucky, University of Louisville, and Western Kentucky University.
All rights reserved.

Editorial and Sales Offices: The University Press of Kentucky
663 South Limestone Street, Lexington, Kentucky 40508-4008
www.kentuckypress.com

17 16 15 14 13   5 4 3 2 1

Maps and illustrations by Dick Gilbreath, University of Kentucky Cartography Lab.

Library of Congress Cataloging-in-Publication Data

Kentucky government, politics, and public policy / edited by James C. Clinger and Michael W. Hail ; forewords by Senator Mitch McConnell and Trey Grayson.
        pages cm
    Includes bibliographical references and index.
    ISBN 978-0-8131-4315-6 (hardcover : alk. paper) — ISBN 978-0-8131-4316-3 (epub) — ISBN 978-0-8131-4317-0 (pdf)   1. Kentucky—Politics and government.   I. Clinger, James C., 1958–
    JK5316.K48 2013
    320.4769—dc23

                                                                        2013022983

Manufactured in the United States of America.

Member of the Association of
American University Presses

Sponsors

A special thank you to our generous sponsors:

Mark Davis

Virginia G. Fox

Bill and Ann Giles

Lawrence and Sherry Jelsma

James H. and Martha C. Johnson

Elizabeth Lloyd Jones

Melanie J. Kilpatrick

Mark and Kate Neikirk

Northern Kentucky University

Jack and Carol Russell

Alice Stevens Sparks

Myra Leigh Tobin

TOYOTA Toyota Motor Manufacturing, Kentucky, Inc.

Contents

Foreword
Senator Mitch McConnell

Suffering as I do from a lifetime addiction to American history—especially Kentucky history—I must confess, I could not find a better place to work than the United States Senate. In the halls of Congress, the history of the Bluegrass State comes alive every day.

In my office in the Capitol hang not one but two portraits of Henry Clay, one of the greatest Kentuckians to serve in Congress. A bronze bust of Clay stands near my desk. Serving in the same Senate seat that he once held and having occupied the famous Henry Clay Senate Desk, I cannot help but imagine Clay rising to speak from his desk against a backdrop of one of the most tumultuous times in American history: the years just before the Civil War. In that time Clay helped craft three major legislative compromises to stave off war and keep a young, fragile America united.

Of course, a major figure in that war—Abraham Lincoln—also happens to be the greatest leader Kentucky or any other state in the Union ever produced. A portrait of Lincoln also hangs in my office, again to remind me of Kentucky's incredible political legacy. The likenesses of such men as Lincoln and Clay on display in the Capitol give me an indissoluble link to Kentucky and to our state's proud history whenever I am there.

Now those of us who love Kentucky and its fascinating political culture have a great new resource: this book. Professors James Clinger and Michael Hail have assembled the most in-depth and comprehensive study of political science in Kentucky I have come across.

For the first time, readers from the casual history buff to the tenured scholar have together in one place the keys to better understand Kentucky's political culture and institutions. You will also learn about the leaders who harnessed the powers of those institutions in the name of the people.

In so doing, Professors Clinger and Hail have collected valuable contributions on such important topics as Kentucky's General Assembly, its executive branch, its judiciary, and the state's relationship with the federal government, as well as such current pressing issues as city-county merger, education reform, and health care. First-rate scholars have contributed to make this a tremendous resource for any political science student interested in learning what makes our special Commonwealth tick. Whether readers agree or disagree with the individual authors' conclusions, they will certainly find their conclusions thought provoking and worthy of discussion and analysis.

In fact, the next great statesman from Kentucky may be reading these words right now. If so, he or she can only benefit from soaking in the lessons of this insightful study of the unique political culture in the Commonwealth of Kentucky.

Foreword

Trey Grayson

Director, Harvard Institute of Politics, Harvard University,
and former Kentucky Secretary of State

I had the distinct honor of serving as Kentucky's Secretary of State from 2004 to early 2011. My office, located in the corner of the first floor of the Capitol—the executive floor of the Capitol—gave me a unique vantage point. I was both a participant and an observer in an exciting and interesting, if not entirely productive, period in Kentucky politics. As I think back on those years and the periods before and after, it is clear to me that a book like this is needed and in fact overdue to put that time in perspective. After all, so much has happened since the last comprehensive Kentucky politics book was published in the early 1990s.

A few broad themes have dominated that period. One of the biggest is that the General Assembly is now ascendant in policy making, and the past few governors have had very little success in implementing their legislative agendas. Indeed, it is not much of a stretch to observe that the most relevant comments on the night of the governor's State of the Commonwealth address are actually the comments by the Speaker of the House and the president of the Senate upon the conclusion of the governor's remarks.

Another recurring theme is the continued squeeze of the state's budget by recessions and rising health-care costs. In particular, the resulting budget cuts, combined with the resulting tuition increases, have threatened one of the most significant policy successes of the past two decades, 1997's Post-secondary Education Act. Meanwhile, the state's pension obligations have risen to such harrowing heights because of generous benefits and inadequate funding that investments in education, transportation, and health care will be squeezed even more in the future.

Finally, since 2000 our state has struggled with divided government, with Republicans dominating the Senate and Democrats dominating the House of Representatives, and neither party has figured out how to work together. The resulting gridlock has exacerbated the state's ability to address its long-term economic, education, and health needs.

As this book goes to press, recent developments have placed Kentucky in the national political spotlight. Mitch McConnell is the current Republican leader in the United States Senate and is gearing up for his 2014 reelection to extend Kentucky's longest tenure in the Senate—thirty years at the conclusion of his current term. His reelection campaign will certainly be the most expensive and possibly the most difficult of his career.

His counterpart in the Senate, Rand Paul, fresh off a thirteen-hour filibuster protesting President Obama's drone policy, is now considered one of the leading Republican candidates for president in 2016. Not bad for a Bowling Green physician who had never run for office before 2010. We will have to leave to the next book how their respective futures play out.

In many ways Kentucky is a state of contrasts. We are neither midwestern nor southern. Our state motto is United We Stand, Divided We Fall, but division has been present for most of the state's history. After several decades of being a battleground state in presidential elections, we have become a solidly "red state," with Republican candidates handily winning the past three presidential contests. Despite that, the Democratic Party still outnumbers the Republican Party three to two and continues to hold the most elected offices.

A book like this is needed to examine these contrasts and to place these recent developments in broader historical perspective. This is important for all Kentuckians regardless of audience. For those with a general interest in Kentucky politics and history, it can be valuable to step back from the day-to-day news stories to put events in a proper context. History can illuminate and provide a necessary perspective.

For government officials and politicians, this book can serve as a reminder that the fights and frustrations of today are often part of a broader trend. That may help them better navigate tough issues and perform their jobs more effectively.

I particularly like that each chapter in this book has different authors, allowing for more subject-matter specialization and balance. This will give academics and others an opportunity to explore additional works by these authors.

In summary, this book is overdue and much appreciated. It deserves a place on the bookshelf of everyone who seeks a better understanding of our Commonwealth.

Introduction
Taking Kentucky Politics Seriously
James C. Clinger and Michael W. Hail

Kentucky politics has been a source of amusement for residents of the Commonwealth for generations, as illustrated by the famous Kentucky orator Judge James Hillary Mulligan, who wrote in his often quoted poem "In Kentucky" for the legislature in 1902, "The landscape is the grandest—and politics—the damnedest . . . . In Kentucky."[1] Citizens of other states, who only occasionally hear of the goings-on in Frankfort or in the city halls and county courthouses of the Bluegrass State, also seem to be somewhat entertained by the colorful, often scandalous, and rarely dull escapades of Kentucky politicians, partisans, and interest-group leaders. Those who teach Kentucky politics, either in high schools or in colleges and universities, often regale students with humorous and outrageous anecdotes about the Commonwealth's government. Some of these stories are true. Nevertheless, it is the premise of this book that Kentucky politics should be taken seriously. Anecdotes, storytelling, or folklore can sometimes be entertaining, but they are not appropriate for serious students of politics. Systematic political science scholarship can and should inform citizens about the nature of their government, the consequences of their policy choices, and the implications of their political processes. As such, this book is intended to investigate the core institutions of Kentucky government and also to examine a number of particular political topics and policy issues of interest to Kentuckians and citizens of other states. The core task of this book is explanation, with explanatory political science that is broad in scope, ambitious in purpose, grounded in history, and theoretically informed. This is a book that seeks to explain trends, patterns, and the direction of political and policy change. The issues, institutions, and policy problems covered here are not likely to go away. The personalities and power brokers may change from one decade to the next, but the topics addressed herein will still remain with us. Many of these topics are not unique to Kentucky but are faced in other states throughout the nation. The comparative approach is used throughout the book to contextualize Kentucky government within the laboratory of federalism and to assess comparatively the issues addressed by political institutions.

This book is intended to fill a significant void in the study of Kentucky politics and to add to a tradition of single-state politics research within the discipline of political science. Like many studies of single states, this book emphasizes a sense of the unique place that is Kentucky. But that sense of place can be understood only in comparison with other places and times that have their own political institutions, public policy traditions, and cultural characteristics. Kentucky is a border state, situated at the northern rim of the southern states and carved out originally from the westernmost counties of old Virginia. It is in many ways southern in its political culture and in its framework of government. But the Commonwealth also borders the midwestern states of Ohio, Indiana, Illinois, and Missouri. Some major Kentucky cities on the Ohio River, such as Louisville and Covington, resemble Cincinnati and St. Louis in their layout and architecture more than they do the prominent cities of the Old South. Kentucky also shares a border with West Virginia, which, like Kentucky, was originally part of the Old Dominion. Eastern Kentucky is as characteristic of Appalachian traditions as is West Virginia and eastern Tennessee.

Among the most significant and enduring studies of state political culture was that conducted by political scientist Daniel Elazar. Elazar categorized states by three ideal types: moralistic, individualistic, and traditionalistic. Political culture is defined as "the pattern of orientations toward government and politics within a society. Political culture generally connotes the psychological dimension of political behavior—beliefs, feelings, and evaluative orientations. A political culture is the product of historical experience of the whole society as well as the personal experiences that contribute to the socialization of each individual."[2] The distribution of political culture in the United States is understood as a historically conditioned process of value transmission and expression.[3] Kentucky's political culture is a hybrid: the eastern section is more individualistic, while the western section is more traditionalistic. The result is a combination of attributes that looks a lot like Kentucky's mother state of Virginia. These political culture variables and the relationship to federalism and intergovernmental relations are discussed more fully in chapter 2.

As a border state, Kentucky has been crossed by people and goods that have traversed the nation. Some of this movement has followed the path of the major rivers (e.g., the Ohio, the Mississippi, the Cumberland, and the Tennessee) that have moved cargo north and south since the late eighteenth century. Railways crossed the Commonwealth throughout the nineteenth and twentieth centuries. Today, interstate highways primarily provide north-south pathways for automobile drivers and truckers. These transportation networks that cross Kentucky have connected industrial and agricultural regions of the country, but they have not always led to the development of a diverse economy in the Commonwealth.

As a border state, Kentucky has also taken part in many of the sectional conflicts in American history. Most obviously, the Civil War was fought in and around Kentucky, and Kentucky is distinctive for being the state that produced two concurrent presidents, Abraham Lincoln and Jefferson Davis. Kentucky never left the Union and never experienced Reconstruction, but it was a slave state and did have many Confederate sympathizers. Its cultural and economic affinity for the South led to a number of political and legal institutions emerging over time.

Kentucky's constitution reflects its political development, and a careful study of the constitution is essential to understand institutional development in the Commonwealth. In chapter 1, Robert M. Ireland, a historian and legal scholar, identifies the southern influences in each of the four state constitutions that have provided the framework of government in Kentucky. The last of these, ratified in 1891, established a limited government that often chafes at its constitutional restrictions. Constitutional amendments and creative court interpretations have permitted the state to circumvent many of the restrictions, but the constraints on governmental activity and sometimes business organization still remain.

In chapter 2, Michael W. Hail discusses how Kentucky fits within the nation's federal and intergovernmental system. The types of governmental institutions that operate in Kentucky are defined and their intergovernmental behavior is examined, both in cooperation and in conflict. The changes in the balance of federalism for states in general, and Kentucky in particular, are examined. The role of political culture and fiscal federalism issues are also discussed. The federal and state constitutions are comparatively examined and their roles under federalism discussed, with important constitutional powers examined such as the separation of powers and the system of checks and balances. In chapter 3, James C. Clinger describes the institutional structure and the internal workings of Kentucky's state legislature, the General Assembly. This chapter covers how the institutional arrangements of the legislature affect how it operates and what kind of legislators are attracted to serve in its chambers. In chapter 4, Kendra B. Stewart and Thomas M. Martin examine many of the formal and official powers of another major actor in Kentucky government, the chief executive. They contrast the formal authority of the governor with the informal powers that the governor can wield. Using interviews with former governors, current and former staff members, and legislators, Stewart and Martin suggest that the formal powers of the chief executive are not necessarily as effective in promoting the governor's agenda as the more informal and personal attributes of the governor. The struggle between Kentucky's governors and the General Assembly is the subject of chapter 5. Paul Blanchard describers how governors, who once were said to dominate the General Assembly, have lost influence over the legislature. Constitutional changes and the institutionalization of the chamber have led to the General Assembly becoming an independent policy-making body that need not cater to the chief executive.

Another independent branch of state government, the judicial branch, is the subject of Bradley C. Canon's chapter 6. Canon discusses how the Kentucky courts have asserted their prerogatives and now operate as independent players in Kentucky government. The constitution often puts some stringent limitations on Kentucky government, but the Kentucky courts have devised creative ways to circumvent those limitations. The courts also have imposed limitations on Kentucky's government at times when doing so promotes the court's views on the proper role of the state and the civil liberties of individuals.

In chapter 7, Murray S. Y. Bessette covers the individuals and agencies of Kentucky's state and local governments that actually implement state policy. Bessette discusses the formal structure of agencies and of local governments and shows how formal arrangements, including procedural constraints on agency action and legal requirements of the merit system, shape administrative behavior. Bessette also notes how Kentucky government has responded to recent calls for privatization of state and local services and to citizen demand for e-government.

How states manage budgeting and financing government is one of the most important topics in state politics. In chapter 8, Lisa A. Cave focuses on raising, borrowing, and spending money for Kentucky government. Constitutional limits constrain how and for what purposes money can be raised, but political expediency and fiscal pressure affect taxing and budgeting decisions. Cave illustrates how the state generates revenue, and she identifies the changing spending priorities of the Commonwealth. She also evaluates the revenue system from the standpoints of both equity and efficiency.

Change in partisan affiliations, organization, and electoral outcomes is the focus of chapter 9 by Joel Turner and Scott Lasley. They discuss how and why the Commonwealth changed from a one-party-dominated Democratic state to one with viable two-party competition and a tendency to be carried by Republican candidates in presidential elections. Although recent years have seen increased competition between the parties, in most instances there is now less competition within the parties. This is evidenced by an increase in uncontested primary elections. Furthermore, the dominance of local party leaders in many areas of the state has been swept away by national and statewide political forces, such as the Tea Party movement.

Campaign finance is the topic of chapter 10 by Donald A. Gross. Gross covers the regulations that apply to the raising and spending of money in state campaigns in Kentucky. Especially noteworthy is the collapse of the public financing system for gubernatorial elections and the rising cost of elections in general in the Commonwealth. Gross also discusses the effects of federal court decisions on state attempts to regulate campaign finance.

Efforts by legislators and governors to affect state bureaucratic agencies are the subject of James C. Clinger's chapter 11. Specifically, Clinger focuses on the use of legislative rule review to reverse or revise agency decisions and on gubernatorial efforts to direct and reorganize state agencies using executive orders. Clinger finds that the General Assembly's use of legislative rule review to shape agency action has decreased over time. Although no extremely obvious trends are observable, it appears that the use of rule review declined after partisan control of the legislature was divided between Democrats and Republicans. Use of gubernatorial executive orders also has varied over time and across the administrations of different governors.

Two chapters that deal with relationships among local governments in Kentucky follow Clinger's study of oversight. In chapter 12, H. V. Savitch, Ronald K. Vogel, and Lucas Elliott describe the efforts to consolidate the governments of Kentucky's largest city, Louisville, and Jefferson County. The consolidation presumably took place to realize certain efficiencies in service delivery, but, as the authors point out, the consolidation had some political implications as well. By combining the city's largely minority, socially liberal, Democratic-leaning residents with the largely white, middle-class, somewhat conservative citizens from outside the city, consolidation changed the constituency of the resulting metro government. The new governmental institutions also changed the representation of urban interests.

In chapter 13, Julie Cencula Olberding presents a somewhat more upbeat account of local government collaboration—not consolidation. She discusses the long history of collaboration among local governments in northern Kentucky and recent developments there. These communities are situated just across the Ohio River from Cincinnati. For years the parochialism and limited vision of individual communities have been said to hinder economic development. Olberding discusses how recent collaboration efforts have promoted the region and, it is hoped, have improved the quality of life.

In chapter 14, Richard E. Day and Jo Ann G. Ewalt examine K–12 education reform. Day and Ewalt describe the long history of efforts to reform the financing and governance and to professionalize the operation of Kentucky's public schools. Substantial progress was not achieved until the Kentucky Supreme Court decision in *Rose v. Council for Better Education* in 1989. In response to that court opinion, the General Assembly enacted the Kentucky Education Reform Act, which created new sources of funding to provide for an adequate education for all public school students and established a system of test-based accountability that preceded the federal No Child Left Behind program.

The prevalence of problems in public ethics is the focus of chapter 15 by Steven G. Koven. The political culture of the Commonwealth tolerates a number of practices that would not be acceptable elsewhere. Despite this, Kentucky has adopted a number of laws regulating conflicts of interest and aimed at preventing improprieties in public office. Scandals still plague Kentucky government. Koven highlights the violations of merit-hiring laws during the Fletcher administration, as well as the misuse of funds by the Kentucky League of Cities.

In chapter 16, Edward T. Jennings Jr. and Jeremy L. Hall focus their attention on policies regarding developmental disabilities in Kentucky. They cover the history of policy making in the Commonwealth and in the nation over a number of years. In explaining policy change regarding the disabled, Jennings and Hall apply three theoretical perspectives used by political scientists to account for policy choices. One perspective is incrementalism, which contends that for various reasons, in the American political system change occurs slowly in small steps over a period of time. The second framework, punctuated equilibrium, argues that most policy change is incremental, but on rare occasions disruptions in policy subsystems are followed by sudden and dramatic change. A third perspective, the advocacy-coalition framework, contends that policy changes occur after one advocacy coalition, made up of individuals and groups with particular deep core beliefs and policy preferences, displaces another coalition. Jennings and Hall apply each of these perspectives in accounting for how Kentucky programs and agencies have dealt with intellectual and developmental disabilities.

In chapter 17, Jeremy L. Hall and Michael W. Hail analyze attempts by Kentucky governments to promote economic and community development in the Commonwealth.

All states and many communities in the country engage in some economic development activities, but in Kentucky some particular development strategies to encourage home-grown economic activity have been adopted. In addition, a number of innovative community and regional development organizations have been developed to deal with the unique challenges of development in local areas.

Health-care policy in Kentucky is the focus of chapter 18 by Ann Beck. She begins with a discussion of the health-reform program considered and enacted in modified form during the administration of Governor Brereton Jones. That debate set the tone for subsequent disputes in Kentucky and around the nation. Much of the rest of Beck's analysis focuses on how the provisions of the federal Affordable Care Act will affect Kentucky residents.

Jeffery C. Talbert and Amie Goodin examine another policy area, pharmaceutical regulation, in chapter 19. The misuse of prescription drugs has become a serious issue across the United States in recent years, and many states have developed policies to curb improper use of these drugs. At the same time, many states, including Kentucky, have made it easier to administer certain kinds of drugs by expanding prescription authority to advanced registered nurse practitioners and other medical professionals. Kentucky and other states have also begun to permit pharmacists to administer certain kinds of immunizations. Talbert and Goodin focus on how different combinations of medical professionals politically opposed or supported policy changes to expand or contract the use of pharmaceuticals.

In the concluding chapter 20, the editors, James C. Clinger and Michael W. Hail, review some of the findings presented in this book and the enduring issues that confront Kentucky. Political forces and prominent figures from Kentucky's past and present are identified. The authors finally offer some conjectures about what the future will hold for Kentucky government.

The appendices of this volume contain some descriptive information and valuable data on the Commonwealth. In order to add some historical perspective, the appendices also contain some historical documents such as the constitution of Kentucky and writings by prominent Kentuckians, including Henry Clay and Abraham Lincoln. These readings demonstrate the fascinating contributions that Kentuckians have made to American political history, through their oratory, their legislative leadership, and their political theory.

NOTES

1. James Henry Mulligan, "In Kentucky," http://www.uky.edu/KentuckyCulture/in-kentucky.html.

2. Jack C. Plano and Milton Greenberg, *Political Science Dictionary* (Hinsdale, Ill.: Dryden Press, 1973), 287.

3. Daniel J. Elazar, *American Federalism: A View from the States* (New York: Thomas Y. Crowell, 1972), 1–8.

Part I

State and Local Institutions

1

The Kentucky Constitution
Robert M. Ireland

The Kentucky Constitution, drafted in 1890–1891 and ratified in 1891, is the last of four constitutions of the state. The first was adopted in 1792 as part of the Commonwealth's admission to the Union. George Nicholas, a transplanted Virginia lawyer and a delegate to the 1792 convention, wrote most of the document. He took 75 of the 107 sections, verbatim or substantially, from the Pennsylvania Constitution of 1790, including 27 of 28 sections of the Bill of Rights. The Bill of Rights included many of the same freedoms recently appended to the U.S. Constitution, such as freedom of and from religion, right to jury trial, freedom from unreasonable search and seizure, and prohibition of double jeopardy, ex post facto laws, and laws impairing the obligation of contracts. All these rights are found in Kentucky's subsequent constitutions, including the current one.[1]

THE FIRST CONSTITUTION

The first constitution established a popularly elected lower house of the legislature and specified that the representatives would serve one-year terms. Electors chosen by the voters would elect the state senate and the governor, both for four-year terms. Because the governor could succeed himself and appoint most state and local officials, he would be one of the most powerful state chief executives in the nation. Overriding the governor's vetoes required a two-thirds majority in each legislative house. The constitution created only one court, a supreme court known as the Court of Appeals, and left it to the legislature to establish such inferior courts as it deemed necessary. Although the Court of Appeals was primarily an appellate court, it was given original jurisdiction over land cases in the hope that it could equitably settle the many competing claims to the Commonwealth's real estate. Judges would be appointed by the governor (with the consent of the Senate) for life on condition of good behavior. In each county, voters would elect sheriffs and coroners for three-year terms, and the former were prohibited from succeeding themselves. Despite the efforts of a determined minority, a solid majority of proslavery delegates powerfully endorsed the institution of slavery. Article IX prohibited the legislature from emancipating slaves without the consent of, and full compensation to, the slave owner.

The delegates to the 1792 convention did not submit their new constitution to the voters for ratification and did not regard their document as anything more than an experiment that would soon have to be revised. To that end they provided that if a majority of those voting for representatives in 1797 and 1798 favored calling a constitutional convention, one would be called by the legislature at its next session. Only a convention could revise or replace the first constitution, which did not provide for adding individual amendments. Controversies involving each branch of government ensured that such a call would be made in 1798.

A public outcry greeted a two-to-one decision of the Court of Appeals in 1794 that the Virginia Land Commission had exceeded its authority when it determined the rights to numerous land disputes in Kentucky in 1779–1780. Because this decision undermined the land titles of thousands of Kentuckians, the legislature attempted to remove the two majority justices of the Court of Appeals by joint address to the governor. The removal resolution failed to receive the necessary two-thirds majority in the Senate, and the House contented itself with a resolution of censure that branded the judges unfit for office. In 1795 the legislature took more decisive action when it removed the original jurisdiction of the Court of Appeals over land cases and transferred it to six newly created district courts. In the same year one of the two majority judges of the Court of Appeals reversed his opinion in the controversial land case and thereby quieted much of the public outrage.

A disputed gubernatorial election in 1796 embroiled the executive branch in controversy. In that year the electoral college failed to give any of the four candidates for governor a majority vote and, instead of declaring the recipient of the plurality of votes the winner, conducted a second ballot between the two highest vote getters. The second-place choice on the first ballot emerged victorious on the second ballot and was declared by the college to be the next governor. Benjamin Logan, the first choice on the first ballot, protested, and his protest was endorsed by the state attorney general. In the interests of governmental stability, Logan eventually abandoned his protest. The state senate also created controversy when it approved a disputed land sale, delayed passage of a popular land-claimants statute, and approved an unpopular pay raise for itself.

THE SECOND CONSTITUTION

The voters overwhelmingly endorsed a convention call in the legislatively decreed referenda of 1797 and 1798. Meeting for just twenty-seven days in the summer of 1799, the convention fashioned a constitution that provided for the direct election of the governor, the lieutenant governor (a newly created office), and state senators (thereby abolishing the electoral college) and prohibited the governor from succeeding himself but continued most of the chief executive's patronage powers, including the appointment of judges. The new constitution did not provide for an amendment process but rather continued the tradition of legislatively sanctioned popular convention-call referenda. Antislavery forces elected only two delegates to the convention, which incorporated almost verbatim the first constitution's slavery protections.

A decision of the Court of Appeals caused the greatest constitutional crisis of the period of the second constitution. In 1819 a major economic depression afflicted the nation as a whole and Kentucky in particular, prompting the legislature in 1820 to enact a debt-relief statute. In 1823 the Court of Appeals declared this statute to be in violation of both the state and federal constitutions, a decision that provoked the Relief Party to wage war against the high tribunal. Failing to muster enough votes in the legislature to remove the justices of the Court of Appeals, the relief partisans by statute purported to abolish the offending tribunal and to create a new Court of Appeals. The members of the old court refused to vacate their offices, and for two years the Commonwealth suffered the indignity of having two functioning supreme courts, each issuing opinions that one or the other political party refused to recognize. In 1826 the antirelief forces gained control of the legislature, which abolished the new court and thereby ended the constitutional farce.

During the period of the second constitution and the second American political party system, the Whigs controlled the governorship and legislature of Kentucky, which meant that they also controlled the appointed judiciary, including the Court of Appeals, the newly created circuit courts (the primary trial courts), and the constitutionally established county courts (which were the primary institutions of county government). This political judicial monopoly, which largely excluded the rival Democratic Party, and the Whig-dominated legislature's gerrymandering of legislative and congressional districts produced almost continuous Democratic demands for a new constitution.

THE THIRD CONSTITUTION

A split in the majority Whig Party in 1847 caused enough Whigs to vote with the Democratic minority in the legislature to approve a referendum on a convention call, which the voters endorsed in 1847 and 1848. The Democrats secured a narrow majority of convention delegates, who, with the support of a number of insurgent Whigs, wrote a reformist constitution at the 1849–1850 convention. The new constitution removed most of the governor's patronage powers, continued the prohibition of gubernatorial succession, and, following a national trend, provided for the popular election of all judges and all county officers for limited terms (sheriffs could serve for only two successive two-year terms). Voters would also elect all state officers except the secretary of state. In response to a large state indebtedness that had been contracted during the period of the second constitution to finance transportation projects that had sometimes failed, the new constitution (also following a national trend) limited state indebtedness to $500,000. Voters needed to approve all other debts except those dealing with certain specified emergencies, such as invasions. Antislavery candidates had failed to win any delegate positions, and the solidly proslavery convention, in order to protect the peculiar institution further, added a section to the Bill of Rights that declared that not even "the largest majority" could exercise "arbitrary power over the lives, liberty, and property of freemen." As with the second and probably the first constitution, the third constitution restricted the right to vote to white male adults (some have argued that the first constitution enfranchised free black males).

After the Civil War complaints about the third constitution began to surface, many of which had to do with railroad corporations and the legislature. Railroad mileage in Kentucky tripled between 1865 and 1880, with the powerful and incredibly profitable Louisville and Nashville Railroad leading the way. Shippers, especially farmers, complained that the railroads charged too much and discriminated in favor of large shippers and against smaller ones. The powerful railroad lobby outflanked agrarian forces that attempted to persuade the legislature to enact reforms that would curb the power of the Louisville and Nashville and other corporations. The lobby rewarded legislators with free railroad passes, whiskey, and other forms of remuneration and thus ensured that even when the legislature created a Railroad Commission, that agency lacked meaningful authority. In 1884 the legislature enacted a statute that granted new railroad construction a five-year tax exemption. The lobby also defeated efforts to strengthen the Railroad Commission and to enact tort reform, including an enhanced opportunity to sue railroads for wrongful death.

Critics especially complained about the legislative preoccupation with local, private, and special legislation to the detriment of statutes that applied to the Commonwealth in general. As an example of the legislative imbalance, the General Assembly of 1887–1888 enacted 1,403 local and private statutes and only 168 general statutes. There was no general law that classified and empowered municipalities, which meant that towns and cities had to obtain their charters from the legislature, and these charters differed in their powers and limitations. The lack of a married women's property act meant that wives needed to secure private legislation if they wished to have control over their own property. Sheriffs often secured special laws that extended periods of tax collection. Individual counties received legislative permission in the form of local statutes to punish certain crimes in special ways, such as whipping those found guilty of petit larceny. Consequently, there were so many exceptions to the general statutes that even lawyers were uncertain about what the law of Kentucky was on many subjects. Another grievance concerned the tendency of the legislature to create special criminal or civil courts to compensate for the constitutional limitation on the number of circuit courts. Critics argued that the time the legislature devoted to private, local, and special legislation led to inordinately lengthy and expensive legislative sessions and statutes that were frequently enacted without having been debated or even read. The constitution limited each session to sixty days unless two-thirds of the membership of each house voted to extend a session, but extensions were easily and routinely approved.

Although the third constitution limited state borrowing, there was no limitation on county indebtedness, and many counties borrowed heavily to attract railroads, which were regarded as the key to economic progress. Not a few of these transportation ventures failed and left the counties without a railroad but with a legally binding debt. This indebtedness rendered a few counties insolvent and caused taxpayer revolts that bordered on anarchy and demands for constitutional limits on local indebtedness. Another financial scandal involved the oft-elected state treasurer, James W. "Honest Dick" Tate, who absconded in 1888 with almost the entire state treasury in the amount of $247,000, prompting demands for a constitutional reform of Tate's office, as well as that of state auditor.

The constitutionally mandated method of casting votes by voice rather than by secret ballot constituted another grievance. Critics argued that the public nature of voice voting led to the commonplace practice of buying and selling votes (because voice voting occurred in public, vote buyers could readily determine whether vote sellers had fulfilled the sales contract), a defect that could be cured only by a constitutional requirement for a secretly cast written ballot (if voting was done alone in secret, it would be theoretically impossible for vote buyers to know for certain that the seller had fulfilled the sales agreement). The third constitution, as well as the previous charters, placed no limits on the number of counties in Kentucky, which by 1890 had 119 of these local governmental units. A majority of counties could not support themselves and required state funds to function. Observers contended that the number and small size of counties contributed to the outbreak of feuds in eastern Kentucky after the Civil War. Labor leaders demanded constitutional reform to prohibit the employment of children in dangerous occupations, such as mining, and to prohibit mining companies from paying their employees in company scrip that was legal tender only in company stores that charged exorbitant prices. Reformers also demanded the constitutional prohibition of lotteries, which were said to extract money primarily from poor wage earners and to exaggerate their promises of payoffs.

Despite these constitutional deficiencies, voters in five referenda between 1875 and 1885 rejected convention calls, in large part because of a controversial method that the legislature had devised to ascertain the number of voters that were needed to approve such a call. Reform of that method in 1887 facilitated voter approval of a convention call in a referendum of that year and another in 1889. The constitutional convention convened in September 1890.

THE FOURTH AND CURRENT CONSTITUTION

A major objective of the convention, which did not adjourn until April 1891, concerned the drafting of provisions that limited the legislature. The constitution prohibited most private, local, and special legislation, limited legislative sessions to once every two years and to only sixty days, required bills to be read at least once in their entirety to the full House and Senate, and specified that no law could be amended by reference to its title only; rather, a bill needed to be published in its entirety so that legislators would know what and how they were amending. For the first time in the state's constitutional history the governor could exercise a line-item veto on appropriation measures, and population, not the number of voters, determined legislative representation. The constitution also provided for the secret printed Australian ballot; abolished tax immunities for corporations; strictly regulated railroads; limited local taxation and indebtedness; established more circuit (trial) courts; and eliminated legislatively created courts, including the Superior Court, which had been established by the legislature in 1880 as an intermediate appellate court designed to relieve a temporary burden on the Court of Appeals. The constitution eliminated a provision found in the previous two constitutions that prohibited clergymen from serving as governor or as a member of the General Assembly. The constitution made it nearly impossible to create new counties and limited the fees and salaries of local officials, the existing fee system having unduly enriched some of the officers of Louisville and other cities and having led to abuses by certain county officials.

The new constitution also limited the salaries of most public officials to $5,000 annually, made all elected state executive officers ineligible for successive terms, provided for stricter audits of the treasurer's office, mandated legislative prohibitions of child labor and company scrip, abolished lotteries, protected suits for personal injury and wrongful death, forbade slavery (which already had been prohibited by the Thirteenth Amendment to the U.S. Constitution), provided for racially segregated public schools, and rendered another constitutional convention less likely but made constitutional change easier by providing for the first time that individual amendments could be proposed by the legislature (two per legislative session) and adopted by popular vote.

Some proposed constitutional reforms failed to be adopted, especially on women's rights. Arguing that such a proposal would threaten the sanctity of the home and marriage, the all-male delegates voted down a provision that would have given married women some control over their property. For much the same reason they also rejected provisions that would have empowered the legislature to grant women the right to vote, whether generally or only for school officers and on school matters (and to be eligible for any school office). However, the constitution did implicitly authorize the legislature to continue to allow women to vote for school trustees.

Critics of the newly drafted constitution argued that it resembled a code of laws rather than a basic frame of government, a charge echoed by some modern scholars. Supporters of the document rightly countered that a more detailed and lengthy constitution was necessary, given the unwillingness of the legislature to reform itself and government in general and to effectively regulate abusive corporations. They also pointed out that the newly minted constitutions of other states were likewise lengthy and detailed for the same reason. After voters overwhelmingly ratified the new charter, the convention reassembled, supposedly only to make minor clarifying revisions of the new constitution. However, minor revision sometimes turned into substantive changes, such as making the Railroad Commission elective instead of appointive. Soon after the convention adjourned sine die and issued a final version of the constitution, opponents sued to invalidate the charter because of the substantive revisions made after popular ratification. The Court of Appeals rejected this challenge, holding in 1892 that the constitution was valid despite the postratification alterations.[2]

CONSTITUTIONAL REVISION

Constitutional reformers have used amendment rather than a convention to change the constitution. Voters rejected convention calls in legislatively directed referenda conducted in 1931, 1947, 1960, and 1977. In an attempt to draft and adopt a new constitution, the legislature in 1964 invoked Section 4 of the constitution, which gives the "people" the "right to alter, reform or abolish their government in such manner as they deem proper," and established a Constitutional Revision Assembly composed of fifty legislatively selected delegates, one each from the state's thirty-eight senatorial districts, seven former governors, and five at-large members, including the mayor of Louisville and the county judge of Jefferson County. In early 1966 the assembly proposed a constitution of 13,500 words, 8,000 fewer than the existing charter. The document provided for sweeping reforms that included a unified judiciary; some popularly elected state officers, such as governor and lieutenant governor, who could serve two consecutive terms; other state officers, such as superintendent of public education and secretaries of state and treasury, who would be appointed; the elimination of most county officers as constitutional positions; and elections to be held in even-numbered years only. It raised the state debt limit, facilitated constitutional amendments, abolished the Railroad Commission and state governmental salary limits, and made wiretaps unconstitutional. The proposed new constitution secured legislative approval, withstood a legal challenge to its constitutionality, and received support from many newspapers, scholars, and political leaders. However, other politicians, including gubernatorial candidates from both parties and many city and county officials who feared a loss of power or even of office opposed the document, which the voters overwhelmingly rejected by a vote of 517,034 to 143,133.

Proposed legislative amendments to the constitution have met with more success and have accomplished many of the revisions proposed by the rejected assembly constitution of 1966. Since 1891 the legislature has approved and submitted to the voters seventy-nine proposed amendments for their ratification, of which forty-four have been approved and thirty-three rejected. The Court of Appeals kept two amendments off the ballot because their provisions had not been publicized in the manner specified by the constitution and invalidated three of the forty-four amendments that had been ratified, two because they were not validly publicized and one because the subject of the amendment was properly addressed by statute rather than by constitutional amendment.

Local government and taxation constitute the categories that are most frequently the subject of proposed amendments. Thirteen proposed amendments have concerned local government, six being ratified and seven rejected. In 1903, having rejected a similar proposal in 1897, voters approved an amendment empowering the legislature to authorize cities and counties to levy license and franchise taxes based on income. In 1909 voters approved an amendment permitting the state to lend its credit to counties for public road purposes and authorizing counties to levy voter-approved taxes for roads and bridges. Ten years later, voters ratified an amendment increasing the legislative power to remove local law enforcement officers. In 1937 they rejected a proposed amendment empowering the General Assembly to reorganize local government and to consolidate cities and counties. In 1984, after similar proposed amendments had been rejected in 1959, 1973, and 1981 (the latter amendment would also have permitted statewide constitutional offers to serve two successive terms), voters ratified an amendment permitting sheriffs to succeed themselves in office. Two years later, they approved an amendment allowing mayors of first- and second-class cities to serve three successive terms. In 1931 voters rejected a proposed amendment that would have raised the debt limits of cities and counties in certain cases. In 1994, after rejecting a somewhat similar proposal four years earlier, voters ratified an amendment authorizing the legislature to grant city governments more independence ("home rule") and allowing counties and cities to incur long-term debt without voter approval. Two years later, the Clark County Circuit Court ruled against the attorney general's petition to invalidate this constitutional amendment on the grounds that it had not been adequately publicized, a decision affirmed by the Court of Appeals.

Seven of ten proposed taxation amendments concerned exemptions. Voters approved amendments that exempted household goods from taxation (1955), created a homestead exemption of $6,500 for single-family residences of persons sixty-five or older (1971) and extended it to other residences (1975), established the homestead exemption for those classified as totally disabled by the federal government or the railroad retirement system (1981), exempted religious property (1990), and authorized the General Assembly to exempt motor vehicles and any other class of personal property from the levy of all or any portion of the property tax (1998). In 1933 voters rejected a proposed amendment that would have authorized the General Assembly to exempt real and personal property from taxation by the state. In 1914 the Court of Appeals invalidated an improperly publicized amendment, ratified in 1913, that authorized the legislature to classify property for tax purposes, but the voters ratified a similar amendment offered in 1915. In 1969 voters ratified an amendment requiring agricultural land in urban areas to be assessed at its value for agricultural purposes and permitting local governments to tax real property at different rates according to governmental services rendered.

Eight proposed amendments related to voting. In 1941, 1945, and 1955 voters approved amendments permitting voting machines, authorizing absentee voting, and enfranchising eighteen-year-olds, respectively; in 1905, 1907, and 1927 they rejected a return to voice voting, tax payment as a prerequisite of voting, and absentee voting. In 1923 voters rejected a proposed amendment that would have eliminated the word "male" from the suffrage clause of the constitution (the Nineteenth Amendment to the U.S. Constitution made this amendment unnecessary), an elimination accomplished by the 1955 amendment, and in 1939 the Court of Appeals, because of inadequate publicity, removed from the ballot a proposed amendment that declared that women were eligible to hold public office (the Nineteenth Amendment likewise rendered this amendment unnecessary).

In 1992 voters approved an omnibus amendment reforming the executive branch that permitted statewide officers, including the governor, to serve two consecutive terms; provided for the joint election of the governor and the lieutenant governor; changed the duties of the lieutenant governor; dealt with gubernatorial disability; and abolished the superintendent of public instruction as an elected state officer. Four times previously (1921, 1957, 1973, and 1986) voters rejected proposed amendments that would have made the superintendent of public instruction an appointive statutory officer, and they twice (1953 and 1992) turned down proposed amendments removing that office and the offices of secretary of state, treasurer, and commissioner of agriculture, labor, and statistics from the list of elective offices. In 1981 they rejected a proposed multi-purposed amendment that would have allowed all statewide officers to serve two consecutive terms.

Five times (1925, 1927, 1929, 1943, and 1963) voters rejected amendments that would have completely or partially altered limits on the salaries of public officials, but they ratified a 1949 amendment that substituted higher limits for these salaries. Another rejected amendment would have authorized the General Assembly to enact a compulsory workers' compensation statute (1943). In 1939 the Court of Appeals kept off the ballot an inadequately publicized amendment that directed the General Assembly to provide aid to dependent children and the needy blind, and in 1960 it invalidated a ratified amendment that would have established a sales tax to fund a veterans' bonus because the objective was properly addressed by a statute.

Four proposed amendments concerned appropriations for education. In 1941 and 1949 voters approved amendments that reduced the percentage of state-appropriated funds to be divided among county school districts on a per capita basis; they had rejected such a proposal in 1921. In 1953 voters ratified an amendment that repealed provisions mandating per capita educational appropriations.

Two ratified amendments specified that legislators (1979) and all officials except for state officers (1992-anomnibus reform) be elected in even-numbered years. The former amendment also authorized the legislature to stretch its regular sixty-day session over a period of three and one-half months. In 2000 voters approved an amendment that provided for annual legislative sessions after rejecting such an amendment in 1969, 1973, and 1998. Voters also rejected amendments allowing the legislature to call itself into extraordinary session (1990) and permitting the legislature to reject administrative regulations issued by the executive branch (1990).

After rejecting amendments that repealed the two-amendment restriction (1929, 1937, and 1951) and an amendment that would have increased the restriction to five (1963), voters in 1979 ratified an amendment that increased to four the number of amendments that could be voted on in a single election and provided that a single amendment could cover several related subjects and alter more than one section of the constitution.

An amendment ratified in 1975 abolished the old court system and established one of the nation's most modern and efficient unified judiciaries. In 2002 voters approved an amendment to Section 112 that permitted the Kentucky Supreme Court to designate one or more divisions of a circuit court within a judicial circuit as a family-court division.

Two ratified amendments concerned alcoholic beverages, the first prohibiting their manufacture, sale, and consumption (1919) and the other repealing that prohibition (1935). Two other ratified amendments concerned gambling; one authorized the legislature to establish a lottery (1988), and the other permitted the legislature to establish and regulate charitable gaming (1992).

In 1915 voters ratified an amendment permitting the use of prisoners for roadwork; the Court of Appeals had declared a similar previously approved amendment invalid in 1914 because it had been invalidly publicized. Other ratified amendments authorized telephone companies to buy or lease competing companies under certain conditions (1917), directed the legislature to authorize old-age pensions (1935), and guaranteed that receipts from certain tax sources should be placed in the highway fund (1945). In

1988 voters ratified an amendment that limited the use of the broadform deed as a legal way to strip-mine coal.

In 1996 voters approved an amendment that eliminated from Section 180 of the constitution language that authorized local governments to levy poll taxes and also deleted language from Section 187 that provided for the maintenance of racially segregated schools. The Twenty-Fourth Amendment to the U.S. Constitution and several U.S. Supreme Court cases made this amendment symbolic.

In 2000 voters ratified an amendment that abolished the Railroad Commission (they had rejected a similar amendment in 1973). An amendment ratified in 2002 modernized Section 190, which deals with corporations, and repealed other antiquated sections that concerned corporations. In 2004 voters ratified an amendment that declared marriage to be between a man and a woman, thereby in effect prohibiting same-sex marriages. The amendment also prohibited "a legal status identical or substantially similar to that of marriage for unmarried individuals." In 2012 voters ratified an amendment declaring that citizens of Kentucky have the personal right to hunt, fish, and harvest wildlife, subject to conservation and preservation laws, and that public hunting and fishing shall be the preferred means of managing and controlling wildlife.

Forty-four of the 263 original sections of the constitution of 1891 have been amended (some more than once), 16 sections have been repealed and reenacted (the judiciary sections by virtue of the judicial amendment of 1975), 34 sections have been repealed (1 of these was revived), and 9 sections have been added (1 of these being among the 34 that have been repealed). These changes have considerably streamlined the document and achieved not a few of the reforms incorporated into the abortive constitution of 1966. The judiciary has also adapted the constitution to modern times by its liberal interpretation of certain potentially restrictive provisions of the state charter. For example, the Court of Appeals ruled in *Matthews v. Allen*, 360 S.W.2d 135 (1962), that cost-of-living adjustments based on the consumer price index did not violate salary restrictions found in Section 246.

JUDICIAL INTERPRETATION OF THE CONSTITUTION

In the words of Robert F. Stephens, the late chief justice of the Kentucky Supreme Court, "In recent years, the constitutions of the various states have become increasingly important in the jurisprudence of those states as tools in the practice of law. This growth has been given impetus by several decisions of the U.S. Supreme Court, which not only recognized the sovereignty of the states, but arguably encouraged the use of those state constitutions. See, for example, *Oregon v. Hass*, 420 US 714 (1989) and *Michigan v. Long*, 463 US 1032 (1983)."[3] An examination of the leading constitutional opinions of the Kentucky Court of Appeals (the supreme court of Kentucky until 1975) and the Kentucky Supreme Court (created as the supreme court of Kentucky by the judicial amendment of 1975) provides evidence of this increased significance, as well as the overall importance of the constitution and its practical meaning and application.

The first 26 sections of the Kentucky Constitution constitute the Bill of Rights. The language of these sections was taken largely from the Pennsylvania Constitution of

1790 but borrowed some verbiage from the Declaration of Independence and the Virginia Declaration of Rights of 1776. Framers of the third constitution and the current constitution added one section each (in the third constitution, Section 2, which denies absolute and arbitrary power, and in the current constitution, Section 25, which forbids slavery). The framers of the third constitution added subsections to Sections 1 (authorizing the legislature to enact laws to prevent persons from carrying concealed weapons) and 11 (authorizing the legislature to enact a general change-of-venue law), and in 1988 voters ratified a legislative addition to Section 19 (in effect prohibiting strip mining under broadform deeds unless such mining is specifically agreed to by the parties to the deed). The Kentucky Constitution's Bill of Rights guarantees all the freedoms guaranteed by the U.S. Constitution's Bill of Rights and in some instances expands those freedoms. For example, the Kentucky Supreme Court has found in Section 5, which guarantees the right of religious freedom, together with Section 189, which prohibits the use of public school money to support religious schools, a higher wall separating church and state. In *Fannin v. Williams*, 655 S.W.2d 480 (1983), the court held unconstitutional a statute that authorized the state librarian to supply textbooks to children in parochial schools, a church-state relationship that had been upheld by the U.S. Supreme Court in a case concerning the First Amendment to the U.S. Constitution.[4]

In 1992 the Kentucky Supreme Court cited language in Section 1 that referred to "inalienable rights," "the right of enjoying . . . their lives and liberties," and "the right of seeking and pursuing their . . . happiness" to find a right to privacy that was violated by a state statute that punished consensual deviate sexual intercourse with another person of the same sex.[5] Six years before this decision the U.S. Supreme Court had upheld a similar state statute that was challenged under the federal constitution in *Bowers v. Hardwick*, 478 U.S. 186 (1986), a decision that was not overruled by that court until 2003 in *Lawrence v. Texas*, 539 U.S. 558. The Kentucky Supreme Court has also found in Section 1 a natural right to pursue a legitimate business or profession, which was violated by Kentucky's compulsory medical malpractice insurance statute.[6]

The framers of the third constitution added Section 2 to the Bill of Rights as an attempt to prevent a future legislative majority from emancipating Kentucky's slaves without compensation to slave owners. More recently, non-slave-owning property owners have found the section's language ("Absolute and arbitrary power over the lives, liberty, and property of freemen exists nowhere in a republic, not even in the largest majority") to be a more effective weapon against certain regulations of the economy than the U.S. Constitution. Thus the Kentucky Supreme Court used Section 2 to invalidate Kentucky's Milk Marketing Law, which, in an effort to prevent monopolies and unfair practices in the sale of milk and milk products, prohibited retailers from selling milk below cost.[7]

The Kentucky Supreme Court has ruled that Section 3 of the Bill of Rights, which declares in part that "all men, when they form a social compact, are equal," together with Sections 1, 2, and 59, embraces the equal protection clause of the Fourteenth Amendment to the U.S. Constitution and might provide greater protection of individual liberties than the federal equivalent.[8]

The Kentucky Supreme Court has generally embraced a generous view of Section 8's guarantee of freedom of speech and press (for example, see *Ashland Publishing Co. v. Asbury*, 612 S.W.2d 749 [1980]), but lately it has taken a less libertarian view of freedom from illegal search and seizure, duplicating somewhat the recent trend of the U.S. Supreme Court (see, for example, *Estep v. Commonwealth*, 663 S.W.2d 213 [1983]). The Kentucky Supreme Court also has not enlarged the freedom from self-incrimination beyond that guaranteed by the U.S. Constitution.[9] Resembling the federal Bill of Rights, Kentucky's Bill of Rights prohibits double jeopardy (Section 13), guarantees the right to bail and habeas corpus (Section 16), restricts imprisonment for debt (Section 18) and standing armies (Section 22), guarantees free emigration (Section 24) and the right to trial by jury (Section 7), and prohibits ex post facto laws and laws that impair the obligation of contracts (Section 19). The Kentucky Supreme Court has upheld the amendment to Section 19 that prohibits strip mining under the broad-form deed unless such mining is specifically agreed to.[10] The Kentucky Court of Appeals ruled that Section 4, which gives the people the right "to alter, reform or abolish their government in such manner as they may deem proper," authorized the legislature to establish in 1964 the Constitutional Revision Assembly that drafted the voter-rejected constitution of 1966.[11]

Section 14 of the Bill of Rights states that "all courts shall be open and every person for an injury done him in his lands, goods, person or reputation, shall have remedy by due course of law, and right and justice administered without sale, denial or delay." The Kentucky Supreme Court has ruled that this section, together with Section 54 (first found in the current constitution, which states that "the General Assembly shall have no power to limit the amount to be recovered for injuries resulting in death, or for injuries to person or property") and Section 241 (also first found in the current constitution, which enlarges the right to sue for wrongful death), serves as a barrier to statutory tort reform and substantially enhances the rights of those who are suing to recover damages for personal injury or wrongful death by prohibiting the legislature from abolishing or diminishing rights to sue that existed before the adoption of the current constitution. For example, the Kentucky Supreme Court invalidated a statute that made it more difficult to secure punitive damages in personal injury cases on the grounds that the legislation sought to diminish a right established before the adoption of the current constitution.[12]

Sections 27 and 28 of the constitution provide for the separation of powers. Citing these sections, the Kentucky Supreme Court invalidated most of the legislation that empowered the Legislative Research Commission to veto administrative regulations issued by the governor, to approve or disallow gubernatorial orders reorganizing the executive branch, and to nominate persons for gubernatorial appointment to certain executive agencies. The statute also authorized the Speaker of the House and the president pro tempore of the Senate to appoint members of certain executive boards and agencies, appointed certain legislators to executive boards and agencies, and designated the Legislative Research Commission as an independent agency of state government, thus making it exempt from the governor's control and reorganization.[13]

Sections 29–62 concerning the legislative branch have been the subject of a number of significant rulings. In 1900 the Court of Appeals invalidated Governor William S. Taylor's attempt amid the turmoil after the controversial gubernatorial election of 1899 and the assassination of the Democratic candidate, William Goebel, to adjourn the General Assembly and to reconvene it in London, Kentucky. The Court of Appeals ruled that the governor had encroached on the prerogatives of the General Assembly as guaranteed by Sections 36 and 41, both of which in part concern legislative adjournment. In the same case the Court of Appeals, citing Section 40, which requires each legislative house to keep and publish a journal of its proceedings, rejected a petition alleging that the legislative journals had been tampered with in order to support J. C. W. Beckham's claim to the governorship. The court decided that the judiciary must presume that entries in legislative journals are valid and cannot launch an inquiry regarding their integrity.[14]

As an example of the judiciary interpreting the constitution in a flexible fashion to adapt it to modern times, the Court of Appeals ruled that revenue bonds, interest-bearing warrants, and holding-company bonds that are not guaranteed by the full faith and credit of the Commonwealth but are funded solely by the revenue generated by the projects the bonds are sold to finance do not constitute debts covered by Section 49, which limits the amount of legislative contracts of indebtedness to $500,000.[15]

In *Stephenson v. Woodward*, 182 S.W.3d 162 (2005), the Kentucky Supreme Court ruled that Section 38, which empowers each legislative house to judge the qualifications, elections, and returns of its members, does not authorize the state senate to seat a candidate who received the most votes in a contested election where that candidate was not qualified because she had not lived in the senatorial district for the required number of years.

Section 59, which prohibits specific kinds of private, local, and special legislation that preoccupied the legislature before the adoption of the current constitution, has been the subject of more published appellate-court adjudication than any other section applying to legislative powers. The Kentucky Supreme Court has declared that the primary purpose of Section 59 is to prevent special privileges, favoritism, and discrimination and to ensure equality under the law. The court has held that this section, together with Sections 1, 2, and 3, invalidated a statute of limitations that immunized from personal injury liability persons who designed, planned, supervised, inspected, or constructed improvements to real property after the expiration of five years following the completion of the improvement.[16]

The framers of the current constitution added Section 61 during the revisory session of the convention in response to complaints from temperance forces that the new constitution was proliquor because Section 59, Subsection 27, forbade the General Assembly from enacting local or special laws authorizing local-option elections. Section 61 empowers the General Assembly to enact a general law that authorizes such elections.

The Kentucky Court of Appeals strictly enforced Section 63, which prohibits the creation of counties less than four hundred square miles in area (*Zimmerman v.*

Brooks, 80 S.W. 443 [1904], invalidated the creation of Beckham County because its area was less than four hundred square miles), Section 64, which requires approval of a majority of all the legal voters to move a county seat (*Hogg v. Baker*, 31 S.W. 726 [1895]), and Section 65, which makes territory stricken from a county liable for its share of the indebtedness of the country from which it was stricken (*Whitley County v. Wood*, 170 S.W. 622 [1914]).

One of the most significant judicial rulings about the executive department (Sections 69–108) interpreted the legislative implementation of Section 90, which states that "contested elections for Governor and Lieutenant Governor shall be determined by both Houses of the General Assembly, according to such regulations as may be established by law." The issue in this case was the constitutionality of the process by which the General Assembly determined the winner of the controversial gubernatorial election of 1899. The Court of Appeals upheld that process, which involved a contest board that was chosen by lot but was heavily Democratic and found for the Democratic candidate, a decision unsurprisingly endorsed by the heavily Democratic General Assembly.[17]

The Kentucky Supreme Court ruled in 2010 that by virtue of Section 93, the state senate possesses the exclusive right to confirm gubernatorial appointments to the Council for Postsecondary Education, and therefore Governor Ernie Fletcher's appointment of Virginia Fox to the council was valid even though only the Senate had confirmed her appointment; there was no vacancy for Governor Steve Beshear to fill.[18] Section 77 grants the governor very broad power to pardon both before and after conviction, a power the Kentucky Supreme Court confirmed when it upheld the constitutionality of Governor Ernie Fletcher's blanket pardon of members of his administration who were under investigation by a grand jury for alleged violations of the state merit system.[19]

Sections 109–24, 140, 142, and 144, which concern the judicial branch, have been the subject of relatively few Kentucky Supreme Court cases. The 1975 judicial amendment created a modern unified judiciary described in Section 109 as "the judicial power of the Commonwealth . . . vested exclusively in one Court of Justice which shall be divided into a Supreme Court, a Court of Appeals, a trial court of general jurisdiction known as the Circuit Court and a trial court of limited jurisdiction known as the District Court." The Kentucky Supreme Court held unconstitutional a statute that prohibited the judiciary from enjoining an order of the Alcoholic Beverage Board that revoked a liquor license while that order was being appealed, in part because the statute violated Section 109, which vests judicial powers exclusively in the court of justice.[20] The court has ruled that Section 110, which deals with its jurisdiction, gives it exclusive jurisdiction to hear and determine any cause that has as its ultimate objective a judgment declaring what the court must do or not do, and therefore that it could hear a case involving a petition brought by a public defender to inspect data assembled by the court concerning the imposition of the death penalty in Kentucky.[21] The Court ruled in *Ex parte Auditor of Public Accounts*, 609 S.W.2d 682 (1980), that Section 116 gave it exclusive authority over the State Bar Association, and therefore the auditor of public accounts had no authority to audit the association's books.

The constitution's Sections 145–55 about suffrage and elections have produced few decisions, one of the most interesting of which concerned an effort by the state attorney general pursuant to Section 150 and legislation enacted under its authority to have the charter of the Kentucky Jockey Club forfeited and substantial fines imposed because the club had allegedly engaged in corrupt political activities and unlawful (pari-mutuel) gambling. Shortly after the filing of this lawsuit the club transferred its assets (Churchill Downs and Latonia racetracks) to a Delaware corporation. The attorney general pursued his lawsuit, asserting that the transfer was a sham to avoid prosecution. The Court of Appeals affirmed the circuit court's dismissal of the lawsuit, ruling that pari-mutuel gambling was legal and that the alleged political transgressions were insufficient to warrant forfeiture or a fine.[22]

Framers of the constitution wrote the sections on municipalities (Sections 156a–68) in order to provide for efficient urban governments and to limit municipal and county indebtedness. Local governments evaded limitations imposed by Section 158 ("Cities, towns, counties and taxing districts shall not incur indebtedness to an amount exceeding . . . maximum percentages on the value of the taxable property therein, to be estimated by the last assessment previous to the incurring of the indebtedness") by selling revenue bonds financed by the revenue of the facility under construction and not guaranteed by the government itself, a mechanism declared constitutional by the Kentucky Supreme Court.[23]

Revenue and taxation sections (169–82) sought to limit statutory tax exemptions and to provide for uniform tax assessments. Amendments that exempted household goods, created and enlarged a homestead exemption, and exempted religious property undermined somewhat the effort to limit tax exemptions. The Court of Appeals ruled that license taxes must be uniform but need not be levied on all trades, occupations, or professions and that different fees may be imposed on each class into which a trade, occupation, or profession may fairly be divided.[24]

County tax assessors ignored Section 172's requirement that all taxable property be assessed "at its fair market value" until the Court of Appeals mandated strict compliance with this section in *Russman v. Luckett*, 391 S.W.2d 694 (1965). Thereafter, most tax assessors made a good-faith effort to comply with the section. Section 177 prohibits the Commonwealth from owning all or part of any company or corporation, but the Kentucky Supreme Court has ruled that a state sale of revenue bonds to finance a private industrial development as an incentive for Toyota Motor Corporation to build an assembly plant in Scott County did not violate this section.[25]

By far the most significant decision concerning the constitution's education sections (183–89) was the ruling in *Rose v. Council for Better Education*, 790 S.W.2d 186 (1989), that Section 183's requirement that the General Assembly "shall, by appropriate legislation, provide for an efficient system of common schools throughout the State" obligated the legislature to provide adequate funding for all school districts and to monitor the school districts to ensure that they were providing an adequate education. This case provides another example of the Kentucky Supreme Court finding a right in the state constitution that the U.S. Supreme Court has not found in the U.S. Constitution.[26]

In 2002 voters ratified an amendment that repealed ten antiquated regulatory sections relating to corporations and revised Section 190 to declare that the General Assembly would provide for "the formation, organization and regulation of corporations except as otherwise provided by the Constitution of Kentucky," a revision that had been recommended by the Special Commission on Constitutional Review of 1987. Most of the appellate jurisprudence that the repealed sections engendered occurred early in the twentieth century.

In 2000 voters ratified an amendment that abolished the Railroad Commission (Section 209) but left in place the other sections of the constitution that dealt with railroads. What few appellate cases these sections have produced were mostly decided in the early twentieth century. An exception is *Commonwealth ex rel. Luckett v. Louisville & Nashville Railroad Co.*, 479 S.W.2d 15 (1972), cert. denied, 409 U.S. 949 (1972), wherein the Court of Appeals ruled that Section 210 prohibits a railroad from establishing an independent securities business.

Sections 219–23 concerning the militia have been the subject of few appellate decisions, one of which involved a ruling by the Court of Appeals that Section 221 authorizes the General Assembly to provide by statute that under certain circumstances militia officers should receive the same rate of pay as corresponding officers in the U.S. Army.[27]

The general provisions (Sections 224–55) cover a variety of empowerments and limitations. Two of the most controversial are Sections 228 and 239. The former requires legislators and attorneys before taking office or being admitted to practice to take an oath that they have neither "fought a duel with deadly weapons . . . nor . . . sent or accepted a challenge to fight a duel with deadly weapons, nor . . . acted as a second in carrying a challenge, nor aided or assisted any person thus offending." The latter disqualifies from "any office of honor or profit in this Commonwealth" persons who present or accept a challenge to a duel with deadly weapons. These sections have almost never been litigated, and many would-be reformers have called for their repeal.

The Kentucky Supreme Court has ruled that Section 230, which declares that all money drawn from the state treasury be appropriated "by law," prohibits the governor from withdrawing funds to finance executive functions when the legislature has adjourned without enacting such appropriations.[28]

Section 231 authorizes the General Assembly to enact laws concerning "the manner and in what courts suits may be brought against the Commonwealth." Pursuant to this section, the legislature has enacted statutes that waive sovereign immunity for certain governmental acts of negligence and breach of contract. The Court of Appeals ruled that a city is liable for injuries caused by negligence except in the performance of legislative, judicial, quasi-legislative, or quasi-judicial functions (*Gas Service Co. v. City of London*, 687 S.W.2d 144 [1985]), but it continued to maintain the general immunity of counties from liability for injuries caused by negligence.[29]

Section 242, which provides for just compensation for governmental takings of private property for public use, has been the subject of much litigation. For example, the

Court of Appeals has ruled that Section 242 subjects cities and counties to liability for damage to private property by public works projects.[30]

Section 246 limits the annual salaries of state public officers, the mayor of Louisville, certain judges, and "all other public officers" to amounts ranging from $12,000 to $7,200. The Court of Appeals, in an example of a decision that adapted the constitution to modern reality, ruled that Section 246 permits salaries to be adjusted to reflect the purchasing power of the dollar as of 1949, the year in which the section was amended.[31]

Constitutional framers adopted Section 251 to settle the ownership of lands granted under the laws of Virginia before Kentucky's statehood or before 1820 under the laws of Kentucky. The section specifies that persons claiming land under such grants "against any person claiming such lands by possession to a well-defined boundary under a title of record" need to commence an action to recover such land "within five years after this Constitution shall go into effect, or within five years after the occupant may take occupation." The Court of Appeals undermined Section 251 until 1941 by decisions favoring absentee Virginia land-title claimants (for example, *Warfield Natural Gas Co. v. Danks*, 112 S.W.2d 674 [1938]) but reversed itself in 1941 when it ruled in a conflict between absentee owners claiming title under Virginia grants and occupants with a later Kentucky grant that Section 251 gave title to the latter.[32]

In an effort to put an end to ongoing efforts to move Kentucky's capital from Frankfort to another location (usually Lexington or Louisville), the framers of the constitution provided in Section 255 that Frankfort would remain the capital unless two-thirds of "each House of the first General Assembly which convenes after the adoption of this Constitution" should vote for removal. At that first session legislators waged a fierce battle over the capital-removal question, and proremoval forces garnered more than two-thirds majority support in the House of Representatives but failed to muster such a majority for any single alternative location. Therefore, the capital remained in Frankfort.[33]

The final sections of the constitution (256–63) concern the mode of revision of the constitution. The current constitution is the first Kentucky constitution to provide for revision by individual amendment. Previous charters did not provide for this process, probably because their drafters feared that slavery might be abolished or compromised by an amendment. Section 256 requires that three-fifths of all the members of each house propose amendments. Proposed amendments (up to a maximum of four) are submitted to the voters at the next general election for members of the General Assembly, and if a majority of voters vote to ratify, a ratified amendment becomes part of the constitution. The Court of Appeals ruled that the submission of proposed amendments cannot be postponed until a later general election for representatives.[34]

Sections 258–63 concern legislative proposals to call a constitutional convention and require the support of a majority of all members of each house for two successive sessions. If a convention call is proposed, a majority of the voters ("equal to one-fourth of the number of qualified voters who voted at the last preceding general election") in the next regular election to be held for state officers or House members must approve the call in order for a convention to be convoked. Voters have rejected all four convention calls proposed under the current constitution.

Kentucky's constitution, understandably detailed given the unwillingness of the legislature to reform itself during the period of the third constitution and given the complexities of governance that had emerged by 1890, has through amendment and judicial interpretation become a more efficient charter that is generally well suited to meet the challenges that confront the twenty-first-century Commonwealth. During the first century of Kentucky's statehood, reformers were able to cure constitutional deficiencies by drafting and adopting entirely new constitutions. The framers of the fourth constitution wisely provided for an amendment process of legislative-popular ratification that has facilitated periodic modernization of the charter, which would have been difficult to achieve by the nineteenth-century convention process given the reluctance of post-nineteenth-century voters to approve convention calls. Flexible judicial interpretation of the current constitution has also helped modernize the charter, as well as establish certain personal liberties not found in the U.S. Constitution. Just as Kentucky's constitutions borrowed from and in many ways resembled the constitutions of other states, so too its revisions, such as an integrated judiciary and the elimination of superfluous sections on corporations, likewise fit within the mainstream of recent state constitutional reform. The decisions of the Kentucky Supreme Court that have found rights in the state constitution not found in the federal charter also fit within the mainstream of state judicial rulings nationally. In short, the Kentucky Constitution occupies a significant place in the legal fabric of the Commonwealth, a significance that is shared by virtually all the state charters of the nation.[35]

NOTES

1. For discussion of the drafting and adoption of Kentucky's first three constitutions, as well as the drafting, adoption, and amendments of the current charter, see Robert M. Ireland, *The Kentucky State Constitution*, 2nd ed. (New York: Oxford University Press, 2012), 3–23. Readers might wish to consult this book in general for a more complete discussion of the specific sections of the current constitution.

2. *Miller v. Johnson*, 18 S.W. 522 (1892).

3. Robert F. Stephens, foreword to Ireland, *The Kentucky State Constitution*, xxv.

4. *Board of Education v. Allen*, 392 U.S. 236 (1968).

5. *Commonwealth v. Wasson*, 842 S.W.2d 487 (1992).

6. *McGuffey v. Hall*, 557 S.W.2d 401 (1977).

7. *Kentucky Milk Marketing & Antimonopoly Commission v. Kroger Co.*, 691 S.W.2d 893 (1985).

8. *Tabler v. Wallace*, 704 S.W.2d 179 (1986), cert. denied, 479 U.S. 822 (1986); *Perkins v. Northeastern Log Homes*, 808 S.W.2d 809 (1991).

9. See, for example, *Commonwealth v. Ellis*, 716 S.W.2d 224 (1986).

10. *Ward v. Harding*, 860 S.W.2d 280 (1993).

11. *Gatewood v. Matthews*, 403 S.W.2d 716 (1966).

12. *McCollum v. Sisters of Charity of Nazareth Health Corp.*, 799 S.W.2d 15 (1990).

13. *Legislative Research Commission v. Brown*, 664 S.W.2d 907 (1984).

14. *Taylor v. Beckham*, 56 S.W. 177 (1900).

15. *J. D. Van Hooser & Co. v. University of Kentucky*, 90 S.W.2d 1029 (1936).

16. *Tabler v. Wallace*, 704 S.W.2d 179 (1986), cert. denied, 479 U.S. 822 (1986).

17. *Taylor v. Beckham*, 56 S.W. 177 (1900).

18. *Fox v. Grayson*, 317 S.W.3d 1 (2010).

19. *Fletcher v. Graham*, 192 S.W.3d 350 (2006).

20. *Smothers v. Lewis*, 672 S.W.2d 62 (1984).

21. *Ex parte Farley*, 570 S.W.2d 617 (1978).

22. *Commonwealth v. Kentucky Jockey Club*, 38 S.W.2d 987 (1931).

23. *Baker v. City of Richmond*, 709 S.W.2d 472 (1986).

24. *Hager v. Walker*, 107 S.W. 254 (1908).

25. *Hayes v. State Property & Buildings Commission*, 731 S.W.2d 797 (1987).

26. *San Antonio Independent School District v. Rodriguez*, 411 U.S. 1 (1973); *Kadrmas v. Dickinson Public Schools*, 487 U.S. 450 (1988).

27. *James v. Walker*, 132 S.W. 149 (1910).

28. *Fletcher v. Commonwealth ex rel. Stumbo*, 163 S.W.3d 852 (2005).

29. *Cullinan v. Jefferson County*, 418 S.W.2d 407 (1967).

30. *Layman v. Beeler*, 67 S.W. 995 (1902). Indirect takings are also subject to Section 242. *City of Henderson v. McClain*, 43 S.W. 700 (1897).

31. *Matthews v. Allen*, 360 S.W.2d 135 (1962).

32. *Warfield Natural Gas Co. v. Ward*, 149 S.W.2d 705 (1941).

33. Robert M. Ireland, "Capital Question: Efforts to Relocate Kentucky's Seat of Government," *Register of the Kentucky Historical Society* 104 (Spring 2006): 249–83.

34. *Harrod v. Hatcher*, 137 S.W.2d 405 (1940).

35. For an excellent exposition of the history, development, and significance of state constitutions, as well as their similarities and dissimilarities and their relationship to the U.S. Constitution, see G. Alan Tarr, *Understanding State Constitutions* (Princeton, N.J.: Princeton University Press, 1998).

2

Federalism and Intergovernmental Relations in the Commonwealth of Kentucky

Michael W. Hail

This chapter covers American federalism with a focus on Kentucky politics. The politics of federalism is examined from a comparative perspective for purposes of institutional analysis with other states. The founding and historical development of the Kentucky Constitution are described, including the parallels with national federalism, such as the separation of powers and the system of checks and balances. The government structures of the Kentucky Constitution and the institutional relationships to substate governmental units of city, county, and special-district governments are examined in this regard. Intergovernmental relations among levels of government are described with regard to public policy making in Kentucky. Issues that are addressed include interjurisdictional competition, unfunded mandates, interlocal agreements, and intergovernmental management.

Federalism Scholar David Walker has identified institutions of American federalism and intergovernmental relations as including the executive, bureaucratic, congressional, judicial, and state institutional components, each with its own role in "federalism."[1] The dynamics of the federal system include institutional behavior in terms of "cooperation, competition, conflict, and conflict resolution."[2] The definition of federalism is "a form of government in which a union of states recognizes the sovereignty of a central authority while retaining certain residual powers of government."[3] The term "intergovernmental relations" is defined in this research as "a body of activities and interactions occurring between governmental units of all types and levels within the U.S. federal system."[4] In examining federalism in Kentucky, the relations between the Kentucky state government and the U.S. federal government will be the primary focus, and with regard to intergovernmental relations, that federal-state analysis is expanded to include Kentucky state government and its relationship to other state governments, as well as local and regional subunits of government.

FEDERALISM AND STATE SOVEREIGNTY

The U.S. Constitution provides for dual sovereignty, meaning that ultimate power and authority are held simultaneously by both national and state governments. As the U.S. Supreme Court stated in *Texas v. White,* "The preservation of the States, and the maintenance of their governments, are as much within the design and care of the Constitution, as the preservation of the Union. . . . The Constitution, in all its provisions, looks to an indestructible Union, composed of indestructible States."[5]

The source of substantive constitutional authority is contained in the Tenth Amendment, which states, "The powers not delegated to the United States by the Constitution, nor prohibited by it to the States, are reserved to the States, respectively, or to the people." This establishes what are called the "reserved powers," which are not stated in the U.S. Constitution as federal powers or which are not prohibited to states. These are state constitutional powers because the supremacy clause applies only to those powers that are constitutionally federal. This means that there are expansive areas that are not constitutionally federal. Some examples of these types of traditional state authority are found in policy-making areas, such as education, health, police, fire, elections, and economic development. Respecting dual sovereignty was underscored by the Eleventh Amendment, which extended sovereign immunity by protecting states from action in federal courts by citizens of another state without the consent of that state. The Eleventh Amendment struck down judicial interpretation of state sovereignty in *Chisholm v. Georgia.*[6] The Eleventh Amendment is one of the few instances where the amendment process has countermanded the judicial interpretation of the constitution. And with the Eleventh Amendment, the dual sovereignty of the states was affirmed.

As Supreme Court Justice Hugo Black wrote in *Younger v. Harris* (1971), federalism is "a proper respect for state functions, a recognition of the fact that the entire country is made up of a Union of separate State governments, and a continuance of the belief that the National Government will fare best if the States and their institutions are left free to perform their separate functions in their separate ways."[7] The federalism jurisprudence of the Court is consistent with the original intent of the Founding Fathers, such as that expressed in *The Federalist* 45 by James Madison: "The powers delegated by the proposed Constitution to the Federal government are few and defined. Those which are to remain in the State governments are numerous and indefinite."[8]

The federal and state governments both hold intrinsic and independent sovereignty. Two examples illustrate that concurrent power. Dual citizenship reflects the dual sovereignty of American federalism, which is demonstrated in the existence of separate constitutions that operate on citizens concurrently. All Americans are U.S. citizens and state citizens at the same time. The U.S. government issues one a passport, and the states issue one a birth certificate and a driver's license; each government provides legitimacy to our identification as persons under the concurrent constitutional authority of each government. Likewise, each government can independently exercise the con-current power of taxation, so, for example, one can pay an income tax to each.

Kentucky has at times been a leader in federal and state relations. Early in Ken-tucky's history, the Kentucky legislature passed the famous Kentucky Resolutions, which were drafted in part by Thomas Jefferson. These resolutions exercised Ken-tucky's sovereignty in an attempt to nullify a federal act of Congress that Kentucky and other states thought was outside the authority of Congress. The Kentucky Resolution stated that the Alien and Sedition Acts were unconstitutional. After this early period of constitutional conflict in which Kentucky and Virginia were states that led in asserting state powers of constitutional interpretation, Kentucky has been a leader in cooperative federalism. Kentucky has sought a variety of partnerships with federal agencies for ev-erything from biolabs to transportation stations to energy pipelines, but the approach has been partnership oriented under a policy-making model of cooperative federalism.

To facilitate constructive engagement with federal government agencies and policy makers, Kentucky has followed the model of other states by establishing a lobbying center in Washington, D.C. Kentucky houses its lobbying efforts in the Hall of the States on Capitol Hill in Washington. The states increasingly lost power throughout the twentieth century and effectively had to lobby the U.S. government in a fashion similar to interest groups. One of the most significant changes to the balance of feder-alism was the result of the Seventeenth Amendment, which effectively removed the direct representation of the states in the U.S. Senate. The representation of the states in the Senate was an essential part of the original Constitution and was the central foundation of American federalism.[9] Kentucky had sent instructions to its U.S. sena-tors directing them how to vote on legislation in Congress since famously doing so with the Kentucky Resolutions (see appendix E).[10] Kentucky, like other states, used this power under the original federalism to direct its U.S. senators on a variety of is-sues ranging from the admission of states to internal improvements, but the practice of instruction essentially ended since the adoption of the Seventeenth Amendment.[11]

During the recent federalism "era of devolution," the national government devel-oped policies increasingly designed to devolve power and policy making to the states.[12] The present era of devolution began with President Reagan's New Federalism initiative and continued through the administration of President George W. Bush.[13] Kentucky exhibited institutional behavior that sought to maximize policy outcomes through en-gagement with federal initiatives, as exhibited by data reflecting its relative and better-than-average success in leveraging federal funding.[14] Establishment Kentucky politicians from both parties define engagement with federal agencies and work to obtain federal funding to advance Kentucky projects, priorities, and programs as a substantial part of their service to their constituents and to the Commonwealth. In almost all cases these efforts are intergovernmental, with the strong support of governors and county judge-executives. Kentucky has an active Tea Party movement, and it can be expected that federal-state relations will be a lively topic in Kentucky's political future.

One final aspect of Kentucky is that it is not a true "home-rule" state but maintains a constitutional relationship whereby county and local governments are extensions of state authority. The Kentucky Constitution provides no structural establishment for substate governments and thereby leaves these as creatures of the state that are subject to state regulatory and statutory direction.

KENTUCKY INTERGOVERNMENTAL RELATIONS

Kentucky has numerous governments that engage in a matrix of policy making similar to the institutional policy network in other states. Kentucky ranks fourth among the states as Kentucky has 120 counties, and various groups often see them as "little kingdoms" or generally as being too numerous. There is no empirical evidence that the number of counties has any relationship to economic growth or good government in general.[15] In most cases the goal of county consolidation is really to break down parochial localism by trying to make broader, more regional policy making possible and fundamentally transform the style of Kentucky politics from its foundational political culture. Kentucky's political culture is a hybrid of individualism and traditionalism in the typology estab-

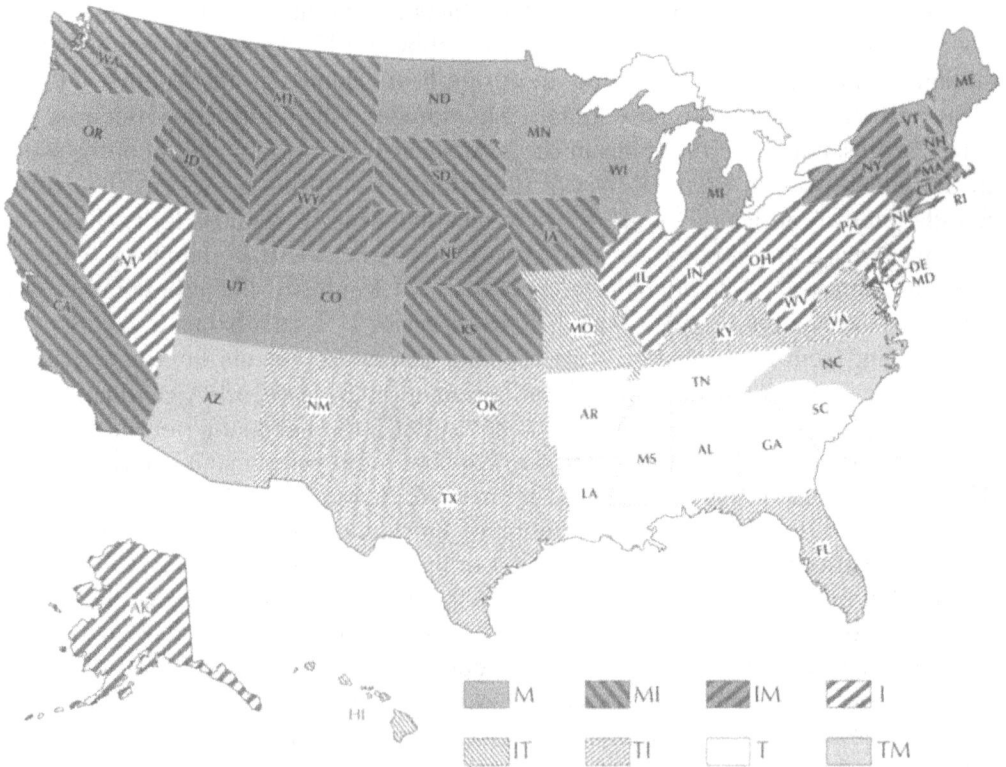

Moralistic (M): views politics as pursuing the common public interest.
Individualistic (I): views politics as a marketplace, as a means of advancing private interests.
Traditionalistic (T): views politics as a means of maintaining the existing order.

Map 2.1. Elazar's state political cultures. Source: Adapted from Daniel J. Elazar, *American Federalism: A View from the States* (New York: Thomas Y. Crowell, 1972), 117.

lished by Daniel Elazar's research on states. The eastern region of Kentucky is more individualistic, and the western region of Kentucky is more traditionalistic. Kentucky's political cultures, as well as those of other states, are displayed in map 2.1.

Daniel Elazar identifies three main political cultures in the United States: moralistic, individualistic, and traditionalistic.[16] Under moralistic culture, politics means pursuing the common public interest, with all citizens having the duty to participate, and there is much government intervention across a broad spectrum of policy. Under individualistic culture, politics is libertarian, with an emphasis on individual rights and on participation that is generally self-interested, and the size and scope of government should be minimized. Under traditionalistic culture, politics is a means of maintaining the existing order; power and decision making are exercised by elites, governmental action is driven by tradition, hierarchy, and broad citizen participation, and innovation is rare and not generally desired. Kentucky is a hybrid of individualistic and traditionalistic. What is typical of local Kentucky politics is a small-government orientation in general and a local elite controlling the political and economic decision making, with self-interested individuals entering and exiting local politics as their interests are addressed. Consistent with that environment of local political culture, voter participation rates have typically been very modest to low, and the nonprofit sector is very small compared with other states and is disproportionately located in the metropolitan areas. Kentucky in 2007 had just over 12,000 nonprofit organizations, an increase of 30 percent since 2000.[17] Figure 2.1 displays the growth in nonprofit organizations.

Kentucky has a relatively large number of counties with 120, but these have remained largely unchanged since the early twentieth century. The only exceptions are Fayette and Jefferson, where the cities of Louisville and Lexington have merged local city and county governments. Table 2.1 shows the number of governmental entities by type in Kentucky; they number approximately 1,698.

Kentucky has 419 cities, which are then classified, customarily by request of the city, into the six classes of city under Kentucky law. The most common type of special district in Kentucky remains the school district, of which Kentucky had 174 in 2012.

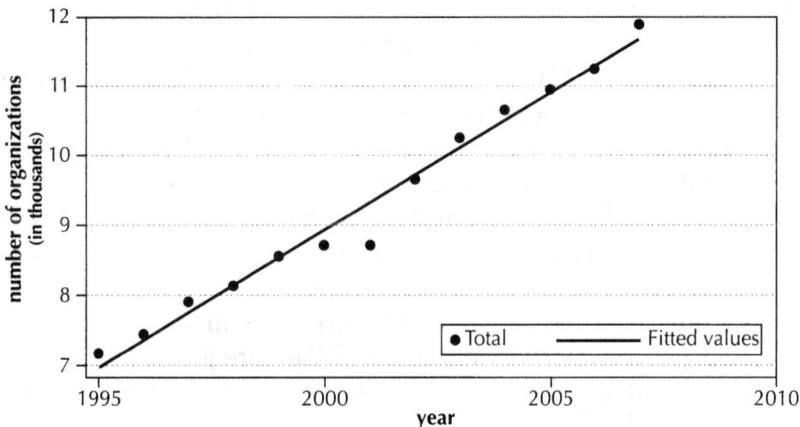

Figure 2.1. Kentucky nonprofit organizations

Table 2.1. Kentucky Governments

Counties	120		
Magistrate fiscal courts		105	
Commissions		15	
Cities	419		
1st class		1	
2nd class		13	
3rd class		19	
4th class		107	
5th class		116	
6th class		163	
Public schools	174		
County schools		121	
Independent city schools		53	
Homeschools			10,252
Special districts—state			1,161
Taxing		797	
Nontaxing		364	
Special districts—federal			809
Special districts average	985		
Total substate governments	1,698		

Source: Author tabulations from U.S. Census of Governments and LRC data on Kentucky governments.

The number of school districts has been decreasing over the past several decades, but there has been continued and sustained growth of other special-district governments. There are between 809 and 1,161 special districts in Kentucky, with an average between the two customary calculation methods of 985.

Kentucky was a part of Virginia before statehood, and the constitution and local government institutions are significantly framed by the Virginia government. Indeed, Kentucky political culture mirrors its origins from the Old Dominion, with a mountain and planter divide between east and west. Kentucky has had four constitutions since becoming a state, but the core institutions remain (see the Kentucky Constitution in appendix K). Kentucky has three branches of government, a governor and an elected executive-branch cabinet, a bicameral legislature, and a judicial system with a supreme court. Kentucky has no home-rule provisions in its constitution, and thus Kentucky county governments are extensions of the state government. Cities in Kentucky are incorporated as independent jurisdictions by the state government and are regulated by the state by class (size) of city.

Kentucky has several intergovernmental measures of government interaction, some of which are illustrated in table 2.2. These data are from the Kentucky Department of

Local Government's database and reflect officially recognized public organizations operating or agreements between them in effect in 2012.

Table 2.2. Kentucky Intergovernmental Relations

Interlocal agreements	569
State-regulated public corporations	45
State authorities	25
Public boards	10
Interagency organizations	424

Source: Kentucky Department of Local Government.

Ann O'M. Bowman has remarked about intergovernmental cooperation that "although the states are increasingly interconnected, the likelihood of sustained cooperative action is tempered by competitive pressures."[18] Of the three areas analyzed, Kentucky ranked average to low in measures of interstate cooperation, as reflected in table 2.3.

Table 2.3. Interstate Cooperation Measures in Kentucky

Membership in interstate compacts	Average to low	22
State involvement in joint legal action	Low	>12
State adoption of uniform laws	Average	8

Source: The Council of State Governments.

Regional government in Kentucky is by Area Development Districts (ADDs), of which there are fifteen (see map 2.2). The ADDs are governed by boards appointed by the county governments in each district, with the county judge-executive serving in most cases. They are financed by intergovernmental revenue from both federal and state governments and are regulated by the Kentucky Department of Local Government. The ADDs perform critical support functions for county governments in such areas as grant development and GIS mapping.

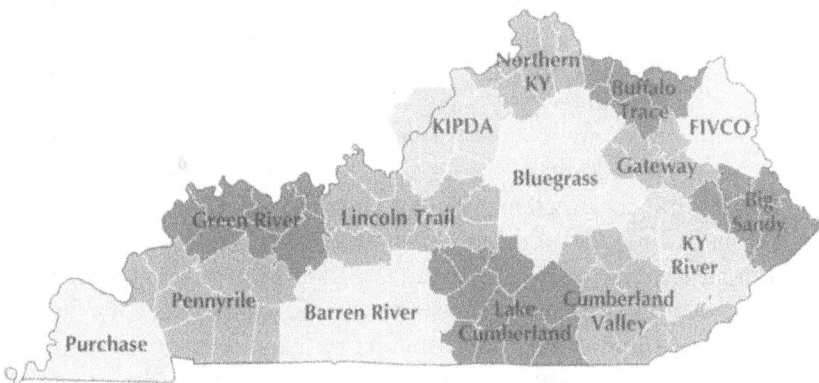

Map 2.2. Kentucky Area Development Districts

PUBLIC PERSPECTIVES ON KENTUCKY GOVERNMENTS

Studies of public attitudes about federalism reveal consistent attitudes on the part of elected officials, as well as the public.[19] Kentucky citizens reflect similar views toward the various levels of government (figure 2.2).

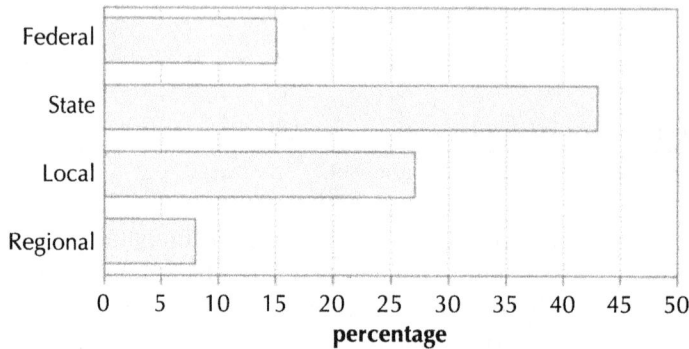

Figure 2.2. Public attitudes about Kentucky

Kentuckians were asked what levels of government had been most effective at addressing their community's needs.[20] Eight percent of Kentuckians voiced approval of the federal government, while 27 percent supported state government, and 15 percent favored regional governments, such as ADDs. But the most significant portion of Kentuckians, 43 percent, responded that local government was the most effective at addressing the needs of their community. This overall approval of local government performance resonates with the national trend for devolutionary policy preferences.

KENTUCKY: RURAL VERSUS URBAN

One of the enduring intergovernmental challenges in Kentucky involves rural versus urban interests. These intergovernmental cleavages break down other dominant political alignments (Democrat-Republican, East-West, conservative-liberal) according to the political issues. One of the most prominent political reference points to this conflict is the term "the Golden Triangle."[21] The Golden Triangle is the most urban area of Kentucky and holds numerous political advantages, from wealth to large legislative delegations with crosscutting influence. Map 2.3 illustrates the rural and urban distribution across the United States.

The changes in demographic trends that have affected shifts in U.S. politics have been slower to transform Kentucky politics. Whereas the United States shifted from a predominantly rural to an urban population over a hundred years ago, the same shift occurred only a few decades ago in Kentucky. These changes marginalize the economic competitiveness of rural areas and also diminish their political clout. Following this population shift was a movement within federalism to governance of persons more than simply places, and thus rural clout was further diminished by procedural changes in representation and electoral systems as the reapportionment

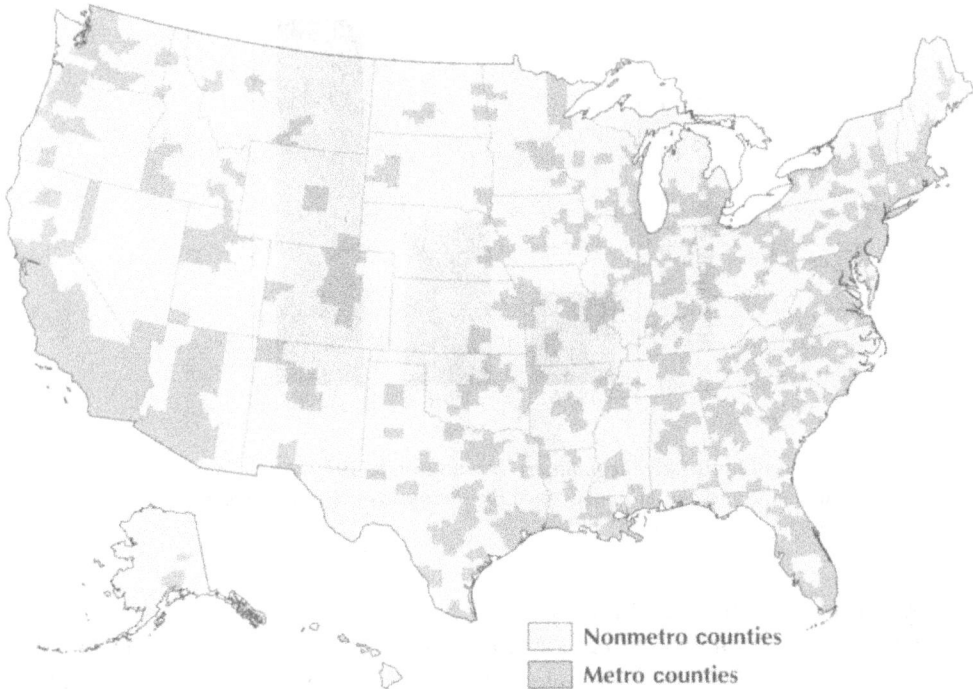

Map 2.3. Nonmetro and metro counties in the United States

revolution of the 1960s (Supreme Court cases such as *Baker v. Carr* and *Reynolds v. Sims*) unfolded. "The cumulative effect of the new population-based paradigm that increasingly looked at individuals in the system of federalism rather than states resulted in a shift in power toward urban areas. The politics of population prevailed over the politics of place, and the current period of devolution that characterizes the American intergovernmental landscape today continues to search for means that reestablish place-based federalism and returns the American intergovernmental system to the era of dual federalism."[22] In Kentucky the decline in the economic and political importance of tobacco made these broader national trends even more significant. Rural members of the General Assembly still maintain significant influence, and the leadership of both chambers remains with rural leaders from Prestonsburg and Burkesville. That influence is a significant counterweight to the continued urbanization of Kentucky and the increasing political and economic clout of cities and the Golden Triangle.

INTERGOVERNMENTAL REGULATORY POLICY IN KENTUCKY

The devolutionary-era approach was statist and reacted to a period of federalism described as co-optive or coercive federalism.[23] The new intergovernmental relationships are less cooperative than client oriented, and the federal aid process accords former cooperative partners a political status more accurately understood through an interest-group exchange framework.[24] This framework makes the regulatory process critical for policy makers to exert policy co-option.

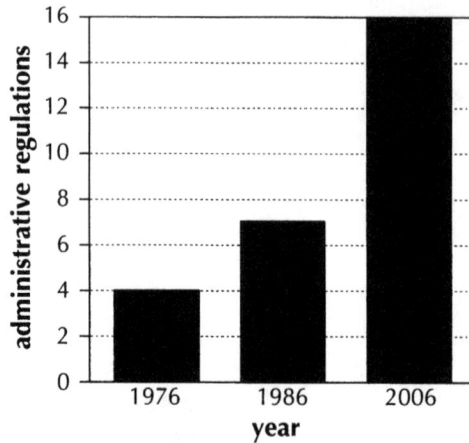

Figure 2.3. Kentucky administrative regulations: growth trends, 1976–2006. Source: Legislative Research Commission, *Kentucky Administrative Regulations Service* (Frankfort, Ky.: Legislative Research Commission, 1976, 1986, and 2006).

Regulations are growing at an expansive rate across all levels of government. The last two years of the Obama administration have seen over 400 new major regulatory policy initiatives, and as the fiscal interdependence increases, federal regulatory expansion carries a concurrent subnational regulatory response. But even considering the national growth, Kentucky has been expanding state regulation at an increasing rate, as illustrated by figure 2.3.

In 2006 Kentucky had 118 titles in the Kentucky Code of Administrative Regulations.[25] The 2006 Kentucky administrative regulations reflected a steady growth that was four times greater than in 1976 and more than twice the volume of 1986. If this rate continues, Kentucky will be one of the most regulated states in the next decade.

KENTUCKY AND FISCAL FEDERALISM

Fiscal federalism refers to financial relations between and across levels of governments. Political scientists measure the amount of funds that flow across levels of government and the regulatory requirements that often come with the transfer of these funds. Governments at all levels count on ever-larger amounts of intergovernmental revenue from other governments. Financing government, like policy making in general, increasingly requires cooperative and coordinated action across levels of government to achieve effective policy making in most areas of concern. As government spending, budgets, and the overall economy have continued to grow over time, intergovernmental fiscal interdependence has consequently increased. But this growth has increased intergovernmental revenue and expenditure at all levels of government even as our leaders continue to debate the balance of federalism and the appropriate scope of government. The data on fiscal federalism in figure 2.4 illustrate the correlation between federal and state funds as a function of intergovernmental revenue flow.

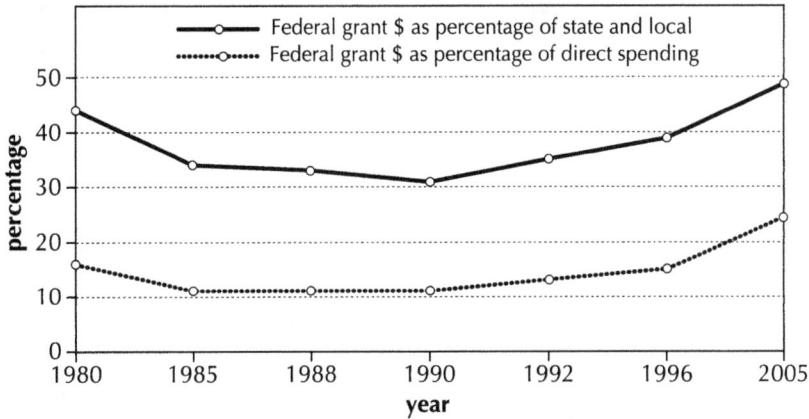

Figure 2.4. Fiscal federalism. Source: Federal Census of Governments 1980–2005.

In fiscal federalism, as in most areas of policy, the supremacy clause of the Constitution provides an uneven playing field where national policy authority trumps state and local authority. The result of this in regulatory policy making is a range of requirements by the national government with which subnational governments must comply. These requirements take many forms, most often what are called "crosscutting regulations" issued by the federal government and sometimes other regulatory actions, such as mandates (funded and unfunded), co-options, and preemptions. These regulatory policy tools are most often tied to funding, and as funding expands at the national level, with corresponding intergovernmental fiscal growth, the power of the national government to use these regulatory tools also expands.

Kentucky political leaders of both parties have expressed continued concern over the national government's expansion of the regulatory powers of government and the adverse conditions for economic growth these powers cause. "Anything we can do to slow down, deter or impede their ability to engage in this kind of oppressive overregulation which is freezing up our economy would be good for the country," Senator Mitch McConnell noted at a Washington policy meeting in 2011.[26]

As Congressman Harold Rogers noted in supporting deregulation legislation, "I applaud Kentucky's own Congressman Geoff Davis for his tireless effort to win passage of the REINS Act, which stops the onslaught of federal regulations and gives our job creators confidence to hire Kentucky workers and spend more, invest more, and produce more. This commonsense legislation is a win-win and will put us one step closer towards restoring our economy." Rogers also noted congressional statistics that reflect "an estimated $1.75 trillion regulatory burden, and yet in 2010 and 2011, the Obama Administration introduced 410 new major rules that have cast additional uncertainty into an already unstable economy."[27]

There is relative bipartisan agreement among most Kentucky politicians that regulatory reform is needed. A good illustration of that can be seen in an exchange between challenger Andy Barr and Congressman Ben Chandler, in which both recognized the importance of addressing the regulatory burden of government and its adverse effect on the economy and job growth. As Congressman Chandler noted in his editorial in the *Lexington Herald-Leader*, "Small businesses currently face an annual regulatory burden of around $10,000 per employee," and there are over "8,000 regulations issued annually."[28] In similar fashion, Andy Barr included government debt and spending in the fiscal equation and concluded that "the best way to get our economy moving again is to get the government out of the way."[29] But despite the recognition by Kentucky politicians that there is too much regulation and that the size and scope of government require reduction, the expansion of government regulations continues at all levels.

Kentucky continues to rely on intergovernmental resources from the national government at an increasing rate, and with the difficult economic times of the past few years and the related budget pressures, these trends will only grow stronger. The continued regulatory burden imposed by the national government through direct mandates, crosscutting regulations, and requirement provisions in grants and contracts has only increased the fiscal cost to the states. With the end of the devolution era and the beginning of a period of new nationalism, there will likely be more co-options and preemptions of state policy as national policy making expands authority across more policy areas more comprehensively. Additional compression of policy authority will likely continue for state and local governments from federal regulation. These trends are expected to continue as the period of economic stress affects resource capacity at all levels of government.

NOTES

1. David B. Walker, *The Rebirth of American Federalism* (Chatham, N.J.: Chatham House, 1995), 26–29. The role of these institutional players in the federal system has received such designations as "executive federalism" or "judicial federalism."

2. Vincent Ostrom, *The Intellectual Crisis in American Public Administration*, 2nd ed. (Tuscaloosa: University of Alabama Press, 1989), 144.

3. Deil S. Wright, *Understanding Intergovernmental Relations* (North Scituate, Mass.: Duxbury Press, 1978), 17.

4. Ibid., 8.

5. *Texas v. White*, 74 U.S. (7 Wall.) 700, 19 L. Ed. 227 (1868).

6. Michael W. Hail, "The Eleventh Amendment," in *The Encyclopedia of United States Civil Liberties*, ed. Otis H. Stephens, John Scheb, and Kara E. Stooksbury (Westport, Conn.: Greenwood Publishing, 2007). *Chisholm v. Georgia*, 2 U.S. 419, 2 Dall. 419, 1 L.Ed. 440 (U.S. 1793).

7. *Younger v. Harris*, 401 U.S. 37, 91 S. Ct. 746, 27 L. Ed. 2d 669 (1971).

8. *Federalist* 45. James Madison, *The Federalist Papers*, ed. Clinton Rossiter (New York: Nal Penguin Mentor Books, 1961), 292.

9. Michael W. Hail, "Seventeenth Amendment," in *Encyclopedia of American Parties and Elections*, ed. Larry J. Sabato and Howard R. Ernst (New York: Facts on File, 2006), 427–28.

10. Ralph Rossum, *Federalism, the Supreme Court, and the Seventeenth Amendment* (Cumnor Hill, Oxford: Lexington Books, 2001), 96–111.

11. Ibid., 96–99. See also George H. Haynes, *The Senate of the United States: Its History and Practice* (Boston: Houghton Mifflin, 1938).

12. Michael W. Hail, "Devolution," in *The Encyclopedia of Political Science*, ed. George Thomas Kurian (Washington, D.C.: CQ Press, 2011), http://library.cqpress.com/teps/encyps _423.3.

13. Michael W. Hail, "Bush's New Nationalism: The Life and Death of New Federalism," in *Perspectives on the Legacy of George W. Bush*, ed. Michael O. Grossman and Ronald E. Mathews Jr. (Cambridge: Scholars Press, 2009), 73–95.

14. Michael W. Hail and Jeremy L. Hall, "County Consolidation and State Rural Economic Development Strategies," in *Public Administration, NGO's and Public Debt: Issues and Perspectives*, ed. Marcel Kratochvil and Valentin Pokorny (New York: NOVA Science Publishers, 2010), 241–56.

15. Ibid.

16. Daniel J. Elazar, *Cities of the Prairie* (Lanham, Md.: University Press of America, 1970), 256–81.

17. As measured by 501(c)3 filings; IRS.gov.

18. Ann O'M. Bowman, "Trends and Issues in Interstate Cooperation," in *The Book of the States* (Lexington, Ky.: Council of State Governments, 2004), 18.

19. *Federal Statutory Preemption of State and Local Authority: History, Inventory, Issues* (Washington, D.C.: Advisory Commission on Intergovernmental Relations, 1992); *Changing Public Attitudes on Government and Taxes* (Washington, D.C.: Advisory Commission on Intergovernmental Relations, 1993).

20. Data developed by Michael Hail using the 2004 Kentucky State Survey by the University of Kentucky Survey Research Center, a semiannual phone survey of randomly selected Kentucky adults.

21. The term "Golden Triangle" refers to a geographic area bounded by Louisville, Lexington, and Cincinnati. This urban triangular area has been home to the most economic growth and features higher educational attainment and other demographic indicators of higher levels of development.

22. Holly R. Barcus and Michael W. Hail, "Rural Policy and Federalism," in *Federalism in America*, ed. Joseph R. Marbach (Westport, Conn.: Greenwood Publishing, 2005), 2:551.

23. Timothy Conlan, *New Federalism* (Washington, D.C.: Brookings Institution, 1988). Conlan notes that even though there have been indications of a "new cooperative federalism" found in some "recent implementation studies," this federalism is more accurately characterized as "co-optive federalism" (236). See also Paul E. Peterson, Barry G. Rabe, and Kenneth K. Wong, *When Federalism Works* (Washington, D.C.: Brookings Institution, 1986), chap. 6.

24. The regulatory model is suggested for understanding the current arrangements of federalism. George E. Hale and Marian Lief Palley, *The Politics of Federal Grants* (Washington, D.C.: CQ Press, 1981).

25. Legislative Research Commission, *Kentucky Administrative Regulations Service* (Frankfort, Ky.: Legislative Research Commission, 1976, 1986, and 2006).

26. Dow Jones On-Line News, accessed June 27, 2011, http://www.nasdaq.com/aspx/stock-market-news-story.aspx?storyid=201106221156dowjonesdjonline000516.l.

27. Office of Honorable Harold D. Rogers, "Rogers Supports 'REINS Act' to Rein in Federal Red Tape," press release, December 7, 2011, http://halrogers.house.gov/News/Document Single.aspx?DocumentID=271781.

28. Ben Chandler, "Needless Regulations Strangle Businesses, Hurt Our Economy," *Lexington Herald-Leader*, September 27, 2011, A9.

29. Andy Barr, "Chandler Supports Policies That Hurt U.S. Economy," *Lexington Herald-Leader*, October 10, 2011, A13.

3

The Kentucky General Assembly
Divided by Party, United by Necessity
James C. Clinger

The two chambers of the Kentucky General Assembly, like the state legislatures of many other states, have been divided in party control in recent decades. In the Kentucky legislature the Republican party has held a majority in the Senate since 2000, while the Democrats have held a majority in the House of Representatives for as long as any living Kentuckian can remember. The two chambers enjoy an uneasy coexistence. Each has its own constitutional qualifications for officeholding, its own electoral cycle, and its own constituencies of different scale and scope. The chambers are related, however, in governing purpose and in the career ladders of politicians who seek to extend or advance their public careers.

This chapter will address several issues regarding the Commonwealth's state legislature, including its constitutional authority, membership characteristics, organizational structure, career opportunities, and legislative procedure. Each of these features interacts with others to shape the operation of the institution.

CONSTITUTIONAL POWERS

The Kentucky Constitution states that the "legislative power shall be vested in a House of Representatives and a Senate, which, together, shall be styled the General Assembly of the Commonwealth of Kentucky" (Section 29). Notably, the constitution does not say, as the federal constitution does, that "all legislative power" is vested in the legislature. Nonetheless, the grant of authority in the constitution and the apparent protections against the intrusions of other branches found in the separation-of-powers provisions (Sections 27 and 28) appear to give the General Assembly substantial power to make policy for the Commonwealth. In practice, however, various restrictions on taxing, spending, and legislative sessions have imposed some limits on policy making. The restrictions on fiscal decisions are detailed elsewhere in this volume (see chapter 8 by Lisa A. Cave), so attention here will focus on time constraints placed on the General

Assembly. Regular sessions of the General Assembly were once held only every other year, and the number of legislative days was limited. Under an amendment to the constitution approved in 2000, the legislature may meet in odd-numbered years for a total of thirty days, and for sixty days in even-numbered years. In the short sessions in odd-numbered years, revenue-raising bills can be passed only by a three-fifths vote of the members of each chamber. Special or "extraordinary" sessions may be called by the governor, but not by the General Assembly. The subjects to be addressed in extraordinary sessions are limited to those specified by the governor (Section 80).

Members of the legislature are elected in plurality-winner elections from single-member districts, unlike the legislators in thirteen states, some of whom are elected from multimember districts. In keeping with Duverger's law, the legislature is populated with members of only two political parties. One lone independent, Bob Leeper, serves in the Senate after winning office earlier as a Republican and earlier still as a Democrat. The state is divided into thirty-eight senatorial districts and one hundred House districts. Each district is approximately the same in population size as any other district from the same chamber, although the constitution stipulates that district boundaries should avoid division of counties as much as possible without violating the equal-population standard.

Members of the House of Representatives serve two-year terms and are elected in November of even-numbered years. The members of the House select their presiding officer, the Speaker of the House (currently Greg Stumbo, a former attorney general). Members of the Senate serve four-year terms and are also elected in even-numbered years. Senate terms are staggered so that half of the thirty-eight senators are elected in any even-numbered year. Prior to a 1992 constitutional amendment, the lieutenant governor served as the Senate's presiding officer, but since 1993 the members of the Senate have selected their presiding officer, the Senate president. The governor, lieutenant governor, and other statewide executive officers are elected in odd-numbered years, so legislative elections are not particularly influenced by gubernatorial coattail effects resulting from the presence of a popular (or unpopular) candidate of the same party at the top of the ballot. Popular or unpopular presidential candidates may still have some impact on legislative candidates' electoral outcomes.

Section 47 of the constitution stipulates that revenue-raising bills must originate in the House of Representatives. Section 93 of the constitution assigns the Senate the responsibility for approving gubernatorial appointments, a point challenged unsuccessfully in *Fox v. Grayson* (see the discussion in chapter 1 by Robert Ireland in this volume).[1] On other matters, the House and Senate share responsibility, although each chamber is permitted to develop its own rules of procedure. With differences in qualifications for office, constituencies, terms of office, numbers of members, and partisan control, it is not surprising that the House and Senate sometimes appear to be separate institutions that share the function of lawmaking.

QUALIFICATIONS

The constitution requires that members of the House of Representatives must be, at the time of election, at least twenty-four years of age and Kentucky citizens who have resided in the Commonwealth for at least two years preceding election. House members must also have resided in the county or city from which they have been chosen. Senators must be at least thirty years of age and also Kentucky citizens who have resided in the Commonwealth for at least six years and in their senate districts for at least one year before election. The residency requirement became a contentious issue in the elections of 2004 when the six-year Kentucky residency of one candidate, Dana Seum Stephenson, was challenged in court the day before the election by her electoral opponent, Virginia Woodward. Evidence was presented that Stephenson had resided in Indiana until shortly before filing for the senate race. Stephenson remained on the ballot and won more votes than Woodward. Nonetheless, the Franklin County Circuit Court ruled in summary judgment in favor of Woodward. Stephenson, along with Senate president David Williams, appealed the case all the way to the Kentucky Supreme Court, claiming that the courts lacked jurisdiction because Section 38 of the constitution stipulates that each house is to be the judge of the qualifications, elections, and returns of its members.[2] The court ultimately ruled against Stephenson and Williams, claiming that a lower court had ruled on the case before Stephenson became a member of the Senate.[3]

In practice, most members of the General Assembly are considerably older than the constitution requires, and most have been long-term residents in their districts. In the House, Representative Michael Lee Meredith at age twenty-seven in 2012 was the youngest legislator serving in the General Assembly. At age eighty-one, Representative Tom Burch and Senator Julian Carroll, a former governor, were the oldest in the legislature in 2012.[4] With respect to other demographic characteristics, the General Assembly has an interesting collection of diverse members, although it is still not particularly close to a proportionate representation of the entire population of the state (see Table 3.1). Approximately 81 percent of the General Assembly membership is male, obviously a

Table 3.1. Chamber Characteristics of the General Assembly (2011)

	House	*Senate*
Number of members	100	38
Term length	Two years	Four years
Percentage having prior elected office	18%	47%
Average years of service in General Assembly	10.1	12.6
Average age	55.4	58.2
Number of women	20	6
Number of veterans	20	7
Number of minorities	7	1
Number of attorneys	17	11
Number of Democrats	58	15
Number of Republicans	42	22

Source: Calculated by the author from data at Legislative Research Commission web pages, http://www.lrc.state.ky.us/home.htm.

much greater percentage than that of the state's population as a whole. Prior research has indicated that southern states, more ideologically conservative states, and states without legislative term limits tend to have fewer women serving in the legislature.[5] With those factors all working against the representation of women in the General Assembly, it is not surprising that the number of female state legislators is low. Nonetheless, the number has been growing over time.

With regard to the representation of racial and ethnic minorities, the General Assembly also has relatively low numbers. Fewer than 6 percent of the members of the legislature are African American.[6] However, it is also important to note that Kentucky is a predominantly white state, so it is not surprising to find that the number of minorities in the General Assembly is low.

PROFESSIONALISM

The study of state legislatures has often focused on the level of professionalization that exists within the institution. For many years state legislatures were sometimes regarded as "sometime governments."[7] Members served a term or two, often at low pay and with little staff support, and then left the legislature, often to return to private life. Legislatures met for short sessions, frequently on a biennial basis, with little time to develop new policies and scant opportunity to oversee existing programs. Most state legislatures, including the Kentucky General Assembly, have moved in the direction of professionalization. In more and more legislatures service is considered a full-time job, and there are improved salaries (and other forms of financial compensation), more staff support, and longer, annual sessions. The Kentucky General Assembly also benefits from the services of the Legislative Research Commission (LRC), which is headed officially by the leaders of each chamber but maintains a professional staff made up of a number of analysts with graduate degrees in political science, economics, law, and public administration. The LRC provides policy research and oversight functions, as well as assistance in bill drafting. The agency has existed since 1948 but has grown in stature and prestige over time, particularly since its 1997 reorganization in the wake of a scandal involving an LRC House operations manager.

The professionalization of the General Assembly may be one of the trends that is reshaping the institution into a body dominated by ambitious, careerist legislators, many of whom expect to make public service a long-term commitment. Politicians in general are considered to be ambitious people. Few shy, introverted people are likely to run for public office. But many political scientists, beginning with Joseph Schlesinger, have contended that there are different kinds of political ambition, and that political leaders motivated by different kinds of ambition will behave in different, albeit predictable, ways.[8] Schlesinger argued that some politicians are motivated by what he called "discrete" ambition. These are public leaders who are willing to serve in a public office for a brief while, often at the urging of others, but who have no desire to pursue long-term officeholding. They may act out of a sense of duty to their communities or out of a strong sense of moral purpose, but they are not election seeking or power hungry. As a result, they are not frightened by the prospect of being kicked out of office in the next election if they vote contrary to their constituents' wishes or if they say or do something that will enrage party leaders or important interest groups. Financial compensation in office does not particularly interest them because they do not plan to stay in office long, although some minimum level of pay may be necessary to support their families even for a short stay in public office.

Schlesinger also wrote of another kind of ambition, which he termed "static." Politicians motivated in this way desire to acquire public office and stay there for a long time, but they may be satisfied to rise only to a particularly modest place in the political hierarchy. For example, they may be content to run and win a seat in the state house of representatives but may never aspire to serve in the state senate or run for a statewide office. Such legislators must win elections again and again to build the kind of career that they crave. This may entail voting the way their constituents demand, even if doing so violates their own conscience. It also means that they will be attracted to and in fact will seek to establish rules in their chambers that reward seniority. For example, they would hope that the longest-serving members would get their preferred committee assignments and gain appointments as chair of the most prestigious or constituency-pleasing committees.

The third kind of ambition that Schlesinger spoke of is "progressive" ambition. Politicians motivated in this way do not desire to win just one office and stay in that position but would like to rise to higher and higher office. Presumably this will require winning many different elections while pleasing different, ever-expanding constituencies. Sometimes this will entail appealing to a larger, presumably more diverse set of interests representing an expanded future electoral constituency even when doing so might not please current constituents.[9] This might also require access to resources from party leaders and interest groups in order to rise to higher office. Current constituents in the district might not get as much attention as the interests that in the future might be useful in rising higher. Legislators with progressive ambition will wish to serve in chambers in which seniority is not a priority. They might prefer that committee assignments be made at the discretion of party or chamber leaders. They also might like to serve in a legislature in which the size of the membership of the state senate is as large as possible in comparison with that of the lower chamber or in a state with many statewide offices and several seats in the U.S. House of Representatives. The greater the number of higher offices that are available to pursue, the more opportunities ambitious legislators will have to fill them.[10] In Kentucky there are almost three times as many House seats as Senate seats, so advancement from the House to the Senate is not easy. The limited number of U.S. House of Representatives seats and statewide elected executive offices may also frustrate legislators with progressive ambition.

SALARY

Financial support for Kentucky legislators is also not high enough to encourage most successful professionals and business people to seek out and stay in a career in the General Assembly. Nonetheless, the compensation is much higher than it once was. As of 2010, Kentucky legislators received a per diem salary of $186.73 for each calendar day, plus an unvouchered per diem of $119.90 for days of legislative service.[11] Because the per diems are not constitutionally limited, they are much easier to change than in states in which legislative compensation is fixed in the state constitution. The members of the General Assembly also are eligible for state pensions after five years of legislative service, with a benefit formula designed to reward legislators who serve a greater number of years in the body. Some observers have argued that the level of legislative compensation is desirable for a number of reasons. First, a higher level of compensation promotes professionalism and a career commitment. Of course, some critics claim that the careerist motivation actually is an undesirable trait. Second, a higher level of compensation makes legislative service more attractive and, in fact, practical for people from various walks of life. When little or no compensation is provided, legislative service becomes the province of independently wealthy individuals or professionals, such as attorneys, who can manage to take extended periods of time from their main occupations to devote attention to public affairs. A final reason for higher compensation is the belief that a better-paid set of legislators will be less susceptible to corruption. In the early 1990s, during the undercover sting operation known as Operation BOPTROT, FBI agents posing as lobbyists for gambling interests were shocked to learn how little money was needed to bribe Kentucky state legislators.[12] The investigation netted twenty-one convictions on federal corruption charges, including a conviction of the sitting Speaker of the House and fourteen other members of the General Assembly.

THE COMMITTEE SYSTEM

The committee system in the Kentucky General Assembly is a crucial part of the legislative process and a critical aspect of how power is shared among individual legislators. Each chamber sets its own rules regarding many committees, although a few committees are so-called statutory committees, which are established by statute, not internal chamber rules, and have jurisdictions and powers defined by statute. Statutory committees also have some citizen members. There are nineteen standing committees (as of 2011) in the House and fifteen in the Senate (table 3.2).[13] In addition, there are fifteen interim joint committees that include members from both chambers and meet, usually once a month, during the interim between regular legislative sessions (table 3.3). The interim committees conduct oversight over state agencies and also review, but not approve, bills that have been prefiled. Members of the legislature are assigned to particular committees by a Committee on Committees in each chamber. In the House the Committee on Committees is made up of five members of the majority party (i.e., the Democratic Party), including the Speaker, and one member of the minority party (the GOP). In the Senate the membership is less slanted in favor of the majority. Five members of the committee, including the Senate president, are Republicans, and three are Democrats.

Recent scholarship on committee assignment in legislatures often tries to explain assignment decisions in one of three ways. One perspective argues that seniority dominates these decisions. In short, the most senior members of the legislature, particularly the most senior members of the majority political party, are assigned to their

Table 3.2. 2012 Standing Committees

House committees	Senate committees
Committee on Committees	Committee on Committees
Rules	Rules
Enrollment	Enrollment
Agriculture and Small Business	Agriculture
Appropriations and Revenue	Appropriations and Revenue
Banking and Insurance	Banking and Insurance
Economic Development	Economic Development, Tourism, and Labor
Education	
Elections, Const. Amendments, and Intergovernmental Affairs	Education
Health and Welfare	Health and Welfare
Judiciary	Judiciary
Labor and Industry	Licensing, Occupations, and Administrative Regulations
Licensing and Occupations	Natural Resources and Energy
Local Government	State and Local Government
Natural Resources and Environment	Transportation
State Government	Veterans, Military Affairs, and Public Protection
Tourism Development and Energy	
Transportation	
Veterans, Military Affairs, and Public Safety	

preferred committees. Furthermore, the most senior members of the majority party become the majority members of the committees to which they are assigned. This perspective generally contends that seniority is a relatively noncontroversial, easily measured characteristic that provides a simple rule for assigning members. Seniority as a basic decision rule also serves to weaken the role of the legislative membership and to reward rank-and-file legislators who have proved themselves by standing for and winning election several times by giving them preferred positions in the body that will allow them the opportunity to serve their constituents or to advance their policy goals. The seniority explanation is probably not particularly well supported by contemporary empirical research on state legislatures.[14]

A second approach is often termed the legislative leviathan perspective. This perspective argues that the majority party runs the legislative chamber and stacks the committees with members who will pursue party goals.[15] In many cases, of course, it is difficult to distinguish loyalty to party goals from personal loyalty to party leaders.

Table 3.3. Statutory and Interim Joint Committees

Statutory committees	Interim joint committees
Legislative Research Commission	Agriculture
Administrative Regulation Review	Appropriations and Revenue
Capital Planning	Banking and Insurance
Capital Projects and Bond Oversight	Economic Development and Tourism
Education Assessment and Accountability Review	Education
	Energy
Government Contract Review	Health and Welfare
Medicaid Oversight and Advisory Committee	Judiciary
Program Review and Investigations	Labor and Industry
Tobacco Settlement Agreement Fund	Licensing and Occupations
	Local Government
	Natural Resources and Environment
	State Government
	Transportation
	Veterans, Military Affairs, and Public Protection

Source: http://www.lrc.state.ky.us/home.htm.

Members who are out of the mainstream of their respective party will be given unattractive committee assignments and will not be named as chairs, at least of important committees. A third perspective, often described as an informational theory, contends that committees work to process legislation on the part of the chamber as a whole. In order to reach decisions that are consistent with the preferences of the chamber as a whole, assignments to committees are made so that the overall composition of each committee is fairly representative of the chamber as a whole. Each committee will be broadly representative of the ideology of the chamber, with few outliers in any committee. This pattern is quite different from what the leviathan model of committee assignment would predict.

Committee assignment in the Kentucky General Assembly does not appear to be strongly associated with seniority. In the House, where Democrats hold a majority of the seats, committee chairs in 2011 on average had just over twelve years of service in the General Assembly, compared with a little over nine years of service for the average nonchair and just under twelve years of service for the average Democrat. In the Senate, committee chairs on average had just under twelve years of legislative service, compared with almost thirteen and a half years for the average nonchair. This seems to reflect the less experienced nature of the majority party in the Senate. The average Republican in the chamber has just eleven years of service.[16]

Determining whether the leviathan model or the informational theory better reflects the common practice of committee assignment in the General Assembly is a bit more difficult. No one expects committee membership to be perfectly representative of the overall membership of each chamber, but then again not many observers would believe that members are extreme outliers relative to their colleagues in the chamber. Research by L. Marvin Overby, Thomas A. Kazee, and David W. Prince and by Prince and Overby indicated that no committees in the House and only a few committees in the Senate could be considered ideological outliers.[17] These scholars used rankings by the National Federation of Independent Business in forty-five states, including Kentucky, that were based on roll-call votes on issues of concern to the federation. These scholars then calculated NOMINATE scores, a scale used in much legislative scholarship to measure the ideological content of the voting behavior of individual members across time and sometimes across legislative chambers. They then compared the NOMINATE scores of individual committees with those of the party delegations of their chamber. On the basis of these findings, the committees in the Kentucky General Assembly seem fairly representative of the overall membership of their chambers.

LEGISLATIVE PROCEDURE

As in almost all state legislatures, the passage of legislation in the Kentucky General Assembly requires two basic constitutional steps: bicameral passage of a legislative proposal and presentment of the proposal to the chief executive. In the first step, each chamber must approve the proposal by a majority vote (and at least two-fifths of the chamber's membership). The proposal as approved in each chamber must be identical in all respects, even in title and identifying number. In the second step, the proposal may become law after the chief executive signs the proposal or after ten days (Sundays excepted) if the governor takes no action. If the governor chooses to veto the proposal, the General Assembly may override the veto by a simple majority of the members of both chambers (twenty members in the Senate and fifty-one members in the House).

The constitution also places some additional restrictions on the legislative process that are not always found in the constitutions of other states. The constitution explicitly mentions the role of committees in Section 46, where the text reads, "No bill shall be considered for final passage unless the same has been reported by a committee and printed for the use of the members." Hence there is no way under the constitution to circumvent the legislative committees. Other restrictions include a prohibition on local or special legislation (Sections 59 and 60) and a ban on the release of debt owed to the Commonwealth or to any city or county (Section 52). The General Assembly also cannot diminish the resources of any sinking fund used to repay the debts of the Commonwealth (Section 48).

Legislative proposals can take the form of bills or resolutions. Bills are more general statements of policy. Resolutions apply to more specific official acts. Simple resolutions are introduced and approved by only one chamber. Concurrent resolutions are passed in each chamber and are presented to the chief executive but are not subject to signature or veto. Joint resolutions are passed in each chamber and are presented to the governor for signature or veto, with the exception of joint resolutions that propose constitutional amendments. Those are not subject to gubernatorial signature or veto but are presented to the voters for ratification. Only bills and joint resolutions are considered legally binding. However, rules for each chamber are established by simple resolution and are binding within the chamber.

Most bills or resolutions can originate in either chamber, but the constitution requires that bills to raise revenue must originate in the House. When a bill is proposed, it is assigned a number, read by title and sponsor, and then referred to a standing committee by the Committee on Committees, the same body that makes committee assignments of members and appoints committee chairs. The bill may or may not have a hearing. That decision is largely made by the committee chair. If a hearing is scheduled, the bill may be amended or reported out as originally written. The report may be favorable, unfavorable, or without opinion. A bill that is not reported out of committee dies at the end of the session. Interestingly, committees in each chamber are more likely to report a bill favorably when the bill originates in the other chamber than when the bill originates in their own chamber.[18]

Bills that are reported out favorably are placed in the legislative calendar for the following day. This reporting out is called "first reading." Bills that are recommended unanimously out of committee can be placed on the consent calendar, which should speed their eventual passage. After being reported out of committee, bills are read by title a second time and sent to the Rules Committee. The Rules Committee can place the bill in the Orders of the Day for a particular legislative day or can recommit the bill to the committee of origination. The majority floor leader makes a motion to have a bill taken from the Orders of the Day, read by title only, and placed on the floor for debate and possible passage. This motion, if approved (usually by voice vote), constitutes the third reading. Once on the floor, a bill or resolution can be debated and amended. For normal legislation, passage requires approval by at least two-fifths of the members of the chamber and a majority of those present and voting. Appropriations legislation requires a majority of those elected to the chamber (fifty-one in the House and twenty in the Senate). Emergency legislation, which can take effect immediately after enactment, requires approval from a majority of those elected to the chamber.[19]

Proposals that are defeated usually will not be brought up again during the same legislative session. Bills that pass in one chamber must go to the other chamber for consideration and approval. The process of committee referral, chamber consideration, and passage after third reading is much the same as if the proposal had originated in the second chamber. If the bill is approved in exactly the same form in which it was approved in the first chamber, it is sent to the governor for signature. If the bill passes in a different form, the differences must be eliminated before presentment can take place. One or both chambers can voluntarily and unilaterally accept the other chamber's version of the bill, or a conference committee can be assembled to iron out the differences in the bills. The conference committee is made up of members chosen from each chamber by the Committee on Committees of each chamber. After the conference committee reports a revised version of the bill, each chamber must approve the bill before presentment. The governor may approve the bill, veto the bill in its entirety, or veto particular portions of appropriations bills. The General Assembly may override the veto by a simple majority of the members elected to each chamber. Although vetoes are not common events, the veto process in Kentucky is procedurally much less difficult than in many other states and in the federal Congress.

The process of passing legislation seems complicated, with many opportunities for opponents of bills and resolutions to thwart passage. There are many steps in the process where interest groups and their lobbyists, as well as interested constituents, can intervene. But despite all the complexities of passage, quite a number of bills and resolutions are enacted into law. In recent years, over six hundred House bills and over two hundred Senate bills have been introduced each session (figures 3.1 and 3.2). Of these, about two hundred bills were passed (figure 3.3). Interestingly, the percentage of introduced bills that are passed has declined over the past decade (figure 3.4). Of the bills that are passed, most pass by overwhelming margins in each chamber. Although there is substantial party unity (with the notable exception of the Democrats in the Senate in the 2003 session), on the vote on third reading most bills pass by large margins with bipartisan support.[20] In short, it appears that most of the contentious issues never get to a vote on the floor of the chamber. Only about one-fifth of the bills that are introduced will pass (often in heavily amended form), but those that do will pass by a large vote margin.

Partisanship does emerge in the process of legislating, even if most roll-call votes on third reading do gain bipartisan support. Often that partisanship appears in hammering out differences in legislation that passes each chamber and sometimes in the disputes between the General Assembly and the governor (see chapter 5 by Paul Blanchard in this volume). One example is the relatively recent battle over funding of the state Medicaid program. In March 2011 Governor Steve Beshear called the General Assembly into special session to deal with a $139 million shortfall in the Medicaid

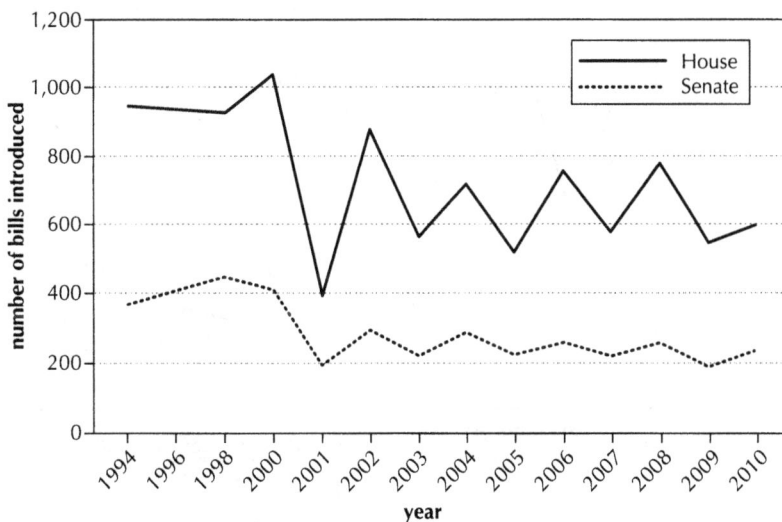

Figure 3.1. Bills introduced, by session

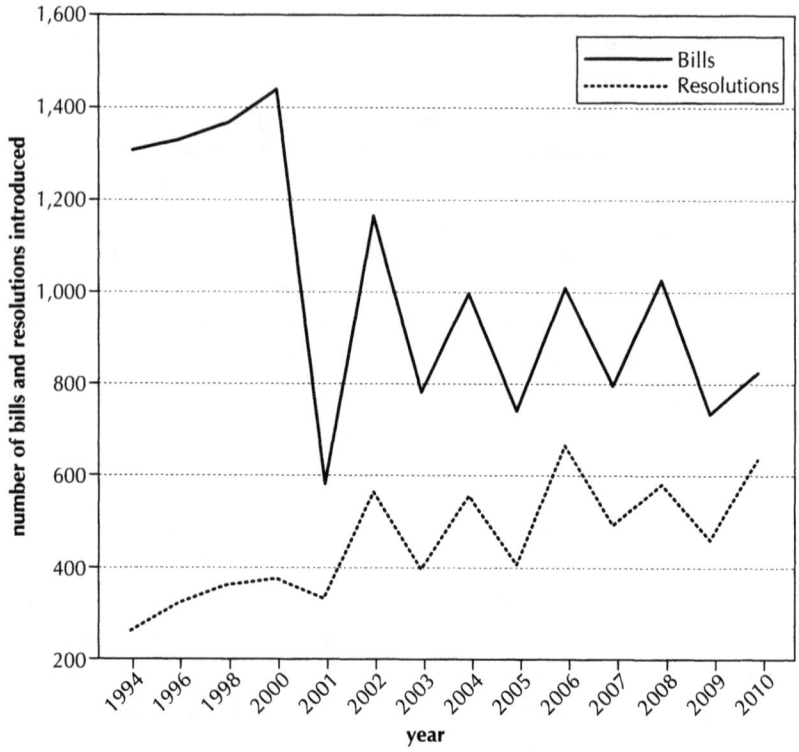

Figure 3.2. Bills and resolutions introduced, by session

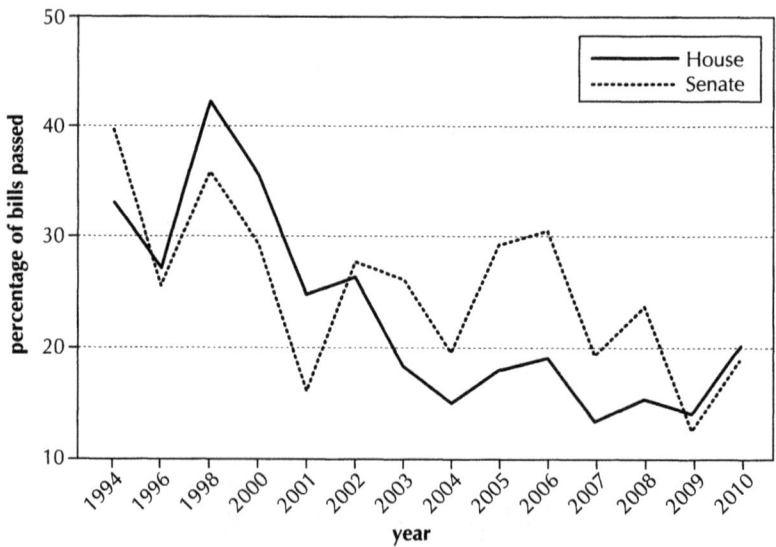

Figure 3.3. Percentage of House and Senate bills passed, by session

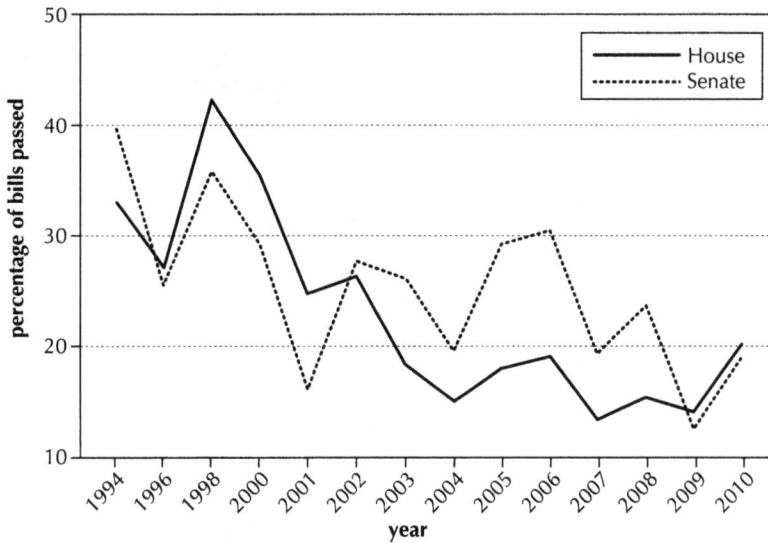

Figure 3.4. Percentage of introduced House and Senate bills passed, by session

budget. The Democratic governor and the House wanted to fill the gap by moving Medicaid money from the next fiscal year to the current fiscal year with the promise that cost-saving measures would cover the future cuts. The House initially adopted a bill that did essentially that. The GOP-controlled Senate, however, approved a bill that cut spending in various parts of state government to provide more spending on Medicaid if the governor could not generate documented savings in Medicaid for the next fiscal year. The House and Senate did not appear to be close to a solution for the impasse as the end of the special session approached, but eventually the House considered the Senate bill on the floor, at which time the Democratic majority floor leader, Rocky Adkins, read a letter from the governor. In the letter the governor pledged to prevent cuts in certain categories of state spending, particularly education, if the Senate plan passed.[21] The House voted to accept the Senate plan, whereupon the governor used his line-item-veto authority to remove the provisions that would have cut spending in areas outside Medicaid. Rather than consider an override of the governor's veto, the House adjourned. The Senate's Republican leadership tried to respond to the veto, but because the other chamber had adjourned, the Senate could not take any effective action before the special session expired. The budget crisis was averted, at least temporarily, but many Senate Republicans contended that the House vote was not made in good faith, and that the deal that the governor made only postponed the crisis for a year.[22]

The Kentucky General Assembly operates under a number of constraints imposed by constitutional restrictions and political realities. The structural constraints have been addressed to some extent in this chapter but are covered at greater length elsewhere in this volume (see chapter 1 by Robert Ireland). What is striking about these structural features is that they interact with political considerations to determine how the legislative

institution operates. For example, the bicameral design of the legislature and the constitutional requirement that new law be made only after approval by each chamber has
made it possible for one party or one strong ideological faction in one chamber to hold
new legislation hostage. If new law is to be made, as most observers would say it must,
proposals must garner support from diverse sets of policy makers seated in both ends
of the capitol. The constitutional design also requires that legislative proposals be presented to the governor. This adds one more step and one more opportunity for partisanship and ideology to shape the final outcome. In the case of the disputed Medicaid
budget, the additional institutional feature of the line-item veto made it possible for
the governor to circumvent the Senate's insistence on wide-ranging spending cuts in
several parts of state government. In effect, the governor's strategic action moved the
adopted policy back to a position close to that of the House bill that the Senate had
modified. This may have been necessary for the short-term budget crisis in Medicaid
to be averted, but it may be long remembered by the Senate. In the future, the Senate
may approve only bills that are written in a way that defies the use of the line-item
veto. In doing so, the partisans of one chamber may be preventing the partisans in the
other chamber or in the governor's mansion from manipulating the rules in their favor.

NOTES

1. *Fox v. Grayson*, 317 S.W.3d 1 (2010).

2. See *Stephenson v. Woodward*, 182 S.W.3d 162 (2005).

3. Paul E. Salamanca and James E. Keller, "The Legislative Privilege to Judge the Qualifications, Elections, and Returns of Members," *Kentucky Law Journal* 95 (2006–2007): 241–
383.

4. Calculated by the author from data at LRC website, http://www.lrc.state.ky.us/home
.htm.

5. Peverill Squire and Gary Moncrief, *State Legislatures Today: Politics under the Domes*
(Boston: Longman, 2010).

6. Calculated by the author from data at LRC website, http://www.lrc.state.ky.us/home
.htm.

7. Citizens Conference on State Legislatures, *The Sometime Governments: A Critical
Study of the 50 American Legislatures* (New York: Bantam Books, 1971).

8. Joseph Schlesinger, *Ambition and Politics: Political Careers in the United States* (Chicago: Rand McNally, 1971), 10.

9. Arthur T. Denzau and Michael C. Munger, "Legislators and Interest Groups: How
Unorganized Interests Get Represented," *American Political Science Review* 80 (March
1986): 89–106.

10. Peverill Squire, "Member Career Opportunities and the Internal Organization of Legislatures," *Journal of Politics* 50 (August 1988): 726–44.

11. Council of State Governments, *The Book of the States, 2010* (Lexington, Ky.: Council of
State Governments, 2011), http://knowledgecenter.csg.org/drupal/system/files/Table_3.9.pdf.

12. Martin Booe, "Ethics: Kentuckians Amazed That $400 Can Buy a Lawmaker," *Los
Angeles Times*, April 13, 1993, accessed June 4, 2013, http://articles.com/print/1993-04-13
/news/mn-22398_1_harness-racing-industry.

13. Calculated by the author from data at LRC website, http://www.lrc.state.ky.us/home.htm.

14. William J. Keefe. and Morris S. Ogul, *The American Legislative Process: Congress and the States* (Englewood Cliffs, N.J.: Prentice Hall, 1993), 197–98.

15. Gary W. Cox and Mathew D. McCubbins, *Legislative Leviathan: Party Government in the House* (Berkeley: University of California Press, 1993).

16. Calculated by the author from data at LRC website, http://www.lrc.state.ky.us/home .htm.

17. Marvin L. Overby, Thomas A. Kazee, and David W. Prince, "Committee Outliers in State Legislatures," *Legislative Studies Quarterly* 29 (February 2004): 81–107; David W. Prince and L. Marvin Overby, "Legislative Organization Theory and Committee Preference Outliers in State Senates," *State Politics and Policy Quarterly* 5 (Spring 2005): 68–87.

18. Malcolm E. Jewell and Penny M. Miller, *The Kentucky Legislature: Two Decades of Change* (Lexington: University Press of Kentucky, 1988), 115–30.

19. Legislative Research Commission, Commonwealth of Kentucky, http://www.lrc.ky.gov/ legproc.htm.

20. Joseph Gershtenson and Dennis L. Plane, "Polarization in American State Politics: The Case of Kentucky" (paper prepared for delivery at the annual meeting of the Southern Political Science Association in New Orleans, January 4–7, 2007).

21. Beth Musgrave and Jack Brammer, "Governor Gets His Way on Medicaid Fix: Beshear's Line-Item Vetoes Eliminate Spending Cuts, Enrage David Williams," *Lexington Herald-Leader*, March 3, 2011, A-3.

22. Ronnie Ellis, "Sorting Out Winners and Losers 3/27/11," *Richmond Register*, March 27, 2011, http://richmondregister.com/viewpoints/x1623045072/Sorting-out-winners-and-losers.

4

The Kentucky Executive Branch
Kendra B. Stewart and Thomas M. Martin

The second most powerful man in the United States, after the President of the United States, is the Governor of Kentucky.
—Attributed to Ed Prichard, 1970s

Since the early days of the Commonwealth, the Kentucky executive branch has been riddled with assassination, political scandal, and even a coup d'état. This chapter will explore both the institutional and personal aspects of the evolution of the Kentucky executive branch. The state has witnessed changes in organization, mission, and capacity of this important branch of government over the past hundred years. First, the electoral process and the political aspects of the state's chief executive officer will be analyzed. Next, this chapter examines the roles, functions, and powers (both formal and informal) of the Commonwealth's governor through a comparative perspective that identifies the similarities and differences between Kentucky's executive and that of other states. An often overlooked aspect of state government, the bureaucracy, will be introduced through an organizational and political perspective. Finally, after perspectives from a series of in-depth interviews with past governors and other lawmakers, this chapter brings to life the reality of how the Kentucky governor's office actually operates. The overarching question will be how all these players work together to wield the power of the state's executive branch of government.

ELECTING THE GOVERNOR

The first governor of Kentucky was elected in 1792 by electors chosen by the state senate. A second constitution was written and adopted just seven years later that provided for popular election of the governor and lieutenant governor. Over the next century two more constitutions were adopted. The fourth constitution, adopted in 1891, is the constitution under which the state operates today. The past several decades have witnessed increasing significance in the chief executive position in the fifty states. The twentieth century also demonstrated the importance of the governor's office as a launching pad for the White House. These two factors have led to greater interest and competition in seeking this statewide office. In general, the race for governor is the most competitive in a state, and Kentucky is no exception.

Nationwide, governors are almost twice as likely to lose their reelection campaigns as U.S. senators. In both incumbent and open-seat elections, the race for the top seat in the state is more likely to be hard fought than a Senate election.[1] The office of governor is at the top of the power structure and is highly sought after because of the recognition it provides to the officeholder. The citizens of a state are more likely to recognize their governor than either of their U.S. senators.[2]

Qualifications

To be eligible for the office of governor in Kentucky, a candidate must be at least thirty years of age and a citizen and resident of the state for at least six years. Until 1992 governors were ineligible to run for reelection for at least four years. The state constitution was amended at that time to allow governors to run for a second consecutive term. The only other limitation on holding this office is an anachronistic one that applies to all state offices in Kentucky and forbids anyone from holding office who has "either directly or indirectly, give[n], accept[ed] or knowingly carr[ied] a challenge to any person or persons to fight in single combat, with a citizen of this State, with a deadly weapon, either in or out of the State" (Kentucky Constitution of 1891, Section 239). On taking office even today, the governor must swear in the oath of office to have not partaken in a duel of any nature.

The American governorship is an office dominated by white men, and this is the case in the Bluegrass State as well. All but one of the fifty-seven Kentucky governors have been men, and all have been white. In general, this is a well-educated, politically connected, and wealthy group of individuals. See appendix A for a list of Kentucky's governors, their terms, and their political party affiliation.

The Election Process

Kentucky is one of only five states that hold gubernatorial elections in odd-numbered years, when there is no other national election taking place. The governor and lieutenant governor are elected on the same ticket, which is a recent phenomenon. According to Penny Miller, succession saves tax dollars and eliminates transition costs while reducing the constant change of focus and new agendas.[3] Gubernatorial candidates are selected by the parties through primary elections. Kentucky has a closed primary system, which requires voters to be registered for a party by December 31 of the previous year in order to vote in that party's primary. This is the most rigid form a primary can take and makes participation more difficult. Eleven other states also use this model to nominate candidates.[4]

Turnout for primary elections is quite low compared with that for the general election. For example, in the 2007 election approximately 550,000 voters turned out to cast ballots in the primary election. This number doubled for the general election less than six months later. The primary election generally takes place in May, with the general election following in November. The two major parties automatically receive a place on the ballot. Third-party candidates, however, must file a statement of candidacy and a nominating petition with the secretary of state's office no later than April 1 of the year in which the general election will be held if they would like to appear on the ballot. The nominating petition must be signed by at least 5,000 registered voters.

GUBERNATORIAL ROLES

The past several decades have seen an expansion in gubernatorial powers across all areas in each of the states.[5] These changes are a result of the devolution of federal government powers to the state and local levels that began in the 1980s. As federal funding for various programs decreased, state governments were forced to pick up the slack and therefore exert more power and control over various issues previously under the jurisdiction of the national government. Today governors are more concerned about the "substantive work of the office than its ceremonial aspects"[6] and "occupy a central position in domestic policymaking."[7]

Modern governors must "step into myriad roles," including chief legislator, chief executive, chief of state, chief of the party, and commander in chief.[8] These roles come with both formal and informal powers, and the capacity of the governor to perform in these roles essentially determines success in office. Governors who make the most of their time in the executive office understand what they are good at and focus on those roles that allow them to capitalize on their strengths.

Chief Legislator

Along with chief executive, chief legislator is considered one of the primary and essential roles of the governor.[9] It is in this capacity that the governor takes the lead in policy making. Although governors are not legislators and do not have the ability to introduce or vote on legislation, their ability to influence this process can determine how successful they are at accomplishing their agendas. Gubernatorial powers such as the ability to introduce the budget, deliver the state-of-the-state message, call the legislature into special session, and veto legislation provide the governor with a legal and formal role in the process. However, many argue that it is actually the informal powers that governors possess that most determine their success in this arena. These include the power to persuade, the governor's popularity with the people, the cohesiveness and influence of the governor's party, and a strong professional staff.[10]

Governors are most influential during the agenda-setting and policy-formulation phases of the process. More than any other actor, the governor is able to have something placed on the agenda because of the formal powers (delivering a state-of-the-state address and calling special sessions) and the informal powers (media attention, public popularity) of the office.[11] The public and the media look to the governor as the single leading actor in the state to set the course for Kentucky. The only formal power the governor has in the policy-formulation stage comes at the end of the process with the power to veto. The governor is totally reliant on the legislature to develop, revise, and pass policy. Throughout this part of the process the governor has to rely on the informal powers of persuasion and bargaining to wield influence. Governors do this by calling on members of their party for support, building coalitions, and offering favors to lawmakers such as constituent services, appointments, and political support. Success in this role is complex and is influenced by many factors. Bernick and Wiggins found in their study of executive-legislative relations that "governors do not define their roles and act in a vacuum," and that "consideration must be given to other factors including the behavior of lawmakers, as well as their perceptions of the appropriate gubernatorial role."[12] See chapter 5 by Paul Blanchard for more about how the Kentucky governor has evolved in this role.

Chief Executive

The Kentucky Constitution states that "the supreme executive power of the Commonwealth shall be vested in a Chief Magistrate, who shall be styled the 'Governor of the Commonwealth of Kentucky'" (Kentucky Constitution of 1891, Section 69). It is the job of the governor to ensure that "the laws be faithfully executed" (Section 81). This is the role that is most closely associated with the governor's office and the one that leads to the greatest challenges. In order to carry out the laws, the governor must rely on the bureaucracy to implement the policies. The size and complexity of the executive branch make this a difficult task. However, governors use their formal powers of appointment and reorganization to manage the bureaucracy effectively. Later in this chapter and in chapter 5 the bureaucracy will be explored in greater depth. One of the major powers the governor possesses to manage the executive branch is the executive order, which allows the governor to pass policy related to the executive branch without legislative approval. For a further discussion of the executive order, see chapter 11 by James C. Clinger.

Chief of State

Chief of state is the symbolic role the governor plays as the head of the state. Traditionally this was the major role of the governor—to serve as the official representative for the state, the "focal point for internal and external observers."[13] As chief of state, the governor takes care of ceremonial duties, such as ribbon cuttings, school openings, state celebrations, and greeting foreign delegates. Governors often enjoy this role because the events are generally uncontroversial and allow them the opportunity to receive media attention and remain in front of the public.

One example of the governor acting in this role is the power he has to award an individual the status of a Kentucky colonel (in conjunction with the secretary of state). The governor serves as commander in chief of this honorary organization and since 1813 has been signing the certificates to honor worthy men and women with this status.

Chief of Party

The governor is generally considered the head of his party. Although this is not an official job, it does stem from being the party's highest elected official at the state level.[14]

How successful the governor is in this role can often determine how successful he is in office. Because governors are now elected through the primary process rather than through a party meeting, the nomination of a gubernatorial candidate on behalf of a party no longer guarantees that that candidate is actually the preferred representative of the party. Before this process, when parties selected candidates, it was more likely that the nominee was the person whom the party viewed as its leader. Today this role is something that must be cultivated over time and regularly attended to while the governor is in office.

Governors can increase their value to the party by assisting with constituent services, ensuring that their agenda aligns with the party platform, campaigning and fund-raising on behalf of party members, and building strong coalitions to assist party members in achieving their goals. Having a united party is crucial for a governor in getting legislation passed and accomplishing his policy agenda.[15]

Commander in Chief

According to Kentucky law, "The Governor shall be commander in chief of the Kentucky Active Militia" (Kentucky Revised Statues [KRS] 37.180). This is a common duty of state governors, mirroring that of the U.S. president. Governors are responsible for the health and safety of their citizens and therefore during a crisis are able to exert extraordinary powers.[16] In Kentucky the adjutant general is the executive officer responsible to the governor for the "effective functioning of the Kentucky active militia" (KRS 37.180). The adjutant general oversees the Department of Military Affairs with over 8,400 soldiers and airmen. What makes the National Guard unique is its dual mission to serve both the state and federal governments. The governor has the power to call out the guard during times of crisis in Kentucky and to assist communities in disaster recovery. In addition, the guard trains to assist the federal government in combat and peacetime missions.[17] The importance of the National Guard has become more visible since September 11, 2001, because of the role it has played in deploying troops to support the U.S. military in Afghanistan and Iraq.

During man-made and national disasters the state looks to the governor to step forward and lead. In Kentucky the governor is granted far-reaching power during times of crisis. The governor has the power to declare, in writing, a state of emergency and at that point may assume direct operational control of all disaster and emergency response activities in the state, require all state and local agencies to respond to the disaster as directed, seize property—including firearms, ammunition, means of transportation, medicines, and fuel—for public protection, impose curfews, give pharmacists emergency authority to issue prescriptions, and, on the recommendation of the secretary of state, reschedule the time and place of elections in the affected areas (KRS 39A.100).

Although declaring a state of emergency is not a common event during a governorship, it does happen. For example, Governor Steve Beshear declared a state of emergency in Kentucky on July 21, 2010, after severe storms struck Pike and Shelby Counties. The storms caused flash flooding, evacuations, and water rescues in several northeastern Kentucky counties. President Obama granted federal disaster assistance for Pike County two days after the governor's declaration. Over the next several days he also granted relief for Shelby, Carter, Lewis, Elliott, Madison, Mason, and Rowan Counties. Federal assistance included "grants for temporary housing and home repairs, low-cost loans to cover uninsured property losses, and other programs to help individuals and business owners recover from the effects of the disaster."[18]

GUBERNATORIAL POWERS

The American distrust of executive powers is reflected in the lack of formal powers possessed by early governors. State constitutions severely limited gubernatorial power and forced governors to use their informal powers in order to be effective. Since 1985 every state has made statutory or constitutional changes granting their governors more formal powers.[19] Because of this growth in formal powers, along with a surge in prestige and media attention, there has also been an increase in the informal powers of state chief executives. Gubernatorial powers exist to ensure that the chief executive has the ability to fulfill the above-mentioned roles successfully. Although both formal and informal powers play a critical role in gubernatorial success, environmental conditions can have significant influence as well.

Formal Powers

Formal powers are those granted to the office through the state constitution or statutes. Political scientist Joseph Schlesinger developed an index to measure gubernatorial powers in order to rank state governors on the basis of the formal powers granted to them.[20] This index measures only four formal powers: budgetary power, appointment power, tenure, and veto power. Although this index has been criticized over time, it still remains a widely used lens for understanding the official power of a state's chief executive. Today this index does not reflect the broadened range of powers granted to modern governors. According to Schlesinger, the governor of Kentucky fell somewhere in the middle (twenty-second) of the fifty states regarding the amount of power the office possessed. In this section seven measures of formal powers will be explored: appointment, budget, tenure, veto, reorganization, pardons and clemency, and the election of other statewide officials.

Appointment In order to execute the laws of the state successfully, a modern governor needs a bureaucracy to manage and oversee the process. Although the majority of public servants in the bureaucracy do not serve at the will of the governor and are protected from losing their jobs because of partisan loyalty, the governor does have the authority to appoint a large number of individuals to executive agencies and boards and commissions. This power allows the governor to infuse his political ideology and policy platform into the state bureaucracy with the hope of accomplishing what he promised during his campaign for the office. The appointment power has traditionally been recognized as a strength of the Kentucky governor because many appointments do not need legislative approval. According to the Kentucky Office of Boards and Commissions, the governor appoints over 6,000 positions, with Governor Beshear having appointed 2,800 in his first three years (a ten-page list of board and commission appointments can be found at the Office of the Governor's website).

Governors use a variety of criteria in determining their appointees, such as party, demographics, geography (where appointees are from in the state), expertise, and political and personal support. Appointments can often be used as rewards for campaign work or favors in exchange for support from state legislators.

Budget The ability to craft a statewide spending plan is an important power of any governor. The state budget sets out financial priorities and shapes public discussion on the policies for the year. An executive budget also forces all state agencies to go through the governor's office to request funding. According to early studies, the Kentucky governor has traditionally been viewed as very strong in this aspect.[21] The governor proposes a biennial budget every two years to the General Assembly, and until just a few decades ago the governor's budget was often approved with very little change.[22] Today the state legislature has unlimited power to change the budget regardless of the governor's proposal. However, in the end it is the governor who both has the veto power and is charged with administering the majority of the budget through state agencies. Enabling legislation is generally broad and lacks specifics on how programs should be carried out in spending the funds provided. Therefore, the governor of Kentucky is able to influence the state budget at both the beginning and the end of the process.

Tenure Schlesinger included tenure in office in his index, arguing that the length of time a governor can serve in office influences his power.[23] As previously mentioned, the governor of Kentucky can serve up to two four-year terms. Before 1992 the governor was not eligible to run for consecutive terms in office but could run again after sitting out a term. This was one of the weaker areas for the Kentucky governor in the power index. Governors with unlimited tenure are able to exert greater influence on the legislature and are not riddled with lame-duck years near the end of their term. Instead of preparing a budget in his first month in office and then becoming a lame duck after the first legislative session, Kentucky's governor now has the "luxury of thinking and planning beyond the four-year horizon of a single term."[24] The succession amendment also enhanced the governor's power by providing that the governor retains his or her power while out of the state, as well as putting the governor and lieutenant governor on the same ticket, reducing conflict between the two offices. As of the writing of this book, only two governors (Paul Patton and Steve Beshear) have been elected to serve two consecutive terms in the chief executive's office.

Veto The final power on Schlesinger's index is the power to veto legislation. It is the single most important power the governor possesses in influencing state legislation.[25]

As Charles Cameron notes, although the veto is rarely used, it does help the executive shape the content of important legislation.[26] When the government is divided, the executive has a strong incentive to use the veto because different policy preferences are on the table. With the veto the executive can shape or block legislation—shape legislation in the sense that the executive impresses his preferences on policy with the veto threat, block legislation in the sense that the legislature cannot override the veto threat. If the executive threatens a veto from a position of power, the general assembly can craft legislation to head off a veto threat but has to address the executive's preferences to do so.

At the end of the twentieth century every state offered its governor some type of veto power (North Carolina was the lone holdout until 1995). In determining the strength of a veto, several factors are considered: line-item or package veto, majority or supermajority to override, and the ability to pocket veto. A package veto is an all-or-nothing approach—the governor either vetoes the entire bill or accepts it. A line-item veto allows the governor to reject just parts of a bill. The 1891 constitution grants the governor of Kentucky the line-item veto, but only in appropriation bills. The greater the number of votes needed by the General Assembly to override a gubernatorial veto, the more power granted to the governor in this arena. Thirty-seven states require a supermajority of two-thirds or three-fifths of both houses to override a governor's veto. Kentucky requires a simple majority of those elected in both houses, so it is easier for the state legislature to overcome the governor's rejection. If the governor does not sign nor veto a bill within ten days (Sundays excepted) of receiving it, the bill automatically becomes law. If the legislature adjourns within the ten days, the bill still becomes law unless the governor vetoes it within ten days of adjournment. Under Schlesinger's index, it appears that the veto power of the governor of Kentucky is relatively moderate in influence compared with the powers of other states' governors.

The gubernatorial veto is generally most effective when it is used sparingly. It is most often used as a threat before legislation is passed to send a message to the General Assembly about some aspect of a bill the governor does not support. However, once a veto threat is made, the governor must stand by it if the bill is passed in order to use the threat viably again in the future. The overall popularity of a governor can often be seen in the number of his vetoes that stand—the weaker the governor, the more likely a veto will be overridden.

Reorganization The power to reorganize allows a governor greater control over the executive branch and is possessed by only about half the governors in the United States. This power provides the governor the opportunity to arrange the bureaucracy in a manner that will give him the greatest political influence. The governor of Kentucky has the right to reorganize and reduce the size of government and number of state employees. The major reorganizations of the Kentucky bureaucracy are discussed at the end of this chapter. Many governors come into office with a view about the role of government in Kentucky and use this power to organize the bureaucracy around that view. For example, Governor Ernie Fletcher had nine cabinet agencies in 2006, which Governor Beshear expanded to eleven when he took office in 2007. Governor Beshear changed Fletcher's Commerce Cabinet into the Tourism, Arts, and Heritage Cabinet, added a Labor Cabinet, and created two separate agencies (Energy and Environment Cabinet and Public Protection Cabinet) out of Fletcher's Environmental and Public Protection Cabinet.

Pardons and Reprieves Before states created pardon and parole systems, the only way for a prisoner to be released early from his sentence was through a gubernatorial pardon. The majority of states (thirty-three) give their governors exclusive and unconditional power to grant pardons or reduce prison sentences.[27] A pardon is a get-out-of-jail-free card that releases a convicted criminal from jail and clears his record. This is traditionally seen as the executive branch's check on the judiciary and has on occasion been used illegally.

According to the Kentucky Constitution, the governor has the "power to remit fines and forfeitures, commute sentences, grant reprieves and pardons, except in case of impeachment" (Kentucky Constitution of 1891, Section 77). A governor who does so must issue a statement of the reasons for his decision, which is to be posted with the secretary of state for public examination. Although the governor has the power to remit fines, this does not apply to fees of the clerk, sheriff, or attorney general in penal or criminal cases.

Statewide Elective Offices An additional measure of formal power is how many other constitutional officers are elected statewide. These positions hold power separate from the governor and often compete with the governor over control of various issues. Other offices potentially elected separate from the governor include the lieutenant governor, secretary of state, attorney general, state auditor, treasurer, comptroller general, secretary of agriculture, and adjutant general.

Citizens in Kentucky elect the governor and the lieutenant governor on the same ticket, and thus the governor has the opportunity to exert influence over this office. In addition, five other officers are elected: the attorney general, the commissioner of agriculture, the state auditor, the secretary of state, and the treasurer. Since the 1990s the power of these state constitutional offices has begun to erode slightly.

Other Formal Powers Other formal powers exist that strengthen the governor's ability to be influential. The constitution gives the governor the sole power to call the General Assembly into session on "extraordinary occasions" and set the agenda. Members can take into consideration only the subjects set forward in the governor's convening written proclamation (Kentucky Constitution of 1891, Section 80). Although there can be negotiation between the governor and General Assembly in setting the agenda, the governor does have the power to prevent action preferred by the legislature by not permitting an issue to be considered. The governor also delivers a state-of-the-commonwealth message annually to the General Assembly in order to "recommend to their consideration such measures as he may deem expedient" (Kentucky Constitution of 1891, Section 79). These two powers allow the governor to exert influence on the legislative process. The state constitution also allows the governor to "require information in writing from officers of the Executive Department upon any subject relating to the duties of their respective offices" (Kentucky Constitution of 1891, Section 78).

The governor has several institutional advantages that can help him further his preferences.[28] First, the governor has unity of direction—one voice—his or her own. The governor has to convince only himself of a policy or program that he wants to pursue and is not constrained by having to persuade other political actors, for example, another legislator, to support a policy. Consider for a moment the difference between a state representative or state senator wanting to get legislation passed and a governor. Whom do you have to get on board for your idea? What coalitions will it require to guarantee smooth sailing through the legislative process? How do you get the governor on board?

Second, the governor is always in session, unlike the General Assembly, which meets for several weeks at the beginning of the year. This year-round job description provides the governor with an additional advantage: information asymmetry—having information at his disposal that the legislative branch does not have simply because the legislators are not in Frankfort to have access to the information. They are back in their districts, doing the things they do for the other forty-odd weeks of the year.

Third, the governor has information about the entire state. Representatives represent only certain districts and could care less about other districts because those districts cannot get them elected, but the governor's constituency is the entire state.

Finally, the governor has first-mover advantage over the legislative branch and benefits from the collective-action problem of the General Assembly. Howell contends that the ability to move first and act alone is distinguished from "all other sources of influence . . . the virtual antithesis of bargaining and persuading."[29]

Informal Powers

In addition to formal powers that are associated with the office, governors have informal, personal powers that are "resources related to the person holding the office rather than the office itself."[30] In studying the U.S. chief executive, Richard Neustadt found that one of the president's greatest tools is his power to persuade.[31] Governors with weak formal powers are sometimes able to compensate when they are effective at using their informal powers. These powers differ substantially from governor to governor and are difficult to measure. It is important to note that formal and informal gubernatorial powers interact, and that a governor with a "strong personal power base can make far better use of the formal powers."[32] Scholars do not agree on a single list of informal powers, so they vary from one author to another. The following are some of the more common informal powers frequently discussed in studies of the state chief executive officer: knowledge and skill, public popularity, and communication and the media.

Knowledge and Skill The background experience and capabilities a governor brings to the office can provide one source of informal power. Expert knowledge in a particular subject area can lead others (such as lawmakers) to defer to the governor on specific issues. Additionally, governors with general knowledge about the system and how it works are at an advantage compared with governors who lack this understanding. For example, a governor with legislative experience will have a better appreciation for and awareness of what makes a governor effective in influencing legislation.[33] Governors bring different types of knowledge to the office, which can help determine in which roles they will be most successful.

It also takes a variety of skills to navigate the various roles and responsibilities of the governor's office. These skills come from both a governor's natural abilities and past experiences. Most governors come to the office unprepared and are forced to learn fast. Therefore, those with a bigger bank of skills tend to be more successful.[34] One skill in particular that has been studied is management. In his analysis of this role in gubernatorial leadership, Raymond Cox found that the "management skill now is recognized as an interpersonal quality that must be present in the governor, rather than as an attribute of the structure of government," and that "success as a manager is a necessary, though not sufficient, condition for overall success in the office."[35]

The most common skill referenced in studies of informal powers is that of persuasion. A governor's ability to bargain and persuade others to support his perspective can play a crucial role in both policy making and implementation. This is especially important when a governor lacks formal powers and has no authority to force various actors to comply with his agenda. The power of persuasion was first studied in regard to the presidency,[36] but now it is widely recognized as an essential skill for gubernatorial success as well.

Public Popularity Governors often use their popularity as leverage, especially with the legislature. On the same note, legislators may not want to associate themselves with the policies of an unpopular governor. Popularity is regularly measured through public opinion polls by various polling and media organizations. The most commonly asked question is whether one approves or disapproves of the job the governor is doing. Generally, the higher the approval rating, the more likely the legislature is to support the governor's initiatives. Popularity is usually highest during the governor's honeymoon period when he is first elected to office. It then tends to decline slowly through the remainder of the term, occasionally picking back up near the end. So many factors affect a governor's popularity that it is often beyond his control, although some circumstances, such as a scandal, can have a severe effect on a governor's popularity.

Communication and the Media It was the evolution of television that helped launch chief executives (at both the federal and state levels) onto the center stage of politics. The governor is an easy target (both good and bad) for the media as the single head figure of the executive branch. Press coverage can influence public opinion both negatively and positively. Governors need to be good communicators to come across well in the press. The media allow the governor an opportunity to address the citizens of the state directly. Effective governors selectively use these opportunities to try to sway public opinion in favor of a particular issue they are supporting.

EVOLUTION AND STRUCTURE OF THE EXECUTIVE BRANCH

Although the constitution of 1891 designates the governor as the chief executive officer, it is very vague about what actual powers come with this charge. To address this issue, the constitution authorizes the General Assembly to determine the governor's administrative powers. This did not come to fruition until the twentieth century with the passage of the 1936 Reorganization Act.[37] Before this legislation the structure of the executive branch was set forth in the evolving state constitutions and was composed mostly of boards and commissions not accountable to the governor. In 1934 the Kentucky executive branch consisted of sixty-nine different boards, commissions, and agencies in addition to the constitutional offices.[38] All this changed two years later. The passage of the Reorganization Act of 1936 is a good example of a governor using his formal powers in a significant way. Governor A. B. Chandler called the state legislature into special session with the directive of bringing together in a systematic and orderly way the multiplicity of boards and commissions that were scattered across the executive branch.[39] The General Assembly complied with the governor's proclamation and passed the first major statewide reorganization effort. As a result, the majority of the boards and commissions were abolished, over fifty agencies were organized into ten departments, and a gubernatorial cabinet was created. This legislation provided the Kentucky governor, for the first time, with the statutory authority needed to manage the executive branch effectively.

As the demand for government services grew, so did the executive branch. From 1944 through 1960, fourteen new departments were created. By 1972 Governor Wendell Ford found himself in a situation similar to that of Governor Chandler thirty-six years earlier. At this time the executive branch had grown to over 60 departments and agencies and 210 boards and commissions falling under the jurisdiction of the governor.[40] Governor Ford issued a reorganization report creating six cabinet departments and a framework for an executive branch that would be more manageable and accountable. As of 2012 this has grown to eleven cabinet departments with three additional cabinet-rank members under the office of Governor Beshear.[41] Each cabinet agency is headed by a secretary who serves at the will of the governor. Several Kentucky statutes (KRS 12.029, 12.040, 12.050, 12.060, and others) give the governor the authority necessary to appoint agency directors and board and commission members; appoint advisory committees; prescribe rules of conduct for agencies; resolve conflicts among agencies; and oversee the executive branch with authority. More on public administration in Kentucky can be found in chapter 7 by Murray Bessette.

Although the governor today does have the appropriate and necessary authority to supervise the state bureaucracy, it is still a daunting task to reconcile citizen demands with gubernatorial services. In his book on state governors, Robert Behn observes, "The ultimate challenge of being a governor is to discover, among competing and often conflicting demands for service and within constrained resources and powers, the opportunity for state government to deliver those public services that the citizens most want and need."[42]

KENTUCKY GOVERNORS' PERSPECTIVES

By studying the Commonwealth's governing documents and statutes and scholarly research, we can develop a good understanding of the institutional aspects of the Kentucky executive branch. However, only from the experiences of inside players can we appreciate the true workings of the office. In order to address this, we conducted a series of in-depth interviews with past governors, lawmakers, and staffers to contrast the theories of executive power with the realities of that power for Kentucky's governor. We were interested in knowing how the Kentucky governor went from being one of the most powerful politicians in the United States to a governor who has been neutered by the legislative branch. From there, we identified which formal powers worked for the executive, which did not, how important bargaining and persuasion were, and how the political actors work together—and at odds—to shape the power of the state's executive branch of government.

Every living governor was asked for an interview. The following governors graciously agreed to be interviewed: Wendell Ford (who served from 1971 to 1974), Julian Carroll (who served from 1974 to 1979 and is now a member of the Kentucky Senate), John Y. Brown (1979 to 1983), Brereton Jones (1991 to 1995), Paul Patton (1995 to 2003), and Ernie Fletcher (2003 to 2007). Two prominent legislators were interviewed to gain their perspectives on executive power. Senator Ed Worley served as a member of the Kentucky Senate from 1999 to 2010, representing the Thirty-Fourth District, and was minority floor leader from 2003 to 2010. Senator R. J. Palmer succeeded Senator Worley as minority floor leader and has served in the Kentucky Senate since 2001. He also served in the House from 1999 to 2001. We also interviewed Tom Dorman, the chief of staff for Rep. Rocky Adkins, majority floor leader in the House of Representatives. Dorman's institutional knowledge of Frankfort stretches back to the early 1970s. Finally, Trey Grayson, Kentucky secretary of state from 2003 to 2011 and currently the director of the Harvard Institute of Politics at Harvard University, was interviewed.

LEGISLATIVE INDEPENDENCE

Before 1980 the governor of Kentucky could be said to rule with an iron fist. As Governor Patton noted, legislators did not have the institutional capacity to compete with the governor; they "just had the desks on the floor and that was it." Legislators had no staff to speak of except for the leadership, whose staff was basically "inconsequential." The legislature had neither the capacity to do research nor the administrative help that the governor had. Therefore, governors were able to wield substantial power because of this inherent weakness in the legislature.

The institutional structure at the time also tilted decisively toward the executive branch. Governor Carroll recalled, "When I was Speaker of the House, I wrote all the rules in the House—I appointed all the committee chairmen in the House. Then I go to the Senate as president of the Senate as lieutenant governor and rewrite the rules of the Senate and appoint the chairmen in the Senate. When I get to the governor's mansion, the chairs I appointed are still there generally, and they were all my friends. As governor, I got what I wanted. I won all the battles."

Governor Ford suggested that the governor had still another institutional advantage. Because the governor could use the veto within the last nine days of the session, "He could veto and the legislature could not come back into session and override his veto if the governor waited until the last nine days. . . . You didn't have time to override. So, if the governor wanted something and you wanted something you probably yielded to the governor and the governor signed your bill" that was crafted toward his preferences. Today, however, the General Assembly generally passes all the bills that it plans on passing in a given session ten days before the constitutional session limit, leaving time to convene to override any gubernatorial veto.

From the legislative perspective, Ed Worley added that "the legislature didn't have a Legislative Research Commission, they had no brains other than 138 laypeople that showed up in Frankfort and out of that 138 you might have 10 percent of them that would spend enough time and energy and work with the administration, work with the cabinet secretaries, and have enough longevity in Frankfort where they could compete and debate the role of state government." Because of that institutional weakness in the General Assembly, the governor and the governor's staff had greater influence.

Tom Dorman noted that ". . . during Wendell Ford's administration, if a legislator wanted to pass a bill he had to go ask the governor for permission to pass it. Legislators used to carry around little slips into committee meetings that were instructions from the governor on what they should do in that committee meeting."

According to Governor Carroll, the critical moment in the changing dynamics of gubernatorial-legislative relations occurred when John Y. Brown became governor.

> The seed of change really took off when he [Governor Brown] was governor, because he told the leadership they could pick their own members. He wasn't very involved in the legislative process. The legislature had so much freedom, they enjoyed their new power and they started to whittle away at the power of the governor. For example, I had . . . a $2 million discretionary fund in the governor's office that was not designated for any purpose other than for me to spend. I sent ball teams on trips, I sent marching bands to Washington, D.C.— I've bought vehicles for senior citizens. If I had a legislator that came to me that had a request that made sense, that sounded reasonable to me, then I would write a check out of my contingency fund. One of the first things that John Y. [Brown] said was, "I don't want a contingency fund," and the legislature took it out of the budget. Do you think one has been back since?

Senator Worley added that Governor Brown "didn't want to get involved in the election of legislative leaders and for the first time it was truly an independent process. When [that happened,] the legislature decided to provide themselves offices, facilities, technology, the research ability and a committee system that was structured to compete with the governor."

Governor Patton argued that there was another factor working when Governor Brown came into office.

> At the same time there was brewing in the legislature an independent streak by some very capable legislators, particularly in the Senate . . . calling themselves the "Black Sheep."[43] When Brown came into office, a lot of people think that he

voluntarily released the legislature. From my information . . . that wasn't the case. The Black Sheep already had enough votes to control leadership and Brown didn't have the political experience or will to try to fight that. . . . There used to be prelegislative conferences down at the Kentucky Dam Village. All the legislators would go down there, the lobbyists would go down there and have a weeklong party and elect their leadership. Typically, the governor would be working the halls to get the right leadership in place. Brown came into one of the cabins where several of the Black Sheep were staying and said, "Well, do you have the votes?" and Ford [Senator Ed Ford] suggest [sic] he had them and Brown said, "Well if you got them, you got them." From that point on the legislature now had the capacity to exert the authority that it has.

Governor Brown's philosophy of the role of the governor was fundamentally different from that of other governors. "I get along with all the governors. I just disagree with their approach. I had a great distaste for politics and the way it was run. . . . I did not want to be kingmaker." Governor Brown also had a unique perspective on what the governor should accomplish, arguing that the executive branch does not have the expertise or the time to run the state, as had been done before him. "I had a lot of people that thought like I did—we all had a distaste for politics, for the dishonesty, the deal making, so we didn't want to tolerate anything that had any kind of political overtones. When working with the legislature, they always wanted me to promise them a road or a bridge and I wouldn't do any of that, that which had been done before."

EXECUTIVE POWER

Although scholars do not have a definitive list of informal powers available to the governor, it is clear that the work originated by Neustadt and continued by others has sparked debate throughout the entire political system.[44] Neustadt observed when describing executive power that "'weak' remains the word with which to start."[45] Because of the institutional weakness of the executive, Neustadt theorized that the essence of a president's persuasive task in an environment of separate institutions sharing power was to bargain with his counterparts.

Formal Powers

When interviewees were asked about the formal powers of the Kentucky governor, there was no consensus about which constitutional or statutory power of the governor was his most effective weapon. Secretary Grayson considered several to be influential. "One lever that the Kentucky governor can use is the appointment power. There are so many people who serve on certain boards, there are so many certain constituencies that are influenced by boards or governed by boards, that the ability to put people on those boards and get 'paid back'—not illegally or unethically—but then to take the political capital and use it for other purposes like reelection or to help him get a bill passed." Governor Carroll echoed the significance of the appointment power, commenting that "the appointing authorities that the governor has, banking, medical board, CPE [Council on Postsecondary Education], racing, etc., is around five thousand appointments [Governor Carroll was not far from the mark; the number is six thousand]. I would make ten appointments per day. Sometimes I would have to take them home with me at night, there were so many. The reason I mention that is that legislators are notorious for wanting someone appointed to those positions and you can use that as leverage for bargaining." This is a prime example of a gubernatorial formal power being enhanced by the informal power of bargaining.

Governor Fletcher believed that the governor has tremendous constitutional power because the budget is not self-actuating, which means that when the legislature leaves town, the governor has full discretion to implement the budget in any way he or she sees fit, within spending limits. The governor cannot spend more than is authorized, but he can spend it on his own timeline and does not have to spend it all. "The governor also has a plethora of choices of projects to choose from. That power can conceivably be used to either reward or punish legislators, although there is not a lot of that done these days because of increased scrutiny. . . . I think it's the most overriding power that the governor has."

Although Governor Patton was generally disdainful of his constitutional powers, he agreed with Governor Fletcher about the influence that control over the budget could provide. Patton explained, "When the 1998 session came, we had money . . . the revenue was much higher than expected. We had money in the bank, we had that uncommitted recurring spending capacity, and that precipitated an increased bonding capacity. We had cash to spend, new programs to implement, and we had ongoing money that we could spend—I introduced pork to Frankfort." Tom Dorman, Governor Patton's legislative liaison, added: "In one of his budgets, Governor Patton allocated so many hundreds of thousands of dollars for Senate members and so many thousands of dollars for House members and we were in charge of calling these legislators to find out what they want to spend this money on. And no surprise, they passed Patton's budget."

Governor Jones's assessment of his formal power was similar to the way scholars might teach it in class, where the governor impresses his preferences on the legislative branch.

The ability to call the General Assembly back into session. Legislators like to say, "Well, he can call us in, but we'll just adjourn"—and that is fine, but I found it to be very effective. They don't want to be bothered as part-time legislators, having to keep coming back for special sessions. Second, it communicates to the voting public that my legislator doesn't want to go to work. If the legislator complains, that sends a message to the public that they don't want to go to Frankfort to do something to help make the state better or make my life better and my legislator is balking. That is a real negative for the next election for that legislator. The governor should never allow anyone—the press or members of his own party—to talk him out of using that power as an important use of his authority.

Like those of Governor Jones, Senator Worley's comments on executive power read like a discussion of information asymmetry and first-mover advantage, those unilateral powers that are reserved for the executive just by the nature of the office. The governor has expertise, experience, and information—both in the institutional structure and the bureaucracy—that the legislative branch cannot match, and the ability to act first and alone allows the governor to be the first to reveal his preferences, not only to the General Assembly but also to the press and the public:

> The most powerful document in Frankfort is developing the budget outside of any legislative agenda that the governor may have. Whether a student can drop out of school at sixteen or eighteen, those are philosophical positions that are significant to people in Kentucky, but nothing is more significant or has more far-reaching implications as the budget. The governor has first run at the budget and has access to the information. He has the cabinet secretaries, the budget office, the state budget director, he has all the initial information. The legislature has the LRC [Legislative Research Commission] that has a lot of smart people, but they are always chasing the information, to determine whether it's accurate or inaccurate.
>
> He gets the first shot at establishing the priorities of the administration and where money should be spent and allocated. This reaches into all aspects of education, Medicaid, Medicare, the whole medical infrastructure of rural Kentucky, all the prisons. So the governor's formal power is that he has immediate access to all information regarding receipts and expenditures within state government and gets to use it twice in his administration and in the annual sessions. He actually has the ability to set off alarms, to convince the legislature and convince the media and convince the people across Kentucky that there needs to be tweaking of those budgets, and while annual sessions were never intended to have budget implications, they are turning that way, because of the executive branch.

Having said that, Senator Worley affirmed that although the ability to propose a budget is theoretically beneficial and has practical, significant application, it is still a function of separate institutions that share power. "In the 2010 and '12 sessions, the governor submitted his budget request, but I don't think anyone looked at it. It is only a budget of recommendation." Once the budget is passed, the power can strategically flow back to the governor. Senator Worley continued, "When we leave Frankfort, the advantages switch back to the governor because he gets to implement the budget. A lot of governors will interpret the legislative intent to mean what they want it to mean instead of what it was intended to mean." He says that the legislature has adjusted for the governor's strategy, and the result has been a budget memorandum "that has grown 100 percent in the last ten years, because the legislature does not buy into the governor's game of 'I didn't know what you wanted me to do.' The budget memorandum carries very explicit written instructions to what the governor is supposed to do with that money so the governor does not have the latitude to broadly interpret legislative intent."

Governor Patton was the most cynical regarding his constitutional powers. He emphasized this by explaining,

> I can propose the first budget but they don't have to go by that. Calling the legislature to special session doesn't work unless you have the executive and the legislature agreeing on the agenda. The pardon has no effect whatsoever. The veto is practically worthless. Any veto I made was for the leadership to come to me and say, "We made a mistake with this bill—would you veto it? There will not be any resistance." There were a couple of issues that I knew were going to be overridden, but just on a matter of principle I vetoed it. Otherwise the veto has very little significance for the governor.

Governor Patton's comments and those of the other former governors and political actors emphasize that over the past several decades the Kentucky chief executive office has experienced a loss of power that has enabled the legislative branch to exert more influence on the political landscape of the Commonwealth.

Informal Powers

Unlike the discussion of formal power, there was unanimous consent about bargaining and persuasion—they were critical to impress a governor's preferences on the legislature. Governor Carroll got right to the point when he said, "Constitutionally, [the governor] is the chief executive . . . *but in my opinion, his strength was not of the constitution as such, so much as his persuasive power.* . . . The constitutional powers of the governor are important, but the General Assembly is looking over the governor's shoulder more. *The real power base of the governor is his persuasive ability, the building of relationships with the legislature and the public, strengthens your persuasive power. The constitutional power of the governor alone is not sufficient to get accomplished what is necessary.*"

Senator Palmer agreed, "Bargaining and persuasion—that's what the process is. Government works best when you have three branches of government that are independent and separate. We do the same thing in the legislative branch—trying to convince the executive branch to view our agenda favorably and help us move it forward." Governor Ford added more context: "If you're able to persuade, it matters little what other powers you have, if you can persuade people to agree with you or pass laws. Henry Clay said that compromise was 'negotiated hurt.' If you get something where you could pass it and it hurts you a little bit and it hurts your partner a little bit—because you're giving up something and your negotiating partner's giving up something—and want to get the agreement, then you move forward with the legislation that's in front of you."

Governor Patton's years as county judge-executive in Pike County helped him understand the role of a public official who has to share power and the need for persuasion to get one's goals accomplished:

Well my view is that the governor's office has two purposes—one is to administer the public policy that has been established by the legislature, whether you
agree with that policy or not, and the second is to attempt to change the public
policy if you think change is warranted by convincing the people, then convincing the legislature to change the policy. The legislature's authority is clear and
that is to establish the public policy of the commonwealth. Its second responsibility is to oversee the governor and administration of that policy. That's the
part the governors don't like too well, but that's a fact of life.

Now, how each branch executes those responsibilities is up to them. The most
important thing that the governor has to understand is the legislature makes the
final decision and once you get that in your head, then you try to use your areas of
influence and powers of persuasion to get them to agree to what you want.

I think I understood that going into office because I had been county judge
for ten years. I learned real quick that I had to have the votes of the members of
the fiscal court. The county judge works totally on the orders of the court . . . the
authority to hire somebody, the authority to spend money . . . those orders . . .
[came from] the court. And that helped me to have a relatively good relationship
with the legislature.

One feature of Kentucky politics that may have diminished the governor's informal
powers was mentioned by Secretary Grayson, who suggested that the decline of statewide media coverage of politics limited the chief executive's power to persuade legislators. "If you are in Murray, Kentucky, you are closer to the St. Louis media market
than you are to Frankfort." Secretary Grayson hails from northern Kentucky, where
there is little or no coverage of Frankfort politics. "The whole media market [in northern Kentucky] is anchored around what happens in Cincinnati. The local television
stations and the radio stations never cover Frankfort. The local newspaper doesn't
have a dedicated reporter to Frankfort; they get most of their news from the Associated Press." If the governor's speeches, press releases, and public pronouncements are
not even covered in some legislators' districts, the governor cannot expect his or her
views to have an impact on public opinion. If the public cannot be persuaded that the
governor is right, the governor cannot expect the public to persuade their representatives to support the governor.

THE EFFECTIVE EXECUTIVE

From this field research, we know that for the Kentucky governor, bargaining and
persuasion not only complement the formal powers but are the main weapons that the
governor uses to accomplish his goals. With that in mind, we now consider the most
important characteristics necessary to be an effective governor. The four skills most
mentioned in the interviews include a willingness to work hard, the ability to surround
oneself with good people, the aptitude to work with the legislature, and an eagerness
to meet with constituents, the people of Kentucky.

Working Hard

According to Governor Jones, "First you need to be willing to work. It's not a social activity, it's a hard-working job and you need to be focused on it every day. You have to be willing to study at night and prepare yourself for what you're going to do the next day."

Competent Staff

Governor Carroll claimed, "You also have to surround yourself with a good staff to be an effective governor. It doesn't matter how much knowledge or experience you have, if you do not have a good staff, you cannot be an effective governor. Wendell Ford had a great staff—Paul Patton had a great staff." Governor Ford always asked his staff to disagree with him if they did, but the final decision was his. "I wanted to know how they felt, because I had a variety of people who were helping me with the various and sundry groups of people from health care to business to you name it, and they all had responsibilities and needs and an understanding of the issues." However, once he made a decision, Governor Ford wanted them to give a full-throated defense of that decision. "I wanted them to follow my lead, and if they couldn't do that, then they should put their resignation on the table."

Governor Brown put together what many observers consider a legendary cabinet and gave those cabinet secretaries free rein to do the jobs that they were appointed to do, versus running the agenda from the governor's office. "You need entrepreneurs that have the independence to make tough decisions like entrepreneurs make on a daily basis, taking a lot of risk and not being afraid to do it."

Working with the Legislature

Senator Palmer said that a good governor needs to build and maintain relationships with the legislature. "What gets lost in Frankfort is the ability to disagree without being disagreeable, because I do believe at the end of the day, we all have similar goals. We have different means to which we will reach those ends and that's called politics and that's how the process works. Focus on the agenda, the policy side, and leave the personal out of it."

According to Governor Patton, there was a small office off of the governor's office that was not much bigger than ten feet by ten feet. Legislators would come back there and meet with the governor for "two or three minutes and we would try to get what they wanted done worked out. David Williams [former president of the Senate, 2000–2012] was a frequent visitor and was our man in the Republican caucus. He would come by all the time and tell us what was going on and asked for favors." Governor Patton firmly believed that legislators represented their constituents, and if a legislator "felt like a particular road needed to be worked on, for example, the Transportation Cabinet ought to pay attention to that."

Senator Worley was always impressed by how Governor Patton made himself available for any legislator, regardless of party or rank:

If you went down to see Paul Patton you would walk in and say, "Sally [Sally Flynn, Governor Patton's executive assistant], I need to see the governor for a second." She would take you to an office behind the governor's office to wait. She would walk into [Patton's] office and hand him a note that there was a legislator waiting to see him. It didn't have to be the president of the Senate, it didn't have to be a leader. If he was meeting with every university president in the state, he would excuse himself, he would . . . speak to that legislator, because he understood their time was valuable. They were only there for the session, for ninety days. They have a lot of stuff that they have to do, so the governor would come and receive whatever the concern was and he would deal openly and honestly with the legislator, telling the legislator either I can do that or I can't do that.

Secretary Grayson recalled a story that Representative Lonnie Napier of House District Thirty-Six told him about working with Governor Patton. "There was somebody in Gov. Patton's office that was lobbying him about the importance of a road or bridge. Well, that project was in Lonnie's district, so the governor called Lonnie to get his opinion, to find out if he thought that this bridge or road was important for his district. What's unique about that story is that Lonnie Napier is a Republican in the House and this was a period in Kentucky when were very few Republicans in the House."

Serving Constituents

Governor Ford insisted that one has to like people and be able to discuss their needs, be knowledgeable about their issues, whether they are industry leaders or rural farmers.

When you are talking about Kentucky and you start over in the mountains, you talk about coal or to a patch farmer; then you have the bluegrass area with the horse industry; then you have the Golden Triangle of northern Kentucky, Louisville, and Lexington and then in western Kentucky you have a mixture of coal operations, farmers, the Tennessee Valley Authority and so you have a mix. You have to understand that mix and be able to talk to those people about their issues. If you can do that without selling your soul, then you can have the opportunity to be a good governor.

According to Senator Worley, Governor Patton worked with anyone who was going to be affected by government action. He noted that Patton "listened to people in various fields, he sought the expertise of the people in the coalfields about coal issues; he sought the expertise of transportation experts on the capacity to build roads and bridges."

Certainly, the governor's institutional powers are important. The governor has the formal authority to appoint over six thousand positions throughout the state; the governor can call the legislature back into an extraordinary session that forces the legislature—whether it adjourns or not—to deal with his preferences. And the governor, with the state-of-the-state address, is the first elected official to formally signal his agenda to the citizens of Kentucky in a statewide broadcast. No other political actor in state government commands that type of attention at any time for the rest of the legislative session.

But these formal powers are enhanced or weakened by the governor's ability to successfully use the informal powers of bargaining and persuasion to impress his preferences on the general assembly. The governor's formal powers alone, according to both theory and practice, are not sufficient for one to be an effective executive.

As noted above, Governor Carroll summarized the theory and the practice of executive power quite nicely: "Constitutionally, [the governor] is the chief executive . . . *but in my opinion, his strength was not of the Constitution as such, so much as his persuasive power. . . .* The constitutional powers of the governor are important, but the General Assembly is looking over the governor's shoulder more. *The real power base of the governor is his persuasive ability, the building of relationships with the legislature and the public, strengthens your persuasive power. The constitutional power of the governor alone is not sufficient to get accomplished what is necessary.*"

NOTES

The authors would like to thank Tom Dorman, Chief of Staff to Rocky Adkins, Majority Floor Leader in the House of Representatives; Mike Hazelwood, owner/agent, E. M. Ford and Company; Christy Fields, Administrative Assistant to Senate President David Williams; B. R. Masters, Deputy Chief of Staff, Senate Democratic Caucus; and Joe Geglio, graduate student at the College of Charleston, as well as Dr. James Clinger, for helpful guidance.

1. David L. Leal, *Electing America's Governors: The Politics of Executive Elections* (New York: Palgrave Macmillan, 2006), 148.

2. Sarah McCally Morehouse and Malcolm E. Jewell, *State Politics, Parties, and Policy*, 2nd ed. (Lanham, Md.: Rowman and Littlefield, 2003), 147.

3. Penny M. Miller, *Kentucky Politics and Government: Do We Stand United?* (Lincoln: University of Nebraska Press, 1994), 130.

4. Margaret R. Ferguson, ed., *The Executive Branch of State Government* (Santa Barbara, Calif.: ABC-CLIO, 2006), 141–42.

5. Thad Beyle, "Governors," in *Politics in the American States*, 5th ed., ed. Virginia Gray, Harold Jacob, and Kenneth Vines (Boston: Little, Brown, 1990).

6. Larry Sabato, *Goodbye to Goodtime Charlie: The American Governorship Transformed* (Washington, D.C.: Congressional Quarterly Press, 1983), 2.

7. Russell Hanson, "The Interaction of State and Local Governments," in *Governing Partners: State-Local Relations in the United States*, ed. Russell Hanson (Boulder, Colo.: Westview Press, 1998), 20.

8. Ferguson, *Executive Branch of State Government*, 32.

9. Ibid.

10. Ibid., 56–74.

11. Ibid.

12. E. Lee Bernick and Charles W. Wiggins, "Executive-Legislative Relations: The Governor's Role as Chief Legislator," in *Gubernatorial Leadership and State Policy*, ed. Eric B. Herzik and Brent W. Brown (Westport, Conn.: Greenwood Press, 1991), 89.

13. Ferguson, *Executive Branch of State Government*, 42.

14. Ibid., 52.

15. Morehouse and Jewell, *State Politics, Parties, and Policy*, 185.

16. Ferguson, *Executive Branch of State Government*, 54.

17. The Kentucky Department of Military Affairs, http://www.dma.ky.gov/.

18. Kentucky Division of Emergency Management, *July Flooding*, 2010, accessed February 25, 2011, http://kyem.ky.gov/currentdisasters/.

19. Ferguson, *Executive Branch of State Government*, 22, 23, 25, 26, 27, 28, 31, 33, and 34.

20. Joseph A. Schlesinger, "The Politics of the Executive," in *Politics in the American States*, ed. Henry Jacob and Kenneth N. Vines (Boston: Little, Brown, 1965), 207–37.

21. Ibid., 227; Thad Beyle, "The Governor's Formal Powers: A View from the Governor's Chair," *Public Administration Review* 28, no. 6 (1968): 540–45.

22. Paul Blanchard, "The Office of the Governor," in *The Kentucky Encyclopedia*, ed. John Kleber (Lexington: University Press of Kentucky, 1992), 380.

23. Schlesinger, "Politics of the Executive," 228.

24. Miller, *Kentucky Politics and Government*, 322.

25. Ferguson, *Executive Branch of State Government*, 57.

26. Charles Cameron, *Veto Bargaining: Presidents and the Politics of Negative Power* (Cambridge: Cambridge University Press, 2000).

27. Ferguson, *Executive Branch of State Government*, 49.

28. William Howell, *Power without Persuasion: The Politics of Direct Presidential Action* (Princeton, N.J.: Princeton University Press, 2003), 14.

29. Ibid., 15.

30. Ferguson, *Executive Branch of State Government*, 69.

31. Richard Neustadt, *Presidential Power: The Politics of Leadership from FDR to Carter* (New York: Wiley, 1980), 31.

32. Nelson C. Dometrius, "The Power of the Purse," in *Gubernatorial Leadership and State Policy*, ed. Eric B. Herzik and Brent W. Brown (Westport, Conn.: Greenwood Press, 1991), 93.

33. Alan Rosenthal, *Governors and Legislatures: Contending Powers* (Washington, D.C.: Congressional Quarterly Press, 1990), 122.

34. Ferguson, *Executive Branch of State Government*, 70.

35. Raymond Cox III, "The Management Role of the Governor," in *Gubernatorial Leadership and State Policy*, ed. Eric B. Herzik and Brent W. Brown (Westport, Conn.: Greenwood Press, 1991), 68.

36. Neustadt, *Presidential Power*.

37. Gregory Friedman, *The Executive Branch of Kentucky State Government*, Informational Bulletin no. 171 (Frankfort, Ky.: Legislative Research Commission, 2002), 1–7.

38. Ibid., 3.

39. Ibid., 3–4.

40. Ibid., 6.

41. For more information, see Governor's Office of Kentucky, http://governor.ky.gov/office/Pages/cabinet.aspx.

42. Robert Behn, ed., *Governors on Governing* (Lanham, Md.: University Press of America, 1991), 6.

43. "The Black Sheep Squadron was a term applied during the 1978 session to a group of senators who were identified as mavericks. They were supporters of greater legislative

independence and critics of the Carroll administration. Some of them had been strong supporters of Governor Ford and had lost major committee assignments when Governor Carroll took office." Malcolm E. Jewell and Penny M. Miller, *The Kentucky Legislature: Two Decades of Change* (Lexington: University Press of Kentucky, 1988), 185.

44. Neustadt, *Presidential Power*; Dometrius, "Management Role of the Governor"; Ferguson, *Executive Branch of State Government*; Bernick and Wiggins, "Executive-Legislative Relations: The Governor's Role as Chief Legislator."

45. Neustadt, *Presidential Power*, 31.

5

Gubernatorial-Legislative Relations
Executive Dominance No Longer
Paul Blanchard

Until 1980 Kentucky's legislative branch was clearly dominated by strong governors. Governors like Wendell Ford and Julian Carroll were able to have virtually all their major legislative proposals passed and to block virtually every bill they opposed. Their budget proposals were routinely passed with little or no change, usually by a unanimous vote. In addition, because of both constitutional and political factors, overriding the governor's veto was almost impossible. Finally, governors normally handpicked legislative leaders, not only from their own parties but from the opposing party as well.

In 1980 this lopsided balance of power began to change. Some of the changes that culminated in the 1980s, however, actually began earlier, during the Louie Nunn administration (1967–1971) and the Carroll administration (1974–1979). Nunn's election in 1967 produced Kentucky's first Republican governor since Simeon Willis's election in 1943. It also prompted the creation of a more effective and longer-lasting leadership for the Democratic majorities in both chambers. Notable examples were House Speaker Julian Carroll and House Majority Leader Terry McBrayer. After serving as lieutenant governor under Wendell Ford, Carroll was fortunate enough to serve five years as governor when Ford was elected to the U.S. Senate in 1974. However, Carroll's highhandedness as a five-year governor irritated legislators who had tasted independence under Nunn. That and his involvement in a federal corruption investigation prompted creation of the Black Sheep Squadron in the Senate, the first sign of real legislative independence.[1]

The Black Sheep Squadron was even more influential during the administration of John Y. Brown Jr. Governor Brown, elected in 1979, had little practical experience in the rough-and-tumble world of Kentucky politics and seemed at a loss about how to have his will prevail in the legislative process. For example, he made no attempt to influence the selection of legislative leaders as his predecessors had done. Perhaps more important, significant constitutional changes that were instituted the year Brown was elected had a major impact on executive-legislative relations. Under the so-called

83

Kenton Amendment, named after former Speaker William Kenton, legislators for the first time had some control over their schedule during a very limited biennial sixty-day session. Another provision of the Kenton Amendment changed the electoral calendar by providing for legislative elections one year before gubernatorial elections, giving the legislative branch a one-year head start on a newly elected governor. This change proved to be very important (and detrimental) to governors like Martha Layne Collins and Wallace Wilkinson in the 1980s. Besides giving newly elected legislators a head start on a governor who would be elected a year later, the amendment separated legislative and gubernatorial elections. Once they were not on the same ballot, lawmakers and gubernatorial candidates made fewer electoral alliances, and candidates for the House and half the Senate were no longer dependent on help from gubernatorial campaigns.[2]

Governor Collins was the first governor to face a General Assembly that, by virtue of the new legislative election cycle, effectively had a one-year head start.[3] The legislature that met in 1984 was organized and established its leadership and committees in January 1983, more than eleven months before she took office in December of that year. As a result of this and other changes, along with her lack of experience in legislative relations, the 1984 session was very difficult for Governor Collins. Her education-reform proposals, along with the increased revenues to pay for them, were "turned down flatly by the legislature."[4] In fact, the legislature responded to her less-than-skillful leadership by passing what was essentially a legislative budget, a major milestone in the development of legislative independence.

Governor Collins's response to the disastrous 1984 session arguably was one of the most significant developments of the 1980s, both for executive-legislative relations and the education-reform process. Rather than reacting with bitterness or hostility toward a legislature that had caused her to be defeated, if not disgraced, she set about creating positive, working relationships with legislative leaders, particularly those legislators who had developed expertise in educational policy.[5] What resulted was unprecedented cooperation between the governor and the legislature that continued throughout much of the last three years of the Collins administration. These cooperative relationships contributed to important education-reform policies that the General Assembly enacted in 1985 and 1986. They focused primarily on educational inputs, including class size, teacher pay, and teacher preparation, particularly a new teacher internship program. These reforms were supported by a relatively small but significant revenue-enhancement package but no major tax increase. When the Collins administration ended, then, legislators, as well as the governor, were pleased with the substantial progress they felt they had made in improving education in Kentucky. More important for the discussion here, legislators were also pleased with the process by which these improvements had been enacted. The legislature had achieved equality—a partnership, if you will—in the development of meaningful educational policy. In the opinion of this writer, Martha Layne Collins, along with Paul Patton, were the two most effective governors over the past thirty years in dealing with the Kentucky General Assembly.

Wallace Wilkinson's election as governor in 1987 added an important new dimension to the education-reform picture in Kentucky, as well as a different style of executive-legislative relations. His views on education were overshadowed by his strong (and electorally popular) advocacy of a state lottery. But Wilkinson did have a rather well-developed position on education reform and the direction it should take, and this created conflict with the legislature. For Wilkinson, the entire educational system needed to be revamped. In this regard, his position anticipated some of the substance of the landmark 1989 Kentucky Supreme Court decision on education. It was also consistent with a number of reform themes discussed in the major national education report issued in 1983, *A Nation at Risk*, and with reform proposals being considered in other states.[6]

But Wilkinson's views on education, along with his views on most matters, were not well received by the 1988 General Assembly. Wilkinson's confrontational style of dealing with legislators would likely have been counterproductive during any session, but it was particularly inappropriate in 1988, given what had been occurring in executive-legislative relations during the previous three years. Wilkinson's entire posture toward the legislature seemed to reflect a total lack of awareness of how the legislature had evolved into a more independent and equal branch of government. His attitude toward the recently enacted reforms of 1985–1986 was especially offensive to legislators. His lack of commitment to these reforms and the funding necessary to continue them was consistent with his position on restructuring, but it reflected a lack of appreciation of all that they symbolized for the General Assembly. Legislators not only had invested considerable emotional and political resources in these reforms, such that they claimed ownership and pride of authorship, but they also were committed to the procedural partnership that these reforms represented and viewed Wilkinson's education proposals as a threat to all that they had achieved. Although the governor probably did not intend to be viewed in this way, both the style and substance he projected were perceived by many legislators as a threat to the legislature as an institution. Thus, from their perspective, they needed to resist this threat with all the energy and resources available to them.

With this level of mutual distrust, often approaching outright hostility, little was accomplished during the 1988 session, not only on education reform but on substantive legislation of any kind. The legislature acceded to the governor's wishes on one major proposal, the lottery amendment. In action reflecting the budget-making process of four years earlier, what was essentially a legislative budget was enacted. Executive-legislative relations had reached a stalemate between the two branches.

The judicial branch provided the action necessary to break this stalemate insofar as education reform was concerned.[7] The Kentucky Supreme Court issued a far-reaching decision in June 1989 in *Rose v. Council for Better Education*. Chief Justice Robert Stephens's majority opinion effectively declared Kentucky's entire school system unconstitutional. The court ruled that the legislature was primarily responsible for correcting these deficiencies and that the necessary corrections had to be made before the beginning of the 1990–1991 school year. This decision ensured that education reform would be the central item on the General Assembly's 1990 agenda. It also signaled the need for more cooperative relations between the executive and legislative branches if the court's mandates were to be addressed in a satisfactory manner.

Although some legislators believed that it would make sense to consider a comprehensive response to the court's *Rose* decision in a special session, it soon became clear that the legislature would not wait for a special session in 1990 to consider education reform. The major reason was the theme of this chapter—legislative independence and equality. As a result of severe animosity between legislators and Governor Wilkinson, which surfaced during the early weeks of the session, a serious lack of trust developed among legislators regarding the governor. They realized that in a special session they would lose control of the agenda to him, and they were unwilling to risk the consequences of this lack of control. Put simply, during the regular session legislators could deal with the governor as equals, but in a special session they would become captives of the governor's agenda.

HB 940, which became the Kentucky Education Reform Act (KERA), was not introduced until March 9, 1990. Once it was introduced, legislators had less than three weeks to move it through both chambers. This would be a formidable challenge for any major piece of legislation, much less the nine-hundred-page bill that many were calling the most important legislation to be considered by the General Assembly in the twentieth century. After less than a week of consideration, the House Education Committee reported the bill favorably with thirty-nine committee amendments.

The pace accelerated as HB 940 moved to the Senate. The Senate Education Committee took less than three days to report the bill favorably, with one amendment, whereupon the bill was recommitted to the Appropriations and Revenue Committee, which added another amendment. Both of these committee amendments had the effect of largely restoring the bill to its original version as proposed by the Education Reform Task Force (ERTF), thus undoing what several legislators saw as damage done in the House. It was this restored version that passed the Senate on March 28, by a vote of 30–8.[8]

By this time members of both chambers were exhausted, and few House members were committed, at this late hour, to go to battle with the Senate over the changes made in the House.[9] Consequently, on March 29 the House concurred in all amendments added to the bill by the Senate. Thus it was the Senate version of the bill that went to the governor for his signature. Finally, on April 11, Governor Wilkinson signed HB 940, and it was enacted into law.

Although the final version of KERA reflected, for the most part, the work of the ERTF, a major goal of which was to remove local politics from the schools, it is clear that politics of another kind, related to executive-legislative relations, was extremely significant in the process of enacting HB 940 into law. This observation can be illustrated by at least two major decisions made by the General Assembly and its leaders. One was the decision not to allow legislators the option to vote separately on education reform and the increased taxes required to pay for it. Legislators who, for political reasons, decided to vote against the massive tax increases were also forced to vote against education reform, which was risky, given the reform environment that seemed to be pervasive among many of Kentucky's citizens. This was a difficult choice indeed, as later legislative elections were to demonstrate. Although a relatively large number of incumbents were later defeated, at least in part because of their vote for higher taxes, almost as many incumbents were defeated who had voted against HB 940, presumably because voters may have perceived that they were antieducation.

More significant was a related decision through which the legislature added $300 million to the governor's proposed tax increase of approximately $1 billion. This was the much-maligned "pork-barrel" portion of the tax increase, which provided funding for dozens of major state projects, such as buildings, swimming pools, and parking garages. The money available for such projects was promised as an enticement to reward those legislators who voted in favor of HB 940 while those who chose to vote in opposition realized their districts would get little or nothing in the way of "pork barrel" projects. Obviously, these promises were not made in writing but nevertheless they were clearly understood. Certainly, then, one of the major ironies in the process of enacting education reform in 1990 was that the most blatant form of patronage politics was used at the state level to pass a package that had as one of its major goals the elimination of blatant patronage politics at the local level.

The passage of a major education-reform bill in Kentucky provided a major boost to the state's educational process, and the law received positive attention in education circles across the country. But how did the 1990 session affect the ever-changing balance between Kentucky's governor and legislature? Clearly Governor Wilkinson played an important leadership role at several points in the process, but he was unable to dominate the legislative process as he would have desired. The governor was never quite able to achieve the trust necessary for close working relationships with legislators. For the first time in memory, Kentucky's judicial branch played an important role in setting the legislature's agenda (normally a gubernatorial role), and a unique and unprecedented decision-making body (the ERTF) artificially forced legislative-executive cooperation on one important bill.

Wilkinson's successor was Brereton Jones, who had been his lieutenant governor. Jones enjoyed a more congenial relationship with the General Assembly than Wilkinson had, but he demonstrated relatively little persuasive skill in getting his legislative agenda enacted. His top priority was health-care reform, and after receiving recommendations from two reform study commissions, he called a special session in 1993 to consider universal health-care legislation. Not surprisingly, especially given the experience with Obamacare in 2010, he experienced great difficulty in getting substantial reform through the legislature. His bill was not passed in 1993 but was introduced again in the 1994 regular session. According to Penny Miller, the 1994 bill was "amended, compromised, and attacked; and it was pronounced dead many times in its rocky road to passage."[10] Miller describes Jones's strange and inconsistent strategy, in which he first lobbied the House to kill his bill and then criticized the legislature on television for not passing a stronger bill before finally signing the bill two weeks after trying to get it killed.[11]

In general, the legislative branch was probably stronger, relative to the governor, during the Jones administration than in any previous administration. Executive-legislative "equality" sometimes bordered on legislative preeminence. Because of the legislators' relative lack of respect for Governor Jones, "a good working relationship between the executive and legislative branches never really developed."[12] Despite this, however, the Jones administration and the General Assembly had some significant accomplishments. One of the strongest ethics laws in the country was passed (the main reason is discussed in the following paragraph), a runoff primary was enacted, and a constitutional amendment allowing gubernatorial succession was approved.[13]

The end of the Jones administration also coincided with a startling new development in executive legislative relations: the BOPTROT investigation, which focused on illegitimate and often illegal actions by lobbyists and interest groups. The increasing power, independence, and professionalism of the legislature had attracted more spending from lobbying interests and had created a cozy culture where lobbyists began operating out of legislative leaders' offices and running open tabs at restaurants and bars near the Capitol, where lawmakers could eat and drink for free. This behavior ended only after a federal investigation, operating under the label Operation BOPTROT, resulted in the arrest and conviction of several prominent legislators, including the House Speaker, and the passage of one of the nation's strongest legislative-ethics laws.[14]

Paul E. Patton was elected Kentucky's governor in 1995 and was reelected in 1999. Although one other governor, James Garrard, also served two consecutive terms (1796–1804), Patton was the first Kentucky governor ever elected to two consecutive four-year terms.[15]

Paul Patton demonstrated an essential leadership skill, agenda setting, when he began his administration in late 1995. It is clear from study of successful presidents and other executives that to be an effective legislative leader, a governor must begin with a short, clear, and focused agenda. Patton seemed to understand that a new chief executive must avoid trying to do too many things at once or focusing on issues early on that are not at the top of his agenda. He made it clear that his top priority would be the reform of Kentucky's higher-education system. Throughout his entire eight years in office, this issue remained at or near the top of his policy agenda.

Patton was highly successful during his first four-year term. Some observers suggested that Patton dominated state government unlike any governor since the 1970s.[16] This was particularly true of the governor's relationship with the General Assembly. Governor Patton won major legislative victories throughout the 1996 and 1998 regular sessions and especially during two special sessions in 1996 and 1997. At the end of the 1998 session, longtime Senate president John "Eck" Rose concluded, "Governor Patton was much stronger in the '98 session than any previous governor since Julian Carroll," who served in the late 1970s.[17]

It is clear that Patton's most pivotal legislative victories throughout his eight years in office occurred during the two special sessions in 1996 and 1997. This illustrates a long-held belief about gubernatorial power in Kentucky—namely, that governors are better able to win legislative victories in special sessions than in regular sessions. If they are effective, they are able to focus legislators' attention on one major issue and mobilize public opinion and the support of influential interest groups on that particular issue.

The 1996 session was devoted to reform of the workers' compensation system. Patton and many others considered workers' compensation in Kentucky too expensive and unfavorable to Kentucky's business climate. The reforms advocated by the governor and approved by the legislature substantially reduced workers' compensation benefits, particularly to coal miners with black-lung respiratory problems. Patton's victory on this issue was politically costly because many of his natural constituents in eastern

Kentucky's coal-mining communities felt that he had betrayed them. He was never again as popular in his home area as he had been in 1995, when he was the first eastern Kentuckian to be elected governor since the 1950s.[18]

The 1997 higher-education session was an even more impressive performance because Patton was forced to take on opponents representing some of Kentucky's most politically powerful institutions. He had proposed to change the mission of the University of Kentucky away from administering the state's community colleges in order to allow it to become a more successful and respected ("Top 20") research university. But this proposal generated strong opposition from many of the community colleges and community leaders from their areas of the state, as well as many of the legislators who represented these areas. In addition, the University of Kentucky itself was an ardent opponent, especially its president, Charles Wethington, who had been in charge of the university's community colleges before he ascended to the presidency.

Patton was surprised that the university and Wethington did not support a plan to make it a great research institution. Instead, the university and the community colleges ran what the governor characterized as "mean" ads on television and in newspapers against him and his higher-education reforms. He was also disappointed by the opposition of influential House leader Greg Stumbo, who represented the interests of Prestonsburg Community College, near where he lived. Patton remembered that Stumbo had been in favor of independent community colleges before 1996, but he believed that Stumbo was still smarting over the workers' compensation legislation, which he had also opposed.

How was Patton able to win the General Assembly's approval for his controversial higher-education reform proposal, the top priority of his entire administration, in the face of substantial opposition from such influential individuals and groups?[19] For an individual who was arguably the most politically skillful and persuasive governor in a quarter century, it is clear that it took every bit of skill and persuasion that he had. Even though he had help from competent advisers like former legislators Ed Ford and Kenny Rapier, Patton personally lobbied scores of legislators, convincing them of the need for the kind of higher-education reform he was proposing. From all reports, he was extremely effective one on one. He had already demonstrated to legislators that he was willing to involve them in the decision-making process (especially on matters related to the budget). The fact that he had established friendly relationships with most legislators, both Democrats and Republicans, and that he had consulted with them on important decisions certainly made him a more influential governor during the special session on higher education and indeed throughout his first term.

Patton's success in dealing with legislators in 1996 and 1997 continued in 1998, when he reached the apex of his influence. He was able to secure legislative support for the major items on his policy agenda, particularly his crime package and legislation in the areas of economic development, Medicaid, and higher education (again). This happened at a time when the governor, who would seek a second term the following year, could have been politically vulnerable. Potentially, this legislative session provided a visible opportunity for the governor's enemies and potential opponents to attempt to discredit him. But it became clear in 1998 that Paul Patton's influence with legislators was enhanced, at least in part, because they expected to see him back in office in 2000 and 2002.

Patton was extremely successful during his first term in office because of several other strengths he demonstrated. One was his work ethic; like successful governors of the past, Patton mastered the details of policies and budgets and was willing to work as hard as necessary to see them succeed; he had a habit of arriving early and working late that was well known. He also was a governor who genuinely loved serving in this capacity, at least until his last year or two in office.

Finally, the 1998 session illustrated one other factor—luck—that has a major impact on leaders and their ability to be effective. In 1998 and through most of his first term, Patton was incredibly lucky, especially with regard to Kentucky's revenue situation. Although his luck in this area certainly ended during the recession years of his second administration, during the 1998 session a $200 million budgetary surplus gave Patton the opportunity to offer his legislative allies, both Democrats and Republicans, something tangible for their districts. He was skillful in distributing surplus revenue, and that gave him substantial leverage in dealing with legislators and allowed him to achieve approval of the major items on his agenda. In addition, because of his advantageous budgetary position, legislators were less willing to oppose or criticize the governor. In explaining this situation, one Democratic legislative leader was heard to say, "Money buys a lot of silence."[20] In this regard, things changed dramatically for Governor Patton during his second term, when some of his most vocal critics were members of the General Assembly.

In 1999 Patton was unopposed in the primary and defeated an extremely weak Republican candidate, Peppy Martin, by an overwhelming margin in the November election. Patton had more than 60 percent of the vote (352,099), while his Republican opponent had only 22 percent (128,788), only slightly more than a third-party candidate, Gatewood Galbraith, who had 15 percent (88,930).

But before the fall gubernatorial election, events during the summer of 1999 changed the political landscape of Kentucky state government dramatically. Two Democratic state senators, Dan Seum of Louisville and Bob Leeper of Paducah, publicly switched parties and became Republicans. This changed the narrow 20–18 Democratic senate majority to an equally narrow but significant Republican majority. This was the first time Republicans had ever controlled the Kentucky Senate.

Thus when Paul Patton began his unprecedented second consecutive term, his convincing electoral victory was overshadowed by the fact that he would face a politically divided General Assembly at the beginning of the twenty-first century. A formidable Republican opponent quickly emerged from the Senate in the person of Senator David Williams, of Burkesville, who became the Senate president. Even though Patton had worked well with Republicans during his first term, he seemed to have a very difficult time adapting to one house being controlled by what had always been the minority party in the legislature. Williams showed considerable skill in holding together his razor-thin majority in the Senate and became the dominant figure in the General Assembly throughout Patton's second term.[21]

The governor's influence waned considerably during the legislative sessions of 2000 and 2001. The latter session was the first short (thirty-day), odd-year General Assembly session after voters approved a constitutional amendment in November 2000 providing for annual sessions. Few of Patton's proposals received significant attention by the legislature, and he accomplished relatively little in the way of new initiatives. By the 2002 legislative session Patton had almost no influence at all, and the Democratic House and the Republican Senate failed to agree on a budget for the 2002–2004 biennium. This legislative impasse did give him increased power temporarily because he was forced to run state government for nearly a year without a budget.

Governor Patton reached his political and personal nadir when it was revealed in September 2002 that he had been involved in an extramarital affair with Tina Conner, the owner of a bankrupt nursing home in western Kentucky, during his first term in office. Conner accused Patton of providing her business with regulatory favors during their affair and then seeking revenge against her after the affair ended by trying to ruin her business through a state investigation. After first denying the affair, Patton admitted it on September 20, 2002: "I apologize to the people of Kentucky for my failure as a person. I have already apologized to Judi and my family. I'm also sorry that I initially denied mistakes I made in my private life."

Patton made his extraordinary confession in an afternoon press conference held at the Kentucky History Center that was widely covered by news organizations from across the state. His remarks were broadcast live and replayed countless times on most major Kentucky television and radio stations. As a result, the governor became the subject of ridicule, not only in Kentucky but across the country. In particular, he was the subject of numerous jokes by Jay Leno, the famous late-night television personality, whose program was watched by millions of Americans.

Patton clearly understood how his actions had rendered him ineffective in his ability to lead. In an interview with the author in April 2003, the governor said, "My ability to lead has been compromised and totally destroyed. There is not much more leading to do." Regarding his relations with the General Assembly, he said that his behavior "has made it legitimate to criticize me. I have lost any ability to influence the legislature." Surprisingly, the governor made no claims that he had been treated unfairly by the news media. In this regard, he said, "I deserve anything I get."

Criticism of Paul Patton intensified in the months after he admitted his affair. During the 2003 legislative session a *Lexington Herald-Leader* columnist wrote that the governor was so far beyond "lame duck" status that legislators from his own party considered him an "irrelevant" dead duck.[22] As that session ended, one reporter wrote that the legislators were hammering out an agreement on a state budget without any interest in the governor's views on anything.

It is somewhat ironic that the first governor in two hundred years to serve two successive terms in office made it appear almost as if two different governors were serving.[23] The Paul Patton of 1995–1999 was persuasive, skillful, and extremely effective, and had his time in office ended after his first term, he would likely be remembered as one of the most successful governors of the past fifty years. His higher-education reforms alone would have assured him a lasting and positive legacy. But his second term in office (1999–2003) will be remembered as a time of uncertain leadership, inability to adjust to a changing political environment, several allegations of highly unethical behavior, and an embarrassing personal scandal. Unfortunately for Patton, he is more likely to be remembered for the failures of his second term than for the successes of his first.

Paul Patton's problems during his second term created problems for the Democratic candidate in 2003, Attorney General Ben Chandler, who was defeated by Congressman Ernie Fletcher. Fletcher capitalized on the Patton sex scandal and the predicted $710 million shortfall in the upcoming budget, promising to "clean up the mess in Frankfort." Fletcher won the election easily, receiving more than 55 percent of the vote.[24]

Republicans had controlled the Kentucky Senate since 2000 and continued to do so during Fletcher's term of office, while Democrats continued to control the House. Consequently, Fletcher had a difficult time getting legislation passed in the General Assembly. Early in the 2004 legislative session Fletcher presented a plan for tax reform that he claimed was "revenue neutral" and would "modernize" the state tax code. As the session wore on, Republicans insisted on tying the tax-reform package to the proposed state budget, while Democrats wanted to vote on the measures separately. Despite last-minute attempts at a compromise as the session drew to a close, the General Assembly passed neither the tax-reform package nor a state budget.[25]

The 2004 session marked the second consecutive session in which the General Assembly failed to pass a biennial budget. When the fiscal year ended without a budget in place, responsibility for state expenditures fell to Fletcher. As had happened in 2002 under Patton, spending was determined by an executive spending plan created by the governor. Democratic attorney general Greg Stumbo filed suit, asking for a determination on the extent of Fletcher's ability to spend without legislative approval. A judicial ruling by a Franklin County circuit-court judge approved Fletcher's spending plan but forbade spending on new capital projects and programs.[26] In 2005 the Kentucky Supreme Court made a more definitive ruling that a governor can spend money without a budget, but only on items directly mentioned in the constitution and state statutes.[27]

Fletcher's plan for tax reform in 2004, which failed in that year, was proposed again during the 2005 short session, and late in the session, both houses passed it. The plan raised taxes on cigarettes and alcohol, as well as increased taxes on satellite television service and motel rooms. Businesses were also subjected to a gross-receipts tax. In exchange, corporate taxes were lowered, as were income taxes for individuals who earned less than $75,000 annually; 300,000 low-wage earners were dropped from the income-tax rolls altogether.[28]

During the spring of 2005 Governor Fletcher and his staff became embroiled in scandal when Attorney General Greg Stumbo began investigating allegations that rank-and-file state jobs were being filled by political cronies instead of hiring based on merit, as state law required.[29] A grand-jury investigation into charges against the Fletcher administration returned indictments against nine administration officials, including state Republican Party chairman Darrell Brock Jr. and acting transportation secretary Bill Nighbert.[30]

How did Fletcher's merit-system problems affect his influence over the 2006 General Assembly?[31] That question was complicated by serious health issues Fletcher faced in early 2006, when he was diagnosed with an inflamed pancreas, as well as gallbladder disease, which required surgery to remove the gallbladder. Then Fletcher developed a blood infection that slowed his recovery, and soon after he was found to have a blood clot that had to be dissolved, which resulted in another five-day stay in the hospital. Fletcher's staff insisted that his absence did not have a negative impact on his ability to get legislation passed during the session, but several proposals he supported failed early in the session. Among the bills that did pass the session were a mandatory-seat-belt law, a law requiring children under sixteen years old to wear a helmet when operating an all-terrain vehicle, and legislation allowing the Ten Commandments to be posted on the grounds of the capitol in a historical context.

The General Assembly approved a biennial budget but did not allow enough time in the session to reconvene and potentially override any of Fletcher's vetoes. In an attempt to avoid what he called "excessive debt," Fletcher used his line-item veto to trim $370 million in projects from the budget passed by the General Assembly. Although he fell far short of his initial prediction of vetoing $938 million, Fletcher used the line-item veto the most in the state's history.[32]

One of Fletcher's priorities that was not resolved during the session was the correction of unintended tax increases on businesses that resulted from the tax-reform plan passed in 2005. Fletcher called a special legislative session for mid-June so that the legislature could amend the plan and also authorize tax breaks designed to lure a proposed FutureGen power plant to Henderson. Republican Senate president David L. Williams asked Fletcher to include tax breaks for other businesses as well, but Fletcher insisted on a sparse legislative agenda. The session convened for five days and passed the tax breaks and amended tax-reform plan unanimously in both houses. Fletcher applauded the legislature's efficiency.[33]

Obviously, Fletcher's merit-system problems would affect his chances for reelection in 2007. After defeating two challengers in the Republican primary, he faced Democrat Steve Beshear, a former lieutenant governor, in the general election.

In the midst of the primary campaign, the 2007 General Assembly convened. Legislation passed during this session included bills raising the state's minimum wage to $7.25 per hour, increasing the speed limit on major state highways to seventy miles per hour, and implementing new safety requirements for social workers and coal miners. Negotiations over how to make the state's retirement system solvent reached an impasse that stalled other proposed legislation. In July Fletcher called the legislature into special session and included sixty-seven items in his call. Democrats in the House argued that none of the items were urgent enough to warrant a special session and claimed that the call was an attempt by Fletcher to boost his sagging poll numbers against Beshear. The House adjourned after only ninety minutes without acting on any of Fletcher's proposals. Nevertheless, Fletcher insisted that a tax-incentive program was needed immediately to keep the state in the running for a proposed coal-gasification plant to be built by Peabody Energy. After negotiating with legislators, Fletcher called another session for August that included only the tax-incentive program, which passed the General Assembly.[34]

In the general election campaign Fletcher tried to draw attention away from the merit-system investigation by making Beshear's support of casino gambling the central

issue. Beshear supported holding a referendum on a constitutional amendment to allow expanded casino gambling in the state, while Fletcher opposed casino gambling,
arguing that it would bring an increase in crime and societal ills. However, the voters
seemed more focused on the hiring scandal than the gambling issue, and Beshear defeated Fletcher by more than 180,000 votes, receiving almost 59 percent of the total.

In spite of this overwhelming rejection of an incumbent, Fletcher had modest success with the legislature, even with its partisan division and with relatively weak support from Republican Senate president David Williams. His chief legislative victories
were the tax-reform package passed during the 2005 session (shortly before the merit-
system charges emerged) and the tax-incentive program to boost economic-development
efforts passed in the second special legislative session he called in 2007. Fletcher at
first seemed to have a difficult time mastering the persuasive skills needed during the
legislative process, even though he had been a legislator, both in Kentucky and in the
U.S. Congress. However, Fletcher became more skillful and effective in legislative
leadership as his term progressed. He received high marks from legislators on both
sides of the aisle for his sincerity and for consistently trying to do the right thing. Legislators, for the most part, believed that they could trust him to do what he said he
would do. He was willing to reach out to Democratic legislators, and over time he
learned how to compromise and became more likely to do so.

Fletcher's replacement, Democrat Steve Beshear, seemed not to have made much
progress as a persuasive legislative leader as his first term neared an end.[35] As *Courier-
Journal* columnist Al Cross wrote in 2008, early in Beshear's term: "So far Beshear
and his team have not demonstrated the skill that will be required to win this uphill
fight. That was demonstrated by Beshear's first political defeat as governor, which displayed weakness at a time when strength—and the image of it—are needed to get
legislators and lobbying interests on board his bandwagon."[36] Cross was referring to
the defeat of the Beshear-supported candidate in a special election to fill the Kentucky Senate seat of the new lieutenant governor, Dan Mongiardo. Both Beshear and
Mongiardo campaigned heavily for the Democratic nominee, Scott Alexander, but
Republican Brandon Smith won the open seat by 401 votes.

Then, as negotiations began over the 2008–2010 biennial budget, Beshear expressed surprise that budget issues consumed so much of the General Assembly's time
during the session, but he admitted that the legislature had become much more independent of the governor than it had been when he was a legislator three decades earlier. In reporting the governor's revelation about the changing legislature, *Lexington
Herald-Leader* reporter Ryan Alessi referred to Beshear, who had first been elected to
the Kentucky legislature some thirty-five years earlier, as a "rookie."[37]

Beshear lost more battles than he won in his first legislative session. He announced
that his proposal for a constitutional amendment to allow for casinos, a major priority
for him, was dead for the regular session in late March 2008. Among the other proposals favored by the governor that failed to pass in the session were an ethics-reform
measure Beshear proposed in the wake of the investigation of the Fletcher administration, a plan to reduce the projected shortfall in the state's pension system, and a
proposed tax increase of seventy cents per pack on cigarettes.

Beshear was able to get a biennial budget passed, but many agreed with columnist Al Cross that the budget was "pitiful": "As the legislature sent Gov. Steve Beshear a pitiful budget last week, he and fellow Democrats who voted for and against it agreed that the budget process is 'dysfunctional.' . . . The Democrats have a governor who won in a landslide but seems to have little or no influence over the General Assembly. They have a House leadership that was the antithesis of the word as it mishandled the governor's main initiative. They have a House budget committee chairman, Harry Moberly of Richmond, who voted against the budget that he spent marathon days negotiating."[38]

Beshear was more successful later in 2008. He was dissatisfied because the General Assembly had not acted in its regular session to shore up the state pension system, so he called a special legislative session for July 2008 after House and Senate leaders informed him that they had reached an agreement on a plan after the regular legislative session's end. The legislation was passed in a session that lasted five days, the minimum amount of time required to maneuver the bill through the legislature.[39]

Early in 2009, during its organizational session of the 2009 General Assembly, House Speaker Jody Richards was ousted by House Democrats by a three-vote margin in favor of former Majority Leader and Attorney General Greg Stumbo. The primary issue facing the legislature for the 2009 session was a $456 million budget shortfall. Expanded gambling was again proposed as a possible source of revenue, and a bill to allow slot machines at the state's racetracks passed the House Licensing and Occupations Committee but died in the House Appropriations and Revenue Committee. Speaker Stumbo expressed doubt that he had enough votes to pass the measure even if it were brought to the House floor. Instead, the General Assembly passed a series of tax bills to deal with the shortfall. The legislature also began the process of reforming the state's system of school accountability testing, a move advocated by Beshear. But for the most part, legislators gave little credit to the governor for what they accomplished.[40]

Events near the end of the 2009 session reinforced the governor's difficulties in legislative leadership. The rules of the House of Representatives required that the final two days of the chamber's session be reserved for overriding any vetoes by the governor, but Beshear hoped that the House would suspend the rules, as it had in previous years. He wanted the House to consider bills he supported to increase funding to public defenders, create a transportation authority to oversee bridge-building projects in Louisville and Henderson, and provide various economic incentives, including a package intended to attract a NASCAR race to Kentucky. The House refused to suspend the rules, however, and adjourned one day early, allowing Beshear's one veto to stand.[41]

The governor was unsuccessful in persuading the legislature to approve an expanded gambling bill in another special session he called in June 2009. Although the bill passed the House, it died in the Senate Appropriations and Revenue Committee. However, an economic-incentives bill and an amended budget passed during the ten-day session.

In the days leading up to the 2010 session, Beshear adopted a new and rather innovative but risky strategy to strengthen his potential success with the Republican Senate. He attempted to chip away at the Republican majority by appointing a few Republicans to desirable positions outside the legislature. First, he appointed Republican senator Charlie Borders, who had chaired the Senate Appropriations and Revenue Committee that voted down Beshear's expanded gambling bill, to the state Public Service Commission. That appointment meant that a special election would be held to fill Borders's seat, which was won by Democrat Robin Webb, reducing the Republican majority to 20–17 (with one independent, Bob Leeper, who usually voted with the Republicans). After Webb's victory Beshear appointed Republican senator Dan Kelly to a circuit judgeship, but Republicans held on to that seat in a special election.[42]

Shortly after Beshear presented his biennial budget proposal to the 2010 General Assembly, which proposed to use revenue from expanded gambling to make up a projected $1.5 billion shortfall, both House Speaker Stumbo and Senate president Williams declared all gambling legislation dead for the session, saying that there was no political will in either chamber to pass such legislation ahead of the legislative elections in November.[43] Although legislators worked on the budget throughout the sixty-day session, no budget agreement had been reached when time ran out.

Beshear blasted the leadership of both chambers for failing to consider his budget proposal. He mocked the legislators for claiming that writing their own budget would be their "defining moment." He stated, "Well, it was. A moment of abject failure."[44] Beshear called the legislature into special session in May, and legislators agreed on a biennial budget. Beshear exercised his line-item veto on nineteen items in the budget, claiming that they restricted his ability to implement the reduction in executive expenses mandated by the budget. Legislators were unable to override the vetoes because the special session had already adjourned.

In general, Beshear has been relatively ineffective in his legislative leadership. To legislators, he seemed disengaged from the process and had limited communication with legislators, even compared with his predecessor, Ernie Fletcher. Both his words and actions, especially when he tried to reduce the number of Republican senators through the appointive process, indicated to some legislators that he had little respect for the General Assembly and a limited understanding of the legislative process. He seemed willing to level public and severe criticism at both Democratic and Republican legislators, especially during the 2010 session. Several of these criticisms were summarized by CNHI columnist Ronnie Ellis early in 2010:

> His attitude toward legislators has gone from dismissive to disgust—and lawmakers feel much the same about him. . . . They say Beshear makes no attempt to work with them, not even bothering to round up votes for his gambling-dependent budget proposal. Now Beshear has gone out of his way to take a shot at lawmakers with sarcastic comments about lawmakers' investigation into causes of a prison riot last August at the Northpoint Training Center. . . . Beshear said lawmakers should focus on "our real problems" rather than catering to criminals "who wish they could go to Wendy's." That doesn't sound like a governor trying to mend fences. Predictably, lawmakers aren't pleased.[45]

What can be learned from this overview of executive-legislative relations in Kentucky over the past thirty years? In general, "executive dominance no longer" is an accurate but incomplete summary. Clearly, some governors were more effective in providing effective and persuasive leadership than others. As noted earlier, in the view of this observer, the two most effective governors during this period were Martha Layne Collins and Paul Patton. Ironically, these two governors followed quite different trajectories through their tenures in office. Collins had major difficulties early in her term but became more and more effective the longer she served. She worked as cooperatively with legislators as any governor ever had, providing necessary executive leadership while demonstrating respect for the legislative process and an appreciation of the General Assembly as a coequal branch of government. In contrast, Paul Patton began as a strong and effective leader and continued in that role throughout his first term, but his second term, a historically unprecedented opportunity for a Kentucky governor, was a different story. A personal scandal was a major problem for Patton, but more significant, perhaps, was his inability to deal with the General Assembly when the Republicans gained control of the Senate, beginning a period of divided control of the legislature that has lasted for more than ten years.

Governors Brown, Wilkinson, Jones, Fletcher, and Beshear were much less successful in dealing with the legislative branch. Brown, Wilkinson, and Jones, none of whom had served in the General Assembly, seemed to have a difficult time understanding, much less mastering, the unique political nuances of the legislative process in Kentucky. Both Fletcher and Beshear had the additional handicap of dealing with a divided legislature, a problem not encountered by Brown, Wilkinson, and Jones. And Steve Beshear faced one additional hurdle, trying to deal with a severe recession, which made it even more difficult to find adequate revenue to fund necessary state services.

It seems clear from my examination of the seven governors who have served since 1980 that those who have been most successful in their dealings with the General Assembly have exhibited these relatively simple and straightforward characteristics: a respect for legislators and the legislative process, an inclination to work hard, a willingness to initiate and engage in meaningful communication with legislators of both parties and to compromise when necessary, and always to act in such a way that legislators can trust the governor to fulfill and follow through on statements and promises he has made. Obviously it also helps to have some luck, especially related to economic conditions. Will the next seven governors exhibit more of these characteristics and be more successful? We will see.

NOTES

1. Malcolm E. Jewell and Penny M. Miller, *The Kentucky Legislature: Two Decades of Change* (Lexington: University Press of Kentucky, 1988), 185–86.

2. This observation and several other perspectives in this chapter have been suggested by former *Courier-Journal* columnist Al Cross, currently director of the Institute for Rural Journalism and Community Issues at the University of Kentucky. Cross is a longtime and astute observer of Kentucky politics, especially of executive-legislative relations.

3. Many of these comments about Collins and Wilkinson are drawn directly from the author's earlier article, Paul Blanchard, "Education Reform and Executive-Legislative Relations

in Kentucky: HB 940 as the Culmination of Legislative Independence, 1980–1990," *Journal of Kentucky Studies* 10 (September 1993): 66–74.

4. Jewell and Miller, *Kentucky Legislature*, 231.

5. See ibid., 129 and 273, for a discussion of the "young turks" who were so important as Collins developed a cooperative relationship with the legislature. See also Lowell H. Harrison and James C. Klotter, *A New History of Kentucky* (Lexington: University Press of Kentucky, 1997), 419–20, for another positive picture of Collins's skillful leadership of the General Assembly.

6. "A Nation at Risk." A report by the National Commission on Excellence in Education, April 26, 1983. U.S. Department of Education, Washington, D.C.

7. Because chapter 14 in this book deals with education reform, that topic will not be discussed in any detail in this chapter.

8. Paul Blanchard, "Education Reform and Executive-Legislative Relations in Kentucky, 71–73. The entire article gives details about various steps in the passage of the Kentucky Education Reform Act of 1990.

9. Ibid., 72–73.

10. Penny M. Miller, chapter on Brereton C. Jones, in *Kentucky's Governors*, updated ed., ed. Lowell H. Harrison (Lexington: University Press of Kentucky, 2004), 249.

11. Ibid. One highly respected legislator interviewed by this writer, who served with seven governors, ranked Jones and Steve Beshear as the two least effective governors in dealing with the legislature.

12. Harrison and Klotter, *New History of Kentucky*, 423.

13. Ibid.

14. BOPTROT was named for the legislature's Business and Organizations and Professions Committee (BOP), where much of the most egregious behavior occurred, and the trotting-track involvement (TROT), which was the focus of some of this behavior. See ibid., 422.

15. Garrard's initial selection in 1796 was by "electors" from various districts, and he was elected to a second term in 1800 after a new Kentucky constitution provided for the popular election of governors. See H. E. Everman, chapter on James Garrard, in Harrison, *Kentucky's Governors*, 7–11.

16. Paul Blanchard, chapter on Paul Patton, in Harrison, *Kentucky's Governors*, 251–63, from which much of the discussion of Patton here is drawn.

17. Ibid., 256.

18. Ibid., 256–57.

19. See ibid., 257–58.

20. Ibid., 258–59.

21. Ibid., 259–60.

22. Larry Dale Keeling, "How Patton Has Fallen—Mistakes, Bad Timing Hurt His Budget Call," *Lexington Herald-Leader*, February 9, 2003, D1.

23. Paul Blanchard, chapter on Paul Patton, in Harrison, *Kentucky's Governors*, 251–63, from which much of the discussion of Patton here is drawn.

24. Al Cross, chapter on Ernie Fletcher, in Harrison, *Kentucky's Governors*, 267.

25. Jack Brammer and Ryan Alessi, "Legislators Fail to Pass a Budget—Tax Plan Feud Puts Spending Power in Fletcher's Hands," *Lexington Herald-Leader*, April 14, 2004.

26. Amanda York, "Ruling Allows Fletcher Plan to Proceed," *Kentucky Post*, July 1, 2004.

27. *Fletcher v. Commonwealth*, No. 2005-SC-0046-TG (KY 5/19/2005).

28. Jack Brammer, "Tax Overhaul Passed 96–4 by House—Approval Is Major Step after Years of Efforts; Some Changes Expected in Senate," *Lexington Herald-Leader*, February 19, 2005.

29. Jack Brammer and Ryan Alessi, "Defiant Fletcher Blames Politics—Says Inquiry Starts '2007 Governor's Race'; Stumbo Rejects Criticism, Claims No Plans to Run," *Lexington Herald-Leader*, May 28, 2005.

30. Jack Brammer and Ryan Alessi, "Druen Accused of 21 New Felonies—More Indictments in Hiring Inquiry; Allegedly Shredded Evidence," *Lexington Herald-Leader*, May 28, 2005. See also Mark Chellgren, "Fletcher Signs Blanket Pardons—Investigation Will Continue," *Kentucky Post*, August 30, 2005.

31. Because chapter 15 in this book discusses the Fletcher hiring scandal, few details about related events and actions are provided here.

32. Ryan Alessi, John Stamper, and Jack Brammer, "Money for Baptist College Stays In—Projects Slashed to Lessen Debt but Nothing Will Be Spent Until Case Is Heard in Courts," *Lexington Herald-Leader*, April 25, 2006.

33. Jim Jordan and Alex Fontana, "Fletcher Signs Tax Relief Bill—Will Ease Burden on Smaller Businesses," *Lexington Herald-Leader*, June 29, 2006.

34. Jack Brammer, "Senate Passes Energy Measure—Fletcher Says He'll Sign Bill Next Week," *Lexington Herald-Leader*, August 25, 2007.

35. This chapter was written in 2011 before that year's gubernatorial election was held.

36. Al Cross, op-ed column, *Courier-Journal*, February 7, 2008.

37. Ryan Alessi, "Rocky Start a Surprise to Rookie Governor; The First 100 Days—Gov. Steve Beshear; Budget Strife Sidelines Other Issues, and Casino Plan Is Stalled," *Lexington Herald-Leader*, March 19, 2008.

38. Al Cross, op-ed column, *Courier-Journal*, April 6, 2008.

39. Ryan Alessi, "Assembly Passes Pension Reforms—Special Session Addresses Funding for Retirement System," *Lexington Herald-Leader*, June 28, 2008.

40. Owen Covington, "Short Session Garners Strong Reviews; State Lawmakers Praise Their Work on Key Issues," The Owensboro *Messenger-Inquirer*, March 29, 2009.

41. Beth Musgrave and Jack Brammer, "Session Ends by the Rules—No Additional Legislation; NASCAR Bill Left in Dust," *Lexington Herald-Leader*, March 27, 2009.

42. Beth Musgrave, "Beshear Gives Kelly Judgeship—Appointment Second to Threaten GOP Majority in State Senate," *Lexington Herald-Leader*, October 27, 2009; Jack Brammer, "14th Senate Seat Stays in Republican Column," *Lexington Herald-Leader*, December 9, 2009.

43. Ryan Alessi and Jack Brammer, "Gambling Bills Dead for Session—Williams, Stumbo Also See Little Chance of Overhauling Tax Code," *Lexington Herald-Leader*, January 23, 2010.

44. Beth Musgrave and Jack Brammer, "Session Ends with No Budget—Beshear to Call Lawmakers Back for Another Try in May," *Lexington Herald-Leader*, April 16, 2010. See also Ronnie Ellis, "The Genie's Back in the Bottle," CNHI News Service column, April 2, 2010.

45. Ronnie Ellis, "Hard Times, Hard Choices, Hard Feelings," CNHI News Service column, January 29, 2010.

6

The Kentucky Judicial System
Bradley C. Canon

Kentucky has adopted four constitutions, in 1792, 1799, 1850, and the current one in 1891. The first two created a judicial system much like that of Virginia, which had furnished a plurality of settlers to the new state. They established the Court of Appeals as the only appellate court. Multicounty circuit courts handled major civil and criminal cases. The governor appointed Court of Appeals and circuit judges for life. The constitutions empowered the General Assembly to establish inferior courts, and that body created county courts to try minor cases. However, a county court's main function was to serve as the county's legislative body.

The 1850 constitution created the office of county judge, who tried small civil and misdemeanor cases alone in quarterly courts (originally they met four times a year) rather than with the county court. Even so, the county judge's primary duty was to serve as the county's chief executive and preside over the county court (now only a legislative body and later renamed the fiscal court because of its taxing and appropriations functions). However, members of the county court were automatically justices of the peace. The 1850 document also reflected Jacksonian populism and provided for the election of all judges and magistrates. Court of Appeals and circuit judges had to be attorneys, but county judges and magistrates were most often not attorneys.

The 1891 constitution largely left the state's judicial system intact, although it authorized cities to establish police courts to try misdemeanor charges and violations of municipal ordinances. Judges of both police and quarterly courts initially examined felony charges and set bail for defendants. The Court of Appeals was the only appellate court, and after World War II its docket became so crowded that two or three years might pass before a decision was rendered.

In 1975, to the surprise of many, the legislature proposed and the voters ratified extensive amendments to the judicial sections (109–24) of the state constitution.[1] Kentucky's judiciary went from a loosely organized, quasi-medieval system of nearly one thousand separate courts to a centrally managed four-tier system in which all courts were courts of record and all judges had to be attorneys. The old Court of Appeals was renamed the Supreme Court, and a new intermediate Court of Appeals was created.[2] The circuit courts remained Kentucky's courts of general jurisdiction, trying felony charges and civil suits where the amount in controversy was $4,000 or more and all civil suits in equity. The amendment also established a new set of district courts with limited jurisdiction that handled the functions of the old quarterly and police courts. In addition to misdemeanors and initial felony-charge appearances, district courts also consider probate, traffic, small-claims (up to $1,500), and juvenile cases.

The 1975 amendment also created a state Administrative Office of the Courts (AOC). With the participation of the state's chief justice, it prepares the judicial budget requests to the General Assembly and supervises budgetary implementation. The current budget is approximately $300 million (plus construction projects of county judicial centers). The judicial payroll covers about 3,300 employees, including judges and court personnel, as well as those working directly for the AOC. The AOC also collects data on filings, charges, case outcomes, etc.; handles money collected by the courts; arranges continuing-education programs for judges and court clerks; maintains a website of laws, policies, and manuals that assist judges, clerks, and court workers in their duties; helps courts develop and maintain drug-diversion programs for those convicted of drug crimes; assists with pretrial and juvenile services; monitors foster care; and arranges for the assignment of judges in cases of recusal and overloaded dockets. The AOC's director, currently Laurie K. Dudgeon, is appointed by the Supreme Court justices.

STRUCTURE OF THE CURRENT JUDICIAL SYSTEM

As a whole, Kentucky's judicial system is called the Court of Justice and contains four levels of courts. Justices and judges are elected on a nonpartisan ballot in even-numbered years (in contrast to state officers, who are elected in odd-numbered years) for terms noted below. The chief justice of the Supreme Court manages the Court of Justice and can assign judges on one tier to hear cases in another tier as conditions require.

The Supreme Court

This court is composed of seven justices, each of whom is elected by the voters in each of seven appellate districts.[3] The districts are not necessarily equally populated. The justices serve staggered eight-year terms. In 2012 they earned about $135,500 annually. The chief justice is elected by his or her colleagues for a four-year term. The current chief justice is John D. Minton of Bowling Green, first elected in 2008. Joseph E. Lambert of Mt. Vernon served from 1998 until he retired in 2008, and before that Robert F. Stephens of Lexington held the position from 1982 to 1998.

The court sits at the state capitol building in Frankfort and hears all cases en banc.[4] In the latter part of the first decade of the twenty-first century, about 1,100 cases appeared annually on its docket on average. About 35 percent of these were mandatory under the 1975 judicial amendment. These are appeals from criminal convictions involving the death penalty or sentences in excess of twenty years (these bypass the Court of Appeals) or State Bar Association disciplinary actions against attorneys.

In the remaining 65 percent of the docket, the Supreme Court has discretion in choosing what cases to consider on their merits. Nowadays there are around three thousand requests for discretionary review each year. They are examined by the court's staff counsels (experienced attorneys) who make accept or decline recommendations to the justices. The court grants about seven hundred. Usually these cases involve constitutional interpretation, the meaning of new statutes, legal issues heretofore undecided in Kentucky, conflict of precedents, abuse of discretion by a lower-court judge, or important issues of public policy or public interest. In cases selected for review, the lower-court decision is overturned much more often than not. The court sets some cases for oral argument, but more are decided on the briefs and the written record. On rare occasions the Supreme Court takes a case directly from a circuit court, bypassing the Court of Appeals. This happens when the case is of obvious and major importance (e.g., the case challenging the state's school-financing system) and will get to the high court anyway.[5] Also, if time is of the essence, the Supreme Court may take a case directly from a circuit-court decision.

The court decides cases in conference shortly after the argument. Sometimes the discussion in conference is lively and contentious. The chief justice assigns someone to write the majority opinion, although occasionally a justice volunteers for the task. Other justices may write concurring opinions or dissenting ones if they disagree with the reasoning or outcome. The court designates perhaps 20 percent of its opinions for publication in the *Southwest Reporter*.[6] These are official precedents that serve to guide future Supreme Court decisions and are binding on the state's lower courts.[7] Unpublished opinions are not official precedents, but those rendered after January 1, 2003, may be considered by a court if there is no published opinion that adequately addresses the issue before the court.

The Court of Appeals

This court is composed of fourteen judges. Two members are elected from each of the seven appellate districts used for the state Supreme Court and serve staggered eight-year terms. They earn $130,000. A chief judge is elected by his or her colleagues for a four-year term. He or she appoints three-judge panels each month to decide its cases and names one of the three as presiding judge, who usually writes the opinions. The Court of Appeals has no home courtroom; the panels hear arguments in courthouses around the state.

The Court of Appeals considered about 2,600 cases annually in the years 2005–2008. It has little discretion about what it considers because appeal from an adverse circuit-court holding is a matter of right.[8] Slightly more than 25 percent of them are criminal cases. It also must hear some appeals from administrative agency decisions, particularly workers' compensation cases—about 10 percent of its docket. Approximately 60 percent of the Court of Appeals's cases are announced in written opinions, and the remainder are disposed of by orders of a few sentences. Around 20 percent are decided after oral argument, and decisions in the rest are based on the parties' briefs. About 15 percent of its opinions are published in the *Southwest Reporter*. The Court of Appeals has discretion about hearing appeals from circuit-court decisions that are based on appeals from a district court.

Circuit Courts

There are fifty-seven circuits in Kentucky, served in 2012 by 146 judges, 51 of whom preside over family courts. Circuits can cover from one to four counties and be staffed by one or more judges. Jefferson County has 17 judges, while the Fifty-Sixth Circuit, composed of Trigg, Caldwell, Lyon, and Livingston Counties, has one judge. The judges are elected for eight-year terms with a salary of $124,600. Circuit courts are the workhorses of the system, handling all felony charges, common-law suits in excess of $4,000, cases in equity, divorce, adoption, and termination of parental rights, contested probate cases, and appeals from some administrative decisions. (The Franklin Circuit Court in Frankfort is especially busy in the last category because it hears challenges to decisions or policies of state agencies.) They also hear appeals from district-court decisions. In fiscal year (FY) 2012 the circuit courts disposed of approximately 31,000 felony charges, 54,000 civil suits, 7,000 divorce or other family cases (from non-family circuit judges), and 7,000 other types of cases for a total of 100,000 cases. This amounts to over 1,100 cases per judge. About 17,000 came from Jefferson County.[9]

Of course, only a small number of cases filed go to trial. Juries have twelve members. Verdicts must be unanimous in criminal cases, but the agreement of only nine jurors suffices in a civil case.

Many circuits have family courts. A pilot family-court project began in Jefferson County in 1991. It was quite successful, so in 2002 the legislature proposed and the voters adopted an amendment to the state constitution authorizing them throughout Kentucky. In 2012 they were in place in seventy-two counties. In circuits with such courts, one judge (more in urban areas) hears only cases involving family issues. The basic idea behind the court is that the family is not shuttled among judges, which can result in uninformed or conflicting decisions, but has one judge who learns its needs over time and fashions orders to accommodate them. In circuits without family courts, matters such as domestic violence, paternity, dependency, child abuse and neglect, and status offenses such as truancy, children beyond control, and habitual runaways are heard in district courts, and matters such as divorce, support, custody, visitation, adoption, and termination of parental rights are heard in circuit courts. In some circuits without a family court, the judge can appoint a domestic-relations commissioner who will conduct hearings for the judge on family matters and write a recommendation to the judge. In FY 2012 family courts disposed of over 72,000 cases, the great bulk of which involved divorce, custody, child support, and domestic violence.

Some family courts had family drug courts to handle substance abuse problems in families or among juveniles. Because of recent budget cuts, however, these courts are not being funded (a few have obtained temporary private funding). Their revival in better fiscal times is uncertain.

District Courts

These courts constitute the lowest level of the judicial system. There are sixty districts. Most are coterminous with the circuits (and share the same elected clerk), but there are 116 district judges. They are elected for four years and have a current salary of $112.667.52. District courts handle misdemeanor cases (including violations of city or county ordinances), traffic offenses, and monetary claims of less than $4,000 (if the amount is less than $1,500, the district court goes into a small-claims mode where parties do not need lawyers and often do not have them); serve as juvenile courts in non-family-court circuits; and handle uncontested probate filings. District judges hold initial hearings in felony charges, set bail, issue emergency protective orders (EPOs) or other orders in domestic-relations disputes, and, like circuit courts, can issue search and arrest warrants. They also establish guardianships and conservatorships and issue involuntary-mental-commitment orders. In sparsely populated counties without a district judge in residence, a trial commissioner (who is not necessarily an attorney) is appointed to set bail and issue EPOs.

In FY 2012 district courts disposed of approximately 150,000 misdemeanor cases, 349,000 traffic cases, 29,000 juvenile cases, 33,000 probate cases, 125,000 civil cases involving amounts between $1,500 and $4,000, 15,000 small-claims cases, 8,000 domestic-relations orders, 56,000 felony arraignments, and 16,000 other types of cases for a total of 749,000, or somewhat more than 7,100 cases per judge. Nearly 155,000 were in Jefferson County.

District-court juries have six persons and require unanimity in misdemeanor cases but only five votes in civil disputes.

Court Clerks

The Supreme Court and the Court of Appeals choose their own clerks. Circuit clerks were untouched by the 1975 judicial amendment and are still elected on a partisan basis for six-year terms. There is one circuit clerk for each of the state's 120 counties, and they also serve as clerks of the district courts. Clerks have some patronage opportunities and perform some nonjudicial functions, such as issuing drivers' licenses.

Legal Training and the Bar

There are three law schools in Kentucky. The one at the University of Kentucky in Lexington has the largest regular faculty and library. The Louis D. Brandeis School of Law is at the University of Louisville and is named for the famous U.S. Supreme Court justice, who was a native of that city. The Salmon P. Chase Law School, long a proprietary law school in Cincinnati, became part of Northern Kentucky University in the 1970s. The last two schools have night divisions. Each school graduates in the neighborhood of 125 students annually.

The Kentucky Bar Association is unified; that is, all attorneys licensed to practice in the state must be members. The association had over 15,000 members in 2010, although not all of them practice law or even live in the state. A Bar Association disciplinary committee hears complaints of unprofessional behavior against attorneys and metes out disciplinary punishment (e.g., disbarment, suspension from practice) in accord with rules established by the Supreme Court. Such punishments are appealable to the Supreme Court.

HOW JUDGES COME TO AND LEAVE THE COURTS

Judicial Elections

The 1975 amendment switched the election of all judges in Kentucky from a partisan to a nonpartisan basis. This probably reduced the number of contested elections, and many incumbent judges are returned unopposed. Even so, perhaps a third of circuit and district judges are opposed by serious challengers. Challenges are more frequent at the appellate levels. Since 1980, five sitting Supreme Court justices (three of whom came to the court by gubernatorial appointment) have been defeated after aggressive campaigns by their opponents, and at least that many have been vigorously challenged. Nearly half of the Court of Appeals judges also undergo serious opposition. Open judgeships at all levels are almost always contested.

Judicial elections are sometimes just contests between attorneys who want the judgeship (if three or more file for the position, the top two vote getters in the May primary are placed on the November ballot unless one receives a majority of the votes in the primary). At times, however, judicial elections can have ideological or even partisan overtones, especially in appellate-court contests. Such issue-oriented contests may well increase in the coming years. In 2008 a Kentucky federal district judge, ruling on a lawsuit by a candidate for the Supreme Court, cited the First Amendment's guarantee of freedom of speech to strike down portions of the state's Code of Judicial Conduct that prohibited candidates for judgeships from raising money themselves, indicating how they stood on political issues, or identifying with a political party.[10] Thus future candidates for judgeships may give speeches or run advertisements about their stands on issues such as abortion, same-sex marriage, and posting the Ten Commandments and may state what party they prefer. At this writing it is not clear just how far judicial candidates can go in acting like candidates for nonjudicial office, but they clearly have considerably more leeway than they did a decade ago. The federal court ruling obviously defeats, at least in part, the intention of the drafters of the 1975 amendment to remove politics from judicial elections.[11] The 2006 election for the Kentucky Supreme Court's Fifth District seat (the bluegrass area) had a partisan flavor. Here John C. Roach, appointed to the court by Republican governor Ernie Fletcher (from a position as counsel to the governor) sought unsuccessfully to stave off the candidacy of Fayette Circuit judge Mary Noble, a Democrat.

Some races are expensive. Over $300,000 was spent in the Seventh District (eastern Kentucky) in 2012 when the Court of Appeals judge Janet Stumbo unsuccessfully challenged incumbent Will Scott for his seat. (This was a rematch of their also expensive 2004 contest when Scott narrowly defeated Stumbo, then the incumbent.) Almost that much was spent in the 2000 race between incumbent John Keller and challenger

Larry Forgy (the 1995 Republican gubernatorial nominee, who narrowly lost to Paul Patton) for the Fifth District seat, which Keller retained. Over a quarter of a million dollars was spent in the 2008 race between incumbent Lisabeth Abrahamson and James Shake for Jefferson County's Supreme Court seat. Abrahamson won a close race. However, unlike some states, national big business or notable social conservative groups have not directly targeted a sitting appellate judge for defeat by backing or even seeking out an opponent and pouring large sums of money into his or her campaign.[12]

Filling Vacant Judgeships

Many judges first reach the bench by nominating-commission recommendation and gubernatorial appointment when a midterm vacancy occurs. The 1975 amendment established a merit-plan mechanism that operates in this situation. Close to 10 percent of Kentucky's judges resign, retire, die, become disabled, or are removed each year. Some resignations occur when a lower-court judge is elected or appointed to a higher court. When a vacancy occurs, the amendment provides for judicial nominating commissions as the first step in filling the vacancy. There is one commission for both appellate courts and one for each circuit- and district-court jurisdiction. The chief justice of the Supreme Court presides ex officio over all commissions. Two members are elected by the bar association (the state bar for the appellate commission, the local bar for the circuit/district), and the governor appoints four nonattorney members, two from each political party. Commission members serve four years. The commission notifies all attorneys in the state or affected circuit, considers those who apply, and contacts those who are nominated by others. It then forwards three nominees without indicating any preference to the governor, who must appoint one of them. If the governor fails to do so after sixty days, the chief justice is empowered to make the appointment. The person named serves until the next regular election (not necessarily the end of the term).

Membership Turnover on the Courts

There has been considerable turnover in membership on the Supreme Court. Two justices, Joseph Lambert (1987–2008) and Donald Wintersheimer (1983–2006), served for over twenty years, and Robert Stephens (1983–1999) served for sixteen years, but most justices hold office for shorter periods, and a few, like gubernatorial appointee John Roach, serve just a few months. Some justices accept other political positions (e.g., Stephens became secretary of the Justice Cabinet under Governor Paul Patton). More often they come to the court around age sixty and retire after a term or a bit more. Some are defeated for reelection. Three justices (along with about 30 percent of judges on other courts) retired on June 30, 2006, before the General Assembly's downward revision of judicial retirement-system pensions took effect the next day. In 2013 none of the justices were really old hands—the member with the greatest seniority, Will Scott, had served only eight years. Three justices, John Minton (chief justice), Bill Cunningham, and Mary Noble, were elected in 2006 for terms ending in 2014. Lisabeth Abrahamson was appointed in 2007 and elected to a full term in 2008 for a term ending in 2016, and Daniel Venters, appointed in 2008, was elected in 2010 to serve through 2018. Michelle Keller was appointed in April 2013 to replace Will Schroder who had retired. Court of Appeals judges also have considerable turnover. Circuit- and district-court judges usually have greater longevity, but some are ambitious and move up in the judicial or political world or leave the bench for a more lucrative law practice.

Diversity

Until recently, Kentucky's judiciary was pretty much an all-male club. The dramatic increase of female attorneys over the past thirty to forty years has naturally led to more women becoming judges. In 2013 three of the seven Supreme Court justices, six of the fourteen Court of Appeals judges, thirty-seven circuit judges, and forty-two district judges were female. In 2013 a majority of the district judges in Jefferson County were women. Governor Paul Patton was particularly instrumental in increasing their number; 27 percent of his judicial appointments were women.[13] The Supreme Court had its first woman justice in 1993 when Governor Brereton Jones named Sara Combs to fill a vacancy in the Seventh District (eastern Kentucky). Shortly afterward, ironically, Combs was defeated for reelection by another woman, Janet Stumbo.[14] Subsequently, two other women have been elected to the high court, Mary Noble of Lexington and Lisabeth Abrahamson of Louisville.

William McAnulty, an African American circuit judge, was elected to the Court of Appeals from the Jefferson County district. In June 2006 Governor Fletcher appointed him to the district's vacant position on the Supreme Court. Sadly, a year later he was diagnosed with fatal lung cancer and had to resign. Denise Clayton, an African American woman, is serving on the Court of Appeals. There is a smattering of African American judges on the circuit and district courts around the state.

The Judicial Conduct Commission

This commission was established as part of the 1975 amendment. It considers complaints that judges have behaved unprofessionally. It has six members, one each selected by the Court of Appeals, circuit and district judges , one elected by the state bar association, and two nonattorney citizens appointed by the governor. Complaints that make a facial case of misconduct are investigated by the commission staff. If the investigation does not resolve the issue, a formal hearing is set in which the commission's attorney presents its case and the judge, likely represented by an attorney, presents a defense. Complaints are not made public unless they reach the hearing stage. In several instances judges have resigned after complaints rather than go to a hearing before the commission.

When the commission finds that a judge has engaged in misconduct, it has several options. The most severe is removal from office—a rarity. Or the commission can suspend a judge without pay for a given time period. This punishment has been meted out to several judges, including one Supreme Court justice, Jack Dan Combs, for improper campaigning (it was later overturned by the Supreme Court). Finally, the commission may reprimand a wayward judge. Reprimands come in three forms. In a public reprimand the finding is made public and the judge is identified; one or two of these occur each year. When the complaint is resolved without a hearing, a private reprimand is issued; the finding is made public, but the judge is not identified. The weakest and most frequent sanction is a private admonishment where the commission sends the judge a letter, but it is given no publicity. All punishments are subject to review by the Supreme Court if the judge involved appeals, and the court has reduced or overturned commission sanctions several times. The commission may also force a judge to retire for a disability that affects his or her ability to handle judicial duties fairly and efficiently.

APPELLATE COURTS IN STATE POLITICS AND POLICY

The highest court in each state sometimes makes decisions that affect public policy in its state. A few such decisions can have a substantial influence on what happens in education, taxation, finance and economic development, controversies over social issues, governmental powers, and other policy areas. Numerous state supreme courts, for example, have ruled that their state constitutions require significant alterations in the ways public schools are financed. In 2008 and 2009 respectively, the supreme courts of California and Iowa ruled that their state constitutions accorded marriage rights to same-sex couples. Of course, a state supreme court takes a political risk if it changes public policy in an unpopular manner; California voters explicitly added a ban on same-sex marriages to their state constitution after the court ruling, and the three Iowa justices who were seeking reelection were defeated in 2010.

Kentucky is no exception, and its highest court has a long history of making important decisions, especially in light of some seemingly rigid restrictions found in the 1891 constitution. The pre-1977 Court of Appeals (then the highest court), for example, made the so-called rubber-dollar decision in 1962.[15] This ruling gutted Section 246 of the constitution, which limited state officers and employees to a salary of no more than $12,500 annually. The court held that the salaries could be multiplied by the difference between the dollar's 1949 (when Section 246 was revised) value and its current value. Obviously, by the 1960s a strict reading of this limit would prevent the state government from having competent personnel. The old court also allowed city and county income taxes despite the state constitution's explicit prohibition of them by designating them as occupational licensing fees.[16] These license fees have become a major source of revenue for cities and counties. The full-value-assessment decision in *Russman v. Luckett* (1965) is another important case.[17] It required county property-valuation assessors to assess property at its full value. Previously, property had often been assessed at 50 percent or less of fair market value, and sometimes there were big differences in the valuation of similar properties depending on who an assessor's friends and enemies were.

Here I discuss some of the major appellate decisions affecting Kentuckians that have been rendered since the new court system became operational in 1977.[18] Most are by the Supreme Court. Few have been unanimous, and dissents have sometimes been passionate.[19] Although frequent turnover of justices and the nonideological nature of most of its cases have foreclosed any visible and consistent voting blocs on the court—unlike the U.S. Supreme Court—the justices do have differing points of view about such issues as business regulation, economic development, social issues, constitutional and statutory interpretive philosophies, and the like. Some justices have been noted for their positions on particular issues. Most notably, Donald Wintersheimer rarely voted to overturn criminal convictions, William Cooper was quite friendly to business when regulation, labor relations, or consumer issues came up, and Jack Dan Combs tended to be sympathetic with plaintiffs in tort cases, workers' compensation claims, and criminal defendants' claims that due process was violated.

Education

Since the Supreme Court's inception in 1977, its most important case making public policy involved the way public schools were financed. In *Rose v. Council for Better Education* (1989),[20] the court by a 5–2 vote found the state school system unconstitutional because it was not an "efficient system of common schools throughout the state," as required by Section 183 of the constitution. The council, an ad hoc group, had challenged the state's uniform funding per pupil policy, arguing that it led to an unequal education for students in poorer districts that could not put as many of their own resources into education as could more prosperous districts. In the following year, after much wrangling, the General Assembly passed the Kentucky Educational Reform Act. This law not only equalized financing so that poorer districts received more state funding than more prosperous ones but also significantly revamped the curricular requirements and administrative structure of local school systems. The educational reforms considerably changed the management of Kentucky's schools and garnered considerable national attention and approval when they were adopted.

A later legislative initiative aimed at lowering high-school dropout rates was adoption of a "no pass, no drive" law that prevented dropouts or those failing in high school from obtaining a driver's license before their eighteenth birthday. In 2003 the state's high court found this measure unconstitutional.[21] It held that the law violated the U.S. Constitution's equal protection clause because in some districts students could pursue an alternative education program, but in others such a program was not available.

Three Supreme Court decisions rejected attempts to have the state fund religious schools directly or indirectly. A law authorizing the state to give secular textbooks for use in private schools was struck down in 1983, and a law allowing public school buses to transport pupils to religious schools was voided in 1994.[22] Both were held to violate Section 189 of the constitution, which prohibits public funding of "any church, sectarian or denominational school." This section applies at the collegiate level as well. In 2006 the legislature appropriated $10 million (plus $1 million in scholarships) for the construction of a pharmacy school at the University of the Cumberlands, a Southern Baptist school in Williamsburg. Again, the court struck down the funding.[23]

Social Issues

The Supreme Court has considered several cases involving what might be considered moral or social conservative issues. Most spectacularly, in a 4–3 vote in *Commonwealth v. Wasson* (1992),[24] the court struck down Kentucky's 194-year-old prohibition of homosexual sodomy, holding that it violated the state constitution's guarantee of individual liberty found in Sections 2 and 3. The majority noted that Kentucky had a long history of protecting individual privacy from state intrusion. *Wasson* was a highly controversial decision at the time—and a pioneering one in that it was just the third state Supreme Court decision striking down such laws (several state legislatures had repealed laws against homosexual behavior). *Wasson* also extended the right of personal privacy beyond that guaranteed by the U.S. Supreme Court, which several years earlier had declined to find such a right in the U.S. Constitution.[25] Surprisingly, although *Wasson* was widely criticized by social conservatives, it did not become an issue in subsequent contests for Supreme Court seats.

Given its subject matter, *Wasson* attracted a great deal of attention both in Kentucky and throughout the nation—it had considerable symbolic importance. But because sodomy laws were difficult to enforce and attempts to do so were rare, the case had little real impact on Kentuckians' lives. In 1997 the Court of Appeals rendered a decision with somewhat greater impact when it interpreted the state's 1992 domestic-violence statutes to include gay and lesbian couples living together, as well as heterosexual couples.[26] And in 2010 the Supreme Court allowed the non-birth-mother partner to seek custody and visitation rights when a lesbian couple broke up.[27] There has been no appellate consideration of a right of homosexual marriage in Kentucky, and with the 2004 adoption of a specific state constitutional prohibition (Section 233A), such a claim is not likely to arise in the state's courts.

The Supreme Court has made no significant decisions related to abortion. However, it did hold in 2004 that a homicide prosecution could be brought against a driver who was at fault in the death of a viable fetus, thus overturning the common-law rule that a fetus has no legal existence until it is born alive.[28] In two cases it also rejected a suit for "wrongful life" against medical providers who failed to prevent contraception or diagnose catastrophic fetal illnesses because, among other reasons, such a cause of action reeked of eugenics.[29] But the court did adopt a "right-to-die" policy allowing a competent individual to refuse hydration and nutrition when a fatal and irreversible illness is certified.[30]

In 1980 the state high court gutted Kentucky's long-standing "blue laws" that prohibited most businesses from operating on Sunday.[31] Blue laws were hotly debated in the 1970s (and in earlier periods as well), but the General Assembly, fearing the political consequences of repeal, did not act. The court overturned them through a clever interpretive device. A few years earlier the legislature had exempted businesses that were in "continuous work scheduling" from the blue laws. The exemption's purpose was to keep industrial production that occurred on a 24/7 basis going (e.g., it was inefficient to bank steel-mill furnaces on Saturday and restart them on Monday). But the Supreme Court interpreted the word "continuous" to mean that if a business was open the other six days of the week, even if only on a nine-to-five basis, it was operating continuously. So as long as employees got at least one day of rest each week, the business complied with the law. Little serious protest followed this decision, and the General Assembly made no attempt to rewrite the statute.

The sale of alcoholic beverages has been a contentious issue in Kentucky for well over a century. By and large the rules concerning wet/dry elections or other aspects of liquor sales have been the province of the General Assembly, but the Supreme Court upheld legislation forbidding precincts in dry counties to vote themselves wet but allowing those in wet counties to vote themselves dry.[32] The court also held a state law preventing the sale of alcohol within two hundred yards of a church unconstitutional as a violation of the U.S. Constitution's prohibition of the establishment of religion.[33] In another decision more related to economics than to the morality of alcohol, the court in 1982 struck down the state's half-century-old "fair-trade" law, which set minimum prices that retailers must charge for various kinds of liquor, as a violation of the Sherman Antitrust Act.[34]

Most challenges to regulating strip clubs are taken to federal court, but the state Supreme Court upheld a Newport ordinance forbidding nude dancing in so-called private clubs and later ended a long battle about near nudity by upholding a McCracken County minimum-clothing and no-touching ordinance.[35]

Although smoking is less a matter of morals than a health concern nowadays, the court upheld Lexington's smoking ban in businesses, restaurants, and bars, rejecting the owners' argument that only the state legislature could do this.[36] Several other counties and cities later passed similar laws.

In pending litigation of some interest, Kentucky is trying to seize about 140 Internet domain names pertaining to online gambling sites on grounds that they violate the state's laws prohibiting gambling. The Court of Appeals held that the state lacked jurisdiction to seize such property. In March 2010 the Supreme Court reversed the Court of Appeals on a technicality, holding that the gaming association lacked standing to sue because it did not own any domain sites. The suit was later amended by including some owners among the plaintiffs. The case has not been litigated on its facts, so it may be a few years before this intriguing question involving issues of federalism and freedom of speech is decided.[37]

Taxes and Economic Development

The Supreme Court rendered a landmark decision in 1987 when it upheld the state's condemnation of homes and farms and transfer of them to Toyota for construction of its large manufacturing plant in Scott County. The justices rejected an argument that the forced transfer of property from one private owner to another was not a public purpose condemnation, holding that the plant's economic benefits to the state's citizens made the state's assistance a public purpose.[38] The decision also upheld state tax-exemption incentives to the automobile manufacturer. Other state high courts had been making similar decisions. This ruling set the precedent that has enabled Kentucky to compete and sometimes win battles with other states in an ongoing effort to attract manufacturing firms to relocate there or to build other revenue-producing entities, such as shopping malls and amusement parks. There was a strong adverse reaction nationally to state condemnation of private property (including homes) and transfer of it to another private owner for economic development after the U.S. Supreme Court held in 2005 that this did not violate the U.S. Constitution.[39] Many states passed laws constraining such transfers, but this negative reaction did not arise in Kentucky.

Coal has a mixed record in the high court. In 1984 the General Assembly passed legislation effectively voiding the "broad-form-deed" interpretation long upheld by the state's highest court. This interpretation of mineral deeds that landowners sold to coal companies in the late nineteenth and early twentieth centuries, when strip mining was unknown, allowed this form of mining to flourish after World War II. The court struck the legislation down in 1987.[40] The following year the legislature overwhelmingly adopted and the voters overwhelmingly approved an amendment to the state constitution prohibiting such an interpretation of mineral deeds. In 1993 the Supreme Court upheld the constitutionality of the amendment against arguments that it violated the U.S. Constitution's clauses on obligation of contract and deprivation of property without due process.[41] In 1988 the court found unconstitutional a state law allowing unmined coal to be taxed at one mill (one-tenth of one cent per hundred dollars in assessment), a drastically lower rate than taxes on other property.[42]

Governmental Powers

Legislative Research Commission v. Brown (1984) is probably the most important case in the area of governmental powers.[43] The General Assembly had authorized the commission, composed of legislative leaders, to delay or reject administrative regulations that various executive agencies adopted. The court held the delegation invalid as a violation of separation of powers. It said that the General Assembly had authorized executive-branch agencies to adopt regulations. The legislature can pass laws to rewrite or void these regulations when it is in session, but the court held that it cannot delegate legislative powers to anyone else. This ruling weakened the ability of the legislative leaders to counteract agency rules that they disliked or that were unpopular with some interest groups. The decision gives various executive-branch cabinets or officers more real power because alteration of regulations is less likely to occur in a short and busy legislative session. *Brown* aside, however, the Supreme Court is often reluctant to trim legislative power and sometimes will uphold a law while noting that the General Assembly has overstepped its bounds.[44]

Kentucky has had divided government since the Republicans took control of the state senate in 2000, so adopting a state budget has become more difficult in recent years. When the 2004 General Assembly failed to do so, Governor Ernie Fletcher drew up a budget plan himself. The court struck it down, ruling that under Sections 27 and 28 (separation of powers) and 230 (no expenditure of funds except as authorized by the legislature) of the state constitution, only the legislature can approve budgets.[45] If no budget is adopted, the governor can spend only continuing appropriations already authorized by the General Assembly.

The court did uphold a sweeping gubernatorial power to pardon under Section 77 of the state constitution. The issue arose in the wake of a grand-jury investigation of Governor Fletcher's appointment of political supporters to merit-system positions and his pardon of those arranging this before any indictments. The court held that Section 77 did not limit the governor's power to issue pardons before an indictment or to a class of individuals not fully known, as well as particular persons.[46]

In 2010 the court struck down legislation that required some gubernatorial appointees to be approved by both houses of the General Assembly. The Court cited Section 93 of the constitution, which requires only Senate confirmation of such appointees.[47]

The court also got into the reapportionment business, usually the domain of the federal courts. After the legislature reapportioned itself following the 1990 census, the court required it to redo the apportionment because too many counties were divided contrary to Section 33 of the state constitution, which mandates the minimum necessary division of counties.[48] Using the same rationale, the court struck down the 2012 redrawing of legislative districts.[49]

Public Safety

When revenues fell during the great recession, the legislature, in an effort to save money, authorized early release from prison or termination of parole for some nonviolent offenders. Some Commonwealth attorneys and other peace officers sought to block the law's implementation, arguing that such action endangered public safety. The court ruled that it was the legislature's duty to make such a choice in times of budget shortfall, and the courts could not second-guess it.[50]

In 2012 the court held that the state's law permitting licensees to carry concealed weapons allowed them to have handguns in their vehicles when they were parked on public or private property even if weapons were otherwise banned on such property (e.g., educational institutions, hospitals).[51]

Athletics

Little is more important to Kentuckians than athletics, especially basketball. In the 1990s the state's courts were occasionally asked to rule on eligibility questions about both secondary-school and collegiate players. The most notable case came in 2001 when a Jefferson County circuit judge enjoined the NCAA from declaring a University of Louisville basketball recruit ineligible to play. When the case reached the Supreme Court, it lifted the injunction and said that courts should refrain from second-guessing athletic-association decisions.[52] Subsequently, few eligibility cases have gone to the courts.

NOTES

Bradley Canon would like to acknowledge assistance from Jason Fleming, a judge on the Christian Circuit Court and a former student.

1. For a discussion of the adoption of the amendments, see Kurt X. Metzmeier, Michael Whiteman, and Jason Nemes, *United at Last: The Judicial Article and the Struggle to Reform Kentucky's Courts* (Frankfort, Ky.: Administrative Office of the Courts, 2006).

2. In this chapter I use "Supreme Court" and "Court of Appeals" to refer to those in Kentucky. When referring to the federal courts of those names, I will precede the reference with "U.S." or "federal."

3. See http://courts/ky.gov/supremecourt/mapsupreme.htm for a map of the districts.

4. It will occasionally hear a case elsewhere in the state for legal educational purposes.

5. *Rose v. Council for Better Education*, 790 S.W.2d 186 (1989). I will omit the name of the state in cases cited from Kentucky's courts.

6. The West Publishing Company prints designated state appellate-court decisions in seven regional reporters. Kentucky's decisions appear in the *Southwest Reporter.*

7. Data on Supreme Court and Court of Appeals caseloads come from Kentucky Administrative Office of the Courts 2012 Statistical Report (http://courts.ky.gov.aoc.statisticalreports). Much of my description of the court's operation comes directly or inferentially from retired justice Donald Wintersheimer's book *Secrets of the Kentucky Supreme Court* (Covington, Ky.: Adams Ave. Books, 2010), 56–68. Wintersheimer served from 1983 to 2006.

8. Acquittals in criminal cases and decrees of divorces cannot be appealed, although custody- and property-division rulings are appealable.

9. Caseloads for the circuit and district courts come from the AOC report cited in note 7.

10. *Carey v. Wolnitzek*, 2008 WL 4602786 (E.D. Ky. 2008). The judge applied the U.S. Supreme Court's decision in *Republican Party of Minnesota v. White*, 536 U.S. 765 (2002). In July 2010 the federal Court of Appeals for the Sixth Circuit, which includes Kentucky, affirmed the ruling but asked the federal district court to determine the meaning of the word "issues" in the state's Code of Judicial Conduct. *Carey v. Wolnitzek*, 614 F.3d 189 (2010). In 2004 the Sixth Circuit refused to stay a federal district-court order enjoining the Judicial Conduct Commission from enforcing these canons against a judicial candidate. *Family Trust Foundation of Kentucky v. Kentucky Judicial Conduct Commission*, 388 F.3d 224 (6th Cir. 2004).

11. See Metzmeier, Whiteman, and Nemes, *United at Last*, on the importance of this intention, especially Chief Justice Lambert's introduction.

12. This is the theme of John Grisham's novel *The Appeal* (New York: Doubleday, 2008). In West Virginia, Massey Coal Company executives contributed over $3 million to a candidate for the state's highest court, who then provided the crucial vote to reverse a large judgment against Massey. The U.S. Supreme Court held that the newly elected justice had to recuse himself under these circumstances. See *Caperton v. A. T. Massey Coal Co.*, 129 S. Ct. 2257 (2009). The U.S. Supreme Court's decision in *Citizens United v. Federal Election Commission*, 130 S. Ct. 876 (2010), allowed corporations and unions to advertise for or against candidates for office directly, so there may well be an increase in corporate or union advertising in judicial contests.

13. "Patton Legacy: Women as Judges," *Lexington Herald-Leader*, December 5, 2003, A-1.

14. In an ironic twist, both Combs and Stumbo now serve on the state Court of Appeals. Combs, the widow of the late governor Bert T. Combs, was the chief judge of the Court of Appeals from 2004 to 2010. Stumbo lost her Supreme Court seat in 2004 and then was elected to the Court of Appeals in 2006.

15. *Matthews v. Allen*, 360 S.W.2d 135 (1962).

16. *City of Louisville v. Sebree*, 214 S.W.2d 248 (1948). Cities and counties cannot impose the tax on income independent of one's occupation.

17. *Russman v. Luckett*, 391 S.W.2d 394 (1965).

18. I will not cover criminal-law and common-law cases. As noted in the text, the Supreme Court hears many mandatory appeals (and some discretionary ones) from criminal convictions, but almost all are case specific (e.g., Did the prosecutor's closing statement contain inflammatory language?). The court sometimes tweaks the U.S. Supreme Court's interpretations of defendants' rights found in the U.S. Constitution, but it has not created important additional rights under the state constitution. The court also decides many common-law cases (tort, property, and contract disputes), but it is not really innovative in changing the common law.

19. See Wintersheimer, *Secrets of the Kentucky Supreme Court*. He describes the majority, concurring, and dissenting opinions in most important cases and sometimes comments on the arguments in conference as well.

20. *Rose v. Council for Better Education*, 790 S.W.2d 186 (1989).

21. *D. F. v. Codell*, 127 S.W.3d 571 (2003).

22. *Fannin v. Williams*, 655 S.W.2d 480 (1983), and *Fiscal Court of Jefferson County v. Brady*, 885 S.W.2d 681 (1994), respectively. The U.S. Supreme Court has allowed such programs under the U.S. Constitution, which is not as explicit as Section 189. See *Board of Education v. Allen*, 392 U.S. 236 (1968), and *Everson v. Board of Education*, 330 U.S. 1 (1947).

23. *University of the Cumberlands v. Pennybacker*, 308 S.W.3d 668 (2010).

24. *Commonwealth v. Wasson*, 842 S.W.2d 487 (1992).

25. *Bowers v. Hardwick*, 478 U.S. 186 (1986). The U.S. Supreme Court overruled *Bowers* in *Lawrence v. Texas*, 539 U.S. 558 (2003).

26. *Ireland v. Davis*, 957 S.W.2d 310 (Ky. App. 1997).

27. *Mullins v. Picklesimer*, 317 S.W.3d 569 (2010).

28. *Commonwealth v. Morris*, 142 S.W.3d 654 (2004).

29. *Schork v. Huber*, 648 S.W.2d 861 (1983). Twenty years later the court reiterated its position in *Grubbs v. Barbourville Family Health Center*, 120 S.W.3d 682 (2003), reversing a Court of Appeals decision that followed the dissenting opinion in *Schork*. The wrongful-life doctrine has been adopted in some states.

30. *DeGrella v. Elston*, 858 S.W.2d 698 (1993).

31. *Commonwealth v. Sutherland*, 601 S.W.2d 908 (1980).

32. *Howard v. Salyer*, 695 S.W.2d 420 (1985), and *Campbell v. Brewer*, 884 S.W.2d 638 (1994), respectively. The legislature most likely reasoned that allowing a wet precinct in a dry county would defeat the voters' desire for a dry county, but allowing a dry precinct would not hamper voters' ability to obtain alcoholic beverages. *Campbell* allowed precincts to vote themselves dry without regard to the three-year wait that the legislature mandated after a county wet-dry referendum.

33. *Farris v. Minit Mart Foods*, 684 S.W.2d 845 (1985).

34. *Alcoholic Beverage Control Board* v. *Taylor Drug Stores*, 635 S.W.2d 319 (1982).

35. *Hendricks v. Commonwealth*, 865 S.W.2d 332 (1993), and *Commonwealth v. Jameson*, 215 S.W.3d 9 (2006), respectively.

36. *Lexington-Fayette County Food and Beverage Assn. v. Lexington-Fayette Urban County Gov't.*, 131 S.W.3d 745 (2004).

37. *Commonwealth ex rel. Brown v. Interactive Media and Gaming Assn.*, 306 S.W.3d 26 (2010).

38. *Hayes v. State Property and Building Comm.*, 731 S.W.2d 797 (1987).

39. *Kelo v. City of New London*, 545 U.S. 469 (2005).

40. *Akers v. Baldwin*, 736 S.W.2d 294 (1987). Kentucky was the last state to cleave to the broad-form deed. It had been rejected or overturned by the highest courts in all other coal-mining states.

41. *Ward v. Harding*, 860 S.W.2d 280 (1993).

42. *Gillis v. Yount*, 748 S.W.2d 357 (1988).

43. *Legislative Research Commission v. Brown*, 664 S.W.2d 904 (1984). The LRC's main services are bill drafting, research, and monitoring the budget.

44. See, e.g., *Commonwealth v. Reneer*, 734 S.W.2d 794 (1987).

45. *Fletcher v. Commonwealth ex rel. Stumbo*, 163 S.W.3d 862 (2005). Governor Paul Patton promulgated a budget plan after the 2002 General Assembly failed to adopt one, but litigation was mooted when the 2003 session adopted one and retroactively approved the governor's expenditures.

46. *Fletcher v. Graham*, 192 S.W.3d 350 (2006).

47. *Fox v. Grayson*, 317 S.W.3d 1 (2010).

48. *Fischer v. State Board of Elections*, 879 S.W.2d 479 (1994).

49. *Legislative Research Comm. v. Fischer*, order, February 24, 2012, opinion, April 26, 2012.

50. *Commonwealth v. Thompson*, 300 S.W.3d 153 (2009).

51. *Mitchell v. University of Kentucky*, April 26, 2012.

52. *NCAA v. Lasege*, 53 S.W.3d 77. Lasege played on the basketball team for a year while the litigation was in progress.

7

State and Local Public Administration

Murray S. Y. Bessette

Public administration at the state and local levels, as at the national level, is about implementing the programs and policies established by the legislative, executive, and
even (at times) judicial branches of government. Because most programs and policies
are established only in a general and partial form, the bureaucracy is responsible for
the particulars of their complete implementation, and as a result, bureaucrats (who are
rarely, if ever, directly responsible to the people) enjoy considerable and significant
discretion in designing the final look and feel of the programs and policies established
by the people's representatives. What is important to note about the responsibility of the
bureaucrats and the representatives to the people of a town, city, county, state, or nation
is that both the bureaucrats and the representatives are responsible, at least in theory,
to the people; that is, bureaucrats are indirectly responsible to the people through
their responsibility to the people's direct representatives. Given the increase in the
size, scope, and complexity of state and local administration, institutional efforts have
been made to increase the responsibility of public servants to elected officials and,
thereby, to the people.[1] This indirect responsibility, however, can be infringed on by
various policies and procedures designed to improve the quality of administration, for
example, the merit system, tenure, and other forms of job security, which seek to limit
the influence of politics in bureaucratic decision making regarding hiring, firing, and
promotion of civil service staff, on the one hand, and the implementation and operation
of programs, on the other. Furthermore, limits placed on the people's representatives
themselves, especially term limits, make it difficult for elected officials to cultivate the
necessary policy expertise while they are in office to comprehend fully what can and
ought to be done to improve the operation of the government. In short, because civil
servants typically serve the public for much longer periods than do elected officials, they
are able to cultivate greater expertise and, therefore, tend also to have greater influence
on the initial design of policies and, thereby, on their outcomes too.[2]

The foregoing, of course, highlights the importance of properly understanding the character of state and local public administration. Because the behavior of individuals within any organization is the result of the complex interplay of institutions and personalities, such an understanding entails knowledge of both the character of the bureaucrats and the structure and organization of the offices they occupy. This chapter will first sketch the structure of the state administrative apparatus and then describe the various forms of government at local levels, both county and municipal. Then it will examine the character of those who make up the civil service—what they look like and how they are recruited and retained, hired and fired, and paid and promoted—as well as recent developments in public management and their effect on the quality of public administration.

STATE GOVERNMENT

The Kentucky Constitution establishes many of the offices charged with the administration of state policies and programs. In addition to the offices of governor and lieutenant governor, the constitution also sets the qualifications, term of office, mode of election, and compensation for the following constitutional state offices: treasurer; auditor of public accounts; commissioner of agriculture, labor, and statistics; secretary of state; and attorney general (Section 91). All other administrative positions (also known as inferior state officers) are provided for by statute; however, the constitution places certain restrictions on the legislative discretion of the General Assembly. As detailed in Section 93, "Inferior State officers and members of boards and commissions, not specifically provided for in this Constitution, may be appointed or elected, in such manner as may be prescribed by law, which may include a requirement of consent by the Senate, for a term not exceeding four years, and until their successors are appointed or elected and qualified."

Although the constitution establishes certain duties and responsibilities for constitutional officers—for example, "The Secretary of State shall keep a fair register of and attest all the official acts of the Governor, and shall, when required, lay the same and all papers, minutes and vouchers relative thereto before either House of the General Assembly" (Section 91)—it does not organize their internal structure. Rather, the particular organization of each office, whether constitutional or inferior, and its additional duties not specified in the constitution are established and promulgated in the Kentucky Revised Statutes (KRS) and the Kentucky Administrative Regulations (KAR).

Of particular note in this regard is KRS 12.020, which enumerates the departments, program cabinets, and administrative bodies responsible for the administration of policies and programs in the state. For the purposes of classification, there are three main divisions: (1) the cabinet for general government, which comprises the departments headed by elected (i.e., constitutional) officers; (2) the program cabinets, headed by appointed officers; and (3) the other departments, headed by appointed officers. In the first group reside the governor, the lieutenant governor, the Departments of State, Law, the Treasury, and Agriculture, and the auditor of public accounts. In the second group one finds eleven cabinets composed of 157 departments, offices, councils, boards, foundations, commissions, authorities, corporations, unions, and parks, many of which themselves consist of further divisions. The eleven cabinets are (1) Justice and Public Safety; (2) Education and Workforce Development; (3) Energy and Environment; (4) Public Protection; (5) Labor; (6) Transportation; (7) Economic Development; (8) Health and Family Services; (9) Finance and Administration; (10) Tourism, Arts, and Heritage; and (11) Personnel. In the final group there are eight departments, commissions, offices, or councils: (1) the Department of Military Affairs, (2) the Department of Local Government, (3) the Kentucky Commission on Human Rights, (4) the Kentucky Commission on Women, (5) the Department of Veterans' Affairs, (6) the Kentucky Commission on Military Affairs, (7) the Office of Minority Empowerment, and (8) the Governor's Council on Wellness and Physical Activity. With the exception of the Department of Veterans' Affairs, all the members of the third group, together with the Governor's Scholars Program, the Agriculture Development Board, the Kentucky Agricultural Finance Corporation, and the Office of Homeland Security, are attached administratively to the governor's office (KRS 12.023).

The size, scope, and cost of government in Kentucky, as in every other state and the nation as a whole, have grown immensely. In 1792 the budget of the state's first governor, Isaac Shelby, called for state revenues of only $16,400.[3] Adjusted for inflation, this represents approximately $204,241.41 in 2009 dollars.[4] In 2010 the General Fund budget of Governor Steve Beshear called for state revenues in excess of $8.5 billion. When Governor Wendell Ford first established program cabinets in 1973, there were only six: (1) Consumer Protection and Regulation, (2) Development, (3) Education and the Arts, (4) Human Resources, (5) Safety and Justice, and (6) Transportation. In 1982, during the administration of Governor John Y. Brown, the number of program cabinets increased to twelve, and Governor Martha Layne Collins added one more in 1984. In 1996, during the administration of Governor Paul Patton, the number of cabinets was increased yet again, to fourteen. In 2003 Governor Ernie Fletcher cut the number of cabinets to nine: (1) Justice and Public Safety; (2) Education and Workforce Development; (3) Environmental and Public Protection; (4) Transportation; (5) Economic Development; (6) Health and Family Services; (7) Finance and Administration; (8) Commerce (now Tourism, Arts, and Heritage); and (9) Personnel. Governor Beshear increased the number to the current eleven during his administration.[5] The number of cabinets is important because promotion to or demotion from cabinet rank is an indication of the respective importance of programs within the administration of government and thus can be understood as a sign of the understanding of the current administrators of the proper scope and function of state government. It can be said without controversy that today many more subjects are considered to be legitimate areas of governmental responsibility than in the past.

COUNTY GOVERNMENT

The idea of counties has its origin in early English history. Today, Kentucky has 120 counties. When it was first admitted into the Union (on June 1, 1792), Kentucky only had 9 counties, but the number grew to 52 over the subsequent eight years. By the time of the 1850 constitution, merely fifty years later, the state encompassed 100 separate counties. The creation of new counties slowed somewhat thereafter, with only 19 more being created in the years leading up to the 1890 constitutional convention, at which time the creation of new counties was limited by constitutional means.[6] The pertinent constitutional sections, which have remained unamended since passage in 1891, are as follows:

> Section 63: No new county shall be created by the General Assembly which will reduce the county or counties, or either of them, from which it shall be taken, to less area than four hundred square miles; nor shall any county be formed of less area; nor shall any boundary line thereof pass within less than ten miles of any county seat of the county or counties proposed to be divided. Nothing contained herein shall prevent the General Assembly from abolishing any county.
>
> Section 64: No county shall be divided, or have any part stricken therefrom, except in the formation of new counties, without submitting the question to a vote of the people of the county, nor unless the majority of all the legal voters of the county voting on the question shall vote for the same. The county seat of no county as now located, or as may hereafter be located, shall be moved, except upon a vote of two-thirds of those voting; nor shall any new county be established which will reduce any county to less than twelve thousand inhabitants, nor shall any county be created containing a less population.

These restrictions have proved successful in that only one county has been created since 1891: McCreary County in 1912. The complete list of Kentucky counties and their seats can be found in appendix D. The following two interesting facts are worthy of note. First, two counties have two county seats: Campbell (Alexandria and Newport) and Kenton (Covington and Independence). Second, only two counties do not have a classified city, but rather a census-designated place, as their county seat— McCreary (Whitley City) and Boone (Burlington). Both of these facts are largely the result of the difficulties involved in moving county seats once they are established.[7]

The governing offices within each county are established by the Kentucky Constitution. Section 99 sets both the duration of the officials' terms ("four years until the election and qualification of their successors") and the mode of selecting the individuals who will fill the offices (election) for the following county positions: judge of the county court (also known as the county judge-executive), county court clerk, county attorney, sheriff, jailer, coroner, surveyor, and assessor, as well as one justice of the peace and one constable in each justice's district. The districting of counties by the General Assembly for the last purpose is discussed in Section 142, where it is required that each county have a minimum of three and a maximum of eight districts. In other words, each county is required to have at least three and at most eight justices of the peace.

Although the offices and the qualifications for them are established by the constitution (Section 100), the particular responsibilities and authorities of the officials largely are not defined therein. Rather, these responsibilities and authorities are defined statutorily by the General Assembly.

Table 7.1. Differences between Magisterial and Commission Fiscal Courts

Type of fiscal court	Number of officials	Mode of election
Magisterial	4–9	At large and districts
Commission	4	At large

Source: Legislative Research Commission, *County Government in Kentucky*, Informational Bulletin no. 115 (Frankfort, Ky.: Legislative Research Commission, December 2003).

The government of all Kentucky counties takes one of two forms of fiscal court: magisterial or commission. The use of either fiscal-court form is unique to the state. These two forms of fiscal court are distinguished in two ways, which are summarized in table 7.1. First, in light of Sections 99, 142, and 144, magisterial fiscal courts have between four and nine officials (the judge of the county court plus the justices of the peace), whereas commissioner fiscal courts have only four officials (the judge of the county court plus the commissioners). Second, as established in the aforementioned constitutional sections, magisterial fiscal courts have a mixture of an at-large member (the judge of the county court) and members elected from districts (the justices of the peace), whereas all members of commissioner fiscal courts are elected at large.

As of 2003 and as reported by the Legislative Research Commission, most Kentucky counties use the magisterial form of fiscal court: "Of Kentucky's 120 counties, 105 have this type of governing body. However, the 15 counties with the commissioner form include most of the Commonwealth's most populous counties, so nearly half of all Kentuckians actually live in counties with a county commissioner type of fiscal court."[8] It is interesting to note that in counties that have adopted the commissioner type of fiscal court, the justice of the peace must still be elected despite having no official responsibilities or authorities. Finally, counties may change from the magisterial to the commissioner type and vice versa by following the procedures outlined in KRS 67.050.[9]

As in the case of the county offices, the Kentucky Constitution nowhere defines the responsibilities and authorities of the fiscal court. Rather, these responsibilities and authorities again are defined statutorily by the General Assembly.

CITY GOVERNMENT

Kentucky has 419 cities that the state recognizes and classifies. Each of these cities falls into one of six classes depending on its population. The use of population to determine city classification is a practice followed by most states within the United States (only 14 of the 40 states that have a classification scheme do not classify cities in this manner).[10] The population requirements for each of Kentucky's six classes, as well as the number of cities within each, can be found in table 7.2.

Classification of cities and towns within Kentucky is the responsibility of the General Assembly, which has historically reclassified cities only at the request of the local government. As can be seen in table 7.2, the distribution of classifications would change dramatically were cities and towns to be classified according to their actual population. Fifty percent of cities would be placed in the sixth class, rather than the

Table 7.2. Classification of Kentucky Cities

Classification	Population	Current classification	Proper classification
First	100,000 or more	1	2
Second	20,000 to 99,999	13	16
Third	8,000 to 19,999	19	29
Fourth	3,000 to 7,999	107	59
Fifth	1,000 to 2,999	116	105
Sixth	999 or less	163	208

Source: Adapted from Kentucky League of Cities, "Kentucky Cities: The Basics," revised November 2010, 6; and Kentucky Secretary of State, "Frequently Asked Questions," accessed January 3, 2011, http://www.sos.ky.gov/land/cities/landfaqs.htm#cityclass.

current 39 percent, and there would be an increase in the number of first-, second-, and third-class cities as well, a pattern consistent with Kentucky's increasing urbanization.

According to the Kentucky League of Cities (KLC), until 1891 cities in Kentucky operated under individual charters that required them to request specific grants of authority from the state legislature to fulfill necessary functions within their jurisdiction. Recourse to such special legislation was foreclosed in 1891 when the people of Kentucky adopted the current constitution, which established the current classification system on the basis of population.[11] Subsequently, in 1994, the Kentucky Constitution was amended to allow the state legislature to change the basis of classification. According to J. D. Chaney, director of governmental affairs for the KLC, although the change empowered the legislature "to create a city classification system based on any number of factors, including tax base, form of government, geography or any other reasonable basis . . . [it] has never acted to change the system."[12]

The significance of the classification system is found in the duties and authorities that are connected to and vary with each class according to state law. According to research conducted by the KLC, there are "357 statutes applicable to cities of the first class, 85 statutes applicable to cities of the second class, 43 statutes applicable to cities of the third class, 29 statutes applicable to cities of the fourth class, 7 statutes applicable to cities of the fifth class, and 15 statutes applicable to cities of the sixth class."[13] A small sample of the breadth of variety follows: sixth-class cities are the only class that may not levy an occupational license fee as a percentage of either earnings or profits (as all other classes may) but rather are restricted to flat annual rates; fourth- and fifth-class cities may levy a restaurant tax provided they have established a tourist and convention commission; second- and third-class cities must create police and fire departments; first-class cities must create a police merit system; and first- and second-class cities may establish local development authorities.

Despite the existence of six classes, the governments of all Kentucky cities are structured according to one of four organizational plans: the mayor-council plan, the commission plan, the city manager plan, or the city administrator plan.

Mayor-Council Plan

Under the mayor-council plan there is a separation of powers akin to that which the constitution establishes between the governor and the General Assembly, whereby the mayor enjoys substantial and broad executive power (including a veto), on the one hand, and the city council enjoys all legislative authority, on the other (figure 7.1). Unlike the state arrangement, however, the mayor not only chairs council meetings but also votes in the event of a tie. The mayor, moreover, as the chief executive, is responsible for the administration of the city government. The size of the city council depends on the city's classification and generally ranges between six and twelve council members. According to the KLC, "Slightly more than half of the state's cities (57 percent) use the mayor-council form of government."[14]

The KLC also notes that the state's two largest cities, Louisville and Lexington, are governed according to a modified mayor-council plan. In Louisville there are twenty-six council members, each representing a single district. Moreover, it is the Louisville Metro council president, and not the mayor, who chairs council meetings. In Lexington there are fifteen council members, of whom twelve represent a single district, and

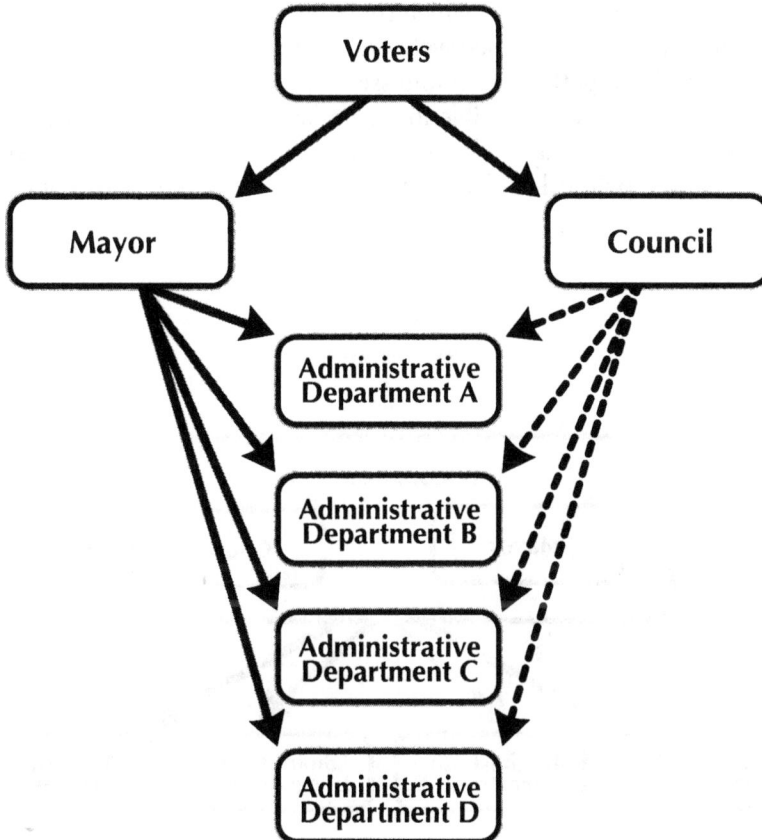

Figure 7.1. Mayor-council plan

the other three serve at-large. The mayor of Lexington chairs council meetings but never votes.

Commission Plan

The commission form of city government is similar to the mayor-council plan in that there is a mayor as well as four other commissioners who together constitute the board of commissioners (figure 7.2). It is in this board that all governmental powers (both legislative and executive) and administrative functions are vested. What distinguishes the mayor from the other four commissioners is that the mayor not only enjoys full voting and participatory rights in board deliberations but also chairs the meetings and has some limited additional powers and responsibilities, which can vary by municipality.

City Manager Plan

In Kentucky the city manager (or commission-manager) form of city government must be adopted via referendum. Nineteen cities have elected to use this governmental form. Unlike either the mayor-council or the commission plans, this form clearly distinguishes between the policy-making and administrative functions of government.

Both the city commissioners (of which there are four) and the mayor are elected to two-year and four-year terms, respectively, and therefore are directly responsible to the people of their locale. Together the commissioners and the mayor constitute the board of commissioners, which is responsible for formulating policy and adopting ordinances (figure 7.3). Although the mayor chairs the meetings of the board and serves as the city's ceremonial and political leader, he enjoys neither any veto power nor any admin-

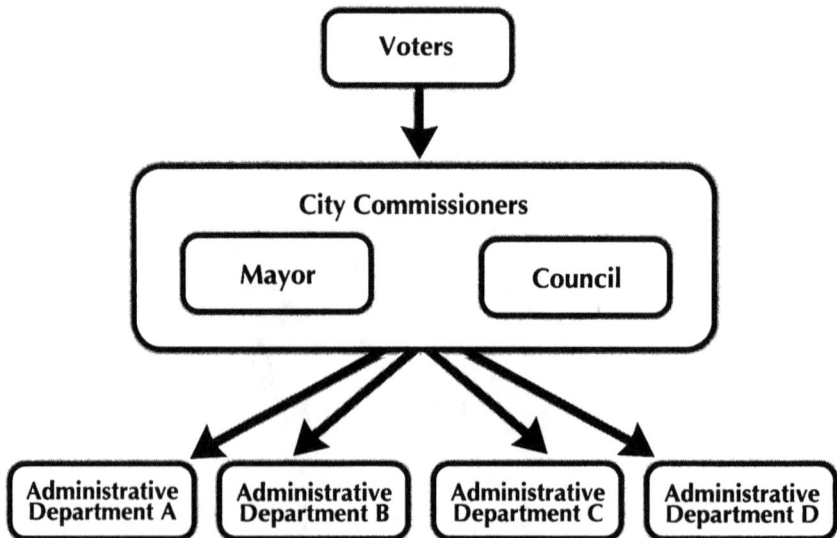

Figure 7.2. Commission plan

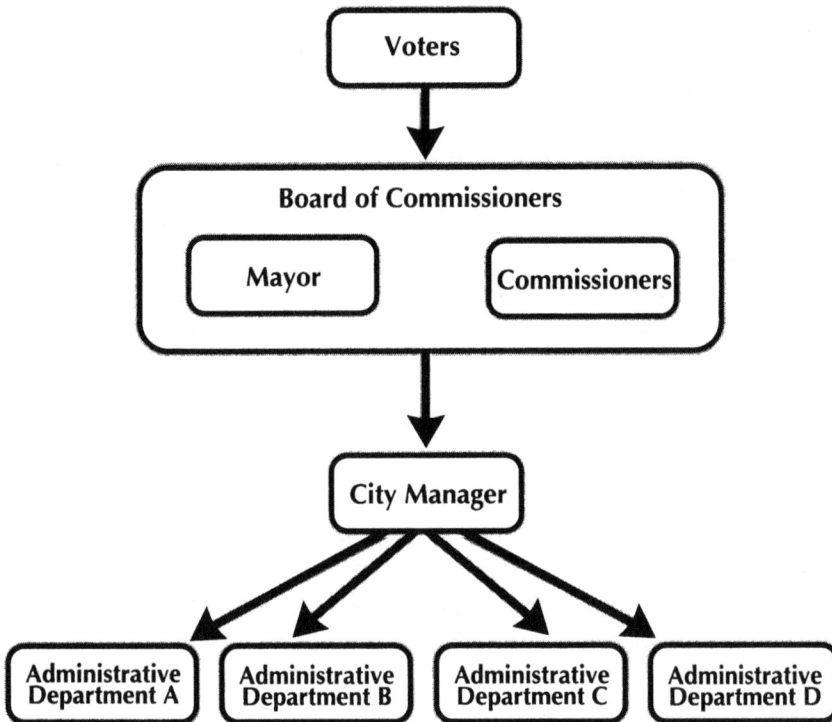

Figure 7.3. City manager plan

istrative authority. The board, moreover, appoints the city manager, who naturally is responsible to it for public administration. According to the Kentucky City/County Management Association (KCCMA), in addition to the daily administration of local government programs and services, the city manager is responsible, according to state statute, for preparing the city budget (which then must be approved by the board of commissioners) and for implementing it on approval. Although the city manager is responsible for public administration, and the board interacts with city departments only through the city manager, the city manager does not enjoy ultimate authority in personnel decisions (i.e., hiring and firing); rather, the board retains this authority.[15]

The Kentucky League of Cities maintains that "this form of government is most often utilized by larger cities with relatively extensive services and programs. More than half of second and third class cities use this form of government."[16]

City Administrator Plan

The city administrator plan, which is used by thirty-two cities in Kentucky, is a modification of either the mayor-council plan or the commission plan for city government organization and was authorized by the General Assembly in 1980. In essence, it allows cities or towns to benefit from a professional, full-time city administrative officer who is not unlike a city manager without going through the necessary referendum process for a city manager plan. According to the KLC, the important difference between a city manager and a city administrative officer is that the latter "position is created by ordinance and is directly responsible to the executive authority instead of the legislative body."

The KCCMA describes the basic responsibilities of the city administrative officer, who is responsible to the mayor or the board as a whole, as both advisory and administrative. That is, the city administrative officer advises the executive in regard to policy development and personnel decisions, prepares and implements the city budget, and carries out duties as established by the legislative body or assigned by the executive. As a result of this combination of legislative ordinance and executive delegation, the administrative functions and responsibilities of city administrative officers can vary widely.[17]

County Administrator Plan

The KCCMA reports that two counties in Kentucky have introduced a novel administrative position into Kentucky, the county administrative officer, who reports to the county judge-executive and whose administrative responsibilities and functions are not defined in statutes but in job descriptions or county ordinances.[18] For example, section 695.0 of the Kenton County Code of Ordinances reads:

> **695.0** COUNTY ADMINISTRATOR
>
> Goals and Objectives: The County Administrator shall be responsible for assisting the Judge/Executive and the Deputy Judge/Executive in administering the county's policies, rules, procedures, etc. as part of running the day to day operation of the various County departments.
>
> **695.1** The Judge Executive, with approval of the Fiscal Court, may hire a County Administrator who shall be responsible to the Judge/Executive.
>
> **695.2** The County Administrator shall be responsible for the administration of personnel and purchasing policies of the county, risk management, insurance matters, grantsmanship, the supervision of all County departments in the absence of the Deputy Judge/Executive, and other duties as may be delegated.

As can be seen in the section above, the general responsibilities and functions of the county administrator can be quite broad, while the particularities of the role are derived chiefly from delegations made by the judge-executive.

STATE AND LOCAL CIVIL SERVANTS

Civil servants include all individuals involved in the implementation of policies, delivery of services, and establishment of programs funded by public funds. In short, civil servants work for the government, whether at the municipal, county, state, or national level. Civil servants are often misidentified as interchangeable with bureaucrats. Bureaucrats, however, work in a bureaucracy, and although the organization of the bureaucracy can be "beautiful,"[19] its activities are perceived to be of a lesser degree of dignity—"pushing paper." Moreover, as a result of the science of administration, the decision making of bureaucrats is often regarded as cold, distant, and indifferent.[20] The police officer walking the beat, the sanitation worker collecting the trash, the maintenance worker repairing the generator, and the teacher teaching the class, however, are by no means distant paper pushers, but they are all civil servants.

Once one recognizes that the public sector includes such a vast, diverse array of jobs, it is easier to understand why the public-sector workforce is so large. In 2010 there were approximately 14.35 million local and 5.13 million state employees (a total of 19.48 million) nationwide. In Kentucky, in 2009 there were 284,300 individuals who were part of the public workforce (down from 284,815 in 2007), of whom the overwhelming majority worked at local levels. The Census Bureau's "Census of Government Employees" surveys the distribution of state and local civil servants across different levels of government according to their different functions.[21] In 2007, the latest year for which complete data are available, it found that approximately two-thirds (186,150) of Kentucky civil servants worked at the local level. Of these, 83.7 percent were full-time. The equivalent percentage for the state government was 73.4 percent. On the surface, there appears to be a significant difference between state and local governments in regard to their respective reliance on part-time employees; however, of the 26,249 part-time civil servants at the state level, fully 88.7 percent (23,282) are in education, with all but 146 serving the public in the state's universities and community colleges. Likewise, of the 30,395 part-time civil servants at the local level, almost 62.2 percent (18,903) are in education, with all but 9 working in the elementary- and secondary-school system. If one removes part-time educators from the numbers, 93.1 percent of local civil servants and 96.1 percent of state civil servants are full-time employees.

Implied in the foregoing is the fact that education is the single greatest function of both state and local governments, representing 53.6 percent and 69.1 percent of all civil servants at the state and local levels, respectively (or 63.7 percent combined). Aside from education, the next five greatest functions of the state government (as measured by number of employees) are public welfare (6.8 percent), judicial and legal (5.6 percent), health (5.0 percent), natural resources (4.5 percent), and corrections (4.3 percent). In looking at local governments, however, one must differentiate among county, municipality, special-district, and school-district levels because each serves a different function. All employees in the school districts work in education. In special districts employment is concentrated in libraries (17.7 percent), hospitals (16.9 percent), water supply (16.5 percent), fire protection (12.5 percent), and health (11.4 percent). In municipalities the top five functions are police protection (20.5 percent), fire protection (11.5 percent), government administration (10.2 percent), parks and recreation (8.0 percent), and water supply (5.5 percent). Finally, in counties one finds the following five priorities: health (19.6 percent), corrections (14.7 percent), hospitals (12.7 percent), police protection (11.9 percent), and highways (9.5 percent).

As reported by the Personnel Cabinet in 2010, of the total number of state employees, 8.67 percent were minorities and 49.03 percent were women, whereas minorities and women make up 11 percent and 51 percent of the state's population, respectively.[22] Depending on how one conceives of representation and responsibility, this discrepancy in bureaucratic representation may or may not have ill effects on the quality of administration.[23] The argument that the bureaucracy ought to mirror the people's demographics is in fact an argument that it ought to mirror their preferences; thus demographic characteristics—such as sexual orientation, ethnicity, age, class, education, religion, and geographic or national origin—serve as proxies for presumed preferences. For instance, research suggests that female child-support enforcement supervisors have different priorities from those of their male counterparts, which may lead to better outcomes for female clients.[24] Although research has shown that higher levels of the bureaucracy are less representative than lower levels,[25] other research also shows that lower-level bureaucrats are more likely to serve as active representatives than are higher-level bureaucrats. As a result, the disparity in representativeness may appear unproblematic from the standpoint of bureaucratic representativeness.[26] In addition, research has shown that civil servants have, on average, higher levels of education than their counterparts in the private sector.[27] Once education and skill level are controlled for, the average compensation of public servants is in fact slightly lower than that for equivalent positions in the private sector; however, this does not take into account the value of either the job security (life tenure) or early-retirement benefits (age fifty or fifty-five with up to 90 percent of final salary) available to public-sector workers that have no counterpart in the private sector.[28] These additional benefits may help recruit the next generation of civil servants.[29]

Regardless, the demographic makeup of the bureaucracy in Kentucky is the result of the human resources system, according to which public servants are recruited and retained, hired and fired, and paid and promoted. It should be unsurprising that Kentucky has an affirmative-action plan (KRS 18A.138), and that the executive branch has taken specific steps to recruit and develop minority managers within state government, including the establishment of the Governor's Minority Management Trainee Program. According to David Hamilton, the general goal of the human resource process is "to obtain the best possible match between job requirements and the person chosen to fill the job, . . . in the public sector. . . . It has been used to further either or both social and political agendas."[30] Affirmative-action programs are an example of using human resource policies and processes to further a social agenda. With regard to seeking to further a political agenda, one typically refers to patronage.

Patronage versus Merit

Generally speaking, the quality of a product is determined by the quality of the materials from which it is made and the skill of those who make it. In the development and implementation of public policy, things are no different. Conventional wisdom seems to suggest that the products produced by the public sector are inherently and inevitably inferior to those produced in the private sector—a "fact" that more often than not is attributed to lack of market competition and the existence of monopoly. The perception of the public, however, does not accord with this nearly as much as one may think, at least not when one probes deeper than the general public-private divide and looks into opinions concerning particular services.[31]

Early in the history of the Republic, civil servants came almost exclusively from the ranks of the educated, wealthy upper class, that is, from among those who one would presume were most fit to discharge the duties and fulfill the responsibilities of the public trust. President Andrew Jackson, seeking to undermine this elitist character of the national administrative apparatus, increased the demographic representativeness of the national government by admitting western frontiersmen via a patronage system.[32] In other words, in President Jackson's administration recruitment and retention, hiring and firing, and pay and promotion could depend on partisan affiliations as opposed to job-related qualifications. The patronage system, however, was not limited to the national government and was, in fact, the dominant means of staffing lower levels as well.[33] This, of course, led to a spoils system. Accordingly, there was a great amount of turnover within the administrative apparatus with every change in administration. Although this political patronage system greatly increased the control of elected officials over those whom they appointed because they had the absolute power of both appointment and removal, and therefore it greatly increased the strength of the indirect responsibility of administrators to the people, it did little to deter corruption and ensure competence in the administration of government.

Civil service reform in the direction of a merit system, that is, toward a system that sought better to attain the general goal of the human resource process—the best possible match between job requirements and the qualifications of the person chosen—truly began with the Pendleton Act of 1883, which was the result of numerous scandals and rampant nepotism within the administration of President Ulysses S. Grant and the assassination of President James Garfield by an individual seeking an appointment in a diplomatic capacity to Europe. The Pendleton Act established the United States Civil Service Commission, which was intended to enforce the merit system in the hiring of federal civil servants. This system was overhauled in 1978 by the Civil Service Reform Act, which abolished the commission and replaced it with the Office of Personnel Management, the Merit Systems Protection Board, and the Federal Labor Relations Authority. The goal of each stage in merit reform was neutral competence; that is, public employees were expected to discharge their duties competently and in a nonpartisan manner. This was to be achieved through the use of testing, a process that continues to be refined.[34] Obviously, merit can come into conflict with both patronage and seniority (which is the outcome of collective bargaining).[35] Such conflicts eventually will work themselves out. The intention that lies behind the reform effort and all the reforms in the process is the goal of better public management and improved delivery of public services.[36]

Immediately after the establishment of the merit system at the national level, like movement began at the state and local levels. The first state to adopt the merit system for public employees was New York in 1883. The very next year Albany, New York, became the first municipality to do so, and in the subsequent year Cook County, Illinois, became the first county to do so. Civil service reform was not uniform across the states. In fact, it took much longer for some states to move away from a reliance on patronage and to establish civil service protections.

The merit system in Kentucky was established by HB 199 and signed into law by Governor Bert T. Combs, who had campaigned on the issue, on March 17, 1960.

Although not all state agencies were included at first, by the time of implementation on July 1, 1961, they all were.[37] In the following decades tensions have continued to exist between merit and patronage in the hiring and firing of civil servants in Kentucky. As evidenced by the 2005 patronage scandal in the administration of Governor Ernie Fletcher, a balance has yet to be struck "between the responsiveness goals of patronage and the competency goals of nonpartisan expertise."[38] That said, institutional mechanisms exist to help reach that balance.

The Quality of Administration in Kentucky

Human resource policy is not the only determinant of quality performance in government. According to the Pew Center for the States, these determinants can be grouped into four categories: money, people, infrastructure, and information. Kentucky's performance (and the national average in parentheses) in each of these categories was C+ (B–), C+ (C+), A– (B–), and B (B–), respectively. The state received an overall grade identical to the national average for all states: B–.[39] The main deficiency identified by the Pew Center was short-term planning, that is, "setting interim objectives for which leaders and managers can be held accountable."[40] However, Kentucky has been a leading state in the development of e-government.[41] This should, in turn, "expand and extend the ability of government organizations to serve their constituencies and to promote a host of other, mainly positive, benefits to both government and its citizens."[42] One of the benefits of e-government is increased service quality at lower cost, a key feature that is often associated with the privatization of government services, which requires monitoring to preserve accountability.[43] Although reducing costs is often cited as a key driver behind privatization (and research supports the view that costs can be lowered via contracting out[44]), a lack of required personnel and expertise can also make it necessary.[45] In furtherance of the goal of quality administration at a lower cost to the public while also maintaining accountability, the state of Kentucky has undertaken a three-part audit of its privatization of commodities,[46] services,[47] and contracts.[48] The final recommendations of each of these audits shared certain emphases. The audits highlighted the need for additional training for state contracting staff and the development of better monitoring systems related to procurement, contracting, and privatization. Moreover, they recommended the identification and adoption of best practices in all these areas.

NOTES

1. Neal D. Woods, "Governors and the Bureaucracy: Executive Resources as Sources of Administrative Influence," *International Journal of Public Administration* 30 (2007): 1219–30.

2. Jeffrey S. Banks, "The Political Control of Bureaucracies under Asymmetric Information," *American Journal of Political Science* 36, no. 2 (May 1992): 509–24.

3. Sylvia Wrobel and George Grider, *Isaac Shelby: Kentucky's First Governor and Hero of Three Wars* (Danville, Ky.: Cumberland Press, 1974), 89.

4. Inflation adjustment (assuming $16,400 in 1800 and an end date of 2009) courtesy of the inflation calculator created by S. Morgan Friedman, available at http://www.westegg.com/inflation/infl.cgi.

5. Legislative Research Commission, *Kentucky Government*, Informational Bulletin no. 137 (Frankfort, Ky.: Legislative Research Commission, February 2003), 86.

6. George Morgan Chinn, *Kentucky: Settlement and Statehood, 1750–1800* (Frankfort, Ky.: Kentucky Historical Society, 1975), 123, 222.

7. Table adapted from the Kentucky Department of Librarians and Archives, "Kentucky County Formation Chart," accessed May 22, 2012, http://kdla.ky.gov/researchers/pages/county formationchart.aspx.

8. Legislative Research Commission, *County Government in Kentucky*, Informational Bulletin no. 115 (Frankfort, Ky.: Legislative Research Commission, December 2003), 8.

9. Ibid.

10. Kentucky League of Cities, "KLC Research Report: Classification of Cities," revised May 10, 2012, http://www.klc.org/userfiles/files/2012_Classification_Report.pdf. See also the Census Bureau's "2007 Census of Governments" description of the organization and structure of state and local government, http://www2.census.gov/govs/cog/all_ind_st_descr .pdf.

11. Kentucky League of Cities, "KLC Research Report: Classification of Cities," 2.

12. J. D. Chaney, "Class Dismissed? The Case for Classification Reform for Kentucky's Cities," *Kentucky City*, July/August 2011, 24.

13. Kentucky League of Cities, "KLC Research Report: Classification of Cities," 6. The report also provides a list of many of the pertinent sections of Kentucky Revised Statutes as an appendix.

14. Kentucky League of Cities, "Kentucky Cities: The Basics," 14.

15. Kentucky City/County Management Association, "About KCCMA," accessed January 3, 2011, http://www.kccma.org/index.php?id=2.

16. Kentucky League of Cities, "Kentucky Cities: The Basics," 15.

17. Kentucky City/County Management Association, "About KCCMA."

18. Ibid.

19. H. George Frederickson, "Can Bureaucracy Be Beautiful?," *Public Administration Review* 60, no. 1 (January–February 2000): 47–53.

20. Charles E. Lindblom, "The Science of 'Muddling Through,'" *Public Administration Review* 19, no. 2 (Spring 1959): 79–88.

21. The data on which the following is based is from the U.S. Census Bureau and can be accessed at https://harvester.census.gov/datadissem/.

22. Personnel Cabinet, "Semi-annual Report on Female and Minority Employment: January 1–June 30, 2010," Frankfort, Ky., September 2010, 7.

23. Kenneth John Meier, "Representative Bureaucracy: An Empirical Analysis," *American Political Science Review* 69, no. 2 (June 1975): 526–42; Antonio Sisneros, "Hispanics in the Public Service in the Late Twentieth Century," *Public Administration Review* 53, no. 1 (January–February 1993): 1–7.

24. Norma M. Riccucci and Judith Saidel, "The Representativeness of State-Level Bureaucratic Leaders: A Missing Piece of the Representative Bureaucracy Puzzle," *Public Administration Review* 57, no. 5 (September–October 1997): 423–30; Vicky M. Wilkins, "Exploring the Causal Story: Gender, Active Representation, and Bureaucratic Priorities," *Journal of Public Administration Research and Theory* 17 (2006): 77–94.

25. Meier, "Representative Bureaucracy;" Riccucci and Saidel, "The Representativeness of State-Level Bureaucratic Leaders: A Missing Piece of the Representative Bureaucracy Puzzle," *Public Administration Review* 57, no. 5 (September–October 1997): 423–24.

26. Kenneth J. Meier, "Latinos and Representative Bureaucracy: Testing the Thompson and Henderson Hypotheses," *Journal of Public Administration Research and Theory* 3, no. 4 (October 1993): 393–414.

27. Joshua M. Franzel, "The Public Sector Workforce—Past, Present, and Future," in *LERA 61st Annual Proceedings* (Champaign, Ill.: Labor and Employment Relations Association, 2009), 147–53; Keith A. Bender and John S. Heywood, *Out of Balance? Comparing Public and Private Sector Compensation over 20 Years* (Washington, D.C.: Center for State and Local Government Excellence and National Institute on Retirement Security, 2010); John Schmitt, *The Wage Penalty for State and Local Government Employees* (Washington, D.C.: Center for Economic and Policy Research, 2010).

28. Adam B. Summers, *Comparing Private Sector and Government Worker Salaries* (Los Angeles: Reason Foundation, 2010), accessed January 23, 2010, http://reason.org/news/show /public-sector-private-sector-salary.

29. Joshua M. Franzel, "Future Compensation of the State and Local Workforce," *Public Manager*, (Summer 2009): 58–64; Beth Almeida and Ilana Boivie, "Recruitment and Retention in the Public Sector: The Role of Pensions," in *LERA 61st Annual Proceedings* (Champaign, Ill.: Labor and Employment Relations Association, 2009), 154–59.

30. David K. Hamilton, "The Staffing Function in Illinois State Government after *Rutan*," *Public Administration Review* 53, no. 4 (July–August 1993): 381.

31. Theodore H. Poister and Gary T. Henry, "Citizen Ratings of Public and Private Service Quality: A Comparative Perspective," *Public Administration Review* 54, no. 2 (March–April 1994): 155–60.

32. Meier, "Representative Bureaucracy," 526.

33. Steven G. Koven, "Patronage in the Commonwealth of Kentucky," *Public Integrity* 9, no. 3 (Summer 2007): 285.

34. Steven W. Hays and Richard C. Kearney, "Anticipated Changes in Human Resource Management: Views from the Field," *Public Administration Review* 61, no. 5 (September–October 2001): 585–97.

35. Joel M. Douglas, "State Civil Service and Collective Bargaining: Systems in Conflict," *Public Administration Review* 52 (March–April 1992): 162–72.

36. J. Edward Kellough and Sally Coleman Selden, "The Reinvention of Public Personnel Administration: An Analysis of the Diffusion of Personnel Management Reforms in the States," *Public Administration Review* 63, no. 2 (March–April 2003): 165–76; Gerald T. Gabris and Douglas M. Ihrke, "Unanticipated Failures of Well-Intentioned Reforms: Some Lessons from Federal and Local Governments," *International Journal of Organizational Theory and Behavior* 6, no. 2 (Summer 2003): 195–225.

37. Larry Gillis, "Merit System Celebrates 50 Years," *Kentucky Personnel Board News and Updates* 1, no. 2 (May 2010): 1.

38. Koven, "Patronage in the Commonwealth of Kentucky," 295. See also Pew Center for the States, "Grading the States: Kentucky," *Governing* (March 2008): 56; Pew Center for the States, "Government Performance Project: Kentucky," *Grading the States* (2008): 3.

39. Pew Center for the States, "Government Performance Project: Kentucky," 1–13.

40. Pew Center for the States, "Grading the States: Kentucky," 56.

41. Darrell M. West, "State and Federal Electronic Government in the United States, 2008," *Governance Studies* (Washington, D.C.: Brookings Institution, 2008). The full report is available at http://www.brookings.edu/~/media/research/files/reports/2008/8/26%20egov ernment%20west/0826_egovernment_west.pdf.

42. Donald F. Norris and M. Jae Moon, "Advancing E-Government at the Grassroots: Tortoise or Hare?," *Public Administration Review* 65, no. 1 (January–February 2005): 64.

43. Jonas Prager, "Contracting Out Government Services: Lessons from the Private Sector," *Public Administration Review* 54, no. 2 (March–April 1994): 176–84; John Rehfuss, "Contracting Out and Accountability in State and Local Governments: The Importance of Contract Monitoring," *State and Local Government Review* 22, no. 1 (Winter 1990): 44–48.

44. Robert Jay Dilger, Randolph R. Moffett, and Linda Struyk, "Privatization of Municipal Services in America's Largest Cities," *Public Administration Review* 57, no. 1 (January–February 1997): 21–26; George A. Boyne, "Bureaucratic Theory Meets Reality: Public Choice and Service Contracting in U.S. Local Government," *Public Administration Review* 58, no. 6 (November–December 1998): 474–84.

45. Keoni S. Chi, Kelley A. Arnold, and Heather M. Perkins, "Privatization in State Government: Trends and Issues," *Spectrum: The Journal of State Government* (Fall 2003): 12.

46. Crit Luallen, *Kentucky's Administration and Management of Master Agreements and Catalog Master Agreements* (Frankfort, Ky.: Auditor of Public Accounts, 2005).

47. Crit Luallen, *State Contracts: Kentucky's Administration and Management of Contracting for Service Workers* (Frankfort, Ky.: Auditor of Public Accounts, 2005).

48. Crit Luallen, *Assessment of Kentucky's Privatization Efforts* (Frankfort, Ky.: Auditor of Public Accounts, 2006).

8

Public Finance and State and Local Budgeting

Lisa A. Cave

The prolonged U.S. recession has had a major impact on state budgets, and Kentucky is no exception. From 2007 to 2009 state revenue has fallen by 5 percent, or approximately half a billion dollars. Projections for the 2010–2012 biennial budget showed a gap of $1.5 billion. The governor, faced with a projected budget shortfall, proposed a budget that relied on the expansion of gaming to reduce the budget gap. Although both the House and Senate dismissed this idea, they were unable to agree on a common budget that eliminated the budget shortfall by the end of the legislative session. Therefore, the governor called a special session during which an amended version of the biennial budget was eventually passed and signed into law.

This chapter examines state and local financing in Kentucky. State and local financing mainly revolves around the taxing and spending of the jurisdiction. This chapter outlines the governor's role in developing and submitting a budget to the General Assembly and the General Assembly's role in enacting the budget into law. It then describes the politics and policies associated with developing optimal taxing and spending levels. This is followed by a discussion of the state's revenue sources and main appropriations. The chapter concludes with a discussion of financing at the local level.

THE BUDGET PROCESS IN KENTUCKY

State and local elected officials are charged with providing services to the constituents they serve. This requires both a political and an economic equilibrium about the level and quality of public goods and services and the distribution of tax shares to pay for these goods and services.

Constituents collectively weigh their desire for individual freedom against social welfare and societal demands. Then, via a series of political interactions with elected officials, they collectively determine the level and quality of services that the government is to provide and how the government will pay for these services.

There are three methods through which the government can pay for the services: imposing taxes, charging fees, or borrowing the funds. Taxes are involuntary contributions that may be levied on the consumption of a specific good, service, or income. In addition to taxes, the government can also impose fees, such as highway tolls, on the use of certain services. The final avenue through which the government can raise revenue to pay for the desired level of services is by borrowing.

Every even-numbered year the Kentucky legislature is required to pass a biennial budget that serves as the state's financial plan for the next two fiscal years. According to the Kentucky Constitution, the General Assembly must pass a balanced budget—spending must equal revenue. The budget outlines the state's plan for spending money on specific or general purposes from a variety of sources.

This process starts with the governor soliciting information from the various state agencies about their expected spending needs for the next two fiscal years. Combining this information with the current economic conditions, public interest, and program priorities, the governor formulates a budget for the executive branch of the government. This budget represents the governor's spending plan for the state for the next two years. The chief justice of the Kentucky Supreme Court and the head of the Legislative Research Commission (LRC) do the same for the judicial and legislative branches.

The governor then submits the budget recommendations to the General Assembly. The Kentucky General Assembly convenes annually on the first Tuesday after the first Monday in January. It convenes for sixty days during even-numbered years, and the constitution requires that the session be completed no later than April 15. In addition to regular sessions, the legislature may also convene extraordinary special sessions at the call of the governor.

The governor's budget recommendations are converted into the form of bills, called appropriation bills, and are introduced into the first chamber of the legislature, the House of Representatives. These appropriation bills authorize a state agency to spend a predetermined amount of public funds during a fiscal year. There are four types of funds from which appropriations are made. The first and most common is the General Fund. This fund contains the majority of the state's tax revenue. The second fund is the Road Fund, which obtains revenue via gas-tax receipts and sales taxes on automobiles. The third fund is the Restricted Fund, which includes revenues from license fees, tuition, and other service charges. The final fund is the Federal Fund. Revenue in this fund is obtained from the federal government in the form of intergovernmental transfers.

Upon entering the House, the budget bills are assigned to the House Appropriations and Revenue (A&R) Committee. The A&R Committee is composed of subcommittees representing the seven major jurisdictional areas: Economic Development, Natural Resources and Tourism; Primary and Secondary Education; Postsecondary Education; General Government, Finance, and Public Protection; Human Resources; Justice, Corrections, and Judiciary; and Transportation. This House committee examines the bills and incorporates the estimates of the Consensus Forecasting Group (CFG). The CFG is an independent group of economists and financial experts whose role is to estimate expected revenues over the next two fiscal years.

Once the bills are introduced, the committee invites experts to testify about specific aspects of these bills. The experts' testimonies typically generate significant discussions that result in numerous amendments to the budget bills before they obtain the majority vote of the committee in order to pass out of committee and be sent to the House floor. When the bills reach the House floor, the process repeats itself. Again, the budget bills require three readings that generate substantial discussions before they obtain a majority vote of the total membership of the chamber (fifty-one members) in order to pass. After passage by the House, the bills are sent to the second chamber of the legislature, the Senate, where they go through the same process.

Sometimes the House and the Senate pass different versions of the budget bills. In these instances a free conference committee composed of members from both chambers is convened to work out the differences in the budget. Typically the conference committee is able to find some middle ground between the two proposed budgets, and these amended bills are then sent to their respective chambers for approval. Once the budget is approved by both the House and the Senate, it is sent to the governor to be signed into law.

The governor has three options upon receiving the budget. He can sign it, let it become law without signature, or use the line-item veto to remove certain items from the budget. The governor's vetoes can be overridden by the General Assembly, but this requires a majority vote of members elected to each chamber.

Before 2000 both the House and the Senate were controlled by the Democratic Party. This control, coupled with a Democratic governor, ensured that the budget passed during the regular sessions. This changed in 2000 when the Republican Party captured the majority and leadership of the Senate. This change in legislative power has greatly influenced the political partisanship surrounding the budget and its passage. Between 2000 and 2010 the legislature failed to pass a budget during the regular session three times.

In 2010 Governor Steve Beshear proposed a budget that partially relied on the expansion of gaming to add $780 million in revenue as a means to reduce the budget gap. Both the Democratic-controlled House and the Republican-controlled Senate dismissed the idea of relying on expanded gaming. However, during this session House and Senate leaders were unable to agree on how to allocate spending within the budget. Primarily, the disagreement centered on a House-backed provision that called for spending hundreds of millions of dollars to bond school-construction projects. The Senate objected to this provision because it would severely increase the state's debt. Unable to overcome partisan differences, the Kentucky General Assembly ended its regular session on April 15, 2010, without passage of a budget.

In order to prevent a shutdown of the government, the governor called for an extraordinary session in May 2010. During this special session disagreements about spending allocations continued. Finally, both chambers agreed on a budget with significant cuts to higher education and most state agencies. However, not all members were satisfied with the final budget and felt compelled to support this plan in order to limit the length of the special session, which was costing taxpayers $64,000 a day.

SOURCES OF REVENUE

State and local governments rely on a diverse variety of revenue streams. Kentucky primarily relies on own-source revenues, such as taxes, charges, and fees.[1] In addition to own-source revenues, the state also receives intergovernmental transfers from the federal government, typically in the form of grants.[2] These grants may be highly restrictive, with specific limits and uses, or they may be general aid that can be used without restriction. The remainder of this section discusses the principles on which revenue may be raised and then explores the main revenue sources of the state of Kentucky.

Principles of Revenue Collection

Government financing is evaluated on the basis of three criteria: equity, efficiency, and ease of government implementation. Equity refers to the fairness of the method of financing. Revenue may be raised according to either the ability-to-pay principle or the benefit principle. The ability-to-pay principle states that as an individual's ability to pay increases, so should the amount that that person contributes (as a percentage of income). A good example of revenue raised according to the ability-to-pay principle is the income tax; as an individual's income increases, so does that individual's marginal tax rate. On the other hand, the benefit principle operates under the assumption that if an individual benefits from the use of a good or service, he should be the one to pay for that good or service. An example of revenue raised according to the benefit principle is park entrance fees.

The efficiency of a revenue source relates to how much the price and quantity of the economic activity from which revenue is being collected are affected. If there are no underlying inefficiencies in the market for the economic activity, then the process of collecting revenue from the activity will prevent the market from achieving an efficient equilibrium. The mechanism through which the revenue is collected will cause a distortion in the market that will affect both the equilibrium price and equilibrium quantity.

The third criterion used to evaluate revenue sources is the ease of government implementation and the acceptability of the mechanism through which the revenue is obtained. Some revenue sources require extensive infrastructure and planning in order to be implemented. For instance, the property tax requires that each property be evaluated every year. This process is time consuming and difficult to monitor. In contrast, the sales tax is significantly easier to implement and collect. The sales tax charges a flat rate on the sale of specified goods and services, and the specified revenue is collected from vendors. Each revenue stream—taxes, fees, and borrowing—is evaluated on the basis of these three criteria.

Taxes

Taxes are the largest source of revenue for the state and are levied on income, consumption, and wealth. The state's ability to tax depends on the tax capacity and tax effort of the tax. Tax capacity refers to the potential to raise revenues from taxes. Higher tax capacities are associated with higher levels of urbanization, per capita income, economic development, and natural resources. Tax effort refers to the degree to which the state exploits its fiscal potential.

In 2010 Kentucky ranked twenty sixth out of all states in state and local tax collections per capita, commonly referred to as the tax burden. Kentucky per capita income was $32,356, of which $3,027 (9.4 percent) went to state and local taxes.[3] In comparison, the national per capita income was $41,146, of which $4,112 (9.9 percent)[4] went to state and local taxes. This indicates that Kentucky places a smaller tax burden on its constituents than more than half of all other states.

The state relies on a wide variety of taxes for revenue. In 2009 tax receipts equaled $9.7 billion.[5] The largest source of state tax receipts is sales taxes (48 percent); the next-largest source of tax revenue is income taxes (38 percent); property taxes, licenses, and other taxes make up approximately 4 to 5 percent of total tax receipts.[6]

The different types of taxes vary in equity, efficiency, and ease of government implementation. Taxes may be implemented on the basis of the ability-to-pay principle, for example, the income tax, or the benefit principle, for example, a unit excise tax. In addition, the equity of a tax depends on whether the tax is progressive, regressive, or proportional. A progressive tax is a tax where individuals with higher incomes pay a higher marginal rate or a higher percentage of their income. A regressive tax is a tax where individuals with lower incomes pay a higher percentage of their income in taxes. A proportional tax is a tax where each individual pays the same proportion of his or her income. Whether a tax is considered equitable depends on the purpose of the tax. If the goal of the tax is to help redistribute income, then progressive taxes are highly equitable.

The second criterion used to evaluate tax revenue is efficiency. If there are no underlying inefficiencies in the market, then the implementation of a tax will prevent the market from reaching an efficient equilibrium. The degree to which the imposition of a tax distorts market decisions varies among the different taxes. The sales tax tends to be less distortional than a unit excise tax. The sales tax, which is imposed on the sale of most goods and services, affects the price of all goods and services together. Therefore, it does not affect the price and quantity of one good relative to other nontaxed goods and services. In contrast, the unit excise tax affects only the market for the specific good being taxed, not only increasing the price of this good but also making it more expensive relative to all other nontaxed goods. Further contributing to the distortional effect of a tax is the underlying price elasticity of demand on the good taxed.[7] If the short-run demand for a good is relatively inelastic,[8] as with motor fuels, for example, then the imposition of a tax will not have as great a distortional effect as if the short-run demand is relatively elastic.[9]

The third criterion used to evaluate tax revenue is acceptability. Acceptability of a tax depends on a variety of factors, such as perceived equity of the tax and its associated pain of payment. For example, constituents largely dislike the property tax because of its somewhat arbitrary evaluation methods, which lead to feelings of unfairness. Further, the tax requires a large lump-sum yearly payment, which increases the perceived pain of payment. In contrast, constituents tend to favor the sales tax, which collects a large amount of revenue but does so only in small increments, so the perceived pain associated with payment is smaller.

Each of the taxes that generate revenue for the state is also evaluated on the basis of one other factor: yield. Yield is a particularly important aspect of taxation because it weighs the amount of revenue expected from the imposition of a tax against the cost of applying this tax. Taxes that have a high yield, such as the income and sales taxes, return large amounts of revenue at low cost and are preferred to taxes with low yields, such as property taxes. The overall yield of a tax depends on three factors: the tax base, the tax rate, and the elasticity of demand.

The tax base is the number of individuals or activities on which the tax is levied. The broader the tax base, the higher the yield; the narrower the base of the tax, the lower the yield. An additional determinant of tax yield is the elasticity of demand for the economic activity on which the tax is levied. The more inelastic the demand for the economic activity, the higher the yield that a higher rate of taxation will provide. If the demand for the economic activity is more elastic, a lower rate of taxation will result in a higher revenue yield. The remainder of this section examines and evaluates the specific types of taxes—sales, unit excise, income, and property taxes—on the basis of equity, efficiency, ease of implementation, and yield.

Although no constituent wants to pay taxes, doing so is necessary for the provision of public services. According to public choice, the level and quality of services and the taxes to pay for these services should mirror the preferences of constituents. Public choice theory assumes that all individuals act in their own self-interest. Each individual desires a given level of public service and the taxes required to provide that level of public service. Collectively, individuals then vote for the politician who best represents their desired level of public service and taxes. Through a series of political interactions, agreement on the level of public services and the accompanying distribution of tax shares among individuals are determined. Taxes are not voluntary contributions; therefore, citizens who vote against this action are still required to contribute.

Sales Taxes   The sales tax is levied at a flat percentage of the price of the good being taxed. In theory, the sales tax should be applied to all goods and services; however, most services are excluded from this tax. Kentucky in particular taxes very few services—37 out of all 183 services—in comparison with a state like Tennessee, which taxes approximately 81 out of 183 services.[10] In addition, there are some goods, for example, grocery foods, that are exempt from the sales tax. This is a common practice among many states as a way to relieve the tax burden on those who spend a relatively large portion of their income on grocery food—the poor. Overall, the sales tax is relatively efficient and easy to implement and has a high yield, but it is inequitable.

Because the sales tax is a flat rate, individuals pay the same percentage regardless of their income. This means that individuals with higher incomes will purchase more goods and services and therefore contribute more to sales tax revenue than their lower-income counterparts. This contribution represents a smaller percentage of their overall income than it does of those with lower incomes—a regressive tax structure—and thus therefore the tax is inequitable.

The sales tax tends to be efficient because all eligible goods and services are taxed at a flat rate. Even though the tax distorts the market equilibrium price and the quantity of goods and services purchased (raising the price and lowering the quantity), it does this for all eligible goods and services and therefore does not distort the relative prices of goods and services. The sales tax has a broad base because it includes the purchase of almost all goods and therefore has a high yield. Because the sales tax is collected from the retailer and is composed of relatively small increments, it is easy to implement and very politically favorable.

State sales-tax rates range from 4 percent to 8 percent. However, the following states do not levy a sales tax: Alaska, Delaware, Montana, New Hampshire, and Oregon. The sales tax was first implemented in Kentucky in 1960 and is currently set at a rate of 6 percent. Kentucky is no different from any of the other state governments that levy sales tax and derives the majority of its revenue from this tax—48 percent (see figure 8.1).

There is one potential area of sales-tax revenue that states still are not able to exploit fully: Internet sales. Initially states imposed taxes or fees on e-commerce activities. However, a U.S. Supreme Court ruling that a state may not require a seller that does not have a physical presence in the state to collect tax on sales in that state severely limited the collection of this tax. The Court's rationale for the ruling was that

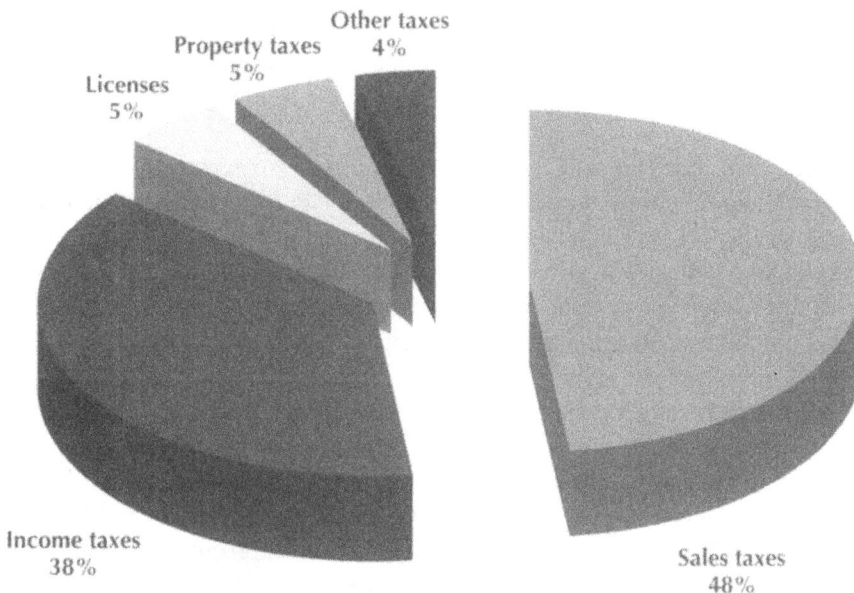

Figure 8.1. Distribution of Kentucky tax receipts in 2009

the existing system of tax collection was too complicated for the collection of Internet sales taxes. This ruling was further augmented by the passage of the Internet Tax Freedom Act (1998), which placed a moratorium on the taxation of Internet sales. In response to the Supreme Court ruling, many states, including Kentucky, have passed streamlined sales tax (SST) legislation. The SST introduces new collection software that reduces the complexities and lays the foundation for the future taxation of Internet sales. Even though steps have been taken to allow for the taxation of these goods and services, it may still be a long way off.

Unit Excise Taxes A unit excise tax is a tax on a specific good or service. Most states employ excise taxes. The goods most often taxed are cigarettes, alcohol, and gasoline. Unit excise taxes tend to raise equity concerns and are inefficient, but they are easy to implement and may result in a high yield.

A unit excise tax raises equity concerns because it taxes only consumers of particular goods. Unless there are underlying reasons, such as negative externalities, these taxes may be viewed as discriminatory. Negative externalities are impacts on a third party because of the consumption of a good or service. For example, the purchase and consumption of cigarettes may impose additional costs on society, such as the harmful effects of secondhand smoke and increased health-care costs that are not captured in the free-market price of cigarettes. In this case the imposition of a unit excise tax on cigarettes may result in the efficient market equilibrium of cigarettes. The case may be made that a unit excise tax is both equitable and efficient, given the existence of negative externalities.

The tax base includes all individuals who consume the taxed goods. The overall yield will depend on the elasticity of demand for these goods. The more inelastic the demand curve, the greater the burden of the tax on consumers. For goods such as cigarettes and gasoline, demand tends to be relatively inelastic, at least in the short run. In this instance state governments can increase revenues by taxing these goods. However, this does raise distributional concerns about whether it is fair to tax these goods at higher rates.

Kentucky, like most states, taxes the consumption of cigarettes, alcohol, and gasoline. Cigarette taxes were first imposed in Kentucky in 1936 and are currently among the lowest in the country. The total tax on a pack of twenty cigarettes is 60 cents, which is well below the national average of $1.32 and ranks the state thirty-ninth highest nationally.[11] Total tax revenue from tobacco and tobacco products was $214 million (4 percent of total sales tax and gross tax receipts) in 2009.[12]

Alcoholic beverages are divided into three categories for taxation: spirits, wine, and beer. Kentucky taxes spirits more heavily than most other states, but wine and beer are taxed at lower rates than the national average. Kentucky levies the following taxes on the different categories of alcoholic beverages: spirits, $1.49 a gallon[13] (national average, $5.89); wine, 50 cents a gallon[14] (national average, 85 cents), and beer, 10 cents a gallon[15] (national average, 27 cents). In 2009 tax revenue from alcohol sales was $111 million (2 percent of total sales tax and gross tax receipts).[16]

The gasoline tax is the most common excise tax and is implemented in every U.S. state. Some states charge as little as 8 cents per gallon (Alaska), while others charge

46.6 cents per gallon (California). The current gasoline tax for Kentucky is 22.5 cents per gallon (national average, 25.96 cents per gallon), ranking the state thirtieth nationally.[17] In Kentucky the gasoline tax is variable and depends on the current price of gasoline. In 2009 motor fuel taxes raised $632 million (14 percent of total sales tax and gross tax receipts).[18] Unlike other tax receipts, the revenue raised through these taxes is allocated to the Road Fund.

Personal Income Taxes   Personal income taxes are taxes that are imposed on all earnings and unearned income. Income taxes are levied at federal, state, and local levels. Not all states levy an income tax. Texas, South Dakota, Nevada, Washington, and Wyoming do not tax personal income, while Tennessee does not tax income other than unearned income. Personal income taxes generate about 22 percent of all state and local tax revenues.

The personal income tax adheres to the ability-to-pay principle, where individuals with higher incomes pay a higher marginal tax rate than individuals with lower incomes—a progressive tax structure. Because of the progressive nature of the tax, the personal income tax is vertically equitable. In addition, the income tax is easy to collect and adjusts to economic conditions. The tax base is net income (gross income adjusted for exemptions and deductions). The tax has a broad base because it encompasses almost all sources of income, so it results in a high yield.

The current Kentucky income-tax rate has remained constant since 2000. Rates vary from 2 to 6 percent depending on the income bracket, with the highest income bracket reaching $75,000. This tax provides the second-largest source of revenue for the state, 38 percent. In addition to state income taxes, eight cities in Kentucky also levy their own tax on income (table 8.1). Residents of these cities pay federal, state, and city income taxes on their income and earnings.

In addition to state and city income taxes, Kentucky cities, counties, and school districts may impose an occupational license tax that operates like an income tax. This tax, the result of *Louisville v. Sebree* (1948), allows the taxing jurisdiction to collect

Table 8.1. Local Income Tax Rates of Selected Kentucky Cities

Kentucky city	Tax rate
Bowling Green	1.85%
Covington	2.5%
Florence	2%
Frankfort	1.75%
Lexington-Fayette	2.25%
Louisville	2.20%
Owensboro	1.33%
Richmond	2%

Source: Tax Foundation, "Local Income Taxes: City- and County-Level Income and Wage Taxes Continue to Wane," accessed June 9, 2013, http://taxfoundation.org/article/local-income-taxes-city-and-county-level-income-and-wage-taxes-continue-wane.

from employers a percentage of any locally earned income. Depending on the taxing jurisdiction, the tax rate ranges from 0.25 to 2.5 percent of earned income.

Property Taxes Property taxes are imposed on the fair cash value that a voluntary sale of real property would be estimated to generate. Property taxes are unpopular among constituents because of very complex, arbitrary methods of assessing the value of the property on which the tax is to be levied, which lead to feelings of unfairness. Reliance on the property tax as a source of revenue has declined in over the past thirty years. The majority of this decline is due to legislation passed in 1979 that limits growth from the tax levied on real property to 4 percent per year. In addition to this legislation, exemptions, such as the homestead exemption and the disability exemption, have been introduced. Under these exemptions taxpayers who are sixty-five years of age or older are classified as disabled and qualify for an exemption that is applied against the value of the tax due.

Kentucky has had a property tax since it became a state in 1792. It is one of thirty-seven states that collect property taxes at both the state and local levels, although the majority of the tax revenue is collected at the local level. The state property tax is a personal property tax that is levied primarily on automobiles. In Kentucky the value of the taxes owed is assessed by the property value administrator (PVA) in each county, and the collection is performed by the sheriff's department. In fiscal year (FY) 2009, the last year for which data are available, Kentucky local governments collected $542.46 per person in property taxes, while the state collected $120.65 per person.[19] Altogether Kentucky collected $663 per capita. This ranks the state forty-sixth, well below the national average.[20]

In order to determine the amount of property tax owed, the property must be appraised at its market value. The method of appraisal is somewhat arbitrary. For example, in Lexington–Fayette County there are several examples of inconsistent property value assessments. In particular, these assessments have occurred in and around the area of Toner Street, a street of almost identical townhomes. In 2004 the Housing and Development Agency sold the residence at 555 Toner for a price of $18,000. Only a year later the Lexington-Fayette PVA reassessed that property at twice the sale value, $36,000. Another property that was sold for $25,000 in 2007 is currently assessed at $36,000, while other properties on that street were sold at a price of $54,000 in 2006 and are currently assessed at that same value. In addition, there is a property that sold for $40,000 in 1984 but is currently assessed at $39,000. These examples highlight the arbitrary nature of this system of appraisal.

In addition, certain types of property are exempt from the tax, such as hospitals, religious buildings, and nonprofit organizations. Further adding to constituents' dislike of the tax is that residential property tax rates vary significantly with respect to property value. In areas where property values are high, the property-tax rates tend to be lower, whereas in areas with lower property values, taxes tend to be higher in order to raise enough revenue to provide the required services. Because high-property-value areas are typically higher-income areas and lower-property-value areas are typically lower-income areas, this method of taxing higher-income individuals at a lower rate is considered inequitable. Altogether, these factors give rise to constituents' view of the property tax as unfair.

The property tax has traditionally been viewed as a reliable source of revenue for state and local governments because of the immobility of the tax base and the fact that as real property values rise over time, revenue will increase without requiring an increase in the tax rate. However, under the current economic climate, with foreclosures on the rise and property values falling, and the passage of legislation both limiting the growth of revenues and increasing the number of exemptions, revenue from this tax is declining and is not as stable as initially thought.

User Charges and Licenses

User charges are categorized under the benefit principle. Individuals who receive the benefits of a service are required to pay for it. User charges may be voluntary, such as entrance to a national park, or mandatory, such as trash collection. They may be applied continuously or just for special occasions. In addition to their efficiency, user fees and licenses are generally politically acceptable.

User fees and licenses made up approximately 5 percent of Kentucky receipts in 2009 and are determined through political rather than market interactions. Current user fees and licenses total approximately $7 billion, with the largest fees and charges coming from hospitals—$1.5 billion, or approximately 21 percent of total fees and licenses. The second-largest category of fees and charges is from universities in the form of tuition—$1.4 billion, representing 20 percent of total fees and licenses received.[21]

User charges and licenses have become more attractive to state and local governments, which have been looking for ways to increase revenue during the economic downturn. User charges and licenses offer a highly equitable and politically acceptable method of revenue generation. In addition, these charges can be imposed or adjusted without legislative action. Therefore, the use of this source of revenue is expected to increase in the future.

Debt Financing

Debt financing is the use of borrowed funds, usually bonds, to finance government expenditures. Typically these borrowed funds are used to finance capital expenditures. The decision to engage in capital financing depends on the size of the expenditure, the duration of the debt, and the method of finance. In some cases state and local governments issue debt for projects whose purpose is less public in nature. These projects are afforded the same tax privileges as debt issued for strictly government-owned and operated projects. The decision about what projects to fund and how much to allocate to these projects is determined by the Private Activity Bond Volume Cap Allocation Committee.

There are several available types of debt financing: state and local bonds, revenue bonds, and tax-incremental bonds. As of June 2009, Kentucky had $6.875 billion in outstanding debt, and interest payments on those bonds consumed 6.43 percent of the state's revenue. By passing the budget in May 2010, the state avoided having to pay $113 million to refinance debt. The federal government subsidizes the use of government bonds by exempting the interest earned by purchasers of government bonds from taxation.

State and local bond financing, sometimes called a general-obligation bond, is a full-faith-and-credit bond. This means that the guaranteed revenues of the issuing jurisdiction are pledged as security. These bonds are used extensively by state and local governments. They indebt the state or local government to the full cost of the capital projected.

A revenue bond is a nonguaranteed bond for which no security is offered. These bonds are obviously more risky than the general guaranteed bonds and offer higher rates of return. State and local governments favor these types of bonds because they allow governments to build infrastructure before sufficient capital has been accumulated.

Tax-incremental financing bonds pledge future increases in property and other tax rates in return for increasing development. This concept of debt financing raises intergenerational equity issues. Capital facilities have long lives and will therefore be enjoyed by future generations. Engaging in debt financing allows the future generation to share in the cost of financing the facilities. By issuing bonds, the current generation has shifted some of the cost of the capital facility to the next generation. However, members of the next generation did not develop or vote on whether they wanted the capital facility.

State and local governments are permitted to use tax-exempt bonds to finance activities that are private in nature. Congress has placed limits on the use of these bonds, both by type of activity and volume of debt that may be issued. The state ceiling on private activity is divided into two pools, with 40 percent allocated for the Local Issuer Pool ($164 million) and 60 percent allocated for the State Issuer Pool ($247 million).[22]

The Private Activity Bond Volume Cap Allocation Committee determines which "qualified private activities" to fund. The state currently funds these tax-exempt bonds and allocates them to private firms and corporations. Examples of firms that receive funding are manufacturing corporations that produce furniture, solid-waste-disposal companies, and the Kentucky Utilities Company.

The size of the state debt has been rising since 2000. Debt capacity, the ratio of net tax-supported debt to personal income, increased from 3.9 percent in 1998 to 5.4 percent in 2010. Kentucky's debt capacity is well above the national average of 3.2 percent and ranks the state eighth nationally.

Enterprise

A final option available to the state to raise revenue is through the sale of private goods and services. An example of such an enterprise is the state lottery. In 2009 the Kentucky state lottery raised $206 million for the state (gross ticket sales less prizes and administration costs).

In addition to state lotteries, a topic that has been discussed the last several legislative sessions is the issue of expanded gaming. There has been a push to legalize gaming in the state as a way to combat the state deficit and increase state revenues. As part of his projected revenue from new sources, Governor Beshear estimated that revenue from the expansion of gaming could provide $780 million in FY 2010–2012. Although gaming can significantly increase state revenues, there are also a number of negative impacts associated with these enterprises, such as compulsive gambling. Legislation legalizing the expansion of this activity has yet to pass both the House and the Senate, although it is likely to continue to be a topic of interest in upcoming legislative sessions.

Intergovernmental Aid

In addition to tax revenues, user charges, and enterprise, Kentucky also relies on intergovernmental transfers. The federal government provides intergovernmental transfers to the states. The goal of intergovernmental transfers is to ensure that state and local governments provide at least minimum levels of public services. Intergovernmental transfers may take several forms: categorical grants, block grants, or general-purpose grants. Categorical grants are the largest source of federal aid to the states. These grants typically have matching requirements and require that specific conditions be met. Matching requires that the federal government match the state payment for a service up to a predetermined percentage. An example of an important categorical grant is Medicaid. The second-largest type of grants is block grants, which are lump-sum grants that are designated for general use, such as community-development grants. The final type of grants is general-purpose grants, which are lump-sum payments that may be used for any purpose.

In 2009 the federal government provided $7.5 billion in intergovernmental transfers to the state of Kentucky. Kentucky is considered a beneficiary state—taxpayers receive more federal funding per dollar of federal taxes paid than the average state. In 2005 Kentucky citizens received approximately $1.51 per federal tax dollar collected, which ranked the state ninth nationally. This is an increase from 1995, when Kentucky received $1.28 per dollar of federal tax collection. In the ten years between 1995 and 2005 the economy was booming, but the state became even more dependent on federal aid.

Overall Revenue

Over the past thirty years revenue collections have been relatively stable as a share of state gross domestic product. Although general and selective sales taxes continue to provide the largest share of state and local tax revenue, the remaining composition of revenue has changed. Less revenue is now received from property taxes and more from charges and miscellaneous revenues.

APPROPRIATIONS FOR GOODS AND SERVICES

The second part of the trade-off between taxes and services in the operation of state and local budgets is the provision of services. Expenditures for services are called appropriations and are paid through one of the aforementioned funds. In the 2010–2012 budget, total appropriations were estimated to be $60.3 billion (figure 8.2).

The size of the state government relative to the state's economy has remained constant since 2000 at approximately 6 percent of gross state product. During this same period state revenue has been growing at the same pace as the economy. Because state revenue has kept pace with the economy, the revenue shortfall in the 2010–2012 budget must be due to increased spending. In particular, spending has increased in the provision of three services: corrections, Medicaid, and public employee health insurance. In the projected 2010–2012 budget the largest appropriation from all funds is Medicaid (19.7 percent), followed by postsecondary education (19.4 percent) and education (17 percent) (figure 8.2). In contrast, the largest appropriation from the General Fund is education (45.1 percent), followed by postsecondary education (13.5 percent) and Medicaid (12.6 percent) (figure 8.3). Although education spending is the largest appropriation from the General Fund and the second-largest from all funds, the appropriation allocations represent a shift away from education toward spending on Medicaid.

These amounts illustrate the differences in the use of funds from different sources. Figure 8.3 depicts appropriations from the General Fund, which is drawn from own-source revenue derived almost exclusively from Kentucky taxpayers. General Fund

Total appropriations—$60.3 billion

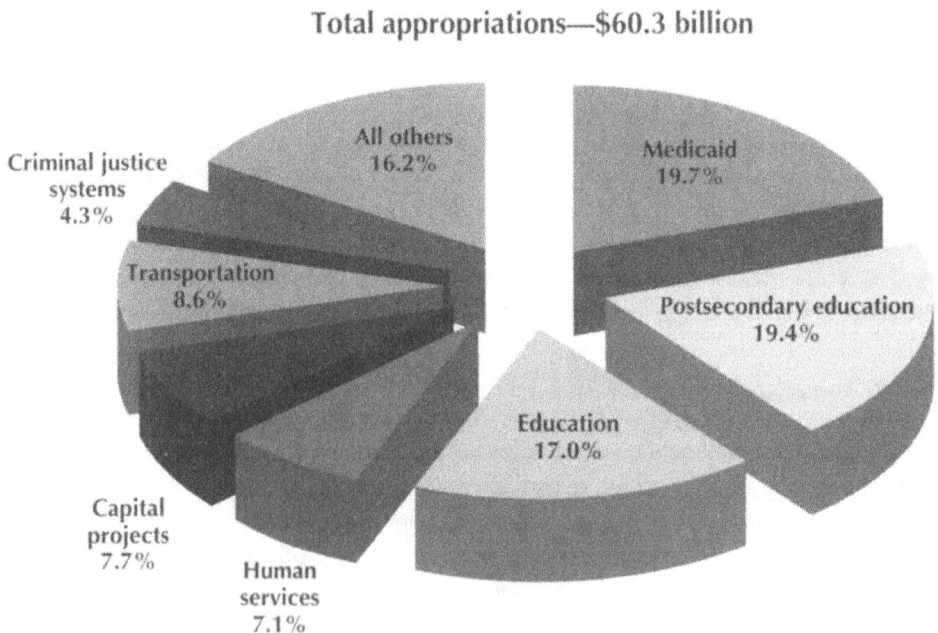

Figure 8.2. Total appropriations as allocated in the 2010–2012 budget

Total General Fund appropriations—$18.1 billion

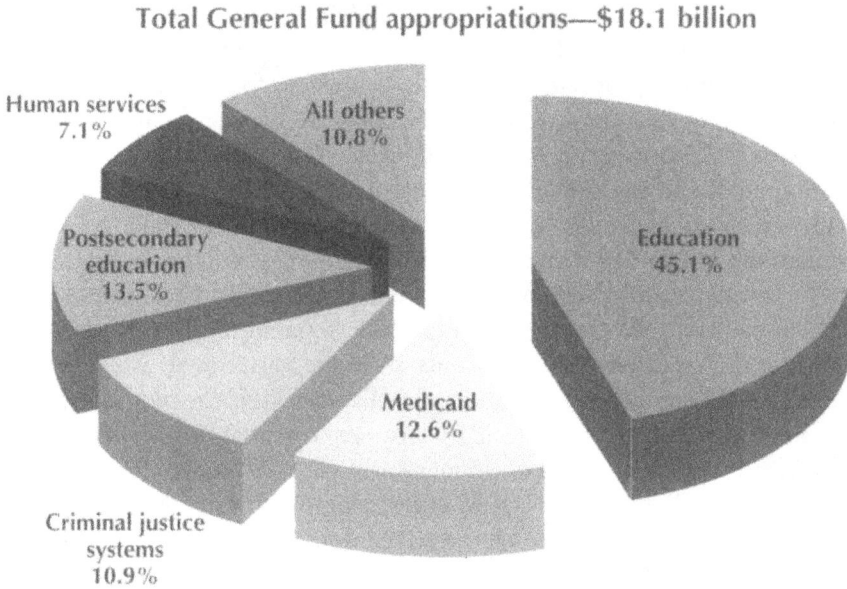

Figure 8.3. Total General Fund appropriations as allocated in the 2010–2012 budget

appropriations are dominated by outlays for education, including both K–12 schools and postsecondary institutions. Medicaid spending from the General Fund, which includes Kentucky's own revenue contributions, is less significant by comparison.

Kentucky General Fund money combined with intergovernmental revenue (primarily federal funds) is depicted as total appropriations in figure 8.2. Education, which is funded from a combination of state, local, and federal sources, remains a big-ticket item, but what is striking about total appropriations is the size of the budget for Medicaid.

Medicaid

Medicaid spending has increased dramatically over the past two decades and is expected to continue rising in future years.[23] Medicaid costs are growing at twice the rate of state budgets. This increase in costs is primarily driven by enrollment, which has increased by approximately 25 percent in the past nine years. In addition to enrollment, inflation in the prices of health-care services and prescription drugs and increases in the use of services by Medicaid enrollees have led to the rising costs of the program.

Medicaid is funded through both the federal and the state governments. The federal government provides funds to the states through a matching grant. The federal matching rate for Medicaid varies across states and ranges from 61.59 percent (California, Colorado, Connecticut, Maryland, Massachusetts, Minnesota, New Hampshire, New Jersey, New York, Virginia, and Wyoming) to 83.05 percent (West Virginia).[24]

Medicaid is one of the fastest-growing categories in the Kentucky budget. It currently accounts for $12 billion, 19.7 percent of all fund appropriations and 12.6 percent of all General Fund appropriations. Although funding for the program is primarily composed of federal aid (approximately 77 percent), General Fund appropriations have increased by 67 percent over FY 2000 levels.

The program currently provides coverage to more than 960,776 persons, 22 percent of Kentucky's population. As stated earlier, the increasing cost of Medicaid is partly linked to rising enrollment. The Kaiser Family Foundation reports a 1 percent increase in the national unemployment rate and an estimated additional 1 million turn to Medicaid for coverage.[25] In the current economic climate, with the unemployment rate at its highest level in twenty-six years, enrollment is expected to continue to rise. Further contributing to rising Medicaid costs is the provision of long-term care and Kentucky's aging population. Twenty-seven percent of Medicaid funding in Kentucky in FY 2010 was allocated to long-term care. Although this is less than the national average of 31 percent, with Kentucky's aging population, the share of long-term care in Medicaid spending is expected to continue to rise in the future.[26]

The federal government passed the American Recovery and Reinvestment Act (ARRA) of 2009 as a way to relieve state budgets in the poor economic climate. Under the ARRA, all states received a temporary increase of 6.2 percent in their federal Medicaid match rate, so Kentucky's matching rate was raised from 70 percent to 80 percent by FY 2010.[27] This temporary increase expired in 2011. Although these stimulus funds were designed to provide relief to the state budget, they were actually a factor in the 2010–2012 budget shortfall. The state expected to receive about $238 million in federal funds and therefore allocated part of the Medicaid budget to fill budget shortfalls in other areas. However, the state received only 58 percent of what it expected—$137 million—and was therefore faced with a $101 million shortfall in Medicaid funding. Because Medicaid is funded at a match rate of approximately 80 percent, this shortfall actually represents a total budget shortfall of $470 million. As a way to combat some of this shortfall in the Medicaid budget, Governor Beshear announced a plan to use private contractors to run managed health-care programs, thus saving $142 million in the Medicaid program over the next two years. Medicaid is the fastest-growing appropriation in the state budget, and given the current economic climate, an aging population, and the rising cost of medical services, it is expected that Medicaid will continue to increase its share of state appropriations in future budgets.

Education

K–12 education and postsecondary education are considered two separate appropriation categories in the budget. Although both provide educational services to the population, they are funded in very different ways. K–12 education is funded primarily through state and local governments. States provide monetary support to local governments through grants-in-aid and revenue sharing. Local governments rely on the revenue from property taxes to make up the remainder of the education budget. In contrast, postsecondary education is funded through the federal and state governments, which provide specific aid to individual universities and colleges. Even though education at the K–12 and postsecondary levels is funded differently, funding for both of these services has declined in recent years.

In Kentucky, K–12 education is the largest appropriation from the General Fund, 45.1 percent, and is 17 percent of total appropriations, $10.3 billion. In recent years the share of K–12 education appropriations from the General Fund has been declining, from a high of 48 percent of General Fund appropriations in FY 1986–1988 to the share in FY 2010–2012 budget of 45 percent.

Postsecondary education's share of General Fund appropriations has also declined, from 17 percent in FY 1986–1988 to FY 2010–2012 share of 13.5 percent. Even though the ARRA provided additional funding of $70 million in FY 2010 and $57.3 million in FY 2011, the FY 2010–2012 budget reduced appropriations for state universities by a further 1.4 percent in 2010–2011 and by 1 percent in 2011–2012. The budgeted appropriation was approximately $1 billion in 2010–2011 and 2011–2012.[28]

The decline in education appropriations characterizes a shift in the state's budget priorities. Spending on education at both the K–12 and postsecondary levels is expected to continue declining and to be replaced with spending on Medicaid and corrections. This shift presents a potential danger. Education represents an investment in the current and future human capital accumulation of Kentucky's children and young adults, and reduction of that investment could cause a decline in the productivity of the future Kentucky population.

Criminal Justice

In Kentucky spending on corrections currently accounts for 11 percent of General Fund appropriations and 4 percent of total appropriations, $2.4 billion. The Kentucky Chamber of Commerce reports that Kentucky's spending on corrections increased by 44 percent between 2000 and 2010 ($619 million in FY 2000–2002 to $894 million in FY 2008–2010).[29] This represents a higher rate of growth than that of general state spending.

Between 2000 and 2009 the rate of imprisonment increased by 250 percent, well above the federal average. This increase led to a rise in the prison population of 50 percent over the same period. This rising rate of imprisonment is the main factor in the increasing cost of corrections, but it has been accompanied by a decline in the crime rate. From 2000 to 2010, while the rate of incarceration grew, the rates of violent and property crimes decreased by 13 and 14 percent, respectively. According to Steven Levitt, the growing prison population is one of four main factors in reducing crime.[30] Earlier research by Marvell and Moody and by Levitt showed a strong positive relationship between increased punishment and lower crime rates, with a higher impact on violent crime than on property crime.[31]

As a way to combat the rising cost of corrections, the General Assembly passed House Bill (HB) 463, which the governor signed into law in March 2011. The bill reduces prison time for nonviolent drug offenders by steering them into alternative sentences and treatment. The new legislation is projected to save the state $422 million over a decade, of which half will be reinvested in treatment and probation and parole programs.

Public Employees

Another important appropriation is the state's commitment to public employees, which includes teachers, state employees, retirees, and their dependents. All state employees are eligible for the Kentucky Employees Health Plan, which currently covers more than 6 percent of all Kentuckians.

Employee health-insurance costs are growing at more than five times the rate of overall state spending. This rise in insurance costs is due to higher premiums and the rising cost of health care. Kentucky pays a higher percentage of premiums than the national average—97 percent versus 88 percent.[32] The average monthly contribution per employee for health insurance has increased by more than 174 percent since 2000, from $221 a month to more than $600 a month in 2010. An estimated 12 percent of the General Fund goes to paying these premium costs.[33]

In addition to health insurance, the state also has an obligation to its retirees. Kentucky, like most states, faces a large aging population. Although health-care costs are the major driver of rising retirement-system costs—55 percent of state contributions—because of previous borrowing from pension funds, Kentucky faces an unfunded pension liability of $23.6 billion, representing more than 50 percent of total liability. Unfunded pension liability is a growing concern across all states in the United States.[34] The Pew Center reports that the number of states that had fully funded pension systems fell from just over half in 2000 to six in 2006 and to only one in 2010—Wisconsin. In contrast, in four states—Connecticut, Illinois, Kentucky, and Rhode Island, less than 55 percent of the liability was funded.[35]

Earmarked Funds

A final topic that needs to be addressed is earmarked funds. Earmarked funds are funds that are reserved and may be spent only on a specified program. In Kentucky earmarked funds are mainly associated with the horse industry, gasoline, and cigarettes. Some examples include the 0.1 percent of all revenues from the imposition of taxes on gasoline, special fuels, and liquefied petroleum that is earmarked for the Kentucky Transportation Center. Another example is the excise cigarette tax, of which one-sixth goes to the tobacco research trust fund.

Overall Appropriations

In May 2010 the General Assembly passed a $17.1 billion supplemental budget. Before passage of this budget, projections for the 2010–2012 biennial budget showed a budget gap of $1.5 billion. The supplemental budget did not raise taxes but did implement budget reductions for many state agencies by 3.5 percent in 2010–2011 and another 1 percent in 2011–2012. This reduction in spending was further compounded by the expiration of the ARRA stimulus in 2011. Although spending has been cut in many state agencies, appropriations for Medicaid, corrections, and public employees continue to rise. The General Assembly passed legislation in 2011 to contain the growth in these three areas; however, the overall impact of this legislation is yet to be seen.

LOCAL GOVERNMENTS

The relationship between state and local governments in regard to financing has always been contentious. Local governments desire autonomy to raise taxes and spending levels according to the wants of their constituents. However, local governments receive almost half of their revenue as intergovernmental transfers from the state. These transfers are usually earmarked for specific purposes, such as education, roads, and public health. Therefore, the ability of local governments to respond to changes in their constituents' requests for public service spending is severely limited. Furthermore, local governments lack the legal ability to raise additional revenues through taxes, although this is changing because the state has authorized an optional income tax for specific local governments.

State and local governments are very different in the composition of their revenue sources and the services that they typically provide. State revenue is approximately double the sum of total local revenue. In 2007–2008 state revenue totaled $20.8 billion, in comparison with total local revenue of $11.9 billion. Local governments rely on the state for approximately 40 percent of their revenue, $4.5 billion. For the remainder of their revenue, local governments rely most heavily on property taxes, which account for 55.5 percent of all local tax revenue, followed by income taxes (26 percent), sales taxes (13 percent), and finally, corporate, and other taxes, constituting the remaining 5 percent of all tax revenue. In contrast, the state relies most heavily on sales-tax receipts (48 percent of total tax revenues), followed by income taxes (38 percent), and property taxes (5 percent of total state revenues), with corporate, motor-vehicle, and other taxes supplying the remaining 9 percent of tax revenue (figure 8.4).

The distribution of state and local government funds is also very different (figure 8.5). Local government appropriations are focused primarily on education (43 percent). The majority of this revenue is allocated to elementary and secondary education. In contrast, the largest state appropriation is for public welfare (37 percent). This appropriation includes the state's contribution to Medicaid. The second-highest appropriation is for education (23.2 percent), of which 71.5 percent is allocated to secondary education.

Even though the state provides a significant amount of aid to local governments, this aid comes with strings attached. In response, local governments chafe at the restrictions placed on them by the state. The existence of a federal system ensures that there will always be tension among the three levels of government.

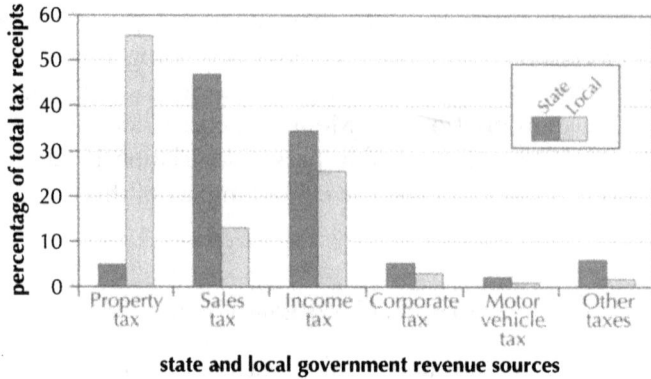

state and local government revenue sources

Figure 8.4. Comparison of tax receipts between the state of Kentucky and local Kentucky governments. Source: Office of State Budget Director, http://www.osbd.ky.gov/.

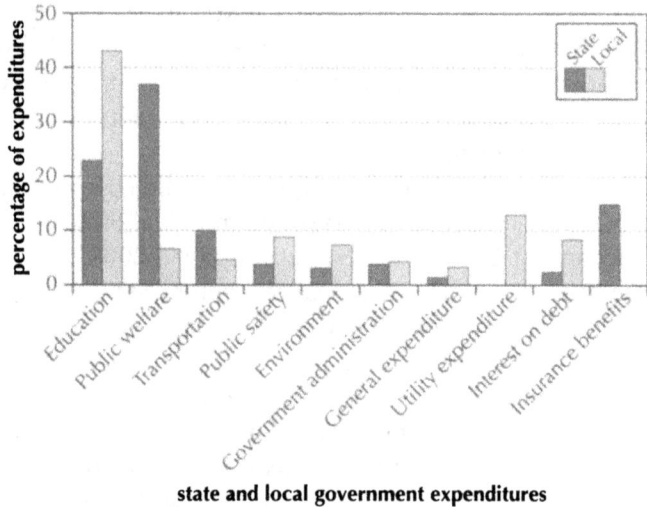

state and local government expenditures

Figure 8.5. Comparison of expenditures between the state of Kentucky and local Kentucky governments. Source: Office of State Budget Director, http://www.osbd.ky.gov/.

FUTURE BUDGETS

The fiscal crisis of the past five years has only worsened the condition of state and local budgets and has placed their continued fiscal sustainability in jeopardy. As budgetary commitments and long-term liabilities continue to grow, outpacing current revenues, this situation is likely to be exacerbated. To try to limit this phenomenon, state and local governments have experimented with a variety of constitutional constraints, such as direct democracy, term limits, debt limits, tax and expenditure liabilities, balanced-budget rules, and rainy-day funds. The evidence is mixed regarding the effectiveness of these constraints to limit state spending, taxing, and debt.[36]

Rainy-day funds have enjoyed the greatest success, while tax and expenditure lim-its (TELs) have been found to be moderately successful in increasing the fiscal sus-tainability of state budgets. The results from the use of direct democracy and debt limits to restrict state spending are mixed. Some studies show that these two con-straints may reduce government spending under certain conditions,[37] while others find the opposite result.[38] The imposition of term limits appears to have the unin-tended consequence of increasing debt and spending.

Most states have a balanced-budget requirement with some degree of stringency. In 2008, forty-four states required their governor to submit a balanced budget to the legislature, forty-one states required their state legislature to pass a balanced budget, and thirty-seven states required their governor to sign a balanced budget. The argu-ment for a balanced budget is that it yields fiscal health. However, there is some evi-dence that balanced-budget rules alone are not sufficient to ensure states' long-term fiscal health because balanced-budget requirements generally apply only to operating budgets—approximately 50 to 60 percent of total state spending. The remainder of state spending is allocated to capital budgets. In 2008 only seven states were legally allowed to carry a deficit into the next fiscal year. All the other states that are required to pass a balanced budget are open to significant shortfalls. Although these states can adjust their revenues and expenditures, they may also decide to issue bonds and use the revenue from their sale to fund the shortfall. At least sixteen states require voter approval to issue general-obligation debt, and at least five states prohibit debt alto-gether. Kentucky has a $500,000 statutory limit for general-obligation bonds; New Hampshire limits this obligation to 10 percent of its general fund. Those states without prohibitions can increase deficit spending and debt issuance for capital projects.

Rainy-day funds are created with excess revenues from the budget set aside for use in times of unexpected revenue shortfalls or deficits. The percentage of annual expen-ditures that states set aside for their rainy-day funds varies widely. In 2009 fund bal-ances ranged from 0 percent in Arkansas, California, Kansas, Michigan, and Wisconsin to 17 percent in Nebraska and nearly 150 percent of annual expenditures in Alaska. Approximately half of all states had rainy-day balances greater than 5 percent of an-nual expenditures. Kentucky is closer to the bottom end of this scale, with a rainy-day balance equal to 2.3 percent of annual expenditures. The fiscal crisis of the past five years has significantly reduced the balances of states' rainy-day funds. Although the majority of research has shown that these funds significantly improve the state's fiscal sustainability and savings, the fiscal crisis that many states continue to face is likely to deplete these funds further.

Tax and expenditure limits (TELs) are designed to restrict the level of growth of government revenues or spending. These rules may limit revenue or expenditures, usually by fixing them to a numerical target or to increases in an index such as popula-tion, inflation, personal income, or some combination of these. In addition, these rules may also restrict appropriations to a percentage of the official revenue forecast or re-quire voter approval or a legislative supermajority to approve tax increases. As of 2008, thirty states had at least one TEL. Twenty-three states imposed state spending limits, four had state revenue limits, and three had both. According to the Tax Policy Center,

Kentucky does not currently have any TELs. Research has shown that these limits may be modestly effective at reducing the growth of government.[39]

Direct-democracy constraints can take the form of a ballot initiative or a referendum. Under a ballot initiative, citizens can propose or vote on specific laws. A referendum requires a prespecified voter majority (or supermajority) to approve a law that has already passed the legislature. There is mixed evidence that these constraints are associated with lower government spending; however, because ballot initiatives have been used to implement a variety of other institutions, such as term limits and TELs, they may be having an indirect effect. Sixteen states have implemented such limits for the passage of new taxes, and forty-six states, including Kentucky, have limited property taxes of state and local governments.

Debt limits may take the form of a debt ceiling, voter referendum requirements, or a legislative supermajority. There is some evidence that debt limits improve the fiscal sustainability of the constituency. Debt ceilings and referenda are associated with lower state debt, while the impacts of requiring a legislative supermajority is more mixed. Conversely, Clingermayer and Wood found that these tools had no impact on the growth of long-term state debt.[40]

Term limits are limitations placed on the duration for which an elected official can retain his or her office. The majority of the research examining the impact of term limits on spending has found that these limits are associated with higher spending. The number of terms allowed is important—spending is higher if there is only one term versus two. Second, term limits shift the balance of power among the political actors, which suggests that spending outcomes may be very different depending on whether these limits are imposed at the gubernatorial level, the legislative level, or together.

Together, these constitutional constraints may be moderately successful at reducing government spending, increasing government saving, and increasing the fiscal sustainability of the state. These constraints have not eliminated the crises that many state governments are now facing. State revenue generation continues to decline for several reasons. The first of these reasons is a shift away from a manufacturing-based economy to a service-based economy. The states, Kentucky in particular, have been slow to adopt taxes that account for the changing nature of the economy. For example, one of the fastest-growing sectors of the economy, e-commerce, is still untaxed.

The decline in the housing market has significantly reduced the property-tax revenues of local governments. In turn, local governments have requested aid from the state in order to meet their balanced-budget requirements, placing a greater burden on the state budget. Although the housing-market collapse may have ended, the impact on tax revenues is expected to continue. Adding further to a decline in tax revenues is the poor economic climate of the past five years, which is expected to continue. Times of economic decline are characterized by higher unemployment levels, increasing demands for benefits, and reduced income-tax collections, which, taken together, significantly reduce the state's revenues.

In conjunction with the poor economic climate, stagnant financial structures, and declining tax revenues, the state is faced with growing expenses. Specifically, state expenses for Medicaid, corrections, and public employees, which currently make up 36 percent of General Fund appropriations, have experienced significant growth in the past decade. Medicaid spending has increased by 67 percent, corrections spending by 44 percent, and spending on public employees by 174 percent. Because of the aging population and high unemployment rates, spending on these three areas is expected to grow significantly in the future. The General Assembly passed legislation in 2011 in an effort to reduce the growth of spending in these areas, but it is too early to tell whether it will be successful. The state is in a difficult position, with declining revenue and rising expenditures. The balances of the rainy-day fund are to be used for economic periods such as this, but that fund is almost depleted, and there will be increasing pressure to find new revenue sources and adapt existing financial structures in order to meet the changing economy.

NOTES

1. Own-source revenues are revenues derived from a government's own taxable resources.

2. An intergovernmental transfer is the transfer of money or resources from one level of government to another.

3. Tax Foundation, "Kentucky's State and Local Tax Burden, 1977–2010," accessed June 9, 2013, http://taxfoundation.org/article/kentuckys-state-and-local-tax-burden-1977-2010.

4. Ibid.

5. U.S. Census Bureau, "2009 Annual Survey of State Government Tax Collections," accessed January 10, 2012, http://www.census.gov/govs/statetax/historical_data_2009.html.

6. Ibid.

7. Elasticity of demand is the responsiveness of the quantity demanded to a change in the price.

8. Demand is inelastic if the quantity demanded changes by less than the change in the price.

9. Demand is elastic if the quantity demanded changes by more than the change in the price.

10. Federation of Tax Administrators, "State Sales Taxation of Services," accessed June 9, 2013, http://www.taxadmin.org/fta/pub/services/services.html.

11. Tax Foundation, "State Cigarette Excise Tax Rates, 2009–2013," accessed June 9, 2013, http://taxfoundation.org/article/state-cigarette-excise-tax-rates-2009-2013.

12. U.S. Census Bureau, "2009 Annual Survey of State Government Tax Collections."

13. Tax Foundation, "State Excise Tax Rates on Spirits, 2007–2013," accessed June 9, 2013, http://taxfoundation.org/article/state-excise-tax-rates-spirits-2007-2013.

14. Tax Foundation, "State Table Wine Excise Tax Rates, 2009–2013," accessed June 9, 2013, http://taxfoundation.org/article/state-table-wine-excise-tax-rates-2009-2013.

15. Tax Foundation, "State Beer Excise Tax Rates, 2009–2013," accessed June 9, 2013, http://taxfoundation.org/article/state-beer-excise-tax-rates-2009-2013.

16. U.S. Census Bureau, "2009 Annual Survey of State Government Tax Collections."

17. Tax Foundation, "State Gasoline Tax Rates, 2009–2013," accessed June 9, 2013, http://taxfoundation.org/article/state-gasoline-tax-rates-2009-2013.

18. U.S. Census Bureau, "2009 Annual Survey of State Government Tax Collections."

19. Ibid.

20. Tax Foundation, "State and Local Property Tax Collections Per Capita by State, Fiscal Year 2009," accessed June 9, 2013, http://taxfoundation.org/article/state-and-local-property-tax-collections-capita-state-fiscal-year-2009.

21. U.S. Census Bureau, "2009 Annual Survey of State Government Tax Collections."

22. Kentucky Cabinet for Economic Development, "Industrial Revenue Bonds," accessed January 10, 2012, http://www.thinkkentucky.com/kyedc/pdfs/irb_2005.pdf.

23. Medicaid is a government program designed to provide medical services to low-income parents, children, seniors, and people with disabilities, including individuals with family incomes up to 400 percent of the federal poverty level (FPL), children with family incomes up to 250 percent of the FPL, and pregnant women with family incomes up to 185 percent of the FPL. Seniors over the age of sixty-five are eligible for nursing-home and long-term care if they meet the income limit, while people with disabilities are eligible for a variety of services.

24. Kaiser Family Foundation, "Federal Medical Assistance Percentage (FMAP) for Medicaid and Multiplier," accessed January 10, 2012, http://kff.org/medicaid/state-indicator/federal-matching-rate-and-multiplier/.

25. Kaiser Family Foundation, "State Fiscal Conditions and Medicaid, accessed January 10, 2012, http://kaiserfamilyfoundation.files.wordpress.com/2013/01/7580-05.pdf.

26. Kaiser Family Foundation, "Distribution of Medicaid Spending by Service," accessed June 9, 2013, http://kff.org/medicaid/state-indicator/spending-by-service-fy2010/.

27. Kaiser Family Foundation, "Federal Medical Assistance Percentage (FMAP) for Medicaid and Multiplier," accessed June 9, 2013, http://kff.org/medicaid/state-indicator/federal-matching-rate-and-multiplier/.

28. Bob King, "D9427-265E-4C9B-889F-DCE7A3F20B10/0/0710postsecondarysubcommittee.pdf" Postsecondary Education Funding Overview," PowerPoint presentation (PDF format), Postsecondary Education Funding Review Subcommittee, Frankfort, Ky., July 2010.

29. Kentucky Chamber of Commerce, "The Leaky Bucket," Leaky Bucket Reports, February 2010, accessed January 10, 2011, http://kychamber.com/sites/default/files/Leaky BucketWhitePaper.pdf.

30. Steven Levitt, "Understanding Why Crime Fell in the 1990s: Four Factors That Explain the Decline and Six That Do Not," *Journal of Economic Perspectives* 18, no. 1 (2004): 163–64.

31. Thomas Marvell and Carlisle Moody, "Prison Population Growth and Crime Reduction," *Journal of Quantitative Criminology* 10, no. 2 (1994): 109–40; Steven Levitt, "The Effect of Prison Population Size on Crime Rates: Evidence from Prison Overcrowding Litigation," *Quarterly Journal of Economics* 112, no. 2 (1996): 319–52.

32. Kentucky Chamber of Commerce, "The Leaky Bucket."

33. Ibid.

34. The Pew Center on States, "Kentucky's Pension Challenges: Opportunities for Real Reform," accessed June 9, 2013, http://www.pewstates.org/uploadedFiles/PCS_Assets/2012/Pew_Kentucky_Pension_Challenges.pdf.

35. The Pew Center on States, "The Widening Gap Update," accessed June 9, 2013, http://www.pewstates.org/uploadedFiles/PCS_Assets/2012/Pew_Pensions_Update.pdf.

36. Shanna Rose, "Institutions and Fiscal Sustainability," *National Tax Journal* 63, no. 4, part 1 (December 2010): 807–38.

37. James Poterba, "State Responses to Fiscal Crises: The Effects of Budgetary Institutions and Politics," *The Journal of Political Economy* 102, no. 4 (1994): 799–21; Alberto Alesina and Tamim Bayoumi, "The Costs and Benefits of Fiscal Rules: Evidence from U.S. States," NBER Working Paper No. 5614, National Bureau of Economic Research, 1996.

38. Susan MacManus, "Special District Governments: A Note on Their Use of Property Tax Relief Mechanisms in the 1970s," *The Journal of Politics* 43, no. 4 (1981): 1207–14; Beverly Bunch, "The Effect of Constitutional Debt Limits on State Governments' Use of Public Authorities," *Public Choice* 68, 1–3 (1991): 57–69.

39. Barry Poulson and Jay Kaplan, "A Rent-Seeking Model of TELs," *Public Choice* 79, 1–2 (1994): 11–34; Dale Bails and Margie Tieslau, "The Impact of Fiscal Constitutions on State and Local Expenditures," *Cato Journal* 20, no. 2 (2000): 255–77.

40. James Clingermayer and Dan Wood, "Disentangling Patterns of State Debt Financing," *American Political Science Review* 89, no. 1 (1995): 108–20; Marvell and Moody, "Prison Population Growth and Crime Reduction"; Levitt, "The Effect of Prison Population Size on Crime Rates." ·

9

Political Parties and Elections
in Kentucky

Joel Turner and Scott Lasley

Kentucky holds a unique place in the political landscape with regard to political parties and electoral outcomes. The overall pattern has been one of Democratic Party dominance, which makes the state similar to many of its neighbors to the south. However, unlike most southern states, the Commonwealth has also always had pockets of Republican Party strength. Parties and elections in Kentucky are also characterized by several prominent personalities. Leaders such as Henry Clay, "Happy" Chandler, and Mitch McConnell have brought attention to the Commonwealth from both state-wide and national observers. Given these and other unique characteristics, it is important to obtain an understanding of both where Kentucky has been and where it may be going with regard to political parties and elections. The purpose of this chapter is to help provide that understanding.

The first half of the chapter will place parties and elections in the Commonwealth in a historical context. This will include an examination of early Democratic-Republican dominance; a chronicle of the rise of the Whigs, led by Henry Clay; a look at the brief emergence of the Know-Nothings and the Constitutional Union Party; and an account of the Democratic factionalism of the mid-1900s, led by Chandler and Earle Clements. The second part of the chapter will examine the state of contemporary parties and elections in Kentucky. This will begin with the end of Democratic factionalism ushered in with the election of Wendell Ford and will include a look at party organization, the party in the electorate, and insights regarding the future of parties in Kentucky.

DEMOCRATIC-REPUBLICAN DOMINANCE

Initially, political parties did not play a significant role in Kentucky politics. The election of the state's first governor, Isaac Shelby, in 1792 featured little of the partisanship that has since come to characterize Kentucky elections.[1] Shortly after this election, however, parties began to exert their influence in the state, and the party that exerted the most influence initially was the Democratic-Republican Party. The strong allegiance to the Democratic-Republicans was largely attributed to two factors. First, the uncertain frontier conditions in Kentucky at the time made the governmental stability trumpeted by the Democratic-Republicans very attractive. The second factor was the state's ties to Virginia. The Jeffersonian idea emerging from Virginia that an aristocracy would naturally lead was an easy sell to Kentucky's economic and political elite.[2]

The early leaders of the Democratic-Republicans in Kentucky were George Nicholas and John Breckinridge. Nicholas, the state's first attorney general, is best known as the architect of the state's 1792 constitution. Breckinridge, a lawyer and horse breeder, held a variety of positions in Kentucky state government before being elected to the U.S. Senate in 1799 and ultimately being appointed U.S. attorney general by Thomas Jefferson in 1805. The opposition to the Democratic-Republicans in Kentucky was the Federalists. For the most part, however, Federalists were minor political players, and members of this party in the state were frequent targets of ridicule and scorn.[3] The most significant victory claimed by the Federalists belonged to Humphrey Marshall, who defeated Breckinridge, John Fowler, and John Edwards for election to the U.S. Senate in 1794. Although Marshall was a well-known politician in the state, it is generally believed that political occurrences at the national level were the primary reason for his election.[4] Victories such as this for Federalists in Kentucky were the exception rather than the rule.

The deaths of Nicholas in 1799 and Breckinridge in 1806 left a leadership vacuum for the Democratic-Republicans in Kentucky that was quickly filled by the legendary Henry Clay, who went on to become one of Kentucky's most famous and beloved political leaders. Clay, a successful lawyer, moved to Lexington from Virginia in 1797. He quickly acquired a vast amount of property in the state, which helped him cultivate a connection with the state's conservative landowning class that would serve him very well politically.[5] Clay took an interest in politics in the early 1800s, voicing opposition to the Alien and Sedition Acts and advocating the emancipation of slaves in Kentucky. Running as a Democratic-Republican, Clay was elected to the Kentucky General Assembly in 1803. He became such a well-liked leader in the General Assembly that he was chosen in 1806 to complete the term of John Breckinridge in the U.S. Senate after Jefferson appointed Breckinridge as attorney general. Upon returning to Kentucky in 1807, Clay was again elected to the General Assembly and was chosen as Speaker of the House. In 1810 Clay was once again chosen to fill an unexpired term in the U.S. Senate when Buckner Thurston resigned to serve as a U.S. circuit-court judge. After his completion of Thurston's Senate term in 1811, Clay was elected to the U.S. House of Representatives.

Clay's career as Speaker of the House was marked by several significant achievements. He remains the only person in American history to be elected Speaker immediately on joining the legislative body. He fostered a reputation as a war hawk because he was one of the leading figures who supported the War of 1812. He was a staunch Americanist, supporting a system of tariffs designed to protect American manufacturing. Perhaps most notably, Clay began to develop his reputation as the Great Compromiser because he was one of the leading figures in the creation of the Missouri Compromise, as well as in brokering an end to the Nullification Crisis of 1850.[6]

WHIG ASCENDANCY IN KENTUCKY

The Whig Party in Kentucky can trace its roots to Andrew Jackson's election as president. The Whigs emerged as the opposition to what they perceived as Jackson's authoritarian policies, specifically his failure to renew the charter of the Second National Bank of the United States and his views regarding Native Americans, the Supreme Court, and war powers.[7] The Whig Party, led by former Democratic-Republican Henry Clay, became influential in Kentucky when a number of Clay loyalists were elected under the Whig banner. By 1834 Whigs had majorities in both houses of the General Assembly, led by former circuit-court judge James Clark, who was elected Senate president, and would follow Thomas Metcalfe and James Turner Morehead as Whig governors. Clark was followed by Whigs Charles Anderson, Robert Letcher, William Owsley, whom many consider the most effective Whig governor, John Crittenden, the second most influential Whig in the state after Clay, John Helm (who was later elected governor as a Democrat, and Lazarus Powell, the last of the Whig governors.

Although the Whigs enjoyed success in Kentucky, nationally they never had the significant presidential achievement their party so desperately needed to entrench them as major players in national politics. Clay received the party's nomination in 1844 but lost. In 1852 Whig Winfield Scott was unable to capitalize on the popularity of the Compromise of 1850 and lost to Franklin Pierce. In addition, the promise of the Whig victories that did occur was never achieved. William Henry Harrison's victory in 1840 was tempered by both his death less than a month after taking office and the fact that most Whigs disliked his replacement, John Tyler.[8] In 1850 Zachary Taylor, the last Whig elected president, died sixteen months into his term.

Although the Whig Party in Kentucky was far more successful than the party at the national level, even its success was relatively short-lived. The last major achievement for the Whigs in the state was gaining control of the General Assembly in 1851, which allowed them to block a number of Democratic governor Lazarus Powell's policy proposals. However, northern Whig dissatisfaction with the Compromise of 1850 led many to start leaving the party, which began to slowly erode the party's viability.[9] What is ultimately seen as the final blow to the Whigs in Kentucky was the death of Henry Clay in 1852, because although a few staunch loyalists remained after his passing, most saw no future in the Whig Party in Kentucky.[10]

THE KNOW-NOTHINGS AND THE CONSTITUTIONAL UNION PARTY

After the death of Clay, most Kentucky Whigs began to explore their political options. Although many joined the Democratic Party, some searched for an alternate way to demonstrate their political opposition. A number of those who refused to join the Democratic Party became involved with the American Party, commonly known as the Know-Nothing Party.[11] The Know-Nothings organized in Kentucky largely around the idea that foreigners and Catholics were the source of the state's problems. The irony surrounding this is that foreigners and Catholics made up a small percentage of Kentucky's population and, for the most part, were viewed as upstanding citizens.[12] Growth of the Know-Nothings in Kentucky was spurred by George Prentice, an influential newspaper editor and former Whig who used his newspaper to launch attacks on Catholics and foreigners.[13] The Know-Nothings made quick political headway, winning local elections in several cities, and in 1855 captured the General Assembly, six congressional seats, and the governorship. Unfortunately for the Know-Nothings, this success was short-lived. The party suffered a major blow to its public perception because of an election-day riot led by Know-Nothing sympathizers in Louisville that resulted in twenty-two deaths, several injuries, and extensive property damage.[14] In 1856 the party suffered another blow when national members split into proslavery and antislavery wings.[15] As a result of these events, the party disintegrated in the state.

The decline of the Know-Nothings left two major parties in the state: Republicans and Democrats. Republicans were viewed in the state as the party of the Civil War victors and the controllers of Reconstruction. A coalition of former Whigs and Union loyalists, the party sought to be a progressive force while taking care to remain more moderate than the Radical Republicans at the national level. The opposition party in the state was the Democratic Party. Painting Republicans as radical on issues of race and governmental power, the Democrats were composed of former Confederates, former Whigs, and disgruntled former Unionists. The extremism of these parties left many moderate Kentuckians without a political home and led to the emergence of the Constitutional Union Party. This party attempted to capitalize on the demise of the Whigs in Kentucky and the dissatisfaction with the extremes represented by the Republicans and the Democrats. The party consisted of old Whigs, former Know-Nothings, and former Union loyalists who were alienated by both of the major parties.[16]

Nationally, the Constitutional Union Party emerged in 1860 with the primary, albeit vague, purpose of preserving the Union by adhering to constitutional principles. The party was attractive to Kentuckians for this reason because the state attempted to maintain the unique position of neutrality during the Civil War.[17] The leader of the party in Kentucky was John Crittenden, whom many supported to receive the party's nomination for president in 1860. The party received a notable victory in Kentucky when General Leslie Combs was elected clerk of the state Court of Appeals over the preferred choice of Southern Democratic Party presidential candidate John C. Breckinridge. The national party lost the presidential election of 1860, and as southern states began to secede, the party lost its purpose and started to disintegrate. The party in Kentucky held on a little bit longer but suffered an overwhelming defeat in the governor's race in 1867 at the hands of John Helm that effectively ended the party.

DEMOCRATIC DOMINANCE AND DESPAIR

Helm died shortly after being sworn in, and his lieutenant governor, John Stevenson, assumed the office and then won a landslide victory in a special election that ushered in an extended period of Democratic dominance. Although there was little interparty competition in the state, philosophical and sectional differences resulted in a tremendous amount of intraparty competition among two competing Democratic factions. The Bourbon Democrats were the more conservative faction. They were strong advocates of a restricted role for government in the Commonwealth. Opposing the Bourbons were the New Departure Democrats, who favored a stronger, more progressive government. Most politicians who served during this period attempted to carve out a middle ground that appeased both of these factions while alienating neither. This middle ground generally consisted of supporting reforms that benefited whites while opposing the extension of civil rights to blacks in the state.[18]

The late 1800s in the state were characterized by victories and difficulties for the Democratic Party in Kentucky, as well as the rise of interest groups in the state. Particularly, the Louisville and Nashville Railroad and the Grange were major players in Kentucky politics at this time. The Grange were so powerful that Governor James McCreary essentially had an agrarian-oriented tenure.[19] Subsequent governors continued their allegiance to these groups, which in the short term helped them but hurt the party over time. McCreary was followed in office by Luke Blackburn, who was noted for his somewhat successful efforts at prison reform and his ability to alienate almost every faction in his party. Blackburn was followed by J. Proctor Knott, who was hamstrung by a powerful General Assembly, and Simon Buckner, whose administration was dealt a major setback by an embezzlement scandal involving treasurer "Honest Dick" Tate. The subsequent election of John Brown was marked by the fact that it was the first time in recent memory that a Democrat was elected with less than 50 percent of the vote. This downward trend resulted in what was once unthinkable in Kentucky: the election of a Republican governor in 1895 and 1899, which, combined with the assassination of William Goebel in February of 1900, the leader of the Democratic Party at the time, meant that Kentucky Democrats found themselves in a state of disarray at the turn of the century.[20]

INTERPARTY COMPETITION IN THE COMMONWEALTH, 1900–1931

The assassination of Goebel resulted in nearly twenty years of controversial legal wrangling regarding the leadership of the state, as well as who the conspirators behind Goebel's assassination actually were. In the immediate aftermath Republican legislators set up in London, Kentucky, while Democratic lawmakers conducted business in various locations around Frankfort. Eventually, Democrats were able to capitalize on popular sentiment, and disqualify enough opposing votes, to give the disputed election to Goebel and ultimately to his lieutenant governor, J. C. W. Beckham, who was sworn in after Goebel's passing. Although Beckham was an able politician who won reelection, the Goebel assassination is perhaps most significant for helping usher in a period of increased interparty competition in Kentucky during the early part of the twentieth century. Partisanship solidified in the state because Republicans felt that Democrats stole the election from William Taylor, while Democrats portrayed Republicans as the ones who took down Goebel.[21]

Although Beckham was relatively popular, his actions in two policy areas drove a wedge into the Democratic Party. First, Beckham refused to send troops to stop the Black Patch Tobacco Wars in the western part of the state, which was not a popular move in the eyes of a state electorate concerned with violence. Second, he supported Prohibition, also not a popular position in the state that is the home of bourbon production. These controversial stances led to the election of Republican Augustus Willson in 1907. Willson attempted to stop the Tobacco Wars and was thought to be an adequate leader, but the credit for many of the achievements during his administration went to the Democratic-led General Assembly. Willson was followed by Democrats James McCreary and Augustus Stanley.[22] These administrations were characterized by progressive economic policies. Stanley was followed by Edwin Morrow, a Republican, who campaigned and governed on a platform of eliminating corruption and violence in Kentucky. He was succeeded by Democrat Jason William Fields, who is best remembered as the primary political enemy of J. C. W. Beckham. Early Republican success and this period of increased interparty competition came to an end with the election of Flem Sampson, who encountered economic turmoil, as well as problems with appointments and a Democratic General Assembly.

DEMOCRATIC DOMINANCE AND FACTIONALISM

The 1931 election ushered in a return to Democratic dominance in Kentucky for the next forty years, during which time only two of the ten men who served as governor were Republicans. This occurred despite the fact that the Republicans were strongly unified, while the Democrats during this time period were largely bifactional, with politicians falling into either the A. B. "Happy" Chandler camp or the Earle Clements faction. Although Democratic factionalism is commonly associated with Chandler and Clements, it actually traces its roots to the governorship of Ruby Laffoon. Specifically, Laffoon benefited from the electoral coalition put together by administration members Tom Rhea and Earle Clements. Laffoon and Clements supported Rhea in the subsequent election, but he was defeated by Happy Chandler, the lieutenant governor who served under Laffoon and relentlessly criticized his actions as governor.

Subsequent Democratic governors elected through 1967 fell into one of these two factions. Early Democratic victors emerged from the Chandler faction. Lieutenant Governor Keen Johnson, a Chandler loyalist, became governor after Chandler's appointment to the U.S. Senate and was elected to his own term in office in 1939. Lyter Johnson, another member of the Chandler faction, received the Democratic nomination in 1945 but lost to Republican nominee Simeon Willis, a rare victory for the Republican Party. Donaldson's loss, combined with Chandler's acceptance of a position as commissioner of major-league baseball, brought at least a temporary end to the dominance of the Chandler faction.[23]

Into this leadership void stepped Earle Clements. Clements continued to build the coalition he had helped start while he was a member of the Laffoon administration, and he parlayed it into support that helped him get elected to the state senate and the U.S. House and ultimately as governor in 1947. After being elected to the U.S. Senate in 1950, Clements was succeeded by faction loyalist Lawrence Wetherby. Politically things looked very good for the Clements faction, but after the conclusion of his tenure as baseball commissioner, Happy Chandler returned to Kentucky and was once again elected governor in 1955. However, the Chandler faction did not become as dominant as it once had been, because he was followed as governor by Clements' loyalists Bert Combs and Ned Breathitt. Clements-faction member Henry Ward was the Democratic nominee in 1967 but lost to Republican Louie Nunn, who, in a demonstration of the hostility that existed between factions, was endorsed by Chandler. The election of Wendell Ford in 1971 essentially ended this period of factional politics within the Democratic Party because Ford emerged despite opposition from Combs and with no serious opposition from the Chandler faction.

Aside from who won and who lost, several characteristics of Democratic factionalism make it one of the more interesting periods of party politics in Kentucky. First, it was characterized by a high level of fluidity. Candidates were elected with the support of different factions in different years, former allies often ran against each other in later elections, and in 1967 Clements supported Chandler in the governor's race against someone from his own faction. Second, factionalism was based on the various personal characteristics of politicians. People were drawn to Chandler because of his infectious personality, which allowed him to have broad popular appeal. Clements's main strengths were his skill as a political organizer and his ability to parlay that into political power. Third, and perhaps most surprising, these factions maintained power without strong evidence of voter loyalty to either. Jewell and Cunningham find that only 53 of the 120 counties in Kentucky consistently voted for the same faction's candidate.[24] They speculate that at the individual level, sectional interests, allegiance to a specific candidate, and strength of party organization were just as important as factional loyalty with regard to vote choice.

CONTEMPORARY PARTY COMPETITION IN KENTUCKY

The past four decades have seen an evolution in partisan competition across Kentucky. Although national politics in the state has trended sharply to the right, Democrats have generally managed to win in state and local elections. Once considered to be one of several bellwether states for national politics, Kentucky has emerged as solidly red in the past several presidential elections. Kentucky's status as a bellwether state stemmed primarily from the fact that the presidential candidate who won Kentucky went on to win the presidency in eleven consecutive elections from 1964 through 2004.[25] For many of the early elections during that period, the statewide vote share won by the Republican candidate was within just a few percentage points of the national vote share. Kentucky was a frequent stop for presidential candidates, their running mates, and their spouses. In the run-up to the 2000 presidential election, it was considered to be a swing state that would draw significant attention from Texas governor George W. Bush and Vice President Al Gore. For example, in May 2000 Governor Bush participated in a bus tour that stopped in Paducah, Hopkinsville, and Bowling Green. When George Bush scored a decisive victory that fall, winning 56.5 percent of the vote, Kentucky saw its status as a swing state and bellwether for presidential politics diminish.

The past three presidential elections also saw Republican presidential candidates post impressive victories in the state. President Bush won 59.6 percent of the vote in his 2004 reelection bid against Massachusetts senator John Kerry, in 2008 Arizona senator John McCain won 57.4 percent of the vote against Illinois senator Barack Obama, and in 2012 Massachusetts Governor Mitt Romney won 60 percent of the vote against President Obama's 38 percent. Bush's statewide vote share was roughly 9 percent higher than his national tally (50.7 percent), McCain performed nearly 12 percent better than his national performance, and Romney performed roughly 13 percent better than his national vote total. Bush, McCain, and Romney also managed to win almost every county across the state. Barack Obama won just 8 of Kentucky's 120 counties in 2008 and only 4 counties in 2012. He did, however, post victories in Fayette and Jefferson counties, the two most populous counties in the state. Bush won 105 and 108 counties in his two presidential races. With the significant exception of Jefferson County, the majority of the counties he lost were in eastern Kentucky.

Republicans have also done very well in congressional elections over the past couple of decades. Since January 1997 Republicans have made up at least 75 percent of Kentucky's congressional delegation.[26] Currently, Republicans hold five of the six U.S. House seats and both U.S. Senate slots. Republicans scored a major victory in May 1994 when religious bookstore owner Ron Lewis upset state senator Joe Prather in a special election to replace William Natcher in Kentucky's Second District. Prather was the heavy favorite to replace Natcher, who had served over forty years in the U.S. House until his death in March 1994. Lewis was just the second Republican to represent the Second District in Congress and the first in over 120 years (Samuel McKee had served a two-year term as a Republican in the 1860s). Lewis successfully linked Prather to President Bill Clinton, who was viewed unfavorably by voters at the time. The victory by Lewis contributed to the bellwether status conferred on Kentucky because it foreshadowed the Republican takeover of Congress in November. It also gave Kentucky's U.S. House delegation an equal number of Democrats and Republicans. Republicans Jim Bunning and Hal Rogers represented the Fourth and Fifth Congressional Districts, while Tom Barlow (First), Ramono Mazolli (Third), and Scotty Baesler (Sixth) made up the Democratic half of the House delegation.

Nationally, the 1994 midterm election saw the Republicans win a majority in Congress. At the state level, Kentucky voters also sent a delegation consisting of a majority of Republicans to Washington for the first time since Herbert Hoover was president. Ed Whitfield, who had previously served as a Democrat in the Kentucky House, became the first Republican elected to represent Kentucky's First District. Whitfield's victory gave Republicans four of the six congressional seats. Republicans added a fifth seat in 1996 when Anne Northup won in the Democratic-leaning Third District. After the 2010 midterm elections, Republicans represented four of Kentucky's six congressional districts. Whitfield and Rogers continued to serve the First and Fifth Districts, respectively. When Ron Lewis retired in 2008, state senator Brett Guthrie from Bowling Green defeated fellow Senator David Boswell from Owensboro in the Second District. Geoff Davis defeated Nick Clooney, a local broadcaster and father of actor George Clooney, in 2004 and continued to represent northern Kentucky's Fourth District until his retirement in 2012. Despite Davis's announcement in December 2011 that he was not going to seek reelection, Republicans were all but assured of holding on to the seat. Lewis County judge executive and Tea Party favorite Thomas Massie emerged the winner in a multi-candidate Republican primary and coasted to an easy victory in the general election.

Prior to the 2012 election Democrats held Kentucky's two other House seats. John Yarmuth regained the Third District for Democrats by defeating incumbent Anne Northup in 2006 and joined Ben Chandler, the only Democrat in Kentucky's congressional delegation in the preceding Congress. In an ironic twist, after losing to Ernie Fletcher in the 2003 gubernatorial election, Chandler won a 2004 special election to fill the Sixth District seat vacated by Fletcher. Chandler narrowly held on to his seat in 2010 with a 648 vote margin over Lexington attorney Andy Barr. Results from the 2012 election provide a good snapshot of the competitive balance of the six congressional districts. Incumbents Whitfield (First), Guthrie (Second), and Rogers (Fifth) all scored decisive victories in districts where Republicans should have an advantage in federal elections. As mentioned above, Thomas Massie won easily in the Republican-friendly Fourth District. John Yarmuth coasted to a comfortable win in the Democrat-friendly Third District. As expected, the Sixth District featured the only competitive House election in 2012 and was the only federal race to receive any serious attention during the campaign. Following Ben Chandler's narrow victory in 2010, the Sixth District was modified slightly during redistricting. The changes to the Sixth District were expected to give Chandler a slight boost in his efforts to hold on to his seat in a much anticipated rematch against Barr. The small changes to the composition of the Sixth were not enough to help Chandler overcome President Obama's unpopularity in most of the district. Chandler failed to win the newly added portions of the District. Ultimately, Barr's winning margin reached almost 4 percent. National politics should provide an advantage to Barr in his efforts to retain the seat, but the Sixth is likely to remain the closest thing to a swing district that Kentucky has. Barr's win gives the Republicans control over five of the six congressional districts.

In addition to success in U.S. House elections, both of Kentucky's U.S. senators have been Republican since 1999. Mitch McConnell, first elected in 1984, is serving his fifth term in the Senate. Hall of Fame pitcher Jim Bunning joined McConnell in the Senate when he won a closely contested election against former University of Kentucky basketball player Scotty Baesler in a battle featuring incumbent members of the U.S. House. In a race that was surprisingly close, Bunning was reelected in 2004 in a contest against state senator Daniel Mongiardo. Bunning survived a shaky campaign riddled with several missteps. Bowling Green ophthalmologist Rand Paul, son of Texas Congressman Ron Paul, was elected to replace Bunning in the U.S. Senate in 2010. Paul scored a fairly decisive victory over Attorney General Jack Conway, winning 55.7 percent of the vote and carrying 93 counties. Like Kerry and Gore in previous presidential elections, Conway's greatest support came from counties in Appalachia.

Overwhelming Republican success in federal elections has not translated into similar success in state and local elections. Since Louie Nunn's victory in 1967, Republicans have won only one gubernatorial election. Congressman Ernie Fletcher defeated "Happy" Chandler's grandson, Attorney General Ben Chandler, by a relatively comfortable 10 percent margin in 2003. The future looked promising for the Republican Party after Fletcher's victory. In addition to the governorship, Republican Trey Grayson was elected secretary of state, and former University of Kentucky basketball player Richie Farmer was elected commissioner of agriculture. The momentum that Republicans enjoyed in statewide elections after Fletcher's victory was short-lived. An investigation into administration hiring practices led to Fletcher being indicted and undermined much of his term as governor. It also led to a primary challenge from former U.S. representative Anne Northup and a fairly sizable defeat at the hands of recycled Democratic gubernatorial candidate Steve Beshear.[27] Beshear, a former state representative, attorney general, and lieutenant governor, had lost a previous bid for the Democratic gubernatorial nomination in 1987 and had been defeated by Mitch McConnell in a U.S. Senate bid in 1996. Despite relatively few identifiable legislative accomplishments in his first term as governor, Beshear coasted to an 18-point general-election victory over the Republican nominee, Kentucky Senate president David Williams, in 2011. In addition to being a stinging rebuke of Williams, the election highlighted the futility that Republicans have encountered in gubernatorial elections.

With the exception of a hotly contested matchup between Democratic lieutenant governor Paul Patton and Republican Larry Forgy in 1995, Democratic candidates won gubernatorial elections between Nunn's and Fletcher's victories by comfortable margins. It was during this period that there was a transformation in the nature of Democratic nomination battles. En route to his election as governor in 1971, Wendell Ford defeated former governor Bert Combs in the primary. In the general election Ford also beat two-time former governor "Happy" Chandler, who was running as an independent. Ford's victories over Combs and Chandler signaled a decline in the factionalism that had defined Democratic Party politics in the middle of the twentieth century. No longer were Democratic primary battles between the two major factions within the party. Consequently, Democratic governors during this period followed both traditional (Ford, Julian Carroll, Martha Layne Collins, Patton) and nontraditional (John Y. Brown and Wallace Wilkinson) routes to office.

Results in state legislative races have been mixed over the past few decades. Republicans have been able to gain and maintain a majority in the Kentucky Senate but have not been able to change the balance of power in the House. The partisan tide at the national level that led to the Republican takeover of Congress in 1994 also influenced state legislative elections across the state. Heading into the general election, Democrats held a 24–14 advantage in the Senate and had over 70 seats in the Kentucky House. After the dust settled in November, Republicans gained 3 seats in the Senate and 8 in the House.[28] After the 1994 gains, Republicans continued to chip away at the Democratic majority in the Kentucky Senate but earned their most significant victories behind closed doors rather than at the ballot box. After Republicans picked up another state senate seat in 1996 to narrow the Democratic majority to 20–18, they partnered with five Democrats to oust Democratic Senate president John "Eck" Rose from Winchester by electing Louisville Democratic senator Larry Saunders. As part of the agreement between Saunders and Republican members, Republicans gained a voting majority on a couple of committees and additional seats on other important committees.

In 1998 Democrats held on to their slim majority in the Senate. They were not, however, able to hold the majority through the following year. In July 1999 Democratic senator Dan Seum from Louisville announced that he was switching parties. The announcement came after a meeting with key Republican leaders at Senator Mitch McConnell's home. McConnell was among those in attendance at the press conference announcing the switch. Seum's party switch evened the partisan makeup of the Senate at 19 for each party. The even split in the Senate raised several operational questions that ultimately went unanswered. In August, Bob Leeper from Paducah became the second Democratic senator to defect to the Republican side, which gave Republicans a narrow majority. McConnell again played a role in this process. Despite the best efforts of Democrats, Republicans have been able to maintain their Senate majority. After the 2012 elections Republicans enjoyed a 23–14 advantage over the Democrats, with one independent. In early 2005, Leeper left the Republican Party to serve as an independent member of the Senate. He has continued to caucus with Republican senators, giving them a working majority of 24 members for the 2013 legislative session.

Although Republicans have been able to cut into the size of the Democratic majority in the Kentucky House, Democrats have continued to maintain control of the chamber. Democrats enjoyed majorities of 70 members or more during a large part of the twentieth century, up to as late as 1994. Republican gains in the 1994 midterm cut the majority to 63 seats. Twice since then, Republicans have been able to get the Democratic majority under 60. In 2004, the first legislative election held after Ernie Fletcher's election as governor, Republicans won 43 House seats. Fletcher's troubles after the 2004 elections, paired with a tough election climate nationally for Republicans, helped the Democrats push their majority back over 60 in 2006 and 2008. Republicans were able to get back to 41 seats with a strong showing in 2010. In redistricting efforts during the 2012 legislative session, House Democrats aggressively pursued a new legislative map that would help ensure a Democratic majority in the chamber for the next couple of election cycles. Franklin Circuit Court judge Phillip Shepherd threw out the new map, along with controversial new Senate districts drawn by the Republican-led Senate. The 2012 legislative elections were run using the old district, but legislative candidates will run in new districts that will be in place for the 2014 elections. Although Republicans seem to have a lock on holding their majority in the Senate, they held 45 seats in the House after the 2012 election.

In addition to looking at partisan composition of the legislature over time, it is important to look at a couple of additional trends in Kentucky legislative elections. Like many states to its south, Kentucky has a history of having state legislative elections that are not particularly competitive.[29] It is not uncommon to have over half of state legislative races go uncontested. More than half the races since 1973 for the Kentucky House of Representatives have failed to have both a Republican and a Democratic candidate running. In several years, under a third of all House races were contested by both parties. For the majority of the period, most of the uncontested matchups consisted of Democrats who did not face Republican opposition. Recently, Republicans have made a concerted effort to put up more candidates. In particular, Republicans made efforts in 2010 and 2012 to increase the number of House races that they contested, with the result that there were more Republicans who did not face a Democratic opponent than vice versa. This is consistent with the general trend that more Republicans are running uncontested than in the past.

In addition to changes in interparty competition, there has been change in intraparty competition. Comparatively, the Democratic Party has seen greater change in intraparty competition than have Republicans. As noted earlier, the decline in the two dominant factions within the Democratic Party changed the dynamics of nomination politics. Open-seat gubernatorial and U.S. Senate primaries continue to see spirited competition, but intraparty competition is primarily ad hoc and centered on personal rivalries. As is the case nationally, modern elections tend to be candidate-centered affairs. Perhaps the greatest change in intraparty competition on the Democratic side is the decline in contested primaries for legislative contests. There has been a clear decline in the number of Kentucky House districts with a Democratic primary during this period. Through the mid-1980s it was common for at least forty House districts to feature a Democratic primary. That number has declined to the low double digits over the past ten years. There were just twelve Democratic primaries for state House elections in 2012.

One area to watch with regard to intraparty competition in both the Republican and Democratic Parties is whether regional factors become more pronounced over time. The 2010 Democratic U.S. Senate primary between Daniel Mongiardo and Jack Conway illustrates the potential for a regional split. The bulk of Conway's support came from the Golden Triangle and down the I-65 corridor, while Mongiardo ran well in the more rural eastern and western parts of the state.[30] A similar pattern emerged in the 2011 Republican gubernatorial primary as well. Tea Party candidate Phil Moffett faired very well in the Golden Triangle, but Senate president David Williams was strongest in counties outside the Triangle, especially in the Old Fifth Congressional District.[31] As in trends in national politics, it is likely that there is a sharper contrast between urban and rural regions of the state.

PARTIES IN THE ELECTORATE

Kentucky regulations that govern political parties significantly affect party and electoral politics in the Commonwealth. The net effect of regulations governing political parties is the reinforcement of a two-party system that makes the emergence of third parties difficult. KRS 118.015 defines a political party as an affiliation or organization of electors representing a political policy and having a constituted authority for its government and regulation. To achieve and maintain official designation as a party, a party's designated presidential candidate must receive at least 20 percent of the total vote cast in the general election. Ballot access is automatically granted to the nominees of political parties that meet this official definition. As is the case in most states, these ballot access rules favor the Republican and Democratic Parties in Kentucky. State law governing Kentucky's primary elections also favors the two established parties. KRS 115.055 establishes a closed primary system, in which only registered partisans are able to participate in their particular primary. As has been seen in presidential politics, whether a primary is open or closed can have a substantial effect on who wins and who loses. The presence of a closed primary also influences voter-registration patterns. Because only Republicans and Democrats are able to participate in Kentucky's closed primary, almost all voters register as a Republican or a Democrat. Before the

May 2012 primary, just under 93 percent of registered voters were registered as Democrat or Republican.[32]

The Democratic Party has long enjoyed a registration advantage across most parts of the state. Despite Republican gains in registration numbers over the past couple of decades, registered Democrats outnumber Republicans in all six of Kentucky's congressional districts and in 86 of 120 counties. In 46 counties at least two-thirds of voters have registered as Democrats. On the other end of the spectrum, at least two-thirds of voters are registered as Republicans in 17 of the 34 counties where Republicans have the registration advantage. Overall, 55.2 percent of registered voters in Kentucky are registered as Democrats, while 37.7 percent are registered as Republicans. Although Democrats still hold a substantial advantage that has an impact on the composition of many state boards, the registration gap between Democrats and Republicans has shrunk over the past several decades. By comparison, over two-thirds of registered voters in 1982 were registered as Democrats.

Although the Democratic registration advantage does reflect genuine partisan preferences in some cases, the numbers are also influenced by a number of other factors. Because there is a significant partisan advantage in many of the 120 counties, many political races, especially local ones, are decided in the primary. Historically, wanting to vote in state legislative races or county judge-executive contests meant registering as a Democrat. In some counties, particularly those in parts of southeastern Kentucky, the Republican primary determined the general-election winner. Anecdotal evidence also indicates that in counties with a significant Democratic advantage, county clerks would frequently suggest registering as a Democrat when they were asked by young voters registering for the first time. Once registered as a partisan, voters seldom change their registration. In some states presidential primaries provide incentives for voters to shift their voter registration. However, because Kentucky's presidential primaries typically occur well after the nomination has been decided, there has been little reason to switch party registration.

In discussing party loyalties within the electorate, it is important not to focus exclusively on voter-registration data. Political scientists generally find that voter registration is not a particularly accurate tool to measure partisan identification. Political scientists view party identification as a psychological attachment that reflects how a voter feels about political parties. One way to measure party identification is to ask voters which party they feel closer to. A 2010 general-election survey conducted by Braun Research highlights the difference between party registration and party identification. Survey respondents were asked two questions related to party affiliation.[33] First, they were asked whether they were registered as a Democrat, a Republican, or something else. Overall responses generally reflected the official registration data from the office of the secretary of state. Among the eight hundred respondents, Democrats enjoyed a registration advantage of more than 16 percent over Republicans and held the advantage in all six congressional districts.

The second question tapped more directly into the question of party identification rather than registration. To measure party identification, respondents were asked, regardless of how they were registered, whether they thought of themselves as closer to the

Democratic Party or to the Republican Party. Responses to this question resulted in an 11-point advantage for Republicans. In this particular survey Republicans enjoyed an identification advantage in five of the six congressional districts. The only district where Democrats had an identification advantage was the Third District in Jefferson County.

Registration data hold some clear advantages over survey-based identification data. Registration data are easy to collect and are generally stable over time. Because party-identification measures rely on survey responses, data are more likely to fluctuate over time. Although one might quibble about the exact measure of partisans in the Commonwealth, it is clear that party-registration data significantly overstate Democratic strength in the Kentucky electorate. It is also possible to piece together data from multiple surveys to provide a better picture of party preferences among Kentucky voters. Kentucky's Third District (Jefferson County) is clearly the most Democratic of the six congressional districts. Republicans seem to have an advantage, particularly in national politics, in four (First, Second, Fourth, and Fifth) of the districts. The Sixth District in central Kentucky, which includes Lexington and Frankfort, falls somewhere in between. The most dynamic difference between registration and identification data is found in western Kentucky's First Congressional District, which includes the eight counties that make up the area known as the Jackson Purchase.[34] The Jackson Purchase, an area once considered to be solidly Democratic, has trended sharply Republican over the past decade or so.

PRIMARY TURNOUT

In addition to enjoying a significant registration advantage over Republicans in the state, Democrats have generally turned out in greater numbers to participate in primary elections. In the twenty-four primaries held between 1982 and 2008, Democratic turnout outpaced turnout in the Republican primary. The 2010 Republican U.S. Senate primary between Bowling Green ophthalmologist Rand Paul and Secretary of State Trey Grayson saw Republicans post slightly higher turnout (34.7 percent) than the Democratic primary (33.9 percent) featuring Attorney General Jack Conway and Lieutenant Governor Daniel Mongiardo. Republicans also had slightly higher turnout in 2011 and 2012 primaries. Republican turnout benefited from a gubernatorial primary in 2011 and competitive primary in the U.S. House race in Fourth District in 2012. Overall, the gap between Democratic and Republican turnout has declined over the past thirty years. The decrease in the turnout advantage in primary elections enjoyed by Democrats stems primarily from a decline in Democratic turnout rather than a surge in Republican turnout.

A quick look at turnout data for primary elections during this period suggests that turnout is often driven as much by local factors as by statewide and presidential contests. Turnout also tends to be lower in more heavily populated counties. Voter turnout is highest in years when county and local officials, including judge-executives, appear on the ballot. The timing of the presidential primary limits Kentucky's influence in the nomination process and does little to stimulate turnout in presidential years. A recent exception to the lack of interest in the presidential primary was the 2008 nomination battle on the Democratic side between Barack Obama and Hillary Clinton. Although the race was essentially decided by the primary date, it was close enough to bring both candidates to the state for several campaign appearances. Turnout in the 2008 Democratic primary was more than double the turnout for the 2000 and 2004 primaries.

Primaries for statewide offices, highlighted by the gubernatorial primaries, have been notable for their relatively low turnout. Even in years with contested primaries on both sides, turnout has been modest. Turnout did not crack 20 percent for either Republicans or Democrats in the 2003 primary, but Democrats did reach 22.4 percent in 2007. Turnout was particularly low for the Republican primary in 2011, barely reaching the low double digits. Low-information and low-participation primaries can lead to unpredictable results, particularly in races far down the ballot. The 2003 primary for attorney general provides a classic example that led to an unfortunate result for Kentucky Republicans. Former judge Jack Wood won the Republican primary even though the state judicial-discipline commission had suspended his pay twice after concluding that he had violated conduct rules.[35] Just a year before the 2003 primary, Wood had run unsuccessfully as a Democrat for a city-county council seat in Jefferson County. In the primary Wood upset state representative and presumptive favorite Tim Feeley and attorney Jack Kimball but went on to lose the general election to Democrat Greg Stumbo even though Ernie Fletcher became the first Republican to win the governorship in thirty-six years. Wood's primary win and subsequent loss in the general election had a significant impact on Fletcher's term as governor. As attorney general, Stumbo led an investigation of Fletcher administration hiring practices. Charges against Governor Fletcher and members of his administration led to several indictments, including three misdemeanor indictments against Fletcher himself.

Democratic primaries have changed over time. During the middle part of the twentieth century gubernatorial primary battles typically featured candidates from the major factions within the Democratic Party. More often than not, primary elections featured a candidate from the "Happy" Chandler faction running against the choice of the Clements/Combs camp. As the factions withered away during the 1970s, Democratic primaries for governor often resembled a free-for-all. For example, the 1987 Democratic gubernatorial primary featured eight candidates, including two former and two future governors.

PARTY ORGANIZATIONS

The role that formal party organizations play in Kentucky reflects the patterns that have been observed nationally and in other states.[36] Party organizations continue to be important pieces of the electoral puzzle but lack the direct influence they once enjoyed. In an era dominated by candidate-centered campaigns, party organizations tend to supplement candidate activities. The use of the direct primary to nominate candidates for office takes control out of the hands of party leaders and shifts it to candidates and voters. The 2010 Republican U.S. Senate primary provides a clear case study of how the direct primary can produce results different from a system dominated by party leaders. Rand Paul was able to use his father's political organization to generate resources necessary to topple the perceived establishment choice, Secretary of State Trey Grayson. Despite broad support from Republican elected officials, including Senator Mitch McConnell, Grayson was soundly defeated by Paul.

Although parties lack control over the nomination of candidates, they continue to serve a number of electoral functions. Among key activities performed by the Kentucky Democratic Party (KDP) and the Republican Party of Kentucky (RPK) are fund-raising, mobilizing voters, supplementing campaign efforts for candidates, and coordinating efforts among different levels of party organization. In addition to the state party organizations, both parties have established legislative campaign organizations within the Kentucky House and Senate. For example, House Democrats have established the Kentucky House Democratic Caucus Campaign Committee. Because fund-raising provides the resources necessary to carry out party organizations' other functions, it is their primary activity. Significant funds need to be raised to fuel get-out-the-vote drives and other electoral activities, so fund-raising is a year-round activity.

Over the past decade both parties have flexed their fund-raising muscle. Although sources of money vary, contribution data indicate that the RPK outraised the KDP for the two-year election cycles running from 2003 to 2008, but the KDP had the upper hand before and after.[37] The legislative campaign committees tell a tale of two chambers. Since 2006 Republicans have held a modest edge over Democrats on the Senate side, but House Democrats have a significant money advantage over House Republicans. One challenge faced by both state parties is adjusting to the impact of the Bipartisan Campaign Reform Act of 2002 (BCRA) passed by Congress. The BCRA placed limits on the flow of soft money that many state parties received before its passage. The BCRA also placed a cap on the size of the contributions that can be given to state and local parties. Unlike most other contributions under the BCRA, the contribution limit for state and local parties was not indexed for inflation.

The KDP and the RPK have spent significant resources in recent elections implementing aggressive get-out-the-vote efforts.[38] Parties typically add staff in Frankfort and across the state for campaign season. To mobilize turnout in recent elections, both parties have opened campaign offices across the state to coordinate mobilization efforts. These mobilization efforts typically involve party organizations at the local, state, and national levels. Voter-mobilization efforts coordinated through these campaign offices typically rely on volunteers who spend tens of thousands of hours making hundreds of thousands of phone calls and knocking on well over one hundred thousand doors. In addition to voter-mobilization efforts, party organizations typically supplement the campaign efforts of candidates. It is common for the state parties to send mail pieces or make phone calls in support of candidates. Legislative campaign committees also get involved in sending mail pieces. It is not atypical for the parties to send out millions of mail pieces in support of candidates.

The party organizations are somewhat similar in structure. Both organizations are guided by executive committees that serve as the primary governing boards for the parties. The state party chair serves as the public face of the party and plays a significant role in the day-to-day management of the party organization. When a party controls the governorship, the governor plays a key role in organizing the state party and charting its course. The party chair is typically a close ally of the governor. The governor is also a valuable resource for the party, particularly for fund-raising efforts. Democratic dominance in gubernatorial elections has provided the KDP an important strategic advantage over the past four-plus decades. On the Republican side, U.S. senator Mitch McConnell has played a role for the RPK similar to the one governors have played on the Democratic side. McConnell has clearly been the dominant influence on the development of the Republican Party in the state over the past two decades. Although the past couple of election cycles showed some limitations of his influence, McConnell's interest and investment in the Republican Party of Kentucky have been central factors in its growth and success.

Although both parties have made efforts to strengthen themselves institutionally over the past couple of decades, local party organizations are relatively weak compared with many other states.[39] Two factors that have helped diminish local party strength are the dominance of the Democratic Party during the bulk of the twentieth century and the strength of local political figures. States where one party dominates electoral politics tend to have underdeveloped party organizations because intraparty conflict replaces interparty competition. The large number of counties in Kentucky promotes the emergence of political fiefdoms where one or two officeholders can often dominate local politics. One consequence of a dominant local politician is that this person tends to develop his personal organization and constituency rather than building and relying on the local party.

CHANGING GEOPOLITICAL LANDSCAPE

The past few decades have seen significant changes in electoral politics across the Commonwealth. Although some changes have been predictable, many others would have been difficult to forecast. Many of the changes in party politics in Kentucky reflect national trends. Republicans have made gains in almost all rural areas across the state. Counties in which Democrats once enjoyed a virtual stranglehold have voted Republican in recent elections. Nowhere is this more evident than in the eight counties that make up the Jackson Purchase in western Kentucky. Once viewed as the Gibraltar of Democracy for its overwhelming support for Democratic candidates, all eight Purchase counties went Republican in the 2004, 2008, and 2012 presidential elections and the 2010 U.S. Senate race. More significantly, Purchase counties are now routinely sending Republicans to Frankfort to represent them in the state legislature.

Republicans not only have made tremendous gains in former Democratic strongholds but also have maintained strength in many areas in which they have traditionally been strong. One such stronghold consists of the 27 counties that make up the area referred to as the Old Fifth in southern Kentucky. The Old Fifth has been reliably Republican and is the home to approximately two-thirds of the Kentucky counties that have more registered Republicans than Democrats. John McCain won all 27 counties in the Old Fifth with at least 65 percent of the vote in the 2008 presidential election, while Rand Paul won at least 60 percent of the vote in 25 of those counties during the 2010 Senate election. In 2012 Mitt Romney won at least 70 percent of the vote in all but two counties in the Old Fifth. Even when Republicans struggle statewide, they generally perform well in the Old Fifth. Twenty-one of the 28 counties carried by Ernie Fletcher in 2007 were in the Old Fifth. As expected, a disproportionate number of Republican primary votes come from this region. David Williams relied on large margins in this district to ensure his victory in the 2011 gubernatorial primary. The Old Fifth offers some degree of strategic advantage for Republicans because it provides them a reliable base of support on which they build for statewide elections.

As Republicans solidify their support in rural corners of the state, the Golden Triangle likely will be the most competitive battleground between the two parties in upcoming elections. Seven of Kentucky's 10 most populous counties are located in the Golden Triangle, while, roughly speaking, the 4 most populous counties (Jefferson, Fayette, Kenton, and Boone) make up the corners of the triangle. Over half the voters in the state who participated in the 2010 U.S. Senate election came from these 23 counties. The Golden Triangle includes solidly Republican and solidly Democratic counties. Most counties in the region have voted Republican in recent elections, but as a whole the Golden Triangle is fairly competitive. Democrat Jack Conway performed almost 5 percent better in the Triangle than he did in the rest of the state in the 2010 U.S. Senate contest, while Barack Obama performed about 10 percent higher in the region than statewide. In national politics Jefferson County has emerged as perhaps the most reliable Democratic county in the state. After going Republican in the six presidential contests between 1968 and 1988, it has gone Democratic in the past five elections. Only Elliott County in eastern Kentucky has a longer streak. Although a strong showing for Democrats in the Golden Triangle is far from a foregone conclusion, success in the region, particularly in Jefferson and Fayette Counties, will be a prerequisite for Democratic success statewide.

Looking Back, Looking Ahead

Perhaps just as interesting as what did happen in Kentucky politics over the past decade is thinking about what did not take place in Kentucky politics. Things looked particularly bright for Republicans after the 2003 gubernatorial and 2004 presidential elections. Republicans had continued their domination of federal elections in Kentucky and made significant advances at the state level. Ernie Fletcher was the first Republican governor elected in thirty-six years. Republicans controlled the Kentucky Senate and had made gains in the House. With forty-three members of the House, Republicans could envision achieving a majority in the not-so-distant future. Republicans also had a folk hero in Richie Farmer, a former University of Kentucky basketball player, serving as commissioner of agriculture, and a rising star in Secretary of State Trey Grayson, who were potential candidates for future statewide contests. Republican momentum vanished when Ernie Fletcher and his administration became embroiled in the hiring scandal that sidetracked his term as governor. In Jefferson County's Third Congressional District, Republican Anne Northup was swept out of office as part of the national Democratic tide in 2006. Democrats also made gains in the state legislature that year and regained the governorship in 2007.

Republicans regained some momentum in the 2010 elections. Rand Paul posted a decisive victory in the U.S. Senate race, and Republicans picked up seats in the Kentucky House and Senate. Republicans also posted impressive gains in local elections by picking up judge-executive positions in counties that had always elected Democrats. Although the victories of 2010 were significant, they were largely just a return to where things had stood six years earlier. The effects of the Fletcher scandal were significant and continue to linger. The scandal led to a tough Republican primary in 2007 that promoted and exposed divisions within the party. The healing has not been quick. Fletcher's fall also knocked him from being a favorite to follow U.S. senator Jim Bunning when he retired. With Fletcher out of the picture in 2010, a series of events was set in motion that ultimately led to Rand Paul's victory in the Republican primary and his election to the U.S. Senate. Paul's support for and from the Tea Party movement exposed potential ideological rifts within the Republican Party. These splits were on display as they played out in the 2011 primary between state senate president David Williams and businessman Phil Moffett. Moffett pitched himself, with some success, as a Tea Party alternative to Williams, the establishment candidate. Despite raising only a modest sum of money, Moffett came within 10 percentage points of the better-funded Williams. In the general election Williams was unable to shake a likability deficit and perceptions that he was the "bully from Burkesville" and lost quite handily to incumbent Steve Beshear. Williams's crushing defeat headlined a tough night for Republicans. Commissioner of Agriculture James Comer was the only Republican statewide winner in 2011. Democrats swept all other statewide offices and saw the emergence of two potential future stars in Secretary of State Alison Lundergan Grimes and Auditor Adam Edelen.

Republican Party reorganization in 2012 highlighted the continued potential for division within the party. Tea Party organizations made orchestrated and in several cases successful efforts to take over local leadership in many counties across the state. The primary in the Fourth Congressional District to replace retiring Congressman Geoff Davis also featured a Tea Party–versus-establishment narrative. Thomas Massie, a first-term judge-executive from Lewis County, emerged as the Tea Party favorite and earned the support of U.S. senator Rand Paul and Phil Moffett. Congressman Davis and retired U.S. senator Jim Bunning were among those who endorsed state legislator Alecia Webb-Edgington in the race. Boone County judge-executive Gary Moore earned endorsements from many of his colleagues and former Second District Congressman Ron Lewis. In addition to the Fourth District primary contest, several incumbent Kentucky House and Senate members found themselves locked in competitive primaries with Tea Party challengers. Ultimately, the general election did allow the Republicans to regain some momentum heading. Election evening was highlighted by Andy Barr's election to the U.S. House representing the Sixth District. Republicans also added to their majority in the Kentucky Senate and narrowed their deficit in the Kentucky House. The short-term prospects for Republicans in Kentucky remain positive. Despite the possibility that the Tea Party–versus-establishment storyline may continue, U.S. senators Rand Paul and Mitch McConnell have worked together to put forward a unified front in an effort to mitigate intraparty factions.

The 2011 primary between Williams and Moffett also highlighted another possible risk to long-term Republican dominance—geography. The difference that exists between northern and southern Republicans at the national level also exists within the state. The debate on casino gambling has previewed the potential divide. Many key operatives pushing for expanded gaming have backgrounds in Republican politics, but the Republican-led Kentucky Senate has been the roadblock preventing a vote on a constitutional amendment to expand casino gambling. If these potential ideological and geographic divisions are manageable, the early half of the twenty-first century should lead to unprecedented success for Republicans in Kentucky. Of course, if history is a guide, predicting the future of party politics in Kentucky is a theoretical exercise sure to go awry.

NOTES

1. Paul Beasley, "Isaac Shelby," in *Kentucky's Governors*, ed. Lowell Harrison (Lexington: University Press of Kentucky, 2004) 1–7.

2. Lowell Harrison and James Klotter, *A New History of Kentucky* (Lexington: University Press of Kentucky, 1997), 73.

3. William Elsey Connelly and Ellis Merton Coulter, *History of Kentucky* (Chicago and New York: American Historical Society, 1922), 475.

4. Harrison and Klotter, *New History of Kentucky*, 74–75.

5. David Heidler and Jeanne Heidler, *Henry Clay: The Essential American* (New York: Random House, 2010), 31.

6. Ibid., 120–53.

7. Harrison and Klotter, *New History of Kentucky*, 112–15.

8. Ibid., 348.

9. William Gienapp, "Nativism and the Creation of a Republican Majority in the North before the Civil War," *Journal of American History* 72, no. 3 (December 1985): 529–59.

10. Harrison and Klotter, *New History of Kentucky*, 122.

11. John Kelly, *The Constitutional Union Party in Kentucky*, masters thesis in history at Western Kentucky University, Bowling Green, Ky., 1971, 11.

12. Harrison and Klotter, *New History of Kentucky*, 122–24.

13. Kelly, *Constitutional Union Party in Kentucky*, 12.

14. John Kleber, *The Encyclopedia of Louisville* (Lexington: University Press of Kentucky, 2001), 488.

15. Tyler Anbinder, *Nativism and Slavery: The Northern Know-Nothings and the Politics of the 1850's* (New York: Oxford University Press, 1994), 170–73.

16. Kelly, *Constitutional Union Party in Kentucky*, 33–34.

17. Penny Miller, *Kentucky Politics and Government: Do We Stand United?* (Lincoln: University of Nebraska Press, 1994), 25.

18. Harrison and Klotter, *New History of Kentucky*, 242–43.

19. Ibid., 257–58.

20. James Klotter, *William Goebel: The Politics of Wrath* (Lexington: University Press of Kentucky, 1977), 126–31.

21. Harrison and Klotter, *New History of Kentucky*, 271–72.

22. James Black temporarily succeeded Wilson as governor but lost an election for his own term and served less than one year as governor.

23. Penny Miller and Malcolm Jewell, *Political Parties and Primaries in Kentucky* (Lexington: University Press of Kentucky, 1990), 42–43.

24. Malcolm Jewell and Everett Cunningham, *Kentucky Politics* (Lexington: University Press of Kentucky, 1968).

25. Election data come from the Kentucky secretary of state's website, http://www.sos.ky .gov/elections/; and from Dave Leip, *Atlas of U.S. Presidential Elections*, http://uselectionatlas .org/.

26. Information on individuals who have represented Kentucky in the U.S. Congress can be found in the *Biographical Directory of the United States Congress*, http://bioguide.congress .gov/.

27. Ann Northup's running mate was Kentucky House of Representatives Republican Minority Leader Jeff Hoover of Jamestown.

28. Much of the historical record from the past twenty years comes from coverage of Kentucky politics by the *Lexington Herald-Leader*.

29. Thomas Holbrook and Emily Van Dunk, "Electoral Competition in the American States," *American Political Science Review* 87 (1993): 955–62.

30. The Golden Triangle consists of twenty-three counties between Louisville, Lexington, and northern Kentucky. The counties are Anderson, Boone, Bourbon, Bullitt, Campbell, Carroll, Clark, Fayette, Franklin, Gallatin, Grant, Henry, Jefferson, Jessamine, Kenton, Madison, Oldham, Owen, Scott, Shelby, Spencer, Trimble, and Woodford.

31. The Old Fifth refers to twenty-seven counties located in southern Kentucky: Adair, Bell, Casey, Clay, Clinton, Cumberland, Estill, Garrard, Green, Harlan, Jackson, Knox, Laurel, Lee, Leslie, Letcher, Lincoln, McCreary, Metcalfe, Monroe, Owsley, Pulaski, Rockcastle, Russell, Taylor, Wayne, and Whitley.

32. Voter-registration and turnout data come from the Kentucky secretary of state.

33. This survey is one of several conducted by Braun Research for Pure Politics on Insight Channel 2. Copies of survey results can be found at the Pure Politics website, http://mycn2 .com/politics/.

34. The eight counties that make up the Jackson Purchase are Ballard, Calloway, Carlisle, Fulton, Graves, Hickman, Marshall, and McCracken.

35. Jack Wood went on to run unsuccessfully as a Democrat for state treasurer in 2007.

36. For additional information on state and local party strength, see James L. Gibson, Cornelius P. Cotter, John F. Bibby, and Robert J. Huckshorn, "Assessing Party Organizational Strength," *American Journal of Political Science* 27, no. 2 (May 1983): 193–222; and James L. Gibson, Cornelius P. Cotter, John F. Bibby, and Robert J. Huckshorn, "Whither the Local Parties? A Cross-Sectional and Longitudinal Analysis of the Strength of Party Organizations," *American Journal of Political Science* 29, no. 1 (February 1985): 139–60.

37. Financial data for the parties come from the Federal Election Commission and the Kentucky Registry of Election Finance.

38. Information on party get-out-the-vote efforts, including rough estimates of types of activities, come from discussions with party activists and officials.

39. Gibson et al., "Assessing Party Organizational Strength."

Part II

Politics and Public Policy Issues

10

Campaign Finance in Kentucky
Escalating Costs and the Search for Reform
Donald A. Gross

For almost half a century campaign finance reform has seemed to remain an issue that simply will not go away. In the 1960s the Kennedy administration began an examination of ways to deal with the escalation of media costs in federal elections, and in 1974 and 1976 the U.S. Congress passed the most comprehensive campaign finance reform laws in the nation's history. More federal legislation followed, as did efforts by the states to reform their campaign finance laws. In many ways Kentucky has often been at the center of the debate over the merits of campaign finance regulation. Kentucky has adopted one of the more stringent sets of regulations on campaign contributions seen in the country and in 1992 passed one of the more innovative systems of financing gubernatorial elections. At the same time, Senator Mitch McConnell of Kentucky remains one of the most powerful and vocal congressional opponents of reform laws. McConnell has helped stop or at least delay numerous campaign finance reform laws and has joined in court actions to challenge federal campaign finance reform laws. In fact, he is fond of saying that no one has ever been defeated for working against campaign finance reform. David Williams, former president of the Kentucky Senate and a friend of McConnell, led the effort to eliminate Kentucky's system of public financing in gubernatorial elections. Perhaps it is not surprising that debate over campaign finance reform remains so contentious and unending. It is fundamentally linked to some of our most important principles and concerns: free speech, equality, power and influence, the role of money in our society, the integrity of our elections, and our democracy.

In this chapter I begin with an examination of the costs of elections in Kentucky.[1] As is the case throughout the United States, it will be seen that campaign costs continue to escalate almost every election cycle. Particular attention will be paid to the elections of 1995 and 1999, when Kentucky experimented with public funding for gubernatorial elections. I then move to a consideration of the regulatory environment in Kentucky and examine how it compares with that seen in other states. Finally, I briefly consider how the nature of the debate over campaign finance will likely proceed in the immediate future.

Election Campaign Costs in Kentucky

My examination of election campaign costs in Kentucky begins with a consideration of federal elections in Kentucky. State election campaign costs are then considered. Campaign costs in state legislation elections are explored followed by examination of gubernatorial campaign costs.

Federal Elections

It is well documented that elections in the United States at almost all levels have, on average, become more costly over recent years.[2] In fact, this trend has been going on in congressional elections for over fifty years. But even though election costs have risen on average, it is not necessarily the case that any subset of elections will have increased cost.

Table 10.1 shows the average cost of U.S. House elections in Kentucky from 1996 to 2010.[3] It also shows the mean cost of all U.S. House elections nationwide, the cost of Kentucky U.S. Senate races, and the mean cost of all U.S. Senate elections. Column 3 in table 10.1 indicates that with the exception of 1998, the average cost of all U.S. House races has risen in every electoral period from 1996 to 2010. The average cost was $971,637 in 1996 but rose to $1,970,977 in 2010, an increase of over 100 percent. One sees a similar trend in column 5. The average cost of all U.S. Senate races has increased every electoral cycle, reaching an average of over $20 million in 2010, an increase of over 190 percent since 1996.[4]

The information on Kentucky federal elections portrayed in table 10.1 suggests two interesting contrasts. First, the information in column 2 indicates that there is not a clear monotonic trend toward increasingly expensive U.S. House elections in Ken-

Table 10.1. Mean Cost of Federal Elections, Nationwide and in Kentucky, 1996–2010

Year	House mean in Kentucky	U.S. House mean	Kentucky Senate	U.S. Senate mean
1996	$1,106,913	$971,637	$6,743,436	$6,982,424
1998	$1,267,404	$913,154	$7,502,230	$7,328,958
2000	$2,024,231	$1,183,433		
2002	$1,772,296	$1,209,163	$7,983,724	$8,531,206
2004	$2,137,242	$1,336,742	$9,415,129	$10,809,254
2006	$2,883,020	$1,728,115		
2008	$1,808,927	$1,857,475	$31,874,850	$11,798,446
2010	$1,654,380	$1,970,977	$19,527,381	$20,351,344

Source: Kentucky Registry of Election Finance, http://www.kref.ky.gov; Federal Election Commission, http://www.fec.gov; and the National Institute on Money in State Politics, http://www.followthemoney.org.

tucky. The average cost for the last four sets of U.S. House elections, 2004 to 2010, was higher than the average cost for the first four sets of U.S. House elections, 1996 to 2002, but the increase was only about 35 percent. Although the average national cost of all U.S. House elections increased over 100 percent from 1996 to 2010, the average cost increase was just under 50 percent in Kentucky. The U.S. House elections in Kentucky in 2008 and 2010 were, on average, actually less expensive than those in 2004 and 2006. With an important exception in 2008, Kentucky U.S. Senate elections have behaved much like national trends: increasing costs over time, with the U.S. Senate election in 2010 costing almost 190 percent more than the election in 1996.[5]

The second interesting contrast between Kentucky U.S. House elections and national averages is that Kentucky elections have tended to be more expensive. With the sole exception of 2010, Kentucky U.S. House elections have cost more, on average, in every election cycle since 1994. The cost of any given U.S. House election is affected by a number of factors. Research has shown, however, that certain factors tend to be associated with more campaign spending. In the case of Kentucky, three factors are of likely importance: urbanization, competitiveness, and television markets.

Television is a major cost in contemporary congressional elections, and some settings are more desirable than others. In many ways the Sixth Congressional District in Kentucky is an ideal setting for congressional candidates. Advertising rates are not overly expensive, almost all voters in the Sixth District are reached by the Lexington television stations, and one does not reach a significant number of voters outside the Sixth District when one advertises on the Lexington stations. The Third and Fourth Districts present a very different picture. When one is advertising in the Fourth District, one must use the Cincinnati television stations, which tend to be more expensive. More important, a large number of their television viewers cannot vote in the Fourth District congressional election. A similar situation exists in Louisville. Both the Third and Fourth Districts also tend to be urbanized. Finally, both districts had a number of competitive elections during the period 1996 to 2010.[6] If we want to know why Kentucky seems to have more expensive congressional elections, therefore, the Third and Fourth Districts are good places to look.

From 1996 to 2010 every U.S. House race in the Third district cost over $2 million. The elections in 2002 and 2004 cost over $4.5 million, and in 2006 more than $5.5 million was spent on the race. In fact, if one excludes the Third District from one's calculations, the mean value of the other five U.S. House elections in Kentucky exceeded the national average four times and was less than the national average four times. The apparently high cost of Kentucky U.S. House elections seems to have a distinctly Louisville look. In a similar vein, the 2004 U.S. House election in the Fourth District cost over $4 million, and over $5.5 million was spent in 2006. If these two elections are removed from the calculations, mean spending in Kentucky U.S. House races has been below the national average for six of the last eight election cycles.

When one is computing averages with an N of 6, mean scores can be a bit deceptive because any single extreme value tends to have a major impact.[7] The mean of campaign spending in Kentucky U.S. House elections does tend to be higher than the national average, but this is very much the result of a limited number of specific high-spending races. Actually, the "typical" Kentucky U.S. House election tends to be much like those seen in other states. A typical race now costs around $1.5 million to $2 million. If one has a highly competitive race in an urbanized setting with moderate to high television rates, costs can and will skyrocket.

State Elections

Table 10.2 shows the total cost of all Kentucky House races, the mean cost per Kentucky House race, the total cost of all Kentucky Senate races, and the mean cost per Kentucky Senate race for each electoral cycle from 1994 to 2008.[8] There is no doubt that Kentucky House races have tended to become more expensive over time. Although costs did drop for the two electoral periods after 1998, they again began to increase greatly in 2004. If one examines column 3 in table 10.2, one sees that the average cost of a Kentucky House election increased from $22,740 in 1994 to an average of $71,460 in 2008, an increase of over 200 percent.

The pattern for the data on Kentucky Senate races portrayed in table 10.2 is less clear than that for Kentucky House races. There does appear to be an overall pattern of increased costs, but the pattern is less stable.[9] The mean cost of a state senate election was much higher in 2000, 2002, and 2004 than in 1994, 1996, and 1998, but then it dropped dramatically in 2006, only to be followed by the most expensive Kentucky Senate races ever seen, with the average state senate race costing $359,177 in 2008. The cost of Kentucky Senate races in 2008 was over 240 percent more than that of the Kentucky Senate races in 1994.[10]

It is very difficult to compare directly the cost of Kentucky state legislative elections with those seen in other states. State legislative elections differ in numerous ways that make comparisons very difficult and beyond the scope of this chapter: the year when elections are held, the number of legislators being elected, and, very important, the population size of their districts. Finally, unlike Kentucky, a number of states do

Table 10.2. Cost of State Legislative Elections in Kentucky, 1994–2008

Year	Cost of all House races	Mean cost of House races	Cost of all Senate races	Mean cost of Senate races
1994	$2,274,014	$22,740	$1,999,051	$105,213
1996	$3,449,811	$34,498	$3,047,066	$160,371
1998	$3,524,322	$35,243	$2,889,199	$152,063
2000	$2,574,747	$25,747	$5,183,615	$272,821
2002	$2,770,040	$27,700	$4,375,671	$230,298
2004	$5,483,379	$54,833	$5,255,812	$276,622
2006	$5,730,031	$57,300	$2,683,479	$141,236
2008	$7,146,056	$71,460	$6,824,356	$359,177

Source: Kentucky Registry of Election Finance, http://www.kref.ky.gov, Federal Election Commission, http://www.fec.gov, and the National Institute on Money in State Politics, http://www.followthemoney.org.

not elect their state legislators from single-member districts.[11] Nevertheless, the National Institute on Money in State Politics does provide a particular type of campaign finance data for state legislative elections that can be very instructive: (m)c50, which is a measure of the financial competitiveness of a particular state legislative election.[12]

Political scientists often use different measures to measure the competitiveness of an electoral district. However, most traditional measures are based on vote totals. What is unique about the measure developed by the National Institute on Money in State Politics is that it focuses on whether the candidates are financially competitive. The measure is relatively simple and straightforward. One begins by determining whether an election is contested. If the election is uncontested, then the district is specified as noncompetitive. Next, fund-raising for the winner of a contested election is compared with that of the loser who raised the most money. A district is said to be financially noncompetitive if one candidate raised more than twice as much money as the other candidate. One can now determine how many state legislative elections in a given state were financially competitive and how many were not competitive.[13]

Table 10.3 shows the percentage of all Kentucky state legislative elections that were not contested and the percentage that were financially competitive for each electoral cycle from 1994 to 2008. It also shows the means of the financially competitive district percentages for all states having state legislative elections in the same years.[14] The first thing that is evident in table 10.3 is that a large percentage of all Kentucky state legislative races are not contested. With the exceptions of 1996, 1998, and 2004, over 50 percent of all elections were uncontested, with a high of 65.5 percent in 2008. Of equal importance, the vast majority of state legislative elections in Kentucky are not financially competitive. A little over 30 percent of all elections were financially competitive in 1996 and 2004, but in five of the eight election cycles, less than 20 percent of all elections were financially competitive. These percentages themselves can be seen as discouraging to those who view competitive elections as central to the

Table 10.3. Competitiveness of Kentucky State Legislative Elections, 1994–2008

Year	Percent of elections that were uncontested	Percent financially competitive	National mean percent financially competitive
1994	54.1	24.6	24.6
1996	40.8	33.3	25.2
1998	45.4	12.6	22.3
2000	61.3	18.5	24.5
2002	61.3	16.8	23.0
2004	46.2	30.3	25.0
2006	55.5	18.5	23.7
2008	65.5	15.1	23.6

Source: Kentucky Registry of Election Finance, http://www.kref.ky.gov; Federal Election Commission, http://www.fec.gov; and the National Institute on Money in State Politics, http://www.followthemoney.org.

democratic process, but a comparison with nationwide figures is equally discouraging. Again, with the exceptions of 1996 and 2004, a comparison of columns 2 and 4 in table 10.3 indicates that Kentucky state legislative races tend to be less financially competitive than the average seen in other states. In six of the eight election cycles Kentucky was below the national average. The mean across the election cycles is 21.2 for Kentucky and 23.9 for all other states. Finally, there does not appear to be any trend toward greater competition either at the national level or in Kentucky.

The trends for Kentucky state legislative elections are not especially encouraging. Over time, Kentucky House and Senate elections are becoming more expensive. At the same time, elections do not seem to be becoming more competitive. A significant number of the elections are not contested, and the vast majority of elections are not financially competitive. There is no trend toward improvement, and Kentucky continues to lag behind national averages.

Table 10.4 presents data on spending levels in gubernatorial elections from 1979 to 2007.[15] The data in column 2 represent total spending for all candidates running in the Kentucky governor's race. The data in column 3 portray the national four-year running means, or running averages, for all gubernatorial elections from 1979 to 2007. For example, the figure in column 3 for 1983 provides the mean cost per state for all gubernatorial elections from 1980 to 1983, while the figure for 2007 provides the mean cost per state for elections from 2004 to 2007.[16] As shown in previous research,[17] the data in column 3 clearly show that the cost of gubernatorial elections nationwide has continued to rise over the years. The mean cost per state for all gubernatorial elections has increased during every four-year election cycle, with an increase of over 475 percent from 1997 to 2007.[18]

The data on Kentucky indicate a picture that is somewhat different from that seen nationwide. The cost of gubernatorial elections rose in Kentucky from 1979 to 1991 and then dropped dramatically in 1995 and 1999. It then took a dramatic jump upward in

Table 10.4. Spending Levels in Kentucky Gubernatorial Elections, 1979–2007

Year	Spending in Kentucky	National four-year mean spending
1979	$9,382,261	$3,543,912
1983	$9,473,018	$5,213,748
1987	$18,366,985	$6,857,872
1991	$19,595,885	$9,061,017
1995	$10,910,380	$10,373,129
1999	$1,779,081	$11,552,476
2003	$25,038,520	$20,060,113
2007	$33,938,499	$20,499,538

Source: Kentucky Registry of Election Finance, http://www.kref.ky.gov; Federal Election Commission, http://www.fec.gov; and the National Institute on Money in State Politics, http://www.followthemoney.org.

2003 and 2007. From 1979 to 1991 Kentucky gubernatorial elections were much more expensive than the running averages of all gubernatorial elections in the United States, generally costing more than twice the national average.[19] Kentucky races were close to the national average in 1995 and well below the average in 1999. In 2003 Kentucky again began to exceed the running average of all gubernatorial elections in the nation.[20]

It is clear that Kentucky gubernatorial elections in 1995 and 1999 departed from the trend toward more expensive elections in Kentucky and a similar trend nation-wide. It is likely that this seeming aberration was the result of Kentucky's experiment with public financing. The story of this experiment shows both the promise and the limitations of campaign finance reform. It is a story of importance to both proponents and opponents of campaign finance reform.

In 1992 the Public Financing Campaign Act was signed into law in Kentucky. The act had three major components. It placed strict new limits on the size of contributions to gubernatorial campaigns. It created the Registry of Election Finance to receive campaign finance reports from candidates and then make them public. Most impor-tant, the legislation created a system of public financing for gubernatorial elections with associated spending limits.[21] The initial voluntary expenditure limits were set at $1.8 million for the primary and $1.8 million for the general election. These limits were to be adjusted by the consumer price index before each election. Once a candi-date achieved a minimum threshold of $300,000 in private contributions, the state began to match each private contribution at a rate of 2 to 1 to a maximum state subsidy of $1.3 million, providing that the candidate agreed to the spending limit. As an incen-tive to induce all candidates to accept the spending limit, if any one candidate ex-ceeded the limit, all other candidates could then exceed the limit and still receive matching funds. Finally, the law required each candidate receiving public funds to participate in up to six public debates.

Before the passage of the 1992 reform act, Republicans in gubernatorial elections had been consistently underfunded relative to their Democratic opponents. In addi-tion, since the beginning of the 1970s Democratic candidates had tended to win the gubernatorial election easily. After the 1995 election proponents of reform felt vindi-cated. Expenditures had been reduced compared with recent gubernatorial elections, and the Democratic primary had been competitive, as in prior gubernatorial elections. Serious candidates did not seem to have great difficulty reaching the $300,000 thresh-old for receiving matching funds despite the new limits on contributions. All major candidates voluntarily accepted the spending limits. Voter turnout was higher than in the previous two gubernatorial elections, and the election was very competitive, with the Democrat winning with less than 51 percent of the vote.

As well as the law seemed to work in 1995, it appeared to be a complete failure in 1999. The 1999 election was also the first in over one hundred years in which the in-cumbent governor could run for reelection. At the beginning of the electoral season the Republicans were confronted with a popular incumbent governor running for re-election, and no major figure in the Republican Party sought the nomination for gov-ernor. Peppy Martin, the eventual Republican nominee, got little help from the state party. Mitch McConnell, a major national Republican figure and fund-raiser, refused to endorse her. She could not even approximate the $300,000 minimum threshold to receive funds from the state. As election day neared, only two questions remained: Would Peppy Martin end up in third place behind independent Gatewood Galbraith, and how big would Governor Paul Patton's victory be?

After the 1999 election proponents and opponents of public financing continued to argue over the consequences of Kentucky's law. Independent of the merits of each side in the argument, the 1999 election was the last Kentucky gubernatorial election for the foreseeable future with a public financing provision. Republicans had taken control of the Kentucky Senate, and the leader of the Republicans, Senator David Williams, blocked all attempts to fund the public financing system before the 2003 election. Eventually the public financing provision of Kentucky's law was repealed.

The merits and problems associated with the public financing of gubernatorial elections are not the focus of this chapter. Nevertheless, it is clear that the public financing provisions of the 1992 law did work to reduce the cost of gubernatorial elections in Kentucky and temporarily reverse the trend toward significantly more expensive elections. Once public financing ended, expenditures grew dramatically, and the trend toward more expensive gubernatorial elections began anew.

In many respects the cost of elections in Kentucky for the past fifteen to twenty years has behaved much as seen in the rest of the nation: costs continue to rise over time. The cost of a U.S. House or Senate race in Kentucky appears to be very similar to that seen in other states. The higher-than-average cost of a U.S. House election in Kentucky seems to be very much the result of a limited number of very expensive races in the Third and Fourth Districts. The cost of state legislative elections in Kentucky has continued to rise over the years even though Kentucky tends, on average, to have fewer financially competitive state legislative elections. And even though Kentucky's experiment with public financing of gubernatorial elections did temporarily reduce the cost of these elections in Kentucky, Kentucky gubernatorial elections continue to become more expensive every electoral cycle and continue to be more expensive than the national average.

CAMPAIGN FINANCE LAW IN KENTUCKY

Campaign finance law covers a wide range of activities associated with a given set of elections. It can include such activities as the prohibition of alcohol sales on election day and prohibitions on vote buying, or bribery. But for the purposes of this section, I will focus on the regulatory environment that surrounds the flow of money in electoral campaigns. As a point of departure, it is most important to understand that the regulatory environment for any given election depends on the governmental body that has jurisdiction over the election. Federal law governs federal elections, such as those for the U.S. House and Senate. The regulatory environment specified by the state of Kentucky governs Kentucky state elections. Local elections can specify their own campaign finance laws.[22] The Kentucky regulatory environment is the focus of this section.[23]

Although campaign finance reform has long been an issue at both the state and national levels, the Watergate scandal focused the nation's attention on issues of campaign finance to a comprehensive degree never before seen in America. Most previous reform efforts tended to focus on specific practices. Watergate raised questions about the entire system of financing elections. Since Watergate over two-thirds of the states, including Kentucky, have passed some campaign finance reform legislation. Some efforts have been minimalistic, while others have been very comprehensive. Five characteristics of the regulatory environments seen in the states have been of central interest in the campaign finance debate: (1) reporting and disclosure requirements, (2) limits on contributions, (3) spending or expenditure limits, (4) public financing, and (5) enforcement provisions.

Reporting and Disclosure Requirements in Kentucky

Reporting and disclosure requirements, also called publicity requirements, have long remained the cornerstone of all state reform efforts. These laws are based on a democratic faith in an informed citizenry as a powerful weapon to minimize the potentially corrupting influence of money in elections. Many states have had publicity laws for over one hundred years, and today all fifty states have some form of reporting and disclosure requirements. Of course, having a law on the books does not guarantee that citizens actually have useful and timely information.

States' reporting requirements basically differ in who or what must report campaign finance activities and what information must be reported. In Kentucky all candidates for state or local office must report campaign financial information. This requirement includes, but is not limited to, candidates for state executive offices, state legislative offices, city council and mayoral offices, and school boards. In addition, state and local party executive committees, political issue committees, permanent political action committees (PACs), and caucus campaign committees must also file reports with the state.

In most cases in Kentucky, individuals and organizations must itemize contributions and expenditures.[24] For example, candidates must itemize all contributions over $100 and must include employer and occupation data. All expenditures over $25 must be itemized. Candidates and organizations are given the option to report in either paper or electronic formats. Reports are submitted to the Kentucky Registry of Election Finance, which is also responsible for the disclosure of campaign finance information.[25] Kentucky law also specifies specific dates for the filing of reports that differ depending on whether the financial activities take place in an election year.

In 2008 the Campaign Disclosure Project evaluated the quality of state reporting and disclosure laws, and Kentucky generally fared quite well in the evaluations.[26] The basic campaign disclosure and reporting law in Kentucky received a B+, which placed the state eleventh in the nation. Kentucky received a B– for disclosure content accessibility (twenty-sixth), a B– for online contextual and technical usability (sixteenth), and an F for its electronic filing program (thirty-first). Kentucky's low ranking for electronic filing was a direct result of the state's refusal to mandate electronic filing.

As the report mentioned in the previous paragraph points out, Kentucky has a solid set of campaign finance reporting and disclosure requirements. Nevertheless, debate will likely continue on a number of contentious issues: electronic filing, reporting requirements for so-called 527s and related organizations, and the development of more user-friendly databases.

Contribution Limits in Kentucky

Other than reporting and disclosure laws, limits on campaign contributions are the most prevalent characteristic of states' campaign finance laws. Limits on campaign contributions tend to differ in three basic characteristics: (1) differences in who or what organizations that make contributions, (2) differences in who or what organizations that receive contributions, and (3) differences in the dollar amounts of specific types of contributions. Not only do these characteristics differ among the states but they can also differ across different electoral offices within a given state.

Kentucky has a fairly extensive list of contribution limits. Individuals, permanent PACs, and contributing organizations are limited in the amount of money that they can contribute to a candidate or slate of candidates, PACs, executive committees, and caucus committees.[27] Corporations are prohibited from contributing to candidates or slates of candidates, PACs, executive committees, or caucus committees. The specific amount of the contribution limit depends on who or what is giving the contribution and who or what is receiving the contribution. For example, the limits on individual contributions are set at $1,000 per election for contributions to a candidate and $2,500 per year for contributions to a caucus campaign committee.[28]

Kentucky is much like many other states with regard to contribution limits. Kentucky is one of thirty-six states that place a limit on the amount that an individual can contribute to a candidate or slate of candidates. It is one of thirty states that place a limit on state party contributions. Thirty-five states place a limit on PAC contributions. And Kentucky is one of forty-one states that place some limit on union contributions and one of twenty-two states that ban corporate contributions.

Spending or Expenditure Limits in Kentucky

Spending or expenditure limits are a mechanism that many saw as a way to reduce, or at least slow down, the ever-escalating cost of elections. In addition, it was often argued that spending limits could reduce the disparity in spending between candidates and increase electoral competition and voter turnout. But in 1976 the U.S. Supreme Court put forward a decision in *Buckley v. Valeo* that effectively prohibited the use of mandatory spending limits by either the federal government or state governments. Spending limits had to be voluntary, although states could put forward public subsidies to encourage the acceptance of spending limits.

In the late 1990s thirteen states had some type of expenditure limit that was a condition for receiving public funds. In most cases these limits were related to gubernatorial elections. As discussed earlier in this chapter, Kentucky experimented with expenditure limits during the gubernatorial elections of 1995 and 1999. As originally written, the expenditure limits were initially set at $1.8 million for the primary and $1.8

million for the general election and were to be adjusted by the consumer price index before each subsequent election. Whether this experiment was a success or a failure is subject to debate. Nevertheless, the law was eventually repealed, and expenditure limits are no longer part of Kentucky's campaign finance regulatory environment.

Public Financing in Kentucky

There are basically two types of public financing used in the states. One alternative provides money to political parties, while the second provides money to candidates for office. Approximately twenty states have some type of public financing system. Some give money exclusively to political parties, some give exclusively to candidates, and some give money to both political parties and candidates. As discussed earlier, Kentucky experimented with public subsidies for gubernatorial candidates in 1995 and 1998 but eventually repealed the law. Kentucky continues to subsidize political parties.

Among the states that provide funds to political parties, approximately one-half rely on a taxpayer checkoff system whereby a taxpayer can designate part of his or her tax liability for the public funding system. This is the system used in Kentucky. Each year each taxpayer in Kentucky is allowed to check a box on his or her state income tax form that will designate $2 of the tax liability for either the Kentucky Democratic Party or the Kentucky Republican Party, of which $1.50 goes to the state party organization and 50 cents goes to the local party organization.

As in most states with similar systems, participation in Kentucky's voluntary check-off system is not particularly high. Significantly less than 10 percent of all taxpayers use the system each year. Each party tends to receive about $100,000 each year, with the Republican Party averaging less money than the Democratic Party. Depending on the year one examines, this amount tends to represent approximately 5 percent of the funds raised by each party.[29]

Enforcement Provisions

As one might expect, there is a great deal of diversity among the states in the enforcement provisions and the implementation of campaign finance law. In most cases there appears to be little effort to systematically cross-check the validity of the information provided by candidates and organizations. In fact, enforcement tends to rely on complaints from individuals and groups outside the state agency charged with enforcing the law.

The Kentucky Registry of Election Finance is the state agency in Kentucky that has prime responsibility for the enforcement and administration of Kentucky's campaign finance laws. It ensures that all reports related to campaign finance activities are filed within proper time periods. It attempts to ensure that all information is complete, accurate, and in compliance with Kentucky law. It is also responsible for maintaining all campaign finance information submitted to the state and for making this information available to the public.

Beyond the collection and dissemination of campaign finance information, the Registry of Election Finance has ultimate responsibility for all policy and enforcement decisions concerning the regulation of campaign finance. It prepares documents to help candidates comply with campaign finance regulations. It can issue advisory opinions, promulgate administrative regulations, and conduct audits of the receipts and expenditures of candidates. It adjudicates administrative charges of violations of campaign finance laws. It can investigate potential violations of campaign finance law and then report potential violations to the appropriate law enforcement authorities. Finally, it can undertake court action to enforce its authority.

The Kentucky Registry of Election Finance is a prime actor in Kentucky's efforts to regulate campaign finance. As stated earlier in the discussion of Kentucky's reporting and disclosure requirements, it has generally received good grades compared with those seen in other states. At the same time, to date there has been no systematic analysis of the accuracy of its reports or of its other major functions. As in other states, action against those violating Kentucky campaign finance laws continues to be heavily reliant on complaints arising from those outside the Registry of Election Finance.

I stated earlier that Kentucky has often been in the middle of the nationwide debate over campaign finance reform. This is partly because of the personalities involved, especially Mitch McConnell. At the same time, the issues confronting Kentucky are much like those confronting the rest of the nation: seemingly unending increases in the cost of elections, perceptions of corruption, the role of money in political decision making, free speech, the competitiveness of elections, and the future of democracy. What are we to do next?

Current trends do not bode well for those wishing to expand the regulatory environment governing campaign finance in Kentucky and for those concerned about the influence of big money in elections. The recent Republican surge in Kentucky, led by individuals generally opposed to further significant campaign finance reform, makes it politically unlikely that we will see any new major initiatives, such as the reintroduction of public funding for election campaigns. In addition, recent U.S. Supreme Court decisions, such as *Randall v. Sorrell* (2006) and *Citizens United v. Federal Election Commission* (2010), have placed proponents of reform, nationwide and in Kentucky, on the defensive.

In *Randall v. Sorrell* the Court declared Vermont's expenditure and low contribution limits unconstitutional. In *Citizens United* the Court argued that the First Amendment prohibited the government from restricting political expenditures by corporations and unions. It was not long before we began to see the direct consequences of these decisions. Citing the *Randall* decision, a federal judge declared Kentucky's $100 contribution limit on individual contributions to school-board candidates unconstitutional. The state merely accepted the decision and did not submit an appeal. Perhaps more important, unfettered by government restrictions because of *Citizens United*, unions and corporations could now engage in independent spending in political campaigns with funds from their own treasury. The direct result is what has come to be known as "super PACs," which are independent expenditure committees that can raise unlimited sums from individuals, corporations, unions, and other organizations.[30] The only real restriction on these committees is that they cannot coordinate their activities with any candidate for office. Although super PACs were effectively unheard of before *Citizens United*, they spent over $65 million during the 2010 electoral season and over $567 million during the 2012 electoral season.[31] The day of the so-called fat-cat contributor, which many thought had ended with the passage of federal legislation in the 1970s, is back once again.

Beyond the specifics of these cases, proponents of campaign finance reform fear what they see as a lethal trend on the Court toward a more interventionist and deregulationist stand. Before *Randall* the Court had shown a tendency to defer to the legislature in specifying contribution limits.[32] A plurality in *Randall*, however, indicated a clear concern over the potential negative effects of contribution limits, particularly the argument that contribution limits have a negative effect on the ability of challengers to mount an effective campaign against incumbents.[33] Because the Court viewed it as its responsibility to protect the structural integrity of the democratic process, so the argument goes, it would be the Court and not the legislature that would determine if a contribution limit was too low. In addition, at least three justices (Thomas, Scalia, and Kennedy) indicated a clear deregulationist stand that called into question the constitutionality of any contribution limit. As proponents of reform shuddered at the thought, opponents of reform looked to the day when all contribution limits might be eliminated.

Even though we seem to be in an era of retrenchment from the campaign finance reform experiments of the past forty years, the debate on campaign finance reform is not going to go away. As the cost of elections continues to rise, the same questions will continue to be raised, and new experiments will be tried. The slim majorities reflected in the current deeply divided U.S. Supreme Court may change, as might the political atmosphere in Kentucky. Both sides on the campaign finance reform debate know that the fight will continue.

NOTES

1. Most of the data used in this chapter were obtained from the website of the Kentucky Registry of Election Finance, http://www.kref.ky.gov. Additional data were obtained from the Federal Election Commission, http://www.fec.gov; and the National Institute on Money in State Politics, http://www.followthemoney.org.

2. Anthony Carrado, Thomas E. Mann, Daniel R. Ortiz, and Trevor Potter, *The New Campaign Finance Sourcebook* (Washington, D.C.: Brookings Institution Press, 2005); Robert K. Goidel, Donald A. Gross, and Todd G. Shields, *Money Matters: The Consequences of Campaign Finance Reform in U.S. House Elections* (Boulder, Colo.: Rowman and Littlefield, 1990); Donald A. Gross and Robert K. Goidel, *The States of Campaign Finance Reform* (Columbus: Ohio State University Press, 2003); and Norman J. Ornstein, Thomas E. Mann, and Michael J. Malbin, *Vital Statistics on Congress, 2008* (Washington, D.C.: Brookings Institution Press, 2008).

3. It is important to recognize that the figures in table 10.1 are based on the total amount of real dollar spending by all candidates in the primary and general elections.

4. Although the increased costs seen in table 10.1 are partly due to inflationary effects in the economy, even if one examines constant dollars, which control for simple inflationary effects,

from 1996 to 2010 the increase in the cost of an average U.S. House election was around 46 percent, and the increase in an average U.S. Senate race was about 109 percent.

5. The 2008 U.S. Senate race in Kentucky was the most expensive in Kentucky history and cost well above the national average. Much of this is likely because Mitch McConnell was on the ballot and was facing a well-funded challenger. McConnell is the minority leader in the Senate and is widely regarded as one of the best fund-raisers in the nation. Again, if one examines constant dollars, the increase in the cost of the 2010 race over that seen in 1996 was well over 100 percent.

6. It has long been known that electoral competition is directly related to campaign spending; there tends to be more spending in highly competitive races (Goidel, Gross, and Shields, *Money Matters*; Gross and Goidel, *States of Campaign Finance Reform*). A question of major debate, however, is whether more spending results in more competitive races or whether more competitive races simply attract more contributors.

7. This is a simple fact that can be found in any introductory statistics book. The easiest way to think about this is that when one only has 6 cases, each case contributes 1/6th to the mean score; when one has 435 cases, each case contributes only 1/435th to the mean score.

8. The figures in table 10.2 represent total spending by all Democrats and Republicans in both the primary and general elections. There were one hundred Kentucky House races in each electoral year and nineteen Kentucky Senate races. Data for 2010 were not included because final figures were not available at the time this chapter was being written.

9. The greater instability in the pattern of spending in state senate races is partly the result of having only nineteen races per election.

10. If one looks at constant dollar figures, the increase in cost for Kentucky state House races was around 116 percent, while it was about 135 percent for Kentucky state senate races.

11. The necessary data for all states and all years were not available to undertake the necessary analyses.

12. For further discussion of this measure and additional information, see National Institute on Money in State Politics, http://www.followthemoney.org/database/graphs/competitive /index.phtml.

13. Use of this measure has a number of advantages. It is unaffected by district size, district population size, inflation, and other considerations. Further, it is adjusted to take multi-member districts into account.

14. Data were not available for all states and all years, so the Ns for each year are not equivalent.

15. The figures reported in table 10.4 represent the total spent in both the primary and general elections.

16. States differ a great deal in the year in which they hold gubernatorial elections. Using a four-year average, therefore, allows one to compare Kentucky with the average of all other states.

17. Gross and Goidel, *States of Campaign Finance Reform*.

18. This represents an increase of almost 350 percent in constant dollars.

19. This was not exactly true in 1983, when it was slightly less than twice the national average.

20. Kentucky has traditionally had relatively expensive gubernatorial elections even when one controls for the size of the state. See Malcolm Jewell and David Olson, *Political Parties and Elections in American States* (Chicago: Dorsey Press, 1988); and Penny M. Miller and Malcolm E. Jewell, *Political Parties and Primaries in Kentucky* (Lexington: University Press of Kentucky, 1990).

21. All spending limits were voluntary but were a condition for accepting public funding.

22. A local government's degree of latitude in establishing campaign finance laws is specified by the state.

23. A specification of federal campaign finance law can be found at the Federal Election Commission's website, http://www.fec.gov.

24. In Kentucky a candidate can opt out of specific reporting requirements if he agrees to spend less than a given amount of money. For example, school-board candidates must agree to spend less than $100.

25. The website for the Kentucky Registry of Election Finance is http://www.kref.gov.

26. The website for the Campaign Disclosure Project is http://www.campaigndisclosure .org.

27. The term "slate of candidates" refers to the situation when the governor and lieutenant governor run together on the same ticket or slate.

28. Until 2010 court action, Kentucky law placed a $100 limit on individual contributions to school-board candidates.

29. The amount of money raised by each party in any given year differs a great deal and is especially dependent on the electoral cycle.

30. *Speechnow v. Federal Election Commission No. 08-5223—F.ed—, 2010, WL 1133857* (D.C. Cir. March 26, 2010) was also significant in the development of super PACs because it removed limits on contributions to independent expenditure committees.

31. These figures were obtained from the Center for Responsive Politics, OpenSecrets.org, and the Wall Street Journal. A related problem resulting from these decisions involves the use of 501(c)4 organizations, which are public advocacy groups that can make expenditures in political races. These organizations need not disclose the source of their contributions, including those from corporations and unions, a provision that undermines transparency in the electoral process.

32. This general deference to the legislature can be traced back to *Buckley v. Valeo* 242 U.S. 1 (1976).

33. Justices Thomas and Scalia would go so far as to see contribution limits as a type of incumbent-protection plan. The problem with this view is that it views the relationship as an established fact when it is actually a highly debated point in the social science literature. Some recent literature suggests that contribution limits actually help challengers. In particular, see Kihong Eom and Donald A. Gross, "Contribution Limits and Disparity in Contributions between Gubernatorial Candidates," *Political Research Quarterly* 59, no. 1 (2006): 99–110; and Thomas Stratmann, "Do Low Contribution Limits Insulate Incumbents from Competition?," *Election Law Review* 9 (2010): 125–40.

11

Intermittent Attention
Political Oversight of Kentucky Regulatory Agencies
James C. Clinger

The Kentucky Constitution, like the constitutions of many states, provides for a very explicit separation of powers among the different "departments" (i.e., branches) of government.[1] This complicates oversight of state bureaucracies by elected leaders in the executive and the legislature. In any separation-of-powers system both legislators and elected executives have both the incentive and, to some extent, the power to exert pressure on bureaucratic agencies. In the case of regulatory policy, where costs are often concentrated and policy benefits are diffuse, there may be particular motivation for elected officials to make considerable efforts to shape agency behavior. Legislators who enact laws often object to the way in which the executive branch or independent regulatory commissions carry out policy, and executives often wish to carry out policy in ways that serve their interests but not necessarily those of legislators.

The analyses reported in this chapter examine two conditions that may affect the contest for control over policy. The first is the partisan division of government, referring to control of one branch of government (either executive or legislative) by one party and control of another branch by another party. The other condition is the existence of institutional arrangements, legislative review of administrative rules and gubernatorial executive orders, that may increase political control over bureaucracies. The chapter examines the review of proposed administrative regulations by the Kentucky General Assembly and the use of reorganization orders by Kentucky governors.

The chapter proceeds as follows. In the first section the significance of divided government for bureaucratic control is discussed, as well as the mechanics of legislative rule review. The review of administrative regulation proposals in Kentucky will then be described in the following section. The next section will examine how this review has been used since the mid-1990s. The focus then shifts to the study of gubernatorial attempts to control the Commonwealth's bureaucratic agencies through the use of executive orders. The trends in executive orders issued by Governor Steve Beshear and Governor Ernie Fletcher will be examined first, followed by summaries of the patterns in reorganization orders issued by Kentucky governors who have served since the late 1970s.

DIVIDED GOVERNMENT, RULE REVIEW, AND INFLUENCE OVER ADMINISTRATIVE AGENCIES

Partisan division among the branches of government presents many different challenges for the adoption and the implementation of policy. When different branches of government are controlled by different parties, each having different interests, ideologies, values, and favored clienteles, policy agreement may become difficult. Although some scholars have found that divided government does not prevent passage of significant legislation at the federal level,[2] other researchers have found that partisan division may prevent the enactment of policy regarding controversial issues, at least at the state level.[3] Some scholars have claimed that partisan division causes greater delegation of policy authority to agencies, largely because legislators wish to pass off conflictual and controversial issues to bureaucrats.[4] Other scholars have argued that divided government creates opportunities for bureau autonomy, primarily because agency actions that are not consistent with preferences of one elected branch of government cannot be overturned except by joint action of the legislature and the chief executive. When the legislature and the chief executive belong to different political parties, such joint actions may be difficult to achieve.[5]

Once policy is enacted and authority is delegated to agencies, the struggle over the concrete application of the law to actual circumstances continues. Even without partisan division of government, there may be conflict between the legislative and executive branches over the details of implementation. The executive or independent commissions are authorized to carry out policy, but legislators have a variety of means at their disposal to exert control over the agencies. Legislators may conduct oversight hearings, engage in casework, and make use of the appropriations process to influence implementation. They also may simply rewrite enabling legislation, although that is a high-cost strategy.[6]

A somewhat more direct, issue-specific way to shape agency decisions is through review of administrative rule making. Using this procedure, the legislature, or at least a committee assigned responsibility for review of administrative regulations, is given the power to review each specific rule promulgated by agencies, usually after the rule has been finalized after completing the notice-and-comment process. Not all state legislatures have this procedure available, and the specific power of review varies from state to state—some legislative committees have only advisory authority, while others have the power to reverse or amend rules approved by agencies. Because this procedure often applies before the rule goes into effect, it has been called "ex ante" control over the bureaucracy, but in some states the rule-review process applies even to existing rules, which suggests that it permits the legislature to exert fine-tuned control both ex ante and ex post.[7] Because the rule-review process does not generally involve policy-specific committees, the review may not be affected by the clientelistic politics that are characteristic of some kinds of policy subsystems. That, however, does not mean that rule review results in greater stringency in regulations. Marcus Ethridge's research in three states found that in two legislatures the rule-review process actually reduced the regulatory vigor of regulations.[8]

It seems likely that the review of regulatory proposals may depend on the political circumstances in the state. A state with Democratic dominance in its legislature may be expected to use rule review, ceteris paribus, to increase the stringency of regulation. In those legislatures where Republicans (or conservative Democrats) are in control, one might expect to find less stringent regulation. In states with divided government, we expect to find legislative rule review used frequently to thwart the initiatives of the rival party. In instances where there is a partisan split between the chambers of the legislature, we should expect to see less concerted activity to change administrative actions, simply because the legislature itself may be unable to come to agreement. Kentucky has not experienced pure divided government, with the governorship held by a member of one political party and both chambers of the General Assembly controlled by another, but it has experienced split partisan control of the legislature, with one party controlling one chamber and another party controlling the other. This phenomenon will get particular attention in the following examination of the review of proposed regulations and the use of gubernatorial executive orders in the Commonwealth.

LEGISLATIVE REVIEW OF PROPOSED ADMINISTRATIVE REGULATIONS IN KENTUCKY

In the Commonwealth of Kentucky, what would be called "legislative rule review" is described as the review of administrative regulations, probably because "rule making" is a power reserved to the Court of Justice, not to any agency. The Kentucky legislature, known as the General Assembly, has delegated its reviewing authority to the Administrative Regulation Review Subcommittee (ARRS), which is a unit within the Legislative Research Commission (LRC), and to the standing committees with oversight responsibility for a particular kind of regulatory measure. The ARRS is composed of eight legislators. Three of these are chosen by the Senate president (the presiding officer and de facto leader of the majority party in the chamber), one member from the minority party is selected by the minority party's floor leader, three members from the House majority party are picked by the Speaker of the House, and one member of the minority party is chosen by the minority party's floor leader in the House.[9]

The ARRS is authorized to conduct continuous study of the need for new legislation and the needs of administrative agencies and to make new recommendations based on that study. The subcommittee is also empowered to comment on proposed regulations submitted to the LRC. The ARRS is also authorized to make "non-binding determinations of deficiency" on a number of grounds.[10] Until January 2002 such determinations of deficiency were essentially binding because deficient regulations would expire at the end of the legislative session unless they were accepted by statute in the General Assembly or the administrative agency acted to remove the offending provision in the regulation, thus removing the deficiency. A nonpublished court opinion, *Patton v. Sherman*,[11] declared that this invalidation of regulations violated the separation-of-powers provisions of the Commonwealth's constitution.[12] Amendments to the statute since 2002 have modified the review process to remove the constitutional problem.

The ARRS review process begins after the regular notice-and-comment process for proposed regulations. This notice-and-comment process roughly resembles the comparable process for administrative rule making in the federal government and in most states. At the end of that process, the agency promulgating a regulation must issue a "statement of consideration" of the final regulation that discusses issues covered during the comment period. The statement is then forwarded to the ARRS, which holds hearings on the proposals at monthly meetings. At the meetings the ARRS makes findings and issues recommendations and comments that are then sent to the LRC, which is headed by the leaders of each chamber of the General Assembly. The findings of the ARRS are published in the *Administrative Register.* The LRC then assigns the proposed regulation to a standing committee of appropriate jurisdiction in the General Assembly. The standing committee can amend the regulation or declare it deficient, just as the ARRS can. Proposed regulations can be found to be deficient for any of eight specific reasons, including exceeding statutory authority or because they "appear to be deficient in any other manner."[13] A deficient regulation can be withdrawn, but it can also take effect if the governor determines that it shall take effect notwithstanding the finding of deficiency.[14] The power of the governor to override the ARRS's or standing committee's determinations of deficiency probably allows the process to withstand court challenges on the basis of a separation-of-powers violation.

EXAMINING LEGISLATIVE ACTIVITIES

To examine efforts to influence regulatory proposals in the Kentucky General Assembly, various records published by the Legislative Research Commission were studied. Most of these records were published as information bulletins for each legislative session since 1994. Some of the minutes of the ARRS are posted online at the LRC website but are not printed in any document. After consideration of the trends of behavior of the ARRS, activities of one standing committee, the Interim Joint Agriculture and Natural Resources Committee, will be presented and discussed.

Figure 11.1 is based on data derived from the *Final Reports of the Interim Joint, Special, and Statutory Committees* from various legislative sessions, beginning with the 1992–1993 session.[15] Before 2002 the General Assembly met in biennial sessions in even-numbered years. A constitutional amendment that took effect in that year permitted annual sessions, although one regular session is much shorter than the other. Significant committee work continues even when the legislature is not in session. Particularly important is the work of the ARRS, which continues irrespective of the meeting of the General Assembly. Figure 11.1 displays the number of administrative regulations filed with the ARRS from the 1992–1993 session until the 2008 session. During that time Democrats retained control of the House of Representatives, with their numbers varying from a high of seventy-four seats in the one-hundred-seat body to a low of fifty-seven seats in the middle of the first decade of the twenty-first century. Republicans took control of the Senate in 1999 after slowly gaining ground on the Democrats throughout the 1990s. Throughout this period Democrats controlled the governor's mansion with the exception of the period from 2003 to 2007, when Republican Ernie Fletcher held office. In assessing the arguments about divided government and split legislative control, the trends in oversight activities after the Republican takeover of the Senate in 1999 and after the election of Governor Fletcher are particularly important.

Figure 11.1 indicates that there was an overall downward trend in the number of regulations reviewed by ARRS from 1992 to 2004. Of course, the earlier sessions lasted two years rather than one. It is noteworthy that there was a slight two-year increase in regulations under review after Republicans took control of the Senate, but then there was a dramatic decrease until 2005, when the number began a comparably dramatic rise. It is also significant that there was a downward trend in the number of regulations reviewed during the first year of the Fletcher administration, but a sharp increase thereafter. During the first year in office of Fletcher's successor, Democrat Steve Beshear, the number of regulations reviewed dropped significantly.

Figure 11.2 displays the number of regulations ruled deficient by the ARRS. The data for this figure are also taken from the annual committee reports alluded to earlier. The percentage of filed regulations ruled deficient has never been a large percentage of the total, but the absolute number of regulations found deficient was certainly nontrivial in the 1992–1993 session. Afterward, however, the numbers dropped. There was an increase in the 2003 session, the first year in which Governor Fletcher was in

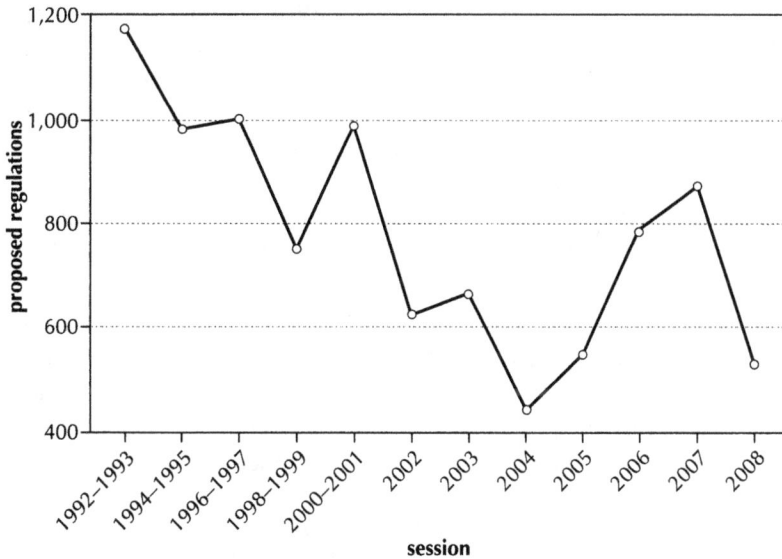

Figure 11.1. Proposed regulations filed with the Administrative Regulation Review Subcommittee (ARRS). Source: *Final Reports of the Interim Joint, Special, and Statutory Committees*, http://www.lrc.ky.gov/lrcpubs/info_bulletins.htm.

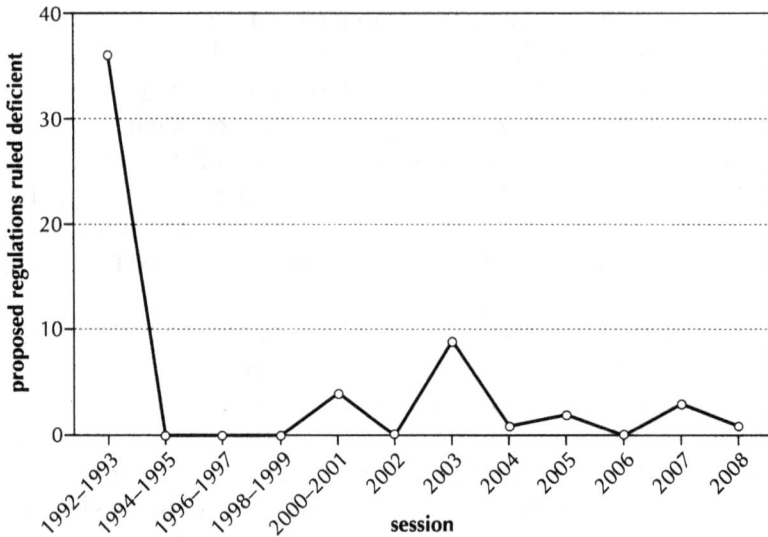

Figure 11.2. Proposed regulations ruled deficient by the Administrative Regulation Review Subcommittee (ARRS). Source: *Final Reports of the Interim Joint, Special, and Statutory Committees*, http://www.lrc.ky.gov/lrcpubs/info_bulletins.htm.

office and ironically immediately after the constitutionality of the review process was questioned in *Patton v. Sherman*, but that brief blip did not represent a continuing trend. In recent years rulings of deficiency have been rare indeed. In fact, it appears that the General Assembly has either little inclination or little authority to overturn proposed regulations as it did in the early 1990s. Even with the advent of annual legislative sessions, the General Assembly has not exercised these powers with great frequency.

Although rulings of deficiency are relatively uncommon, amendment of proposed regulations is a continuing activity of the ARRS. To depict this activity over time, figure 11.3 was derived from the minutes posted online for every monthly meeting of the ARRS.[16] Minutes from meetings before 2000 are not available online. The information contained in the minutes is not entirely consistent over time. Throughout the period, however, there are data on the number of regulations amended and the number ruled deficient. Those trends are depicted in figures 11.2 and 11.3.

Figure 11.3 indicates that the number of regulations amended slowly trended downward from the spring of 2000 to the spring of 2004. These trends are not necessarily substantively or statistically significant. There was a slow upward trend in amended regulations after April 2004, the first full year of the Fletcher administration and the second session in which Republicans controlled the Senate, but the increase was not dramatic.

Figure 11.4 depicts the activity of one committee with a substantive interest in a particular policy area, the Interim Joint Agriculture and Natural Resources Committee. This committee reviews proposed regulations dealing with agriculture, natural resources, and environmental issues after the notice-and-comment period is completed and after the ARRS considers them. Figure 11.4 is derived from data taken

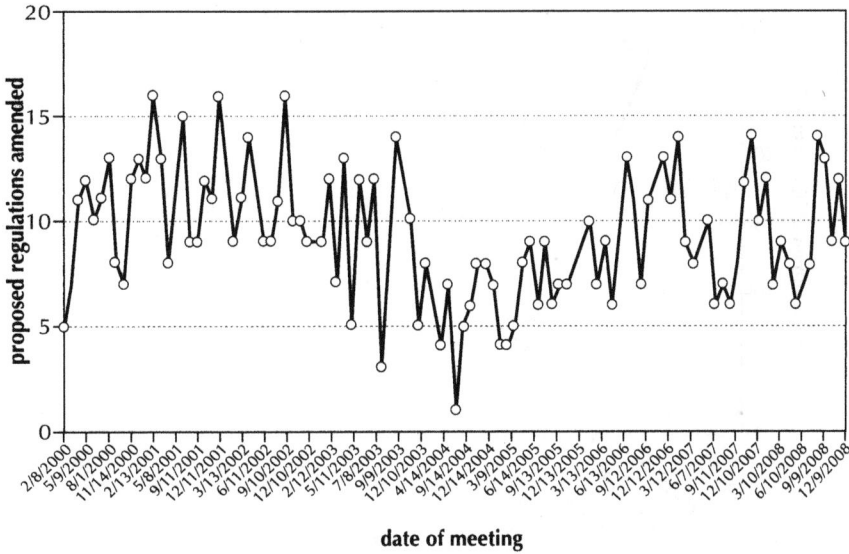

Figure 11.3. Number of proposed regulations amended. Sources: http://www.lrc.ky.gov/Committee _Prior_Interim/Statutory/Admin%20Regs/minutes_old.htm; and http://www.lrc.ky.gov/Committee_Prior _Interim/Statutory/Admin%20Regs/minutes.htm.

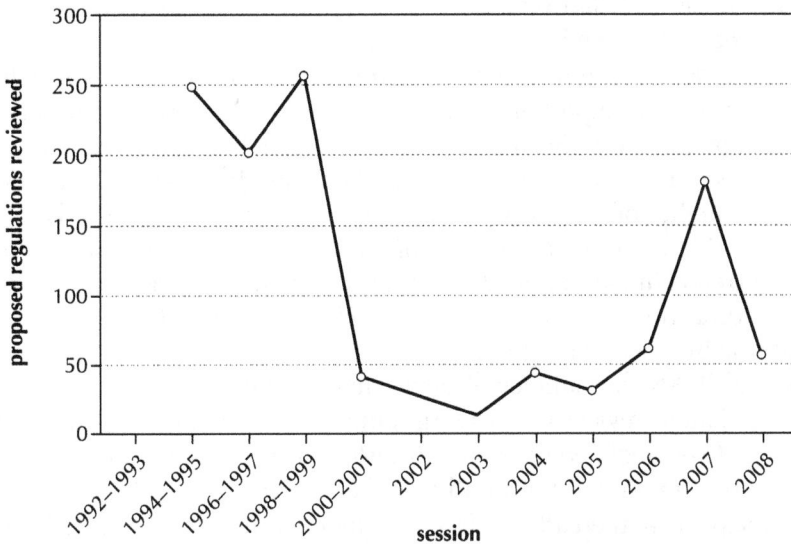

Figure 11.4. Proposed regulations reviewed by the Agricultural and Natural Resources Committee. Source: http://www.lrc.ky.gov.

from the annual committee reports published by the LRC. These data begin in 1994 and continue to 2008.

The number of regulations dropped substantially in 2000, just as the number did for the ARRS. This was the year after Republicans began to gain a Senate majority. The number of administrative regulations reviewed by the committee increased

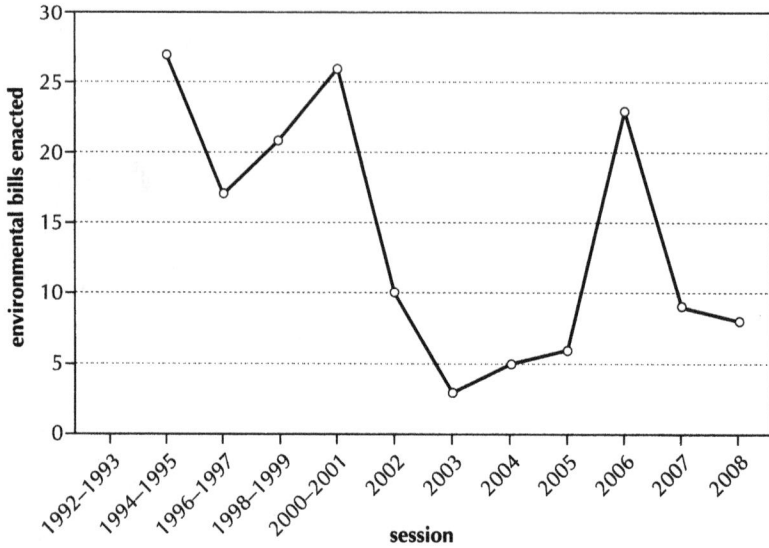

Figure 11.5. Number of environmental bills enacted. Source: *Action of the General Assembly*, http://www.lrc.ky.gov.

dramatically in 2007, the last year of the Fletcher administration, but then declined in the first full year that Steve Beshear served in office.

Figure 11.5 depicts the number of environmental and conservation bills enacted during this period. It is important to understand that the legislature can supervise the bureaucracy not only by reviewing specific regulations but also by enacting new laws that change the authority of agencies. The data used in figure 11.5 are derived by counting the number of bills enacted, as indicated in the index of the LRC information bulletins, titled *Action of the General Assembly*, for various years.[17] Figure 11.6 overlays the trends in environmental bills and regulations reviewed by the Agricultural and Natural Resources Committee, which is the committee with oversight authority over environmental programs.

In the mid-1990s the number of environmental bills passed and the number of proposed regulations reviewed by the Agriculture and Natural Resources Committee were both relatively high, compared with historic trends. The number of regulations reviewed by the committee hit an all-time high in the 1998–1999 session but then dropped precipitously thereafter. After the Republican takeover of the Senate both the number of environmental bills enacted and the number of proposed regulations reviewed remained low until 2006, when legislative activity increased, followed by a sharp increase in regulations reviewed in 2007.

The only significant predictor of the number of regulations reviewed by the committee is the number of Democrats in the Senate. Statistically, neither the Fletcher administration nor the number of environmental bills nor the partisan makeup of the House of Representatives seems to matter in affecting the oversight activities of this committee. The partisan makeup of the Senate does make a difference. This suggests

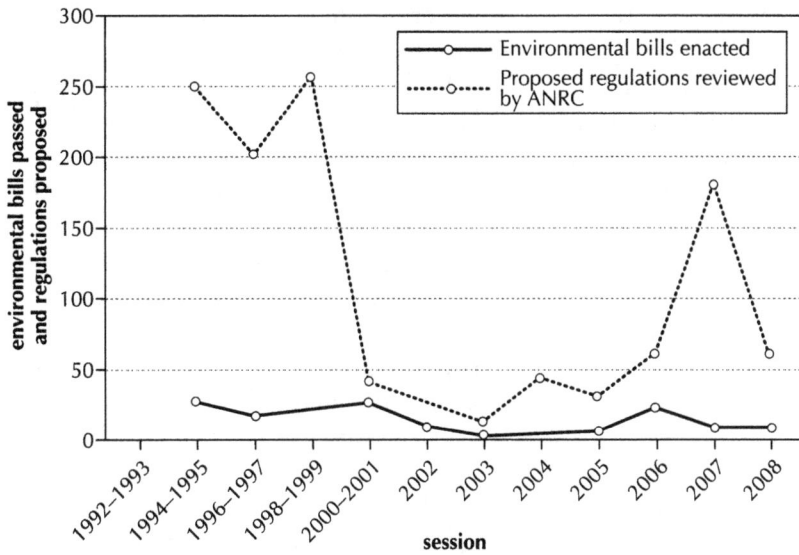

Figure 11.6. Environmental bills passed and regulations proposed by session. Source: *Action of the General Assembly*, http://www.lrc.ky.gov.

that the sessions with split legislative control of the General Assembly affected the workload of the committee, represented by the number of regulations reviewed.

EXECUTIVE ORDERS

Executive orders are not referred to in the U.S. Constitution and are not always found in state constitutions. These orders are directives from an executive (frequently the chief executive) that an officer of government take particular action. They are presumed to be legally binding, although the legal authority for the orders is not always clear, and ex post it may appear that the chief executive has exceeded his or her proper authority. President Franklin Roosevelt used executive orders to send Japanese nationals and some Japanese Americans to internment camps during World War II. President Reagan ordered Office of Management and Budget review of major regulatory proposals during the 1980s. President Obama has used executive orders to direct that the Guantanamo Bay detention facility for suspected terrorists be closed. At the state level governors have ordered public health commissioners to see that teenage girls receive HPV vaccination and have established (or removed) sexual orientation as a suspect classification from public employment antidiscrimination policy. With regard to the last, Kentucky governor Paul Patton used an executive order that added sexual orientation to the list of protected categories by executive order; Governor Fletcher rescinded that order by executive order, but Governor Beshear reinstated Patton's original order.[18]

Governors sometimes have constitutional authority for these orders, but it is more common for legislatures to delegate such authority to governors with respect to particular kinds of decisions. It is perhaps most common for governors to claim that some such authority is inherent in their position as chief executive or is implicit in their general power to see that the laws of the state are executed. This kind of justification has not been available to recent Kentucky governors, however, because the Kentucky Supreme Court ruled in *Royster v. Brock* that the governor may exercise only powers specifically designated by the constitution or the General Assembly.[19]

Much of the literature dealing with the governorship has presumed that the power of the state chief executive was rooted in his or her ability to persuade other institutional actors, notably state legislators, to support the governor's policy agenda. Through bargaining, arm-twisting, and threats to use political as well as formal powers, governors were thought to influence legislators who might otherwise oppose the governor's program or ignore his or her agenda. Such arguments are basically the state-level version of the long-revered view of the presidency proposed by Richard Neustadt, who famously said that the main power of the president was the "power to persuade."[20] This view, however, has been challenged by presidential scholars who have argued that many presidents exert power unilaterally, with "the stroke of a pen."[21] These scholars contend that actions by the president that do not require congressional action or cooperation give the president considerable power to accomplish his goals. Among these actions are executive orders, which presidents use for various purposes, including efforts to shape the direction of regulatory policy, to reorganize existing agencies, and to provide concrete benefits to supportive interest groups.

What is less obvious is why presidents or governors make use of executive orders, or more precisely, why some chief executives use executive orders more than others and under what conditions these orders are most commonly used. One explanation suggests that chief executives act opportunistically, when their political position is strongest. Normally, these opportunities occur when the chief executive's political party has sizable majorities in each chamber of the legislature, or shortly after winning a landslide election, or when public popularity is high. Another explanation suggests that chief executives use executive orders as acts of desperation when they cannot accomplish their policy objectives in any other way because they are constrained by circumstances.[22] According to this view, governors resort to executive orders when the opposing party is in power, when chief executives are confronted by other hostile elected executives, or when the economy is in a severe crisis. In addition, there may be a number of practical considerations regarding the management and sometimes the reorganization of bureaucratic agencies that are relevant to the decision to make use of these orders. Executive orders are often used to change the structure and procedures of bureaucratic organizations. Arguably, states with larger state bureaucracies might need more formal direction from the governor. Hypothetically, states with more professionalized and capable bureaucracies will need less direction. Little research on the use of executive orders at the state level has been done, but that little indicates that governors are more likely to use executive orders when their party controls the legislature (i.e., when they can act from a position of partisan strength) and when state bureaucracies are relatively large.[23]

KENTUCKY ANALYSIS

The following analysis examines the use of executive orders by governors in the Commonwealth of Kentucky over the past thirty years. Copies of recent executive orders were taken from the secretary of state's website, specifically the link to the *Executive Journal*, which is the online publication that publishes executive orders.[24] Unfortunately, the online postings cover only the administrations of Governor Ernie Fletcher and current governor Steve Beshear. The executive orders of previous Kentucky governors are available in the secretary of state's Frankfort office in the basement of the state capitol in printed form. Because the online data and those gleaned from the printed documents may not be completely comparable, the analysis will focus first on the trends in issuance of executive orders by Governors Fletcher and Beshear and then examine the patterns of the use of executive orders by earlier governors.

Kentucky governors are inaugurated in the December after their November election. Hence Governor Fletcher assumed office in December 2003, and Governor Beshear began his duties in December 2007. Figure 11.7 displays the number of executive orders from 2004 to 2009. Governor Fletcher did issue a handful of executive orders in 2003, but the bulk of those in that year were issued by his predecessor, Governor Paul Patton. Likewise, the bulk of the executive orders in 2007 were issued by Governor Fletcher, although a few were issued at the end of 2007 by Governor Beshear. A few executive orders were issued in 2010, but to make the data more comparable, only executive orders for entire years are presented here.

In figure 11.7 it seems clear that Governor Fletcher did not begin his term in office by issuing a large number of executive orders. When he entered the governor's mansion, he enjoyed fairly high popularity after a fairly tough electoral race against his opponent, Attorney General Ben Chandler. Although the campaign seemed close for much of the race, Fletcher prevailed by a larger margin than was initially predicted. Governor Fletcher, a Republican, still faced a Democratic majority in the state house

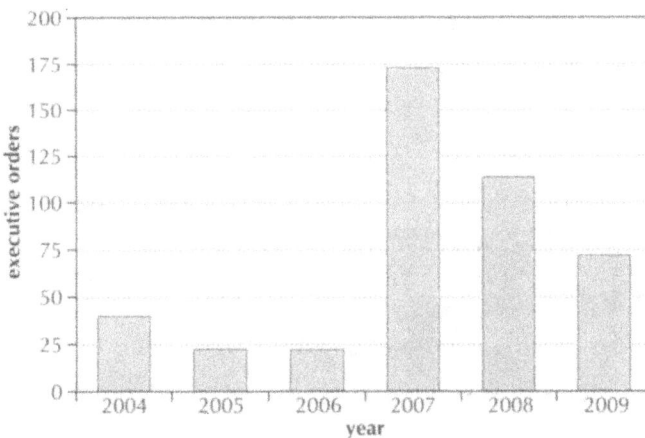

Figure 11.7. Total number of Kentucky executive orders by year. Source: http://www.sos.ky.gov/.

of representatives, although the GOP controlled the state senate. His honeymoon period was short-lived because less than two years after he assumed office, a scandal broke out involving political appointments made to merit positions in state government. Governor Fletcher was indicted in May 2006 on three counts of criminal conspiracy, official misconduct, and political discrimination. The charges were dropped in August 2006 after the governor admitted to some wrongdoing.[25] Ironically, the bulk of the executive orders during the Fletcher administration were issued during 2007, after the indictment was dismissed, but during the time at which the governor was attempting a reelection bid that ultimately proved unsuccessful. Governor Steve Beshear, who prevailed against Fletcher in the 2007 election, has not faced a scandal comparable to that plaguing his predecessor, but he has been rebuffed several times by a state legislature that has resisted the governor's attempts to expand legalized gaming as a way of generating state revenue. Governor Beshear, like Governor Fletcher, faces a legislature with a partisan split between the two chambers. What is notable is that the number of executive orders issued during his administration has trended downward during the course of his term. In Governor Fletcher's case, the number increased, with a particularly large increase during his last year.

Figures 11.8 and 11.9 display the trends in issuance of two particular kinds of executive orders, those classified as "miscellaneous" and those involving appointments to boards and commissions. The former are depicted here in large part because an employee in the secretary of state's office indicated that he believed that the "miscellaneous" orders, as well as those dealing with administrative reorganization, were those that were most pertinent to the governor's efforts to control state agencies. Figure 11.9 reveals that 2007 was a huge year for the Fletcher administration in issuing orders involving appointments to boards and commissions. That may have been due to the number of vacancies occurring during that year, or there may be some other reason. It is also noteworthy that Governor Fletcher made most of these 2007 appointments during his last days in office. In any case, Governor Beshear, unlike Governor Fletcher,

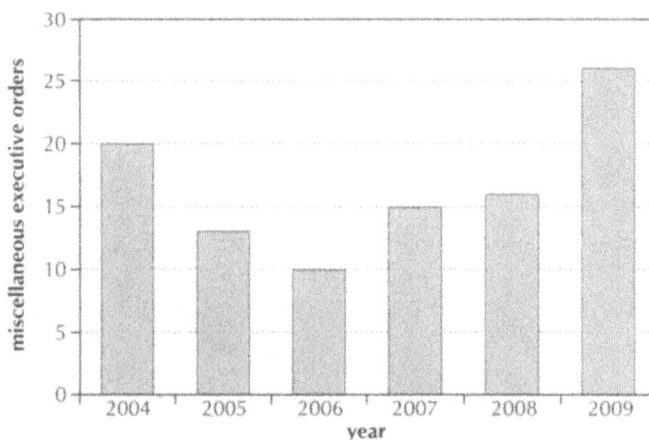

Figure 11.8. Number of Kentucky miscellaneous executive orders by year. Source: http://www.sos.ky.gov/.

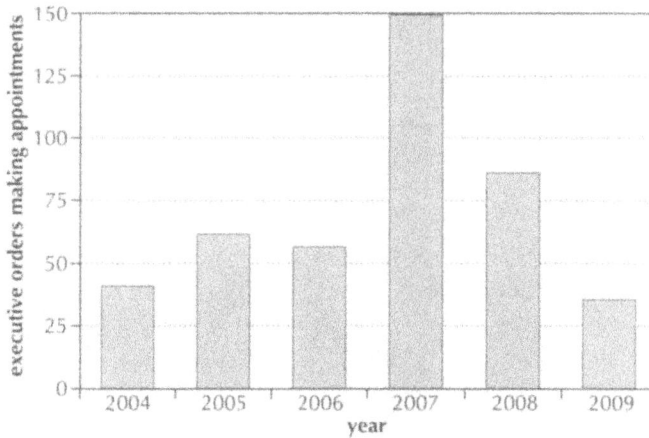

Figure 11.9. Number of Kentucky executive orders making appointments to boards and commissions by year. Source: http://www.sos.ky.gov/.

made a significant number of such appointments in his first full year in office and then somewhat fewer in 2009. In examining figure 11.8, it is interesting to note that Governor Fletcher issued a large number of miscellaneous orders in his first year in office, but considerably fewer in his second year and fewer still in his third year. The trend shifted in his final year in office. Governor Beshear did not issue a large number of miscellaneous orders in 2008, his first full year in office, but issued a large number of these orders in 2009.

Executive orders for many years before 2003 were also examined, again using data from the secretary of state's office. However, those data are not available in electronic form on the secretary's official website. The author examined hard copies of the indexes of gubernatorial executive orders in the basement of the secretary's office in the state capitol. Those indexes were not organized and categorized in the same way in which the orders on the secretary's website are classified. For that reason, those orders are examined separately from the recent orders for the Fletcher and Beshear governorships. All orders that were classified in the indexes as reorganizations or that appeared to reorganize a state agency were classified as reorganizations. The totals were then coded electronically and used to produce figure 11.10.

Figure 11.10 reveals that the use of reorganization orders increased dramatically during the administration of John Y. Brown Jr. Early in that administration the governor made many attempts to control the state bureaucracy. The number of orders dropped almost as precipitously to quite low levels after the governor's first year in office. It was during the Brown administration, in 1982, that the Kentucky Supreme Court limited the powers of the governor to reorganize state offices that were headed by a constitutional officer.[26] The data indicate that the number of reorganization orders had begun to decline even before that ruling. Later governors never exercised their powers of reorganization as extensively as Brown did in his first year in office. Governor Martha Layne Collins used executive reorganization orders quite infrequently,

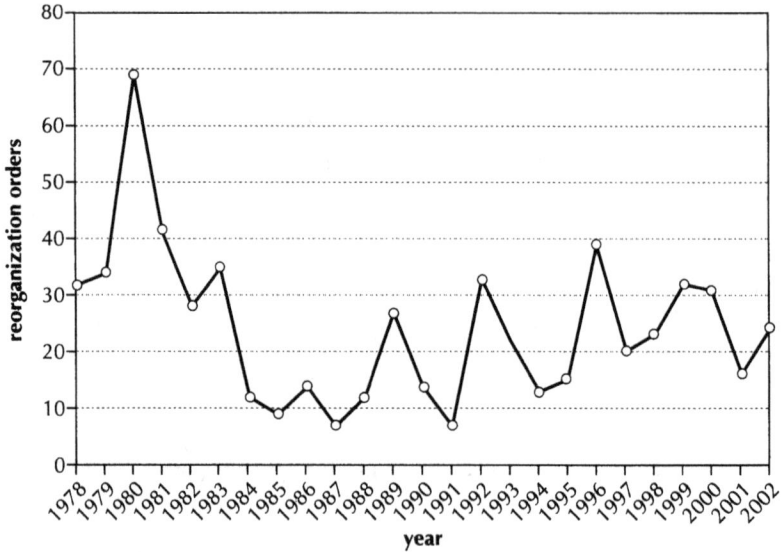

Figure 11.10. Number of reorganization orders. Source: http://www.sos.ky.gov/.

while her successors used them somewhat more often. It is also interesting to note that most governors made use of executive reorganization orders most frequently in the first or second full year of their terms, presumably when they were trying to assume control of the state bureaucracies. In most instances the number of reorganization orders declined in the last two years of a governor's term.

The attempts by Kentucky's elected representatives to control administrative agencies by executive order and by review of administrative regulations have not been constant over time. Instead, they have been intermittent, without easily explainable patterns. But some generalizations can be made. Over the past three decades there has been a substantial decrease in the use of both legislative rule review and gubernatorial reorganization orders. Part of the explanation for the change in gubernatorial activity might be the Kentucky Supreme Court's decision in *Brown v. Barkley*, but that is probably not the only reason for the change. Other reasons probably are related to the general changes in gubernatorial-legislative dynamics, which are described in other chapters in this volume. The governor is probably less involved in attempts to shape bureaucratic behavior after the legislative branch has already asserted itself. There was a brief upturn in executive orders during the later years of the Fletcher administration, but that trend was quickly reversed after Governor Beshear took office. Many of Fletcher's orders involved appointments to boards and commissions, and many of the reorganization orders were repeated attempts to make permanent changes in the structure of agencies after the General Assembly had refused to give its approval.

It should also be recognized that legislative review of proposed administrative regulations has changed dramatically since the early 1990s. The number of proposed regulations that were ruled deficient decreased substantially during the 1994–1995 session, rose slightly in 2003, and then dropped into single digits again. The actual number of environmental regulations reviewed by the legislature's oversight committee dropped substantially after 1999. The number of environmental regulations issued by state agencies remained low after the GOP takeover of the Senate in 2001 (and the enactment of environmental bills remained low for a few years as well). Again, oversight activities by the General Assembly increased briefly during the later part of Governor Fletcher's term in office, just as executive orders briefly increased in frequency at the same time.

In short, the attempts to control the bureaucracy appear to be part of the inter-branch dynamics that have characterized Kentucky's politics and the policy-making process. Significant changes took place in the early 1980s, when the conflict between Governor Brown and the General Assembly resulted in dramatic changes in the institutions of the chief executive and the legislature. Other departures from the trends examined here occurred after partisan changes. Oversight of proposed regulations appears to have decreased in frequency and stringency after Republicans gained a majority in the Senate. Changes in the trends for both the governor's executive orders and the review of regulations took place after the first GOP governor in decades assumed office. It is not clear that simple partisanship accounts for most of the changes in oversight activities, but it is more than plausible that considerations of party advantage affected many of the trends during the past decade.

NOTES

1. Constitution of the Commonwealth of Kentucky, Sections 27 and 28.

2. See, for example, David Mayhew, *Divided We Govern* (New Haven, Conn.: Yale University Press, 1999).

3. See, for example, Cynthia Bowling and Margaret R. Ferguson, "Divided Government, Interest Representation, and Policy Differences: Competing Explanations of Gridlock in the Fifty States," *Journal of Politics* 63 (February 2001): 182–206.

4. See, for example, David Epstein and Sharyn O'Halloran, "Divided Government and the Design of Administrative Procedures: A Formal Model and Empirical Test," *Journal of Politics* 58 (May 1996): 373–97.

5. Thomas H. Hammond and Jack H. Knott, "Who Controls the Bureaucracy? Presidential Power, Congressional Dominance, Legal Constraints, and Bureaucratic Autonomy in a Model of Multi-institutional Policy-Making," *Journal of Law, Economics and Organization* 12 (1996): 119–65.

6. John D. Huber, Charles R. Shipan, and Madelaine Pfahler, "Legislatures and Statutory Control of Bureaucracy," *American Journal of Political Science* 45 (April 2001): 330–45.

7. Brian J. Gerber, Cherie Maestas, and Nelson C. Dometrius, "State Legislative Influences over Agency Rule-Making: The Utility of Ex-Ante Review," *State Politics and Policy Quarterly* 5 (Spring 2005): 24–46.

8. Marcus E. Ethridge, "Consequences of Legislative Review Of Agency Regulations in Three U.S. States," *Legislative Studies Quarterly* 9 (1984): 161–79.

9. Kentucky Revised Statutes (KRS) 13A.020.

10. KRS 13A.030.

11. *Patton v. Sherman*, Civil Action No. 01-CI-00660 (Franklin Cir. Ct., January 2002).

12. Personal communication from John Schaaf, legal counsel, Legislative Ethics Commission, 2009.

13. KRS 13A.030(2)(a).

14. KRS 13A.330.

15. The reports are posted as informational bulletins and can be found at the Legislative Research Commission website, http://www.lrc.ky.gov/lrcpubs/info_bulletins.htm.

16. These minutes are posted on the LRC website at http://www.lrc.ky.gov/Committee _Prior_Interim/Statutory/Admin%20Regs/minutes_old.htm and http://www.lrc.ky.gov/Com mittee_Prior_Interim/Statutory/Admin%20Regs/minutes.htm.

17. Posted online at http://www.lrc.ky.gov/lrcpubs/info_bulletins.htm.

18. See Executive Order #2008-047, http://apps.sos.ky.gov/Executive/Journal/execjournal images/2008-MISC-2008-0473-195680.pdf. See also Joanne Deschenaux, "Executive Order Bans Sexual Orientation Bias in State Government," Society for Human Resource Management, June 16, 2008, http://www.shrm.org/LegalIssues/StateandLocalResources/Pages/Executive OrderBansSexualOrientationBiasinStateGovernment.aspx.

19. *Royster v. Brock*, 79 S.W.2d 707 (Ky., 1935).

20. Richard Neustadt, *Presidential Power and the Modern Presidents* (New York: Free Press, 1990), 29–49.

21. See Kenneth R. Mayer, *With the Stroke of a Pen* (Princeton, N.J.: Princeton University Press, 2001); and Kenneth R. Mayer, "Executive Orders and Presidential Power," *Journal of Politics* 61 (May 1999): 425–66.

22. George A. Krause and David B. Cohen, "Presidential Use of Executive Orders, 1953–1994," *American Politics Quarterly* 25 (October 1997): 458–81; and George A. Krause and David B. Cohen, "Opportunity, Constraints, and the Development of the Institutional Presidency: The Issuance of Executive Orders, 1939–96," *Journal of Politics* 62 (February 2000): 88–114.

23. James C. Clinger, "Opportunism and Desperation? The Use of Gubernatorial Executive Orders in Kentucky and the Nation" (paper presented at the annual meeting of the Kentucky Political Science Association, Murray, Ky., March 2010). See also Margaret Ferguson, "Unilateral Decision-Making in the American Governorship" (paper presented at the State Politics and Policy meeting, Austin, Tex., February 22–25, 2007, http://www.olemiss.edu/depts /political_science/ . . . /Ferguson%20Paper.do).

24. Secretary of State, Commonwealth of Kentucky website, http://www.sos.ky.gov/executive /journal/.

25. See Ian Urbina, "Kentucky Governor Signs Agreement Citing Wrongdoing in a Hiring Scandal," *New York Times*, August 25, 2006, http://www.nytimes.com/2006/08/25/us/25 kentucky.html.

26. *Brown v. Barkley*, 628 S. W. 2d 616 (1982).

12

Look before You Leap
Louisville's Merger and Its Aftermath
*H. V. Savitch, Ronald K. Vogel,
and Lucas Elliott*

REFORM AND CITY-COUNTY CONSOLIDATION

The Appeal of Change

Americans revere change. We are a dynamic people—always moving and always struggling to "keep up with the times." Indeed, the idea of change is a popular political slogan. In 1960 John F. Kennedy ran for the presidency on the platform that we must "get America moving again." Nearly a half century later Barack Obama won the presidency on a promise of change. Every industry from high tech to music posits change as a central value, and we as people have come to believe that if we do not grow we die. Change has become so omnipresent in our society that it is sometimes pursued for its own sake.

The idea of government reform epitomizes the positive values associated with political change. In most places and most times, to be a "reformer" is to want good things. Historically, it has often meant cleaning up government, doing away with corruption, and most of all the introduction of meritocracy into the public realm. Reform also meant that government could be run "more like a business" than a political entity. A familiar reformist expression was that there was no Democratic and no Republican way to pave a street, only the right way.

To "reform" also means to reorganize government—effectively reconfiguring it so that its rules, procedures, and scope of activity undergo dramatic change. At a local level, city-county consolidation fit the reformist agenda. It united fragmented local governments into a single encompassing unit; it streamlined a cumbersome bureaucracy; it broadened the territorial net over which public policy was exercised; and it simplified the jurisdiction of public officials so that voters could directly evaluate their performance.

Ideally, city-county consolidation worked to achieve two central goals: (1) to make local government more efficient and (2) to achieve greater accountability for government so citizens could make informed choices at election time. Efficiency is evaluated as a ratio of inputs to outputs. That is, for every investment of money and personnel, one hopes to get more out of a service. For example, $100 of expenditure on roads may yield two miles of pavement, but the same investment under different circumstances might also produce four miles of pavement, thereby increasing efficiency by 100 percent. Although it was not always possible to measure efficiency in precise numbers, reformers believed that they could make educated assessments in furtherance of their objectives. By implication, at least, reformers were not only efficient but had a sense of value. They could hold down budgets, keep payrolls within limits, and through efficiencies invest in worthy causes like "making the city beautiful."

Accountability was also consistent with efficiency. As the theory went, if public servants were held accountable, their performance would improve. Clear lines of authority would allow voters to dispense with politicians who did not perform and elect those who did perform. More than anything else, accountability hinged on democratic processes. The only things needed were clearly designated responsibilities, an educated citizenry, and honestly run elections. The process would then take care of itself. Running a city like a business also had an analogy in the form of government adopted by city-county consolidation. The top-down approach of consolidation saw the mayor functioning as a chief executive, the metro council as a board of directors, and the bureaucracy as a workforce with staff and line operations.

Before we turn to Louisville, we put that city's experience in context by pointing to other city-county consolidations. In recent decades a number of publications began to advocate city-county consolidation as a way to overcome severe urban problems, including racial segregation, central city decline, and sprawl.[1] This led to a resurgence of interest in city-county consolidation across the United States. Despite the resurgence, Louisville is the only major metropolis to have consolidated in recent years, and it drew its inspiration from two previous consolidations, the merger of Indianapolis and Marion County, adopted in 1969, and the merger of Jacksonville, Florida, and Duval County in 1967. Table 12.1 compares Louisville's consolidation with those of Indianapolis and Jacksonville.

As can be seen, the rationales for merger differed but could be reduced to the common denominators of a quest for better economic development, greater service efficiency, and enhanced governmental accountability. These consolidations were laden with political implications that included the fortunes of Democrats and Republicans, as well as future advantages to central cities and suburbs. Last, we should add that even today merger remains a hot political issue in metropolitan areas around the United States, including Buffalo, Charlotte, Cleveland, Memphis, Pittsburgh, St. Louis, and even Detroit.

For these reasons alone, Louisville's experience with reform is valuable to other cities.

Louisville seemed like the perfect venue for government reorganization. It was a city that prided itself on meeting challenges, it had a strong and vibrant business com-

Table 12.1. Comparison of Consolidations in Louisville, Indianapolis, and Jacksonville

	Year	Metropolitan reform	Rationale	Assessment
Louisville	2003	• Consolidate city and county legislative and executive • Exempt suburban cities	• Economic development • Maintain city as largest in state	• Minority dilution • No evidence of gains in efficiency, effectiveness, economic development • Rise of suburban power
Indianapolis	1969	• Reduce number of cities to five with Unigov mayor over economic development and land use	• Republican power grab with no referendum • Make Indianapolis something special	• Minority dilution • Enhanced downtown development • Suburban takeover
Jacksonville	1967	• Consolidate city and county government and add new independent agencies • Exempt affluent suburban cities	• Economic development • Reform to end political corruption • Breakdown in services (e.g., education accreditation threatened, sewage system inadequate) • Fear that city would become black	• Minority dilution • No improvement in tax revenue • Decline in voter turnout • Suburban takeover

Sources: R. K. Vogel and J. J. Harrigan, *Political Change in the Metropolis* (New York: Pearson Longman, 2007), chap. 9; D. Phares, ed., *Governing Metropolitan Regions in the 21st Century* (Armonk, N.Y.: M. E. Sharpe, 2009); M. S. Rosentraub, "City-County Consolidation and Rebuilding of Image: The Fiscal Lessons from Indianapolis's UniGov Program," *State and Local Government Review* 32, no. 3 (2000): 180–91; and B. E. Swanson, "Quandaries of Pragmatic Reform: A Reassessment of the Jacksonville Experience," *State and Local Government Review* 32, no. 3 (2000): 227–38.

munity, and its seemingly archaic institutions were ready for a radical overhaul. Louisville before the merger was governed by an old-fashioned board of aldermen, while Jefferson County was run by even more quaint institutions, consisting of a fiscal court with a county judge-executive presiding over three county commissioners. Moreover, Louisville had always sought to change with the times and today parades the slogan "possibility city."

In 2000 what seemed improbable became possible. The voters approved city-county consolidation, or, as it was locally called, "merger," in a general election. Within two years merger between the city and the county was implemented, making Louisville the first large-scale city-county consolidation in over thirty years.[2] We should mention that the merger was not entirely complete. More than eighty suburban municipalities were able to continue as separate entities, and their prerogatives were left intact. What were effectively merged were the area within the former city of Louisville and the county's unincorporated areas. A decade after Louisville first voted for consolidation, newly inaugurated mayor Greg Fischer called for a second look at what locals call "Merger 2.0." The new mayor and others were anxious about Louisville's future and, we might surmise, about the performance of "Merger 1."[3] We now put the current situation in context by examining the initial efforts at merger.

HISTORY OF THE MERGER

The Compact

Louisville has sought to reorganize its government for over fifty years; the roots can be traced back to a proposed expansion of the city's boundaries in 1956.[4] In 1956 local citizens defeated a proposal, the Mallon Plan, to expand the city's boundaries to include all urbanized areas within the county. The Mallon Plan sought to provide suburban residents with urban services. Passage of the proposal was conditioned on approval of both county and city voters. Although a majority of city residents voted in favor of the expansion, the measure failed to attract suburban residents, who voted against the Mallon Plan.[5]

From 1960 through 2000 cultural and economic developments transformed the landscape of Louisville. Deindustrialization spurred an exodus to the suburbs. The city of Louisville's population declined between 1960 and 2000 from 390,000 to 256,000.[6] In contrast to the city's diminishing population, the suburbs in the rest of Jefferson County saw their population escalate from 221,000 in 1960 to 438,000 in 2000.[7] Much of the county's growth can be attributed to citizens seeking open space, bigger housing, and the tranquility of suburbia. Businesses followed the movement of population, and malls and edge cities sprang up in the suburbs.

The exodus of many of Louisville's residents transformed its social composition and racial complexion. In 1950 Louisville was 15.6 percent African American; by 2000 that proportion had nearly doubled to 33 percent. Although the rest of Jefferson County was heavily white, it did see an increase in African American residents between 1950 and 2000 from 4.4 percent to 10.6 percent.[8] Seen as a whole, Louisville and Jefferson County have been sharply divided by social class and race. Today the larger metro area has a racial dissimilarity index of .59, which means that in order to achieve real integration, 59 percent of the population living in segregated neighborhoods would have to be evenly distributed throughout the area.[9] Within the city the West End is primarily black and poor, the South End is populated by white, blue-collar residents, and the East End is predominantly white and affluent.[10]

Territorial divisions by race and class sometimes worried community leaders who prided themselves on being a "single community." Besides this, leaders saw the ever-looming prospect of a city that was becoming increasingly black and some day could elect a black mayor and board of aldermen. Racial tensions were always a latent factor in Louisville politics, and politicians were careful to keep that motive under wraps. But in a 2009 interview the metro's normally cautious mayor, Jerry Abramson, let it slip that without merger Louisville was becoming "poorer, blacker and older."[11] Abramson later apologized for this remark, but he unintentionally confirmed what everybody knew. Consolidation seemed like a political avenue toward unifying a disparate metropolis. And although no one would readily admit it, consolidation was also a way of ensuring a white-majority government.

At least among the city's political and business communities, merger had appeal, and they were determined to pursue it. By 1982 the mayor, the county executive, and local business leaders were ready for action. They petitioned the state government to create a charter commission to study a possible merger. Within a short time the commission developed a proposal for city-county consolidation that would be submitted to the voters. The outcome was close. Louisville's black West End and white, blue-collar South End voted in opposition. With the slightest of margins the merger plan was defeated by 50.4 percent to 49.6 percent. Out of 182,000 votes, a mere 1,450 votes accounted for the merger's defeat. Nevertheless, proconsolidation groups were encouraged. Just one year later a revised consolidation plan was submitted to the voters. This time the margin of defeat grew to 5,600 votes.[12]

Throughout the 1980s the suburbs continued to prosper, while the city struggled to keep business and the middle class within its boundaries. A good part of this struggle involved efforts to keep the existing revenue base. Approximately half of the revenue was derived from the occupational tax, which is essentially a tax on wages based on place of work. With businesses spreading into the suburbs, the city was losing potential revenue, and political leaders sought to remedy this situation by annexing unincorporated sections into the city. This amounted to a zero-sum contest with the county because a successful annexation would entail consequent losses for the county.

Notwithstanding the political and legal obstacles, the city readied itself to annex outlying areas. In 1985 the Louisville Board of Aldermen passed legislation under which all unincorporated areas would become attached to the city. Thus began various annexation wars between the city and the county. The county staunchly opposed the city's actions, and legal battles ensued. The annexation wars resulted in a good deal of tension between the city of Louisville and Jefferson County.

Eventually, both the county and the city grew weary of the conflict and sought to resolve their differences. In 1986 a new city mayor, Jerry Abramson, and a new county judge-executive, Harvey Sloan, agreed on the Louisville–Jefferson County Compact. The compact provided for a division of occupational tax revenues between the city and the county, each receiving 55 percent and 45 percent, respectively. In addition to this unique tax-sharing arrangement, the compact created an interlocal service agreement under which services could be jointly undertaken or divided. For instance, a joint board was established for services like planning and zoning. Other services called for a division of labor: the city was responsible for the zoo and emergency services, while the county was accountable for air quality and planning.[13]

The compact was set for twelve years but was renewable. In 1998 the compact was given a continuance with only minor changes. The success of the compact demonstrated that the two governments could work together. For more than ten years the compact gave the city and the county a sense of stability and shared prosperity. Leaders within the area, however, insisted that Louisville and Jefferson County could do better. Many leaders, including members of the Chamber of Commerce, the mayor, and the county judge-executive, viewed the compact as a bandage measure and a temporary fix. For them, only city-county consolidation would enable the area to speak as a single body.

Winning at the Polls: UNITY versus COST

In 1994 the Jefferson County Governance Project established a study of local governance and a Citizen Task Force. After a two-year study the task force determined that a reorganization of government would be more advisable than attempting another full-blown effort at city-county consolidation.[14] However, by September 1999 the recommendation had been reversed. Another proposal for consolidation soon followed, led by two newly elected heads of the city and the county, Louisville mayor David Armstrong and county judge-executive Rebecca Jackson. In January 2000 a state task force endorsed a consolidation proposal. The following spring the General Assembly passed a merger bill. Consolidation was slated for a vote in the general election of November 2000.

Once again the residents of both the city and the county were politically divided. Proponents of consolidation founded a group called UNITY, which was established by the Chamber of Commerce (now called Greater Louisville Inc. or GLI) and a coalition of leading politicians. UNITY prided itself on being bipartisan, with recognizable members such as former mayor Jerry Abramson and then mayor Dave Armstrong, both Democrats. Joining them were two Republicans, county executive Rebecca Jackson and Senator Mitch McConnell. The city's newspaper, the *Courier-Journal*, also supported UNITY.

The prospect of still another merger attempt engendered opposition. A new coalition readied itself for an extended campaign. A popular county commissioner named Darryl Owens led this group, called Citizens Organized in Search of the Truth (COST). Its membership consisted of labor unions, civil rights groups, gay rights advocates, members of the Board of Aldermen, and neighborhood associations.[15] The group's message was spread through a grassroots campaign that warned of increased taxes and diminished local democracy.

Within a month of the general election, it was clear that the opposition was at a financial disadvantage. COST had raised only $41,000 compared with UNITY's reported $700,000, a ratio disparity of 17 to 1.[16] The financial imbalance was reflected in the voting. COST received support from voters in both the South End and the West End, but in lower numbers than in the 1982 and 1983 votes. Proponents of consolidation finally celebrated their victory when merger passed by a margin of 55 percent to 45 percent.[17] The consolidated Louisville–Jefferson County government began operation in January 2003.

Institutional Change and Merger

Consolidation had a profound effect on the organization of Louisville and statistically transformed the area. Louisville's boundaries increased from 62 square miles to over 380 square miles, and its population went from 256,000 to 558,389. Table 12.2 shows the basic elements of how Louisville changed and what it looks like today.

The merger as passed in 2000 provided only for the new city council and mayor. The mayor and council would have to work out the details. There was a transition process, but it was very incomplete and was largely disregarded. When the merged government

Table 12.2. Louisville before Merger, after Merger, and Today

	Before merger (city)	After merger	Today
Land area (sq. miles)	62	386°	386°
Total population	256,231	558,389°°	566,503°°
White	161,261 (62.9%)	432,193 (77.4%)[2]	381,375 (72.7%)[2]
Black or African American	84,586 (33.0%)	105,535 (18.9%)[2]	112,167 (19.8%)[2]
Median household income	$28,843	$39,457°	$44,493°°
Unemployment rate	7.4%	5.8%[1]	10.2%°°°
Homeownership rate	52.5%	64.9%	67.7%°°°°
Median house price	$82,300	$103,000	$131,200°°°°

Source: U.S. Census Bureau, Decennial Census 2000; city data are from http://censtats.census.gov /data/KY/1602148000.pdf (accessed June 1, 2007).

Other sources for *After merger* and *Today*

°Louisville government after consolidation, http://www.louisvilleky.gov/NR/rdonlyres/177354E3 -E933-432E-A880-4CE6FDFCFD42/0/MergerSummary.pdf.

°°Data per July 1, 2009, http://factfinder.census.gov/servlet/GCTTable?_bm=y& geo_ id=04000US21&-_box_head_nbr=GCT-T1-R&-ds_name=PEP_2009_EST&-_lang=en&-format =ST-9S&-_sse=on.

°°Data per July 1, 2009, detailed information available via State of Metropolitan America, Brookings Institution Metropolitan Policy Program, http://www.brookings.edu/metro/StateOfMetro America/Profile.aspx?fips=31140#/?fips=31140&viewfips=31140C&subject=10&ind=113& year=2009&geo=city.

°°°Data per November 2009, available at U.S. Department of Labor, Bureau of Labor Statistics, http://www.bls.gov/lau/laucntycur14.txt.

°°°°Data per 2010 available at U.S. Census Bureau, Housing Vacancies and Homeownership, http:// www.census.gov/hhes/www/housing/hvs/annual09/ann09ind.html.

1. Historical data obtained through Bureau of Labor Statistics, http://data.bls.gov/pdq/SurveyOutput Servlet?series_id=LAUMT21311403&data_tool=XGtable.

2. The percentages are obtained from State of Metropolitan America, Brookings Institution Metropolitan Policy Program, http://www.brookings.edu/~/media/Files/Programs/Metro/state_of _metro_america/metro_america_profiles/louisville.pdf. Because the Brookings report uses Jefferson County as the primary city for the Louisville, KY-IN MSA, we have adjusted the figures by applying those percentages to total population as it is listed in the American Community Survey (ACS), U.S. Census Bureau.

began operating, the mayor decided to merge the city and county police departments immediately under a new chief hired from outside. This resulted in changes in the number and organization of police districts and reassigning city officers to patrol the county and vice versa. Transition costs for consolidating police were approximately $9.4 million.[18] Harmonizing the two departments led to significant morale problems in the merged police department. The city and county had vastly different police cultures and standard operating procedures.[19] The city was oriented toward urban policing, including minority and poor neighborhoods. The county was oriented toward suburban policing, and officers had little experience in urban areas. The forces attracted different types of officers and emphasized different training and practices. Many officers felt that police consolidation had been done haphazardly.[20] The police experience was repeated across the new government in other agencies. There was no comprehensive strategy to consolidate city and county government agencies.

EVALUATING THE MERGER'S RESULTS: EFFICIENCY

Promises

Consolidation was lauded as a cure that would not only heal the ailments of the community but also provide the stimulus to reach previously unattainable success. Politicians who campaigned for merger claimed that it would make Louisville more efficient by avoiding duplication of services and reaping the benefits of economies of scale.[21] One of the campaigners for the merger, Jerry Abramson, stated that the merger would eliminate many top government positions and thin out middle management, as well create savings.[22] Whether these promises were borne out is the subject of our next section.

In accordance with the reformist model, merger enthusiasts reasoned that a unified government under a single executive commanding a single bureaucracy would be swifter, more transparent, and more efficient. They believed that merged government would save money and even improve services.[23]

Budgets and Public Employees

We now take up these propositions by examining budgets, personnel, and expenditures. The reader should bear in mind that data for the fiscal years from 1997 to 2002 represent Louisville and Jefferson County before the merger, while data for 2003 to 2010 are for the merged metropolis of Louisville and Jefferson County.[24]

Figure 12.1 shows Louisville and Jefferson County budgets from 1999 through 2010. The budgets have been adjusted to constant dollar values for 2009 (based on the consumer price index) or CPI to account for inflation.

If the government was working more efficiently, one indicator should have been an overall decrease in total budget. In the first fiscal year studied, 1999–2000, the total budget was $835.3 million. Between 1999 and 2000 and the first merger year the budget had decreased by 3.49 percent to a total of $806.1 billion. The budget continued along the same path, hitting a low of $784.2 million for the 2006–2007 fiscal year. At

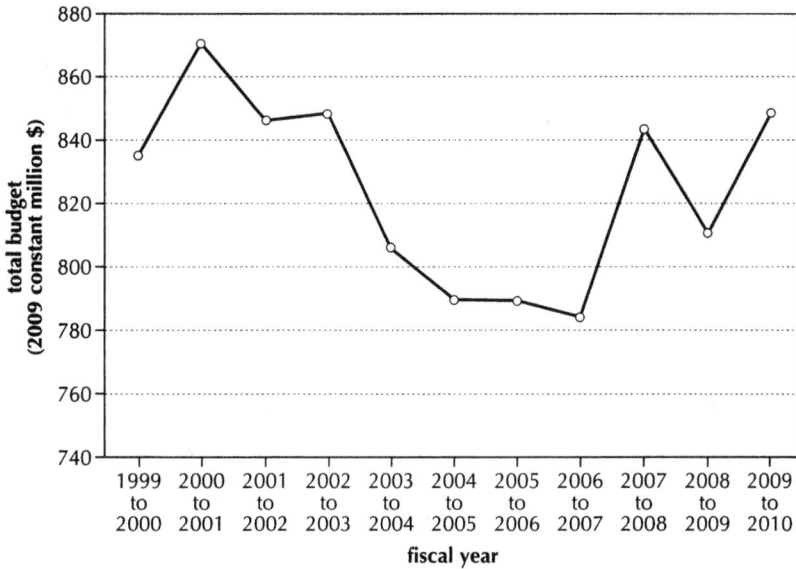

Figure 12.1. Louisville—Jefferson County budgets, fiscal years 1999–2000 to 2009–2010. Source: Louisville and Jefferson County Executive Budget.

first sight it would appear that the merger had produced lower budget expenditures, but on further examination we note that the total budget also had begun to decrease during the premerger period 2000–2001. The real story lies in the most recent years of the merger period. By the 2007–2008 fiscal year the total budget had increased to $843.4 million. Comparison of the 1999–2000 budget with the 2009–2010 budget of $848.8 million makes it clear the budget did not decrease but actually increased by 1.6 percent. In fact, the postmerger period, 2003–2004 to 2009–2010, witnessed an increase of 5.29 percent.

Although the total budget data did not show savings, other fiscal aspects are also important. One of these is whether the merger eliminated duplication and brought about reductions in public employment. Another is whether the cost of municipal employees increased or decreased. Figures 12.2 and 12.3 show data for Louisville–Jefferson County for the years 1999 through 2010.[25] Both of these figures address the broader issue of efficiency.

In the 1999–2000 fiscal year, total employees were 7,177. There was a slight increase in 2000–2001, but in the remainder of the period before the merger there was a slight employment decrease each year for an overall decrease of 1.84 percent. In 2003, after the merger, there was a slight decrease in personnel of 50 to a total of 6,995. From 2007–2008 until 2009–2010 the number of personnel fell to 6,631. Throughout the postmerger period the number of personnel has declined by 5.88 percent. Overall, the workforce has been reduced by 546 over the course of the study period. Since its inception, the new metro government reduced its total number of employees.

However, there is another side to this reduction, the expenditures per employee. Although the number of personnel has drastically decreased, it does not necessarily

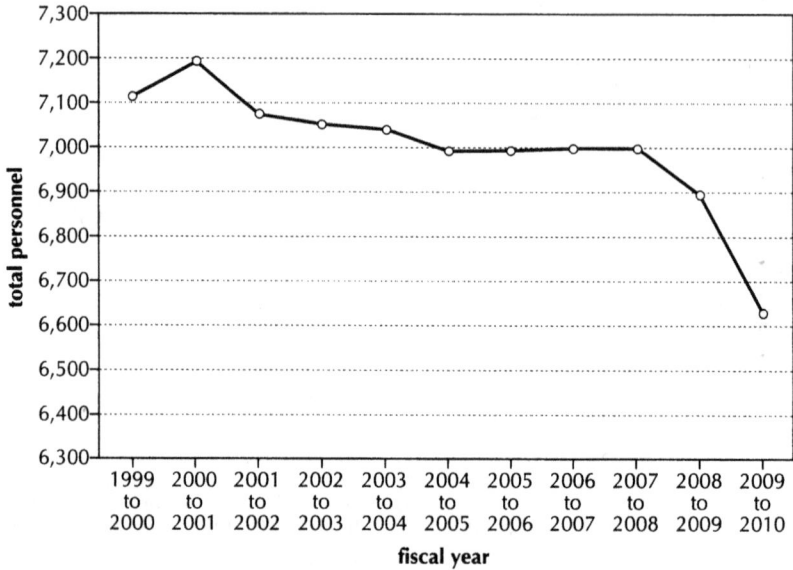

Figure 12.2. Louisville—Jefferson County personnel, fiscal years 1999–2000 to 2009–2010. Source: Louisville and Jefferson County Executive Budget.

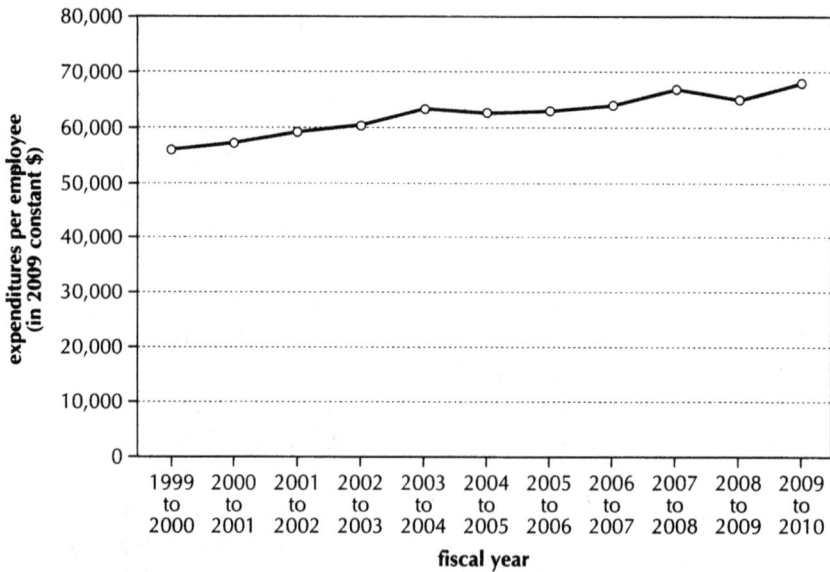

Figure 12.3. Louisville—Jefferson County expenditures per employee, fiscal years 1999–2000 to 2009–2010. Source: Louisville and Jefferson County Executive Budget.

follow that the metro government has reduced the cost of government. During the premerger period per employee expenditures steadily increased until the year of the metro-Louisville merger. In the first year of the merger per employee expenditures were $63,705. The next year the amount dropped but soon began to ascend again to new records in cost. From 2003–2004 to 2009–2010 per employee expenditures rose

7.16 percent, a modest amount compared with the premerger increase of 13.49 percent. Consolidation has not reduced the amount spent on each employee, although it may have slowed the rate of increase.

What might explain the decreased personnel but the rise in the costs of existing personnel? Before the merger there had been a large disparity between salaries for city and county employees. Merger required salary adjustments across jurisdictions so that compensation for all employees is equal—referred to as a "ratcheting upward of salaries." The new government thus found itself paying more for fewer employees.

On the basis solely of these indicators we find no overall increased efficiencies. Louisville metro is running at a record-high total budget. Whether the reduction in employees has affected the delivery of services is another question. Although we cannot account for all or most service outputs, we can present data in a few critical areas, such as road condition, air quality, and crime.

Performance (Road Maintenance, Air Quality, and Crime)

Road Maintenance Maintaining a safe transportation network is vital to the livelihood of a city. Employees, goods, and customers all must travel as part of the business process. Local governments bear the entire responsibility of maintaining the roadways. If a consolidated government is more efficient, it follows that road conditions should have improved with the top-down management of metro government.

Table 12.3 presents Louisville's performance in maintaining its roads between 2001 and 2008. The report defines roads as "good," "fair," "mediocre," or "poor."

With only a few years of premerger data to study, it is difficult to determine whether those two years are an anomaly or an indication of a trend. In 2003 roads were mostly "mediocre"; 24 were classified as "good," 23 as "fair," and 12 as "poor." Conditions remained mostly stable throughout the years. Overall, between 2003 and 2008, road conditions fluctuated, but we discern no dramatic changes one way or another.

Air Quality Environmental quality is important for a locality, both to protect the health of its citizens and as a way of improving local amenities in order to attract productive

Table 12.3. Road Maintenance in Louisville–Jefferson County, 2001–2008

	Year	Poor	Mediocre	Fair	Good
Premerger period	2001	16	33	28	22
	2002	17	40	17	26
Postmerger period	2003	12	41	23	24
	2004	12	41	25	22
	2005	11	40	21	28
	2006	14	40	24	22
	2007	14	37	21	29
	2008	13	39	22	26

Source: The Road Information Program (TRIP), Washington, D.C.

residents. In the past Louisville has not fared well on this count and was placed among the twenty-five most polluted localities in the United States in 2006.[26] Although the regulation of Louisville's air quality is in the hands of a special district, the newly consolidated government exercises considerable influence on this condition. Metro government has made clean air a priority, and its first mayor, Jerry Abramson, vowed to take on this challenge.[27]

Table 12.4 displays Louisville–Jefferson County air-quality data from 1998 to 2008. Each day is labeled either "good," "moderate," or "unhealthy." Also shown are the differences between premerger and postmerger years.

As the table shows, premerger Louisville averaged a total of 171.2 good days, while postmerger Louisville increased those good days to 181.2. This is clearly an improvement, and metro government should be given credit for making headway on this issue. The criterion of "moderate" days can be interpreted as the air quality being "fair" or "acceptable." Here the premerger period registered an average of 159.2 moderate days, while the postmerger period increased that number to 168.6 moderate days. The critical criterion is unhealthy days, and here too metro government does better. During the premerger period the average number of unhealthy days was 34.8, compared with the postmerger average of 15.4 unhealthy days. Since the merger Louisville has experienced a 50 percent decrease in unhealthy days.

Crime Public safety is an important factor in evaluating urban life. First, crime control absorbs a considerable part of a city's budget. Second, safe streets are a high priority for city residents and are often a factor in the kinds of neighborhoods people choose. For this reason crime affects not only quality of life but also property values.

Table 12.4. Air Quality in Louisville–Jefferson County, 1998–2008

	Year	Good	Moderate	Unhealthy
Premerger period	1998	254	74	37
	1999	148	164	53
	2000	147	197	22
	2001	142	199	24
	2002	165	162	38
Postmerger period	2003	182	170	13
	2004	195	169	2
	2005	157	181	27
	2006	191	166	8
	2007	181	157	27
	2008	183	118	5

Source: U.S. Environmental Protection Agency, *Air Quality Report* (Washington, D.C.).
    Note: Data for 2008 are reported for only 306 days. Unhealthy days include days classified unhealthy for both sensitive groups and the general population.

Last, a safe city attracts investors and business, while a dangerous city drives commerce away.

We should also point out that crime rates hinge on many factors that are exogenous to police performance. High levels of poverty, low educational achievement, and broken families influence crime rates. Nevertheless, good policing can reduce crime, sometimes to minimal levels. During the 1990s the New York Police Department (NYPD) employed a number of innovative techniques to reduce crime. Among these techniques was a computerized system for deploying police into hot spots. The NYPD also implemented a "no-tolerance" policy for minor infractions. The techniques were effective enough to be copied in smaller cities and achieved national recognition.[28] Although we cannot determine whether these techniques would have the same effect in Louisville, we can say that more effective crime fighting was a part of consolidating into a single police force.

With this in mind, we present figure 12.4, which shows crime rates in Jefferson County between 1997 and 2009. The figure displays two line graphs representing violent and property crimes.

By 2003 the trend line for violent crime began to rise. Between 2006 and 2008 violent crime rose above 4,500 per 100,000 residents before dipping a bit in 2009. At the same time the trend line for property crime continued to crawl below the 1,000 mark. These figures can be looked at in another way. By taking averages for the pre- and postmerger periods, we come to a different result. For the premerger period, 1997 through 2002, the yearly averages were 681 violent crimes and 3,867 property crimes per 100,000 populations. After the merger, from 2003 to 2009 the yearly average of violent crimes decreased to 606 per 100,000 residents, but during the same period the yearly average of property crimes increased to 4,422 per 100,000 residents.

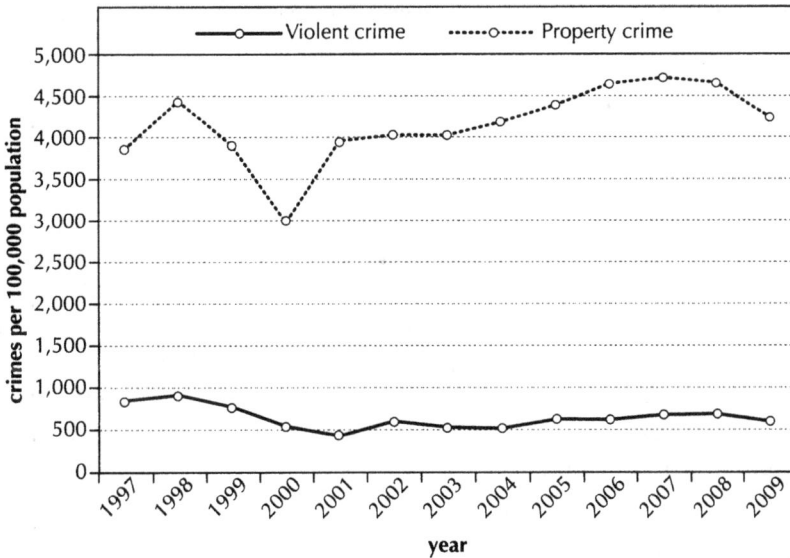

Figure 12.4. Violent and property crime in Louisville—Jefferson County, 1997–2009. Source: Federal Bureau of Investigation, Uniform Crime Reporting (UCR), http://www.fbi.gov/ucr/ucr.htm#cius.

However one interprets the results, the crime rates did not dramatically change between periods. Contrary to expectations, we detect no improvement in the metro police force's ability to reduce crime.

EVALUATING THE MERGER'S RESULTS: ACCOUNTABILITY

Promises

Merger was supposed to make citizens more invested in the electoral process and hold elected officials more accountable for their actions. Premerger Louisville was served by aldermen who represented the central city. A smaller land mass also meant that neighborhoods were closer together and as a consequence held more issues in common. All this changed after merger. A much-enlarged metro area now meant that the central city would compete with the suburbs.

City-county consolidation also meant that new districts would have to be drawn, and the new area was divided into twenty-six metro council seats. Nearly two-thirds of the council seats came from suburban districts, while the remaining third were in the former city. African American representation was also down from approximately a third of the board of aldermen to less than a quarter of the metro council. Residents of the old city would have to struggle to maintain a modicum of influence on the new metro council.[29]

Despite these disadvantages, politicians who advocated the merger promised that council members elected from smaller districts would increase accountability. With roughly 23,000 constituents from distinctly drawn districts, council races were thought to be more competitive. After all, the coherence and familiarity of a neighborhood were supposed to contribute to more citizen interest, more and better candidates for office, and greater familiarity with the issues. Did these claims materialize?

Voter Turnout

Figure 12.5 illustrates voter turnout in primaries for both premerger and postmerger periods. After the merger voter turnout initially dropped from 19.7 percent in 2003 to 15.9 percent by 2005. The great exception here is the escalation to 39.4 percent in 2008. Turnout in this particular year was extremely high and was attributed to the presidential race, in which both Republican and Democratic candidates were vying for nomination in very well-publicized races. As expected, by 2010 the voter turnout decreased to 27.7 percent. Here too, Louisville went through hotly contested mayoral primaries, engendering greater turnout. Thus far, the postmerger period has seen increased voter turnout. Only time will tell whether this is an artifact of particular circumstances or a durable trend.

Campaign Finance

Merger was supposed to bring about campaign finance reform, making the election process less expensive and opening up the system to newcomers.[30] Thus far this expec-

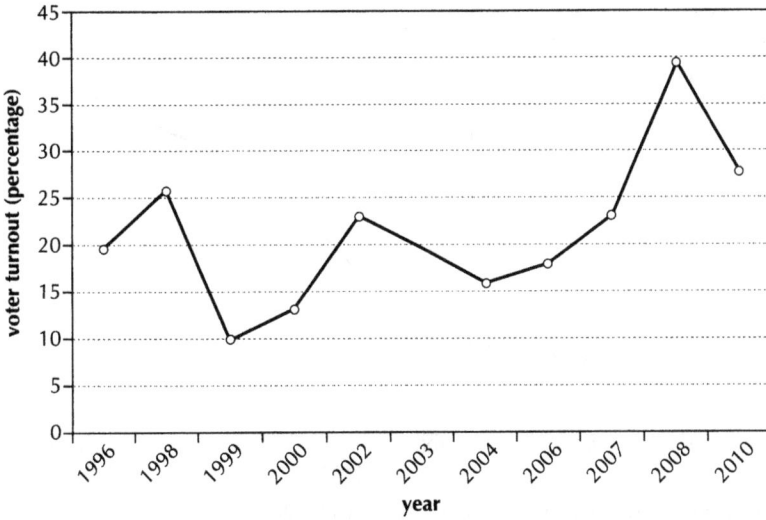

Figure 12.5. Louisville—Jefferson County primary-election voter turnout. Source: Kentucky State Board of Elections, "Turnout Statistics," http://elect.ky.gov/stats/turnout.htm.

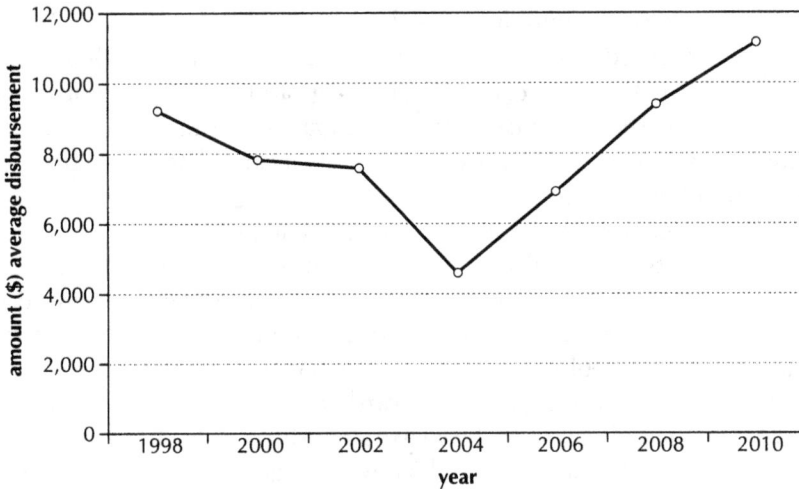

Figure 12.6. Campaign finances for Board of Aldermen and Metro Council, 1998–2010 (constant 2009 dollars). Source: Kentucky Registry of Election Finance, http://www.kref.state.ky.us/krefsearch/.

tation has not been met. The cost of elections has dramatically increased since the merger, and the trend toward more expensive elections seems well set. Figure 12.6 displays the average spending in aldermanic and council elections from 1998 to 2010.

In 2000 the average amount spent in the aldermanic election was nearly $8,000 (in 2009 constant dollars). In 2010, after the merger went into effect, the average amount spent per metro council candidate reached a high of $11,140 (in 2009 constant dollars).[31] Spending on mayoral races provides a clearer picture of candidate spending. Figure 12.7 shows the change in total funds disbursed from 1998 to 2010.

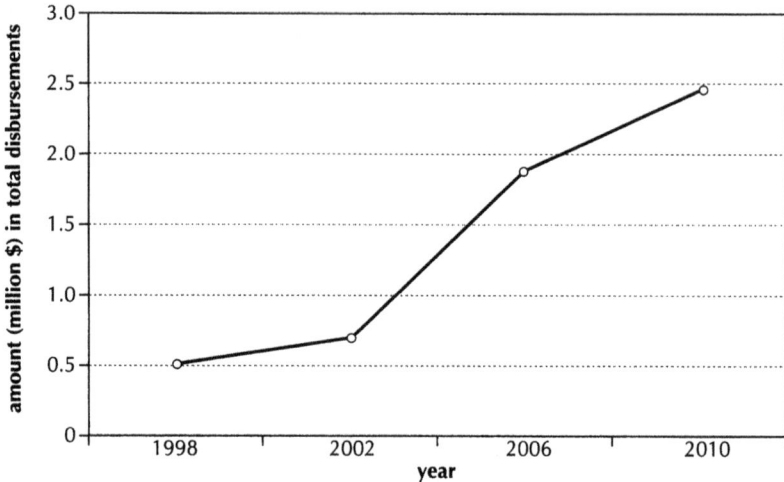

Figure 12.7. Campaign finances for mayoral elections, 1998–2010 (constant 2009 dollars). Source: Kentucky Registry of Election Finance, http://www.kref.state.ky.us/krefsearch/.

During the last premerger mayoral election in 1998 the total amount spent was $501,431, but in 2006 the amount more than doubled to $1,880,386. In 2010 total disbursements increased once again to $2,449,725 (in constant 2009 dollars). The mayoral race is not getting less expensive, as suggested by merger proponents, but it has become more difficult for candidates without heavy financing because of the metro's much larger territory. Gone are the days when candidates could base their campaign on neighborhood coffee klatches.

The 2010 election was also important because it showed that Republicans had the potential to control the mayoralty via the suburban vote. The Democratic candidate, Greg Fischer, received 51 percent of the votes, winning the election by just 6,100 votes out of more than 256,000 cast. Democrats overwhelmingly drew their support from the central city, while Republicans garnered a majority of the suburban vote. As Louisville's demography continues to slip toward the suburbs, Republican candidates stand a better chance of carrying the mayoralty. Merger also has paved the way for larger campaign budgets and more media advertising. The increased cost of mayoral campaigns puts city hall at the disposition of those who contribute most to candidates and their parties. Although one might argue that metro Louisville has become more competitive between Democrats and Republicans, both parties are now more dependent on big money from the business community. At the broadest level, accountability to the mass of citizens is very much in question.

The merger of Louisville and Jefferson County was passed more than a decade ago, and its implementation is now past the ten-year mark. At least by the criteria of efficiency and accountability, we find that promises made on the merger's behalf have not been realized. On one measure of efficiency the number of metro personnel was lower than the previously combined total for Louisville and Jefferson County, but that reduction has been more than offset by rising budgets and higher personnel costs. Indeed, it could be argued that fewer workers earning more may have damaged service delivery rather than improved it. With the exception of air quality, metro's performance also falls short. Road conditions are disappointing, with only a quarter evaluated as good. Depending on how one looks at changes in crime rates, the results may vary. One thing is certain, the conclusion that a merged police department has not made a significant dent in crime. Accountability fares little better. More citizens have gone to the polls since merger, and that is a good sign. However, voter participation has been stymied by the costs of running for office, particularly the costs of running for mayor.

We opened this chapter with the observation that the newly elected mayor of the metro has called for an examination of Merger 1 with an eye toward improving it through Merger 2. We trust that our work on Merger 1 can be put to use in the efforts to come.

NOTES

1. David Rusk, *Cities without Suburbs* (Washington, D.C.: Woodrow Wilson Center Press, 1993); G. Ross. Stephens and Nelson B. Wikstrom, *Metropolitan Government and Governance* (New York: Oxford University Press, 2000).

2. H. V. Savitch, Ronald. K. Vogel, and Y. Lin, "Louisville Transformed but Hardly Changed: A Survey of a City before and after Merger," in *Governing Metropolitan Regions in the 21st Century*, ed. Don Phares, 164–84 (Armonk, N.Y.: M. E. Sharpe, 2009); H. V. Savitch, Ronald K. Vogel, and Lin Ye, "Beyond the Rhetoric: Lessons from Louisville's Consolidation," *American Review of Public Administration* 40, no. 1 (2010): 3–28.

3. Sheldon S. Shafer, "Mayor Greg Fischer Forms Task Force to Study Louisville Metro Merger," *Louisville Courier-Journal*, January 6, 2010, accessed January 12, 2011, http://www .courier-journal.com/apps/pbcs.dll/ article?AID=/201101061741/NEWS0106/301060048.

4. Savitch, Vogel, and Ye, "Louisville Transformed but Hardly Changed."

5. Ibid.; R. K. Vogel, *Local Government Reorganization* (Louisville, Ky.: League of Women Voters of Louisville and Jefferson County; Department of Political Science, University of Louisville, 1994).

6. H. V. Savitch and R. K. Vogel, "Suburbs without a City: Power and City-County Consolidation," *Urban Affairs Review* 39, no. 6 (2004): 758–90.

7. U.S Census Bureau, 1960 and 2000, http://www2.census.gov/prod2/decennial/documents /41557421v3p2ch09.pdf.

8. U.S Census Bureau, 1950 and 2000, http://www2.census.gov/prod2/decennial /documents/41557421v3p2ch09.pdf.

9. Censusscope, "Segregation: Dissimilarity Indices," accessed December 20, 2010, http://www.censusscope.org/us/rank_dissimilarity_white_black.html.

10. Savitch, Vogel, and Ye, "Louisville Transformed but Hardly Changed."

11. WLKY, 2009; *Louisville Eccentric Observer,* 2009, accessed February 3, 2010, http:// blogs.wvgazette.com/watchdog/2009/07/10/metro-government-louisville-mayor-jerry -abramson/#comments.

12. Savitch, Vogel, and Ye, "Louisville Transformed but Hardly Changed."

13. Ibid.

14. Jefferson County Governance Task Force, *Final Recommendations* (Louisville, Ky., 1996).

15. Savitch, Vogel, and Ye, "Louisville Transformed but Hardly Changed."

16. *Louisville Courier-Journal*, October 7, 2000, 1; *Louisville Courier-Journal*, October 12/13, 2000, 1.

17. Savitch, Vogel, and Ye, "Louisville Transformed but Hardly Changed."

18. D. Greenwell, "The Transitional Costs of Police Consolidation in the Louisville Metro Area," unpublished manuscript, University of Louisville, Ky., 2004.

19. A majority of the city police favored (80 percent) while a majority of the county police (85 percent) opposed it. Kristen Clarke, "Voting Rights and City-County Consolidations," *Houston Law Review* 43 (2006): 659.

20. Edward Daniel Blaser, "Police Consolidation and Job Satisfaction: Louisville, Kentucky," unpublished manuscript, University of Louisville, Ky., 2006.

21. Dave Armstrong, "County Promises More Cooperation with City to Work toward 'Speak with One Voice' Goal," *Business First*, October 10, 1997; Dave Armstrong and Rebecca Jackson, *A Blueprint for City of Louisville and Jefferson County Government Reorganization* (Louisville, Ky.: City of Louisville and Jefferson County, 1999); Rebecca Jackson and Dave Armstrong, "Jackson, Armstrong Make Case for City-County Merger," *Voice Tribune*, November 10, 1999, A10.

22. Jerry Abramson, "Louisville Merger: A Community Conversation?," *KET 2*, August 23, 2000, http://www.ket.org/merger/.

23. Savitch, Vogel and Lin, "Louisville Transformed but Hardly Changed."

24. Data before 1999–2000 were not available in complete form, and therefore the beginning date is the fiscal year 1999–2000. Note that fiscal years run from July 1 to June 30 and cover two calendar years.

25. As can be seen in each figure, amounts are adjusted for inflation.

26. American Lung Association, *State of the Air*, 2006, accessed January 21, 2011, http://www.lungusa.org/assets/documents/publications/state-of-the-air/state-of-the-air-report-2006.pdf.

27. *Louisville Courier-Journal*, 2003, http://pqasb.pqarchiver.com/courier_journal/access/1828583701.html.

28. David Weissburd, Stephen D. Mastrofski, Rosann Greenspan, and James J. Willis, *The Growth of Compstat in American Policing* (New York: Police Foundation, 2001); W. Bratton, *Crime and Restoring Order: What America Can Learn from New York's Finest* (Washington, D.C.: Heritage Foundation, 1996).

29. Under Section 5 of the Voting Rights Act, some, but not all, states with a history of racial discrimination in voting must gain preclearance from the federal government before making changes in voting qualifications, electoral constituencies, and/or voting procedures. Because Kentucky is not a preclearance state, the Section 5 voting rights provisions were not available to African Americans to block the merger on the basis of minority dilution. Kristen Clarke argues that it might be possible to challenge the consolidation on the basis of Section 2 of the Voting Rights Act in "Voting Rights and City-County Consolidations."

30. Jackson and Armstrong, "Jackson, Armstrong Make Case for City-County Merger."

31. Although not visible on the line graph, this amount has decreased over the past elections and reached an average of $11,140 spent per candidate in 2010. The data, however, do not take into account the many candidates who are on the ballots but do not raise or spend money. Recently, more third-party candidates have been placing their hats in the race and using a grassroots style of campaign, making the averages lower.

13

From Fragmentation to Collaboration
The Evolution of Interlocal Relations
in Northern Kentucky
Julie Cencula Olberding

Over the years interlocal government relations in northern Kentucky have evolved from disunity and fragmentation to regional cooperation and collaboration. This chapter begins with a discussion of a conceptual framework of interlocal relations based on the literature. The next section provides background information on northern Kentucky, including the number of local governments in the region, the long history of a vice economy in the region and cross-jurisdictional efforts to change it, and state legislation and programs that have supported norms of cooperation and cross-jurisdictional efforts. The chapter then focuses on regional visioning and planning processes that have occurred in northern Kentucky in more recent decades—the 1980s, the 1990s, and the first decade of the twenty-first century—including key differences among these three processes. It then discusses key outcomes of regional collaboration in northern Kentucky, along with some challenges. The chapter concludes by trying to distill a few lessons that may be helpful for government leaders and citizens who may be interested in enhancing regional cooperation and collaboration in other areas of Kentucky and beyond.

A CONCEPTUAL FRAMEWORK OF INTERLOCAL RELATIONS

In the political science, economics, and public administration literature, there are a number of concepts and theories about interlocal government relations. One of the clearer and more concise ways to conceptualize interlocal relations is three models on a continuum. At one extreme is decentralization with fragmented local governments, and at the other extreme is centralization with regional government (see figure 13.1).

Fragmentation	Regional governance	Regional government

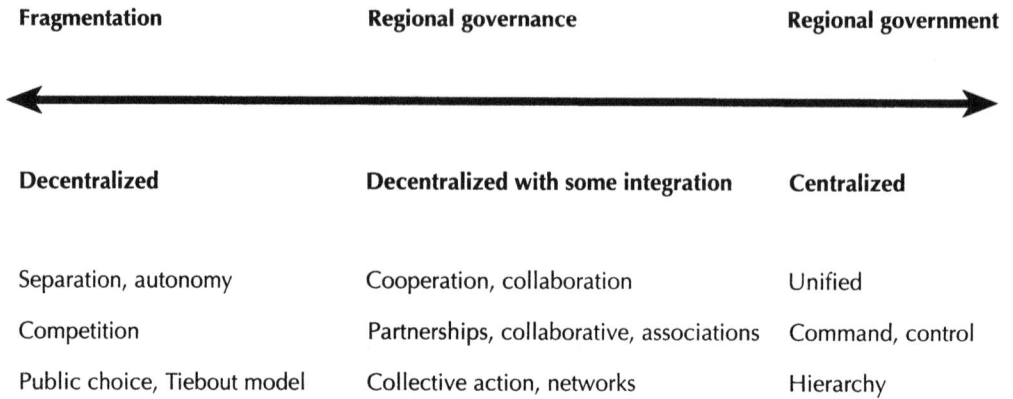

Decentralized	Decentralized with some integration	Centralized
Separation, autonomy	Cooperation, collaboration	Unified
Competition	Partnerships, collaborative, associations	Command, control
Public choice, Tiebout model	Collective action, networks	Hierarchy

Figure 13.1. A basic conceptual model of interlocal government relations

In the middle is some decentralization with integration, which can be considered regional governance. Each of these three points on the continuum will be described in greater detail later.

A general definition of "fragmentation" is "a state or situation in which there are small parts that are separated and possibly isolated from one another." Thus at one extreme of the continuum is local government fragmentation, which can be characterized by a number of small local governments making and implementing policies and programs in a separate and isolated manner. Further, some scholars observe that this fragmented state results in competition among local governments. This conceptualization is often framed in terms of public choice theories, particularly the Tiebout model. Tiebout asserts that there is an optimal amount of residents and businesses at which communities produce a bundle of public services at the lowest average cost. Communities at the optimum try to maintain their residents and businesses, and communities below the optimum try to attract more of them.[1] Proponents argue that multiple cities offering various public services and different tax rates result in an efficient outcome because this enables citizens and businesses to choose jurisdictions with public services and taxes that most closely match their preferences.

Some scholars have raised doubts about Tiebout's core assumptions that citizens are knowledgeable about the tax and service levels of local governments[2] and that they are mobile.[3] In addition, some have said that this model can result in a bidding war among local governments for a finite number of residents and businesses. They argue that this competition is a zero-sum game because businesses, jobs, and income are just shifted or shuffled from one jurisdiction to another.[4]

At the other extreme of the continuum is a model in which authority is more unified and centralized in a regional government, such as a metropolitan government or a consolidated city-county government. Public administration traditionalists have asserted that a more unified government results in greater authority and ability to address significant problems, more accountability of elected officials and public administrators, more equitable treatment of citizens across the region, and the opportunity for economies of scale that enable services to be provided at lower costs.[5] These broad-sweeping efforts to institute a metropolitan government or consolidate governments have not been popular in the United States. For example, voters have rejected proposals to consolidate city and county governments nearly one hundred times but have approved them only about twenty times, so the success rate is only about 20 percent.[6]

In the middle of the continuum is regional governance, which is characterized by independent local governments with some cooperation and coordination. "Governance" has been conceptualized as political processes that generate a community identity and shared values[7] and as a network of individuals across sectors that share resources and deliver public services.[8] Proponents of regional governance have asserted that a more optimal outcome is achieved when local governments recognize their interdependencies and act in a coordinated way.[9] In many cases local governments cooperate or collaborate on only one or a few policy areas, such as economic development, transportation, or environmental management. Techniques that are used to collaborate in targeted areas are special districts, written agreements among local governments, and regional partnerships.

Regional governance seems to be increasing, while regional government seems to be on the decline, according to scholars.[10] "The federally mandated regional planning efforts and the consolidation proposals of the past three decades are being replaced by voluntary cooperation among governments and sectors through public-private, 'inter-community partnerships.'"[11] Scholars describe these changes in interlocal government relations as the emergence of a networked society, in which private and nonprofit organizations share an equal part in governance with government agencies.[12]

Why and how do local governments move from acting in a fragmented and isolated manner to a cooperative and collaborative manner? Olberding put forth a collective-action framework to study the movement from local government fragmentation to regional governance,[13] based on seminal work asserting that cooperative norms are key determinants in collective action.[14] Olberding found some evidence that norms of regional cooperation—measured as the strength of regional councils of government (COGs)—were positively related to the formation of regional partnerships for economic development. In addition, the author found that fragmentation of local government—measured as the number of general-purpose local governments in a metropolitan area and the number of special districts—were negatively related to the formation of these regional partnerships. Feiock, Tao, and Johnson also used collective-action theory as a framework, but they distinguished between external constraints on collective action and endogenous factors related to social capital.[15] The authors asserted that external constraints on regional partnerships, which include local government fragmentation, may be overcome by endogenous social capital factors, such as experience with interlocal agreements.

INTERLOCAL RELATIONS IN NORTHERN KENTUCKY

It is fairly well known that Kentucky is a state with a large number of general-purpose county governments—120 of them, to be exact. Only Texas and Georgia have more counties. The region known as northern Kentucky traditionally has been defined as consisting of three counties—Boone, Campbell, and Kenton—that are at the north-ernmost point of the state, along the southern bank of the Ohio River.[16] In addition to these three county governments, northern Kentucky is made up of 36 general-purpose local governments.[17] A number of these local governments seem to be small parts or pieces—that is, fragmented—in that they represent a small number of citizens. Only 3 of the 36 municipalities have a population of 20,000 or more: Covington, Independence, and Florence (table 13.1). Many of the municipalities in northern Kentucky have fewer than 3,000 residents, and some have significantly fewer, including California, 83; Fairview, 143; Kenton Vale, 144; Mentor, 167; Woodlawn, 252; Melbourne, 450; Crestview, 455; Bromley, 774; and Ryland Heights, 817.

Table 13.1. Municipalities by Population in the Three Traditional Counties of Northern Kentucky

County and municipality	Population	County and municipality	Population
Campbell County			
Newport	15,721	Wilder	2,974
Fort Thomas	15,413	Silver Grove	1,165
Alexandria	8,002	Crestview	455
Bellevue	5,943	Melbourne	450
Highland Heights	5,754	Woodlawn	252
Dayton	5,508	Mentor	167
Cold Spring	5,480	California	83
Southgate	3,311		
Boone County			
Florence	26,929		
Union	3,479		
Walton	2,935		
Kenton County			
Covington	42,797	Ludlow	4,766
Independence	20,254	Crescent Springs	3,983
Erlanger	16,965	Crestview Hills	3,482
Edgewood	8,869	Park Hills	2,776
Elsmere	7,884	Lakeside Park	2,672
Villa Hills	7,707	Ryland Heights	817
Fort Mitchell	7,554	Bromley	774
Taylor Mill	6,715	Kenton Vale	144
Fort Wright	5,420	Fairview	143

Source: U.S. Census Bureau, "2007 Governments Integrated Directory."

In addition to general-purpose local governments, northern Kentucky has a number of special districts. Most notably, it has 23 fire-protection (or ambulance) districts and 13 school districts. It also has 3 countywide library districts, 3 countywide soil conservation districts, 2 water supply districts, 1 flood-damage-prevention district, and 1 housing- and community-development district.[18] In all, northern Kentucky has a total of 85 local governments, serving about 350,000 residents.

Historically, most important political decisions and actions tended to happen within the boundaries of each county government or each municipal government in northern Kentucky. However, community organizers and leaders began working across jurisdictional lines more and more in the late 1950s and continued to do so during the decades that followed. These cross-jurisdictional activities are discussed in the next few sections.

Government Fragmentation Fosters a Vice Economy

This section provides some historical context about an important part of the region's economy for 150 years and also some insight on early collective action across local government jurisdictions. From the early 1800s through the 1970s, northern Kentucky had a national reputation for being a center of gambling and other vices, including bootlegging during Prohibition and prostitution after that. Newport was commonly referred to as "Sin City on the Ohio River."[19]

A key reason was that local government fragmentation on the Kentucky side of the Ohio River enabled crime syndicates, particularly the infamous Cleveland Syndicate, and other vice interests to pay off elected officials and law enforcement officers in the numerous small municipalities. In other words, northern Kentucky was on the extreme end of the continuum, with fragmented, decentralized local governments acting autonomously. On the Ohio side of the river, it was more difficult for vice interests to have influence because Cincinnati was a much larger city that was run by powerful political machines during the late 1800s and early 1900s and then, after the Progressive movement in the 1920s, by a cadre of more professional public administrators. At that time a common expression in Cincinnati was that things are "a bit looser on the other side of the river."[20] Further, the economy of gambling was able to flourish in this region because it was part of the Commonwealth of Kentucky, which was the national center for horse racing and which never outlawed gambling on this particular sport. In addition, although Cincinnati kept much illegal gambling out of its own jurisdiction, the city had hundreds of thousands of citizens who were potential consumers of gambling and vice, as well as excellent transportation hubs for tourists from outside the region.[21]

Gangs, Gambling, and Crime Encourage Cross-Jurisdictional Efforts

Beginning in the 1950s, illegal gambling became the target of reformers from various local jurisdictions in northern Kentucky who, interestingly, felt that it was a barrier to the region's long-term economic development. At that time the traditional economic base of the region was located in Cincinnati, and 90 percent of northern Kentucky residents commuted across the Ohio River for work.[22] In Campbell County, in particular, community leaders believed that large corporations would not move to or invest in Newport and surrounding communities because vice interests had corrupted local politicians so that they did not support new businesses and industry. Community leaders and citizens from various jurisdictions in Campbell County, especially Ft. Thomas and other suburban jurisdictions, formed the Committee of 500. This group "focused on cleaning up Newport not for any altruistic reform purpose, but because they wanted to replace the political economy of gambling and corruption with the political economy of the modern corporation and jobs."[23]

The first accomplishment of the Committee of 500 was to elect George Ratterman as Campbell County sheriff in 1961. Ratterman brought some fame to the campaign because he had been a four-letter athlete at the University of Notre Dame and had played football with the Cleveland Browns and Buffalo Bills, among other NFL teams. This strong reputation may have helped him win the election despite the syndicate's attempt to frame him and force him out of the race by drugging him, putting him in bed with a local showgirl, and prearranging a police raid with photographs. After taking office, Sheriff Ratterman worked with U.S. attorney general Robert Kennedy and federal agents to enforce antigambling laws at state and federal levels, and they were able to shut down most gambling, prostitution, and vice businesses in Newport and the rest of the county.[24]

Thus local leaders' actions in the 1950s and 1960s—envisioning the region's long-term economic development and working across jurisdictions to address a crisis or serious problem—helped pave the way for regional planning and action in the years to come.[25] In other words, collaboration and cooperation across jurisdictions in the 1950s may have strengthened norms of regional cooperation, which supported regional planning and visioning in the 1980s, the 1990s, and the first decade of the twenty-first century.

State Legislation and Programs Promote Regional Cooperation

Another important factor related to interjurisdictional cooperation in northern Kentucky is state legislation and programs that supported it. Specifically, in the 1970s the Kentucky General Assembly created Area Development Districts (ADDs) that covered the Commonwealth—fifteen of them in all—to bring local government officials and community leaders together to solve common problems and to speak to the state and federal government in a unified manner. The Northern Kentucky Area Development District (NKADD) covers eight counties, including Boone, Kenton and Campbell— the three counties at the core of the region—as well as Carroll, Gallatin, Grant, Owen, and Pendleton.[26] "As a result of its creation, local leaders from across northern Kentucky came together for the first time in a spirit of cooperation that set the stage for many of the regional and cooperative approaches to problem-solving that have defined the region."[27] Its community-development services include economic and commercial development, recreation, water and sewer services, transportation, and historic preservation. Its public administration services help local governments and nonprofits in the region be more efficient and effective, for example, by providing assistance with budget preparation and personnel policies.

In 1982 the General Assembly established the Kentucky Enterprise Zone Authority (KEZA) to concentrate government incentives in economically depressed areas for a set time—twenty years—in order to attract private investment and jobs. State incentives included exemption from sales tax for new construction or renovation, sales tax for the purchase or leasing of equipment, and usage tax of business-related motor vehicles. In most cases local incentives were also added, including exemptions from the business license fee, rebates in payroll taxes, and a reduction in property taxes.[28] Of the ten enterprise zones established throughout the Commonwealth, two were in northern Kentucky—one in Covington and another in Campbell County. The Campbell County zone was "unusual in that it originally covered a number of governmental units, including the cities of Bellevue, Dayton, Highland Heights, Newport and Southgate, as well as county acreage."[29] One of the biggest impacts of the enterprise zone was development of the Newport Aquarium and Newport-on-the-Levee.

THREE WAVES OF REGIONAL PLANNING IN NORTHERN KENTUCKY

This section describes three continuous waves of regional visioning and planning that occurred in northern Kentucky during the 1980s, the 1990s, and the first decade of the twenty-first century. The first of these processes in the 1980s was initiated at the state level, like the actions described in the previous section; however, although the governor created a regional planning task force, it was not supported by state legislation or funding, and it was led by leaders from various local jurisdictions. The two regional processes that followed were even more driven by local leaders, who worked not only across jurisdictional boundaries but also across sectors. That is, these processes were driven by regional public-private partnerships that continued to involve various county and municipal governments and that increasingly represented private corporations, religious institutions, foundations, nonprofit organizations, colleges and universities, neighborhood groups, and individual citizens. This section provides a brief overview of each of these regional governance efforts.

Regional Planning Task Force in the 1980s

When John Y. Brown was elected governor of Kentucky in 1979, he soon became frustrated with the fact that elected officials from all the local jurisdictions in northern Kentucky would approach him with funding requests on an individual basis. "Governor Brown said that as far as he was concerned, northern Kentucky was a region. 'Until they come together, I'm not doing anything,'" retold Mike Hammons, who previously served as executive director of both Forward Quest and Vision 2015, two nonprofit organizations responsible for implementing initiatives from the subsequent regional planning processes in the 1990s and 2000s.[30] In 1981 Governor Brown appointed a task force, which published a report titled *Northern Kentucky's Future*. The report focused on concerns of "fragmentation" and "disunity" in the region and contained a list of eighteen recommended actions, including the following:

- Forming a regional legislative caucus and a consensus process for securing state funds for northern Kentucky
- Mapping a single congressional district for the region, distinct from Louisville and Lexington
- Consolidating water and sanitation districts
- Creating a tricounty economic-development agency
- Investing in the urban core

Ten of the report's eighteen recommended strategies were completed by the second round of planning in the mid-1990s.[31] Two strategies—a collector road and an urban-redevelopment challenge grant—resulted in development of River Place in Newport and the Northern Kentucky Convention Center and RiverCenter Towers in Covington. These projects were the first new developments in northern Kentucky's urban center in seventy-five years, and many say that they fueled redevelopment in these two cities on the Ohio River. In addition, local leaders created the Tri-County Economic Development Corporation (Northern Kentucky Tri-ED), which has been credited with helping attract six new corporate headquarters, including Toyota Motor Manufacturing North America, Fidelity Investments, and Heinz/Starkist Foods.

Forward Quest in the 1990s

In contrast to the first planning process, which was driven by the governor, the second planning process in 1995 was locally initiated, organized, funded, and staffed. Known as Quest, this effort to develop a twenty-five-year strategic vision had the following mission statement: "We will paint a picture of what we want the future to be."[32] Cochairpersons of Quest were William Butler, founder and chairman of Corporex Companies, and Father Bill Cleves, rector of the Covington Cathedral Basilica of the Assumption. The process received financial support from Northern Kentucky Tri-ED and staff support from the Northern Kentucky Chamber of Commerce. Quest involved more than one hundred meetings and about one thousand citizens during an eighteen-month period. "Public forums, letters, phone calls, faxes and emails were used to assemble the insights and aspirations of the people of our community."[33]

The outcome of this second planning process was a forty-page report with colorful maps, illustrations, and photographs. The report identified six action areas and forty-four initiatives. The two action areas identified as the highest priorities were governance and education. Other action areas were regionalism, growth and development, human services, and culture and entertainment. Many of the forty-four initiatives and ideas were aimed at changing the physical environment, such as the following:

- An international executive conference center for training activities and smaller meetings near the Cincinnati/Northern Kentucky International Airport, which is in Hebron, Kentucky

- The Freedom Tower, which was conceptualized as a six-hundred-foot tower that would mark historic crossings along the Underground Railroad with an overlook on the Ohio River toward the new National Underground Railroad Freedom Center in Cincinnati
- Grant's Lake, which was envisioned as a huge lake created by a dam on the Licking River that would serve as a recreational amenity that would spawn new residential development
- The Sky Loop, which was an idea for an elevated "personal rapid transit" system—a network of podcars—that would link the downtown and riverfront areas of northern Kentucky to Cincinnati, Ohio[34]
- A high-speed monorail that would go from the Cincinnati/Northern Kentucky International Airport to the urban center, with linkages to the Sky Loop[35]

The Quest report also proposed a number of strategies that were designed to affect the political environment, such as the following:

- Consolidating Covington, Newport, and at least one other municipality to create one city with a population of 100,000
- Merging the three county governments in northern Kentucky—Boone, Campbell, and Kenton—into one county government
- Creating a nonprofit organization to work with community leaders representing government agencies, businesses, and foundations to implement the initiatives in the Quest report

Committees studied many of these recommendations, and some were implemented, including the METS conference center near the airport and the creation of a nonprofit organization, called Forward Quest, to work on the report's initiatives. However, the bolder and more controversial recommendations have not been implemented. These include the Sky Loop and the monorail, as well as the consolidation of city governments and the merging of county governments.

Vision 2015 in the First Decade of the Twenty-first Century

In 2004, Forward Quest recommended that "the community revisit the Quest vision and launch a new community plan for the next decade."[36] A consulting firm, Collaborative Economics, was hired to guide the planning process. Five action teams were formed to identify goals and develop action plans to achieve those goals. Forward Quest was able to garner a broad base of funding for the third planning process. Funders included the following:

- Foundations, such as the Gannet Foundation, the Greater Cincinnati Foundation, and the Scripps Howard Foundation
- Corporations, including Citigroup, Delta Air Lines, Fidelity Investments, Great American Financial Resources, and Toyota Motor Manufacturing North America

- Nonprofit organizations and institutions, such as the Northern Kentucky Chamber of Commerce, Northern Kentucky University, and Thomas More College
- Individual donors

"Vision 2015" is the name of two things: (1) "the public plan [that] represents the region's priorities"[37] and (2) the organization that is managing that public plan or call to action. The plan identifies a "common purpose" for northern Kentucky that is rooted in developing the regional economy: "To ensure Northern Kentucky is capable of competing in a global economy, with our citizens benefitting from the prosperity and opportunity this creates."[38] The plan defines six "strategic directions": competitive economy, effective governance, educational excellence, livable communities, urban renaissance, and regional stewardship. Some of the strategies recommended in the report are the following:

- Forming a "Regional Stewardship Council," supported by a small professional staff, to catalyze existing organizations to implement strategies in Vision 2015
- Creating a regional park system for the nine counties in northern Kentucky to increase access to the Ohio and Licking Rivers and to develop the "southern-tier" counties as the region's premier outdoor recreation venue
- Developing a nationally recognized "culture of contribution" through service learning in schools and the full engagement of the community in the schools

Differences among the Three Regional Planning Processes

The three planning processes in northern Kentucky were similar in that they identified local government fragmentation as a key issue and called for regional solutions; however, the types of solutions identified by each process varied quite a bit. The first process in the early 1980s called for creating a tricounty economic-development agency and consolidating water and sanitation districts. In other words, it called for collaboration that targeted particular public services and programs.[39] In contrast, the second plan included recommendations to consolidate city governments—that is, Covington, Newport, and one other city—and to merge the three county governments in northern Kentucky, Boone, Campbell, and Kenton. In other words, it called for consolidating general-purpose local government—the "broad-sweeping" approach of regional government.[40] But proponents were not successful in getting local leaders and citizens to accept the idea of regional government. In this sense northern Kentucky is like most other regions of the country that have resisted regional government.[41] Probably because of limited success with regional government, the third regional plan did not call for consolidation or merger of general-purpose local governments. Rather, it recommended that a Regional Stewardship Council work through existing organizations to implement Vision 2015 initiatives, which is a regional-governance approach.

Another key difference across the three planning processes was that the definition of northern Kentucky expanded significantly. For the first two processes, the northern Kentucky region was defined as only the three northern counties along the Ohio

River, Boone, Campbell, and Kenton. During the third planning process, Vision 2015, organizers and leaders expanded the definition to nine counties—the three along the Ohio River plus six more counties to the south—Bracken, Carroll, Gallatin, Grant, Owen, and Pendleton. Participation by leaders in nine counties is one of the most significant aspects of Vision 2015, according to Hammons. "We're interconnected and growing together," he said. "We need to plan together and maximize that."[42]

Also, a major distinction of Vision 2015 is that it involved a broader group of individuals, both community leaders and grassroots citizens. Vision 2015 organizers were determined to move beyond the old-boy network, so they made a conscious effort to have men and women from Generation X, born between the mid-1960s and the early 1980s. In order to achieve this, organizers worked with Legacy, a leadership group of twenty- to forty-year-olds that was inspired by one of the initiatives of the Quest process in the mid-1990s. Organizers asked A. J. Schaeffer, a Legacy member and an attorney from Boone County, to cochair Vision 2015 with Dr. James Votruba, president of Northern Kentucky University. Five other Legacy members cochaired the action teams, each with an older and more established community leader. "I don't know of any regional planning process in the United States that has been this bold in including 30- to 35-year-olds," said Votruba.[43]

In all, the third planning process received input from about two thousand citizens—about twice as many as the second planning process in the 1990s and at least ten times as many as the first planning process in the 1980s. Vision 2015 organizers increased public engagement through a number of strategies, including a Regional Summit, at which hundreds of citizens used handheld electronic voting devices to register their preferences about the future of northern Kentucky; a public survey, based on the electronic survey used at the Regional Summit, which companies administered to employees and which government agencies and nonprofits administered to clients; a Young Adult Summit, which attracted nearly one thousand high-school students and other youths; meetings in urban neighborhoods, convened by African American pastors in their churches; and meetings convened by a nonprofit organization dedicated to assisting the Hispanic population in the region. According to Hammons, there were two reasons to get input from the many different groups within the community: "We know that the community is made up of many parts, so we were trying to get these perspectives. I think we accomplished that. The other reason is to build buy-in. That remains to be seen."[44]

KEY OUTCOMES IN NORTHERN KENTUCKY

In essence, there have been three regional planning processes in northern Kentucky, running consecutively in various stages for about thirty years, from the early 1980s until the present day. Some strategies and actions that came out of these plans have been more successful than others, both in implementation and, ultimately, in outcomes. The more successful efforts have led to developments in the physical, economic, political, and social environment in the region. As discussed earlier, ideas from the first two planning processes resulted in new roads, commercial buildings, and a convention center in the urban core, which have helped revive and redevelop Bellevue, Covington, Newport, and other cities along the Ohio River. Also, ideas from the three planning processes led to a regional legislative caucus and consensus process for securing state funds for northern Kentucky and consolidated water and sanitation districts. This section describes in greater detail a few of the most successful examples that have supported regional cooperation and resulted in noteworthy changes in the physical, economic, political, and social environment in the region.

Tri-County Economic Development Corporation

The Tri-County Economic Development Corporation, or Northern Kentucky Tri-ED, was created as a nonprofit organization in 1987, based on an idea from the first regional visioning process. This public-private partnership serves as the primary economic-development marketing agency for Boone, Kenton, and Campbell Counties, and its seventeen-member board consists of judge-executives and corporate leaders from these three counties.[45] Initially, local governments and the private sector funded Tri-ED, but in 1995 state legislation provided it with an additional and more permanent funding source from rental-car license fees.[46] Tri-ED has been credited with helping in the location or expansion of 540 companies in northern Kentucky, accounting for 51,750 new primary jobs and $5.2 billion in capital investment.[47] *Site Selection* magazine has named it one of the top ten economic-development organizations in the United States at least five times during the past decade. "Perhaps Northern Kentucky Tri-ED's most enduring legacy will be how its creation ushered in an age of unprecedented community-wide cooperation."[48]

Southbank Partners

The impetus for Southbank Partners began with the desire to bring a convention center to downtown Covington rather than an alternative plan to locate it in suburban Fort Mitchell. In 1995 the Kentucky General Assembly awarded $40 million for the convention center in Covington, and construction was completed in 1998.[49] Southbank Partners was founded to provide more attractions for conventioneers and other visitors to northern Kentucky's urban core, which includes the cities of Bellevue, Covington, Dayton, Fort Thomas, Ludlow, and Newport. Its mission is to assist these cities in "creating their vision for a vibrant riverfront community and helping them to bring vision to reality by promoting and coordinating economic development, facilitating teamwork and collaboration, and providing a unified voice to represent the common needs and interests."[50] In addition to the convention center, another successful project was the saving and renovation of an old railroad bridge across the Ohio River. The Purple People Bridge has become a popular pedestrian link between Newport and Cincinnati and an icon of the urban core's renewed vitality. Southbank Partners' biggest project to date is the Riverfront Commons trail project, a $50 million, four-mile walking and biking path connecting Covington to Bellevue.[51]

Licking River Greenway and Trails

The Licking River spans multiple counties and cities in northern Kentucky, running between Covington and Newport, where it joins the Ohio River. During the regional planning processes in the 1990s and the first decade of the twenty-first century, local leaders identified the Licking River as a prime recreation resource for northern Kentucky if the banks could be cleaned up and access improved. In 2008 the Vision 2015 organization published a master plan for the Licking River Greenway and Trails, and in 2010 local government officials, consultants, and volunteers finalized design standards to assure consistency for the trails.[52] Three local governments along the Licking River—Covington, Taylor Mill, and Wilder—have signed an interlocal agreement to develop 5.2 miles of multipurpose trail. The City of Covington is funding a portion of the trail development out of its general fund and allowing city employees to do some of the work "in-house."[53] There are some significant barriers to extending the trail all along the Licking River, including factories built along its banks during the 1800s and 1900s, but the City of Covington, Campbell County, and the NKADD are working together to apply for state grants for brownfield cleanup.

Regional Stewardship

Participants in both Forward Quest and Vision 2015 looked not only at the local government systems in northern Kentucky but also at the broader political and social context. Specifically, the Vision 2015 report stated, "We must cultivate the next generation of regional stewards who are civic entrepreneurs, integrators, and coalition builders . . . leaders at every level and across every sector who care deeply about overall regional progress and are committed to turning *Vision 2015* into reality."[54] Some strategies include creating a Regional Stewardship Council to lead the implementation of Vision 2015; building and sustaining a culture of civic volunteerism and philanthropy; expanding leadership-development opportunities throughout the region; and increasing the number of women, minorities, and young people in key leadership positions. "Every parent, educator and community member wants Northern Kentucky kids to grow up to be prepared, well-rounded, and civic-minded adults."[55] Children Inc., a nonprofit organization serving young children in northern Kentucky, initiated and led a service learning program that "connects meaningful community service experiences with academic learning, personal growth and civic responsibility"[56] To date, more than 2,400 teachers in northern Kentucky have been trained in service learning principles, and 18,000 children have completed a service learning project.

CHALLENGES IN NORTHERN KENTUCKY

Although there have been some successes of regional visioning and planning in northern Kentucky, there also have been some challenges. According to a few observers, the most important challenge is that not enough has been done to address local government fragmentation, duplication of services, and resulting inefficiencies. In other words, some people want to see further movement toward the merger or consolidation of local governments—that is, regional government. After Quest, the second regional planning process, local government leaders in the city of Florence and Boone County considered the idea of merging, but they "passed on it," according to Votruba, Vision 2015's cochair. In addition, the judge-executives of Campbell and Kenton Counties considered merging their two jurisdictions, said Votruba. "They ran the flag up the pole, but it didn't get anywhere."[57] Mike Hammons, former executive director of Forward Quest and Vision 2015, expressed some regret about not being more assertive in pushing for mergers and consolidations in northern Kentucky. "I think that we backed off too quickly. We avoided tough conversations with those vested in government, such as elected officials and top administrators. We felt like we were going to lose them if we talked about merged government."[58]

It has been very difficult to implement a merger or consolidation strategy even for narrowly defined public services for which a strong rationale or need has been identified. In particular, in the late 1990s Forward Quest's Regional Governance Committee commissioned a study of fire service in northern Kentucky relative to comparable regions. The study, conducted by the NKADD, concluded that northern Kentucky had a large number of fire departments and high per capita spending on fire service relative to other benchmark regions. On the basis of the report, Forward Quest recommended the reduction of the number of fire departments through consolidation and mergers. This became the topic of some controversial stories in the local media, arousing resistance to the idea among local government officials and even questioning of Forward Quest as an organization. Since 2000 there has been only one significant merger of fire departments—Bellevue and Dayton in 2002—although some other lower-level types of cooperation and collaboration have occurred.

In addition, there have been resistance and roadblocks to the implementation of regional approaches for public services that citizens called for during the regional planning processes. For example, one of the key strategies identified in the Vision 2015 process was a regional park system. As discussed earlier, some progress has been made in establishing linear parks and trails along the Licking River. However, there have been some challenges to the implementation of a regional park system on another front. In 2008 the Boone County Fiscal Court put a countywide parks tax on the ballot, which was 2.2 cents for every $100 of assessed value on all taxable property ($22 per year for a $100,000 home). The proposal was tax-rate neutral because other special districts reduced their rates by a total of 2.2 percent, and it would have generated about $2.5 million annually to build and maintain parks and preserve green space across the county. But a grassroots group called Citizens for Lower Taxes was formed specifically to defeat the parks tax, and the levy ended up failing by a huge margin.

Another challenge is that some of the regional approaches and strategies can be seen as adding to the fragmentation—or at least the complexity—of local government in northern Kentucky. As discussed earlier, the Vision 2015 process added six southern-tier counties, expanding the region from three counties to nine. These six counties have a total of twenty municipalities (table 13.2). Most of these local governments represent a small number of citizens; therefore, they can be seen as small parts or

Table 13.2. Municipalities by Population in the Six Additional Southern-tier Counties of Northern Kentucky

County and municipality	Population
Bracken County	
Augusta	1,250
Brooksville	609
Germantown	152
Carroll County	
Carrollton	3,885
Ghent	389
Sanders	256
Worthville	225
Prestonville	174
Gallatin County	
Warsaw	1,834
Glencoe	250
Sparta	211
Grant County	
Williamstown	3,435
Crittenden	2,573
Dry Ridge	2,174
Corinth	189
Owen County	
Owenton	1,476
Monterey	177
Gratz	95
Pendleton County	
Falmouth	2,123
Butler	645

Source: U.S. Census Bureau, "2007 Governments Integrated Directory."

pieces that increase fragmentation, particularly if they operate in a separated, detached, or isolated manner. With only two exceptions (Carrollton and Williamstown), the cities in the six southern-tier counties have fewer than 3,000 residents, and some have many fewer: Gratz, 95; Germantown, 152; Monterey, 177; Corinth, 189; Sparta, 211; Worthville, 225; Glencoe, 250; Sanders, 256; and Ghent, 389.

Further, the various new organizations designed to enhance regional governance may also be adding to the complexity of providing public services and enhancing quality of life in northern Kentucky. During the past twenty-five years a number of re-gional organizations have been created, such as Vision 2015 (formerly known as Forward Quest), the Tri-County Economic Development Corporation (Northern Ken-tucky Tri-ED), Southbank Partners, and Licking River Greenway and Trails. Each of these regional organizations focuses on a targeted area—for example, economic de-velopment for the region, improvement of cities along the Ohio River, or expansion of parks and green space. It should be emphasized that these newer entities have been created on top of existing regional organizations, most notably the NKADD, the Northern Kentucky Area Planning Commission, and even the Northern Kentucky Chamber of Commerce.

LESSONS FROM THE NORTHERN KENTUCKY EXPERIENCE

This chapter has presented a case study of one region in one state—northern Kentucky—where efforts have been made during the past thirty years to move from local govern-ments that are fragmented and autonomous to regional governance that is more cooperative and collaborative. This section offers a few lessons from northern Ken-tucky's experience that could be useful for other regions in the state and the country.

Be as Inclusive as Possible

An important lesson of the second regional planning process in the 1990s was that it should have included a broader group of stakeholders from the beginning. One spe-cific part of the Quest report demonstrates this lesson: an illustration of a proposed marina on the Ohio River in the city of Covington. The marina looked very aestheti-cally appealing, but it was drawn in place of an existing lower-income neighborhood called Eastside. "Eastside residents were shocked to see an artist's rendering had re-placed housing projects with a marina."[59] The proposed marina created considerable controversy and, of course, ended up being the part of the Quest report on which the local media chose to focus. This resulted in negative publicity for the Quest planning process and report.

This was a tough lesson for Forward Quest organizers and leaders, but it was one that they took to heart for the third planning process, Vision 2015. They made sure to invite religious leaders and community organizers from urban neighborhoods in Cov-ington and Newport. As mentioned earlier, Vision 2015 organizers worked with Afri-can American pastors and with leaders of Hispanic nonprofit organizations to convene meetings that would include groups who were not part of the first two regional plan-ning processes.

Another group that was left out of the first two regional planning processes was representatives of the southern-tier counties. Henry Bertram, judge-executive of Pendleton County, said that the six counties south of Boone, Campbell, and Kenton often are treated like a "redheaded stepchild."[60] Vision 2015 organizers made a point of including Bertram and other judge-executives in the third planning process.

Think Big Even in Good Times

In discussing regional visioning and planning, organizers and leaders in northern Kentucky agreed that "big ideas" and "big change" tend to happen in regions that are experiencing crisis or on the verge of crisis. Hammons, former executive director of Vision 2015 and Forward Quest, cited the consolidation of Louisville and Jefferson County as an example. "Louisville was able to achieve consolidated government because it was facing a problem of losing its status as the largest city in Kentucky," he said. "This was the catalyst for change."[61] But northern Kentucky was not facing such a crisis. The region has been strong economically relative to many other regions in the state and the country. Votruba, cochair of Vision 2015, agreed. "Northern Kentucky is a self-satisfied community. Generally, this is a good place to be. It's comfortable; it's affordable," he said. "How do you create a sense of urgency?"[62]

To counter the inertia of a "self-satisfied community," Votruba said that he and other leaders tried to approach the regional visioning and planning process in terms of opportunity cost or foregone alternatives. He said, "The most important question is: Is everything that we now invest in more important than everything we want to invest in?"[63] When Votruba met with community leaders and citizens, he would ask them to consider whether they wanted to continue paying many local governments to provide similar public services or would rather have fewer local governments providing these services more efficiently and invest more public resources in big projects that would make northern Kentucky an even better place to live, work, and play. An example of such a big project is the expansion of outdoor recreation in the region by creating linear parks along the Licking and Ohio Rivers.

Settle for Regional Governance, at Least in the Short Term

Some community leaders in northern Kentucky have felt compelled to address local government fragmentation through merger and consolidation. They believe that regional government is necessary to address significant problems in the region and achieve economies of scale in government. As discussed earlier, Hammons believed that organizers and leaders should have pushed harder for merger of county governments and consolidation of city governments. But scholars have observed that merger and consolidation proposals are being replaced by voluntary partnerships among governments, nonprofit organizations, and the private sector. Northern Kentucky seems to be part of this national trend toward regional governance in lieu of regional government. And it may be that regional government—consolidated governments or metropolitan government—is possible only in times of crisis or near crisis.

After a bad experience with recommendations of regional government during the second planning process in the 1990s, Vision 2015 organizers have decided to move forward with the Regional Stewardship Council as the solution or strategy, at least in the short term. Of course, this council is another form of regional governance, not regional government. But as Votruba indicated, it may offer opportunities for thinking about and discussing regional government in a safer and more thoughtful manner, possibly incorporating the ideas of opportunity cost or foregone alternatives.

NOTES

1. Charles M. Tiebout, "A Pure Theory of Local Expenditures," *Journal of Political Economy* 64, no. 5 (October 1956): 416–24.

2. Paul Teske, Mark Schneider, Michael Mintrom, and Samuel Best, "Establishing the Micro Foundations of a Macro Theory: Information, Movers, and the Competitive Local Market for Public Goods," *American Political Science Review* 87, no. 3 (1993): 702–13; William E. Lyons, Davie Lowery, and Ruth Hoogland DeHoog, *The Politics of Dissatisfaction: Citizens, Services, and Urban Institutions* (Armonk, N.Y.: M. E. Sharpe, 1992).

3. E.g., David C. Saffell and Harry Basehart, *Governing States and Cities* (New York: McGraw-Hill Companies, 1997); Lyons, Lowery, and DeHoog, *Politics of Dissatisfaction*; David Lowery and William E. Lyons, "The Impact of Jurisdictional Boundaries: An Individual-Level Test of the Tiebout Model," *Journal of Politics* 51, no. 1 (February 1989): 73–97; Paul E. Peterson, *City Limits* (Chicago: University of Chicago Press, 1981).

4. E.g., John P. Blair, *Local Economic Development: Analysis and Practice* (Thousand Oaks, Calif.: Sage Publications, 1995); Phillip W. Roeder, *Public Opinion and Policy Leadership in the American States* (Tuscaloosa: University of Alabama Press, 1994).

5. Lyons, Lowery, and DeHoog, *Politics of Dissatisfaction*.

6. Charles S. Clark, "Revitalizing the Cities: Is Regional Planning the Answer?," *CQ Researcher* 5 (October 1995): 897–905; David B. Walker, "Snow White and the 17 Dwarfs: From Metro Cooperation to Governance," *National Civic Review* 76, no. 1 (January/February 1987): 14–27.

7. James G. March and Johan P. Olsen, *Democratic Governance* (New York: Free Press, 1995).

8. H. Brinton Milward and Keith G. Provan, "How Networks Are Governed," in *Governance and Performance: New Perspectives*, ed. C. J. Heinrich and L. E. Lynn Jr., 238–91 (Washington, D.C.: Georgetown University Press, 2000); Laurence J. O'Toole Jr., "Treating Networks Seriously," *Public Administration Review* 57, no. 1 (1997): 45–52.

9. William R. Barnes and Larry C. Ledebur, *The New Regional Economies: The U.S. Common Market and the Global Economy* (Thousand Oaks, Calif.: Sage Publications, 1997); William Dodge, "Regional Problem Solving in the 1990s: Experimentation with Local Governance for the 21st Century," *National Civic Review*, July/August 1990, 354–66; William Dodge, *Regional Excellence: Governing Together to Compete Globally and Flourish Locally* (Washington, D.C.: National League of Cities, 1996); Allan D. Wallis, "Evolving Structures and Challenges of Metropolitan Regions," *National Civic Review* 83, no. 1 (Winter/Spring 1994): 40–53; Neal R. Peirce, *Citistates: How Urban America Can Prosper in a Competitive World* (Washington, D.C.: Seven Locks Press, 1993); Jan Grell and Gary Gappert, "The New Civic Infrastructure: Intersectoral Collaboration and the Decision-Making Process," *National Civic Review* 82, no. 2 (Spring 1993): 140–48; William R. Barnes and Larry C. Ledebur, "Toward a New Political Economy of Metropolitan Regions," *Environment and Planning C* 9 (1991): 127–41.

10. Julie Cencula Olberding, "Diving into the 'Third Waves' of Regional Governance and Economic Development Strategies: A Study of Regional Partnerships for Economic Develop-

ment in U.S. Metropolitan Areas," *Economic Development Quarterly* 16, no. 3 (2002): 251–72; Dodge, "Regional Problem Solving in the 1990s."

11. Dodge, "Regional Problem Solving in the 1990s," 354.

12. Robert Agranoff and Michael McGuire, *Collaborative Public Management: New Strategies for Local Government* (Washington, D.C.: Georgetown University Press, 2003); Kurt Thurmaier and Curtis Wood, "Interlocal Agreements as Overlapping Social Networks: Picket-Fence Regionalism in Metropolitan Kansas City," *Public Administration Review* 62, no. 5 (2002): 585–98; Milward and Provan, "How Networks Are Governed"; O'Toole, "Treating Networks Seriously"; Eugene Bardach, *Getting Agencies to Work Together: The Practice and the Theory of Managerial Craftsmanship* (Washington, D.C.: Brookings Institution Press, 1998).

13. Julie Cencula Olberding, "Does Regionalism Beget Regionalism? The Relationship between Norms and Regional Partnerships for Economic Development," *Public Administration Review* 62, no. 4 (2002): 432–43.

14. E.g., Elinor Ostrom, "A Behavioral Approach to the Rational Choice Theory of Collective Action," *American Political Science Review* 92, no. 1 (1998): 1–22; Robert Axelrod, "An Evolutionary Approach to Norms," *American Political Science Review* 80, no. 4 (1986): 1095–111; Robert Axelrod, *The Complexity of Cooperation: Agent-Based Models of Competition and Collaboration* (Princeton, N.J.: Princeton University Press, 1997); Peter Smith Ring and Andrew H. Van de Ven, "Developmental Processes of Cooperative Interorganizational Relationships," *Academy of Management Review* 19, no. 1 (1994): 90–118; Andrew H. Van de Ven, "On the Nature, Formation, and Maintenance of Relations among Organizations," *Academy of Management Review* 1, no. 4 (October 1976): 24–36; Mancur Olson Jr., *The Logic of Collective Action* (Cambridge, Mass.: Harvard University Press, 1965).

15. Richard C. Feiock, Jill Tao, and Linda Johnson, *Collective Action in Metropolitan Governance: Conflict, Competition, and Cooperation* (Washington, D.C.: Georgetown University Press, 2004).

16. As will be discussed later in this chapter, the most recent regional planning process has expanded this definition from three counties to nine.

17. U.S. Census Bureau, *Governments Integrated Directory* (Washington, D.C.: U.S. Census Bureau, 2007).

18. Ibid.

19. Robert Gioielli, "Suburbs v. Slot Machines: The Committee of 500 and the Battle over Gambling in Northern Kentucky," *Ohio Valley History* 5, no. 2 (2005): 61–84.

20. Robert Gioielli, "Gambling," in *The Encyclopedia of Northern Kentucky*, ed. P. A. Tenkotte and J. C. Claypool (Lexington: University Press of Kentucky, 2009), 384.

21. Ibid., 384–86.

22. Robert Gioielli, "Newport Reform Groups," in Tenkotte and Claypool, *Encyclopedia of Northern Kentucky*, 660–61.

23. Ibid., 661.

24. Ibid.

25. The Committee of 500 did get rid of most illegal gambling; however, part of the "sin" economy remained at the core of Newport's central business district for a few more decades—especially adult bars and theaters that often involved prostitution—as did the label of "Sin City" (Mike Williams, "Newport Second Cleanup," in Tenkotte and Claypool, *Encyclopedia of Northern Kentucky*, 661–62). Again, reformers believed that these types of businesses and

this image were not healthy for the long-term economic interests of Newport, Campbell County, and northern Kentucky. In the 1980s citizen groups, police detectives, and prosecutors worked together on the so-called second cleanup of Newport.

26. Robert Schrage, "Northern Kentucky Area Development District," in Tenkotte and Claypool, *Encyclopedia of Northern Kentucky*, 668–69.

27. Ibid., 668.

28. J. T. Spence, "Enterprise Zones," in Tenkotte and Claypool, *Encyclopedia of Northern Kentucky*, 305–7.

29. Ibid., 306.

30. Mike Hammons, personal communication.

31. Forward Quest, *Quest: A Vison for Northern Kentucky* (Covington, Ky.: Forward Quest, 1997).

32. Ibid., inside front cover.

33. Ibid., 5.

34. Ibid.

35. The Quest report, 1997.

36. Vision 2015, *Vision 2015: Shaping Our Future* (Covington, Ky.: Vision 2015, 2006).

37. Vision 2015 website, http://www.vision2015.org.

38. Ibid.

39. Olberding, "Does Regionalism Beget Regionalism?"; Julie Cencula Olberding, "Toward Evaluating the Effectiveness of Regional Partnerships for Economic Development in U.S. Metropolitan Areas," *International Journal of Public Administration* 32, no. 5 (2009): 393–414.

40. Ibid.

41. Clark, "Revitalizing the Cities"; Walker, "Snow White and the 17 Dwarfs."

42. Hammons, personal communication.

43. Dr. James Votruba, personal communication.

44. Hammons, personal communication.

45. Northern Kentucky Tri-County Economic Development Corporation website, http://www.northernkentuckyusa.com.

46. Dan Tobergate, "Northern Kentucky Tri-ED," in Tenkotte and Claypool, *Encyclopedia of Northern Kentucky*, 675–76.

47. Mark Green, "Northern Kentucky Tri-ED Tallies 28 Industry Company Locations and Expansions in 2011," *The Lane Report*, March 21, 2012, http://www.lanereport.com/3211/2012/03/northern-kentucky-tri-ed-tallies-28-industry-company-locations-and-expansions-in-2011/.

48. Tobergate, "Northern Kentucky Tri-ED," 676.

49. Robert W. Stevie, "Southbank Partners," in Tenkotte and Claypool, *Encyclopedia of Northern Kentucky*, 841–42.

50. Southbank Partners website, http://www.southbankpartners.com.

51. Ibid.

52. Vision 2015 website.

53. Ibid.

54. Vision 2015 report, "Regional Stewardship."

55. Vision 2015 website.

56. Children, Inc. website, http://www.childreninc.org/divisions-of-children-inc/.

57. Votruba, personal communication.

58. Hammons, personal communication.

59. Mike Rutledge, "Vision 2015 Offers Strategy," *Cincinnati Enquirer*, April 6, 2006, accessed April 30, 2012, http://news.cincinnati.com/article/20060402/NEWS0103/604020439/Vision-2015-offers-strategy 2006.

60. Ibid.

61. Hammons, personal communication.

62. Votruba, personal communication.

63. Ibid.

14

Education Reform in Kentucky
Just What the Court Ordered
Richard E. Day and Jo Ann G. Ewalt

This chapter discusses primary- and secondary-education policy in Kentucky and the political and environmental forces that have led to significant policy changes over the years. The primary emphasis of our policy coverage is, first, an analysis of the political decision making that led to sweeping policy changes called for in the 1989 Kentucky Supreme Court decision in *Rose v. Council for Better Education* and implemented through the subsequent education-reform legislation, the Kentucky Education Reform Act of 1990 (KERA). Through these actions Kentucky completely overhauled its school finance system and its curricular and assessment processes. The second emphasis of the chapter is on more recent education-reform measures that have significantly altered some policy approaches found in KERA.

Descriptions of Kentucky's educational system portray a state with great promise that sadly fails time and again to live up to its potential. One observer has noted that the Commonwealth's "one step forward, one step back" approach to education policy demonstrates that the social, political, and legal components of the policy process are almost never fully aligned, and thus substantial educational improvements are rare and largely unsustainable.[1] As we demonstrate, the Kentucky Supreme Court decision declaring the entire public school system in the Commonwealth unconstitutional and the school-reform legislation that followed were significant exceptions to this pattern of uneven gains in school policy and in education finance. Their achievement was due in large part to the synchronization of critical policy elements.

We begin with a brief historical overview of Kentucky's approach to education to provide a backdrop for consideration of the more recent school reforms. We then turn to the political and environmental forces that led to the enactment of KERA. An examination of the transition from the reforms of the 1990s to more recent education policy changes in the Commonwealth follows, and the chapter concludes with a discussion of policy implications of the current state of education reform in Kentucky.

EARLY EDUCATION POLICY IN KENTUCKY

Kentucky was America's first frontier state. Those seeking religious freedom and opportunity flooded the beautiful land with an independent and self-sufficient spirit that spilled over into every aspect of life. Land disputes and dueling were common in the early days as class stratifications emerged. These settlers were not necessarily indifferent about the education of their children, but it was hard for the vast majority who would live their days on the family farm to see the relevance of book learning. The scarcity of qualified teachers and textbooks made it difficult to build good schools, particularly in remote locations.[2] In the cities of the bluegrass region in central Kentucky, where good teachers could more readily be found, public schools were the pride of the community. A formal education in Greek and Latin was left for the children of aristocrats who would grow up to govern this paternalistic border-southern society.[3]

After a handful of failed attempts, a rudimentary tuition-based system of common schools for white children was established. That system was made free by 1848, and a free system for black children was developed by 1874. Kentucky's funding plan was twice ruled unconstitutional in 1882 and 1883 and led to changes in the Kentucky Constitution. Weak public support for taxation and low attendance rates contributed to the slow development of an inequitable system of "good schools" and "bad schools" that compared poorly with schools in the northern states but less poorly with those in other southern states. The impact of the Industrial Revolution caused an increased demand for skilled laborers, but by the late 1800s only 42 percent of Kentucky children were enrolled in school. Knowing that a grammar-school education could no longer provide the skills and knowledge Kentucky's citizens needed in an industrialized society, the so-called Educational Legislature of 1908 passed the County School District Law, which required a high school in every county and compulsory attendance for city children and provided for improved teacher training. Despite these improvements, Kentucky's educational attainment was outpaced by most other states throughout the twentieth century.[4]

Part of the problem was systemic. Until the mid-1900s the Kentucky Constitution required that school funds be distributed on the basis of the school-age population in each district. This requirement ensured more funds for larger, more urban areas. A prevalent disinclination to raise taxes in support of education and a citizenry, at least in rural areas, that demonstrated little concern for its poor educational performance further limited Kentucky's capacity to support primary and secondary education.

EARLY ENVIRONMENTAL FACTORS LEADING TO EDUCATION REFORM

Inequities in Kentucky's school funding laws were deliberately designed into the system from the start. The first law addressing the education of blacks, after the Civil War in 1866, mandated that only taxes collected from blacks could be used to support the education of black children. Because newly emancipated slaves had only recently been considered property themselves, few possessed sufficient wealth from which adequate support could be drawn.

But inequities among the schools were not exclusively the product of racial discrimination. Inequities between white city schools and white country schools persisted as well. For example, Lexington, known as the "Athens of the West," was fortunate for its ability to attract good teachers, which was a major stumbling block for much of the rest of the state. The inability to attract and retain excellent teachers has kept many of Kentucky's rural schools, particularly in the Appalachian region, from matching the progress of other sections.

In *Kentucky v. Jesse Ellis* (1882) a U.S. federal court declared the 1866 law unconstitutional. The General Assembly responded with a funding system that used the same per capita rate for black and white schools, but that plan covered only state funds. Local school districts could still discriminate with their local funds.

When African American taxpayers sued over the continued discrimination, U.S. Circuit Judge John W. Barr ruled in *Claybrook v. Owensboro* (1883) that such discrimination violated the Fourteenth Amendment to the U.S. Constitution. The two systems could remain separate, but funding must be equal, at least on the surface. This case prompted the legislature to amend Section 183 of the state constitution in 1891 to declare, "The General Assembly shall, by appropriate legislation, provide an efficient system of common schools throughout the state." This remains the constitutional mandate today, although, as an earlier treatment of Kentucky politics notes, "This ancient provision was observed principally in the breach, until the Supreme Court of Kentucky in 1989 took the word *efficient* and construed it broadly to mean both equal and adequate."[5]

The U.S. Supreme Court ruling in *Plessy v. Ferguson* (1896) threw the nation into the Jim Crow era with its approval of de jure segregation, which persisted until it was overturned by *Brown v. Board of Education* in 1954. Schools for blacks were funded at roughly one-third the level of white schools. Rural schools were not supported as well as city schools.

At the same time, in Kentucky the General Assembly was establishing a new school funding formula called the Minimum Foundation Program (MFP). The MFP was designed to provide an adequate level of state financial support, but it allowed school districts to sweeten the pot by adding local tax dollars on top of state dollars. But in order for the MFP to work as designed, property in the state had to be assessed at 100 percent of its fair market value, and the program had to be adequately funded. That was not the case in Kentucky.[6]

The undervaluation of property by county tax assessors was such that in one school district it took a tax rate of $1.77 to produce what a $1.10 rate should have produced. As a result there was court action. In *Russman v. Luckett* (1965) the Kentucky Court of Appeals ruled that all property had to be assessed at its fair market value. On average, property in Kentucky was being assessed at 27 percent of its fair market value, so that decision would have had the effect of immediately tripling taxes for every property owner in the state, all of whom had previously benefited from the artificially low assessments.[7]

Convinced that they would lose their elected offices if they were perceived to have raised taxes, the legislature decided to change the tax structure of the Commonwealth instead. Intending that *Russman v. Luckett* would not produce an additional penny of new taxes, the General Assembly passed House Bill 1, known as "the Rollback Law." The act required a lowering of the tax rate to offset any gains through the new assessments and prohibited any local board of education from submitting a budget that would require more revenue than the preceding year.[8]

Intending to equalize school funding, Governor Julian Carroll (1974–1979) was successful in securing passage of House Bill 4, which created the Power Equalization Program (PEP). In 1976 Kentucky's school finance policies were trending toward disequalization when the legislature added the PEP as a second tier to the MFP. The PEP was simply a formula that distributed state funds to school districts in a manner that was inversely proportional to the fiscal capacity of the district, but the PEP lacked sufficient funding to reverse the trend. To participate in the PEP, districts were required to levy taxes at a rate of 25 cents per $100 of assessed property valuation, but state aid assured an equivalent ability to generate revenue up to about half that rate. For example, by the 1985–1986 school year, the equalization rate was 9 cents and grew only to 13 cents in 1986–1987, not enough to alter the trend.[9]

Because the MFP and the PEP were producing modest amounts of support, districts looked for ways to supplement their budgets. But the ability of a local superintendent to raise money locally was dependent on local wealth, so some of Kentucky's poorest districts made the lowest tax effort. At the same time, some of Kentucky's wealthiest districts made the greatest tax effort, a fact that would later prove influential to the courts.[10]

But a more powerful legislative action soon locked the existing inequities in place. During Carroll's absence from the state, Lieutenant Governor Thelma Stovall called a special session of the General Assembly, during which House Bill 44 was enacted. This law required school districts to reduce their tax rates on real property each year such that current revenue could not exceed the previous year's revenue by more than 4 percent. As a direct result, property-tax rates declined 33 percent statewide from 1979 to 1981, even though total assessed value increased.

The impact of property-tax cuts and other factors was that by the 1980s Kentucky had compiled a depressing list of deficiencies: the most illiterate citizenry in the United States (48.4 percent literacy in Appalachia) and a host of dismal education rankings, including forty-third in per pupil expenditure, forty-seventh in per capita spending by state and local governments, forty-ninth in the nation in college attainment, and dead last in adults with a high-school diploma.[11]

The hope of school superintendents in poor districts lay with the PEP, but the lack of funding for the program during the administration of Governor John Y. Brown (1979–1983) failed to reduce disparities between poor and wealthy districts.[12] Patience was growing short.

POLICY INPUTS: SUPPORTS FOR EDUCATION REFORM

On December 31, 1983, incoming state school superintendent Alice McDonald released veteran school administrator and financial expert Arnold Guess from the Department of Education. This freed Guess to act on his long-standing irritation over the inequitable school funding that he knew well but could do nothing about while he was employed by the state. Guess called together a group of superintendents under the name Council for Better Education, and together they challenged the legislature to do more for Kentucky's children. The council lobbied the legislature for change to the education funding system while simultaneously threatening to sue. To fund the potential suit, the council charged the "66" member districts 50 cents per child in average daily attendance (ADA).[13]

The council's members were local leaders, but they held little sway in Frankfort, where some members of the General Assembly considered them "ungrateful" for asking for more money. In fact, the education leaders worried about their own legitimacy, considering themselves "rabble-rousers" who lacked the necessary status to create change. Persuading Bert Combs to represent them was their solution to that problem. As a former Kentucky governor (1959–1963), Combs was familiar with the constitutional mandate that the legislature must produce good schools throughout the state.

Legitimacy also came from the strength of the council's claims about education deficiencies in the Commonwealth and through the help of powerful friends. In addition to the Kentucky press corps, which generally supported the idea of improving the schools, business support for education reform was significant and consistent. The business community pledged not to oppose tax hikes if substantial changes in school policies were made and if public education was held accountable for the results of school reform. The reason for the support was pragmatic: the poor quality of Kentucky's high-school graduates and the alarming dropout rates in the state meant that employers lacked an adequate supply of well-educated employees.[14]

However, education reform in Kentucky will forever be linked to the contemporaneous emergence of the Prichard Committee for Educational Excellence, which was formed in 1983 as a not-for-profit, independent citizen advocacy group. The committee was named for its chairman, Edward F. Prichard, a Harvard-educated Kentucky native whose intelligence and charisma attracted much attention in the 1930s and 1940s. He rose to power in the Franklin D. Roosevelt administration, fell from grace because of a conviction for stuffing a Bourbon County ballet box, and subsequently redeemed himself as a renowned education leader in Kentucky.[15] The purpose of the Prichard Committee was to publicize and build support for efforts to improve schools in the Commonwealth. Through its mix of highly regarded members, which included former governors, business leaders, education experts, and ordinary citizens, and its participation in the study and dissemination of information on Kentucky's poor educational system, the group provided strong support for the council's position.

When the matter reached trial, Prichard Committee executive director Bob Sexton and others contributed undisputable evidence that Kentucky lagged behind most other states in high-school completion, educational performance rankings, wealth of taxable property, per pupil expenditures, average annual salary of instructional staff, ACT scores, and pupil/teacher ratio. The court considered 30 percent of the state's local school districts "functionally bankrupt."[16] In addition, evidence of funding disparities among school districts was undisputable. Jacob Adams notes in an early recounting of education reform in Kentucky:

> The Kentucky Office of Education Accountability (OEA), for example, reported 1989–90 pre-KERA disparities that included the following: property wealth per pupil varied from $39,138 to $341,707. Levied equivalent tax rates varied from 22.9 cents to 111.9 cents. Local revenue per pupil varied from $80 to $3,716. State revenue per pupil varied from $1,750 to $2,753. In addition, the OEA reported that pre-KERA average per-pupil expenditures for instruction varied from $1,499 to $3,709, average teacher salaries varied from $21,718 to $30,379, the number of classroom teachers per 1,000 students varied from 49.5 to 84.7, and the number of teacher aides per 1,000 students varied from 0 to 40.7.[17]

An equally important contribution to the policy dialogue was the Prichard Committee's publication of *The Path to a Larger Life: Creating Kentucky's Educational Future* in 1985. This report proposed major changes in seven areas, including curriculum, teacher preparation, assessment of student performance, and education finance.[18] A *Louisville Courier-Journal* editorial claimed at the time that "the Prichard Committee is an essential anchor [of educational reform], because it is focused on long-term objectives, and, perhaps more important, because it is free of ties to any special political or educational interest."[19]

POLICY INPUTS: DEMANDS FOR EDUCATION REFORM

Because the Kentucky General Assembly historically had been an unlikely source of educational improvements, it is not surprising that the Council for Better Education sought relief from the courts. However, Bert Combs did not like his options in filing a suit. He greatly preferred to file suit in federal court but was precluded from doing so by the 1973 decision in the *Rodriguez* case.[20] In *Rodriguez* the U.S. Supreme Court had closed its doors to equity suits based on Fourteenth Amendment claims, stating that education was not a fundamental right under the U.S. Constitution. That decision forced Combs into state court, where judges were elected and therefore more acutely subject to political pressures.

Governor Martha Layne Collins (1983–1987) called a special session of the General Assembly in 1985 to consider education improvements, but the council concluded that the legislative effort did little to improve funding equity for Kentucky's schools. In November of that year the council sued Governor Collins, the superintendent of public instruction, and the General Assembly, seeking funding equity for its member schools, in *Council for Better Education, et al. v. Martha Layne Collins, Governor, et al.* (Civil Action No. 85-CI-1759). During the trial phase of the case, which took place in Judge Raymond Corns's Franklin County Circuit courtroom, an election pro-duced new state officers, and Governor Wallace Wilkinson (1987–1991), who had promised no new taxes, replaced Collins as a defendant.

Judge Corns reached his momentous decision on May 31, 1988, declaring the state's system for funding schools unconstitutional. The case was appealed to the Kentucky Supreme Court as *Rose v. Council for Better Education*. The council urged the court to uphold the lower-court ruling and find the state's education finance system unconstitutional.

Both Governor Wilkinson and newly elected State Superintendent of Public Instruction John Brock, himself a plaintiff in the suit and a member of the Prichard Committee, dropped their defenses. Thus the main appellants at the Kentucky Supreme Court level were members of the legislative branch, represented through the suit against the Kentucky Speaker of the House and president of the Senate. The appellants argued that the General Assembly had done the best it could because the people of Kentucky did not want more taxes and that judicial notice should be taken that Kentucky was a poor state.

The court disagreed with the appellants but also took judicial relief far beyond that sought by the council. Amazing appellants and appellees alike, the court ruled in *Rose v. Council for Better Education* that the "entire system" of common schools was unconstitutional.[21]

POLICY OUTPUTS: EDUCATION-REFORM POLICY DECISIONS

The Kentucky Supreme Court came to its landmark decision under the leadership of a self-proclaimed activist chief justice, Robert F. Stephens, who assigned the writing of the opinion to himself. He affirmed and expanded the lower court's opinion. The final opinion changed from one closely crafted to address finance issues only to the broader finding that the entire system was unconstitutional.

The heart of the *Rose* case was the court's definition of an "efficient" system of common schools. The court enumerated characteristics of an efficient system as follows: one that was established and maintained by the General Assembly to be substantially uniform throughout the state, was free to all Kentucky children, and provided equal educational opportunity regardless of place of residence or economic conditions. An efficient system must also be sufficiently funded and free of waste, duplication, mismanagement, and political influence, and it must have as its goal the development of seven specified educational capacities. These capacities, which formed a substantial set of skills that outlined the curriculum that each student must learn, included oral and written communication skills; knowledge of economic, social, and political systems and governmental processes; knowledge of mental and physical wellness; a grounding in the arts; and academic or vocational skills.[22]

Less than a year after the Kentucky Supreme Court ruling, the legislature passed the Kentucky Education Reform Act of 1990. Remarkable for its scope, KERA undertook reforms not only in finance but also in curriculum, assessment and accountability, district employment, and school governance. Among the most significant and controversial changes was the replacement of grades K–3 with the multiage/multiability Primary Program and the replacement of letter grades with a report card using a qualitative assessment of student work. School-based decision-making councils with substantial power over matters of curriculum and instruction were created to ensure representation of parents and teachers in school leadership. Rewards were given to schools that excelled on the Kentucky Instructional Results Information System (KIRIS), which used "performance-based" assessments, including portfolios and "open-response items," to assess school performance more than individual student performance. Antinepotism regulations altered some long-standing employment practices. In 1998 KIRIS was replaced by the Commonwealth Accountability Testing System (CATS), which included a national norm-referenced test, de-emphasized open-response questions, and increased emphasis on multiple-choice items.

POLICY OUTCOMES OF EDUCATION REFORM

According to observers at the time and later, the *Rose* decision was one of the most far-reaching education finance equity opinions ever issued, and it has been cited by numerous other courts in similar suits, including cases in Massachusetts, Alabama, New Hampshire, North Carolina, and South Carolina. For a while Kentucky's progressive judicial review was the talk of the nation because the case addressed the content and process of education, as well as its funding.[23]

The *Rose* case launched a new "third wave" of school-reform litigation based on both equity and adequacy as expressed in state constitutions. As a result, the 1990s were notable for the volume of state-level education policy activity that mirrored Combs's approach. States began to shift away from the historical practice of assessing the quality of a given school by input measures, such as per pupil expenditures, the number of volumes in the library, or the percentage of faculty with advanced degrees. The courts' willingness to accept a standards-based approach as judicially manageable created a shift toward educational outcomes, such as the percentage of students achieving a score of "proficient" on the statewide assessment, as the means of determining the adequacy of the school.[24]

Nationally there was another impetus. Richard Herrnstein and Charles Murray's book *The Bell Curve*, published in 1994, argued that among subgroups of students cognitive inequality was largely explained by genetic inequality. This prompted a strong reaction from civil rights activists who complained bitterly that American schools were failing the same kinds of students over and over again.[25] Kentucky civil rights leaders like Fayette County Urban League executive director P. G. Peeples and Rev. Louis Coleman of Shelbyville pressed for improved results for Kentucky's African American students in the state's school districts. This activity culminated in Senator Gerald Neal's Senate Bill 168, which passed in 2002, requiring that student test scores be reported by subgroups and that targets be set for closing achievement gaps.

Before 1990 education policy in Kentucky was typically derived from the interaction of a host of education interest groups with the governor and the legislature. Citizens were accustomed to the lobbying efforts of the Kentucky School Boards

Association, the Kentucky Education Association, and the Kentucky Chamber of Commerce, to name a few of the groups active in education policy development. However, specific performance data regarding the progress of the schools was largely withheld from public view on the argument that student achievement data were confidential.

To provide strong motivation to the schools, KERA included a new kind of high-stakes accountability system based on student achievement outcomes. Rather than using a student-centered approach, the KIRIS test was designed to measure how well the schools were performing. Previous test-score reporting, which had been limited to schoolwide means, had concealed the substandard performance of as much as a third or more of the school population. The combination of high-stakes state assessments and the new practice of publicly reporting student test-score data that were disaggregated by student subgroups proved to be a powerful tool for driving change.

University of Kentucky professor William Hoyt could not confirm educational progress in his 1999 equalization study of KERA, but he did find that "the most dramatic impact of KERA [may have] been its effect on equalizing spending throughout the state."[26] However, once state education funds were allocated to local districts, there were no controls in place to assure an equitable distribution below that level. The state relied totally on local districts to ensure funding equity within the districts. The Kentucky Office of Education Accountability, a watchdog agency created by KERA and attached to the Legislative Research Commission, has analyzed funding equity almost every year since the passage of education reform. It notes that although there have been variations in the level of funding equity between property-rich and property-poor districts, the equity gap was greater before KERA than it has been since.[27]

Confirmation of educational gains would come later. In October 2007 the Kentucky Long-Term Policy Research Center found that on the basis of its interpretation of various national rankings, Kentucky had improved its national ranking from forty-third in 1992 to thirty-fourth in 2005.[28] These results mirror those of *Education Week*'s Quality Counts 2007 Achievement Index,[29] which ranked Kentucky thirty-fourth, and the Morgan Quinto 2006–2007 Smartest State Index,[30] which ranked Kentucky thirty-first. The policy center noted that this progress was largely due to gains in fourth- and eighth-grade science scores and fourth-grade reading scores and a reduction in the dropout rate from 5.6 percent in 1996 to 3.3 percent in 2004.

FEEDBACK AND THE TRANSITION TO POST-KERA: IMPLICATIONS FOR THE FUTURE OF EDUCATION POLICY IN KENTUCKY

The promise of equality of educational opportunity that had guided American schools for a century was effectively replaced by a new goal, equity of student achievement outcomes. State governments passed legislation, adopted new procedures and standards, and pursued policies in a number of areas that galvanized the new emphasis on outcomes over inputs. The question of what constitutes an adequate education for all students was expanded to include strong measures of equity in student outcomes, otherwise known as closing achievement gaps while maintaining high standards. As the court ordered, an efficient system of schools must be adequately funded. Whenever the system is inadequately funded, excellence and equity are forced to compete.

The policy environment is constantly in flux as it reacts to and reflects changes in public opinion, the impact of federalism, advances in technology, new policy actors, and other factors. As Kentucky worked to improve the educational performance of its students and schools, environmental forces of change continued to influence policy decisions. Several important catalysts for policy modifications have taken education in new directions since KERA was passed. One such impetus was federal education legislation.

In 2002 President George W. Bush signed into law the No Child Left Behind Act (NCLB) of 2001. This reauthorization of the Elementary and Secondary Education Act built on a standards-based reform whose roots were found in policy responses to the 1983 report *A Nation at Risk* decrying mediocrity in public schools.[31] In many ways the law was consistent with KERA's emphasis on performance outcomes, and because Kentucky had already implemented its own standards-based education system, much of the legislation fit fairly well with current practices in the state.[32] NCLB requires states receiving federal funding to implement a system of annual assessment of student progress for schools and districts. As initially enacted, the legislation allowed states to set the standards to which they are held accountable, and parental choice was provided for schools that persistently failed to make adequate progress.

However, one of the most controversial elements of the law continues to trip up many schools in Kentucky and across the nation. In order to live up to its name, NCLB requires that improvements in performance be achieved not just for students as a whole but for each subgroup as well. Subgroups include students identified on the basis of poverty, race, ethnicity, disabilities, and limited English proficiency.[33] As noted, Kentucky had already implemented an assessment process that reported student performance for groups of students, but it had not based overall performance results on the progress of all groups. At this writing it is uncertain what new presidential and congressional leadership will mean for NCLB because critics continue to urge revisions to the measure. But a major accomplishment of the law has been its unapologetic national focus on measuring student outcomes and holding schools and districts accountable for those outcomes—a focus Kentucky began in 1990.

Kentucky's legislators have remained consistent in their emphasis on assessment and accountability measures. However, they have embraced a second theme that cuts at a core element of KERA and has ushered in a new era of education policy in the Commonwealth. In recent years lawmakers have been intent on infusing testing with national instruments, and the state has embraced a focus on college readiness, national norm-referenced testing, and national curriculum standards.

KERA set in place a state assessment system that was not intended to facilitate comparisons of Kentucky's students with the performance of other state's students or, for the most part, to permit comparisons with national averages. By 2008, however, lawmakers desiring such comparisons required all high schools to administer the ACT exam to eleventh-grade students and also required two other ACT-supplied tests, one in the eighth grade and one in the tenth grade.[34] The latest KERA revisions have gone much further: Senate Bill 1, enacted in 2009, completely dismantled the Kentucky-based CATS testing system and is phasing in new standards designed to be shorter, clearer, and better focused on students being ready for college, work, and global competition. In developing its new standards, Kentucky is working with forty-seven other states on "common core" standards in language arts, mathematics, science, and social studies.

The Common Core State Standards Initiative is a state-led effort coordinated by the National Governors Association and the Council of Chief State School Officers. In the next few years the forty-seven states that have currently adopted the Common Core Standards will be developing new, shared methods to test and report student progress to parents, teachers, officials, and the general public.[35] In the interim Kentucky will use a temporary test that state education officials say will match the new standards but will not have all the strengths of the longer-term, multistate testing methods.[36]

Using the educational reforms of Senate Bill 1 and its status as the first state in the nation to adopt the common core standards as the foundation of its application, Kentucky took part in a national grant competition to secure funding to pay for its recently enacted reforms. As part of the Obama administration's economic stimulus policy—the American Recovery and Reinvestment Act of 2009—Kentucky and forty-five other states and the District of Columbia competed in a three-phase, $4.55 billion national education grant program called Race to the Top, whereby the federal government sought to encourage education reforms in four areas: new standards and assessments linking primary and secondary education to success in college and the workplace; improved data systems to measure student performance and contribute to formative assessment; enhanced recruitment and retention of effective school personnel, particularly in poorly performing districts; and reduction of the performance gap for the lowest-achieving schools.[37] Kentucky was a finalist in the competition but failed to attract Race to the Top funds in the first two rounds. It was successful in winning funding in the third competition, which was much less funded. In December 2011 Kentucky was awarded $17 million, much less than the $175 million it requested, to implement reforms designed in part to prepare students for more rigorous science, technology, engineering, and math (STEM) course work.

Education Commissioner Terry Holliday attributed Kentucky's failure to win Race to the Top funding in the first two rounds to the General Assembly's refusal to enact legislation permitting charter schools, a criticism echoed by many of the state's Republican lawmakers. As an alternative to regular public school systems, charter schools are publicly funded but are freed from many curricular and decision-making requirements of traditional public schools. According to the Center for Education Reform, forty states and the District of Columbia permit charter schools,[38] but Kentucky's steadfast refusal to allow charter schools has been blamed on strong lobbying from teachers' unions in the state.[39] Democratic lawmakers point to mixed results from charter schools in other states and also worry that charter schools will not work in rural school districts, a concern that is also voiced by the Rural School and Community Trust, a national nonprofit organization that points out that among the ten states that have not authorized charter schools, nine are predominantly rural.[40] Proponents stress the choice aspect of charter schools and point to the long-term failure of some Kentucky schools to show gains in student performance.[41] The rise of charter schools in other states began in 1992 while Kentucky was fully engaged in implementing KERA, and thus at the time charter policy garnered little attention in the Commonwealth. The current charter-school debate in Kentucky is part of the larger movement of state education reforms promoted by the Obama administration, the Bill and Melinda Gates Foundation, and others to improve student success and increase accountability on the part of teachers and schools.

Regardless of the outcome of future efforts to incorporate charter-school authorization in the state, education reform in Kentucky has been remarkable. In the past twenty years Kentucky has reformed its school finance system, reformed its school governance process, updated and improved its core required curriculum, and implemented a statewide assessment and accountability system. Indeed, Kentucky undertook the largest set of school reforms implemented by any one state at one time. As we have shown, those reforms were surprising in a state known for dragging its heels on education policy, and student performance in the state has clearly improved from pre-KERA days.

On many measures, the Commonwealth has left the bottom of the pack and joined states in the middle. However, like all states, Kentucky has faced significant fiscal challenges brought on by the great recession of the past few years, and consistent gains in educational performance have suffered. *Education Week*'s Quality Counts 2011 Achievement Index placed Kentucky thirty-fourth, precisely where it was in 2007. In addition, the recent push to use ACT tests to compare Kentucky's student achievement with that of other states and the nation has clearly demonstrated how far student performance lags. In 2011 students in Kentucky public high schools received an average composite score of 19.6, compared with 21.1 nationally. Table 14.1 shows the challenges ahead for students, parents, educational leaders, and policy makers in helping prepare Kentucky's graduates. Over 40 percent of the Kentucky students who took the ACT exam in 2010 failed to meet the benchmark score in English, and nearly three in four students failed to achieve the benchmark score in mathematics. Scores for reading (43 percent of students achieving benchmark scores) and science (about one in five

Table 14.1. 2011 ACT Benchmarks and Student Performance in Kentucky

Content area	Benchmark	Percent of students meeting benchmark	Average score
English	18	57	19.2
Mathematics	22	28	19.1
Reading	21	43	20.0
Science	24	21	19.6
All areas	—	16	19.6 (composite)

Source: Kentucky Department of Education.

Table 14.2. Kentucky Students Entering College Ready for College-level Work

	2002–2003	2004–2005	2006–2007	2008–2009
Percent ready	55.2	57.6	58.7	61.8
Number of entrants	20,616	19,920	20,965	22,586

Source: Kentucky Council on Postsecondary Education.

students scoring at or above benchmark) also illustrate the magnitude of Kentucky's students who are unprepared for college.[42]

Despite these challenges, Kentucky is making progress in increasing the number of high-school graduates who go on to college and in decreasing the number of students who require remedial classes, as shown in table 14.2, but there is much work still to do. Although 63 percent of Kentucky's 2008 high-school graduates were enrolled in college the next fall, up from 51 percent in 2004, that is still below the national average of 68.6 percent.[43]

To address these issues, Kentucky policy makers are now emphasizing national curriculum standards and school and district accountability in order to increase the number of citizens who are prepared for and succeed in college and the workplace.[44] Although much progress has been accomplished, a troublesome link remains between Kentucky's educational environment before the enactment of KERA in 1990 and the environment that currently exists.

Three decades ago education leaders were worried about uneven funding for Kentucky's schools and students. Today large variations in student performance across the state dominate the policy debate. For example, Louisville's Dupont Manual High School in Jefferson County had the highest composite score on the 2010 ACT test, 24.8, compared with 14.2 for Cordia High School in rural southeastern Knott County. Perhaps as significant, there are wide variations in performance within school districts as well. The three high schools with the lowest 2010 composite ACT scores were in Jefferson County. Kentucky will need to find a way to maintain educational performance in its high-achieving schools while breaking the bonds of high poverty, high unemployment, low completion rates, and low student achievement found in many other schools across the Commonwealth.

When Kentucky embarked on its pioneering education reforms in the 1980s and 1990s, the effort energized a number of education public interest groups, whose memberships included education experts, parents, average citizens, and political, community, and business leaders. These groups, and especially the Council for Better Education and the Prichard Committee, were largely responsible for creating the demands and supports that caused the nation's most sweeping education reform. They acted at the state level, but they had a profound impact on both state and national education policy as Kentucky became the state to watch.

The school-reform movement that produced KERA was made possible by Kentucky's judicial branch, but it would be naïve to conclude that the judges acted in a vacuum. The court's sweeping opinion and the legislation that followed were part of a "constellation of factors" that included broad collaborations among school leaders, citizen groups, the press, governors, and legislators. Moreover, the court's decision supported the General Assembly's desire to strengthen itself against a historical pattern of gubernatorial control, the public expected the legislature to follow the court's directives, and legislators used that political cover to blame tax increases on the court.[45] However, it remains to be seen whether Kentucky will live up to its lofty aspirations. Will a new school-reform movement provide an adequate education, as measured by performance outcomes, for students in every section of the state?

The next era of education policy in Kentucky comes as advances in communications and technology have raised the demand for a better-educated workforce once again. But this new reform movement will be subject to the expectations and conditions set in place by these earlier pioneers: that an adequate education is the fundamental right of each and every student; that the General Assembly is solely responsible for maintaining an efficient system of schools; and that those schools must be equitable throughout the state and adequate to meet the state's goals.

Notes

1. Scott C. Trimble and Andrew C. Forsaith, "Achieving Equity and Excellence in Kentucky Education," *University of Michigan Journal of Law Reform* 28, no. 3 (1995): 604–5.

2. Daniel Drake, *Pioneer Education and Life* (Cedar Rapids, Iowa: Torch Press, 1939): 141–62.

3. Thomas D. Clark, *A History of Kentucky* (Lexington, Ky.: John Bradford Press, 1954), 213–16.

4. Thomas D. Clark, *A History of Kentucky* (Ashland, Ky.: Jesse Stuart Foundation, 1988), 366–67; Richard E. Day, "Each Child, Every Child: The Story of the Council for Better Education, Equity and Adequacy in Kentucky's Schools," Ed.D. diss., University of Kentucky, 2003.

5. Penny M. Miller, *Kentucky Politics and Government: Do We Stand United?* (Lincoln: University of Nebraska Press, 1994), 249.

6. Richard E. Day, "Bert Combs and the Council for Better Education: Catalysts for School Reform," *Register of the Kentucky Historical Society* 109, no. 1 (Winter 2011): 33–36, http://works.bepress.com/richard_day/4.

7. *Russman v. Luckett*, 391 S.W.2d 694 (1965); Trimble and Forsaith, "Achieving Equity and Excellence in Kentucky Education," 601–4.

8. Kentucky Revised Statutes 160.470 (1965).

9. Trimble and Forsaith, "Achieving Equity and Excellence in Kentucky Education," 3.

10. J. E. Adams Jr. and W. E. White II, "The Equity Consequence of School Finance Reform in Kentucky," *Educational Evaluation and Policy Analysis* 19 (1997): 165–84.

11. *Council for Better Education v. Collins*, No. 85-CI-1759 (Franklin County Circuit Court, Kentucky, October 14, 1988). See also Debra H. Dawahare, "Public School Reform: Kentucky's Solution," *University of Arkansas at Little Rock Law Review* 27 (2004): 39.

12. Day, "Bert Combs and the Council for Better Education," 27–62.

13. The number 66 was somewhat mythical in that it represented the level of philosophical commitment rather than actual membership. The number of paid member districts at the time of the trial was sixty, but several districts that were sympathetic to the cause but could

not afford to join were incorporated into the count. See Day, "Each Child, Every Child," 219, 354–64.

14. Molly A. Hunter, "All Eyes Forward: Public Engagement and Educational Reform in Kentucky," *Journal of Law and Education* 28, no. 4 (1999): 490–91.

15. Tracy Campbell, *Short of the Glory: The Fall and Redemption of Edward F. Prichard, Jr.* (Lexington: University Press of Kentucky, 1998).

16. *Rose v. Council for Better Education*, 790 S.W.2d 186, 60 Ed. Law Rep. 1289 (1989), 10.

17. Jacob E. Adams Jr., "School Finance Reform and Systemic School Change: Reconstituting Kentucky's Public Schools," *Journal of Education Finance* 18 (1993): 331.

18. Prichard Committee for Academic Excellence, *The Path to a Larger Life: Creating Kentucky's Educational Future* (Lexington, Ky.: Prichard Committee for Academic Excellence, 1985).

19. Jacob E. Adams Jr., *The Prichard Committee for Academic Excellence: Credible Advocacy for Kentucky Schools* (New Brunswick, N.J.: Consortium for Policy Research in Education, Rutgers University, 1993), 3.

20. *San Antonio Independent School District v. Rodriguez*, 411 U.S. 1 (1973).

21. Hunter, "All Eyes Forward," 496, quotes Debra Dawahare, counsel to plaintiffs, in a July 17, 1993, interview.

22. *Rose*, 790 S.W.2nd, 212.

23. Hunter, "All Eyes Forward," 497.

24. David Hurst, Alexandra Tan, Anne Meek, and Jason Sellers, *Overview and Inventory of State Education Reforms: 1990 to 2000*, NCES 2003–020 (Washington, D.C.: U.S. Department of Education, National Center for Educational Statistics, 2003).

25. Richard J. Herrnstein and Charles Murray, *The Bell Curve: Intelligence and Class Structure in American Life* (New York: Simon and Schuster, 1994), 105–15. See also Christopher Jencks and Meredith Phillips, *The Black-White Test Score Gap* (Washington, D.C.: Brookings Institution Press, 1998), v.

26. William H. Hoyt, "An Evaluation of the Kentucky Education Reform Act," in *Kentucky Annual Economic Report* (Lexington: Center for Business and Economic Research, University of Kentucky, 1999), 36.

27. Marcia Seiler, Pam Young, Jo Ann Ewalt, and Sabrina Olds, *2006 School Finance Report*, Report 336 (Frankfort, Ky.: Legislative Research Commission, 2006).

28. A. Watts, *An Index of Kentucky's Educational Progress*, Kentucky Long-Term Policy Research Center, Frankfort, Policy Note no. 23 (2007), accessed December 5, 2010, http://kltprc.info/policynotes/ pn0023_education_index.pdf.

29. Education Week's Quality Counts 2007 Achievement Index.

30. Morgan Quinto 2006–2007 Smartest State Index.

31. Carl Kaestle, foreword to *Politics, Ideology, and Education: Federal Policy during the Clinton and Bush Administrations*, by Elizabeth DeBray (New York: Teachers College Press, 2006), xii; United States National Commission on Excellence in Education, (Washington, D.C.: United States National Commission, 1983).

32. Kentucky Department of Education, *NCLB Briefing Packets and Reports 2010*, accessed December 6, 2010, http://www.education.ky.gov/kde.

33. Office of the Undersecretary of Education, *No Child Left Behind: A Desk Reference* (Washington, D.C.: U.S. Department of Education, 2002). For other background information on NCLB, see Paul E. Peterson and Martin R. West, *No Child Left Behind? The Politics and*

Practices of School Accountability (Washington, D.C.: Brookings Institution, 2003), and DeBray, *Politics, Ideology, and Education*.

34. Senate Bill 130, enacted and signed into law in 2006, amends Kentucky Revised Statues 158.6453 and implements and provides funding for a statewide standardized college readiness assessment program, which began in 2008. Currently, only a handful of states require all students to take the ACT.

35. National Governors Association Center for Best Practices and Council of Chief State School Officers, *Common Core State Standards* (Washington, D.C.: National Governors Association Center for Best Practices, Council of Chief State School Officers, 2010).

36. Susan P. Weston, *Kentucky's Next Giant Steps*, Prichard Committee, December 1, 2010, accessed December 5, 2010, http://prichblog.blogspot.com/ 2010_12_01_archive.html.

37. U.S. Department of Education, "Race to the Top Fund," accessed March 10, 2011, http://www2.ed.gov/programs/racetothetop/ index.html.

38. Mississippi authorizes charter schools, but to date none have opened. Center for Education Reform, accessed March 3, 2011, http://www.edreform.com/Fast_Facts/Ed_Reform _FAQs/?Just_the_FAQs_Charter_Schools.

39. Heartland Institute, Center for School Reform, "Kentucky Votes Yes on Federal Money No on Charter Schools," accessed March 3, 2011, http://www.heartland.org/schoolreform-news .org/ Article/26853/Kentucky_Votes_Yes_on_Federal_Money_No_on_Charter_Schools.html.

40. Rural School and Community Trust, "Rural Policy Matters," September 29, 2009, accessed March 5, 2011, http://www.ruraledu.org/ articles.php?id=2298.

41. Heartland Institute, "Kentucky Votes Yes on Federal Money No on Charter Schools."

42. ACT benchmark scores are established by ACT Inc. and relate to the probability of passing an entry-level college course in these content areas with a grade of C or higher. Kentucky Department of Education, "2010 Kentucky Graduates ACT Data Released," August 18, 2010, accessed March 13, 2012, http://www.education.ky.gov/KDE/HomePageRepository/News.

43. Council on Postsecondary Education, *2008 College and Career Readiness High School Feedback Reports*, accessed December 8, 2010, http://dataportal.cpe.ky.gov/hsfr.shtm; U.S. Department of Labor, Bureau of Labor Statistics, "2008 High School Grads and College Enrollment," April 29, 2009, accessed December 8, 2010, http://www.bls.gov/opub/ted/2009 /apr/wk4/art03.htm. Readiness statistics beyond 2009 were not available at the time of this analysis.

44. Kentucky Council on Postsecondary Education, *Stronger by Degrees: A Strategic Agenda for Kentucky Postsecondary and Adult Education* (Frankfort: Kentucky Council on Postsecondary Education, 2011).

45. Day, "Each Child, Every Child," 247–48.

15

Hiring Practices in the State of Kentucky
The Ethical Conundrum
Steven G. Koven

Ideals of ethics are grounded in competing perspectives. Principles such as the greatest good for the greatest number, service to the public, and natural law serve as rough guides for ethical action. Ethics as an academic subdiscipline has gained a respectable degree of attention within the fields of political science and public administration. Much of the work in this area refers to universal theories of right or wrong behavior.

Distinguishing right from wrong is an eternal dilemma. In the United States, at the national level, a large literature has been promulgated that denounces ethical transgressions. For example, in the past much has been written about "dirty tricks" and Watergate during the Nixon administration, the secret sale of arms to Iran (Iran-contra) during the Reagan administration, perjury and the Clinton impeachment, abuse of prisoners at Abu Ghraib prison during the Bush administration, and other violations of ethics. Virtually no national administration has escaped unscathed from criticism regarding actions taken during its watch.

Although an enormous amount of literature concerns ethical violations at the national level, a paucity of literature exists on ethics at the state level, and even less that directly addresses ethics in the Commonwealth of Kentucky. This chapter hopes to fill that void through discussing the case for merit, patronage, and neutral competence before embarking on a description of the ethical environment in the Commonwealth and identifying specific ethical controversies. Conclusions are offered in regard to instilling the ethos of merit in Kentucky and how doing so may change perceptions of government in the state.

THE CASE FOR MERIT

Advocates of merit argue that the spoils system principally advanced the interests of a relatively few individuals without much regard for the welfare of the vast majority.[1]

Merit or an ethos of "neutral competence" was viewed as an antidote to the corruption of spoils. The English scholar Lord James Bryce noted in 1893 that machines in America forged client-patron relationships similar to those that existed in ancient Rome and between vassals and lords in the Middle Ages. Patronage was at the heart of the political machine. Dependents linked to the machine boss desired wealth or at least a livelihood.[2] Machines handed out lucrative contracts and "no-show" jobs.

Over time political machines became synonymous with excessive graft and corruption. For example, Boss Tweed of New York City's Tammany Hall was renowned for his plundering of public funds. In 1861, when Tweed became chair of the New York County Democratic Central Committee, he was penniless. By 1870, however, he claimed to have a net worth of $20 million. Tweed was the third-largest landowner in New York City, occupied a mansion on Fifth Avenue, and owned another expensive home in Greenwich, Connecticut. As his wealth grew, people began to question how a public servant earning a salary of $7,500 a year could afford such an extravagant lifestyle.[3]

The federal Civil Service Act of 1883 (also known as the Pendleton Act) was initiated in an effort to jettison patronage and replace it with the ethos of "neutral competence." Initially the objective of the Pendleton Act was to limit the power of political executives and give authority to experts who, if they did not actually appoint personnel, at least could screen applicants. Eventually the Civil Service Commission extended its influence into dismissals, promotions, and position classification.[4]

The Civil Service Reform Act of 1883 in effect introduced a British type of civil service system into the United States. This reform legislation created the Civil Service Commission to (1) administer competitive examinations, (2) allow for entrance into public service at the bottom, (3) establish a full-scale career service, and (4) disallow the use of offices for political purposes. The Civil Service Act allowed for admission to the federal service on the basis of open, competitive testing. It prohibited firing of federal workers for any reason other than cause and provided that federal employees could not be coerced to make contributions.[5]

Proponents of merit hiring asserted that it would (1) distribute offices more rationally than the spoils system, (2) provide a remedy for corruption, and (3) lay a foundation for the development of technical expertise.[6] Merit supporters derided the spoils system for limiting government effectiveness, raising taxes, and reducing social spending.[7]

During the Progressive Era (1890s–1920s) advocates of reform viewed patronage as an inherently unproductive, destructive, "evil" activity that could not contribute to the progress or improvement of society.[8] Patronage was perceived as constituting a direct challenge to competence.[9] Feeney and Kingsley contend, "Patronage enfeebles, debases, and demoralizes government employees" because even when people hired under patronage are qualified, they may cover up problems to protect political benefactors or fail to work hard because their benefactor will protect them.[10]

Patronage is not a vestige of the past but an ongoing phenomenon. The administration of George W. Bush provides numerous examples of patronage hiring. Michael

Brown, the head of the Federal Emergency Management Agency (FEMA), is widely recognized as the poster child for what can go wrong with patronage appointments. His performance as the head of FEMA during Hurricane Katrina was widely castigated. Brown became the butt of jokes by popular comedians. Comedian Jon Stewart stated, "No word yet on Mr. Brown's future plans, though sources say he does want to spend more time doing nothing for his family." Jay Leno noted, "This is very exciting, you may have heard today President Bush announced a plan to put a man on Mars—the head of FEMA." Damning references to Brown also came from the lips of elected leaders. The president of Jefferson Parish near New Orleans pleaded for Brown's replacement, stating, "Take whatever idiot they have at the top of whatever agency and give me a better idiot."[11]

Other patronage appointments of the Bush administration drew negative attention as well. Monica Goodling, a young attorney who was a graduate of an evangelical law school, was appointed to a powerful position in the Department of Justice. Goodling revealed that while she was at the Department of Justice, she sought information about political leanings of job applicants and asked interviewees about their political beliefs. Highly qualified liberal candidates were more likely to be eliminated for jobs than those with conservative or neutral backgrounds. It was later revealed that candidates who used "leftist commentary and buzz words" in their application essays were disadvantaged.[12]

The hiring of political allies is believed to be relatively common. It has been carried out in varying degrees in the federal government since the beginning of the Republic. Anne Freedman stated, "As long as politicians need to raise money and find workers for campaigns, as long as elected officials have to bargain with legislators and interest groups and work to establish control over the bureaucracy, patronage will exist in one guise or another."[13]

It is interesting that the progressive issue of merit hiring gained so much attention in Kentucky, a state whose image seems to be more tightly associated with moonshine, violence, and tight-knit families than for following the letter of reform legislation. Controversy over hiring nevertheless plagued the administration of Governor Ernie Fletcher (2003–2007). This controversy, however, may have been more about politics than about the desire for ethical purity. Only relatively minor penalties were assessed for merit-law violations discovered while Fletcher was in office. A review of hiring practices and reimbursement at the Kentucky League of Cities is also instructive for mapping the contours of Kentucky's ethical concerns in the early years of the twenty-first century. Both of these affairs addressed monetary issues. One scandal concerned jobs; the second dealt with questionable use of public funds.

It is possible that the socioeconomic conditions of the Commonwealth played a role in the controversies. Jobs with good salaries and benefits are relatively scarce in the Commonwealth. Education levels are relatively low, and poverty rates are relatively high. According to the U.S. Census Bureau, Kentucky's population grew at a slower pace (6.7 percent) between 2000 and 2009 than the total U.S. population (9.1 percent). The proportion of state high-school graduates in 2000 (74.1 percent), as well as the proportion of the population with college degrees or higher in 2000 (17.1 percent), lagged behind respective national averages of 80.4 percent and 24.2 percent. Income levels were relatively low; 2008 median household income was $41,489 in 2000, compared with the national median household income of $52,029. State per capita income in 1999 was $18,093, compared with the national per capita income of $21,587. The proportion of persons living below the poverty level in Kentucky in 2008 (17.3 percent) considerably exceeded the national proportion of 13.2 percent.[14]

Patronage was vigorously attacked by reformers who advanced the case for merit hiring in the public sector. Justification for patronage, however, exists and is an age-old occurrence. Many still adhere to the aphorism "To the victor belong the spoils of the enemy," which U.S. senator William Marcy of New York declared in 1832 in reference to the victory of the Jackson Democrats in the election of 1828.[15]

THE CASE FOR PATRONAGE

Advocates of patronage or the spoils system proclaim that the victors in elections should be able to appoint those who will pursue the winners' priorities and agendas. This allegiance will enhance the ethos of responsiveness to voters' preferences and promote the values of democracy. Andrew Jackson is commonly associated with spoils and ending the rule of the upper classes that followed the American Revolution. Beginning in 1829, Jackson introduced "government by the common man," displacing the "government of gentlemen" that had dominated in the United States since 1789. In making appointments, the nation's first president, George Washington, looked for fitness of character, measured by family background, formal education, and general honor and esteem. Except for education, these traits were based almost entirely on reputation.[16]

When Jackson became president, he replaced many of the nation's bureaucrats with his own appointees. Jackson espoused "democratic republicanism" that stressed the virtue, intelligence, and capacity for self-government of common people. Jackson expressed a deep disdain for the "better classes," which claimed a "more enlightened wisdom" than common men and women. Jackson and his supporters promised to remove impediments to ordinary citizens' opportunities for economic improvement. He advocated free competition in an open marketplace that would ensure wealth distribution in accordance with each person's "industry, economy, enterprise, and prudence." The goal of Jackson was to remove all obstacles that prevented farmers, artisans, and small shopkeepers from earning a greater share of the nation's wealth.[17]

In his first annual message to Congress, Jackson stated that public offices should be rotated among party supporters in order to help the nation achieve its republican ideals. He argued that performance in public office required no special intelligence or training, and that rotation in office would ensure that the federal government did not develop a class of corrupt civil servants set apart from the people. His supporters advocated the spoils system on practical political grounds, viewing it as a way to reward party loyalists and build a stronger party organization. The spoils system opened government positions to many of Jackson's supporters, but critics claimed that the practice was not new, nor was it as sweeping as some desired. Many of the men Jackson appointed to office had backgrounds of wealth and social eminence.[18]

By the time of Jackson's inauguration on March 4, 1829, a number of states, including New York and Pennsylvania, already had well-established political patronage systems in place. For example, in 1828 New York City employees were expected to contribute 6 percent of their weekly pay to the Democratic political organization. In 1882 every employee of the state of Pennsylvania was expected to remit 2 percent of his pay. In the city of Philadelphia expected payments ranged from 3 percent to 12 percent depending on one's salary. In Louisiana state employees contributed a flat 10 percent to the ruling party's campaign chest.[19]

Patronage and its organ of distribution, political machines, have also been defended on the grounds that they (1) humanized assistance to the needy, (2) linked business to government, and (3) provided channels of social mobility for those excluded from typical avenues of advancement.[20] Patronage was also viewed by its supporters as the glue that held political organizations together.[21] At the beginning of the twentieth century Democratic state senator from New York George Washington Plunkitt stated that men were not in politics for "nothin'" and that the republic would fall if the civil service became too powerful. He unequivocally stated that the very thought of a civil service made his "blood boil."[22]

Patronage was viewed by its champions as the "life-blood" of American politics because it promoted intraparty cohesion, attracted voters, and generated campaign contributions.[23] In modern times the use of patronage has been justified because of its ability to overcome what is perceived to be a hostile bureaucracy. In addition, patronage is praised for its ability to facilitate change,[24] for its capability to enhance innovation,[25] for furthering representation,[26] and for mitigating negative perceptions of the civil service.[27] Policy redirection by political appointees is a desirable outcome from the perspective that when the people speak, policies should be implemented that reflect their ideals. According to this mind-set, elected leaders should have latitude in appointing officials to direct unresponsive bureaucrats.

Modern-day leaders have often used patronage in order to further their ideological worldview. For example, the Nixon administration sought to use political appointees to weaken a perceived liberal orientation of Washington bureaucrats. The Reagan administration attempted to weaken the regulatory power of bureaucrats and advance business interests. As an example of such action, Harris and Milkis identify Reagan's appointments of like-minded persons to regulatory commissions (such as the Federal Trade Commission and the Federal Communications Commission) that weakened oversight.[28] Reagan also appointed officials with conservative philosophies (such as James Watt, the antienvironmental secretary of the interior) to important positions. Similarly, the Clinton administration used political appointments to emphasize more liberal priorities, such as limiting the practice of logging on federal land.[29]

In recent years patronage has taken on a clear ideological bent. Conservative think tanks encouraged President Ronald Reagan to appoint officials who were deeply committed to his agenda. The use of ideologically oriented patronage continued unabated throughout the twentieth century. In 2001 the Heritage Foundation advocated the selection of political appointees on the basis of loyalty first and expertise second. The foundation recommended that the whole government apparatus should carefully consider the role of loyalty in making appointments. The administration of George W. Bush embraced these recommendations and increased the number of political appointees. In addition, the Bush administration often gave preference to appointees who lacked backgrounds in the policy areas for which they became responsible but had strong financial or familial connections to the Republican Party.[30]

Criticism of the merit system grew in the later part of the twentieth century. Critics asserted that the modern civil service had made it increasingly difficult to punish poor performers or to reward talented workers. The bureaucracy became politicized, and some states (Texas and Georgia) eliminated civil service protections in the 1980s and 1990s. Florida eliminated protections for middle managers in 2001. Arkansas, Missouri, North Dakota, Oklahoma, and South Carolina abolished their merit systems altogether.[31]

The debate over merit (neutral competence) versus patronage (spoils system) reared its head in Kentucky during the administration of Governor Ernie Fletcher. The debate appeared to be partisan and politically motivated; however, it revealed attitudes about the acceptability of patronage in the state.

NEUTRAL COMPETENCE IN THE COMMONWEALTH?

Indictments resulting from state hiring practices in 2005 and an audit of spending at the Kentucky League of Cities in 2009 indicate that ethical violations periodically become high-profile issues in the Commonwealth. Viewed from the prism of a political culture with a relatively high tolerance for corruption, the Fletcher patronage scandal seems relatively insignificant. The small fines assigned to the two state officials (Basil Turbyfill and Richard L. Murgatroyd) who were sanctioned by the Kentucky Executive Branch Ethics Commission reflect this perspective. Rather than pushing the ethical envelope, the Republican Fletcher administration appeared simply to be carrying on practices that had been adopted under every Democratic administration in Kentucky since 1971.

Hiring in Kentucky under Fletcher simply adhered to the age-old maxim "To the victor belong the spoils." Governor Fletcher perceived the grave concerns of Attorney General Greg Stumbo as purely political rather than an objective defense of the value of neutral competence. Some indication of the politicization of the hiring scandal is evident in the attorney general's declaration, "I have not in my 20-plus years here in Frankfort seen this type of abuse of the system."[32]

The scandal had notable political ramifications. Governor Fletcher's lieutenant governor, Steve Pence, announced that he would not be the governor's running mate for Fletcher's reelection bid. Fletcher was challenged in the Republican primary by former Congresswoman Anne Northup and businessman Billy Harper. Northup promoted the perspective that Fletcher's involvement in the hiring scandal had made him unelectable. She secured the endorsements of Kentucky senator Jim Bunning and Lieutenant Governor Pence. Fletcher was able to defeat his primary challengers but was soundly defeated in the general election by Steve Beshear, carrying only 41 percent of the vote.

The political ambitions of Attorney General Stumbo became evident when he ran for lieutenant governor with Bruce Lundsford in the 2007 Democratic gubernatorial primary. The Lundsford-Stumbo ticket, however, lost in the Democratic primary to the gubernatorial ticket of Steve Beshear and Daniel Mongiardo. Abuses in hiring receded as an issue of concern after Beshear's election. The one true lesson that appears to have emerged from the patronage scandal is a better understanding of how e-mails may be recovered and used by prosecutors.

Misuse of public funds became an issue in the Commonwealth when the *Lexington Herald-Leader* began to expose spending practices at the Kentucky League of Cities (KLC), an organization that receives public funds. The controversy surrounding the KLC involved the level of remuneration for its officials. In a state where the mayor of the largest city (Louisville) received about $101,000, the executive director of the KLC was receiving an annual salary of $331,000. Conflicts of interest were identified in a report by State Auditor Crit Luallen. The following highlights some of these conflicts:

- The KLC paid $1.4 million for legal services to a law firm where the husband of Sylvia Lovely (executive director of the Kentucky League of Cities) was a partner.
- The KLC spent $28,600 at Azur Restaurant, which was owned, in part, by Sylvia Lovely's husband.
- The KLC made payments of $14,413 to the wife of the chief insurance services officer, who provided decorating services. The spouse was also paid $1,000 to travel to New York City to select artwork.
- The KLC's deputy executive director purchased a vehicle from the KLC vehicle pool for $9,000 when the actual value of the vehicle was at least $15,623.[33]

The state auditor also found that from July 1, 2006, through June 30, 2009, more than $74,000 was charged to credit cards without supporting documentation. Almost $213,000 in KLC spending was questioned on the basis of the documentation provided. Approximately another $13,000 in spending had no documentation at all. It was discovered that KLC staff also benefited from receipt of a retirement bonus that took the form of a "forgivable loan" as an incentive to remain with the organization. It was estimated that the projected monthly pension benefit for Sylvia Lovely at age sixty-five would be $17,725.[34]

The audit led to greater awareness of spending abuses at KLC. This awareness can be viewed as a double-edged sword. One the one hand, exposure can lead to corrective action and behavior more consistent with desires of average citizens. On the other hand, awareness can further alienate citizens from the state or organizations associated with the state. In order to assess the impacts of the hiring and remuneration controversies, a review of the ethical environment of Kentucky is instructive.

ETHICAL ENVIRONMENT IN KENTUCKY

Some literature suggests that a high degree of tolerance for political corruption exists in the Commonwealth of Kentucky. This literature refers to extorting money from bootleggers in the 1970s, mail fraud in the 1980s, and legislative bribery in the 1990s.[35] Images of the Hatfields and McCoys still prevail in many parts of the nation, equating the culture of Kentucky with clannish feuds that produce deadly outcomes.

Some evidence from the first decade of the twenty-first century suggests that the ethical climate may not have changed much from earlier days. For example, the 2002 election in Kentucky gained national attention when two candidates in local sheriff's races were killed. In one of the shootings a political challenger was arrested. In addition to these killings, stories of gunfire, fistfights, and trading OxyContin for votes were reported.[36]

In 2010, eight individuals in Clay County in southeastern Kentucky were convicted of vote buying, mail fraud, extortion, and money laundering. Those convicted included a former circuit judge, a former school superintendent, a county clerk, a county magistrate, a former election commissioner, and a former precinct worker. The vote-buying scheme involved reviewing lists of voters to determine who could be bribed for prices of $30, $40, or $50. Arrangements were made to drive those people to the polls, where precinct workers made sure they voted correctly. According to testimony at the trial, voters were given a sticker or ticket to redeem for payment. The 2010 trial was preceded by earlier convictions in a continuing federal investigation of a county clerk, a mayor of the city of Manchester, a city manager, two council members, an assistant police chief, and a magistrate.[37]

The trading of alcohol and cash for votes is renowned not only in Appalachia but in other areas of the nation. Such selling of votes, as well as promises of jobs or patronage, has traditionally been a staple of well-oiled political machines. In 1832 in New York City, the price for an uncommitted vote was believed to approximate five dollars, which represented two or three days' wages for an ordinary laborer. By 1838 major parties paid nonresidents of the city to vote early and often. Fraud was so rampant that in the 1844 presidential election the combined vote in New York City for the two presidential candidates (James Polk and Henry Clay) was higher than the total number of qualified voters.[38]

During the administration of Governor Ernie Fletcher significant attention was given to abuse of executive power in making appointments. Attention to violations in merit-hiring legislation may be interpreted as a desire to instill greater competence in governance, or charges of violations may simply reflect politics as usual in the state. In the case of politics as usual, charges of abuse serve as a handy mechanism to discredit political opponents. As a prelude to a detailed review of two ethical controversies in the Commonwealth, the following section describes the political culture of the state.

Political Culture of Kentucky

As in other states, some cultural influences are more dominant in Kentucky than others. This cultural imprint is attributed to early patterns of settlement in the state, as well as later patterns of migration. The political culture of Kentucky as well as the culture of other states are depicted in a popular text. Daniel Elazar noted that three qualitatively different subcultures exist in the United States: (1) moralistic culture, (2) traditionalistic culture, and (3) individualistic culture.[39] Many states, including Kentucky, are said to possess a mix of subcultures. In his depiction Elazar characterized Kentucky as a state with a dominant traditionalistic strain but also a strong individualistic strain.[40]

The traditionalistic political culture is viewed as rooted in a paternalistic and elitist conception of the Commonwealth. It reflects an older, precommercial attitude that accepts a hierarchical society as part of the ordered nature of things. The traditionalistic culture authorizes and expects those on top of the social structure to take a special and dominant role in government. This cultural construct tends to be instinctively antibureaucratic because bureaucracies can interfere with the web of interpersonal relationships that lie at the root of the traditionalistic system. Under the paradigm of the traditional culture, bureaucracy should operate under the influence of the established power holders. Power is confined to a relatively small and self-perpetuating group drawn from members of an established elite who often inherit their right to govern through family ties or social position.[41]

In contrast to this view, the individualistic political culture is ambivalent about the role of the bureaucracy. On the one hand, bureaucracy and hiring according to merit are antagonistic to the favor/patronage system that is central to the individualistic culture. On the other hand, organizational efficiency is valued. Such efficiency can result in lower taxes, another outcome that the individualistic political culture values. Under this framework some merit hiring may occur; however, government is still influenced by the appointment of personnel at the upper level. The merit system is molded to meet political demands. Under the individualistic perspective there is likely to be a fairly loose attitude toward the perquisites of office. A fair amount of corruption is expected.[42] Political machines have thrived in jurisdictions noted for their individualistic political culture.

The moralistic political culture emphasizes politics as one of the great activities of humanity in its search for the good society. Good government is measured by the degree to which it promotes the public good in terms of honesty, selflessness, and commitment to the public welfare. Government is considered a positive instrument with a responsibility to promote the general welfare. Under the perspective of the moralistic political culture, the bureaucracy is a useful tool to inculcate desirable political neutrality. A strong merit system is advocated.[43]

Over the years Kentucky has experienced growing pockets of an individualistic political culture in Lexington, along Kentucky's northern border, including Louisville, and in the Kentucky suburbs outside of Cincinnati, Ohio. Moralistic cultural attitudes are thought to be relatively rare in Kentucky and are scattered throughout the Commonwealth.[44]

Cultural differences have been identified not only between states but also within states. For example, in a study of Kentucky, West Virginia, Missouri, and Maryland, three distinct groups were identified as competing for cultural influence: Bourbons, Mountaineers, and small farmers and urban workers.[45] The wealthy Bourbons were descended from settlers who came from the South Atlantic region and cultivated rich agricultural lands. The poor Mountaineers came to eastern Kentucky and southern Missouri from the highlands of western Virginia and North Carolina. Small farmers and urban workers tended to affiliate with the Republican Party in opposition to the plantation-centered Bourbon Democrats.[46] Sharp social and economic distinctions evolved over time, especially with regard to the poverty of mountain dwellers.

Within the cultural context of Kentucky, a state with a dominant traditionalistic strain and a strong individualistic strain, relatively high tolerance for corruption is expected. On the basis of the political culture of the state, one would not anticipate great concern for "progressive" initiatives, such as merit-based hiring. As a reflection of prevailing state attitudes toward merit principles, the extent to which merit-hiring violations were punished is addressed in one of the two controversies discussed in the following section.

ETHICAL CONTROVERSIES IN THE COMMONWEALTH

As previously noted, it is anticipated that the Commonwealth of Kentucky should possess its share of ethical controversies. Two controversies in particular attracted widespread attention at the turn of the twenty-first century. They addressed the long-standing issues of public sector patronage and misuse of public money.

Fletcher Hiring Scandal

In 2005, two state employees filed complaints alleging that the administration of Governor Ernie Fletcher was filling rank-and-file jobs on the basis of politics rather than merit. The Democratic attorney general of Kentucky, Greg Stumbo, vigorously pursued an investigation into the hiring practices of the Republican Fletcher administration. Seized e-mails subsequently revealed that Local Initiative for a New Kentucky (LINK), an office in Fletcher's administration, regularly reviewed candidates for civil service jobs, a violation of the merit-hiring laws.

Kentucky Revised Statutes (KRS) 18A and 11A address these violations. KRS 18A specifically states that "all appointments and promotions to positions in the state classified service shall be made solely on the basis of merit fitness." The intent of this provision is to "improve morale and motivation of state employees and to gain the maximum utilization of human resources." KRS 11A provides that government decisions are to be made through the established process, and that actual or attempted use of one's official position "to secure or create privileges, exemptions, advantages, or treatment for himself or others in derogation of the public interest at large" is prohibited. The patronage hiring scandal seems to have violated these statutes in that the criterion of merit fitness was disregarded, procedures were ignored, and special treatment was extended in order to enhance Republican electoral prospects.

It was reported that during the Fletcher administration an official of LINK was in frequent contact with the Commonwealth of Kentucky's Transportation Personnel Office. It appeared that members of the governor's office were involved in placement of personnel in government jobs. The governor's office, however, denied wrongdoing and claimed that LINK was merely providing constituent services.

Seized documents later revealed that Kentucky Transportation Cabinet officials regularly tracked the status of job candidates and noted party registration and whether candidates had been interviewed by prominent Republicans. Perhaps most damaging, a four-page memo (labeled the "hit list") was uncovered that included the names of thirty-two state employees. This memo recommended transferring, demoting, or firing twenty-three of these employees. Ten of the twenty-three were merit workers.[47]

A former Transportation Cabinet official testified that state officials compiled names of people who should be terminated, and that the names were given to the personnel director in Governor Fletcher's office. The personnel director stated that he briefed the governor, who in turn supported the recommended terminations. The governor subsequently stated that he had never seen the "hit list" until it became public in the summer of 2005.

In June 2005 a grand jury was impaneled, and nine individuals, including two state Republican Party officials, a Transportation Cabinet official, and a former special adviser to the governor, were indicted on a variety of charges relating to merit hiring. The governor, however, pardoned all individuals charged with violating state merit-hiring laws except himself. Fletcher fired nine officials and closed the agency alleged to be at the heart of the patronage controversy.[48]

Governor Fletcher also contended that the charges leveled by Attorney General Stumbo paralyzed his ability to serve the people of Kentucky, that the attorney general was playing a game of political "gotcha," and that he would not stand by and watch tax dollars being wasted.[49] The governor dismissed the hiring scandal as a "witch-hunt." He acknowledged that people had made mistakes, but he insisted that those people were not criminals.

Before the merit-hiring scandal erupted, Fletcher projected an unsoiled image as a former U.S. Air Force fighter pilot who promised to "clean up the mess" from thirty-two years of Democratic rule. Fletcher was a native of Kentucky, earned an engineering degree from the University of Kentucky, participated honorably in the military, received a medical degree from the University of Kentucky, practiced medicine for twelve years, and served as a Baptist lay minister. His clean image helped him defeat the former governor, Paul Patton, who was mired in a scandal concerning allegations about a sexual relationship with the owner of a state-regulated nursing home, in the 2003 election.[50]

Until Fletcher's election in 2003, the Democrats had controlled the Kentucky governorship since Republican governor Louie B. Nunn's term ended in 1971. This produced patronage hiring under the preferences of the Democratic Party. The director of the Institute for Rural Journalism and Community Issues at the University of Kentucky, Al Cross, noted that Democratic Party governors had left a disproportionate number of party loyalists on the payroll, even in predominantly Republican counties. As a result, roads that should have been built were never started in the Republican counties. This dearth of Republicans working even in Republican counties created pressure on Fletcher to remedy the situation quickly. In his haste to remedy this situation, mistakes may have been made. Cross contended that one of the mistakes of the Fletcher administration was systematizing the patronage process, unlike his more ad hoc Democratic predecessors. This systemization produced evidence of wrongdoing that political opponents could use.[51]

Actual penalties handed down after the hiring scandal were relatively benign. As previously noted, in August 2005 Fletcher issued a pardon for everyone involved in the merit-hiring scandal except himself. Fletcher was indicted on three misdemeanor charges, but the charges were dismissed in a settlement agreement with Attorney General Stumbo. In 2010 the Kentucky Executive Branch Ethics Commission approved settlements with Basil Turbyfill, who was director of Fletcher's Office of Personnel and Efficiency, and Richard L. Murgatroyd, who was Fletcher's deputy transportation secretary and deputy chief of staff. Under the agreements Turbyfill was required to pay $1,500 and Murgatroyd $2,000. The ethics commission found probable cause to charge Turbyfill with the crime of considering political influence in personnel actions for workers who were protected under the state merit system. Murgatroyd was charged with facilitating the selection or approval of individuals on the basis of private political interests rather than qualifications.[52]

The merit-hiring scandal produced real political damage. In 2007 Fletcher's challenger, Steve Beshear, carried 59 percent of the vote in the governor's reelection bid. During the campaign Fletcher criticized the challenger, Beshear, for his position in support of casino gaming. Beshear had proclaimed that allowing a limited number of casinos at racetracks and at offtrack sites would generate about $500 million in additional tax revenue that could go toward health care and education. Fletcher aired television ads vilifying casinos, saying that if they were legalized in Kentucky, they would bring a number of social ills, including divorce, suicide, and prostitution. Fletcher claimed that casinos would change the state's values and send the wrong message to children about easy money.[53] The ads were not successful, and Beshear went on to electoral victory. It did appear that the merit-hiring controversy played some role in Fletcher's electoral defeat.[54]

MISUSE OF PUBLIC MONEY AT THE KENTUCKY LEAGUE OF CITIES

Patronage is associated with hiring less qualified friends and relatives for well-paying positions. It is also associated with abusing public money and using one's position of public trust for personal gain. The issue of abuse of one's position and use of public money for personal gain arose in the spending controversy involving officers of the Kentucky League of Cities.

In 2009 the *Lexington Herald-Leader* newspaper requested records of the KLC under the state's Open Records Act. This request followed stories about questionable spending at Blue Grass Airport and the Lexington Public Library, both of which received public money. Four airport officials resigned or were fired after the *Lexington Herald-Leader*'s Blue Grass Airport stories were published.

In contrast to the purely public Blue Grass Airport and Lexington library, the KLC (formed in 1927) engages in both nonprofit and for-profit enterprises. Supporters of the KLC claim that it provides valuable services to Kentucky cities, including legal advice, insurance protection, and lobbying support. Lobbying activities include attempts to protect city revenue and home-rule authority. In addition, training and education opportunities are provided for elected and appointed officials, as well as staffs.

The KLC is funded through city dues, city insurance premiums, and interest from loans.[55] It is not a public agency, strictly defined, although it includes public entities as members and receives public funds.

The *Lexington Herald-Leader* reported that although the KLC warned Kentucky cities that they were on the financial brink, there was little oversight of league employees who enjoyed generous benefits. For example, the KLC's executive director, Sylvia Lovely, received an annual salary of $331,000 in 2009 and a league-provided BMW and traveled with her husband at the expense of the organization. In 2009 the *Herald-Leader* noted that while cities in Kentucky were cutting services, the top three executives of the KLC had charged more than $300,000 for travel, meals, and other expenses. State Auditor Crit Luallen questioned the lack of oversight by the Executive Board of the KLC and asserted that expenditures of the league should be "transparent and reasonable in nature." Furthermore, the state auditor contended that expenditures should be "tied to quantifiable benefits to the public."[56]

The *Herald-Leader* specifically cited three league executives who had spent a large sum of money on meals at Azur, a restaurant in south Lexington that Bernard Lovely, the husband of the executive director, co-owned. In addition, benefits to league officials included a box at Churchill Downs, Ryder Cup tickets, meals at restaurants in New Orleans and Washington, D.C., travel to Alaska, University of Kentucky football and basketball season tickets, and money to attend President Barack Obama's inauguration and the Bluegrass Ball in Washington, D.C. Travel expenses by the executive director and her husband included more than $8,000 for a trip on business to Dublin, Ireland. The executive director defended her conduct, observing that travel was an important part of her job and included mingling, raising Kentucky's profile nationally, and bringing new ideas home.[57]

In August 2009 Sylvia Lovely announced that she would step down from her position as executive director. Lovely accepted responsibility for the loss of credibility that the league had suffered. She admitted that her organization had "missed cues" about the need for transparency and accountability. The Executive Board of the league accepted her resignation, noting that the decision followed a closed personnel meeting between Lovely and the board. The board released a statement that indicated that her departure came "at the right time." The resignation was announced one day before league officials were to appear before the Kentucky General Assembly's Interim Committee on Local Government. State Auditor Luallen supported the resignation of Lovely, stating that it gave the KLC an opportunity to focus on the future.[58]

In December 2009 state auditor Crit Luallen issued her report, which included thirty specific findings and many recommendations for improvements. Among its conclusions were the following: "KLC's leadership lost sight of its fiduciary duty to the members of KLC and allowed KLC to operate without properly scrutinizing all financial activity. These deficiencies and excesses of KLC's leadership are made all the more significant by the public nature of the organization—its members are cities, its elected leaders are public officials, and its revenue originates from taxpayers. Until public scrutiny was applied, KLC leaders, elected and staff, neglected the standards of oversight, accountability, and trust that the organization should uphold."[59] The state auditor's report criticized the Executive Board for its poor governance of financial resources, its lack of compensation guidelines, bonuses and loans made by officials without Executive Board approval, inadequate board control of credit-card spending, excessive spending for travel and entertainment, and conflicts of interest that contributed to the appearance of improprieties, if not actual ones.[60]

In 1956 Herbert Kaufman wrote that disillusionment with government leads to a quest for neutral competence. The core value of this search is the ability to do the work of government expertly and according to explicit, objective standards rather than personal or party loyalties.[61] Rewards for personal and party loyalty, however, have a long tradition in the United States.

The two examples discussed in this chapter (Fletcher and the KLC) suggest that behavior in Kentucky may not be vastly different from behavior in the nation as a whole. Furthermore, the political culture of Kentucky seems predisposed toward patronage. Any movement toward merit-based principles would seem to require a greater embrace of what Elazar characterized as the moralistic culture.

Patronage has been a recurring issue at the federal level, especially under the administration of George W. Bush (e.g., FEMA and Michael Brown). In recent years many private individuals and corporations have benefited enormously from taxpayer money. For example, the value of the services provided in Iraq through no-bid contracts has been questioned by leading members of Congress.[62] The question of when payments using taxpayer money are excessive, however, remains somewhat subjective. What is clearer is that the *Lexington Herald-Leader* and the state auditor perceived payments to officials of the Kentucky League of Cities in 2009 as worthy of exposure.

Ethically, career government officials and elected leaders have an obligation to serve the public in an efficient, responsible manner. To promote more ethical governance in the Commonwealth of Kentucky, a wholesale change in thinking must occur. As a start, citizens should not think of government jobs as a reward for service or campaign contributions. Elected leaders should not think of the bureaucracy as a trough from which to distribute payments. Political appointees should not consider their government positions as sinecures, attained through family connections, personal relationships, or substantial donations. Organizations that accept public money should not misuse the money even if they think that there is little oversight.

The ideal of merit remains essential for the effective continuance of modern organizations. This ideal, as promoted by the Pendleton Act of 1883, was based on three principles: (1) entry to the system by way of competitive examination, (2) promotion and penalty based on performance, and (3) protection from actions based on partisan political pressure.[63] These principles still hold value. If the Commonwealth of Kentucky is to become serious about the value of merit and the efficient delivery of public services, it should look to propriety in hiring not as a political football but as a means to change perceptions about how government works. Perceptions of corruption and incompetence can be altered over time and replaced with more positive imagery.

NOTES

1. Herbert Kaufman, "Emerging Conflicts in the Doctrines of Public Administration," *American Political Science Review* 50, no. 4 (1956): 1060.

2. James Bryce, "Setting the Stereotype" (1893), in *Urban Bosses, Machines, and Progressive Reformers*, ed. B. Stave (Lexington, Mass.: D. C. Heath, 1972), 8.

3. Steven G. Koven, *Responsible Governance: A Case Study Approach* (Armonk, N.Y.: M. E. Sharpe, 2008), 75.

4. Kaufman, "Emerging Conflicts," 1061.

5. Patricia Ingraham, "Building Bridges over Troubled Waters: Merit as a Guide," *Public Administration Review* 66, no. 4 (2006): 486.

6. Paul P. Van Riper, *History of the United States Civil Service* (Evanston, Ill.: Row, Peterson and Company, 1958).

7. Mary K. Feeney and Gordon Kingsley, "The Rebirth of Patronage: Have We Come Full Circle?," *Public Integrity* 10, no. 2 (2008): 166.

8. Domonic A. Bearfield, "What Is Patronage? A Critical Reexamination," *Public Administration Review* 69, no. 1 (2009): 67.

9. Donald P. Moynihan and Alasdair. S. Roberts, "The Triumph of Loyalty over Competence: The Bush Administration and the Exhaustion of the Politicized Presidency," *Public Administration Review* 70, no. 4 (2010): 576.

10. Feeney and Kingsley, "Rebirth of Patronage," 166.

11. Michael J. Brennan and Steven G. Koven, "Hurricane Katrina: Preparedness, Response, and the Politics Administration Dichotomy," in *Bureaucracy and Administration*, ed. A. Farazmand (Boca Raton, Fla.: CRC Press, 2009), 264.

12. Moynihan and Roberts, "Triumph of Loyalty over Competence," 575.

13. Anne Freedman, *Patronage: An American Tradition* (Chicago: Nelson-Hall, 1994), 177.

14. U.S. Census Bureau, "State and County QuickFacts," accessed September 15, 2010, http://quickfacts.census.gov/qfd/states/21000.html.

15. White House, "Andrew Jackson, 1829–1837," accessed April 5, 2012, http://www.whitehouse.gov/about/presidents/andrewjackson/.

16. Dennis L. Dresang, *Public Personnel Management and Public Policy* (Boston: Little, Brown and Company, 1984), 24.

17. Digital History, "The Presidency of Andrew Jackson, Period: 1820–1860," accessed September 15, 2010, http://www.digitalhistory.uh.edu/database/article_display.cfm?HHID=637.2010/.

18. Ibid.

19. Koven, *Responsible Governance*, 47.

20. Robert Merton, "The Latent Function of the Machine: A Sociologist's View," in *City Boss in America*, ed. A. Callow (New York: Oxford University Press, 1976 [1957]), 25–30.

21. Feeney and Kingsley, "Rebirth of Patronage," 166.

22. George W. Plunkitt, "Reciprocity in Patronage" (1905), accessed August 26, 2010, http://www.panarchy.org/plunkitt/patronage.1905.html.

23. Frank J. Sorauf, "The Silent Revolution in Patronage," in *Classics of Public Personnel Policy*, ed. F. J. Thompson (Oak Park, Ill.: Moore Publishing Company, 1979 [1960]), 153.

24. Jack H. Knott and Gary J. Miller, *Reforming Bureaucracy* (Englewood Cliffs, N.J.: Prentice Hall, 1987), 17, 250.

25. David A. Schultz and Robert Maranto, *The Politics of Civil Service Reform* (New York: Peter Lang, 1998), 106; Robert Maranto, "Thinking the Unthinkable in Public Administration: A Case for Spoils in the Federal Bureaucracy," in *Radical Reform of the Civil Service System*, ed. S. E. Condrey and R. Maranto (Lanham, Md.: Lexington Books, 2001), 72.

26. Schultz and Maranto, *The Politics of Civil Service Reform*, 36.

27. Maranto, "Thinking the Unthinkable in Public Administration," 81.

28. Richard A. Harris and Sidney M. Milkis, *The Politics of Regulatory Change: A Tale of Two Agencies*, 2nd ed. (New York: Oxford University Press, 1996), 6, 114.

29. Bearfield, "What Is Patronage?," 70.

30. Moynihan and Roberts, "Triumph of Loyalty over Competence," 574–75.

31. Feeney and Kingsley, "Rebirth of Patronage," 169.

32. Steven G. Koven, "Patronage in the Commonwealth of Kentucky," *Public Integrity* 9, no. 3 (2007): 289.

33. Thomas McAdam, "The Kentucky League of Cities Scandal," *Louisville Public Policy Examiner*, December 18, 2009, accessed September 16, 2010, http://www.examiner.com /public-policy-in-louisville/the-kentucky-league-of-cities-scandal.

34. Ibid.

35. Lovell H. Harrison and James C. Klotter, *A New History of Kentucky* (Lexington: University Press of Kentucky, 1997), 422.

36. Francis X. Clines, "In Eastern Kentucky, Politics Extends a Bloody Legacy," *New York Times*, June 2, 2002, accessed August 23, 2010, http://www.nytimes.com/2002/06/02/us/in -eastern-kentucky-politics-extends-a-bloody-legacy.html.

37. Bill Estep, "Clay Vote-Buying Included Unindicted Co-conspirators, Prosecution Says," *Lexington Herald-Leader*, February 4, 2010, accessed November 3, 2010, http://www.kentucky .com/2010/02/04/1122911/opening-arguments-begin-in-clay.html; Estep, "Former Clay Clerk Describes $100,000 Worth of Vote-Buying in 2002 Primary," *Lexington Herald-Leader*, March 4, 2010, accessed November 3, 2010, http://www.kentucky.com/2010/03/04/1166415 /former-clay-clerk-describes-100000.html; Estep, "Jury Convicts All 8 Defendants in Clay Vote-Buying Case," *Lexington Herald-Leader*, March 26, 2010, accessed November 3, 2010, http://www.kentucky.com/2010/03/26/1197075/jury-convicts-all-8-defendants.html.

38. Koven, *Responsible Governance*, 47, 67.

39. Daniel Elazar, *American Federalism: A View from the States*, 3rd ed. (New York: Harper and Row, 1984), 115.

40. Ibid., 136.

41. Ibid., 119.

42. Ibid., 116.

43. Ibid., 117, 120.

44. Richard C. Fording, Penny M. Miller, and Dana J. Patton, "Reform or Resistance? Local Government Responses to State-Mandated Ethics Reform in Kentucky," *Publius: The Journal of Federalism* 33, no. 2 (2003): 8.

45. John H. Fenton, *Politics in the Border States: A Study of the Patterns of Political Organization, and Political Change, Common to the Border States: Maryland, West Virginia, Kentucky, and Missouri* (New Orleans: Hauser, 1957).

46. Steven G. Koven, *Public Budgeting in the United States: The Cultural and Ideological Setting* (Washington, D.C.: Georgetown University Press, 1999), 44.

47. Koven, "Patronage in the Commonwealth of Kentucky," 289.

48. Ibid., 288.

49. Ibid., 290.

50. Ibid., 287.

51. Louis Jacobson, "Fletcher Struggles to Overcome Hiring Probe," Stateline.org, September 127, 2007, accessed September 7, 2010, http://www.stateline.org/live/details/story?contentID-243760.

52. Jack Brammer, "Two Final Cases in State Hiring Scandal Settled," *Lexington Herald-Leader*, January 29, 2010, accessed September 7, 2010, http://www.kentucky.com/2010/01/29/1116918/two-final-cases-in-state-hiring.html.2010.

53. Jacobson, "Fletcher Struggles to Overcome Hiring Probe."

54. Associated Press, "Democrat Steve Beshear Unseats Troubled Kentucky Gov. Ernie Fletcher," FoxNews.com, November 7, 2007, accessed September 7, 2010, http://www.foxnews.com/story/0,2933,309137,00.html.

55. Linda B. Blackford, "League Prospers as Ky. Cities Struggle," *Lexington Herald-Leader*, June 7, 2009, accessed September 8, 2010, http://www.kentucky.com/2009/06/07/820342/leagueprospers-as-ky-cities-struggle.html.

56. Ibid.

57. Ibid.

58. Linda B. Blackford, "League of Cities' Lovely to Step Down," *Lexington Herald-Leader*, August 26, 2009, accessed September 8, 2010, http://www.kentucky.com/2009/08/26/908616/league-of-cities-lovely-to-step.html.

59. Crit Luallen, *Examination of Certain Financial Transactions, Policies, and Procedures of the Kentucky League of Cities, Inc.* (Frankfort: Commonwealth of Kentucky, 2009), 33.

60. Ibid., ii–ix.

61. Kaufman, "Emerging Conflicts," 1060.

62. Gail R. Chaddock, "Targeting No-Bid Deals," *Christian Science Monitor*, October 10, 2003, accessed September 16, 2010, http://www.csmonitor.com/2003/1010/p02s01-usfp.html.

63. James P. Pfiffner, "Government Legitimacy and the Role of the Civil Service," in *The Future of Merit: Twenty Years after the Civil Service Reform Act*, ed. J. P. Pfiffner and D. A. Brook (Washington, D.C.: Woodrow Wilson Center Press, 2000), 27–28.

16

Developmental Disability Policies in Kentucky

Edward T. Jennings Jr. and Jeremy L. Hall

We are all familiar with at least some aspects of disability policy. When we go shopping, we see accessible parking spaces reserved for individuals with disabilities. In school we have classmates who are receiving special educational services. When we are walking on the sidewalk, we come to curb cuts designed to facilitate the movement of those with mobility impairments. When we enter buildings, we see electronic doorways designed to make it easier for those with disabilities to enter. We may have worked with someone who required an accommodation, such as modifications in equipment, to be able to function effectively in the workplace.

Individuals with intellectual and developmental disabilities constitute a unique subset of individuals with disabilities. They face many of the same challenges as other citizens with disabilities, but they also face unique challenges and require supportive policy if they are to be integrated into the mainstream of society. Their issues involve health, education, employment, transportation, financial security, civic engagement, and social involvement. An array of organized groups and agencies has mobilized to address these needs and pursue public policies to enable those with intellectual and developmental disabilities to participate to their full potential in society. In Kentucky those groups include the 874 K Coalition, Easter Seals, the Commonwealth Council on Developmental Disabilities (formerly the Kentucky Council on Developmental Disabilities), the Arc of Kentucky, the American Association of Retired Persons, the Kentucky Mental Health Coalition, and others.

Disability policy, broadly defined, includes protecting the rights of individuals with disabilities and offering particular services to that population. An example of the former is the Americans with Disabilities Act (ADA), which seeks to guarantee rights to public services and employment opportunities. An example of the latter is the Home and Community Based Services program, which enables individuals with disabilities to stay in their home or the community instead of entering a nursing home or a long-term-care facility. More broadly, we can think of disability policy as the use of a variety of instruments to foster the development and inclusion of individuals with disabilities in society: rights, services, insurance, subsidies, and representation.

Like policy in many other arenas, disability policy in the United States has evolved in fits and starts, with gradual changes in policy preceding and following sharp punctuations. Kentucky faces major challenges in meeting the needs of the disability population because it has a disproportionate number of individuals with disabilities. Although the state has charted its own course on disability issues, it has also been supported and guided by federal initiatives.

This chapter offers a portrait of the disability population in Kentucky, provides a brief overview of some major disability policies, identifies and discusses the institutions that play a central role in disability policy, describes the evolution and current status of disability policy, and analyzes the political forces in this policy arena. Throughout, the chapter gives special attention to intellectual and developmental disabilities.

CHARACTERIZING THE DISABILITY POPULATION

Who are individuals with disabilities, particularly those with intellectual or developmental disabilities? One approach to this question is to look at what the law has to say. The ADA, approved by Congress in 1990, states, "An individual is considered to have a 'disability' if s/he has a physical or mental impairment that substantially limits one or more major life activities, has a record of such an impairment, or is regarded as having such an impairment." The Civil Rights Division of the U.S. Department of Justice further clarifies that definition:

> The first part of the definition makes clear that the ADA applies to persons who have impairments and that these must substantially limit major life activities such as seeing, hearing, speaking, walking, breathing, performing manual tasks, learning, caring for oneself, and working. An individual with epilepsy, paralysis, HIV infection, AIDS, a substantial hearing or visual impairment, mental retardation, or a specific learning disability is covered, but an individual with a minor, nonchronic condition of short duration, such as a sprain, broken limb, or the flu, generally would not be covered. The second part of the definition protecting individuals with a record of a disability would cover, for example, a person who has recovered from cancer or mental illness.[1]

The Developmental Disabilities Assistance and Bill of Rights Act of 2000 defines a developmental disability as a severe, chronic disability of an individual that results from mental or physical impairment, is manifest before age twenty-two, is likely to continue indefinitely, and results in substantial functional limitations in three or more of the following areas: self-care, receptive and expressive language, learning, mobility, self-direction, capacity for independent living, or economic self-sufficiency. For example, individuals with cerebral palsy, autism spectrum disorders, vision impairment, hearing impairment, or intellectual disabilities are considered developmentally disabled.

LIVING WITH DISABILITIES IN KENTUCKY

There are some important facts to keep in mind in discussing disability policy in Kentucky. First, a disproportionate number of Kentuckians have disabilities, 16.9 percent of the population, compared with 12 percent of the national population in 2009.[2] That means that in 2008, 717,397 Kentuckians had a disability. Second, if generally accepted prevalence rates of 1.5 to 2 percent are used, there are an estimated 60,000 to 80,000 persons with developmental disabilities in Kentucky. Third, Kentucky ranks almost at the bottom among the states in the percentage of individuals with disabilities who are working: 31.1 percent in Kentucky, compared with 39.3 percent nationally.

Individuals with disabilities have significantly lower levels of education than the general population in Kentucky. Only 7 percent have a bachelor's degree, compared with 23 percent of the general population; 31 percent have less than a high-school diploma, compared with 11 percent of the general population. Another way to look at this is that Kentucky ranks forty-ninth in the percentage of individuals with disabilities who have a college degree, but first in the percentage of those with less than a high-school diploma.

In 2007–2008 Kentucky schools served 109,187 students with disabilities, about 16.4 percent of the student population. Nationally, the figure was 13.4 percent of the student population.[3] A major goal of disability advocates has been to integrate children with disabilities into the regular classroom. This is one area where Kentucky has been a leader; in Kentucky 69.6 percent of children with intellectual and developmental disabilities (IDDs) are served in the regular classroom, compared with 57.2 percent nationally.

STATE AGENCIES RESPONSIBLE FOR
DEVELOPMENTAL DISABILITY POLICIES

A diverse set of state agencies exists to promote the interests of individuals with developmental disabilities in Kentucky. Three agencies that make up the Kentucky Developmental Disabilities Network, products of federal legislation and funded with federal appropriations, serve as advocates for those with developmental disabilities. The Commonwealth Council on Developmental Disabilities advocates the interests of developmentally disabled individuals with public officials and sponsors demonstration projects to identify ways to better address their needs. Kentucky Protection and Advocacy uses the legal system to protect and promote the rights of the developmentally disabled. The Kentucky Human Development Institute, based at the University of Kentucky, conducts research and offers services to promote the lifelong well-being of individuals with disabilities.

At least eight state agencies deliver services to individuals with IDDs:

• Department for Behavioral Health, Developmental and Intellectual Disabilities
• Department for Medicaid Services
• Department for Aging and Independent Living

- Department of Public Health
- Department for Community Based Services
- Commission for Children with Special Health Care Needs
- Office of Vocational Rehabilitation
- Department of Education

As should be clear from the names of these agencies, none is devoted exclusively to IDDs. Instead, each has programs that serve many Kentuckians, including those with IDDs.

A brief description will help in understanding the bureaucratic milieu of developmental disability services. Most of these agencies are part of the conglomerate Cabinet for Health and Family Services, which includes most of the state's human services and health-care programs. The cabinet has almost eight thousand employees.

The Department for Behavioral Health, Developmental and Intellectual Disabilities (DBHDID) is an important source of advocacy and services for the developmentally disabled (DD) community. It provides information, services, and support for individuals with needs related to mental illness, developmental and intellectual disabilities, and substance abuse. Perhaps its most important services for the DD community are funding and management of ten intermediate-care facilities for individuals unable to live in the community and Supports for Community Living, which enables individuals with disabilities and others to live in the community instead of being confined to an intermediate-care institution.

The DBHDID houses the independent Commonwealth Council on Developmental Disabilities. The DD Council has twenty-six members, including agency representatives and a majority of individuals with developmental disabilities or their family members. It is a major vehicle for the representation of developmental disability interests in the policy system. The council, funded largely with federal funds through the Administration for Developmental Disabilities, advocates on behalf of individuals with developmental disabilities and sponsors demonstration projects to identify effective ways to address particular problems. For example, in recent years it has funded the Future Is Now Project, an initiative to help families plan for the future of family members with developmental disabilities once the parents are deceased. Through its Public Policy Committee the council has tracked legislative developments, provided the General Assembly and administrative agencies with information and analysis bearing on important issues, and advocated solutions to pressing problems.

The Department for Medicaid Services operates the single largest program in the state government, and individuals with disabilities are significant beneficiaries of that spending. The DBHDID administers a variety of waiver programs that supplement the regular Medicaid program. These waivers provide services that help individuals remain in their communities rather than residing in institutions, such as intermediate-care facilities.

The Department of Public Health develops and operates public health programs for the citizens of Kentucky. These include health programs for the detection, prevention, and treatment of physical disabilities and disease. An important service that Public Health offers the DD community is First Steps, an early-intervention system to provide services to children from birth to age three years who have developmental disabilities.

The Department for Aging and Independent Living has a mission of preserving individual dignity, self-respect, and independence for Kentucky's elders and individuals with disabilities. It operates Aging and Disability Resource Center programs to facilitate access to long-term support options. It supports assisted-living and caregiver support services that benefit individuals with developmental disabilities. It also manages the Consumer Directed Option under Medicaid, which allows consumers to choose their own service providers for nonmedical and residential services.

The public invests heavily in programs that serve the needs of individuals with disabilities, but that investment is mingled with funds serving other individuals needing services, so it is often difficult to determine just how much is spent on the IDD population. Governor Steve Beshear's recommendations for funding of the agencies for fiscal year 2013 are included in Table 16.1.

Table 16.1. Governor's Budget Recommendations for Agencies with Programs for Individuals with Developmental Disabilities

Agency	Recommended funding (millions of dollars)
Cabinet for Health and Family Services	7,900
Federal funds	5,000
State funds	2,900
Commission for Children with Special Health Care Needs	16.4
Medicaid	5,909
Behavioral Health, Developmental and Intellectual Disabilities	445.1
Public Health	396.2
Family Resource Centers and Volunteer Centers	3.6
Income Support	109.9
Community Based Services	930.3
Aging and Independent Living	58.9
Department of Education	4,600
Federal funds	800
State funds	3,800
Division of Learning Services	191.6
Vocational Rehabilitation	56.5
Federal funds	43.4
State funds	13.1

Source: Commonwealth of Kentucky 2012–2014 Executive Budget, accessed June 20, 2012, http://www.osbd.ky.gov/NR/rdonlyres/28C22F94-8799-47C4-9627-3CF8B40C388F/0/1214ExecBudBudIn Brief.pdf.

As can be seen, the biggest part of the budget goes to programs that meet the needs of a large population that includes the relatively small number of individuals with developmental disabilities. For example, the Medicaid budget is $5.9 billion; only a portion of this serves individuals with developmental disabilities. The Department of Education has a budget of $4.6 billion; only $191.6 million of that is committed specifically to programs to address the needs of students with learning disabilities. One other thing is clear: funding for services in Kentucky is heavily dependent on federal grants. Sixty-three percent of the budget of the Cabinet for Health and Family Services comes from federal grants.

Thus what we find is a broad array of agencies whose missions and services are critical to the intellectual and developmental disability community. The sharing of responsibilities among a complex set of agencies leads to administrative and policy challenges, including competing priorities and problems coordinating services and activities. The missions of the agencies, particularly with respect to developmental disabilities, have been shaped by shifting conceptions of government's responsibilities and the reflection of those conceptions in public policy, as is discussed in the next section. We turn now to those patterns of policy.

SHIFTING SOCIAL DYNAMICS AND DISABILITY POLICY CHANGE

Over time, as social conditions have changed, our understanding of disabilities has also changed. As a result, the definition of the policy problems or issues surrounding disabilities has shifted, and this shift has led to significant changes in the Commonwealth's approach to assisting this population. The language that we use to identify those with intellectual and developmental disabilities has evolved over time. Part of that change is a product of demands to treat individuals with respect and avoid demeaning language. Part of the transformation of language reflects a change in our understanding of disabilities, particularly developmental disabilities. What is considered demeaning is socially defined and grows out of the way words are used in society. As a result of efforts to find language that is respectful but accurately captures the individual's disabilities, usage changed through the course of the twentieth century from "idiocy" to "mental retardation" to "intellectual and developmental disabilities." A more recent effort to treat individuals with respect involves terminology related to disabilities. People First Language is an "objective way of acknowledging, communicating and reporting on disabilities. It eliminates generalizations, assumptions and stereotypes by focusing on the person rather than the disability."[4] For many years disabilities were regarded as individual deficiencies that required treatment or that left individuals needing protection and unable to participate fully in society. Therefore, we used to talk about the disabled; now we refer to individuals with disabilities.

A definition of disability as socially understood and culturally imposed has come to supplement the traditional medical definition that identified disabilities as defects in individuals and sought to change the individual through treatment or correction. The result of this shift is movement away from a service-based model to one that emphasizes rights and adapting society to the individual instead of adapting the individual to society.

It is useful to consider disability policy changes over time through a few accepted lenses. Three frameworks provide a useful set of ideas or lenses for thinking about the development of disability policy: incrementalism, punctuated equilibrium, and the advocacy-coalition framework. It is also critically important to understand that Kentucky policies respond to and are shaped by programs and policies of the national government, as the preceding discussion of funding indicates and as we will see later.

One policy theory revolves around the generally incremental nature of policy change identified by Lindblom and Woodhouse and other scholars.[5] From this perspective, policy changes gradually over time; it is seldom characterized by sharp departures from past practices, and policy change is seldom all-encompassing. Taking off from this perspective, Baumgartner and Jones developed punctuated-equilibrium theory in a series of works dating back to the 1990s.[6] Policy is generally stable over time. Friction, in the form of cognitive limits of policy makers, barriers to change inherent in the structure of American government, and a stable balance of political power, inhibits rapid policy change. Most adaptation of policy occurs at the margin; policy evolves gradually over time. Sometimes, however, the friction breaks. Advocates of change manage to create a new image of the policy issues, or a new political coalition is voted into power. Under either of these conditions, we can see rapid change in policy as new initiatives punctuate the policy arena.

This has been the case with disability policy. Disability policy in Kentucky has been characterized by long periods of stability. The now-anachronistic definition of disabilities as defects persisted for decades because scientific evidence to the contrary was not available and perceptions of the disabled as unable to participate in society were strongly held. Even after medical research had filled this gap, policies instituted during this period persisted in an incremental fashion because social understanding of such conditions significantly lags behind scientific understanding. In the earliest days individuals living with developmental and other disabilities were cared for in the home by their families. Over time many became wards of the state and were institutionalized in facilities such as Frankfort State Hospital for the "feeble-minded." In the late 1960s Governor Louie B. Nunn pushed for changes to the way these individuals were treated, and large new institutions to provide intermediate care for the "mentally retarded" were developed to better serve their needs, such as Oakwood, located in Somerset. Kentucky took this step just as a national movement to deinstitutionalize the mentally ill and developmentally disabled gained momentum. As we shall see shortly, that movement has dramatically changed the living arrangements of these citizens nationally and in Kentucky.

Legislative committees, administrators, and courts work out the meaning of existing policies. Budgets expand gradually. New initiatives work around the edges of existing regulations and programs. Advocates seek to protect the gains they have achieved and to develop momentum for further advances. The general public pays little attention to disability policy and even less to developmental disability policy. Occasionally, however, the political momentum for change develops and causes punctuations in this equilibrium. Disability issues receive growing attention from the media and the public. Opposition is converted to support, or sympathetic supporters come to power.

Dramatic policy change follows. This was the case with the adoption of the Americans with Disabilities Act in 1990. That legislation, which built on relatively modest and disconnected prior initiatives, like the Architectural Barriers Act of 1968, marked a dramatic departure from the past and opened the doors to accessibility for millions of American citizens.

Harlan Hahn maintains that the major shifts in disability policy, such as those signified by the Rehabilitation Act of 1973 and the Americans with Disabilities Act of 1990, were made possible by changes in the way we think about disabilities.[7] For years disability had been defined as a medical issue involving various conditions, such as deafness, blindness, or cerebral palsy. Because the problem was defined in that way, solutions were sought in finding ways to improve an individual's functioning. Hahn argues that this kept the focus on distinct disabilities rather than on the common traits shared by individuals with disabilities. A shift in national thinking to the barriers that prevented the full inclusion of disabled citizens opened the window to new policy possibilities. If the problems were architectural or institutional barriers, then the solution was policies that would eliminate barriers. One way to do this was by asserting the rights of the disabled to inclusion and integration in schools, workplaces, transportation, and public accommodations of all sorts. This shift in thinking drew together individuals with disparate disabilities and allowed the formation of an advocacy coalition[8] that included many different disability groups.

As Jacqueline Switzer points out, this shift in thinking led to an emphasis on civil rights for those with disabilities.[9] Consistent with this civil rights model of disability policy are

- requirements of the Urban Mass Transportation Act of 1970 that local transit agencies design public transit so as to be accessible to individuals with disabilities;
- the Rehabilitation Act of 1973 provisions for civil rights protections in federal programs and in hiring by federal agencies and most federal contractors;
- the Education for All Handicapped Children Act of 1975 requiring free, appropriate public education for children with disabilities; and
- the Americans with Disabilities Act of 1990, which provided for inclusion and nondiscrimination in such areas as employment, public accommodations, and telecommunications.

These changes in policy can also be explained in terms of the advocacy-coalition framework.[10] The advocacy-coalition framework developed as part of a theoretical and empirical attempt to understand changes in public policy. Its major components are belief systems and advocacy coalitions. In today's highly networked environment, various groups have coalesced to affect varied dimensions of disability policy; moreover, individuals with disabilities are now more empowered than ever and are playing an active role in determining their own fates. Sabatier's advocacy-coalition framework provides a superior model for understanding the way disability policy change occurs today.

Belief systems are the glue that binds different individuals and groups together in the policy world. They are characterized by deep core beliefs, core policy beliefs, and secondary policy beliefs. Deep core beliefs consist of our fundamental understandings of the world, the values that we hold to be important, assumptions about human behavior, and basic orientation toward the role of government in society. Policy core beliefs define the way we think about particular public problems and issues, the values that we believe are relevant to policy issues, and the basic courses of action we believe government should follow in dealing with problems in a particular policy arena. Both deep core beliefs and core policy beliefs are firmly held and are very resistant to change. Secondary policy beliefs relate to particular polices and tools of government. Although they are important, they are more susceptible to change.

Advocacy coalitions consist of groups that are active in a particular policy arena. The coalitions, made up of interest groups, government officials, scholars, think tanks, and others, contend over the definition of problems and the nature of solutions. They struggle to gain power to guide policy in a particular arena. In the disability policy domain there are many interest groups that advocate on behalf of individuals with disabilities. In *Disabled Rights* Switzer identifies seventy-four groups active on disability issues in Washington, D.C.[11] Most of these are highly specialized. Examples include the American Society for Deaf Children, the Arthritis Foundation, and the United Cerebral Palsy Association. Others, such as the Council for Disability Rights, the National Organization on Disability, and the Society for Disability Studies, have a broad orientation that cuts across particular disabilities. These diverse groups often focus on the needs of their particular constituencies, but they also come together in coalitions to promote broader policy initiatives.

Advocacy coalitions operate in policy subsystems that deal with specific types of policies. These policy subsystems are typically composed of legislative committees, executive agencies, interest groups, and other actors interested in the policy issues addressed by the subsystem. For example, in Kentucky much legislation dealing with developmental disability issues engages the Cabinet for Health and Family Services, particularly the DBHDID; the Health and Welfare Committee of the House of Representatives; the Appropriations and Revenue Committee in the Senate; the Kentucky Developmental Disabilities Network; and various interest groups concerned with developmental disability policy. This subsystem was activated, for example, during the 2011 General Assembly session when legislators considered a statutory change (HB 264) to create a Technical Advisory Committee on Intellectual and Developmental Disabilities to offer guidance to the Advisory Council on Medical Assistance as it advises the Cabinet for Health and Family Services about health and medical services. The creation of the Technical Advisory Committee provides the developmental disability community the opportunity to help shape decision making for the Medicaid program, which is a critically important source of services for individuals with developmental disabilities.

The composition of the policy subsystem for developmental disabilities varies with the particular issue. For example, if the issue involves rights or protections, it typically engages the Senate Judiciary Committee, although the legislation may still originate in the Health and Welfare Committee of the House. That was the case for HB 101 of the 2011 session, which would have created an Adult Abuse Registry of persons found to have abused, neglected, or exploited an adult and would have prohibited institutions serving adults, such as nursing homes, from employing individuals on the registry. That legislation did not advance and was submitted for consideration again in the 2012 session of the General Assembly. Again it failed to advance, apparently because of concerns about costs and the due process rights of individuals who might be listed on the registry.

The disability advocacy coalition often finds itself at odds with business interests and conservative groups that come together to form a coalition to oppose changes in policy that would impose new mandates on businesses or require new government spending. When the Americans with Disabilities Act was under consideration by Congress, for example, a coalition of industry trade associations, such as the National Federation of Independent Businesses and the National Hotel and Motel Association, sought to defeat or weaken the bill.[12] Public transit providers also raised questions about the bill.

Evidence increasingly shapes developmental disability policy, and states often adapt their policies on the basis of the experience of others. An example of this is the decision of the Robert Wood Johnson Foundation and the Office of the Assistant Secretary for Planning and Evaluation in the United States Department of Health and Human Services to initiate a Cash and Counseling demonstration project in three states to assess the effectiveness of a self-direction model for service delivery. As the Cash and Counseling website puts it: "Cash & Counseling offers Medicaid consumers who have disabilities more choices about how to get help at home. Specifically, it gives frail elders and adults with disabilities the option to manage a flexible budget and decide for themselves what mix of goods and services will best meet their personal care needs. In some states, children with developmental disabilities are also served."[13]

The evaluation of the demonstration project in three states found that participants in the experiment were much more likely to have their needs met and to be happy with the services than a control group receiving services through the traditional model of Medicaid-certified home-care agencies.[14] That success led quickly to the expansion of the program to an additional twelve states, including Kentucky.

As mentioned earlier, we can think of disability policy as using a variety of tools to foster the development and inclusion of individuals with disabilities in society, including rights, services, insurance, mandates, and representation. Those tools are reflected in major laws adopted at the federal level that shape Kentucky programs and policies for individuals with intellectual and developmental disabilities, some of which we have already mentioned: the Americans with Disabilities Act of 1990, the Developmental Disabilities Assistance and Bill of Rights Act of 2000 (successor to the Developmentally Disabled Assistance and Bill of Rights Act of 1975), the Individuals with Disabilities Education and Improvement Act of 2004 (originally adopted as the Education for All Handicapped Children Act of 1975), the Rehabilitation Act of 1973, and Title XIX of the Social Security Act (Medicaid). These five acts stand out among thirty-five initiatives of the federal government dating back to 1857.[15] They create a set of rights, mandates, insurance, and services, all of which require engagement of state governments. The movement has been consistently in the direction of inclusion.

Kentucky differs from other states in its level of commitment to deal with IDD issues and the approaches it takes to service provision, but it is important to note that the commonwealth is also quite similar to other states in the array of services it offers. The evolution of policy in Kentucky and elsewhere can be seen in changes in how individuals with developmental disabilities are supported and the opportunities that are provided in the workforce. Some of the changes in these areas reflect changes in service-delivery models, but others are a result of rights granted through laws like the ADA.

One long-term trend in the United States has been to move individuals with IDDs needing residential services out of large state institutions, such as Oakwood in Somerset, Kentucky, and to provide for their care at home and in community-based settings. Policy makers have largely done away with traditional state hospitals. They were replaced by intermediate-care facilities for the mentally retarded (ICF/MR), which are steadily giving way to community-based and home support options, such as those supported through the Home and Community Based Services Medicaid waiver and the Cash and Counseling program. Although federal policies have offered financial incentives to move in this direction, individuals with developmental disabilities have also used the rights granted under the ADA to spur reluctant states to move more actively in this direction. For example, in *Olmstead v. L. C. and E. W.*,[16] the U.S. Supreme Court upheld a lower-court decision in a case initiated by two plaintiffs from a large state institution in Georgia. The courts ruled that the state could not force individuals to receive services in institutional settings if they could be served in a more integrated, community-based setting.

Private and nonprofit organizations have emerged to provide community-based services to this deinstitutionalized population. Nationally, the number of persons with intellectual and developmental disabilities in large state institutions fell from 194,650 in 1968 to 131,345 in 1980 and to 33,795 in 2009. In Kentucky, that number fell from 907 in 1980 to 172 in 2009.[17] The transition has not been uniformly simple, nor has either alternative been without its problems. Allegations of resident abuse by caregivers in Oakwood resulted in the state contracting out the facility's management. Similar incidents have been reported by caregivers working in private firms. In spite of tremendous progress, this population includes individuals who are quite vulnerable, and abuse continues to be a concern.

Recognizing inadequacies in Kentucky's policies to serve the developmentally disabled population, the General Assembly approved HB 144 in 2000. This law mandated the creation of a Commission on Services and Supports for Persons with Mental Retardation and Other Developmental Disabilities. The commission was given the responsibility to evaluate the state's services and make recommendations to move the system toward a person-driven, outcome-based model. The twenty-seven-member commission drew on the insights of hundreds of Kentuckians as it developed a plan to guide the state's efforts. The commission developed a series of recommendations to prevent developmental disabilities where possible and to promote choice and quality of services and access to those services for individuals with developmental disabilities. It also made recommendations on how to finance the changes.

Unwilling to wait for the Commonwealth to follow through on this ambitious plan, Michelle Phillips and three other plaintiffs filed suit against the Kentucky Medicaid program in 2002, asserting that it violated the ADA and the Medicaid Act when it failed to provide services to persons with developmental disabilities in a reasonably prompt manner and in a more integrated community setting when that is their choice. The claims were converted to a class-action suit. In a 2006 settlement, *Michelle P. v. Bird-whistell*,[18] Kentucky agreed to substantially expand services for the developmentally disabled, including increases in funding for supports for community living, increased funding for crisis support services, adoption of a Money Follows the Person program for individuals leaving ICF/MR facilities, and a pledge not to backfill the vacated beds. Under the terms of the Michelle P. Waiver approved by the federal government, an additional ten thousand Kentuckians will receive services through this program.

These policy initiatives are consistent with the push by the advocacy community for self-determination. The Center for Self-Determination advocates a policy environment reflecting the following: "I believe ALL people should have the right to live in their own home and control who assists them via Self-Determination."[19]

Employment is another area in which advocates have pushed for change. The ADA provides legal protection that may help some IDD individuals obtain and retain jobs. Traditionally, individuals with developmental disabilities did not work. With growing recognition of their capabilities and, in some case, the development of assistive technology, more are now able to join the workforce. In Kentucky, as elsewhere, sheltered workshops that received state subsidies and were exempt from minimum-wage laws have provided rehabilitation and training services and employment for many individuals. Growing recognition that developmentally disabled individuals can contribute in the regular market economy has led to a de-emphasis on sheltered employment in favor of supported employment. Supported employment provides services that allow individuals to perform effectively in the workplace and enable them to be integrated into the community. Sheltered workshops often fail to move participants toward regular employment and do nothing to promote inclusion, so the Kentucky Office of Vocational Rehabilitation no longer supports them.

Advocacy for children with autism spectrum disorders (ASD) provides an illuminating case of the pathways that advocates can follow to accomplish their goals. Early in the twenty-first century the parents of children with ASD set out to create a venue to bring attention to the needs of children with ASD and a vehicle for promoting attention to their needs. Representative Scott Brinkman, the father of a child with ASD, promoted legislation to create a state commission on ASD to develop a plan to address ASD in Kentucky. His efforts were rewarded with the passage of legislation in 2005 to create the Kentucky Commission on Autism Spectrum Disorders. The commission was charged with developing a comprehensive statewide plan for an integrated system of training, treatment, and services for people with ASD. The commission, composed of five parents of children with ASD, four representatives of ASD service providers, three elected members of the General Assembly, and nine state agency representatives, first met in August 2005 and forwarded its report to Governor Ernie Fletcher and the General Assembly on October 1, 2006.

The Kentucky Council on Developmental Disabilities (KCDD; now the Commonwealth Council on Developmental Disabilities) was charged with monitoring the implementation of the statewide plan. Its Public Policy Committee took on the advocacy of a major goal of advocates for persons with ASD: the adoption of legislation requiring health-insurance providers to include significant coverage for ASD. In a classic pattern of legislative development, bills were submitted for consideration each year from 2006 to 2010. KCDD's Public Policy Committee and the Autism Speaks Kentucky Chapter led advocacy for the legislation from the outside, and Representative Brinkman mobilized support in the General Assembly. The culmination of these efforts was passage of House Bill 159 during the 2010 legislative session. That statute requires large-group and state-employee insurance policies to provide a maximum annual coverage of $50,000 for children aged one to six with ASD. Children aged seven to twenty-one are eligible for a maximum benefit of $1,000 a month, or $12,000 a year, for ASD treatment. As a story in the *Lexington Herald-Leader* noted, it took Representative Brinkman years of quiet work educating legislators alongside advocates' persistent efforts to move this bill to passage.[20]

This case illustrates something important about DD policy. Its advocates are both Republican and Democratic; they come from all walks of life. The issues here affect individuals from all social classes. And the problems can be addressed with regulatory mandates in many cases, meaning that the impact on public budgets is limited. That is a critical insight at a time when Kentucky, like many other states, is confronting severe budgetary difficulties. Although conservatives' support for private-sector solutions and reduced government means that they will sometimes stand on the opposite side of disability issues from liberals, disability is an arena where the two sides often find a way to work together, as is shown by the vote on the ADA, which passed by a 76–8 margin in the U.S. Senate and a 377–28 margin in the U.S. House of Representatives.

THEMES IN KENTUCKY DISABILITY POLICY CHANGE

Several observations stand out in this discussion of intellectual and developmental disability policy. First, policy develops in a pattern that is sometimes incremental and at other times punctuated by sharp change. In Kentucky an example of policy departing from incremental patterns of change was the move to develop intermediate-care facilities in the 1970s. At the national level, the Americans with Disabilities Act was in many ways a major transformation of policy, but it built on earlier initiatives. That act also reflects the bipartisan nature of much disability policy because it was passed by Democratic majorities in both the House and Senate with significant Republican support and was signed into law by a Republican president. On the other hand, the evolution of community-based care in Kentucky has been slow and incremental.

A second observation that stands out is the role of advocacy coalitions in the development of developmental disability policy. An interrelated group of organizations and individuals consistently advocates for changes in policy to bring rights, services, and support to citizens with developmental disabilities to integrate them to more completely into the mainstream of American society. Change often comes slowly, reflecting the balance of competing policy interests. The coalition works over time to shape perceptions, beliefs, and ideas while building political support for change.

This leads to a third feature of policy making illustrated by the discussion here. Ideas and images are critical. Changing disability policy has often required changing the ways in which individuals with disabilities are perceived. Implementation of the

Cash and Counseling program depended critically on the perception that the developmentally disabled had the capacity to make decisions in their own interest. This represented a substantial departure from traditional views of this population.

Finally, it should be clear that Kentucky policy is shaped in critical ways by the federal government. The federal-state Medicaid program is a major source of funding to address health and living needs of the developmentally disabled and provides the framework within which state options for community-based care operate through waivers to Medicaid rules. In arena after arena, the federal presence shapes and constrains what the state does. This federal-state interaction can be seen in the way in which the Americans with Disabilities Act, a federal law, grants rights that are enforced through legal advocacy on behalf of individuals with developmental disabilities by Kentucky Protection and Advocacy, an independent state entity funded through a federal grant.

NOTES

1. U.S. Department of Justice, Division of Civil Rights, "Americans with Disabilities Act Questions and Answers," 2011, accessed January 27, 2011, http://www.ada.gov/q%26aeng02.htm.

2. Rehabilitation Research and Training Center on Disability Statistics and Demographics (StatsRRTC), "Annual Disability Statistics Compendium, 2010," accessed March 17, 2011, http://disabilitycompendium.org/Compendium2010/index.html.

3. U.S. Department of Education, National Center for Education Statistics, "Digest of Education Statistics, 2009," table 52, accessed January 27, 2011, http://nces.ed.gov/programs/digest/d09/tables/dt09_052.asp?referrer=list.

4. Texas Council on Developmental Disabilities, "Describing People with Disabilities," accessed February 3, 2011, http://www.txddc.state.tx.us/resources/publications/pfanguage.asp.

5. Charles E. Lindblom and Edward J. Woodhouse, *The Policy-Making Process*, 3rd ed. (Englewood Cliffs, N.J.: Prentice Hall, 1993).

6. Frank R. Baumgartner and Bryan D. Jones, "Agenda Dynamics and Policy Subsystems," *Journal of Politics* 53, no. 4 (1991): 1044–74; Bryan D. Jones and Frank R. Baumgartner, *The Politics of Attention: How Governments Prioritize Problems* (Chicago: University of Chicago Press, 2005).

7. Harlan Hahn, "Civil Rights for Disabled Americans: The Foundation of a Political Agenda," in *Images of the Disabled, Disabling Images*, ed. Allan Gartner and Tom Joe (New York: Praeger, 1987).

8. Paul A. Sabatier, "An Advocacy Coalition Framework of Policy Change and the Role of Policy-Oriented Learning Therein," *Policy Sciences* 21, nos. 2/3 (1998): 129–68; Paul A. Sabatier and Christopher M. Weible, "The Advocacy Coalition Framework: Innovations and Clarifications," in *Theories of the Policy Process* ed. Paul A. Sabatier, 2nd ed. (Boulder, Colo.: Westview Press, 2007), chap. 7.

9. Jacqueline Vaughn Switzer, *Disabled Rights: American Disability Policy and the Fight for Equality* (Washington, D.C.: Georgetown University Press, 2003).

10. Hank Jenkins-Smith and Paul Sabatier, eds., "Policy Change and Policy-Oriented Learning: Testing an Advocacy Coalition Framework," *Policy Sciences* 21, nos. 2–3 (1988).

11. Switzer, *Disabled Rights*, 71–74.

12. Ibid., 108–11.

13. Cash and Counseling, accessed January 23, 2011, http://www.cashandcounseling.org.

14. Randall Brown, Barbara Lepidus Carlson, Stacy Dale, Leslie Foster, Barbara Phillips, and Jennifer Schore, *Cash and Counseling: Improving the Lives of Medicaid Beneficiaries Who Need Personal Care or Home and Community-Based Services, Final Report* (Princeton, N.J.: Mathematica Policy Research, August 2007).

15. Committee on Disability in America, Institute of Medicine of the National Academies, *The Future of Disability in America* (Washington, D.C.: National Academies Press, 2007), 31–32.

16. *Olmstead V. L. C.* (98–536) 527 U.S. 581 (1999).

17. K. Charlie Lakin, Sheryl Larson, Patricia Salmi, and Amanda Webster, "Residential Services for Persons with Developmental Disabilities: Status and Trends through 2009," Research and Training Center on Community Living Institute on Community Integration, University of Minnesota, 2010, 5, accessed February 1, 2011, http://rtc.umn.edu/docs/risp2009 .pdf.

18. *Michelle P. v. Birdwhistell.* Not Reported in F.Supp.2d, 2008 WL 631202 E.D.Ky. (2008).

19. Center for Self-Determination, "A Call for Self-Determination," 2010, accessed March 17, 2011, http://centerforself-determination.com/Call_To_Action.html.

20. Beth Musgrave, "Autism Bill Puts Ky. at Forefront," *Lexington Herald-Leader*, April 5, 2010, accessed February 1, 2011, http://www.kentucky.com/2010/04/05/1210475/autism-bill -puts-kentucky-at-forefront.html#more.

17

Economic and Community Development in Kentucky

Jeremy L. Hall and Michael W. Hail

The most enduring policy concern in Kentucky politics is economic development. Governors, state legislators, senators, congressmen, mayors, and county judge-executives all give special attention to job creation and business growth. As Congressman Harold "Hal" Rogers, a Republican representing the Fifth District of Kentucky, often states with determination, his goal is that "no young person should have to leave home" to find employment and make his future.[1] The district Congressman Rogers represents has several counties that are among the most economically distressed in the nation, and his aspiration for the young people of the communities across his district echoes the sentiments of local, state, and federal leaders across the political spectrum. Congressman Rogers often works in a bipartisan effort with local legislators like Representative Rocky Adkins, as well as with Democrat Governor Beshear. When economic development is most successful, it is an intergovernmental policy-making exercise. Creating sustainable employment opportunities and business growth is the central strategic imperative of Kentucky politicians.

Economic development is a systematic intergovernmental and intersectoral effort to influence job creation and income positively in a defined geographic region. Economic development is conceptually distinct from economic growth in that it concentrates on altering the mix of goods and services produced in an economy rather than simply the quantity of such goods and services.[2] In policy making, "economic-development policy" refers to public policy "actions that are intended to affect growth in the economy, either through development (a structural change in production) or growth (an increase in output based on existing production)."[3] Innovation and entrepreneurship are thus central to promoting economic development. This conceptual distinction is often lost in the field of economic-development practice, where administrators and politicians compete with their neighbors to generate any positive gains in employment, income, or tax revenue over the status quo.

309

States have long engaged in efforts to stimulate economic activity within their boundaries, but these efforts were expanded and institutionalized in earnest during the "smokestack-chasing" period beginning in the 1970s. A plethora of local government institutions sprung up to lure industry away from the industrial North to Sun Belt states where labor costs were comparatively lower, unions were less common, and the cost of doing business was lower across the board. Local governments compete for jobs and industry within states just as states compete with each other in what is commonly viewed as a zero-sum game that creates winners and losers with each firm location or relocation. Globalization has resulted in a similar shift of manufacturing—particularly heavy manufacturing—from first-world nations to the third world that has left low-skill, low-wage states with employment gaps and little opportunity for generative growth. Globalization's intensification of competitive efforts has led states to abate taxes and provide additional incentives for prospective employers. As Harold Wolman notes, states and their elected leaders feel pressured to "do something" to stimulate the economy or to frame policies and programs in terms of economic-development potential.[4] There have been many critics of these efforts over time, and many studies have examined the effectiveness of industrial recruitment efforts and have found that they cost more than their resulting benefits.

States can be classified according to their predominant economic-development strategies. Traditional states continue to concentrate on recruitment, while more progressive states have expanded into non-zero-sum efforts that focus on development from within, such as entrepreneurship, tourism, or science and technology development. Kentucky's approach to economic development has been predominantly traditional in spite of recent efforts to capitalize on high-tech innovation. This stems in large part from the nature of Kentucky's economy.

One of the enduring questions of economic development is whether public-sector intervention is capable of stimulating economic activity where it is otherwise lacking and sufficient to do so. The answer depends largely on circumstances surrounding the problem and the investment. An absence of private-sector investment and activity likely indicates economic inefficiencies that public-sector investment will not help overcome. For example, labor costs may be too high or workforce skills too low relative to other locations. Likewise, transportation costs of raw products or finished merchandise may be prohibitive. Still, government investment is capable of stimulating activity, sometimes successfully. Government may help remove barriers or obstacles to development. It may mediate collaboration or assist with exports. In some cases government may simply advocate the advantages of a particular location to footloose firms seeking a place to locate.

HISTORY OF KENTUCKY'S ECONOMY

Kentucky was settled as a result of westward expansion beginning in the late 1700s that eventually led to separation from Virginia and statehood in 1792. Kentucky was considered the "happy hunting ground" by numerous Native American tribes that depended on it for food and fur.[5] These abundant natural resources also made the state attractive to settlers, and the rolling hills of the bluegrass region made it attractive for agricultural development. Limestone soil made the state suitable for horses, which have become one of its most internationally recognized industries. Limestone spring water was also an essential contributor to the state's bourbon industry. The climate in Kentucky and portions of a dozen surrounding states make it one of the few places in the world where burley tobacco can be cured naturally. Consequently, small farms were pervasive across the landscape, where a self-reliant people etched out a subsistence living, producing only agricultural products for export.

One of the areas of need for the developing United States was infrastructure for roads, bridges, and canals. One of Kentucky's senior statesmen, Henry Clay, was the author of the Whig political program to address this need, called the "American Plan."[6] This plan called for federal government investment in infrastructure to facilitate commerce and economic growth. Clay and the Whigs led a vigorous battle throughout the early nineteenth century and eventually achieved a policy consensus and constitutional basis for establishing this policy authority.

The eastern coalfields in the Appalachian mountain range provided the cheap energy source to support industrial development—initially through steam but eventually through generation of electricity. Even today, electricity rates in Kentucky are among the lowest in the nation. The combination of a strong work ethic, cheap power, and available labor made Kentucky appealing as a site for large manufacturing companies. Ford Motor Company opened its truck plant in Louisville in 1955, for example.[7] Over time the income that could be obtained from off-farm employment became attractive and led many to supplement their agricultural income with outside employment. In many cases manufacturing employment enabled landownership where agricultural commodity prices were no longer sufficient to sustain themselves and thereby preserved Kentucky's small-farm model.

With the advances in manufacturing, a supportive business services structure emerged to provide legal, accounting, banking, food, medical, and other necessary services. With further development in transportation infrastructure, telecommunications, and information technology after the emergence of microcomputers and later the Internet, service industries expanded to the point that they have now displaced manufacturing as the state's principal economic-growth industrial sector.

STRUCTURE OF ECONOMIC DEVELOPMENT IN KENTUCKY

A number of actors—formal and informal, governmental and nongovernmental—play a role in carrying out economic development in Kentucky. These actors and their varied roles and responsibilities are introduced below.

Key State-level Actors

The governor is the chief economic developer in the state. Because gubernatorial campaigns often hinge on jobs and the economy, governors have a vested interest (reelection) in stimulating economic growth within the state or luring it from elsewhere.

The governor ultimately acts as a figurehead for development efforts, however, and leaves administration to the Cabinet for Economic Development. As a figurehead, the governor is useful in communicating state government support to firms considering the Commonwealth as a home.

The Kentucky Cabinet for Economic Development (KCED) manages the day-to-day operation of development efforts in the state. Firms interested in the state will likely look to the KCED as the first stop for information on state incentives and programs. The KCED has formal authority to issue tax incentives and other benefits necessary to compete for business on the open market. The KCED works closely with local governments and their development authorities to organize packages that reflect the intergovernmental nature of governance today. Firms potentially receive abatements and other incentives from local governments, regional-development-district economic-development programs, the KCED, and often educational institutions and other entities, such as the Center for Rural Development.

The Department of Local Government (DLG; formerly the Governor's Office for Local Development) is the administrative arm through which government efforts are coordinated across the Commonwealth. This office is attuned to economic-development needs on a regional basis. The DLG is the agency to which the Area Development Districts (ADDs) report and therefore the one through which all regional and intergovernmental efforts are coordinated. Transportation, utilities, such as water and sewers, and economic-development tasks, such as regional industrial parks, are vetted through ADDs, and resources are combined to overcome externalities of individual government action. These regional governments have been demonstrated to enhance local government capacity in leveraging federal funds.[8] In particular, the DLG and its administrative ADDs reflect the rural nature of the Commonwealth and seek to improve the economy against great adversity in those places where infrastructure is lacking. The coordinated efforts of this agency allow rural areas to compete more effectively with their urban counterparts. At the regional level the ADDs employ professional economic-development staff who work to coordinate projects, recruit industry, and respond to industry needs through infrastructure and people-based programs and activities. We turn to a closer examination of the ADDs in the following section.

The Kentucky Council on Postsecondary Education (CPE) is the coordinating body for higher education in the Commonwealth. It is the entity to which all of the state's colleges and universities report, from which they receive their budgetary authority, and through which all education policy at the state level is established. Under the CPE are the state's flagship university (the University of Kentucky), its urban research university (the University of Louisville), and six regional universities (Morehead State University, Northern Kentucky University, Eastern Kentucky University, Western Kentucky University, Murray State University, and Kentucky State University). The Kentucky Community and Technical College System oversees thirteen community and technical colleges across the state. Each of these institutions plays a central role in economic development and growth derived largely from differences in their missions. The University of Kentucky and the University of Louisville are large research universities that focus on basic research. As such, they produce scientists and engineers with terminal degrees in their respective fields; these graduates become the engines of innovation through the development of new products and processes through research and development. These universities have recently begun to capitalize on this dimension of their efforts through technology-commercialization programs, such as the Advanced Science and Technology Commercialization Center and the Coldstream Research Farm at the University of Kentucky. These institutions are a source of expertise for businesses of all types, and faculty members consult widely with such firms. Additionally, these institutions tend to be more selective, offering the best and brightest high-school graduates opportunities for education across the full spectrum of academic disciplines. Regional universities, because of their size, location, and mission, serve more of a general education function. They offer primarily four-year degrees and only a handful of graduate degree programs. Because of their size, economy of scale means that the variety of disciplines available for study is also narrower in these schools. Nonetheless, each has a particular specialty that permits it to contribute to economic development. Faculty members in these schools are also experts in their own right and are called on to solve problems for business and industry. They coordinate job-skills training for new employers. Each has a distinctive focus for which it is known across the state. For example, Morehead State University has a program of distinction in regional analysis and public policy. Kentucky State University has a specialty in the field of aquaculture and marine biology. These universities do much more than offer four-year degrees through their outreach and service orientation. The system of community and technical colleges offers basic higher education to overcome geographic obstacles faced by students in many areas. The central component of their mission in economic development, however, is the applied nature of their training programs. Students graduate with the ability to work as nurses, machinists, or aircraft mechanics or in other skilled trades that are in high demand and that offer desirable salaries in Kentucky and beyond.

The Kentucky Cabinet for Travel and Tourism reflects the increasing specialization that is taking place in the economic-development field. This agency concentrates on the existence (rather than the use) value of natural resources. It promotes Kentucky's natural beauty, its history, and its unique industry to tourists. By bringing in external dollars, Kentucky businesses benefit. Moreover, keeping travel dollars from Kentucky residents in the state also helps Kentucky businesses relative to those in other states. Hotels, restaurants, attractions, and theme parks benefit from the activities of this agency. Examples of projects undertaken by this agency include the Kentucky Bourbon Trail, which highlights one of Kentucky's most notable industries. A recent effort through the KCED with significant tourism implications is the Kentucky Creation museum and theme park, which features a full-size model of Noah's ark. This plays to Kentucky's traditional religious values and offers a specialized niche tourism attraction to the Bible Belt's many Christians. The logo/slogan for the agency touches on another of Kentucky's most familiar resources—horses. The stylized horse and "unbridled spirit" slogan market the state to the world. It should be clear that Kentucky's uniqueness plays a significant role in its economy; the traditional aspects of the economy provide gravity, however, making it easy to imagine the state's traditional aspects while overlooking its more innovative and high-tech characteristics.

Regional Actors (Quasi-Nongovernmental Organizations)

Regional ADDs are the conduit between the state and local government entities that translate policy into plans and programs to resolve problems that transcend city and county boundaries. These quasi-nongovernmental organizations operate under the auspice of the DLG but also are incorporated as 501(c)3 nonprofit organizations. This status gives them tremendous flexibility to affect economic-development efforts in the regions they serve.[9] Their boards are composed of local elected officials—mayors and county judge-executives—who are thus ultimately responsive to their stakeholders.

The Center for Rural Development was incorporated in 1996 in Somerset, Kentucky. Like the ADDs, it was originally conceived as an extension of state government through partnership with the University of Kentucky, and it was provided with state funding matched by substantial federal support from Congressman Harold Rogers to establish the partnership. Today the Center operates independently as a 501(c)3 organization serving the counties of southern and eastern Kentucky. Its mission is to support the residents of the region—to provide them with opportunities for a brighter future. However, the Center's programs operate largely through partnerships and in cooperation with local governments and existing educational organizations. As a regionwide entity, the Center provides training, planning, and event-coordination services, as well as telecommunications networking, such as videoconference capabilities, that serve to overcome barriers to industrial recruitment and training for potential employees.[10] The Center was the brainchild of Congressman Rogers, who ultimately ascended to the powerful position of chair of the U.S. House of Representatives Appropriations Committee in 2011. As a nonprofit organization, the Center has worked to realize the vision of Congressman Rogers while organizing local government leaders in an emerging intergovernmental success story. The Center's political founding embodies its philosophy that local elected officials are best equipped to recognize problems and coordinate the development of solutions. This approach has made the Center effective at sustaining intergovernmental partnership as it delivers innovative programs like CenterNet that have been national models for rural development. The Center's board of directors consists of appointees from each of the forty-two counties served. Management is provided by a smaller executive committee of the board and an executive director.

The Center was viewed as a one-stop economic development shop to address the variety of barriers impoverished eastern Kentucky was facing on a daily basis. Not only does it serve a variety of functions within this broad mission but its facility also operates as an umbrella for organizational predecessors with narrowly focused functional responsibilities. These are the Southern Kentucky Economic Development Corporation (SKED), the Southern Kentucky Agricultural Development Association, and the Southern and Eastern Kentucky Tourism Development Association. These organizations, affectionately known within the Center as "the critters," each address problems and offer programs in their narrow functional areas. For example, SKED operates a number of small-business loan programs. Collectively these organizations offer substantial organizational capacity to confront challenges and coordinate programs to affect development in the Commonwealth's Appalachian region.

Other similar organizations also address economic development in a more tangential manner but through the same structure and umbrella. East Kentucky PRIDE (Public Responsibility in a Desirable Environment) offers numerous environmental programs—many through the schools—to help make the region a nicer place to live. Operation UNITE (Unlawful Narcotics Investigations, Treatment and Education) is a drug-abatement program that targets many of the region's more substantial social problems. These organizations target the region's quality of life and its image, which ultimately bear on its attractiveness for development.

Local Actors

One hundred twenty county governments in Kentucky cover the totality of the state's geography and therefore collectively serve all of the state's residents. Counties are the administrative arms of the state, collecting taxes and delivering uniform services, such as vehicle licensing. One of their more complicated roles is competition for precious economic-development activity. Many counties address economic-development issues directly through the fiscal court. Others with greater capacity and more regular activity have chosen to institutionalize their economic-development activities through a formal department with a director and sometimes staff.

Cities, like counties, are engaged in economic-development competition. Whereas counties serve all residents and are geographically determined, cities serve concentrated pockets of residents and are determined by organization of these populations into governments to provide municipal services. Cities are also engaged in competition, but the extent of their involvement is largely a function of city size. Many small cities execute economic development through council action, and the mayor carries out the council's will. Larger cities may establish economic-development departments, and the largest cities may divide the economic-development function into its constituent components, such as tourism, industrial recruitment, and community development (which focuses more on housing and quality-of-life issues).

As extensions of the state, counties and cities are often restricted in what they are allowed under state law to do. Cities and counties that have not attained sufficient economies of scale to implement independent economic-development departments often choose to coordinate their efforts by forming an independent (quasi-autonomous nongovernmental) nonprofit corporation to carry out recruitment and other development efforts. Even cities and counties with sufficient scale often opt for this administrative structure to overcome the restrictions placed on local governments by state law. Such organizations are able to operate with greater flexibility in developing, funding, and implementing projects. These cities and counties often utilize the occupational tax to provide resources for economic development. Both cities and counties can establish occupational taxing districts, cooperatively or independently. The most successful economic development results for local government are through intergovernmental cooperation.

Nonprofit Actors

Nonprofit organizations play an important role in economic development in Kentucky. Often these entities focus on quality-of-life issues, such as addressing poverty through education and other programs. The Mountain Association for Community Economic Development in Berea has offered assistance to the people of Appalachian Kentucky for decades. Forward in the Fifth was a regional program envisioned by Congressman Hal Rogers early in his tenure in the U.S. House of Representatives to stimulate educational improvement in low-performing school districts. The Kentucky Appalachian Commission and Leadership East Kentucky have provided regional leadership in eastern Kentucky, just as Western Kentucky Corporation has for western Kentucky and the Northern Kentucky Regional Partnership has for Covington and northern Kentucky communities.

The organizational framework within which economic development takes place is dictated by structure, but the nature of the problem has resulted in much greater coordination among these various entities through partnerships that seek to affect the regional and state economy in meaningful ways. Although competition is stiff, firms looking at potential sites generally have specific areas in mind within the state, and if they do not, the Kentucky Cabinet for Economic Development offers assistance in identifying sites that meet their criteria. As a result, competition among local governments is usually against local governments in other states. Thus the collective effort becomes one that exhibits strong patterns of coordination originating at the state level. The capability for successful policy making in a government organization is commonly called government capacity.[11] The major factors in assessing capacity are human resources, fiscal resources, and the means to organize these resources effectively. In Kentucky limitations in all three areas of capacity have made competitiveness challenging for economic-development policy makers.[12]

Relevant parties are invited to participate and offer services and incentives that prospective firms might value.[13] To an increasing extent, economic-development efforts have taken a from-within focus that emphasizes entrepreneurship. These programs are noncompetitive because new development is not a zero-sum game but a pie-enlarging endeavor. Once firms are established, they may draw on these extensive state resources to start operation or expand. Incentives for homegrown employment have not been emphasized but are important nonetheless.

POLITICS AND ECONOMIC DEVELOPMENT

Politicians are motivated to act to improve the local economy because it is visible and highly salient to voters.[14] In bad economic times they feel pressure to bring jobs. In good economic times they feel pressure to bring more jobs than their counterparts in other communities. In both cases they will be judged according to their performance at the next election cycle in two to four years. Problematic aspects of this pressure are the limited influence government is able to exert on firms' location decisions and the lengthy time frame within which such decisions can be implemented. Consequently, elected officials often opt to pursue tangible projects, such as roads and speculative buildings, rather than intangible programs, such as education and training. Moreover, physical capital is not mobile, whereas people are, so people-based investments are less appealing.

According to Green and Yanarella's critical assessment of the results of the Toyota industrial recruitment, the trade-offs provided what the Kentucky Chamber of Commerce and business leaders consider the most significant statewide initiative.[15] Manufacturing jobs remain an important component of Kentucky's economy, and Kentucky has a workforce that makes manufacturing a long-term need in economic-development policy making. But those critical of smokestack chasing aspire for Kentucky to have a diversified economic-development approach that moves away from traditional industrial recruitment. The political reality remains clear: Kentucky politicians, whether Republican or Democratic, have a bipartisan commitment to sustained industrial business growth and job creation.

CURRENT ECONOMIC-DEVELOPMENT POLICY

Kentucky's economic-development policy can be readily assessed through a glance at the KCED's website.[16] Providing information about the host of available programs to stimulate development in the state is the site's primary purpose. The programs are broken down conceptually into the traditional program, site selection and expansion, and more entrepreneurial strategies that include small-business support and technology and innovation.

MEASURING KENTUCKY'S PROGRESS

Kentucky is characterized by an average-sized traditional economy. Kentucky's economy is the twenty-seventh largest in the United States, with 2008 gross domestic product of $156 billion (up from $112 billion in 2000, or a growth rate of 4.3 percent per annum).[17] Manufacturing led the state's economy with 18.4 percent of economic output in 2008, while public-sector employment ranked second, contributing 15.7 percent of economic output; health care contributed 8.3 percent.[18] Economic activity in the state is heavily clustered in urban areas. "The three most urbanized regional economies—Louisville, Northern Kentucky, and Lexington—account for 55 percent of the state's population, 60 percent of the jobs, and 65 percent of the payrolls."[19] The 2011 Kentucky unemployment rate was 9.5 percent, compared to 8.9 percent nationally, but the state rate improved to 8.2 percent in 2012 compared to 8.1 percent nationally.[20] As figure 17.1 reveals, Kentucky average unemployment typically exceeds the national average, though recent data suggests that Kentucky may be recovering at an above average pace relative to its state peers.

We have already noted that Kentucky has a traditional economy based on agriculture and manufacturing. It is helpful to break down these sectors further to paint a clearer picture of the types of products the state produces. We begin with the primary economy. Kentucky leads the nation in coal production, although limestone, natural

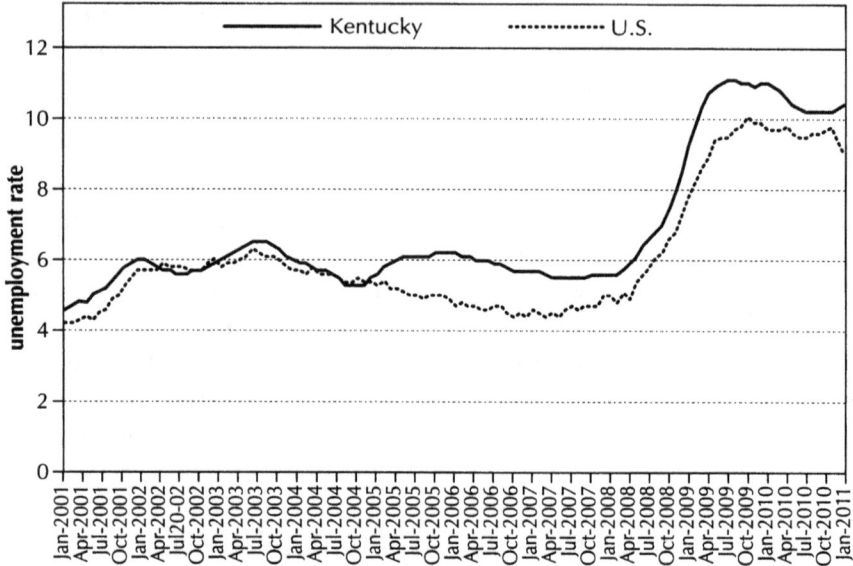

Figure 17.1. Kentucky and U.S. unemployment rate trends, 2001–2011. Source: U.S. Bureau of Labor Statistics.

gas, and petroleum are also extracted there.[21] Kentucky's agricultural economy is currently dominated by livestock (66 percent of agricultural revenues, primarily Thoroughbred horses and beef cattle), with crops such as tobacco, soybeans, and corn making up the balance.[22] Many of these products are central to the state's image in the world—it has long been the Thoroughbred horse capital of the world, the largest burley-tobacco-producing state, and the largest bourbon-producing state. The state's leading vegetable is the tomato, and apples lead fruit sales. In manufacturing, the dominant sector of the economy, transportation equipment leads the way; Ford, GM, and Toyota have major assembly facilities in the state. Chemicals and machinery manufacture are second and third, respectively.[23] In the service area, business and personal services dominate, followed by wholesale and retail trade, with government services ranking third.[24]

Table 17.1 displays, by aggregate industry codes, the number of firms, the number of employees, and the amount of revenue in sales in each industrial category. It is also interesting to reflect on those industries where Kentucky has a comparative advantage in sales nationally. Table 17.2 displays industries in which the state ranked first nationally. A number of Kentucky-grown industries are household names around the world: Humana, Lexmark, Papa John's, KFC, Ashland, and Louisville Slugger.[25]

There has been increasing interest in ranking and assessment across the spectrum of public policy, and economic development has been no exception. A variety of public and private organizations, some issue focused and some general, calculate the rankings. Nonetheless, there "are two common types of ranking systems: one looks at typological definitions (the substance of the policies) and the other looks at relative performance (the outcomes of the policies)."[26] The U.S. Chamber of Commerce ranked Kentucky in the top ten in 2011 because of favorable regulation and tax policies. In

Table 17.1. Industrial Composition of Kentucky's Economy

2007 NAICS code and industry description	Number of establishments	Sales ($ thousands)	Payroll ($ thousands)	Employees
21 Mining, quarrying, and oil and gas extraction	628	7,557,387	1,157,708	21,192
22 Utilities	329	n/a	578,081	8,282
23 Construction	8,615	16,492,910	31,131,470	83,154
31–33 Manufacturing	4,165	119,105,421	10,773,228	247,096
42 Wholesale trade	4,485	94,546,249	3,408,949	70,882
44–45 Retail trade	16,404	50,405,925	4,502,186	214,782
48–49 Transportation and warehousing	3,176	11,790,557	3,516,709	78,936
51 Information	1,594	n/a	1,252,145	33,996
52 Finance and insurance	6,594	n/a	3,076,132	66,825
53 Real estate and rental and leasing	3,898	3,894,326	593,447	20,146
54 Professional, scientific, and technical services	8,114	7,917,131	2,852,056	61,994
55 Management of companies and enterprises	676	615,812	1,989,269	25,180
56 Administrative and support and waste management and remediation services	3,900	5,312,255	20,033,303	96,386
61 Educational services	553	250,352	83,858	4,445
62 Health care and social assistance	10,600	22,151,809	8,395,085	235,282
71 Arts, entertainment, and recreation	1,341	1,205,333	368,118	18,556
72 Accommodation and food services	7,309	6,300,866	1,787,430	151,551
81 Other services (except public administration)	6,150	3,751,120	1,009,328	40,956

Source: 2007 Economic Census.

ranking Kentucky eighth, it comments, "Kentucky's lowest cost of living in the nation helps move it into this year's top 10. In order to further streamline business interactions with state government, the state recently passed legislation that will lead to the creation of a business 'One-Stop' web site. The online interface will simplify business filings and cut down on the need for business owners to complete multiple forms."[27]

Table 17.2. Industries in which Kentucky Ranks First

NAICS code	Description	Total sales/receipts ($ thousands)	Sales/receipts per capita ($)
42494	Tobacco and tobacco product merchant wholesalers	6,162,962	1,507.21
3313	Alumina and aluminum production and processing	3,503,731	856.87
492	Couriers and messengers	2,817,326	689.01
4921	Couriers	2,792,585	682.95
42432	Men's and boys' clothing and furnishings merchant wholesalers	1,582,338	386.98
3255	Paint, coating, and adhesive manufacturing	1,286,064	314.52
32551	Paint and coating manufacturing	790,697	193.37
332999	All other miscellaneous fabricated metal product manufacturing	637,522	155.91
32552	Adhesive manufacturing	495,367	121.15
3326	Springs and wire product manufacturing	462,471	113.10
311911	Roasted nuts and peanut butter manufacturing	458,190	112.05
332611	Spring (heavy garage) manufacturing	256,065	62.62
32192	Wood container and pallet manufacturing	222,182	54.34
213113	Support activities for coal mining	165,998	40.60

Source: 2002 Economic Census.

The state compares favorably with its counterparts in competition for new industry activity. In 2008 Kentucky ranked ninth among the states in *Site Selection* magazine's Governor's Cup ranking—the highest ranking it had ever achieved since the ranking's inception.[28] The ranking is for new and expanding industry projects that exceed $1 million in capital investment, create 50 or more jobs, or add 20,000 square feet of floor space. Kentucky's ranking was based on 280 location or expansion announcements that created 11,536 new jobs and capital investment of $1.7 billion.[29] This is not surprising, given that the state was ranked seventh nationally for business climate in 2006—an improvement from ninth place the preceding year.[30] The Kentucky Long Term Policy Research Center developed an index of state quality of life to assess Kentucky's progress and progress relative to peer states. The State of the Commonwealth Index ranked Kentucky forty-sixth in 1990, but that rank improved to fortieth by 2001.[31]

Where Kentucky's performance in the new economy is concerned, the rankings reveal limited advancement of an otherwise traditional economy. Kentucky ranked thirty-ninth out of the fifty states in a composite score of innovation capacity in 2000.[32] Innovation capacity has been demonstrated to stimulate economic development.[33] The character of innovation capacity is subject to change over time. Kentucky has been classified as having an emphasis on human capacity for innovation in the early 1980s and transitioning to an emphasis on state and local financial capacity for innovation from the late 1980s to the present.[34] Other indexes of new economy performance reveal similar placement for the Commonwealth. Kentucky ranges in rank from thirty-ninth to forty-sixth in indexes generated by the Progressive Policy Institute, the Corporation for Enterprise Development, and the Milken Institute for the same year.[35] Why does the state fare poorly in such high-tech indicators? Investment in science and research and development lag considerably behind national averages for most indicators.[36] In fact, research and development expenditures as a share of gross domestic product are about one-third of the U.S. average.[37]

KENTUCKY'S ECONOMIC DEVELOPMENT FUTURE

The recent recession has affected Kentucky, as it has the nation. Kentucky has not been as negatively affected as some states, but it remains in the middle range of states in most assessments of economic impact from the recession. The energy sector in Kentucky has been among the hardest hit, with coal and gas facing regulatory constraints from the federal government that have resulted in significant job losses and business contraction. Kentucky's orientation toward traditional industrial recruitment and its favorable manufacturing-production factors have made it competitive in some business sectors as the economic downturn has resulted in business realignments domestically. Cooperation among Kentucky universities, and particularly between the University of Kentucky and the University of Louisville, is a hopeful signs of the new economy initiatives yielding new partnerships for twenty-first-century economic growth. Twenty-first-century economic development will require knowledge-based resources, and Kentucky's commitment to higher education will be critical to Kentucky's economic competitiveness. Regional cooperation in northern Kentucky also points to hopeful signs of regional intergovernmental cooperation that can align resources efficiently and make collective policy that attracts business and industry without fundamentally changing the units or structures of government. The traditional approach of Kentucky economic development has yielded sustained success in many economic sectors, and new economy approaches featuring high-tech strategies and innovative partnerships have been demonstrating emerging effectiveness, even in challenging economic times. The political consensus Kentucky government leaders have demonstrated for bipartisan intergovernmental policy making has been important for Kentucky's competitiveness in the past and is an important tradition to maintain for future industrial recruitment and for sustainable economic development.

NOTES

1. Center for Rural Development Leadership, accessed May 31, 2013, http://www.Centertech.com/leadership.

2. Jeremy L. Hall, "Understanding State Economic Development Policy in the New Economy: A Theoretical Foundation and Empirical Examination of State Innovation in the U.S.," *Public Administration Review* 67, no. 4 (July/August 2007): 630–46.

3. Michael Hail and Jeremy L. Hall, "Economic Development," in *Federalism in America: An Encyclopedia*, ed. Joseph Marbach, Ellis Katz, and Troy Smith (Westport, Conn.: Greenwood Press, 2006), 1:163–66, 163.

4. Harold Wolman with David Spitzley, "The Politics of Local Economic Development," *Economic Development Quarterly* 10, no. 2 (1996): 115–50, 132.

5. E. Polk Johnson, *Kentucky and Kentuckians: The Leaders and Representative Men in Commerce, Industry and Modern Activities* (Chicago and New York: Lewis Publishing Company, 1912), 3. Also conceptually discussed in Thomas D. Clark, *A History of Kentucky* (Ashland, Ky.: J. Stuart Foundation, 1988).

6. Michael W. Hail, "The Whig Party," in *Encyclopedia of American Parties and Elections*, ed. Larry J. Sabato and Howard R. Ernst (New York: Facts on File, 2006), 493–94.

7. Ford Motor Company, "Plant Information," accessed April 12, 2011, http://media.ford.com/article_display.cfm?article_id=28696.

8. Jeremy L. Hall, "Assessing Local Capacity for Federal Grant-Getting," *American Review of Public Administration* 38, no. 4 (2008): 463–79; Jeremy L. Hall, "The Forgotten Regional Organizations: Creating Capacity for Economic Development," *Public Administration Review* 68, no. 1 (2008): 110–25; Jeremy L. Hall, "The Distribution of Federal Economic Development Grant Funds: A Consideration of Need and the Rural/Urban Divide," *Economic Development Quarterly* 24, no. 4 (2010): 311–24; Jeremy L. Hall, "Giving and Taking Away: Exploring Federal Grants' Differential Burden on Metropolitan and Non-metropolitan Regions," *Publius: The Journal of Federalism* 40, no. 2 (2010): 257–74.

9. Jeremy L. Hall, "Moderating Local Capacity: Exploring the E.O. 12372's Intergovernmental Review Effects on Federal Grant Awards," *Policy Studies Journal* 36, no. 4 (November 2008): 593–613.

10. Center for Rural Development, accessed April 12, 2011, http://www.Centertech.com.

11. Hall, "Assessing Local Capacity for Federal Grant-Getting," 463–79; Hall, "Forgotten Regional Organizations," 110–25.

12. Michael W. Hail, "Federalism and Government Reform: Assessing Government Performance and Economic Development Policy in Kentucky," *Cities* (Kentucky League of Cities) (Winter 2004): 20–21.

13. Jeremy L. Hall, *Grant Management: Funding Public and Nonprofit Programs* (Sudbury, Mass.: Jones and Bartlett, 2010).

14. Wolman and Spitzley, "Politics of Local Economic Development," 115–50, 132.

15. Ernest J. Yanarella and William C. Green, eds., *The Politics of Industrial Recruitment: Japanese Automobile Investment and Economic Development in the American States* (Westport, Conn.: Greenwood Press, 1990).

16. Kentucky Cabinet for Economic Development, http://www.thinkkentucky.com.

17. Econpost, "Kentucky Economic Development, GDP Size and Rank," accessed April 13, 2011, http://econpost.com/kentuckyeconomy/kentucky-gdp-size-rank.

18. Ibid.

19. Paul Coomes, *Improving Earnings per Job: The New Economic Development Challenge in Kentucky* (Lexington, Ky.: Center for Business and Economic Research, 2002), accessed April 13, 2011, http://cber.uky.edu/Downloads/coomes02.htm.

20. Kentucky Labor Market Information, accessed May 31, 2013, http://www.kylmi.ky.gov/gsipub/index.asp?docid=476.

21. Netstate, "Kentucky Economy," accessed April 13, 2011, http://www.netstate.com/economy/ky_economy.htm.

22. Ibid.

23. Ibid.

24. Ibid.

25. Kentucky Economic Development Guide, "Governor Steve Beshear Welcomes You to Kentucky's Wonders," 2011, accessed April 13, 2011, http://kentuckyeconomicdevelopment .com/node/547.

26. Hail and Hall, "Economic Development," 163–66, 165.

27. U.S. Chamber of Commerce, "Enterprising States: Recovery and Renewal for the 21st Century," 2011, accessed May 31, 2013, http://www.uschamber.com/sites/default/files/reports /ES2011-full-doc-web.pdf.

28. Cabinet for Economic Development, "Kentucky Ranks 9th Nationally for Number of New and Expanding Industry Projects in 2008," 2009, accessed April 13, 2011, http://www .thinkkentucky.com/newsarchive/ArchivePage.aspx?x=03092009_SiteSelection.html.

29. Ibid.

30. Cabinet for Economic Development, "Kentucky's Business Climate Ranked 7th in the Nation by *Site Selection Magazine*," 2006, accessed April 13, 2011, http://www.thinkkentucky .com/cednews/nov2006/enews_nov06_bizclimate.htm.

31. Amy L. Watts, "New Index Measures Well-Being and Ranks Kentucky," *Foresight* 11, no. 1 (2004), accessed April 13, 2011, http://www.kltprc.net/foresight/Chpt_75.htm.

32. Hall, "Understanding State Economic Development Policy in the New Economy," 630–46.

33. Jeremy L. Hall, "Developing Historical Fifty-State Indices of Innovation Capacity and Commercialization Capacity," *Economic Development Quarterly* 20, no. 2 (May 2007): 107–23.

34. Jeremy L. Hall, "Measurement with Meaning: Evaluating Trends and Differences in Innovation Capacity among the States," *Economic Development Quarterly* 23, no. 1 (2009): 3–12.

35. Jeremy L. Hall, "Comparing Indices of State Performance in the Knowledge-Based Economy," *Applied Research in Economic Development* 6, no. 1 (2009): 3–13; Hall, "Distribution of Federal Economic Development Grant Funds," 311–24.

36. Alliance for Science and Technology Research in America (ASTRA), "Kentucky R&D 2011," accessed April 13, 2011, http://www.usinnovation.org/state/pdf_cvd/KentuckyR&D2011 .pdf.

37. Ibid.

18

National Health-Care Reform and Health in Kentucky

Ann Beck

In 1993 Democratic governor Brereton Jones proposed "quality, affordable health care for every Kentuckian."[1] In the early 1990s the Kentucky public overwhelmingly supported such action; about 90 percent of randomly polled Kentuckians believed that health care was a fundamental right, 70 percent were willing to pay higher taxes for universal coverage, and 75 percent favored a payroll tax on companies that did not provide health insurance to employees. The legislation proposed by Governor Jones (but never passed by the state legislature) was remarkably similar to the national health-care reform legislation passed in March 2010. Like the current Patient Protection and Affordable Care Act passed in 2010, the proposed 1993 legislation

- used existing private (profit-based) insurance practices to cover citizens;
- managed competition among health-care providers and insurance companies to control costs;
- required universal health-insurance coverage (all residents were required to have insurance) for Kentuckians to assure access to various medical-care services;
- established set basic benefits for all health-insurance policies to promote basic equity in services available to both rich and poor;
- placed conditions on insurers to use community rating systems that would even out the price that each individual paid and reduce price differences for the old and chronically ill;
- regulated medical charges (discounts from providers for belonging to an insurance network with many potential patients) to hold down the spiraling cost of care and managed care for Medicaid recipients; and
- required larger employers to provide basic medical-insurance coverage for employees or pay a tax to assure employees continued access to medical-insurance benefits through the employer.[2]

Similar to the intent in 2010, the practices proposed in 1993 were primarily designed to assist residents in getting medical services that would help them (1) access reasonable treatment for chronic (long-term) or acute (immediate) injuries or illnesses; (2) avoid individual financial ruin through sharing the risk and costs of providing treatment; and (3) prevent or delay the onset of various chronic or acute illnesses through preventive care, such as immunizations, screening tests, use of pharmaceutical treatments, and periodic evaluations of possible health risks by a health-care professional.

The legislative and public debate over both the proposed 1993 legislation and the 2010 passed legislation has tended to center almost exclusively on the idea that a medical-care system is the same as a health-care system. A medical-care system focuses on who can get access to medical treatment, how the cost of this treatment can be provided for through existing insurance structures and who will pay for this treatment, and how the costs of medical services might be held in check and quality might be maintained. The medical-care model focuses on problems of each individual in isolation and reflects only one of a variety of models that can be used to protect and promote the health of people. The individualized medical-care model gives very little attention to how health is connected to persons' larger physical, social, political, and cultural environment. The medical-care model of health seeks to treat most "illnesses" or health concerns through the use of technical interventions and prescribed pharmaceuticals controlled by an elite set of practitioners. But is this individualized medical model the best model for promoting the health of Kentuckians? In this chapter I explore what is meant by "health," why governments have always been involved in "health" issues in the United States, how the current model of medicalized treatment came to dominate the way we think about health and health care, how Kentuckians currently fare on many measures of health, and what the impacts of the national "health-care" legislation might be on both the medical-care system in Kentucky and the wider conception of health care for the people of Kentucky.

DEFINING HEALTH AND GOVERNMENT INVOLVEMENT IN HEALTH CARE

People rate good health as one of the most important aspects of having a good life and a valuable individual and collective goal. What matters most is not only the length of one's life but also the quality of that life. The World Health Organization defines health as a state of complete physical, mental, and social well-being and not merely the absence of disease or infirmity.[3] The extent of this sense of physical, mental, and social well-being (a dynamic state of health) experienced by a person is a product of individual genetic predispositions and behavioral choices, as well as environmental and social forces that affect behavioral choices and other aspects of people's private and social lives. Over time, as people discovered cause-and-effect relationships between these individual, environmental, and social forces and people's health, they used their governments to help "promote the general welfare" of the community. Local governments in the United States have been involved in working toward healthy outcomes for citizens for over two centuries, while states have been deeply involved since the mid-nineteenth century and the national government since the founding of the Marine hospital service in 1798.[4]

State and local governments traditionally tried to alleviate or lessen the risks and burdens associated with unhealthy and unsafe conditions. Although the Kentucky Constitution does not explicitly spell out the ability of the state government to protect or promote the health of the public, early on, the Kentucky state legislature established authority for local governments to undertake systematic public health activities related to controlling communicable diseases and quarantining persons with such diseases under its police powers to promote public health, safety, and morals and under its historical authority to protect persons under its legal guardianship (children or adults unable to care for themselves). Later, when disease-transmission processes were better understood, local governments began engaging in control of disease-carrying vectors (insects and pest animals), sewage and water treatment to prevent deadly bacteria from infecting the population, safety and fire codes for buildings to prevent deadly fire hazards, occupational health standards to protect people at work, food-inspection and preparation standards, and communicable-disease control through vaccination and treatment. The state legislature authorized the creation of local boards of health and similar local agencies that could levy taxes through public health districts to undertake these important activities, as well as collect information on various life events and the incidence of disease (vital statistics). Other state agencies promoted agricultural research that led to the development and delivery of a wider variety of more nutritious foods for communities.

In time, large-scale outbreaks of infectious and deadly communicable diseases (e.g., typhoid, cholera, diphtheria, whooping cough, and polio) became well controlled, famine was largely prevented, and unsafe labor and living conditions were regulated so that occupational and home deaths and infectious diseases were significantly reduced. Fewer people died of water- and food-borne infections. As a result, people lived longer lives with higher quality. Between the beginning of the twentieth century and its midpoint, the population gained almost twenty years of longevity. In the United States the average life expectancy for a person born in the years 1900–1902 was about forty-nine years. By 1950 the life expectancy was slightly more than sixty-eight years. The rate of increase in longevity slightly decreased over the next half century, and life expectancy was ten years greater in 2004 than it had been in 1950 and stood at almost seventy-eight years for men and women combined.[5]

During the nineteenth and twentieth centuries, as certain risks to health and longevity were reduced, other threats to health became more noticeable. The contemporary factors that are considered to affect health most profoundly in modern (postindustrial) societies include genetic predisposition of individuals in the population to various diseases, social circumstances (e.g., income, education, occupation, and social networking) of individuals in the population, environmental exposure of the population to harmful substances, patterns of personal behavior and risk taking, and access to and use of the clinical screening, prevention, and medical-care systems.[6] Like the historical health risk factors of disease, famine, and injury, the modern risks to the length and the quality of life (well-being) can be reduced through measures taken by individuals, groups, and governments in society.

Although scholars cannot agree on an exact contribution of each of these modern health risk factors to the overall health of a person or a population, there is agreement that some risk factors are much larger contributors to the level of health and well-being than others. For example, genetic predispositions and behavioral patterns of citizens (what they eat, drink, and smoke and how much they exercise) may now contribute over half of the effect on the length of a healthy life. These behavioral patterns are created and changed by an interaction of individual choices and social conditioning practices (family, friends, class membership, genetic predisposition, eating habits, psychological states) that affect such elements as a person's proportionate body weight, amount of physical activity, and tobacco smoking. These three elements, in connection with a person's genetic predispositions, are now viewed as key to predicting health and longevity.[7] Although there is still disagreement on the exact proportion of deaths and disability due to factors such as diabetes, obesity, and smoking within the category of personal behaviors, there is considerable agreement that these modifiable risk factors are the leading behavioral causes of premature death.

In Kentucky over the past seventy years, the state legislature has created various state and local government authorities and agencies to deal continuously and expertly with health, medical-treatment, and risk-sharing issues important to individual residents and to the productivity of the Kentucky population. The efforts of local governments were initially supplemented with state revenues. Through the development and extension of the intergovernmental system with hundreds of grant-in-aid programs in the second half of the twentieth century, the national government significantly enhanced money available for Kentucky state and local government health efforts. These funds have been used by Kentucky state and local government agencies charged with licensing and regulating private and often for-profit health-care practitioners, medical-equipment providers, facilities, transporters, and insurers who provide insurance services and private health-provider treatments to residents. Other Kentucky state and local government agencies using national government grants-in-aid directly treat injuries, acute and chronic illnesses, disabilities, and other causes of premature death. Both the state and local governments in Kentucky have used money from the national government to establish and staff public hospitals, public nursing homes, poor farms, public clinics, and home-visiting health-practitioner services. Still other public agencies at both state and local levels, helped by federal grants, promote health through immunization programs for children and prevention and treatment of sexually transmitted diseases. In a related vein, additional state and local agencies and authorities regulate unsafe behaviors that could lead to injury, illness, disease, disability, loss of functioning, or premature death. These efforts are aimed at regulating harmful substances that affect citizens through various pathways, such as water, air, and food and drink; regulating the sale and use of alcohol and other drugs that are often related to injury and death; and requiring the use of safety equipment and practices at work, at home, on the road, and at play. Still other local and state agencies have been created to regulate and reduce an individual's financial or care risks associated with clinical (hospital or clinic) treatment after a person's health has been compromised.

DEFINING HEALTH AS A MEDICAL PHENOMENON

In the second half of the twentieth century a stronger and richer United States and its national government became more deeply involved in many of the risk-reduction activities surrounding health that had traditionally been designed, financed, and delivered through state and local governments. More important, the idea of "health" became fixed on the provision of clinical medical care or treatment after an injury, illness, disease, chronic condition, or disability had occurred. This medical-care system—the small slice of the pie that represents about 10 percent of the determinants of health—came to be viewed as the primary way of defining "health care." A new commercialized, technology-based, medicalized vision of health care gained rapid hold and provided additional stature and resources to physicians, hospitals, and drug manufacturers. As a result of the public's respect for these providers' expertise and their growing resource base, these provider interests were able to influence significantly the design, direction, and scope of national and state policy on "health care."

By the 1990s "health" activities had become fully dominated by the corporate, for-profit, medicalized, and individually based clinical-care approach to disease treatment rather than the traditionally broader focus on more of the determinants of health. A complex arrangement of providers and payers had emerged during the previous decades, and the for-profit business model came to dominate the approach to health.[8] Despite much higher per capita expenditures on "health" care during previous decades, the United States, in comparison with other rich democracies, has not come as far in improving population health on a wide variety of indicators. For example, life expectancy in the United States increased from an average of slightly more than seventy years in 1960–1962 to an average of almost seventy-eight years in 2003–2005, but the rich democracies of Europe increased their life expectancy from seventy years to eighty years during the same period.[9] Most Organization for Economic Cooperation and Development (OECD) countries have achieved near-universal access to medical care or medical insurance, but about 17 percent of the U.S. population is still without access or insurance.[10] Similarly, the gap in life expectancy between the richest and poorest persons in the United States has also been widening in recent decades.[11] This is the reverse of the trend of closing the gap in life expectancy for people in the United States between 1930 and 1960.[12] The poor performance of the United States on improving health outcomes relative to other rich democracies is, in part, the result of how the United States developed its approach to financing and providing health care.

THE THREE COLLECTIVE FINANCIAL AND DESIGN SPONSORS OF MEDICAL CARE

During the 1950s and 1960s three sets of actors came to share financing of the medicalized vision of health care. These three sets of financiers, along with professional providers of medical care and drug and equipment manufacturers, helped create the systems of delivery of medical care to U.S. residents today. Most important, the medical care that is delivered now is almost exclusively targeted at correcting problems

(1) when health is impaired (a person is ill or injured), (2) when acute or chronic care is needed to prevent death at the end of life, or (3) when it is desired to provide a higher quality of life for a chronically or acutely ill person until that person dies. This emphasis on postproblem correction through medical care became synonymous with the idea of caring for the health of the population. In order to understand the current "healthcare" reforms proposed or implemented at either the national or the state level, one must first understand how the employer and government payer systems developed in the 1950s and 1960s and sowed the seeds for contemporary reform.

The first nonindividual financing system, which rapidly developed and expanded in the 1950s in the United States, was an employer-sponsored system of providing medical-care insurance for employees in larger private and public enterprises. Decisions by the U.S. Supreme Court and the Internal Revenue Service on both negotiability of health benefits by employers and unions and favorable tax treatment of this form of employee compensation led to a rapid expansion of private, voluntary, tax-free, and union-negotiable-but-employer-sponsored health benefits. The "health benefits" were mostly in the form of group medical insurance for full-time employees through private, for-profit insurance companies. Under this scheme, eligibility for coverage by insurance, the types of services to be covered under the medical-insurance plan, and the share of insurance-payment costs between the employer and the employee are developed by each employer acting in isolation or through employer-union negotiation. Although the employer pays the insurance provider, the real cost of the medical insurance is borne by the employees through (1) wage trade-offs in the form of lower growth in wages; (2) employees paying for some part of the medical-insurance "premium" cost out-of-pocket, that is, from their own wages; and (3) consumers paying higher prices for products produced by the employer so that the employer can provide the employees with medical insurance. These costs to employees, employers, and consumers become revenues for mostly private hospitals, physicians, and other providers of health services, drug manufacturers and distributors, insurance providers, and manufacturers of medical equipment and devices. This employer-sponsored insurance covering both private and public employees had an estimated employer cost in 2010 of about $829 billion per year.[13] In 2009 about 55 percent of the entire U.S. population had medical-insurance coverage under this financing system.[14]

The second financing system that developed came through the passage of the national Medicare program by the U.S. Congress in 1965. Medicare became a national (rather than state-by-state) program targeted to reduce medically induced poverty among seniors and to improve access to medical treatment for the elderly. Medicare uses nationally uniform standards of eligibility and medical-insurance coverage for basic services for almost all elderly in the population and for severely disabled nonelderly persons (a later addition to the original system). Like the medical-insurance plans for employers, Medicare operates largely as a fee-for-service reimbursement system for private providers of covered services, supplies, and equipment. Providers are paid according to a fee system established by congressional action under Medicare. Medicare is financed through a combination of a payroll tax on almost all workers, national government general-fund revenues, and "premium" payments by Medicare recipients (almost the entire population of those sixty-five years and older). The cost of this medical insurance is borne by workers, taxpayers, and the elderly recipients. These costs become revenues for the same businesses and persons as in the first system. The Medicare system allowed previously uncompensated care given by various providers to be more fully compensated and shifted a significant portion of medical costs previously borne by individuals receiving care and by states and local governments to the national government. Along with the Social Security pension system, the Medicare system helped reduce (but not eliminate) rates of poverty caused by costs of medical care among the elderly.

The third development, also based on the medicalized view of health care, was the passage of the Medicaid program by the U.S. Congress in 1965. The Medicaid program targeted medical insurance to the poorest families (and later to near-poor children and pregnant women). Unlike Medicare, under Medicaid each state could set different eligibility standards above a minimum floor, authorize fewer or more services that the insurance would cover, and set higher or lower levels of recipient out-of-pocket payments for insurance premiums, co-payments, or deductibles. Medicaid is financed through national government grants to the states funded from general tax revenues of the national government and by formula-based matching amounts from the state governments. The formula takes into account a state's ability and effort to pay. A state government's cost share for Medicaid is paid largely from the general revenues of the state. The total cost of Medicaid is borne mostly by national taxpayers, followed by a smaller part shared by state taxpayers, and a very small part of the cost is borne by recipients of Medicaid through payment of out-of-pocket expenses for co-payments or annual deductibles/fees to participate.

These Medicaid costs become revenues for the same businesses and persons as in the first two systems. Like Medicare, Medicaid allowed previously uncompensated or low-compensated care to become better compensated. It shifted a significant portion of medical costs previously borne by individuals receiving care or by local and state governments to the national government. As with Medicare, the implementation of the Medicaid program increased demand for medical services and equipment, along with demand for nursing-home services. This increased demand rewarded providers of medical services and goods, nursing homes, and drug manufacturers. In 2010 Medicaid served 60 million individuals, and estimated expenditures through this medical-insurance financing system were approximately $427 billion.[15] Nationally, only about one-third of eligible persons actually enroll in Medicaid because social stigma continues to be attached to this program, unlike the Medicare program.[16] In fiscal year 2010 Medicaid and State Children Health Insurance Program (SCHIP) spending was expected to be 8 percent of total federal outlays of approximately $3.5 trillion.

Some persons have coverage under more than one insurance system. For example, millions of poor elderly are covered under both Medicare and Medicaid (dual eligibles). Similarly, there are persons who are still working who may have coverage both under Medicare and under employer-sponsored insurance. In addition to amounts paid under these three major insurance schemes, individuals still finance a significant amount of their own medical-care costs. These are called out-of-pocket expenses.

All medical costs of people who are uninsured are out-of-pocket. No one shares their financial risk.

In the past twenty years, not only has the amount spent on health increased dramatically but also the share of the spending has decreased for businesses and households but increased for government. In 2009 U.S. households paid for about 28 percent of the $2.486 trillion spent on health care. The level of household (and out-of-pocket) contributions has declined over the past twenty years. Businesses now sponsor about 21 percent of national health expenditures, and their proportion relative to total spending has also been falling over the past two decades. The share paid by governments (national, state, and local) has increased over the past two decades, and the national government has assumed a much larger part of the increase than state and local governments. This continues a pattern that has been occurring over the past fifty years since the introduction of Medicare and Medicaid.

SPONSORS' WORRIES ABOUT THE SYSTEM

By 2009 about $2.1 trillion was spent in the United States on personal health-care supplies and services—a subset of total national health expenditures ($2.486 trillion in 2009) that excludes certain public health expenses, as well as research and development expenses of the national, state, and local governments.[17] This $2.1 trillion is about 15 percent of the entire gross domestic product of the U.S. economy and 85 percent of the total health expenditures in the United States. Per capita expenditures on personal health and medical care in the United States are about twice the expenditures in the average rich democracy (i.e., OECD countries) when they are compared in purchasing parity dollars.[18] Again, compared with the average rich OECD country, U.S. sponsors pay about 30 to 50 percent more for prescription drugs, 100 percent more for hospital care, physicians, and ambulatory services.[19] Thus the overall current cost of medical care in the United States is more than double the parity purchasing power price cost of medical care in the average OECD country.[20]

HOW KENTUCKIANS FARE COMPARED WITH OTHER AMERICANS

Despite significant improvements in both the quality and length of life for the average American and Kentuckian by the twenty-first century, Kentuckians continue to be less healthy than other Americans. If Kentuckians have lower levels of physical and mental well-being, there are implications for their economic productivity, their individual and collective quality of life, the lengths of their lives, and the fullness of their years of life. Of the suggested causes for poorer health outcomes, compared with the average American, Kentuckians tend to have higher genetic predispositions for certain diseases and conditions that limit health, higher levels of risky behaviors that may be culturally embedded (e.g., poor diets, higher smoking rates, higher rates of vehicle accidents, and higher obesity rates), lower incomes, and more unhealthy environments (high levels of particulate matter, higher occupational death and injury rates), as well as less access to and lower quality of medical clinical-care services.[21]

Table 18.1 presents selected information on contemporary Kentucky health indicators and outcomes as reported by the United Health Foundation in its annual scorecard publication "America's Health Rankings."[22] This annual assessment of each state's population has been carried out for almost two decades and is a joint effort among three nonprofit organizations—United Health Foundation, the Partnership for Prevention, and the American Public Health Association—and the U.S. Department of Health and Human Services. Findings for various health outcomes are presented from the reports issued in 2008, 2009, and 2010 so that short-term trends can be identified. The outcomes for each year are typically based on information collected in the previous year.

As identified in table 18.1, Kentucky has very poor mental and physical health outcomes relative to the other states in the United States. Kentucky ranks in the bottom fifth of all states on all these health outcomes except the geographic disparity of outcomes. In addition to these state-level outcomes monitored by the United Health Foundation, one can also note that Kentuckians are much more likely than the general U.S. population (1) to be disabled, 26 percent versus 15 percent; (2) to be poor, 22 percent versus 18 percent; and (3) to live in rural areas, 50 percent versus 16 percent.[23] Similarly, the Commonwealth Fund periodically assesses states on their achievement of certain benchmarks for healthy population outcomes. In its 2009 report Kentucky ranked forty-fifth overall, with higher rates of mortality from certain cancers, cardiovascular disease, overall causes of death, asthma, and mortality that is premature.[24] As

Table 18.1. Kentucky Health Outcomes, 2008, 2009, and 2010

Outcome	2008	2009	2010	2010 rank
Poor mental health days/month	3.7	4.6	4.6	50th
Cancer deaths per 100,000 pop.	226	225	227	50th
Premature death years (years lost/100,000 pop)	9,116	8,929	9,059	49th
Health status self-rated fair or poor	23.1%	20.3%	22.7%	49th
Cardiovascular deaths/100,000 pop.	343	332	322.3	43rd
Geographic disparity in health across the counties of the state	12.3	12.2	12.2	31st
Poor physical health days/month	4.8	4.5	5.2	50th
Have cardiac heart disease	5.7%	5.8%	5.9%	49th
Have had heart attack	6.0%	5.4%	5.9%	49th
Are obese	28.7%	30.2%	32.3%	47th
Have diabetes	9.9%	9.8%	11.5%	47th
Have high blood pressure	30.0%	30.0%	36.3%	47th
Have high cholesterol	38.5%	38.5%	41.6%	49th
Overall		41st	44th	

Source: Constructed from information at www.americashealthrankings.org.

noted in table 18.1, many outcomes are not improving but rather are getting worse over time—poor physical health days reported each month, obesity, high blood pressure, and high cholesterol. If these trends continue, they will likely offset other improvements in quality and quantity of life.

As demonstrated in both the United Health Foundation and Commonwealth approaches to evaluating medical illness outcomes for Kentucky, Kentuckians are in greater need of improving both medical care and health outcomes for its citizens. National and state reforms have been proposed to help Kentuckians pursue a healthier life. Some of the activities that are associated with improvements in medical care are addressed in the new national reform legislation of 2010.

The March 2010 U.S. Health Reform Efforts

David A. Reisman describes the U.S. health-care system as surrounded by ignorance, uncertainty, asymmetrical information, professional monopolies, noncompetitive markets in insurance, and poverty.[25] These characteristics make it nearly impossible for an effective market to exist. These same characteristics of the chaotic medical-insurance system also clarify why it is difficult for both elected officials and public administrators to effect comprehensive reform because of various factors, such as bounded rationality, fragmented political institutions, resistance from concentrated interests, and perceived fiscal constraints.[26] Despite these obstacles, sometimes reform is possible when researchers and practitioners, concentrated interests, and the financiers and providers of the health-care systems can agree on some of the broad goals of such reform. Although efforts for reform in the early 1990s failed both in Kentucky and at the national level, in 2010 there was sufficient consensus among the major stakeholders to get a national bill passed.

Two significant elements dominated the most recent debate about "health-care" reform—ensuring access to medical insurance as the primary vehicle for improving population health and controlling the ever-spiraling costs of our medical care system. Neither of these foci reflects much on the larger question whether the extraordinary reliance on the current medical-care and medical-insurance activities is the better or best way to modify the wide range of contemporary health risks. In late March 2010 the Patient Protection and Affordable Care Act (ACA), Pub. L. 111–148 (March 23, 2010), as immediately amended by the subsequent Health and Education Reconciliation Act, Pub. L. 111–152 (March 30, 2010), became law. The implementation of the Affordable Care Act is being fully fleshed out through the codevelopment of regulations by the three federal agencies charged with implementation of the ACA: the Department of Health and Human Services, the Department of Labor, and the Internal Revenue Service. In addition to these actors, there are required tasks for state and local governments, as well as medical-care providers and suppliers.[27]

In general terms, some of the major intentions or desired outcomes of the legislation and its subsequently published regulations to date include the following:

- Provide medical services and prescriptions drugs to those for whom health insurance is unavailable or unaffordable.

- Slow the rate of increase in the cost of medical care and the amount spent on medical care.
- Reduce or eliminate catastrophic financial impacts on persons who need medical care.
- Spread the costs of medical-care insurance so that the impact of the cost on a person's or household's income is less regressive.
- Protect those who need medical care the most from socially unacceptable practices.
- Equalize the playing field for U.S. employers that continue to help finance medical-care insurance for their workers and dependents of those workers.
- Create insurance and reinsurance vehicles that will help better share risk and overcome adverse selection problems.
- Promote illness prevention and wellness efforts.
- Increase the supply of health-care providers and clinics, especially for more vulnerable populations.

Table 18.2 presents a partial list of activities under the ACA and the primary values that each of the actions promotes in the medical-care system.

The most significant changes for Kentucky that will result from the passage and implementation of the ACA are the extension of insurance coverage and greater use of medical services by Kentuckians. The two provisions of the law that have this impact are (1) the expansion of the public Medicaid program to cover more families and single adults up to at least 133 to 138 percent of the federal poverty level (FPL)[28] and (2) the provision of refundable and advanceable premium credits and cost-sharing subsidies to persons with household incomes between 133 percent and 400 percent of the FPL to buy individual or family insurance policies through their employers or through health-benefit exchanges. The amount of the subsidy is based on a determined maximum proportion of income that the family or individual can pay for an individual or group insurance premium.

Other important activities under the law will encourage employers to continue offering medical insurance to their employees. Larger employers have incentives to enroll employees in their own plans or they must pay penalties or provide vouchers to help equalize the playing field among larger employers, most of whom currently offer medical-insurance coverage to their employees and pay a significant portion of the premium cost of that medical-insurance coverage. For the period from 2010 until 2014, when the insurance exchanges will be in place, employers (or their insurance companies) who are providing health-insurance coverage to retirees over fifty-five years of age but less than sixty-five will be able to be reimbursed for 80 percent of the cost of retiree claims between $15,000 and $90,000 in order to lower costs for premiums for all current early retired enrollees. In addition, temporary national- or state-level high-risk insurance pools are being established until 2014 so that persons normally excluded from coverage in the individual market can get insurance coverage at lower cost. These changes are designed to substantially improve access to medical insurance by 2014 and will likely have effects on health outcomes (as well as financial effects) for Kentuckians.

Table 18.2. Patient Protection and Affordable Care Act and Values Promoted

Action	Value(s) promoted
1. Eliminate preexisting and canceling practices	Access/decreases cost to households
2. Require citizens/legal residents to have insurance	Access/equity
3. Establish basic services covered for all and update periodically	Equity
4. Expand Medicaid coverage to more of poor population	Access
5. Premium subsidies for poorer citizens (progressive)	Access/equity
6. Tax credit for small businesses that provide coverage	Access
7. Temporary national reinsurance program for ERs who cover 55–64 retirees not eligible for Medicare	Decrease cost to households and businesses
8. Tax penalty for those who fail to get coverage	Access/revenue
9. Limit maximum annual contribution to FSA/HSA to $2,500	Equity/revenue
10. Create insurance exchanges and have floor standards on accreditation and reporting	Access/decrease cost to households and businesses
11. Restrict most abortions from coverage under insurance	Political agenda
12. Restrict illegal immigrants from coverage	Political agenda
13. Create four benefit levels with different deductibles applied to individual, small group, and exchange markets only	Equity
14. Control out-of-pocket limits	Equity/decrease cost to households
15. Eliminate maximum lifetime limits	Equity/access
16. Allow some variation in costs of insurance	Political agenda
17. Temporary national high-risk pool	Decrease cost to households and businesses
18. Require standards for simplification	Efficiency
19. Require employers to provide coverage if they have more than 50 employees or pay tax/fee. Automatic opt-in for all employees.	Access/revenue
20. Require employers to enroll employees automatically in insurance plan (employee may opt out)	Access
21. Increase age for dependent coverage	Access
22. Allow for creation of transstate insurance compacts	Political agenda
23. Restructure payments for Medicare Medical Advantage plans	Efficiency
24. Provide twelve years of exclusive use of biologic drugs to drug manufacturers	Political agenda
25. Authorize the FDA to approve generic versions of biologic drugs after twelve years	Efficiency

(cont.)

Table 18.2. (*cont.*)

Action	Value(s) promoted
26. Money from national government to support comparative effectiveness research positive outcomes	Effectiveness/efficiency
27. Create incentives for primary care at home for certain high-need Medicare patients	Effectiveness/efficiency
28. Require disclosure of financial relationships among providers	Regulation of "market"
29. Provide funds to create national initiatives in health promotion, prevention, and wellness	Health promotion
30. Create national initiatives and evidence-based programs especially in underserved areas	Access/effectiveness
31. Require chain restaurants and vending machines to provide information disclosing nutritional content outcomes	Health promotion
32. Require any health insurance plans to report medical loss ratio (how much goes to pay claims)	Regulation of "market"
33. Reduce certain Medicaid payments	Efficiency
34. Increase Medicaid drug rebate percentage	Efficiency
35. Create community living assistance services voluntary insurance program with automatic enrollment of all working adults	Access/decrease cost to households and governments
36. Close donut-hole over time in Medicare	Equity/decrease cost to households
37. Establish scholarships and loans for medical trainees	Access/efficiency
38. Address nursing shortage—increase supply of providers	Access/efficiency
39. Create interdisciplinary training models to encourage integration of treatment and/or primary care (medical home) models	Effectiveness/efficiency
40. Increase number and access to community and school-based health centers	Access/efficiency
41. Work on reducing ethnic, racial, gender, language, disability status, and rural status disparities through various actions	Equity
42. Create voluntary national long-term-care insurance program with five-year vesting by payroll deduction with automatic opt-in provisions (employee may opt out)	Access/decrease cost to households and governments
43. Reduce waste, fraud, and abuse in public programs	Efficiency

Source: The Patient Protection and Affordable Care Act as amended by the Health and Education Reconciliation Act.

THE ACA'S LIKELY IMPACT ON KENTUCKY

Under the legislative changes in the ACA, Kentucky, with significantly lower average per capita and family income than the national average, will be eligible for a very large additional injection of both federal Medicaid and federal subsidy funds that will both decrease the rate of uninsured persons in Kentucky and heavily stimulate the medical services sector of Kentucky's economy. In total, the two major reforms—Medicaid expansion and federal subsidies for purchasing insurance through exchanges—are predicted to generate about $4 billion of economic stimulus per year after 2014. This $4 billion will be 90 to 95 percent paid for by people outside Kentucky through tax transfers from richer parts of the country. Table 18.3 shows the distribution of the Kentucky population by age and insurance status and the size and age distribution of the poorest Kentuckians.

Table 18.3. Distribution of Kentucky and U.S. Population by Age Group, Poverty Level, and Insurance Coverage, 2007–2008

	KY	KY	United States
Total population	*Number*	*Percent*	*Percent*
0–18 years old	1,070,800	25	26
19–64 years old	2,599,400	62	61
65 and above	555,900	13	13
All ages	**4,226,100**	100	100
Poor within age group (< 100% FPL)	*Number*	*Percent*	*Percent*
0–18 years old	314,700	29	23
19–64 years old	528,500	20	17
65 and above	65,900	12	13
Total 100% FPL	909,100	21.5	18.3
Poor 101%–133% FPL	279,000	6.6	6.4
Total	**1,188,100**		
Insurance coverage of nonelderly	*Number*	*Percent*	*Percent*
ESI (employer)	2,121,500	57.8	60.9
Individual	169,700	4.6	5.3
Medicaid	618,900	**16.9**	14.9
Other public	140,300	3.8	2.7
Not Insured	**619,800**	**16.9**	**17.4**
Total nonelderly	3,670,200	100	101

Source: Kaiser Family Foundation, KY State Medicaid fact sheet 2007 data.

Before the great recession of 2008 to 2010, about 1.2 million Kentuckians would have been eligible for Medicaid on the basis of income alone under the ACA reform. Additional Medicaid recipients (children and pregnant women) who have incomes above 133 percent of the FPL are also eligible for Medicare under Kentucky regulations. However, the great recession significantly increased the number of unemployed and uninsured in Kentucky and rapidly increased the number of Kentuckians who became qualified for Medicaid under the pre-ACA changes.

According to the later 2009 estimates by Holahan and Blumberg,[29] 70 percent of Kentucky's nonelderly citizens meet the means-test income criteria to qualify for either the expansion of Medicaid coverage or the subsidy under the reform. In Kentucky in 2009, 33 percent of the state's nonelderly residents had incomes less than 133 percent of the FPL; another 37 percent of Kentuckians fell in the income zone between 133 percent and 400 percent of the FPL. Among the 3.7 million nonelderly Kentuckians in 2009, about 17.8 percent are now medically insured through Medicaid and the closely related Children's Health Insurance Program, another 54.2 percent are covered under employer-sponsored group medical-insurance programs, 17.2 percent are not medically insured, and coverage of the remaining 10.8 percent is about evenly divided between the individual insurance market and another public insurance sponsor—military, Veterans' Administration, or Medicare.[30] Because of the nature of income and work arrangements among the uninsured, about 90 percent of the uninsured are eligible for either the Medicaid expansion or the subsidy.

Table 18.4 displays the number of persons who would be newly eligible for Medicaid insurance coverage and the number of persons currently eligible but not yet enrolled in Medicare. Holahan and Blumberg[31] and Holahan and Headen[32] used detailed information from the Current Population Surveys on income, size of place of employment, employment status, and current insurance coverage to estimate how the ACA will likely affect future insurance coverage in Kentucky.

Table 18.4. Approximate Impact of Reform on Kentucky Medicaid Enrollments 0–133% FPL: Average of Various Participation Scenarios

	Number	Percent of population	Percent from uninsured
Medicaid newly eligible	376,000	10	61
Medicaid currently eligible but not covered	294,000	8	40
Total eligible	670,000	18	53
Likely to enroll (75% of total)	502,000	14	

Source: Compiled by the author on the basis of data from John Holahan and Linda Blumberg, "How Would States Be Affected by Health Reform?," Robert Wood Johnson Foundation Report Series, accessed March 1, 2010, http://www.rwjf.org/files/research/55090.pdf; and John Holahan and I. Headen, "Medicaid Coverage and Spending in Health Reform: National and State-by-State Results for Adults at or below 133% FPL," 2010, accessed February 22. 2011, http://www.kff.org/healthreform /upload/Medicaid-Coverage-and-Spending-in-Health-Reform-National-and-State-By-State-Results -for-Adults-at-or-Below-133-FPL.pdf.

The final "likely to enroll" estimates in table 18.4 assume that 75 percent of the newly Medicaid eligible under the ACA reform and those Kentuckians currently eligible under the existing Medicaid provisions would enroll in Medicaid. This percentage is higher than the current takeup rate among eligible persons, but it is likely that extensive marketing and easy enrollment procedures will be used starting in 2014 to help overcome the stigma attached to Medicaid coverage. The demographic composition of the newly eligible will have a large proportion of single adults who have never been eligible for coverage under any program for the poor. The ACA requires that most persons acquire health insurance, and this mandate should also help increase enrollments in the Medicaid program.

About 500,000 more poor Kentuckians under the reform proposal would likely become medically insured through the federal and state publicly funded Medicaid program by 2019. These additional entrants into the Medicaid system would be a 62 percent increase over the approximately 800,000 Kentucky residents enrolled in Medicaid as of July 2010.[33] A majority of these new entrants will be poor adults with children and single poor adults who are currently ineligible for Medicaid under existing rules applied to Medicaid in Kentucky. About one-third of these new entrants will have been previously diagnosed with a chronic condition.[34] If average spending per enrollee is approximately $6,000 annually for these newly covered citizens, the addition of 500,000 entrants will lead to about $3 billion of additional medical spending per year after 2014.

Under the current American Recovery and Reinvestment Act of 2009, the modified Federal Medical Assistance Percentage rate for Kentucky is 80.1 percent for persons currently eligible for Medicaid. This means that for the years 2009, 2010, and 2011, the national government funded a greater portion of Medicaid costs than it had before. The ACA also states that the national government will pay between 90 and 95 percent of the cost of coverage for newly qualified poor persons who were not eligible for Medicaid before the passage of the ACA. Although more federal funds will flow to Kentucky, Kentucky will also have to pay some additional money to cover more of the previously eligible who become covered under Medicaid, as well as about 5 percent of the cost of covering those newly eligible under the ACA. Kentucky's share for funding the new entrants to Medicaid would be about $370 million additional per year at the higher enrollment levels. To fund the Medicaid program at this higher level, about $2.7 billion of federal money will be flowing annually into Kentucky from taxpayers outside Kentucky. The latest estimates from the Kaiser Commission on Medicaid and the Uninsured project that Kentucky spending on Medicaid for the period 2014–2019 will go up about 4 percent, while the federal contribution will increase by 32 percent.[35] These new funds will be going to medical-care providers, drug manufacturers, hospitals and clinics, producers and vendors of medical equipment and supplies, etc.

Table 18.5 provides similar estimates of the impact of the medical-insurance subsidy reforms on those Kentuckians with incomes between 133 percent and 400 percent of the FPL. The number of Kentucky citizens who will likely be eligible and enroll in the subsidy is smaller than the number of those who are eligible and enroll in Medicaid because many of the eligible citizens who fall between 133 percent and 400 percent of the FPL are likely already to have employer coverage at relatively

Table 18.5. Impact of Reform on Kentucky Subsidy Enrollment FPL 133–400%

	Population	Percent of population
Total people 133–400% FPL	1,382,000	37.5
Small-firm employees	332,000	9.0
Self-employed/part-time/unemployed	230,000	6.2
Likely to enroll (60% small-firm, all self-employed/ part-time/unemployed)	369,200	10

Source: Holahan and Blumberg, "How Would States Be Affected by Health Reform," Robert Wood Johnson Foundation Report Series (2010), 13, accessed March 1, 2010, http://www.rwjf.org/files /research/55090.pdf.

affordable rates. Those who have employer coverage may also be eligible for financial assistance to help pay the medical-insurance premium cost if the cost of the employer-sponsored insurance premium to the employee exceeds a set percentage of household income. These subsidies have not been considered in this discussion.

The most likely citizens to make full use of the subsidy option to become medically insured in the private or exchange markets are those who have not been eligible for employer coverage because (1) they work in small firms that do not offer group insurance coverage and nongroup insurance has been too expensive, (2) they are self-employed and could not join a cheaper group insurance plan, (3) they work less than full-time and are excluded from coverage under employer plans, (4) they are unemployed and are not covered by COBRA benefits (postemployment ability to carry medical insurance for a temporary period by paying the entire cost of the premium), or (5) they cannot afford the cost of the COBRA premium. As indicated in table 18.5, almost 370,000 Kentuckians are likely to be eligible for and use the subsidy to provide themselves medical-insurance coverage. Again, the subsidy will be fully financed by the national government and will not require additional Kentucky taxpayer support through a grant formula. I computed an average subsidy based on 50 percent of the current average premium cost for individual group coverage in Kentucky.[36] The 2009 premium rate in Kentucky was $4,337, and half that rate is a subsidy amount of about $2,168. If all 370,000 eligible Kentuckians used that amount to purchase insurance, then about $800 million in new money will flow to Kentucky. This new money is financed by taxpayers from other states. These new dollars would be used to purchase medical insurance that would pay for medical services, drug prescriptions, and medical equipment covered by the insurance. The spending on these goods and services then becomes income for medical services providers, equipment and supply vendors, insurance companies, and other gainers under the existing medical-care provision schemes.

Overall, under the combined reform scenarios of Medicaid expansion and subsidies for families to purchase insurance in exchanges, Kentucky would gain about $3.8 billion annually from amounts paid mostly by taxpayers in other states. In essence, this influx of new spending will be about $1,000 for each resident of Kentucky. In addition to the economic stimulus, the combined reforms will dramatically reduce the level of uninsured Kentuckians by about two-thirds.[37] This insurance effect also has implications for the mental health outcomes of Kentuckians. First, simply possessing medical-care insurance may provide many more Kentuckians with greater peace of mind and a sense of security in these uncertain times. Second, because lack of medical insurance and excessive out-of-pocket costs relative to income are implicated in over 60 percent of all bankruptcies,[38] about 25,000 personal bankruptcies of Kentuckians may be avoided each year. Because states have a strong incentive to manage Medicaid cost growth, it is more likely that costs for medical care will grow more slowly if state governments get involved. Observers have pointed out that Medicaid spending growth per enrollee is lower than employer insurance coverage. Over the past decade the increase in Medicaid per enrollee was 4.6 percent per year, but for employer insurance the growth was 7.7 percent per year.[39] Similarly, others have estimated that if one controls for the age and illness level of the Medicaid population, especially those elderly who are dually covered under both Medicaid and Medicare and who account for about half of Medicaid spending, costs are actually about 7 percent less under Medicaid than under employer-sponsored insurance, and enrollees spend substantially less on additional out-of-pocket costs.[40]

Two groups of Kentuckians are most likely to benefit greatly from the increased Medicaid spending and federal subsidies for lower-income employees. If employers stop providing employer-subsidized health insurance and encourage those previously employer-insured poor to move to the public Medicaid system or to the exchanges, then those employers will enjoy an increase in income because they no longer have to pay as much as they did for insurance coverage for their employees. The sanction, penalty, or fine for not covering one's employees will be significantly less than the actual cost of the premiums that many employers are now paying under the existing system. There will also be a substantial increase in income for medical suppliers and providers in the state. The challenge for Kentucky's voters and legislature will be to determine whether and how to recover some of these windfall increases in income from those who gain from the ACA (hospitals, medical-care providers, medical-equipment vendors, employers who drop medical coverage for employers) to help pay the increased state government share of the formula match for new Medicaid enrollees.

MEDICAL INSURANCE AND IMPROVED HEALTH OUTCOMES

The World Health Organization's definition of health implies that there are two components of health—a sense of physical well-being and a sense of mental well-being. Various scholars have used many techniques to examine whether health insurance improves the quantity and quality of life. Some of the possible measures of better or worse health have included mortality; mental, physical, and social disability and activity limitations in everyday life; feeling well, healthy, and whole; amounts of hospitalization; length of healing period; development of comorbidities (other illnesses); and other factors. There is no consensus among research scholars across the disciplines that having medical insurance significantly improves all the measures equally for all members of the community. A discussion of how insurance may affect the health outcomes of particular groups of Kentuckians is beyond the scope of this chapter. However, in a recent meta-analysis of the evaluation and assessment literature on this topic written since 2002, Dr. J. Michael McWilliams concluded: "To date, numerous studies have found consistently beneficial and often significant effects of insurance coverage on health across a comprehensive set of outcomes and a broad range of treatable chronic and acute conditions that affect many adults in the U.S., including hypertension, coronary artery disease, congestive heart failure, stroke, diabetes, HIV infection, depressive symptoms, acute myocardial infarction, acute respiratory illnesses, and traumatic injuries. . . . Based on the evidence to date, the health consequences of uninsurance are real, and vary in magnitude in a clinically consistent manner."[41]

In particular, after insurance coverage is provided to the previously uninsured, these Kentuckians may well improve both the quality and quantity of their lives through earlier detection and treatment of cancers, reduction in preventable hospitalizations because of efforts to establish medical homes and build more community- and school-based clinics, greater longevity from more effective and earlier treatment of cardiovascular disease, and higher quality of life after motor vehicle accidents. Stan Dorn, in an update of the Institute of Medicine's 2002 study about early death and lack of insurance, reports on research that estimates a 15 percent increase in the mortality rate overall among those who are underinsured.[42] Increased medical-insurance coverage for more Kentuckians, therefore, will likely result in hundreds fewer premature deaths each year. In addition to fewer premature deaths, the lessening of pain, comorbidity, intensive treatment, rehospitalization, and other negative outcomes of seeking and getting treatment late or getting less than the recommended treatment will also lower the suffering and stress of thousands of Kentuckians each year, according to research by various scholars.[43]

There may also be some unanticipated consequences from greater spending through these expanded medical-insurance programs. People in rural areas will have more resources, so practitioners may be more likely to go to those areas. In addition, the ACA also provides direct funding for rural and traditionally underserved areas that may stimulate innovative approaches to providing medical services to people living remotely in Kentucky. Some other provisions of the reform legislation will attempt to increase the number of physicians and nurses. Every new physician who begins practice in Kentucky generates more than $1.7 million of economic activity per year in the local community where the physician practices.[44]

One of the potential problems of the ACA may be that a large number of eligible persons under the act will be churned between Medicaid coverage and subsidized exchange programs. That is, people might work part of a year for an employer, be covered by employer or exchange insurance, and then be laid off or furloughed and lose coverage under the employer's insurance or exchange and have to move to Medicaid coverage or no coverage. Sommers and Rosenbaum have suggested that the churning rates could be as high as 50 percent per year.[45] This shifting of insurance coverage often means having to change providers. This in turn affects continuity of coverage and care because there will be different services offered and different co-payments and coinsurance levels between exchange and Medicaid plans. Disruption of continuity of care can interfere with continuous treatment or prevention and cause problems for individuals suffering from chronic conditions.

Assessing the impact of the ACA on Kentuckians' health will involve determinations of how well the legislation is able to increase access, efficiency, effectiveness, and quality of the medical-care system, as well as improve healthy behaviors and outcomes for Kentuckians over time. Assessing the economic, societal, or individual value of the benefits of health improvements, regardless of the measurements used, can be difficult and politically hazardous. Each level of government—national, state, and local—along with their residents and voters must decide (1) what constitutes the meaning of good health, (2) how we will individually and collectively try to achieve it, (3) who gets to have it, and (4) what portion of our individual and collective resources we wish to devote to its pursuit. Many opponents have claimed that the current ACA creates a major, federally dominated, and federally directed takeover of the medical-care system. The current reform effort does none of that. It is very similar to and expands on the same reforms widely accepted by Kentuckians almost twenty years ago. The current reform, like the previously proposed Kentucky reform, continues all the existing financing and providing systems that have been in place for half a century. Full implementation of the ACA by 2014 will provide much higher levels of financial rewards for providers and suppliers in the current medical-care system, who are mostly private entities. By 2014 the ACA reforms will make a significant number of poor, uninsured, and previously uninsurable Kentuckians eligible to join in financial risk-sharing schemes that most persons enjoy now and have enjoyed for the last half century. These reforms will increase the flow of money and medical economic activity to a poor and unhealthy Kentucky. If we are lucky, they may even improve the health of Kentuckians.

NOTES

1. Penny M. Miller, *Kentucky Politics and Government: Do We Stand United?* (Lincoln: University of Nebraska Press, 1994), 328.

2. Ibid., 330–33.

3. World Health Organization, "Preamble to the Constitution of the World Health Organization as Adopted by the International Health Conference, New York, 19 June–22 July 1946; Signed on 22 July 1946 by the Representatives of 61 States," *Official Records of the World Health Organization*, no. 2 (1946): 100.

4. Bernard J. Turnock, *Public Health: What It Is and How It Works* (Sudbury, Mass.: Jones and Bartlett, 2009); Institute of Medicine and Board on Health Promotion and Disease Prevention, *The Future of the Public's Health in the 21st Century* (Washington, D.C.: Institute of Medicine of the National Academies Press, 2002); and Lawrence O. Gostin, "Legal and Public Policy Interventions to Advance the Population's Health," in *Promoting Health: Intervention Strategies from Social and Behavioral Research* (Washington, D.C.: National Academy Press, 2000), 390–416.

5. U.S. Centers for Disease Control, "Life Expectancy by Age, Race, and Sex: Death-Registration States, 1900–1902 to 1919–1921, and United States, 1929–1931 to 2004," *National Vital Statistics Reports* 56, no. 9 (2007): table 11.

6. Steve Crabtree, "Income, Education Levels Combine to Predict Health Problems," accessed October 6, 2010, http://www.gallup.com/poll/127532/Income-Education-Levels-Com bine-Predict-Health-Problems.aspx; J. M. McGinnis, P. Williams-Russo, and J. R. Knickman, "The Case for More Active Policy Attention to Health Promotion," *Health Affairs* 21, no. 2 (2002): 78–93; Michael Marmot and Richard G. Wilkinson, *Social Determinants of Health* (New York: Oxford University Press, 1999); and G. Dahlgren and M. Whitehead, *Policies and Strategies to Promote Social Equity in Health* (Stockholm: Stockholm Institute for Future Studies, 1991).

7. American Hospital Association (AHA), 2010 Long-Range Policy Committee, John W. Bluford III, Chair, *A Call to Action: Creating a Culture of Health* (Chicago: American Hospital Association, January 2011), accessed February 23, 2011, http://www.hret.org/whatsnew /resources/creating-a-culture-of-health.pdf; Centers for Disease Control, "Table 148: Medicare Enrollees, Enrollees in Managed Care, Payment per Enrollee, and Short-Stay Hospital Utilization, by State: United States, 1994 and 2007," 436, accessed March 1, 2010, http://www.cdc.gov /nchs/data/hus/hus09.pdf.; and Kentucky Institute of Medicine, "The Health of Kentucky: A County Assessment," accessed February 22, 2011, http://www.kyiom.org/healthky2007a.pdf.

8. Paul Starr, *The Social Transformation of American Medicine* (New York: Basic Books, 1982); Bradford H. Gray, *The Profit Motive and Patient Care: The Changing Accountability of Doctors and Hospitals* (Cambridge, Mass.: Harvard University Press, 1991); Howard Wolinsky and Tom Brune, *The Serpent on the Staff: The Unhealthy Politics of the American Medical Association* (New York: Tarcher/ Putnam, 1994); James C. Robinson, *The Corporate Practice of Medicine: Competition and Innovation in Health Care* (Berkeley: University of California Press, 1999); Maggie Mahar, *Money-Driven Medicine* (New York: HarperCollins, 2006); Rosemary Stevens, "A History and Health Policy in the United States: The Making of a Health Care Industry, 1948–2008," *Social History of Medicine* 21, no. 3 (2008): 461–83.

9. David Carey, Bradley Herring, and Patrick Lenain, "Health Care Reform in the United States," Working Paper 665, Economics Department of the Organization for Economic Cooperation and Development (Paris, February 2009), 8; E. Nolte and C. M. McKee, "Measuring the Health of Nations: Updating an Earlier Analysis," *Health Affairs* 27, no. 1 (2008): 58–71.

10. Employee Benefit Institute, "Income and Benefits, I: Health Insurance Coverage," accessed February 27, 2010, http://www.ebri.org/pdf/FFE152.27Jan10.final.pdf.

11. Carey, Herring, and Lenain, "Health Care Reform in the United States," 10.

12. E. M. Kitagawa and P. M. Hauser, *Differential Mortality in the United States: A Study in Socioeconomic Epidemiology* (Cambridge, Mass.: Harvard University Press, 1973), 70–71.

13. U.S. Centers for Medicare and Medicaid Service, "National Health Expenditures Aggregate, per Capita Amounts, Percent Distribution, and Average Annual Percent Growth, by Source of Funds: Selected Calendar Years, 1960–2009," accessed February, 22, 2011, http://www.cms.gov/NationalHealthExpendData/downloads/tables.pdf.

14. U.S. Census Bureau, "Income, Poverty, and Health Insurance Coverage in the United States: Summary of Key Findings," accessed September 16, 2010, http://www.census.gov/news room/releases/archives/income_wealth/cb10-144.html.

15. Kaiser Family Foundation, "Waiting for Economic Recovery, Poised for Health Care Reform: A Mid-year Update for FY 2011—Looking Forward to FY 2012," accessed February 22, 2011, http://www.kff.org/medicaid/upload/8137.pdf.

16. Stan Dorn and Genevieve M. Kenney, "Automatically Enrolling Eligible Children and Families into Medicaid and SCHIP: Opportunities, Obstacles, and Options for Federal Policy

Makers," Commonwealth Fund, accessed February 22, 2011, http://www.commonwealthfund
.org/~/media/Files/Publications/Fund%20Report/2006/Jun/Automatically%20Enrolling
%20Eligible%20Children%20and%20Families%20Into%20Medicaid%20and%20SCHIP
%20%20Opportunities%20%20Obsta/Dorn_auto%20enrollingchildren_931%20pdf.pdf.

17. U.S. Centers for Medicare and Medicaid Service, "Table 1: National Health Expenditures and Selected Economic Indicators, Levels and Annual Percent Change: Calendar Years 2004–2019," accessed February 22, 2011, http://www.cms.hhs.gov/NationalHealthExpend Data/downloads/proj2009.pdf.

18. Carey, Herring, and Lenain, "Health Care Reform in the United States," 13.

19. Ibid., 24; Mark Pearson, "Disparities in Health Expenditures across OECD Countries: Why Does the United States Spend So Much More than Other Countries?," Organization for Economic Cooperation and Development, Paris, France, accessed February 22, 2011, http://www.oecd.org/dataoecd/5/34/43800977.pdf.

20. Organization for Economic Cooperation and Development, "OECD Health at a Glance 2009: Key Findings for the United States," accessed February 22, 2011, http://www.oecd.org /unitedstates/oecdhealthataglance2009keyfindingsfortheunitedstates.htm.

21. Kentucky Institute of Medicine, "The Health of Kentucky: A County Assessment," accessed February 22, 2011, http://www.kyiom.org/healthky2007a.pdf.

22. United Health Foundation, America's Health Care Rankings website, "E-access for Kentucky," accessed March 1, 2010, http://www.americashealthrankings.org/yearcompare /2008/2009/KY.aspx#Sup.

23. Kaiser Family Foundation, "Kaiser Center for Medicaid and Medicare, State Health Facts, Kentucky," accessed February 22, 2011, http://www.statehealthfacts.org/mfs.jsp?rgn=19 &rgn=1.

24. Commonwealth Fund, "State Scorecard," accessed February 23, 2011, http://www .commonwealthfund.org/Maps-and-Data/State-Data-Center/State-Scorecard/DataByState /State.aspx?state=KY.

25. David Reisman, *Health Care and Public Policy* (Northampton, Mass.: Elgar, 2009), 1–7.

26. T. R. Oliver, "The Politics of Public Health Policy," *Annual Review of Public Health* 27, no. 1 (2006): 195–233.

27. U.S. House of Representatives, Office of the Legislative Counsel, "Compilation of Patient Protection and Affordable Care Act [as Amended Through May 1, 2010] Including Patient Protection and Affordable Care Act and the Health-Related portions of the Health Care and Education Reconciliation Act of 2010 through May 2010," accessed June 9, 2010, http://docs.house.gov/energycommerce/ppacacon.pdf.

28. In June 2012 the U.S. Supreme Court ruled in *National Federation of Independent Business v. Sebelius* (132 S. Ct. 2566) that it was not constitutionally permissible for the federal government to withhold all Medicaid funds from states that failed to expand Medicaid eligibility to the level specified in the Affordable Care Act. The federal government can still offer financial inducements to expand the Medicaid program, but it is not clear whether all states, including Kentucky, will expand the program to the extent specified in the legislation.

29. John Holohan and Linda Blumberg, "How Would States Be Affected by Health Reform?," Robert Wood Johnson Foundation Report Series, accessed March 1, 2010, http://www .rwjf.org/files/research/55090.pdf.

30. Ibid., table 1.

31. Holohan and Blumberg, "How Would States Be Affected by Health Reform?"

32. John Holahan and I. Headen, "Medicaid Coverage and Spending in Health Reform: National and State-by-State Results for Adults at or below 133% FPL," accessed February 22, 2011, http://www.kff.org/healthreform/upload/Medicaid-Coverage-and-Spending-in-Health -Reform-National-and-State-By-State-Results-for-Adults-at-or-Below-133-FPL.pdf.

33. Kentucky Cabinet for Health and Family Services, "MS 264 Report and Supplements: Characteristics of Eligible MS Recipients, by County, Table 1: Grand Total Eligible Recipients by Age Group," accessed February 20, 2011, http://chfs.ky.gov/NR/rdonlyres/4BCBDCF8 -6361-4897-9D7B-0481A38FB4D2/0/MS264July10PartA.pdf.

34. Kaiser Family Foundation, "Kentucky Employer-Based Health Premiums," accessed February 22, 2011, http://www.kff.org/healthreform/8052.cfm.

35. Kaiser Family Foundation, "StateHealthFacts.org.," accessed July 1, 2012, http://state healthfacts.org/comparereport.jsp?rep=68&cat=4.

36. Kaiser Family Foundation, Commission on Medicaid Facts, "Medicaid Enrollment: December 2009 Data Snapshot," accessed February 20, 2011, http://www.kff.org/medicaid /upload/8050-02.pdf.

37. Holohan and Blumberg, "How Would States Be Affected by Health Reform?"

38. David U. Himmelstein, Deborah Thorne, Elizabeth Warren, and Steffie Woolhandler, "Medical Bankruptcy in the United States, 2007: Results of a National Study," *American Journal of Medicine* 122 (August 2009): 741–46.

39. Kaiser Family Foundation, "Waiting for Economic Recovery, Poised for Health Care Reform," 2.

40. Center on Budget and Policy Priorities, "Expanding Medicaid a Less Costly Way to Cover More Low-Income Uninsured than Expanding Private Insurance," June 26, 2008, 3, accessed February 23, 2011, http://www.cbpp.org/files/6-26-08health.pdf.

41. J. Michael McWilliams, "Health Consequences of Uninsurance among Adults in the United States: Recent Evidence and Implications," *Milbank Quarterly* 87, no. 2 (2009): 443–94.

42. Stan Dorn, "Uninsured and Dying Because of It," Urban Institute, January 2009, table 3. Dorn's methodology is based on that of P. Franks, C. Clancy, and M. Gold, "Health Insurance and Mortality: Evidence from a National Cohort," *JAMA*, August 1993, accessed February 22, 2011, http://www.urban.org/UploadedPDF/411588_uninsured_dying.pdf.

43. Dorn, "Uninsured and Dying Because of It"; McWilliams, "Health Consequences of Uninsurance among Adults in the United States."

44. Alison Davis and Simona Balazs, "The Economic Impact of the Participants in State Loan Repayment Program on Kentucky's Economy," Kentucky Rural Health Works Program, University of Kentucky, Kentucky Cooperative Extension Service, May 2008, accessed February 23, 2011, http://www.ca.uky.edu/agecon/index.php?p=255.

45. Benjamin D. Sommers and Sara Rosenbaum, "Issues in Health Reform: How Changes in Eligibility May Move Millions Back and Forth between Medicaid and Insurance Exchanges," *Health Affairs* 30 (2011): 228–36.

19

The Politics of Kentucky Pharmacy Regulation

Jeffery C. Talbert and Amie Goodin

This chapter examines pharmaceutical health policy in Kentucky by exploring the political process behind the Commonwealth's implementation of some key pharmaceutical regulations. Pharmaceutical regulations affect the distribution, sale, and access to medications, and are often politically contentious because of the influence of opposing well-financed interest groups, such as medical professional organizations, the pharmaceutical industry, and insurers or third-party payers. This chapter focuses on two themes, the interplay among competing interest groups and regulatory variation across states. State regulations are important because of the U.S. model of federalism, a system of shared governance between the national (federal) government and state governments. Under this framework, some decisions are made and implemented at the national level, some decisions are made and implemented at the state level, and some decisions are shared by both (or more) levels of government. Pharmacy, like most health professions, is licensed and regulated at the state level. Each state has authority to specify how health professionals are regulated, and a licensed pharmacist in one state cannot practice in another state unless that person completes additional licensing requirements. In addition to licensing differences, states specify additional criteria for the practice of pharmacy, such as operation and management rules, regulation of controlled substances, marketing, and dispensing. This chapter focuses on how interest-group influence has produced interesting variations across state regulatory policy with regard to mail-order pharmacies, prescribing authority for physician extenders, immunization authority for pharmacists, and the implementation of state programs to monitor prescription drugs.

MAIL-ORDER PHARMACIES

A mail-order pharmacy is an alternative way to purchase prescription medications. Rather than traveling to a local pharmacy to pick up prescriptions, patients can send prescriptions and verification forms to a central processing pharmacy that packages a bulk supply of medication (usually a three months' supply) and mails the package to individual homes. Most commercial health insurers also contract with a pharmacy benefit manager, such as Caremark, Express Scripts, or Medco, which usually processes and completes the claim forms to simplify the transaction. The key to the mail-order business model is the efficiency gains from high volume and low overhead.

The regulations for licensing and for dispensing medications by mail-order pharmacies are quite complex and vary significantly across states. Before 2007, Kentucky regulations required that any mail-order pharmacy that dispensed prescriptions within the state must be licensed in Kentucky and must report dispensing information on controlled substances to Kentucky's prescription drug monitoring program. The in-state licensing requirement was a disincentive to potential nationally focused mail-order pharmacy businesses, which often use an automated drug dispensing process supervised by pharmacists licensed in other locations. For example, large, high-volume mail-order pharmacies commonly use a warehouse facility specialized to package shipments with great efficiency. This model may use low-cost technicians to complete the majority of the packaging process and have the pharmacists verify the prescription at the end of the shipping process. Advances in Internet technology and communication have allowed remote-location verification, in which a licensed pharmacist checks the package by using a remote video link. This allows maximum efficiency and time use for the pharmacist, who can often cover multiple sites from a single location. However, that is where some state regulations become an issue for this business model. Imagine the Amazon.com business of shipping books all over the United States from regional warehouses, but with each state regulating how the shipping process works and what can be shipped where and by what type of workers. Such rules may reduce the efficiency of this business model to the point where it is no longer effective. The mail-order business in pharmacy is more complicated. Some state regulations allow this business design, while others restrict or exclude some of the required design elements.

In October 2007 Medco Health Solutions announced that it was considering opening a mail-order pharmacy business in Louisville. The site was well suited to the business decision because of the UPS terminal at the Louisville International Airport and Kentucky's central location for much of the eastern United States. But the plan had a critical flaw because current regulations governing the practice of pharmacy in Kentucky prohibited automated-process pharmacies. Medco and the Kentucky state economic development agencies asked the Kentucky Board of Pharmacy to amend the regulations and allow the company to use its automated processes. To make its case, Medco cited Kentucky's "any willing provider" laws, which prevent insurers from excluding coverage for service providers who agree to provide care for the insurers' terms. The Board of Pharmacy agreed to review existing regulations and began an expedited review process to consider regulatory change. The changes considered would have vast implications for pharmacy businesses and patient care. The review process involved notices sent to registered pharmacists in the state and public information meetings to discuss the new regulations.

Independent and chain pharmacy associations responded by mobilizing and sent their representatives to voice opposition to Medco's plans. When the board prepared to review the regulatory change, it was persuaded to consider a more in-depth review process and explore the possible consequences of the regulation change. The extended review period resulted in a delay in approving the operation of the Medco facility. Fearing an extended delay in the Kentucky approval process, Medco abandoned its Kentucky plan and instead opened a new mail-order facility in Indiana.[1]

This case highlights several important factors concerning regulations and politics. Interest group influence is often an important factor in shaping regulations—in this case Kentucky's pharmaceutical regulations. The Medco plan would have diluted the labor power of Kentucky pharmacists, who responded quickly to counter changes in regulation that would shift the rules.

STATE VARIATION IN PRESCRIBING AUTHORITY

Each state has somewhat different regulations governing which types of health-care professionals have the authority to prescribe specific classes of medications. Practitioners are generally required to meet specific certification requirements, and the prescriptions they write must fall within the scope of their practice. Examples of types of practitioners with prescribing authority are physicians, advanced registered nurse practitioners (ARNPs), certified physician assistants, certified registered nurse anesthetists, optometrists, pharmacists, dentists, and veterinarians. Why do states set specific regulations rather than follow a national regulatory framework (for example, ARNPs may not prescribe certain medications, such as controlled substances, in Kentucky without entering into a collaborative agreement with a physician despite having independent authority in most other states)? One answer to this question is the relationship between organized groups and the political framework in the state. The influence of certain professional organizations in Kentucky can be observed through the strict regulation of prescribing and dispensing authority of various health-care professionals in the state.

During the 2005 Kentucky legislative session Senate Bill (SB) 122 included provisions that would grant ARNPs authority to prescribe controlled substances. An exploratory study conducted by Kentucky's Legislative Research Committee reported that 96 percent of ARNPs supported the expansion of ARNP prescribing authority. However, only 31 percent of physicians supported expansion of ARNP authority.[2] The Kentucky Medical Association (KMA), a professional organization representing Kentucky physicians, opposed the bill, citing concerns of increased drug abuse and diversion.[3] The Kentucky Coalition of Nurse Practitioners, a professional organization representing ARNPs, countered by citing problems with access to care in parts of the state and provider shortages in rural areas. After several months of intense lobbying against the bill by the KMA and the Kentucky Board of Medical Licensure, SB 122 passed successfully through both the House and the Senate but was not signed into law, a brief success for the KMA.

Just one year after the defeat of SB 122 a new bill was introduced that included similar provisions to grant ARNPs prescribing authority for controlled substances.

This new bill, SB 65, gained significant momentum when the KMA changed its official position to "neutral" and nursing groups stepped in to lobby in favor of the bill.[4] The KMA cited a divided membership as the reason for relaxing its position. As the bill appeared to gain momentum to pass the Senate and the House, the KMA again changed its position and succeeded in lobbying to add provisions that required ARNPs to enter into collaborative agreements with physicians before they were permitted to prescribe controlled substances. The revised bill was signed into law in 2006.

Four years after ARNPs were granted prescribing authority in Kentucky, the issue returned to the spotlight when two separate bills (SB 75 and House Bill [HB] 556) were introduced to remove the requirements that ARNPs enter into collaborative agreements with physicians. The KMA went back on the offensive, decrying the bills as a way for ARNPs to usurp the role of physicians and calling the bill "egregious."[5] Senator Gary Tapp, who sponsored SB 75, described the intensity of lobbying efforts: "I don't think there's anything I could do with the bill, with the exception of letting it die, that will suit the KMA." The Kentucky Coalition of Nurse Practitioners fired back by restating its original position of problems with access to medical care in rural Kentucky and alleging financial abuses of collaborative-agreement provisions by physicians as reasons for granting ARNPs independent prescribing authority. Both bills passed out of committee and were presented to the full House and Senate in March of 2010, but SB 75 did not come to a vote after it was presented to the full Senate for discussion, and HB 556 was sent back to the House Health and Welfare Committee. Both bills died at the end of the 2010 legislative session and no similar bill has been introduced in legislative sessions since that time.

The political conflict between physician and nursing organizations over ARNP prescribing authority arose because of the desire of both parties to hold the rights to sell prescribing services. This type of behavior, where an individual or group seeks to limit the ability of others to legally provide the same service, is an example of rent seeking. Rent seeking occurs when one group or person tries to obtain selective benefits through the political process. The legal exclusivity granted physicians to perform many types of medical services has provoked criticism of the medical community for quite some time.[6] The medical professional organizations representing both ARNPs and physicians can be described as engaging in rent-seeking behavior. The KMA likely sought to maintain exclusivity in prescribing authority because ARNP prescribing authority could potentially decrease physician earnings by acting as economic competition to physicians, particularly in areas of the state with limited access to medical care.

IMMUNIZATIONS BY PHARMACISTS

Immunizations or vaccinations are a form of medication where patients are given weakened or killed germs (microbes) that are unable to cause disease in order to build immunity. Immunity teaches a person's body how to fight the microbes the next time they are encountered and prevents the microbes from causing disease. Immunizations are generally administered though injections, or shots. In the past, most patients were given vaccinations at their health-care provider's office, usually a primary care physician's office. But other health-care providers, such as physician assistants and ARNPs, can also administer immunizations at locations that are more convenient for patients. As seen in the case of ARNP prescribing regulations, professional organizations and other interest groups can be powerful influences in the legislative decision-making process. Another area of pharmaceutical regulation where interest group influence is apparent is the regulation (or lack thereof) of pharmacist authority to administer immunizations in Kentucky. Pharmacists are now permitted to give immunizations in almost every state, but the right to immunize was a slow fight in most states. This section will explore the lobbying efforts by Kentucky pharmacists to expand the pharmacist's authority to administer immunizations.

Pharmacists were prohibited from providing immunizations in most states until the late 1990s and the early years of the twenty-first century, when national and state pharmacist associations began advocating for immunization authority on the grounds that no other health-care providers are subject to prohibitions on immunization authority. As map 19.1 shows, by 2004 most states had moved to allow pharmacist immunizations.

According to the National Association of Boards of Pharmacy annual law reports, all states had adopted regulations permitting pharmacists to provide immunizations under certain circumstances by 2010.[7] Map 19.2 reflects this change: only three states prohibited pharmacist immunizations by 2009 and those remaining three states

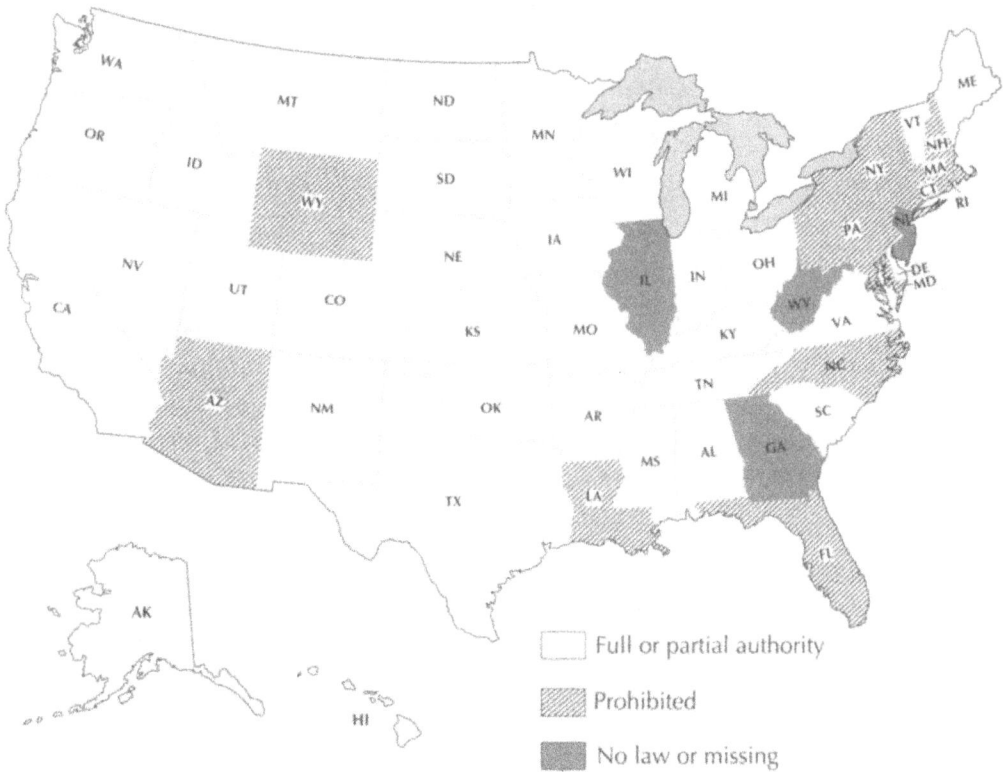

Map 19.1. Pharmacist immunization authority in 2004

moved to grant pharmacist immunization authority by the next year. Even after this large increase in pharmacist immunization authority, several states continue to limit immunization authority in some way, usually by restricting pharmacists from administering immunizations to people younger than eighteen years of age or by limiting immunization authority to the influenza vaccine. This trend toward fewer restrictions on pharmacist immunization authority over time can be observed in figure 19.1.

In Kentucky pharmacist immunization authority began in 2004 with a simple modification to statute that separated the dispensing process of medications from immunizations. This minor change was made to allow pharmacists to provide immunizations in Kentucky after a successful lobbying effort by Kentucky pharmacist organizations, who were advocating for increased authority on the basis of successful authority increases in other regions of the country. The change did not appear to affect other health-care providers and so did not attract opposition from the KMA or other medical interest groups. No complaints were filed during the 2004 trial year after the statute change, and so lawmakers did not pursue further restrictions of Kentucky pharmacist immunization authority.

The 2004 change propelled Kentucky pharmacists to one of the highest degrees of immunization authority in the nation. By 2010 all the states surrounding Kentucky except Ohio had abandoned restrictive regulations in favor of more permissible poli-

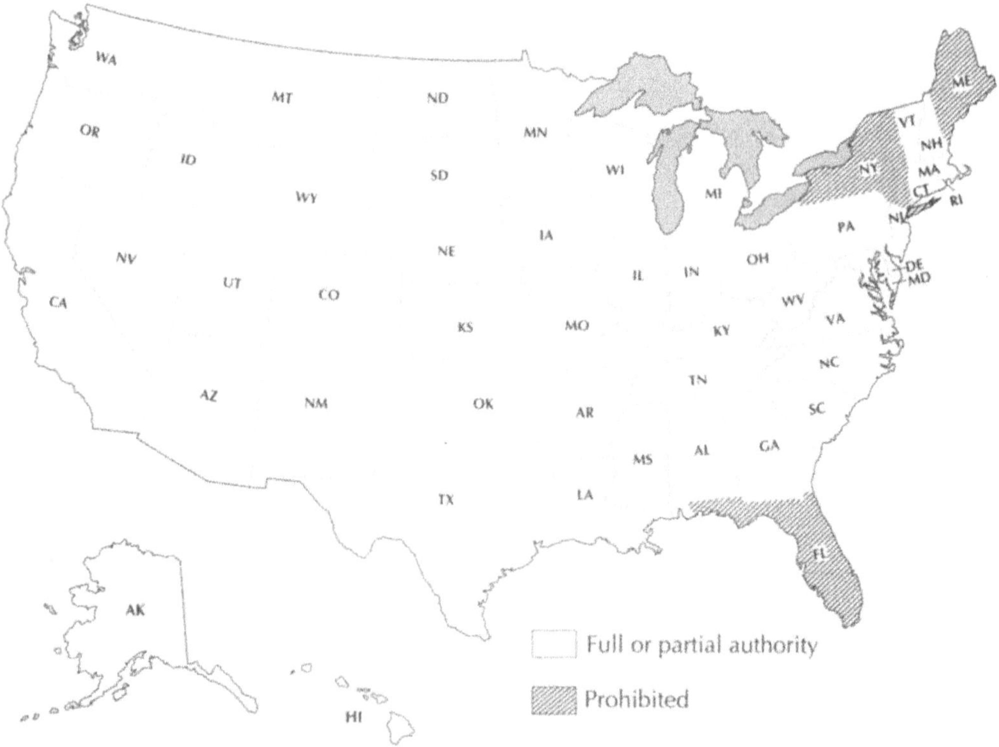

Map 19.2. Pharmacist immunization authority in 2009

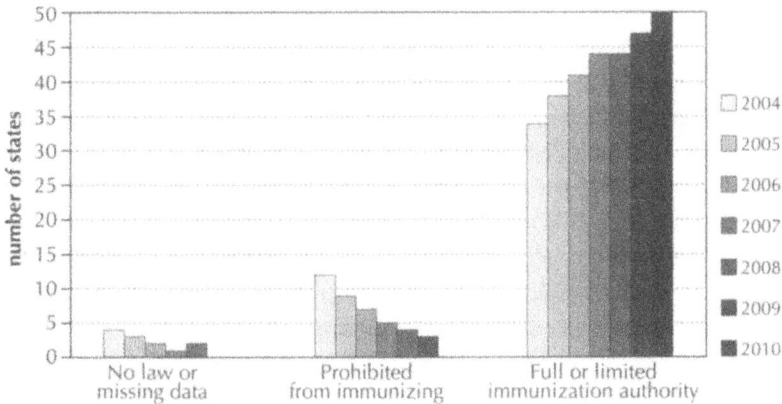

Figure 19.1. ARNP prescribing authority

cies. The state of Kentucky and most surrounding states grant pharmacists full immunization authority, which means that there are no restrictions on the age of the recipient or the type of immunization administered. Many factors influence differences in policy adoption among states, and regulatory variation in pharmaceutical policies across states will be the focus of the next section.

STATE PROGRAMS TO MONITOR PRESCRIPTION DRUGS

Controlled prescription drugs, including opioid pain relievers, tranquilizers, and sedatives, are at the core of a public health crisis facing the United States today: prescription drug abuse. Prescription drug abuse has reached epidemic status and shows no sign of abating.[8] Kentucky has been hit particularly hard by the epidemic of prescription drug abuse. In 2000 only 2.7 percent of substance abuse treatment admissions in Kentucky were for opiate addiction, but by 2009 substance abuse treatment admissions for opiate addiction skyrocketed to 23.5 percent of all substance abuse treatment admissions.[9] If one compares the Kentucky treatment admissions data with national substance abuse treatment admissions trends for opiate addiction (1.6 percent in 2000 and 7.1 percent in 2009), it is clear that Kentucky faces a serious prescription drug abuse problem. In 2011 Kentucky saw another dramatic increase in opiate substance abuse treatment admissions (32.5 percent of total treatment admissions), but national data are not yet available for comparison. According to the 2004 National Survey on Drug Use and Health, Kentucky teens and adults were also more likely to abuse prescription pain relievers than teens and adults in any other state.[10]

Controlled prescription drugs (also referred to as prescription controlled substances) have been regulated by the federal government since 1970; however, individual states have taken the lead in creating programs to reduce prescription drug abuse and diversion by discouraging doctor shopping, inappropriate prescribing, prescription forgery, and inappropriate controlled substance dispensing. Currently, forty-nine states have enacted legislation authorizing prescription drug monitoring programs

(PDMPs), and forty-two of those states have active programs.[11] PDMPs serve both a public health and law enforcement mission. Although model legislation for PDMPs is available, variation exists across states in the enacting legislation, program design, and operations. Ultimately, all programs are designed to fulfill the same mission: to reduce prescription drug abuse and diversion.

The basic program design seeks to facilitate collection, analysis, and reporting of controlled substance use; however, states exhibit considerable variation in their operation. Although the majority of PDMPs are housed within state agencies that are coupled with a public health mission (e.g., health profession boards and departments of health and human services), six states (California, Georgia, New Jersey, Oklahoma, Pennsylvania, and Texas) operate PDMPs from state law enforcement agencies.[12] Some PDMPs, classified as having a mission predominantly oriented to public health, generate solicited (reactive) reports in response to an inquiry by a health-care provider who wishes to check the prescription history of an individual patient. In contrast, PDMPs with a law enforcement focus may generate unsolicited (proactive) reports whenever "suspicious behavior" (of patients, prescribers, or pharmacies) is detected.[13] Map 19.3 shows the variation of the PDMP programs across the United States by type of program: reactive, proactive (letter), proactive (reports), and no program.

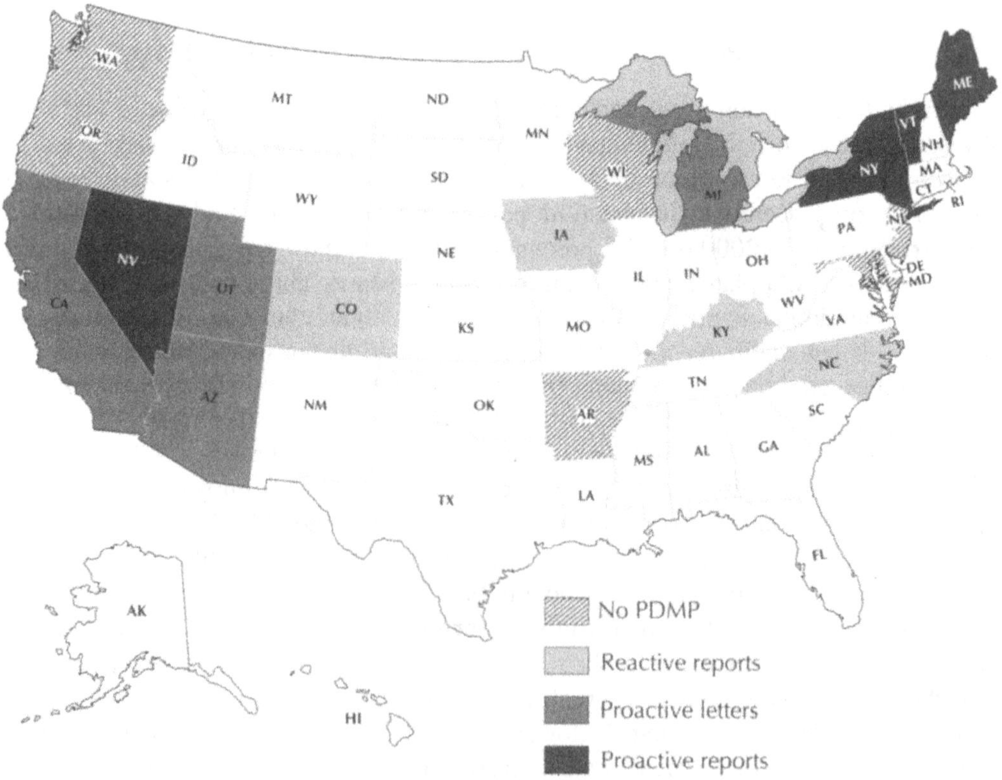

Map 19.3. State prescription drug monitoring programs

We now examine regulatory variation across states in a broader sense by examining the policy differences among states with and without operational PDMPs. As of 2013, Kentucky was one of forty-two states with an operational PDMP.

The Kentucky All Schedule Prescription Electronic Reporting program (KASPER) was enacted in 1999 to monitor the prescription and distribution of controlled substances. The original design of the program required dispensers of controlled substances to report dispensing information to a centralized database every sixteen days. Pharmacists, prescribers, and law enforcement could request information about a patient in the form of a KASPER report, which offers details about the amount of controlled substances prescribed for and dispensed to that patient. In 2005 KASPER regulations were altered to accommodate a more technologically sophisticated version of the program, which allowed KASPER users to receive KASPER reports instantly through a secure website rather than waiting for mail or fax report delivery. Dispensers of controlled substances are now required to submit dispensing information every day.

Kentucky's KASPER program served as a model program for several states. Ohio lawmakers cited the success of KASPER as the reason for modeling Ohio's PDMP after KASPER.[14] Despite the perceived effectiveness of KASPER, no state with an operational PDMP has produced evidence on the effectiveness of PDMPs to reduce mortality from prescription drug overdoses.[15] Kentucky officials cite problems with leakage from other states where easy access to controlled substances allows patients to move large quantities of controlled substances into the state. Several reports note that continued drug-diversion problems in eastern Kentucky are partially due to the lack of a PDMP in Florida, where arrests are often made of patients who traffic in controlled substances and doctor-shop along the so-called pill pipeline that runs along the interstates from Florida to Kentucky.[16]

According to some Kentucky lawmakers, the pill pipeline originated from Florida's lack of regulations that would prevent medical practitioners from selling and dispensing controlled substances without providing adequate medical examinations or supervision. The relative ease of obtaining controlled substances in Florida attracts patients from other states, who then transport the drugs back to Kentucky and other states along the pipeline. Although Florida pharmacists agreed that a PDMP should be implemented in their state,[17] Florida lawmakers have been reluctant to follow through.

The Florida PDMP, enacted in 2009 but not yet operational, was on the chopping block just one year after its adoption. Florida governor Rick Scott proposed cutting the planned Florida PDMP in early 2011. The manufacturer of the controlled substance known as OxyContin stepped in and offered to fund Florida's PDMP. The funding was refused, and the governor's office cited privacy concerns as the reason for repealing Florida's PDMP. The proposed repeal sparked an outcry from Kentucky politicians. In February 2011 Kentucky and Florida news outlets published letters from U.S. representative Hal Rogers of Kentucky and Kentucky governor Steve Beshear to Florida governor Rick Scott that pleaded with him to reconsider the repeal of Florida's PDMP.

The resulting media attention stirred by the controversial proposal resulted in a congressional hearing, in which the governors of Kentucky and Florida were called on to testify about the damages caused to both states by the pill pipeline. By the time of the congressional hearing, which occurred just a few weeks after the initial proposal to cut the program, Florida governor Scott changed his position and agreed to implement a PDMP as planned.[18] Florida's legislature responded to harsh criticism for its inaction by adopting a bill that stiffens penalties for physicians and clinics found to be selling and dispensing controlled substances in a medically inappropriate manner.[19] The Florida PDMP officially began operations on September 1, 2011.

Policies may spread from one government to another via several mechanisms.[20] The spread or diffusion of PDMPs among state governments could have occurred through policy-oriented learning, economic competition, coercion, or imitation. Policy-oriented learning occurs when governments adopt policies that have been successful in other states[21] or test policies in their own state.[22] Ohio's decision to model its PDMP after KASPER because of perceived success is an example of the diffusion mechanism of policy-oriented learning.

Economic competition does not sufficiently explain the diffusion of PDMPs across states because the states without operational PDMPs are scattered throughout the country. If economic competition were a significant factor in a state's decision to adopt a PDMP, then it would be reasonable to assume that the neighbors of states with PD-MPs would also adopt PDMPs, but this has not been the case. It is possible that some states chose to implement PDMPs because of a desire to imitate other state programs, but the practical reasons for cooperating with neighboring states seem to explain the motivations for PDMP implementation more effectively. In other words, states facing similar drug abuse and diversion problems may be more likely to implement PDMPs because they observe success in other states.[23]

In comparisons of states with and without operational PDMPs, there are few characteristics that predict the likelihood of a state having an operational PDMP. Statistical analysis reveals no association between states that have operational PDMPs and the general political leanings of the population (defined here as voting majority Republican in three or four of the last four presidential elections), the current political party control of the state legislature, the regional location of the state (categorized here as Northeast, West, South, and Midwest), and states that have large rural populations (more than 30 percent of the state population is classified as living in a rural area as defined by the 2010 census). There is a statistically significant relationship between having an operational PDMP and having a current Republican governor ($p = 0.091$), although this variable becomes insignificant when all other factors mentioned are controlled for in a logistic regression analysis.

A combination of public support for PDMPs and the political will to address Kentucky's prescription drug abuse and diversion problem created the unique political climate in Kentucky necessary for the program to be implemented successfully. Changes to KASPER and other state PDMPs continue to be proposed. Professional organizations and interest groups representing health-care providers, pharmacists, prescription drug manufacturers, and law enforcement are likely to take more active roles in influencing future policy changes.

All the cases of pharmaceutical regulations discussed in this chapter address in some way the broader question of the more effective level at which to design governance and regulation: the federal level or the state level. Although interest groups are certainly active at the national level, our cases highlight that they are also very active at the state and local levels. The impact of this access to decision makers and governing is not immediately clear, but proponents of the states as laboratories appear to have some support. States do appear to learn from one another and implement programs that appear successful in other states, as demonstrated in the case of state emulation of PDMPs that were perceived to be successful. Without such learning opportunities, governance would seem to be reduced in effectiveness and representation.

Pharmaceutical regulations broadly affect policy actors at different levels of governance: from licensure and prescribing authority at the state and local level to the regulation of interstate commercial activity at the state and national level. This chapter has focused on case examples to demonstrate the interplay between federalism and interest group influence. Under a federalism model, state and federal governance is shared, and as demonstrated in the cases discussed throughout this chapter, shared governance affects the design and organization of pharmaceutical regulations across the states.

NOTES

1. "The Board of Pharmacy, GLI and Medco: Protecting Consumers," *Louisville Courier-Journal*, November 26, 2007, A8; "Medco Chooses Central Indiana," *Louisville Courier-Journal*, November 13, 2007, A1.

2. Legislative Research Commission, *A Study of Expanding Prescriptive Authority for Controlled Substances to Advanced Registered Nurse Practitioners (2004 House Bill 595)*, Research Report 323 (Frankfort, Ky.: Legislative Research Commission, December 2004).

3. Deborah Yetter, "Time Grows Short for Bill on Painkiller Prescriptions," *Louisville Courier-Journal*, March 4, 2005.

4. Laura Ungar, "Some Fear Drug Bill Could Encourage Abuse," *Louisville Courier-Journal*, February 18, 2006, B1.

5. Deborah Yetter, "Battle Brewing over Nurse Practitioners," *Louisville Courier-Journal*, March 4, 2010, A1.

6. Keith B. Leffler, "Physician Licensure: Competition and Monopoly in American Medicine," *Journal of Law and Economics* 21, no. 1 (1978): 165–86.

7. National Association of Boards of Pharmacy, NABPLAW Online, accessed June 7, 2011, http://www.nabp.net.

8. Quiping Gu, Charles F. Dillon, and Vicki L. Burt, "Prescription Drug Use Continues to Increase: U.S. Prescription Drug Data for 2007–08," NCHS Data Brief no. 42, September 2010, accessed June 7, 2011, http://www.cdc.gov/nchs/data/databriefs/db42.pdf; S. H. Hernandez and L. S. Nelson, "Prescription Drug Abuse: Insight into the Epidemic," *Clinical Pharmacology and Therapeutics* 88, no. 3 (2010): 307–17; and Leonard J. Paulozzi, Edwin M. Kilbourne, and Hema A. Desai, "Prescription Drug Monitoring Programs and Death Rates from Drug Overdose," *Pain Medicine* 12 (2011): 747–54.

9. Substance Abuse and Mental Health Data Archive (SAMHDA); Treatment Episode Data Sets-Admissions, 1992 to Present, accessed June 2, 2013, http://wwwdasis.samhsa.gov/webt/NewMapv1.htm.

10. Substance Abuse and Mental Health Services Administration; National Survey on Drug Use and Health (NSDUH) 2004, Table B.8 Nonmedical Use of Pain Relievers in Past

Year, by Age, Group, and State: Percentages, Annual Averages Based on 2003 and 2004 NS-DUHs, accessed June 2, 2013, http://www.samhsa.gov/data/2k4State/appB.htm.

11. Alliance of States with Prescription Monitoring Programs, "Status of PDMPs," May 16, 2011, accessed July 24, 2011, http://www.pmpalliance.org/pdf/pmpstatusmap2011.pdf.

12. Ibid.

13. Carnevale Associates, *Prescription Drug Monitoring Information Brief: State Prescription Drug Monitoring Programs Highly Effective* (Gaithersburg, Md.: Carnevale Associates LLC, August 2007), accessed October 15, 2010, http://www.carnevaleassociates.com /PDMP_Info_Brief.pdf; Nathaniel Katz, Lee Panas, MeeLee Kim, Adele D. Audet, Arnold Bilansky, John Eadie, Peter Kreiner, Florence C. Paillard, Cindy Thomas, Grant Carrow, "Usefulness of Prescription Monitoring Programs for Surveillance—Analysis of Schedule II Opioids Prescription Data in Massachusetts, 1996–2006," *Pharmacoepidemiology and Drug Safety* 19 (2010): 115–23.

14. "Ohio House Passes Drug Control Bill—Database Would Keep Users from Shopping for Prescriptions," *Lexington Herald-Leader*, May 18, 2004, B3.

15. Paulozzi, Kilbourne, and Desai, "Prescription Drug Monitoring Programs."

16. Bill Estep, "Pill Pipeline from Florida Remains Open," *Lexington Herald-Leader*, January 3, 2011, A1.

17. Jennifer A. Fass and Patrick C. Hardigan, "Attitudes of Florida Pharmacists toward Implementing a State Prescription Drug Monitoring Program for Controlled Substances," *Journal of Managed Care* 17, no. 6 (2011): 430–38.

18. Lesley Clark, "Scott Describes Fla. Response to Prescription Drug Abuse to Congress: Rick Scott Joined the Governor of Kentucky to Testify before Congress over the Prescription Drug Abuse Crisis Affecting Both States," *Miami Herald*, April 13, 2011, A1.

19. Arian Campo-Flores, "Florida Targeting 'Pill Mills,'" *Wall Street Journal*, May 9, 2011, accessed June 2, 2013, http://online.wsj.com/article/SB1000142405274870468190457631102 593116480.html#printMode.

20. Charles R. Shipan and Craig Volden, "The Mechanisms of Policy Diffusion," *American Journal of Political Science* 52, no. 4 (2008): 840–57; F. S. Berry and W. D. Berry, "State Lottery Adoptions as Policy Innovations: An Event History Analysis," *American Political Science Review* 84, no. 2 (1990): 395–416.

21. Craig Volden, "States as Policy Laboratories: Emulating Success in the Children's Health Insurance Program," *American Journal of Political Science* 50, no. 2 (2006): 294–312.

22. Craig Volden, Michael M. Ting, and Daniel P. Carpenter, "A Formal Model of Learning and Policy Diffusion," *American Political Science Review* 102, no. 3 (2008): 319–32.

23. Christopher Z. Mooney, "Modeling Regional Effects on State Policy Diffusion," *Political Research Quarterly* 54, no. 1 (2001): 103–24.

Part III

Kentucky Politics:
Past, Present, and Future

20

Future Political Developments in the Commonwealth

James C. Clinger and Michael W. Hail

The review of Kentucky institutions and public policy issues presented in this book reveals a composite picture of challenges similar to those facing other states in the American system of federalism. But challenges are not new, and Kentucky has had a long tradition of producing leaders in national politics who faced challenges and created some new ones of their own. In the nineteenth century several luminaries of national politics—Abraham Lincoln, Jefferson Davis, and Henry Clay—had Kentucky origins. Today Kentucky again is the home of some of the most influential national leaders. Mitch McConnell is Senate Republican leader, and Harold Rogers is chair of the House Appropriations Committee.

But Kentucky politics remains, as Richard F. Fenno Jr.[1] has noted, substantially defined by local politics. The "home style" of Kentucky politics continues to underscore this politics of locality, which is often termed in Kentucky "the courthouse crowd." There are numerous manifestations of the local nature of politics in the Commonwealth of Kentucky, but the consistency of community-level political forces directing state and federal electoral politics is unmistakable. A good example of this is the American Plan of Kentucky's most famous political son, Henry Clay. Clay was the congressional leader of the Whig Party, and throughout his political career he championed the constitutional position that there was a positive role for government to foster economic and community development through what were then termed "internal improvements." The Democrats, most notably James Madison and Andrew Jackson, had opposed this broad understanding of the commerce clause and the use of federal power and had vetoed legislation that would have built roads and bridges to promote commerce as fundamentally unconstitutional. In recent times, of course, it is the Democrats who have supported this broad view of the commerce clause and the expansive use of federal authority.

In the early nineteenth century, however, Henry Clay articulated the constitutional counterview and advocated a stronger role for the national government to promote the general welfare and economic development through these internal improvements. Clay championed several projects in Kentucky that would benefit from federal support under his American Plan, and even though some, like the Maysville Road, were not realized, it is important to note that local political forces were a significant part of Clay's position on this issue. Clay's position was a significant foundation for what would later not only develop into a national consensus on the role of government but also would effectively be the constitutional position on which economic-development policy making would be based during the past century and up to the present. For a careful student of politics, it is essential to understand the role of local politics in shaping the leaders in Kentucky politics.

Another important point to consider is the role that local elective office plays in developing the leadership of Kentucky's most prominent and successful politicians. Senator Mitch McConnell was County Judge-Executive of Jefferson County before his election to the U.S. Senate. His mentor, Senator John Sherman Cooper, was Pulaski County Judge-Executive prior to being elected U.S. senator from Kentucky. The local governments are where essential political experience is gained and grounded.

Regions and political parties are important points around which the geography of local politics aggregates and articulates interests. The basic regions of east, central, and west still hold great significance for Kentucky politics. The northern and southern areas can also be added as geographic political regions that are gaining importance. Additionally, the economic region of the Golden Triangle has gained importance as an economic and political region. The Triangle affects the politics of Kentucky as an extension of the older and enduring conflict of urban and rural interests that has been increasingly cultural rather than economic at its core. Economic sectors that have historically aligned with regions remain significant political influences, with the notable exception of the decline of tobacco and some farming interests. Traditional sectors like the coal, horse, and bourbon industries are among the sectors with significant influence, despite the coal and energy sector and the horse industry experiencing some various struggles.

Significant factionalism remains in the Democratic Party, where interests from these myriad forces create alliances and rivalries. Potential factionalism within the Republican Party is a function of growth in the size of the GOP as realignment trends across the southern states continue to translate traditionally conservative Democrats into Republicans, but even more significant for Republicans is the rise of the Tea Party movement in Kentucky. Kentucky is becoming more two-party competitive even as it retains the character of larger-scale patterns of politics. The future effects of continuing realignment and dealignment, as well as political movements like the Tea Party, will create a political geography that will foster two-party competitiveness where larger political identities become more nationalized for the parties, while the decisive forces of articulation remain local and in traditional Kentucky interest aggregations.

Kentucky, like other states, will be struggling with fiscal pressures. Kentucky must find ways to maintain essential services across a range of typical state responsibilities from education to public safety with a shrinking resource base, as discussed in chapter 8 on public budgeting. Complicating this challenge are the competing pressures of federal devolution and rising interstate program costs. The federal cost shifting of programs without resources and other central government dictates through unfunded mandates, preemptions, and co-optations, as noted in chapter 2 on federalism, continue to be an enduring intergovernmental political trend. Structural changes to health care by the central government, as discussed in chapter 18, or regulatory changes to health care, as discussed in chapter 19, further illustrate the effects of these trends.

In the coming years Kentucky faces many challenges that may be difficult to overcome. Like many states, Kentucky government suffers from serious financial problems. As chapter 8 by Lisa A. Cave explains, whether these problems stem from a lack of revenue or an excess of spending is significantly disputed. What is not in question is that the Kentucky government's fiscal problems have been substantial in recent years and do not seem likely to disappear anytime soon. Medicaid costs have been increasing substantially, and requirements of compliance with the Affordable Care Act will increase the number of households eligible for Medicaid coverage. Furthermore, Kentucky's population is rapidly aging. As the size of the elderly population increases, the number of people on Medicaid for nursing-home care is likely to rise as well. Education costs remain a large component of the budget. At one time, as Richard Day and Jo Ann Ewalt discuss in chapter 14, Kentucky's educational system was poorly funded relative to other states. Over time, however, K–12 education has been substantially reformed and professionalized. More money has been spent, and there has been some subsequent improvement in observable performance. But Kentucky students' test scores, compared with national averages, are still low. More progress needs to be made, but there is little evidence that additional funds will be forthcoming. Kentucky has tried and failed to secure significant funding from the Race to the Top program, which involved competition with other states for limited grant funds. Although correctional costs are still small relative to the overall budget, they have grown dramatically over the past few decades as prison populations have increased. This rate of increase is probably not sustainable, and thus corrections and criminal justice policy will be one area of Kentucky politics in which the coming decade will likely feature conflict and restructuring. In 2011 the General Assembly changed the criminal codes' penalties for many crimes, particularly drug offenses, with the hope that lighter penalties for small-scale, nonviolent drug offenders would keep incarceration rates and costs in check.

Tax reform, a topic that returns to popular debate with great regularity, seems to have wide support, but no one seems to agree what true reform should be. Many of the Democratic members of the General Assembly would prefer a more progressive state tax code with a heavier burden on high-income individuals and corporate taxpayers, and many Democrats would also prefer to boost revenue derived from expanded gaming. Most Republican legislators would prefer a tax system that focuses on consumption and reduced tax burdens for investment and businesses. Many Republicans would also prefer a tax code with lower marginal rates but fewer deductions and credits. With Democrats in control of one chamber and Republicans in control of the other, it will be difficult for the chambers to come to an agreement about tax policy changes.[2] As long as there is divided government in Frankfort, substantial reform seems unlikely without a broad consensus-building, bipartisan approach. Though it should be noted that the recently elected Senate president, Republican Robert Stivers, has already demonstrated leadership that could improve prospects for bipartisanship in the future.

One of the most significant factors that arguably promote economic development is a college education. The Kentucky Long Term Policy Research Center conducted several research studies that underscored the national literature to substantiate the strong correlation between education attainment and economic prosperity. Kentucky has historically lagged behind the rest of the nation in the percentage of its population that has attained the distinction of a college diploma. The Commonwealth's Council on Postsecondary Education has set a goal of doubling the number of college graduates by 2020. The number of Kentuckians completing college has increased in recent decades, and all state universities in Kentucky have adopted ambitious plans for recruiting and retaining students. But the chances of reaching the 2020 goal seem remote. Much of the funding used by Kentucky high-school graduates comes from the Kentucky Educational Excellence Scholarship (KEES) fund, which is funded by proceeds from the lottery, but KEES money is constrained by the fiscal constraints of lottery revenue. Declining appropriations from the General Assembly to the state universities in recent years have stressed each university and have led to tuition increases imposed on students. Enrollments have increased at almost every state institution, and the community college system has grown dramatically. But the goal of doubling the number of graduates by 2020 seems unlikely to be reached despite substantial progress.

In addition to the policy challenges that face the Commonwealth, there are a number of perceived problems with Kentucky's political process that must be confronted in the coming years. As chapter 15 by Steven Koven discusses, Kentucky has been plagued by serious problems of political corruption throughout its history. Kentucky's legislature, its governors, and even its courts have been tainted by various scandals from time to time. Kentucky is not alone in having this problem, as the recent corruption in Illinois illustrates. Often, other states have responded with various types of reform that have included expanded ethics laws, campaign finance regulations, term limitations, and expansion of direct democracy. Just as other states have addressed these problems, the Commonwealth has responded with new ethics rules and campaign finance regulations, and as Koven discusses in his chapter, Kentucky has adopted one of the strictest ethics laws in the nation. As Donald Gross discusses in chapter 10, Kentucky adopted campaign finance regulations, including public financing of gubernatorial elections. Nonetheless, campaign costs have continued to rise, and the General Assembly has refused to continue appropriating money to finance the gubernatorial campaigns.

Future research on state and local politics in Kentucky, as in other states, requires an attention to the increasing interdependence and complexity of the intergovernmental political system. The system of American federalism provides a dynamic market for policy innovation and diffusion. There are no easy solutions to government reform. In most cases the electorate ultimately must take responsibility and participate in the system for any real change or fundamental reforms to be realized. Kentucky has a great tradition of developing prominent national leaders and policies, and Kentucky states-men, both Democrats and Republicans, continue this tradition today. Kentucky leaders most often start in local politics, and state and local politics in Kentucky continues to present serious students of politics substantive material for study and research.

NOTES

1. Richard F. Fenno Jr., *Home Style: House Members in Their Districts* (Boston: Little, Brown and Company, 1978).

2. The Kentucky House and Senate remain very close in their partisan division. The Kentucky House under Republican Minority Leader Jeff Hoover has narrowed the margin to 55–45, and it is the last Democrat-controlled lower chamber in the South.

Acknowledgments

The editors wish to thank all the contributors, students, faculty colleagues, staff, and administrators for their support at Murray State University and Morehead State University and all the contributing authors' institutions of higher education across the Commonwealth. But some contributions should be specifically acknowledged.

James Clinger recognizes the research assistance of Whitney Darnall, Scott Schaefer, Nate Cox, Patrick Griffo, Abby Hart, Abigail Heard, and Janie Stenberg. He particularly wants to thank Dr. Ken Winters, former state senator from the First District, for his comments on the chapter on the Kentucky General Assembly. He would also like to thank Kim, Josh, Renee, Grant, Jacob, and Katie Grace for putting up with him during the ordeal of putting together this book.

Michael Hail wishes to recognize several colleagues at Morehead State University who specifically assisted or encouraged the development of this book, including William Green, Stephen Lange, Christine Emrich, David Campbell, Brian Reeder, David Rudy, and Robert Albert. Some outstanding student research assistants were invaluable to me, including Stephanie Davis, Kaci Foster, Madyson Hutchison, Autumn Baker, and Ashley Ruggiero. In addition, the administration and Board of Regents at Morehead State University provided a sabbatical that greatly assisted completion of this book. And I want to acknowledge the support of my family, Charlotte and my children, Sarah and Allen, as well as my mother, Doris. My late father, Mark, was an elected official who continued the political tradition of service in my family and inspired me with a serious interest in politics from my earliest days.

Finally, we would both like to recognize the outstanding support and service from the University Press of Kentucky. Stephen Wrinn, Allison Webster, and the excellent staff at the University Press of Kentucky were the best editorial and publishing support any faculty could imagine. We also want to acknowledge the faculty and students who regularly participate in the Kentucky Political Science Association, which serves as an ongoing, excellent forum for sharing research on Kentucky politics.

James C. Clinger   Michael W. Hail
Murray, Kentucky   Somerset, Kentucky

Appendix A

Kentucky Governors

Name	County of residence	Political party	Dates of office	Education	Occupation	Religion
Shelby, Isaac	Lincoln County, KY	Jeffersonian-Republican	1792–1796	Rural education	Military-Major General Colonial Army, Founding Board Chairman Centre College	Church of England, later Presbyterian
Garrard, James	Stafford County, VA; Bourbon County, KY	Jeffersonian-Republican	1796–1804	°°°°	Military, Minister	Baptist
Greenup, Christopher	Loudoun County, VA; Fayette County, KY	Jeffersonian-Republican	1804–1808	Law	Military, Clerk, U.S. House Rep	°°°°
Scott, Charles	Goochland County, VA; Woodford County, KY	Jeffersonian-Republican	1808–1812	Rural education	Military	°°°°
Shelby, Isaac	Lincoln County, KY	Jeffersonian-Republican	1812–1816	Rural education	Military-Major General Colonial Army, Founding Board Chairman Centre College; former Governor	Church of England, later Presbyterian
Madison, George	Augusta County, VA; Lincoln County, KY	Jeffersonian-Republican	1816	Rural education	Military	Presbyterian
Slaughter, Gabriel	Culpeper County, VA; Mercer County, KY	Jeffersonian-Republican	1816–1820	Rural education	Farmer, Military, KY House Rep, KY Senate, Lt. Gov	Baptist
Adair, John	Chester County, SC; Mercer County, KY	Democratic-Republican	1820–1824	Public education in NC	Military, KY House Rep, Speaker, U.S. Senate	Protestant
Desha, Joseph	Monroe County, PA; Harrison County, KY	Jeffersonian-Republican	1824–1828	Rural education	Military, KY House Rep, KY Senate, U.S. House Rep	°°°°
Metcalfe, Thomas	Fauquier County, VA; Nicholas County, KY	Whig	1828–1832	Rural education	Stonecutter, Military, KY House Rep, U.S. House Rep	°°°°

Name	Party	Origin	Term	Education	Offices	Religion
Breathitt, John	Jacksonian-Democrat	Henry County, VA; Logan County, KY	1832–1834	Rural education, Law	Teacher, Surveyor, KY House Rep, Lt. Gov	Presbyterian
Morehead, James Turner	Whig	Bullitt County, KY	1834–1836	Transylvania University–Law	Law, KY House Rep, Lt. Gov	Baptist
Clark, James	Whig	Bedford County, VA; Clark County, KY	1836–1839	Pisgah Academy, Woodford County, KY–Law	Law, KY House Rep, U.S. House Rep, KY Senate, Circuit-Court Judge	Protestant
Wickliffe, Charles Anderson	Whig	Washington County, KY	1839–1840	Law	KY House Rep, U.S. House Rep, Lt. Gov	°°°°
Letcher, Robert P.	Whig	Goochland County, VA; Garrard County, KY	1840–1844	Joshua Fry Academy–Law	Masonry, KY House Rep, U.S. House Rep	Presbyterian
Owsley, William	Whig	Lincoln County, KY	1844–1848	Common schools, Law	Teacher, Deputy Sheriff, KY House Rep, Court of Appeals Justice, KY Senate, Secretary of State	Presbyterian
Crittenden, John Jordan	Whig	Woodford County, KY	1848–1850	Pisgah Academy, Washington and Lee University, William and Mary College–Law	Law, Attny Gen. of IL, KY House Rep, U.S. Senate, U.S. District Attny, U.S. Attny Gen.	Presbyterian
Helm, John L.	Whig	Hardin County, KY	1850–1851	Private tutor, Rural schools, Law	Law, KY House Rep, Speaker, KY Senate, Lt. Gov	°°°°
Powell, Lazarus	Democratic	Henderson County, KY	1851–1855	St. Joseph College, Transylvania University–Law	KY House Rep	°°°°

°°°° = No information available

(cont.)

Name	County of residence	Political party	Dates of office	Education	Occupation	Religion
Morehead, Charles Slaughter	Nelson County, KY	American (Know Nothing)	1855–1859	Transylvania College–Law	KY House Rep, Speaker, Attny Gen of KY, U.S. House Rep	°°°°
Magoffin, Beriah	Mercer County, KY	Democratic	1859–1862	Centre College, Transylvania College–Law	KY State Senate	°°°°
Robinson, James F.	Scott County, KY	Democratic	1862–1863	Forest Hill Academy, Transylvania University–Law	Law, KY Senate, Senate President	Baptist
Bramlette, Thomas E.	Cumberland County, KY	Democratic	1863–1867	Law	Judge 6th Judicial District, Military, U.S. Attny Gen of KY	°°°°
Helm, John L.	Hardin County, KY	Democratic	1867	Private tutor, Rural schools, Law	Law, KY House Rep, Speaker, KY Senate, Lt. Gov	°°°°
Stevenson, John W.	Richmond, VA; Kenton County, KY	Democratic	1867–1871	Hampden-Sydney Academy, University of Virginia–Law	Law, KY House Rep, U.S. House Rep, Lt. Gov	Episcopalian
Leslie, Preston H.	Clinton County, KY	Democratic	1871–1875	Rural schools, Law	Law, KY House Rep, KY Senate, Senate President	Baptist
McCreary, James B.	Madison County, KY	Democratic	1875–1879	Centre College, Cumberland University–Law	Military, KY House Rep, Speaker	Presbyterian
Blackburn, Luke P.	Woodford County, KY	Democratic	1879–1883	Public schools, Transylvania University–Medical	KY House Rep, Health officer	Episcopalian
Knott, James Proctor	Marion County, KY	Democratic	1883–1887	Home, Public schooling, Law	MO House Rep, Attny Gen of MO, U.S. House Rep	Presbyterian

Name	County	Party	Years	Education	Offices	Religion
Buckner, Simon Bolivar	Hart County, KY	Democratic	1887–1891	West Point Academy	Military	Episcopalian
Brown, John Young	Harrison County, KY	Democratic	1891–1895	Centre College–Law	Law, U.S. House Rep, Military	Presbyterian
Bradley, William O.	Garrard County, KY	Republican	1895–1899	Private, Law	Military, Prosecuting Attny, RNC	Baptist, later Presbyterian
Taylor, William S.	Butler County, KY	Republican	1899–1900	Law	County Judge, RNC, KY Attny Gen	Presbyterian
Goebel, William	Sullivan County, PA; Kenton County, KY	Democratic	1900	Cincinnati Law School	Law, KY Senate, Senate President	°°°°
Beckham, J. C. W.	Nelson County, KY	Democratic	1900–1907	Roseland Academy, Central University, University of Kentucky–Law	Law, KY House Rep, Speaker, Lt. Gov	Presbyterian
Willson, Augustus E.	Mason County, KY	Republican	1907–1911	Alfred Academy, Harvard University–Law	Law, Clerk, RNC	Presbyterian
McCreary, James B.	Madison County, KY	Democratic	1911–1915	Centre College, Cumberland University–Law	Military, KY House Rep, Speaker	Presbyterian
Stanley, Augustus	Shelby County, KY	Democratic	1915–1919	Gordon Academy (Kentucky Agricultural and Mechanical College), Centre College	Law, Teacher, Principal, U.S. House Rep	Disciples of Christ
Black, James D.	Knox County, KY	Democratic	1919	Tusculum College–Law	Law, KY House Rep, Knox County Superintendent, Asst Attny Gen, Lt. Gov	Methodist Episcopal

(cont.)

Name	County of residence	Political party	Dates of office	Education	Occupation	Religion
Morrow, Edwin P.	Pulaski County, KY	Republican	1919–1923	St. Mary's College, Cumberland College, University of Cincinnati–Law	Somerset City Attorney, Law, U.S. Dist Attny, RNC	Presbyterian
Fields, William Jason	Carter County, KY	Democratic	1923–1927	University of Kentucky–Law	Farmer, Real estate, U.S. House Rep	Methodist
Sampson, Flem	Laurel County, KY	Republican	1927–1931	Union College, Valparaiso University–Law	Law, Judge	Methodist
Laffoon, Ruby	Hopkins County, KY	Democratic	1931–1935	Columbia Law School, Washington and Lee University–Law	Chairman State Insurance Rating Board, Hopkins Circuit Board Bench	Disciples of Christ
Chandler, A. B. "Happy"	Henderson County, KY; Woodford County, KY	Democratic	1935–1939	Harvard University, Transylvania College, University of Kentucky–Law	KY Senate, Lt. Gov	Episcopalian
Johnson, Keen	Lyon County, KY	Democratic	1939–1943	Vanderbilt Preparatory School for Boys, Central College, University of Kentucky	Military, Journalist, Lt. Gov	Methodist
Willis, Simeon	Lawrence County, OH; Boyd County, OH	Republican	1943–1947	Public schools, Law	Principal, Law, KY Court of Appeals Judge	Methodist
Clements, Earle C.	Union County, KY	Democratic	1947–1950	University of Kentucky	Military, Sheriff, Clerk, Judge, KY Senate, U.S. House Rep	Christian

Name	County	Party	Term	Education	Career	Religion
Wetherby, Lawrence	Jefferson County, KY	Democratic	1950–1955	University of Kentucky–Law	Law, Lt. Gov	Methodist
Chandler, A. B. "Happy"	Henderson County, KY	Democratic	1955–1959	Harvard University, Transylvania College, University of Kentucky–Law	KY Senate, Lt. Gov, formerly KY Governor	Episcopalian
Combs, Bert T.	Clay County, KY	Democratic	1959–1963	Cumberland College, University of Kentucky–Law	Military, KY Court of Appeals Bench	Baptist
Breathitt, Edward "Ned"	Christian County, KY	Democratic	1963–1967	University of Kentucky–Law	Military, KY House Rep, Gov Commission	Methodist
Nunn, Louie B.	Barren County, KY	Republican	1967–1971	Bowling Green Business University, University of Louisville–Law	Barren County Judge-Executive	Methodist, later Disciples of Christ
Ford, Wendell	Daviess County, KY	Democratic	1971–1974	University of Kentucky, Maryland School of Insurance	Military, Insurance, Asst to Gov, KY Senate, Lt. Gov	Baptist
Carroll, Julian	McCracken County, KY	Democratic	1974–1979	University of Kentucky–Political science/Law	Military, Law, KY House Rep, Speaker, Lt. Gov	Cumberland Presbyterian
Brown, John Y., Jr.	Fayette Urban County, KY	Democratic	1979–1983	University of Kentucky–Law	Military, KFC co-owner, Pro-team owner	°°°°

(cont.)

Name	County of residence	Political party	Dates of office	Education	Occupation	Religion
Collins, Martha Layne	Shelby County, KY	Democratic	1983–1987	University of Kentucky	Teacher, KY Supreme Court Clerk, Lt. Gov., President St. Catherine's College	Baptist
Wilkinson, Wallace	Casey County, KY	Democratic	1987–1991	University of Kentucky (did not complete degree)	Retail bookstore owner	Christian
Jones, Brereton C.	Mason County, WV; Woodford County, KY	Democratic	1991–1995	University of Virginia–BS Commerce	Real estate, Horse farm, Lt. Gov	Presbyterian
Patton, Paul E.	Lawrence County, KY	Democratic	1995–2003	University of Kentucky–Mechanical engineering	Dpty Sec of Transportation, Pike County Judge/Exe, Lt. Gov, Sec of Econ Dev.	Presbyterian
Fletcher, Ernie	Montgomery County, KY	Republican	2003–2007	University of Kentucky–Engineering, Medicine	Military, Family physician, CEO, KY House Rep, U.S. House Rep	Baptist
Beshear, Steven L.	Hopkins County, KY	Democratic	2007–	University of Kentucky–Law	Military, Attny, KY House Rep, Attny Gen; Lt. Gov	Christian

Appendix B

Kentucky Lieutenant Governors

Name	County of residence	Political party	Dates of office	Education	Occupation	Religion
Bullitt, Alexander Scott	Jefferson County, KY	Jeffersonian-Republican	1800–1804	Rural education	Military, KY Senate/President	°°°°
Caldwell, John	Nelson County, KY	Jeffersonian-Republican	1804–1804	°°°°	Military, KY Senate, KY House Rep	°°°°
Posey, Thomas	Henderson County, KY	Jeffersonian-Republican	1806–1808	Rural education	Military, Farmer, U.S. Senator-LA, KY State Senator, Provisional Governor of Indiana territory	Presbyterian
Slaughter, Gabriel	Mercer County, KY	Jeffersonian-Republican	1808–1812	Rural education	Farmer, Military, KY House Rep, KY Senate, Lt. Gov	Baptist
Hickman, Richard	Clark County, KY	Jeffersonian-Republican	1812–1816	°°°°	KY House Rep, KY Senate	°°°°
Slaughter, Gabriel	Mercer County, KY	Jeffersonian-Republican	1816	Rural education	Farmer, Military, KY House Rep, KY Senate, Lt. Gov	Baptist
Barry, William Taylor	Fayette Urban County, KY	Democratic	1820–1824	Pisgah Academy, Kentucky Academy, Transylvania University, William and Mary College–Law	Law, KY House Rep, U.S. House Rep, U.S. Senate, KY Senate	°°°°
McAfee, Robert Breckinridge	Mercer County, KY	Democratic	1824–1828	°°°°	Military, KY House Rep	°°°°
Breathitt, John	Logan County, KY	Democratic	1828–1832	Rural education, Law	Teacher, Surveyor, KY House Rep, Lt. Gov	Presbyterian
Morehead, James Turner	Warren County, KY	National Republican	1832–1834	Transylvania University–Law	Law, KY House Rep, Lt. Gov	Baptist
Wickliffe, Charles A.	Nelson County, KY	Whig	1836–1839	Law	KY House Rep, U.S. House Rep, Lt. Gov	°°°°
Thomson, Manlius Valerius	Scott County, KY	Whig	1840–1844	Common schools, Transylvania A.B. 1822 J...	Law, KY Senate	°°°°

Name	County	Party	Dates	Education	Offices	Religion
Dixon, Archibald	Henderson County, KY	Whig	1844–1848	Common schools, Law	KY House Rep, Law, KY Senate, U.S. Senate	°°°°
Helm, John LaRue	Hardin County, KY	Democratic	1848–1850	Private tutor, Rural schools, Law	Law, KY House Rep, Speaker, KY Senate, Lt. Gov	°°°°
Thompson, John Burton, Jr.	Mercer County, KY	Whig	1851–1853	Rural education, Law	KY House Rep, KY Senate, Commonwealth's Attny, U.S. House Rep, U.S. Senator	°°°°
Hardy, James Green	Barren County, KY	Know-Nothing	1855–1856	°°°°	Teacher, Surveyor, KY House Rep, Lt. Gov	Baptist
Boyd, Linn	McCracken County, KY	Democratic	1859	°°°°	KY House Rep, Speaker, Farmer	°°°°
Jacob, Richard Taylor	Oldham County, KY	Union Democratic	1863–1864	Law	Farmer, KY House Rep	°°°°
Stevenson, John White	Kenton County, KY	Democratic	1867	Hampden-Sydney Academy, University of Virginia–Law	Law, KY House Rep. U.S. House Rep, KY Gov, Professor	Episcopalian
Carlisle, John Griffin	Kenton County, KY	Democratic	1871–1875	Law	Law, KY House Rep, KY Senate	°°°°
Underwood, John Cox	Jefferson County, KY	Democratic	1875–1879	Rensselaer Polytechnic Institute–Civil engineering	City engineer, Mayor	°°°°
Cantrill, James E.	Scott County, KY	Democratic	1879–1883	°°°°	Military–Capt. Confederate Army	°°°°
Hindman, James Robert	Adair County, KY	Democratic	1883–1887	°°°°	°°°°	°°°°
Bryan, James William	Bourbon County, KY	Democratic	1887–1891	°°°°	°°°°	°°°°
Alford, Mitchell Cary	Fayette County, KY	Democratic	1891–1895	Transylvania University–Law	Commissioner–Fayette County, Law, KY Senate	°°°°

°°°° = No information available

(cont.)

Name	County of residence	Political party	Dates of office	Education	Occupation	Religion
Worthington, William J.	Greenup County, KY	Republican	1895–1899	Public schools	Farmer, Military, Iron company, Greenup County Judge, KY Senate	°°°°
Marshall, John	Jefferson County, KY	Republican	1899–1900	°°°°	°°°°	°°°°
Beckham, J. C. W.	Nelson County, KY	Democratic	1900	Roseland Academy, Central University, University of Kentucky–Law	Law, KY House Rep, Speaker, Lt. Gov	Presbyterian
Thorne, William P.	Henry County, KY	Democratic	1903–1907	Eminence College–Law	Judge, KY House Rep	Presbyterian
Cox, William H.	Mason County, KY	Republican	1907–1911	Private education	Bank president, City council, Mayor, RNC, KY Senate	Episcopalian
McDermott, Edward J.	Jefferson County, KY	Democratic	1911–1915	Harvard University–Law	Law	Roman Catholic
Black, James Dixon	Knox County, KY	Democratic	1915–1919	Tusculum College–Law	Law, KY House Rep, Knox County Superintendent, Asst Attny Gen, Lt. Gov	Methodist Episcopal
Ballard, Samuel Thruston	Jefferson County, KY	Republican	1919–1923	°°°°	Founder and owner Ballard & Ballard Co.	°°°°
Denhardt, Henry H.	Warren County, KY	Democratic	1923–1927	Cumberland University–Law	Prosecutor, Judge, Military, Law	°°°°
Breathitt, James, Jr.	Christian County, KY	Democratic	1927–1931	Centre College	KY Senate	°°°°
Chandler, A. B. "Happy"	Woodford County, KY	Democratic	1931–1935	Harvard University, Transylvania College, University of Kentucky–Law	KY Senate, Gov, Baseball Commissioner	Episcopalian

Name	County	Party	Years	Education	Occupation	Religion
Johnson, Keen	Madison County, KY	Democratic	1935–1939	Vanderbilt Preparatory School for Boys, Central College, University of Kentucky	Military, Journalist, Lt. Gov	Methodist
Myers, Rodes Kirby	Warren County, KY	Democratic	1939–1943	Ogden College, University of Kentucky–Law	Teacher, Law, DNC, KY House Rep, KY Senate	°°°°
Tuggle, Kenneth Herndon	Knox County, KY	Republican	1943–1947	Law	Law	°°°°
Wetherby, Lawrence Winchester	Jefferson County, KY	Democratic	1947–1950	University of Kentucky–Law	Law, Lt. Gov	Methodist
Beauchamp, Emerson "Doc"	Logan County, KY	Democratic	1951–1955	°°°°	Military, KY Senate	°°°°
Waterfield, Harry Lee	Hickman County, KY	Democratic	1955–1959	Murray State University	Newspaper publisher, KY House Rep, Speaker	°°°°
Wyatt, Wilson Watkins	Jefferson County, KY	Democratic	1959–1963	University of Louisville, Jefferson School of Law	Law, Mayor	°°°°
Waterfield, Harry Lee	Hickman County, KY	Democratic	1963–1967	Murray State University	Newspaper publisher, KY House Rep, Speaker	°°°°
Ford, Wendell H.	Daviess County, KY	Democratic	1967–1971	University of Kentucky, Maryland School of Insurance	Military, Insurance, Asst to Gov, KY Senate, KY Gov	Baptist
Carroll, Julian M.	McCracken County, KY	Democratic	1971–1974	Paducah Jr. College, University of Kentucky–Political science/Law	Military, Law, KY House Rep, Speaker, Lt. Gov	Cumberland Presbyterian
Stovall, Thelma L.	Jefferson County, KY	Democratic	1975–1979	LaSalle Extension University–Law	KY House Rep, Secretary of State, KY State Treasurer	°°°°
Collins, Martha Layne	Woodford County, KY	Democratic	1979–1983	University of Kentucky	KY Court of Appeals Clerk	Baptist

(cont.)

Name	County of residence	Political party	Dates of office	Education	Occupation	Religion
Beshear, Steven L.	Fayette Urban County, KY	Democratic	1983–1987	University of Kentucky–Law	Military, KY House Rep, Attny Gen, Gov.	Christian
Jones, Brereton C.	Woodford County, KY	Democratic	1987–1991	University of Virginia–Commerce	Real Estate, Horse farm, Gov	Presbyterian
Patton, Paul E.	Lawrence County, KY	Democratic	1991–1995	University of Kentucky–Mechanical engineering	Deputy Sec of Transportation, Pike County Judge-Exe, KY Gov, Sec of Econ Dev, Pres. Pikeville College	Presbyterian
Henry, Steve	Daviess County, KY	Democratic	1995–2003	Western Kentucky University, University of Louisville–Medicine	Orthopedic surgeon, County Commissioner	°°°°
Pence, Steve	Jefferson County, KY	Republican	2003–2007	Eastern Kentucky University–Business, University of Kentucky–Law	Asst. Attny Gen, Military	°°°°
Mongiardo, Daniel	Perry County, KY	Democratic	2007–2011	Transylvania University, University of Kentucky–Medicine	Physician, KY Senate	Roman Catholic
Abramson, Jerry	Jefferson County, KY	Democratic	2011–	Indiana University Bloomington, Georgetown University–Law	Military, Law, Mayor	Jewish

Appendix C

Kentucky Cities

City	Established	County
Adairville	1833	Logan
Albany	1838	Clinton
Alexandria	1834	Campbell
Allen	1913	Floyd
Allensville	1867	Todd
Anchorage	1878	Jefferson
Arlington	1876	Carlisle
Ashland	1856	Boyd
Auburn	1865	Logan
Audubon Park	1941	Jefferson
Augusta	1799	Bracken
Bancroft	1970	Jefferson
Barbourmeade	1962	Jefferson
Barbourville	1812	Knox
Bardstown	1788	Nelson
Bardwell	1878	Carlisle
Barlow	1903	Ballard
Beattyville	1851	Lee
Beaver Dam	1873	Ohio
Bedford	1816	Trimble
Beechwood Village	1950	Jefferson
Bellefonte	1951	Greenup
Bellemeade	1956	Jefferson
Bellevue	1870	Campbell
Bellewood	1950	Jefferson
Benham	1961	Harlan
Benton	1845	Marshall
Berea	1890	Madison
Berry	1867	Harrison
Blackey	1915	Letcher
Blaine	1886	Lawrence
Blandville	1845	Ballard
Bloomfield	1819	Nelson
Blue Ridge Manor	1964	Jefferson
Booneville	1847	Owsley
Bowling Green	1810	Warren
Bradfordsville	1835	Marion
Brandenburg	1872	Meade

City	Established	County
Bremen	1869	Muhlenberg
Briarwood	1957	Jefferson
Brodhead	1880	Rockcastle
Broeck Pointe	1980	Jefferson
Bromley	1890	Kenton
Brooksville	1839	Bracken
Brownsboro Farm	1966	Jefferson
Brownsboro Village	1940	Jefferson
Brownsville	1828	Edmonson
Buckhorn	1996	Perry
Burgin	1878	Mercer
Burkesville	1846	Cumberland
Burnside	1890	Pulaski
Butler	1868	Pendleton
Cadiz	1822	Trigg
Calhoun	1852	McLean
California	1874	Campbell
Calvert City	1951	Marshall
Camargo	1969	Montgomery
Cambridge	1953	Jefferson
Campbellsburg	1840	Henry
Campbellsville	1817	Taylor
Campton	1870	Wolfe
Caneyville	1880	Grayson
Carlisle	1818	Nicholas
Carrollton	1794	Carroll
Carrsville	1860	Livingston
Catlettsburg	1858	Boyd
Cave City	1866	Barren
Centertown	1890	Ohio
Central City	1873	Muhlenberg
Clarkson	1888	Grayson
Clay	1860	Webster
Clay City	1890	Powell
Clinton	1831	Hickman
Cloverport	1828	Breckinridge
Coal Run Village	1963	Pike
Cold Spring	1941	Campbell

(cont.)

City	Established	County
Coldstream	1983	Jefferson
Columbia	1803	Adair
Columbus	1820	Hickman
Concord	1833	Lewis
Corbin	1902	Knox and Whitley
Corinth	1878	Grant and Scott
Corydon	1868	Henderson
Covington	1815	Kenton
Crab Orchard	1849	Lincoln
Creekside	1977	Jefferson
Crescent Springs	1957	Kenton
Crestview	1950	Campbell
Crestview Hills	1951	Kenton
Crestwood	1970	Oldham
Crittenden	1837	Grant and Kenton
Crofton	1873	Christian
Crossgate	1968	Jefferson
Cumberland	1917	Harlan
Cynthiana	1793	Harrison
Danville	1787	Boyle
Dawson Springs	1832	Caldwell and Hopkins
Dayton	1867	Campbell
Dixon	1861	Webster
Douglass Hills	1973	Jefferson
Dover	1836	Mason
Drakesboro	1888	Muhlenberg
Druid Hills	1950	Jefferson
Dry Ridge	1920	Grant
Earlington	1871	Hopkins
Eddyville	1812	Lyon
Edgewood	1948	Kenton
Edmonton	1836	Metcalfe
Ekron	1906	Meade
Elizabethtown	1797	Hardin
Elkhorn City	1912	Pike
Elkton	1820	Todd
Elsmere	1896	Kenton
Eminence	1851	Henry

City	Established	County
Erlanger	1897	Kenton
Eubank	1886	Lincoln and Pulaski
Evarts	1921	Harlan
Ewing	1880	Fleming
Fairfield	1818	Nelson
Fairview	1957	Kenton
Falmouth	1793	Pendleton
Ferguson	1906	Pulaski
Fincastle	1974	Jefferson
Flatwoods	1932	Greenup
Fleming-Neon	1977	Letcher
Flemingsburg	1912	Fleming
Florence	1830	Boone
Fordsville	1886	Ohio
Forest Hills	1959	Jefferson
Fort Mitchell	1910	Kenton
Fort Thomas	1867	Campbell
Fort Wright	1941	Kenton
Fountain Run	1908	Monroe
Fox Chase	1983	Bullitt
Frankfort	1786	Franklin
Franklin	1820	Simpson
Fredonia	1869	Caldwell
Frenchburg	1871	Menifee
Fulton	1872	Fulton
Gamaliel	1856	Monroe
Georgetown	1784	Scott
Germantown	1795	Bracken and Mason
Ghent	1835	Carroll
Glasgow	1799	Barren
Glencoe	1960	Gallatin
Glenview	1985	Jefferson
Glenview Hills	1972	Jefferson
Glenview Manor	1965	Jefferson
Goose Creek	1969	Jefferson
Goshen	1990	Oldham
Grand Rivers	1890	Livingston
Gratz	1881	Owen

(cont.)

City	Established	County
Graymoor-Devondale	1987	Jefferson
Grayson	1844	Carter
Green Spring	1974	Jefferson
Greensburg	1794	Green
Greenup	1818	Greenup
Greenville	1812	Muhlenberg
Guthrie	1876	Todd
Hanson	1873	Hopkins
Hardin	1952	Marshall
Hardinsburg	1800	Breckinridge
Harlan	1884	Harlan
Harrodsburg	1785	Mercer
Hartford	1808	Ohio
Hawesville	1836	Hancock
Hazard	1884	Perry
Hazel	1911	Calloway
Hebron Estates	1984	Bullitt
Henderson	1797	Henderson
Heritage Creek	1960	Jefferson
Hickman	1841	Fulton
Hickory Hill	1979	Jefferson
Highland Heights	1867	Campbell
Hills and Dales	1976	Jefferson
Hillview	1974	Bullitt
Hindman	1886	Knott
Hodgenville	1839	Larue
Hollow Creek	1971	Jefferson
Hollyvilla	1958	Jefferson
Hopkinsville	1804	Christian
Horse Cave	1864	Hart
Houston Acres	1956	Jefferson
Hunters Hollow	1979	Bullitt
Hurstbourne	1982	Jefferson
Hurstbourne Acres	1963	Jefferson
Hustonville	1836	Lincoln
Hyden	1882	Leslie
Independence	1842	Kenton
Indian Hills	1941	Jefferson

City	Established	County
Indian Hills–Cherokee Section	1955	Jefferson
Inez	1942	Martin
Irvine	1812	Estill
Irvington	1889	Breckinridge
Island	1908	McLean
Jackson	1839	Breathitt
Jamestown	1826	Russell
Jeffersontown	1797	Jefferson
Jeffersonville	1876	Montgomery
Jenkins	1912	Letcher
Junction City	1882	Boyle and Lincoln
Keene	1844	Jessamine
Kenton Vale	1949	Kenton
Kevil	1910	Ballard
Kingsley	1939	Jefferson
Kuttawa	1872	Lyon
La Center	1981	Ballard
La Fayette	1836	Christian
La Grange	1840	Oldham
Lakeside Park	1930	Kenton
Lakeview Heights	1979	Rowan
Lancaster	1793	Garrard
Langdon Place	1977	Jefferson
Lawrenceburg	1820	Anderson
Lebanon	1815	Marion
Lebanon Junction	1895	Bullitt
Leitchfield	1866	Grayson
Lewisburg	1878	Logan
Lewisport	1844	Hancock
Lexington	1782	Fayette
Liberty	1830	Casey
Lincolnshire	1953	Jefferson
Livermore	1850	McLean
Livingston	1880	Rockcastle
London	1836	Laurel
Loretto	1866	Marion
Louisa	1822	Lawrence

(cont.)

City	Established	County
Louisville	1778	Jefferson
Loyall	1924	Harlan
Ludlow	1864	Kenton
Lynch	1963	Harlan
Lyndon	1965	Jefferson
Lynnview	1954	Jefferson
Mackville	1967	Washington
Madisonville	1807	Hopkins
Manchester	1844	Clay
Manor Creek	1972	Jefferson
Marion	1844	Crittenden
Martin	1920	Floyd
Maryhill Estates	1963	Jefferson
Mayfield	1824	Graves
Maysville	1833	Mason
McHenry	1880	Ohio
McKee	1882	Jackson
Meadow Vale	1967	Jefferson
Meadowbrook Farm	1975	Jefferson
Meadowview Estates	1954	Jefferson
Melbourne	1912	Campbell
Mentor	1957	Campbell
Middlesboro	1890	Bell
Middletown	1797	Jefferson
Midway	1846	Woodford
Millersburg	1817	Bourbon and Nicholas
Milton	1846	Trimble
Mockingbird Valley	1940	Jefferson
Monterey	1954	Owen
Monticello	1810	Wayne
Moorland	1959	Jefferson
Morehead	1869	Rowan
Morganfield	1812	Union
Morgantown	1813	Butler
Mortons Gap	1888	Hopkins
Mount Olivet	1851	Robertson
Mount Sterling	1792	Montgomery
Mount Vernon	1818	Rockcastle

City	Established	County
Mount Washington	1822	Bullitt
Muldraugh	1952	Hardin and Meade
Munfordville	1880	Hart
Murray	1844	Calloway
Murray Hill	1982	Jefferson
Nebo	1860	Hopkins
New Castle	1817	Henry
New Haven	1839	Nelson
Newport	1795	Campbell
Nicholasville	1837	Jessamine
Norbourne Estates	1950	Jefferson
North Middletown	1819	Bourbon
Northfield	1965	Jefferson
Nortonville	1873	Hopkins
Norwood	1975	Jefferson
Oak Grove	1974	Christian
Oakland	1977	Warren
Old Brownsboro Place	1977	Jefferson
Olive Hill	1884	Carter
Orchard Grass Hills	1979	Oldham
Owensboro	1817	Daviess
Owenton	1828	Owen
Owingsville	1811	Bath
Paducah	1830	McCracken
Paintsville	1834	Johnson
Paris	1789	Bourbon
Park City	1871	Barren
Park Hills	1927	Kenton
Parkway Village	1940	Jefferson
Pembroke	1869	Christian
Perryville	1817	Boyle
Pewee Valley	1870	Oldham
Pikeville	1824	Pike
Pineville	1781	Bell
Pioneer Village	1974	Bullitt
Pippa Passes	1983	Knott
Plantation	1960	Jefferson
Pleasureville	1842	Henry and Shelby

(cont.)

City	Established	County
Plum Springs	1966	Warren
Poplar Hills	1983	Jefferson
Powderly	1963	Muhlenberg
Prestonsburg	1818	Floyd
Prestonville	1867	Carroll
Princeton	1820	Caldwell
Prospect	1974	Jefferson and Oldham
Providence	1840	Webster
Raceland	1915	Greenup
Radcliff	1956	Hardin
Ravenna	1921	Estill
Raywick	1838	Marion
Richlawn	1948	Jefferson
Richmond	1809	Madison
River Bluff	1980	Oldham
Riverwood	1969	Jefferson
Robards	1997	Henderson
Robinswood	1965	Jefferson
Rochester	1839	Butler
Rockport	1870	Ohio
Rolling Fields	1958	Jefferson
Rolling Hills	1966	Jefferson
Russell	1869	Greenup
Russell Springs	1936	Russell
Russellville	1810	Logan
Ryland Heights	1972	Kenton
Sacramento	1860	McLean
Sadieville	1880	Scott
Saint Charles	1874	Hopkins
Saint Mary	1865	Marion
Saint Matthews	1950	Jefferson
Saint Regis Park	1953	Jefferson
Salem	1813	Livingston
Salt Lick	1888	Bath
Salyersville	1860	Magoffin
Sanders	1871	Carroll
Sandy Hook	1850	Elliott
Sardis	1850	Mason and Robertson

City	Established	County
Science Hill	1882	Pulaski
Scottsville	1817	Allen
Sebree	1871	Webster
Seneca Gardens	1941	Jefferson
Sharpsburg	1825	Bath
Shelbyville	1792	Shelby
Shepherdsville	1793	Bullitt
Shively	1938	Jefferson
Silver Grove	1950	Campbell
Simpsonville	1833	Shelby
Slaughters	1861	Webster
Smithfield	1870	Henry
Smithland	1805	Livingston
Smiths Grove	1871	Warren
Somerset	1812	Pulaski
Sonora	1885	Hardin
South Carrollton	1849	Muhlenberg
South Park View	1961	Jefferson
South Shore	1957	Greenup
Southgate	1907	Campbell
Sparta	1852	Gallatin and Owen
Spring Mill	1983	Jefferson
Spring Valley	1983	Jefferson
Springfield	1793	Washington
Stamping Ground	1834	Scott
Stanford	1861	Lincoln
Stanton	1854	Powell
Strathmoor Manor	1931	Jefferson
Strathmoor Village	1929	Jefferson
Sturgis	1890	Union
Sycamore	1979	Jefferson
Taylor Mill	1956	Kenton
Taylorsville	1829	Spencer
Ten Broeck	1979	Jefferson
Thornhill	1976	Jefferson
Tompkinsville	1819	Monroe
Trenton	1840	Todd
Union	1833	Boone

(cont.)

City	Established	County
Uniontown	1840	Union
Upton	1865	Hardin and Larue
Vanceburg	1827	Lewis
Versailles	1792	Woodford
Vicco	1964	Knott and Perry
Villa Hills	1962	Kenton
Vine Grove	1865	Hardin
Wallins Creek	1925	Harlan
Walton	1840	Boone and Kenton
Warfield	1982	Martin
Warsaw	1831	Gallatin
Water Valley	1884	Graves
Watterson Park	1981	Jefferson
Waverly	1869	Union
Wayland	1914	Floyd
Wellington	1946	Jefferson
West Buechel	1951	Jefferson
West Liberty	1823	Morgan
West Point	1797	Hardin
Westwood	1967	Jefferson
Wheatcroft	1902	Webster
Wheelwright	1917	Floyd
White Plains	1888	Hopkins
Whitesburg	1876	Letcher
Whitesville	1867	Daviess
Wickliffe	1882	Ballard
Wilder	1935	Campbell
Wildwood	1964	Jefferson
Williamsburg	1819	Whitley
Williamstown	1825	Grant and Pendleton
Willisburg	1833	Washington
Wilmore	1890	Jessamine
Winchester	1793	Clark
Winding Falls	1977	Jefferson
Windy Hills	1952	Jefferson
Wingo	1872	Graves
Woodburn	1866	Warren
Woodbury	1854	Butler

City	Established	County
Woodland Hills	1961	Jefferson
Woodlawn	1922	Campbell
Woodlawn Park	1955	Jefferson
Worthington	1920	Greenup
Worthington Hills	1980	Jefferson
Worthville	1878	Carroll
Wurtland	1970	Greenup

Appendix D

Kentucky Counties

County	Established	Seat
Adair	1802	Columbia
Allen	1815	Scottsville
Anderson	1827	Lawrenceburg
Ballard	1842	Wickliffe
Barren	1799	Glasgow
Bath	1811	Owingsville
Bell	1867	Pineville
Boone	1799	Burlington
Bourbon	1786	Paris
Boyd	1860	Catlettsburg
Boyle	1842	Danville
Bracken	1797	Brooksville
Breathitt	1839	Jackson
Breckinridge	1800	Hardinsburg
Bullitt	1797	Shepherdsville
Butler	1810	Morgantown
Caldwell	1809	Princeton
Calloway	1821	Murray
Campbell	1795	Newport
Carlisle	1886	Bardwell
Carroll	1838	Carrollton
Carter	1838	Grayson
Casey	1807	Liberty
Christian	1797	Hopkinsville
Clark	1793	Winchester
Clay	1807	Manchester
Clinton	1836	Albany
Crittenden	1842	Marion
Cumberland	1799	Burkesville
Daviess	1815	Owensboro
Edmonson	1825	Brownsville
Elliott	1869	Sandy Hook
Estill	1808	Irvine
Fayette	1780	Lexington
Fleming	1798	Flemingsburg
Floyd	1800	Prestonsburg
Franklin	1795	Frankfort
Fulton	1845	Hickman

County	Established	Seat
Gallatin	1799	Warsaw
Garrard	1797	Lancaster
Grant	1820	Williamstown
Graves	1824	Mayfield
Grayson	1810	Leitchfield
Green	1793	Greensburg
Greenup	1804	Greenup
Hancock	1829	Hawesville
Hardin	1793	Elizabethtown
Harlan	1819	Harlan
Harrison	1794	Cynthiana
Hart	1819	Munfordville
Henderson	1799	Henderson
Henry	1799	New Castle
Hickman	1822	Clinton
Hopkins	1807	Madisonville
Jackson	1858	McKee
Jefferson	1780	Louisville
Jessamine	1799	Nicholasville
Johnson	1843	Paintsville
Kenton	1840	Covington and Independence
Knott	1884	Hindman
Knox	1800	Barbourville
Larue	1843	Hodgenville
Laurel	1826	London
Lawrence	1822	Louisa
Lee	1870	Beattyville
Leslie	1878	Hyden
Letcher	1842	Whitesburg
Lewis	1807	Vanceburg
Lincoln	1780	Stanford
Livingston	1799	Smithland
Logan	1792	Russellville
Lyon	1854	Eddyville
Madison	1786	Richmond
Magoffin	1860	Salyersville
Marion	1834	Lebanon
Marshall	1842	Benton

(cont.)

County	Established	Seat
Martin	1870	Inez
Mason	1789	Maysville
McCracken	1825	Paducah
McCreary	1912	Whitley City
McLean	1854	Calhoun
Meade	1824	Brandenburg
Menifee	1869	Frenchburg
Mercer	1786	Harrodsburg
Metcalfe	1860	Edmonton
Monroe	1820	Tompkinsville
Montgomery	1797	Mount Sterling
Morgan	1823	West Liberty
Muhlenberg	1799	Greenville
Nelson	1785	Bardstown
Nicholas	1800	Carlisle
Ohio	1799	Hartford
Oldham	1824	La Grange
Owen	1819	Owenton
Owsley	1843	Booneville
Pendleton	1799	Falmouth
Perry	1821	Hazard
Pike	1822	Pikeville
Powell	1852	Stanton
Pulaski	1799	Somerset
Robertson	1867	Mount Olivet
Rockcastle	1810	Mount Vernon
Rowan	1856	Morehead
Russell	1826	Jamestown
Scott	1792	Georgetown
Shelby	1792	Shelbyville
Simpson	1819	Franklin
Spencer	1824	Taylorsville
Taylor	1848	Campbellsville
Todd	1820	Elkton
Trigg	1820	Cadiz
Trimble	1837	Bedford
Union	1811	Morganfield
Warren	1797	Bowling Green

County	Established	Seat
Washington	1792	Springfield
Wayne	1801	Monticello
Webster	1860	Dixon
Whitley	1818	Williamsburg
Wolfe	1860	Campton
Woodford	1789	Versailles

Appendix E

The Kentucky Resolutions of 1798

I. *Resolved*, that the several States composing the United States of America, are not united on the principles of unlimited submission to their General Government; but that by compact under the style and title of a Constitution for the United States, and of amendments thereto, they constituted a General Government for special purposes, delegated to that Government certain definite powers, reserving each State to itself, the residuary mass of right to their own self-Government; and that whensoever the General Government assumes undelegated powers, its acts are unauthoritative, void, and of no force: That to this compact each State acceded as a State, and is an integral party, its co-States forming as to itself, the other party: That the Government created by this compact was not made the exclusive or final *judge* of the extent of the powers delegated to itself; since that would have made its discretion, and not the Constitution, the measure of its powers; but that, as in all other cases of compact among parties having no common Judge, each party has an equal right to judge for itself, as well of infractions as of the mode and measure of redress.

II. *Resolved*, that the Constitution of the United States having delegated to Congress a power to punish treason, counterfeiting the securities and current coin of the United States, piracies, and felonies committed on the High Seas, and offenses against the law of nations, and no other crimes whatsoever; and it being true as a general principle, and one of the amendments to the Constitution having also declared, "that the powers not delegated to the United States by the Constitution, nor prohibited by it to the States, are reserved to the States respectively, or to the people," therefore also the same act of Congress passed on the 14th day of July, 1798, and entitled "An act in addition to the act entitled an act for the punishment of certain crimes against the United States," as also the act passed by them on the 27th day of June, 1798, entitled "An act to punish frauds committed on the Bank of the United States" (and all their other acts which assume to create, define, or punish crimes other than those so enumerated in the Constitution) are altogether void and of no force, and that the power to create, define, and punish such other crimes is reserved, and of right appertains solely and exclusively to the respective States, each within its own Territory.

III. *Resolved*, that it is true as a general principle, and is also expressly declared by one of the amendments to the Constitution that "the powers not delegated to the United States by the Constitution, nor prohibited by it to the States, are reserved to the States respectively or to the people;" and that no power over the freedom of religion, freedom of speech, or freedom of the press being delegated to the United States by the Constitution, nor prohibited by it to the

States, all lawful powers respecting the same did of right remain, and were reserved to the States, or to the people: That thus was manifested their determination to retain to themselves the right of judging how far the licentiousness of speech and of the press may be abridged without lessening their useful freedom, and how far those abuses which cannot be separated from their use, should be tolerated rather than the use be destroyed; and thus also they guarded against all abridgment by the United States of the freedom of religious opinions and exercises, and retained to themselves the right of protecting the same, as this state by a Law passed on the general demand of its Citizens, had already protected them from all human restraint or interference: And that in addition to this general principle and express declaration, another and more special provision has been made by one of the amendments to the Constitution which expressly declares, that "Congress shall make no law respecting an Establishment of religion, or prohibiting the free exercise thereof, or abridging the freedom of speech, or of the press," thereby guarding in the same sentence, and under the same words, the freedom of religion, of speech, and of the press, insomuch, that whatever violates either, throws down the sanctuary which covers the others, and that libels, falsehoods, and defamation, equally with heresy and false religion, are withheld from the cognizance of federal tribunals. That therefore the act of Congress of the United States passed on the 14th day of July 1798, entitled "An act in addition to the act for the punishment of certain crimes against the United States," which does abridge the freedom of the press, is not law, but is altogether void and of no effect.

IV. *Resolved*, that alien friends are under the jurisdiction and protection of the laws of the State wherein they are; that no power over them has been delegated to the United States, nor prohibited to the individual States distinct from their power over citizens; and it being true as a general principle, and one of the amendments to the Constitution having also declared, that "the powers not delegated to the United States by the Constitution nor prohibited by it to the States are reserved to the States respectively or to the people," the act of the Congress of the United States passed on the 22^d day of June, 1798, entitled "An act concerning aliens," which assumes power over alien friends not delegated by the Constitution, is not law, but is altogether void and of no force.

V. *Resolved,* that in addition to the general principle as well as the express declaration, that powers not delegated are reserved, another and more special provision inserted in the Constitution from abundant caution has declared, "that the *migration* or importation of such persons as any of the States now existing shall think proper to admit, shall not be prohibited by the Congress prior to the year 1808." That this Commonwealth does admit the migration of alien friends described as the subject of the said act concerning aliens; that a provision against prohibiting their migration, is a provision against all acts equivalent thereto, or it would be nugatory; that to remove them when migrated is equivalent to a prohibition of their migration, and is therefore contrary to the said provision of the Constitution and void.

VI. *Resolved*, that the imprisonment of a person under the protection of the Laws of this Commonwealth on his failure to obey the simple *order* of the President to depart out of the United States, as is undertaken by the said act entitled "An act concerning Aliens," is contrary to the Constitution, one amendment to which has provided, that "no person shalt be deprived of liberty without due process of law," and that another having provided "that in all criminal prosecutions, the accused shall enjoy the right to public trial by an impartial jury, to be informed of the nature and cause of the accusation, to be confronted with the witnesses against him, to have compulsory process for obtaining witnesses in his favor, and to have the assistance of counsel for his defense," the same act undertaking to authorize the President to remove a person out of the United States who is under the protection of the Law, on his own suspicion, without accusation, without jury, without public trial, without confrontation of the witnesses against him, without having witnesses in his favor, without defense, without counsel, is contrary to these provisions also of the Constitution, is therefore not law but utterly void and of no force.

That transferring the power of judging any person who is under the protection of the laws, from the Courts to the President of the United States, as is undertaken by the same act concerning Aliens, is against the article of the Constitution which provides, that "the judicial power of the United States shall be vested in Courts, the Judges of which shall hold their offices during good behavior," and that the said act is void for that reason also; and it is further to be noted, that this transfer of Judiciary power is to that magistrate of the General Government who already possesses all the Executive, and a qualified negative in all the Legislative powers.

VII. *Resolved*, that the construction applied by the General Government (as is evinced by sundry of their proceedings) to those parts of the Constitution of the United States which delegate to Congress a power to lay and collect taxes, duties, imposts, and excises; to pay the debts, and provide for the common defense, and general welfare of the United States, and to make all laws which shall be necessary and proper for carrying into execution the powers vested by the Constitution in the Government of the United States, or any department thereof, goes to the destruction of all the limits prescribed to their power by the Constitution—That words meant by that instrument to be subsidiary only to the execution of the limited powers, ought not to be so construed as themselves to give unlimited powers, nor a part so to be taken, as to destroy the whole residue of the instrument: That the proceedings of the General Government under colour of these articles, will be a fit and necessary subject for revisal and correction at a time of greater tranquility, while those specified in the preceding resolutions call for immediate redress.

VIII. *Resolved*, that the preceding resolutions be transmitted to the Senators and Representatives in Congress from this Commonwealth, who are hereby enjoined to present the same to their respective Houses, and to use their best endeavours to procure at the next session of Congress, a repeal of the aforesaid unconstitutional and obnoxious acts.

IX. *Resolved lastly*, that the Governor of this Commonwealth be, and is hereby authorized and requested to communicate the preceding Resolutions to the Legislatures of the several States, to assure them that this Commonwealth considers Union for specified National purposes, and particularly for those specified in their late Federal Compact, to be friendly to the peace, happiness, and prosperity of all the States: that faithful to that compact, according to the plain intent and meaning in which it was understood and acceded to by the several parties, it is sincerely anxious for its preservation: that it does also believe, that to take from the States all the powers of self-government, and transfer them to a general and consolidated Government, without regard to the special delegations and reservations solemnly agreed to in that compact, is not for the peace, happiness, or prosperity of these States: And that therefore, this Commonwealth is determined, as it doubts not its co-States are, tamely to submit to undelegated & consequently unlimited powers in no man or body of men on earth: that if the acts before specified should stand, these conclusions would flow from them; that the General Government may place any act they think proper on the list of crimes & punish it themselves, whether enumerated or not enumerated by the Constitution as cognizable by them: that they may transfer its cognizance to the President or any other person, who may himself be the accuser, counsel, judge, and jury, whose *suspicions* may be the evidence, his order the sentence, his officer the executioner, and his breast the sole record of the transaction: that a very numerous and valuable description of the inhabitants of these States, being by this precedent reduced as outlaws to the absolute domination of one man and the barrier of the Constitution thus swept away from us all, no rampart now remains against the passions and the power of a majority of Congress, to protect from a like exportation or other more grievous punishment the minority of the same body, the Legislatures, Judges, Governors, & Counsellors of the States, nor their other peaceable inhabitants who may venture to reclaim the constitutional rights & liberties of the States & people, or who for other causes, good or bad, maybe obnoxious to the views or marked by the suspicions of the President, or be thought dangerous to his or their elections or other interests public or personal: that the friendless alien has indeed been selected as the safest subject of a first experiment: but the citizen will soon follow, or rather has already followed; for, already has a Sedition Act marked him as its prey: that these and successive acts of the same character, unless arrested on the threshold, may tend to drive these States into revolution and blood, and will furnish new calumnies against Republican Governments, and new pretexts for those who wish it to be believed, that man cannot be governed but by a rod of iron: that it would be a dangerous delusion were a confidence in the men of our choice to silence our fears for the safety of our rights: that confidence is everywhere the parent of despotism: free government is founded in jealousy and not in confidence; it is jealousy and not confidence which prescribes limited Constitutions to bind down those whom we are obliged to trust with power: that our Constitution has accordingly fixed the limits to which and no further our confidence may go; and let the honest advocate of confidence read the Alien and Sedition Acts, and say if the Constitution has not been wise in fixing limits to the Government it created, and whether we should be wise in destroying those limits? Let him say what the Government is if it be not a tyranny, which the men of our choice have conferred on the President, and the President of our choice has assented to and accepted over the friendly strangers, to whom the mild spirit of our Country and its laws had pledged hospitality and protection: that the men of our choice have more respected the bare suspicions of the President than the solid rights of innocence, the claims of justification, the sacred force of truth, and the forms & substance of law and justice. In questions of power then let no more be heard of confidence in man, but bind him down from mischief by the chains of the Constitution. That this Commonwealth does therefore call on its co-States for an expression of their sentiments on the acts concerning Aliens, and for the punishment of certain crimes herein before specified, plainly declaring whether these acts are or are not authorized by the Federal Compact? And it doubts not that their sense will be so announced as to prove their attachment unaltered to limited Government, whether general or particular, and that the rights and liberties of their co-States will be exposed to no dangers by remaining embarked on a common bottom with their own: That they will concur with this Commonwealth in considering the said acts as so palpably against the Constitution as to amount to an undisguised declaration, that the Compact is not meant to be the measure of the powers of the General Government, but that it will proceed in the exercise over these States of all powers whatsoever: That they will view this as seizing the rights of the States and consolidating them in the hands of the General Government with a power assumed to bind the States (not merely in cases made federal) but in all cases whatsoever, by laws made, not with their consent, but by others against their consent: That this would be to surrender the form of Government we have chosen, and to live under one deriving its powers from its own will, and not from our authority; and that the co-States recurring to their natural right in cases not made federal, will concur in declaring these acts void and of no force, and will each unite with this Commonwealth in requesting their repeal at the next session of Congress.

Edmund Bullock, S.H.R.
John Campbell, S.S.P.T.
Passed the House of Representatives, Nov. 10th, 1789.
Attest,
Thomas Todd, C.H.R.
In SENATE, November 13th, 1798, unanimously
    concurred in,
Attest,
B. Thruston, Clk. Sen.
Approved November 16th, 1798.
James Garrard, G.K.
By The Governor,
Harry Toulmin,
Secretary of State.

Henry Clay's 1850 Compromise Speech

It has been objected against this measure that it is a compromise. It has been said that it is a compromise of principle, or of a principle. Mr. President, what is a compromise? It is a work of mutual concession—an agreement in which there are reciprocal stipulations—a work in which, for the sake of peace and concord, one party abates his extreme demands in consideration of an abatement of extreme demands by the other party: it is a measure of mutual concession—a measure of mutual sacrifice. Undoubtedly, Mr. President, in all such measures of compromise, one party would be very glad to get what he wants, and reject what he does not desire but which the other party wants. But when he comes to reflect that, from the nature of the government and its operations, and from those with whom he is dealing, it is necessary upon his part, in order to secure what he wants, to grant something to the other side, he should be reconciled to the concession which he has made in consequence of the concession which he is to receive, if there is no great principle involved, such as a violation of the Constitution of the United States. I admit that such a compromise as that ought never to be sanctioned or adopted. But I now call upon any senator in his place to point out from the beginning to the end, from California to New Mexico, a solitary provision in this bill which is violative of the Constitution of the United States.

The responsibility of this great measure passes from the hands of the committee, and from my hands. They know, and I know, that it is an awful and tremendous responsibility. I hope that you will meet it with a just conception and a true appreciation of its magnitude, and the magnitude of the consequences that may ensue from your decision one way or the other. The alternatives, I fear, which the measure presents, are concord and increased discord. . . . I believe from the bottom of my soul that the measure is the reunion of this Union. I believe it is the dove of peace, which, taking its aerial flight from the dome of the Capitol, carries the glad tidings of assured peace and restored harmony to all the remotest extremities of this distracted land. I believe that it will be attended with all these beneficent effects. And now let us discard all resentment, all passions, all petty jealousies, all personal desires, all love of place, all hankerings after the gilded crumbs which fall from the table of power. Let us forget popular fears, from whatever quarter they may spring. Let us go to the limpid fountain of unadulterated patriotism, and, performing a solemn lustration, return divested of all selfish, sinister, and sordid impurities, and think alone of our God, our country, our consciences, and our glorious

Union—that Union without which we shall be torn into hostile fragments, and sooner or later become the victims of military despotism or foreign domination. . . .

Let us look to our country and our cause, elevate ourselves to the dignity of pure and disinterested patriots, and save our country from all impending dangers. What if, in the march of this nation to greatness and power, we should be buried beneath the wheels that propel it onward! . . .

I call upon all the South. Sir, we have had hard words, bitter words, bitter thoughts, unpleasant feelings toward each other in the progress of this great measure. Let us forget them. Let us sacrifice these feelings. Let us go to the altar of our country and swear, as the oath was taken of old, that we will stand by her; that we will support her; that we will uphold her Constitution; that we will preserve her union; and that we will pass this great, comprehensive, and healing system of measures, which will hush all the jarring elements and bring peace and tranquillity to our homes.

Let me, Mr. President, in conclusion, say that the most disastrous consequences would occur, in my opinion, were we to go home, doing nothing to satisfy and tranquillize the country upon these great questions. What will be the judgment of mankind, what the judgment of that portion of mankind who are looking upon the progress of this scheme of self-government as being that which holds the highest hopes and expectations of ameliorating the condition of mankind—what will their judgment be? Will not all the monarchs of the Old World pronounce our glorious republic a disgraceful failure? Will you go home and leave all in disorder and confusion—all unsettled—all open? The contentions and agitations of the past will be increased and augmented by the agitations resulting from our neglect to decide them.

Sir, we shall stand condemned by all human judgment below, and of that above it is not for me to speak. We shall stand condemned in our own consciences, by our own constituents, and by our own country. The measure may be defeated. I have been aware that its passage for many days was not absolutely certain. . . . But, if defeated, it will be a triumph of ultraism and impracticability—a triumph of a most extraordinary conjunction of extremes; a victory won by abolitionism; a victory achieved by freesoilism; a victory of discord and agitation over peace and tranquillity; and I pray to Almighty God that it may not, in consequence of the inauspicious result, lead to the most unhappy and disastrous consequences to our beloved country.

—Henry Clay
Washington, D.C.—February 6, 1850

Appendix G

Abraham Lincoln's Eulogy of Henry Clay

On the fourth day of July, 1776, the people of a few feeble and oppressed colonies of Great Britain, inhabiting a portion of the Atlantic coast of North America, publicly declared their national independence, and made their appeal to the justice of their cause and to the God of battles for the maintenance of that declaration. That people were few in number and without resources, save only their wise heads and stout hearts. Within the first year of that declared independence, and while its maintenance was yet problematical, while the bloody struggle between those resolute rebels and their haughty would-be masters was still waging,—of undistinguished parents and in an obscure district of one of those colonies Henry Clay was born. The infant nation and the infant child began the race of life together. For three quarters of a century they have travelled hand in hand. They have been companions ever. The nation has passed its perils, and it is free, prosperous, and powerful. The child has reached his manhood, his middle age, his old age, and is dead. In all that has concerned the nation the man ever sympathized; and now the nation mourns the man.

The day after his death one of the public journals, opposed to him politically, held the following pathetic and beautiful language, which I adopt partly because such high and exclusive eulogy, originating with a political friend, might offend good taste, but chiefly because I could not in any language of my own so well express my thoughts:

"Alas, who can realize that Henry Clay is dead! Who can realize that never again that majestic form shall rise in the council-chambers of his country to beat back the storms of anarchy which may threaten, or pour the oil of peace upon the troubled billows as they rage and menace around! Who can realize that the workings of that mighty mind have ceased, that the throbbings of that gallant heart are stilled, that the mighty sweep of that graceful arm will be felt no more, and the magic of that eloquent tongue, which spake as spake no other tongue besides, is hushed—hushed for ever! Who can realize that freedom's champion, the champion of a civilized world and of all tongues and kindreds of people, has indeed fallen! Alas, in those dark hours of peril and dread which our land has experienced, and which she may be called to experience again, to whom now may her people look up for that counsel and advice which only wisdom and experience and patriotism can give, and which only the undoubting confidence of a nation will receive? Perchance in the whole circle of the great and gifted of our land there remains but one on whose shoulders the mighty mantle of the departed statesman may fall; one who while we now write is doubtless pouring his tears over the bier of his brother and friend brother, friend, ever, yet in political sentiment as far apart as party could make them. Ah, it is at times like these that the petty distinctions of mere party disappear. We see only the great, the grand, the noble features of the departed statesman; and we do not even beg permission to bow at his feet and mingle our tears with those who have ever been his political adherents—we do [not] beg this permission, we claim it as a right, though we feel it as a privilege. Henry Clay belonged to his country—to the world; mere party cannot claim men like him. His career has been national, his fame has filled the earth, his memory will endure to the last syllable of recorded time.

"Henry Clay is dead! He breathed his last on yesterday, at twenty minutes after eleven, in his chamber at Washington. To those who followed his lead in public affairs, it more appropriately belongs to pronounce his eulogy and pay specific honors to the memory of the illustrious dead. But all Americans may show the grief which his death inspires, for his character and fame are national property. As on a question of liberty he knew no North, no South, no East, no West, but only the Union which held them all in its sacred circle, so now his countrymen will know no grief that is not as wide-spread as the bounds of the confederacy. The career of Henry Clay was a public career. From his youth he has been devoted to the public service, at a period, too, in the world's history justly regarded as a remarkable era in human affairs. He witnessed in the beginning the throes of the French Revolution. He saw the rise and fall of Napoleon. He was called upon to legislate for America and direct her policy when all Europe was the battlefield of contending dynasties, and when the struggle for supremacy imperilled the rights of all neutral nations. His voice spoke war and peace in the contest with Great Britain.

"When Greece rose against the Turks and struck for liberty, his name was mingled with the battle-cry of freedom. When South America threw off the thraldom of Spain, his speeches were read at the head of her armies by Bolivar. His name has been, and will continue to be, hallowed in two hemispheres, for it is

"'One of the few, the immortal names
That were not born to die!'

"To the ardent patriot and profound statesman he added a quality possessed by few of the gifted on earth. His eloquence has not been surpassed. In the effective power to move the heart of man, Clay was without an equal, and the heaven-born endowment, in the spirit of its origin, has been most conspicuously exhibited against intestine feud. On at least three important occasions he has quelled our civil commotions by a power and influence which belonged to no other statesman of his age and times. And in our last internal discord, when this Union trembled to its centre, in old age he left the shades of private life, and gave the death-blow to fraternal strife, with the vigor of his earlier years, in a series of senatorial efforts which in themselves would bring immortality by challenging comparison with the efforts of any statesman in any age. He exorcised the demon which possessed the body politic, and gave peace to a distracted land. Alas! the achievement cost him his life. He sank day by day to the tomb his pale but noble brow bound with a triple wreath, put there by a grateful country. May his ashes rest in peace, while his spirit goes to take its station among the great and good men who preceded him."

While it is customary and proper upon occasions like the present to give a brief sketch of the life of the deceased, in the case of Mr. Clay it is less necessary than most others; for his biography has been written and rewritten and read and reread for the last twenty-five years; so that, with the exception of a few of the latest incidents of his life, all is as well known as it can be. The short sketch which I give is, therefore, merely to maintain the connection of this discourse.

Henry Clay was born on the twelfth day of April, 1777, in Hanover County, Virginia. Of his father, who died in the fourth or fifth year of Henry's age, little seems to be known, except that he was a respectable man and a preacher of the Baptist persuasion. Mr. Clay's education to the end of life was comparatively limited. I say "to the end of life," because I have understood that from time to time he added something to his education during the greater part of his whole life. Mr. Clay's lack of a more perfect early education, however it may be regretted generally, teaches at least one profitable lesson: it teaches that in this country one can scarcely be so poor but that, if he will, he can acquire sufficient education to get through the world respectably. In his twenty-third year Mr. Clay was licensed to practise law, and emigrated to Lexington, Kentucky. Here he commenced and continued the practice till the year 1803, when he was first elected to the Kentucky Legislature. By successive elections he was continued in the Legislature till the latter part of 1806, when he was elected to fill a vacancy of a single session in the United States Senate. In 1807 he was again elected to the Kentucky House of Representatives, and by that body chosen Speaker. In 1808 he was re-elected to the same body. In 1809 he was again chosen to fill a vacancy of two years in the United States Senate. In 1811 he was elected to the United States House of Representatives, and on the first day of taking his seat in that body he was chosen its Speaker. In 1813 he was again elected Speaker. Early in 1814, being the period of our last British war, Mr. Clay was sent as commissioner, with others, to negotiate a treaty of peace, which treaty was concluded in the latter part of the same year. On his return from Europe he was again elected to the lower branch of Congress, and on taking his seat in December, 1815, was called to his old post—the Speaker's chair, a position in which he was retained by successive elections, with one brief intermission, till the inauguration of John Quincy Adams, in March, 1825. He was then appointed Secretary of State, and occupied that important station till the inauguration of General Jackson, in March, 1829. After this he returned to Kentucky, resumed the practice of law, and continued it till the autumn of 1831, when he was by the Legislature of Kentucky again placed in the United States Senate. By a re-election he was continued in the Senate till he resigned his seat and retired, in March, 1848. In December, 1849, he again took his seat in the Senate, which he again resigned only a few months before his death.

By the foregoing it is perceived that the period from the beginning of Mr. Clay's official life in 1803 to the end of 1852 is but one year short of half a century, and that the sum of all the intervals in it will not amount to ten years. But mere duration of time in office constitutes the smallest part of Mr. Clay's history. Throughout that long period he has constantly been the most loved and most implicitly followed by friends, and the most dreaded by opponents, of all living American politicians. In all the great questions which have agitated the country, and particularly in those fearful crises, the Missouri question, the nullification question, and the late slavery question, as connected with the newly acquired territory, involving and endangering the stability of the Union, his has been the leading and most conspicuous part. In 1824 he was first a candidate for the Presidency, and was defeated; and, although he was successively defeated for the same office in 1832 and in 1844, there has never been a moment since 1824 till after 1848 when a very large portion of the American people did not cling to him with an enthusiastic hope and purpose of still elevating him to the Presidency. With other men, to be defeated was to be forgotten; but with him defeat was but a trifling incident, neither changing him nor the world's estimate of him. Even those of both political parties who have been preferred to him for the highest office have run far briefer courses than he, and left him still shining high in the heavens of the political world. Jackson, Van Buren, Harnson, Polk, and Taylor all rose after, and set long before him. The spell—the long-enduring spell—with which the souls of men were bound to him is a miracle. Who can compass it? It is probably true he owed his pre-eminence to no one quality, but to a fortunate combination of several. He was surpassingly eloquent; but many eloquent men fail utterly, and they are not, as a class, generally successful. His judgment was excellent; but many men of good judgment live and die unnoticed. His will was indomitable; but this quality often secures to its owner nothing better than a character for useless obstinacy. These, then, were Mr. Clay's leading qualities. No one of them is very uncommon; but all together are rarely combined in a single individual, and this is probably the reason why such men as Henry Clay are so rare in the world.

Mr. Clay's eloquence did not consist, as many fine specimens of eloquence do, of types and figures, of antithesis and elegant arrangement of words and sentences, but rather of that deeply earnest and impassioned tone and manner which can proceed only from great sincerity, and a thorough conviction in the speaker of the justice and importance of his cause. This it is that truly touches the chords of sympathy; and those who heard Mr. Clay never failed to be moved by it, or ever afterward forgot the impression. All his efforts were made for practical effect. He never spoke merely to be heard. He never delivered a Fourth of July oration, or a eulogy on an occasion like this. As a politician or statesman, no one was so habitually careful to avoid all sectional ground. Whatever he did he did for the whole country. In the construction of his measures, he ever carefully surveyed every part of the field, and duly weighed every conflicting interest. Feeling as he did, and as the truth surely is, that the world's best hope depended on the continued union of these States, he was ever jealous of and watchful for whatever might have the slightest tendency to separate them.

Mr. Clay's predominant sentiment, from first to last, was a deep devotion to the cause of human liberty—a strong sympathy with the oppressed everywhere, and an ardent wish for their elevation. With him this was a primary and all-controlling passion. Subsidiary to this was the conduct of his whole life. He loved his country partly because it was his own country, and mostly because it was a free country; and he burned with a zeal for its advancement, prosperity, and glory, because he saw in such the advancement, prosperity, and glory of human liberty, human right, and human nature. He desired the prosperity of his countrymen, partly because they were his countrymen, but chiefly to show to the world that free men could be prosperous.

That his views and measures were always the wisest needs not to be affirmed; nor should it be on this occasion, where so many thinking differently join in doing honor to his memory. A free people, in times of peace and quiet—when pressed by no common danger—naturally divide into parties. At such times the man who is of neither party is not, cannot be, of any consequence. Mr. Clay therefore was of a party. Taking a prominent part, as he did, in all the great political questions of his country for the last half century, the wisdom of his course on many is doubted and denied by a large portion of his countrymen; and of such it is not now proper to speak particularly. But there are many others, about his course upon which there is little or no disagreement amongst intelligent and patriotic Americans. Of these last are the War of 1812, the Missouri question, nullification, and the now recent compromise measures. In 1812 Mr. Clay, though not unknown, was still a young man. Whether we should go to war with Great Britain being the question of the day, a minority opposed the declaration of war by Congress, while the majority, though apparently inclined to war, had for years wavered, and hesitated to act decisively. Meanwhile British aggressions multiplied, and grew more daring and aggravated. By Mr. Clay more than any other man the struggle was brought to a decision in Congress. The question, being now fully before Congress, came up in a variety of ways in rapid succession, on most of which occasions Mr. Clay spoke. Adding to all the logic of which the subject was susceptible that noble inspiration which came to him as it came to no other, he aroused and nerved and inspired his friends, and confounded and bore down all opposition. Several of his speeches on these occasions were reported and are still extant, but the best of them all never was. During its delivery the reporters forgot their vocation, dropped their pens, and sat enchanted from near the beginning to quite the close. The speech now lives only in the memory of a few old men, and the enthusiasm with which they cherish their recollection of it is absolutely astonishing. The precise language of this speech we shall never know; but we do know we cannot help knowing—that with deep pathos it pleaded the cause of the injured sailor, that it invoked the genius of the Revolution, that it apostrophized the names of Otis, of Henry, and of Washington, that it appealed to the interests, the pride, the honor, and the glory of the nation, that it shamed and taunted the timidity of friends, that it scorned and scouted and withered the temerity of domestic foes, that it bearded and defied the British lion, and, rising and swelling and maddening in its course, it sounded the onset, till the charge, the shock, the steady struggle, and the glorious victory all passed in vivid review before the entranced hearers.

Important and exciting as was the war question of 1812, it never so alarmed the sagacious statesmen of the country for the safety of the Republic as afterward did the Missouri question. This sprang from that unfortunate source of discord—negro slavery. When our Federal Constitution was adopted, we owned no territory beyond the limits or ownership of the States, except the territory northwest of the River Ohio and east of the Mississippi. What has since been formed into the States of Maine, Kentucky and Tennessee, was, I believe, within the limits of or owned by Massachusetts, Virginia, and North Carolina. As to the Northwestern Territory, provision had been made even before the adoption of the Constitution that slavery should never go there. On the admission of States into the Union, carved from the territory we owned before the Constitution, no question, or at most no considerable question, arose about slavery—those which were within the limits of or owned by the old States following respectively the condition of the parent State, and those within the Northwest Territory following the previously made provision. But in 1803 we purchased Louisiana of the French, and it included with much more what has since been formed into the State of Missouri. With regard to it, nothing had been done to forestall the question of slavery. When, therefore, in 1819, Missouri, having formed a State constitution without excluding slavery, and with slavery already actually existing within its limits, knocked at the door of the Union for admission, almost the entire representation of the non-slaveholding States objected. A fearful and angry struggle instantly followed. This alarmed thinking men more than any previous question, because, unlike all the former, it divided the country by geographical lines. Other questions had their opposing partisans in all localities of the country and in almost every family, so that no division of the Union could follow such without a separation of friends to quite as great an extent as that of opponents. Not so with the Missouri question. On this a geographical line could be traced, which in the main would separate opponents only. This was the danger. Mr. Jefferson, then in retirement, wrote:

"I had for a long time ceased to read newspapers or to pay any attention to public affairs, confident they were in good hands and content to be a passenger in our bark to the shore from which I am not distant. But this momentous question, like a firebell in the night, awakened and filled me with terror. I considered it at once as the knell of the Union. It is hushed, indeed, for the moment. But this is a reprieve only, not a final sentence. A geographical line coinciding with a marked principle, moral and political, once conceived and held up to the angry passions of men, will never be obliterated, and every irritation will mark it deeper and deeper. I can say with conscious truth that there is not a man on earth who would sacrifice more than I would to relieve us from this heavy reproach in any practicable way.

"The cession of that kind of property—for it is so misnamed—is a bagatelle which would not cost me a second thought if in that way a general emancipation and expatriation could be effected, and gradually and with due sacrifices I think it might be. But as it is, we have the wolf by the ears, and we can neither hold him nor safely let him go. Justice is in one scale, and self-preservation in the other."

Mr. Clay was in Congress, and, perceiving the danger, at once engaged his whole energies to avert it. It began, as I have said, in 1819; and it did not terminate till 1821. Missouri would not yield the point; and Congress—that is, a majority in Congress—by repeated votes showed a determination not to admit the State unless it should yield. After several failures, and great labor on the part of Mr. Clay to so present the question that a majority could consent to the admission, it was by a vote rejected, and, as all seemed to think, finally. A sullen gloom hung over the nation. All felt that the rejection of Missouri was equivalent to a dissolution of the Union, because those States which already had what Missouri was rejected for refusing to relinquish would go with Missouri. All deprecated and deplored this, but none saw how to avert it. For the judgment of members to be convinced of the necessity of yielding was not the whole difficulty; each had a constituency to meet and to answer to. Mr. Clay, though worn down and exhausted, was appealed to by members to renew his efforts at compromise. He did so, and by some judicious modifications of his plan, coupled with laborious efforts with individual members and his own overmastering eloquence upon that floor, he finally secured the admission of the State. Brightly and captivating as it had previously shown, it was now perceived that his great eloquence was a mere embellishment, or at most but a helping hand to his inventive genius and his devotion to his country in the day of her extreme peril.

After the settlement of the Missouri question, although a portion of the American people have differed with Mr. Clay, and a majority even appear generally to have been opposed to him on questions of ordinary administration, he seems constantly to have been regarded by all as the man for the crisis. Accordingly, in the days of nullification, and more recently in the reappearance of the slavery question connected with our territory newly acquired of Mexico, the task of devising a mode of adjustment seems to have been cast upon Mr. Clay by common consent—and his performance of the task in each case was little else than a literal fulfilment of the public expectation.

Mr. Clay's efforts in behalf of the South Americans, and afterward in behalf of the Greeks, in the times of their respective struggles for civil liberty, are among the finest on record, upon the noblest of all themes, and bear ample corroboration of what I have said was his ruling passion—a love of liberty and right, unselfishly, and for their own sakes.

Having been led to allude to domestic slavery so frequently already, I am unwilling to close without referring more particularly to Mr. Clay's views and conduct in regard to it. He ever was on principle and in feeling opposed to slavery. The very earliest, and one of the latest, public efforts of his life, separated by a period of more than fifty years, were both made in favor of gradual emancipation. He did not perceive that on a question of human right the negroes were to be excepted from the human race. And yet Mr. Clay was the owner of slaves. Cast into life when slavery was already widely spread and deeply seated, he did not perceive, as I think no wise man has perceived, how it could be at once eradicated without producing a greater evil even to the cause of human liberty itself. His feeling and his judgment, therefore, ever led him to oppose both extremes of opinion on the subject. Those who would shiver into fragments the Union of these States, tear to tatters its now venerated Constitution, and even burn the last copy of the Bible, rather than slavery should continue a single hour, together with all their more halting sympathizers, have received, and are receiving, their just execration; and the name and opinions and influence of Mr. Clay are fully and, as I trust, effectually and enduringly arrayed against them. But I would also, if I could, array his name, opinions, and influence against the opposite extreme—against a few but an increasing number of men who, for the sake of perpetuating slavery, are beginning to assail and to ridicule the white man's charter of freedom, the declaration that "all men are created free and equal." So far as I have learned, the first American of any note to do or attempt this was the late John C. Calhoun; and if I mistake not, it soon after found its way into some of the messages of the Governor of South Carolina. We, however, look for and are not much shocked by political eccentricities and heresies in South Carolina. But only last year I saw with astonishment what purported to be a letter of a very distinguished and influential clergyman of Virginia, copied, with apparent approbation, into a St. Louis newspaper, containing the following to me very unsatisfactory language:

"I am fully aware that there is a text in some Bibles that is not in mine. Professional abolitionists have made more use of it than of any passage in the Bible. It came, however, as I trace it, from Saint Voltaire, and was baptized by Thomas Jefferson, and since almost universally regarded as canonical authority 'All men are born free and equal.'

"This is a genuine coin in the political currency of our generation. I am sorry to say that I have never seen two men of whom it is true. But I must admit I never saw the Siamese Twins, and therefore will not dogmatically say that no man ever saw a proof of this sage aphorism."

This sounds strangely in republican America. The like was not heard in the fresher days of the republic. Let us contrast with it the language of that truly national man whose life and death we now commemorate and lament: I quote from a speech of Mr. Clay delivered before the American Colonization Society in 1827:

"We are reproached with doing mischief by the agitation of this question. The society goes into no household to disturb its domestic tranquillity. It addresses itself to no slaves to weaken their obligations of obedience. It seeks to affect no man's property. It neither has the power nor the will to affect the property of any one contrary to his consent. The execution of its scheme would augment instead of diminishing the value of property left behind. The society, composed of free men, conceals itself only with the free. Collateral consequences we are not responsible for. It is not this society which has produced the great moral revolution which the age exhibits. What would they who thus reproach us have done? If they would repress all tendencies toward liberty and ultimate emancipation, they must do more than put down the benevolent efforts of this society. They must go back to the era of our liberty and independence, and muzzle the cannon which thunders its annual joyous return. They must renew the slave trade, with all its train of atrocities. They must suppress the workings of British philanthropy, seeking to meliorate the condition of the unfortunate West Indian slave. They must arrest the career of South American deliverance from thraldom. They must blow out the moral lights around us and extinguish that greatest torch of all which America presents to a benighted world—pointing the way to their rights, their liberties, and their happiness. And when they have achieved all those purposes their work will be yet incomplete. They must penetrate the human soul, and eradicate the light of reason and the love of liberty. Then, and not till then, when universal darkness and despair prevail, can you perpetuate slavery and repress all sympathy and all humane and benevolent efforts among free men in behalf of the unhappy portion of our race doomed to bondage."

The American Colonization Society was organized in 1816. Mr. Clay, though not its projector, was one of its earliest members; and he died, as for many preceding years he had been, its president. It was one of the most cherished objects of his direct care and consideration, and the association of his name with it has probably been its very greatest collateral support. He considered it no demerit in the society that it tended to relieve the slave-holders from the troublesome presence of the free negroes; but this was far from being its whole merit in his estimation. In the same speech from which we have quoted he says:

"There is a moral fitness in the idea of returning to Africa her children, whose ancestors have been torn from her by the ruthless hand of fraud and violence. Transplanted in a foreign land, they will carry back to their native soil the rich fruits of religion, civilization, law, and liberty. May it not be one of the great designs of the Ruler of the universe, whose ways are often inscrutable by short-sighted mortals, thus to transform an original crime into a signal blessing to that most unfortunate portion of the globe?"

This suggestion of the possible ultimate redemption of the African race and African continent was made twenty-five years ago. Every succeeding year has added strength to the hope of its realization. May it indeed be realized. Pharaoh's country was cursed with plagues, and his hosts were lost in the Red Sea, for striving to retain a captive people who had already served them more than four hundred years. May like disasters never befall us! If, as the friends of colonization hope, the present and coming generations of our countrymen shall by any means succeed in freeing our land from the dangerous presence of slavery, and at the same time in restoring a captive people to their long-lost fatherland with bright prospects for the future, and this too so gradually that neither races nor individuals shall have suffered by the change, it will indeed be a glorious consummation. And if to such a consummation the efforts of Mr. Clay shall have contributed, it will be what he most ardently wished, and none of his labors will have been more valuable to his country and his kind.

But Henry Clay is dead. His long and eventful life is closed. Our country is prosperous and powerful; but could it have been quite all it has been, and is, and is to be, without Henry Clay? Such a man the times have demanded, and such in the providence of God was given us. But he is gone. Let us strive to deserve, as far as mortals may, the continued care of Divine Providence, trusting that in future national emergencies He will not fail to provide us the instruments of safety and security.

Appendix H

Jefferson Davis's Inaugural Address

Gentlemen of the Congress of the Confederate States of America, Friends, and Fellow-Citizens:

Called to the difficult and responsible station of Chief Magistrate of the Provisional Government which you have instituted, I approach the discharge of the duties assigned me with an humble distrust of my abilities, but with a sustaining confidence in the wisdom of those who are to guide and aid me in the administration of public affairs, and an abiding faith in the virtue and patriotism of the people. Looking forward to the speedy establishment of a permanent government to take the place of this, which by its great moral and physical power will be better able to combat with many difficulties that arise from the conflicting interests of separate nations, I enter upon the duties of the office for which I have been chosen with the hope that the beginning of our career, as a Confederacy, may not be obstructed by hostile opposition to our enjoyment of the separate existence and independence we have asserted, and which with the blessing of Providence, we intend to maintain.

Our present political position has been achieved in a manner unprecedented in the history of nations. It illustrates the American idea that governments rest upon the consent of the governed, and that it is the right of the people to alter or abolish them at will whenever they become destructive of the ends for which they were established. The declared purpose of the compact of the Union from which we have withdrawn was to "establish justice, insure domestic tranquillity, provide for the common defence, promote the general welfare, and secure the blessings of liberty for ourselves and our prosperity"; and, when in the judgment of the sovereign States now composing this Confederacy, it has been perverted from the purposes for which it was ordained, and ceased to answer the ends for which it was established, a peaceful appeal to the ballot-box declared that, so far as they are concerned, the Government created by that compact should cease to exist. In this they merely asserted the right which the Declaration of Independence of July 4, 1776, defined to be "inalienable." Of the time and occasion of its exercise they as sovereigns were the final judges, each for itself. The impartial and enlightened verdict of mankind will vindicate the rectitude of our conduct; and He who knows the hearts of men will judge of the sincerity with which we have labored to preserve the Government of our fathers in its spirit.

The right solemnly proclaimed at the birth of the United States, and which has been solemnly affirmed and reaffirmed in the Bills of Rights of the States subsequently admitted into the Union of 1789, undeniably recognizes in the people the power to resume the authority delegated for the purposes of government. Thus, the sovereign States here represented have proceeded to form this Confederacy; and it is by abuse of language that their act has been denominated a revolution. They have formed a new alliance, but within each State its government has remained; so that the rights of person and property have not been disturbed. The agent through which they communicated with foreign nations is changed, but this does not necessarily interrupt their international relations. Sustained by the consciousness that the transition from the former Union to the present Confederacy has not proceeded from a disregard on our part of just obligations, or any failure to perform every constitutional duty, moved by no interest or passion to invade the rights of others, anxious to cultivate peace and commerce with all nations, if we may not hope to avoid war, we may at least expect that posterity will acquit us of having needlessly engaged in it. Doubly justified by the absence of wrong on our part, and by wanton aggression on the part of others, there can be no cause to doubt that the courage and patriotism of the people of the Confederate States will be found equal to any measures of defense which their honor and security may require.

An agricultural people, whose chief interest is the export of commodities required in every manufacturing country, our true policy is peace, and the freest trade which our necessities will permit. It is alike our interest and that to all those to whom we would sell, and from whom we would buy, that there should be the fewest practicable restrictions upon the interchange of these commodities. There can, however, be but little rivalry between us and any manufacturing or navigating community, such as the Northeastern States of the American Union. It must follow, therefore, that mutual interest will invite to good-will and kind offices on both parts. If, however, passion or lust of dominion should cloud the judgment or inflame the ambition of those States, we must prepare to meet the emergency and maintain, by the final arbitrament of the sword, the position which we have assumed among the nations of the earth.

We have entered upon the career of independence, and it must be inflexibly pursued. Through many years of controversy with our late associates of the Northern States, we have vainly endeavored to secure tranquillity and obtain respect for the rights to which we were entitled. As a necessity, not a choice, we have resorted to the remedy of separation, and henceforth our energies must be directed to the conduct of our own affairs, and the perpetuity of the Confederacy which we have formed. If a just perception of mutual interest shall permit us peaceably to pursue our separate political career, my most earnest desire will have been fulfilled. But if this be denied to us, and the integrity of our territory and jurisdiction be assailed, it will but remain for us with firm resolve to appeal to arms and invoke the blessings of Providence on a just cause.

As a consequence of our new condition and relations, and with a view to meet anticipated wants, it will be necessary to provide for the speedy and efficient organization of branches of the Executive department having special charge of foreign intercourse, finance, military affairs, and the postal service. For purposes of defense, the Confederate States may, under ordinary circumstances, rely mainly upon the militia; but it is deemed advisable, in the present condition of affairs, that there should be a well-instructed and disciplined army, more numerous than would usually be required on a peace establishment. I also suggest that for the protection of our harbors and commerce on the high seas, a navy adapted to those objects will be required. But this, as well as other subjects appropriate to our necessities, have doubtless engaged the attention of Congress.

With a constitution differing only from that of our fathers in so far as it is explanatory of their well-known intent, freed from sectional conflicts, which have interfered with the pursuit of the general welfare, it is not unreasonable to expect that States from which we have recently parted may seek to unite their fortunes to ours under the Government which we have instituted. For this your Constitution makes adequate provision; but beyond this, if I mistake not the judgment and will of the people, a reunion with the States from which we have separated is neither practicable nor desirable. To increase the power, develop the resources, and promote the happiness of the Confederacy, it is requisite that there should be so much of homogeneity that the welfare of every portion shall be the aim of the whole. When this does not exist, antagonisms are engendered which must and should result in separation.

Actuated solely by the desire to preserve our own rights and promote our own welfare, the separation by the Confederate States has been marked by no aggression upon others, and followed by no domestic convulsion. Our industrial pursuits have received no check, the cultivation of our fields has progressed as heretofore, and, even should we be involved in war, there would be no considerable diminution in the production of the great staples which have constituted our exports, and in which the commercial world has an interest scarcely less than our own. This common interest of the producer and consumer can only be interrupted by external force which would obstruct the transmission of our staples to foreign markets——a course of conduct which would be as unjust, as it would be detrimental, to manufacturing and commercial interests abroad.

Should reason guide the action of the Government from which we have separated, a policy so detrimental to the civilized world, the Northern States included, could not be dictated by even the strongest desire to inflict injury upon us; but, if the contrary should prove true, a terrible responsibility will rest upon it, and the suffering of millions will bear testimony to the folly and wickedness of our aggressors. In the meantime there will remain to us, besides the ordinary means before suggested, the well-known resources for retaliation upon the commerce of an enemy.

Experience in public stations, of subordinate grade to this which your kindness has conferred, has taught me that toil and care and disappointment are the price of official elevation. You will see many errors to forgive, many deficiencies to tolerate; but you shall not find in me either want of zeal or fidelity to the cause that is to me the highest in hope, and of most enduring affection. Your generosity has bestowed upon me an undeserved distinction, one which I neither sought nor desired. Upon the continuance of that sentiment, and upon your wisdom and patriotism, I rely to direct and support me in the performance of the duties required at my hands.

We have changed the constituent parts, but not the system of government. The Constitution framed by our fathers is that of these Confederate States. In their exposition of it, and in the judicial construction it has received, we have a light that reveals its true meaning.

Thus instructed as to the true meaning and just interpretation of that instrument, and ever remembering that all offices are but trusts held for the people, and that powers delegated are to be strictly construed, I will hope by due diligence in the performance of my duties, though I may disappoint your expectations, yet to retain, when retiring, something of the good-will and confidence which welcome my entrance into office.

It is joyous in the midst of perilous times to look around upon a people united in heart, where one purpose of high resolve animates and actuates the whole; where the sacrifices to be made are not weighed in the balance against honor and right and liberty and equality. Obstacles may retard, but they can not long prevent, the progress of a movement sanctified by its justice and sustained by a virtuous people. Reverently let us invoke the God of our Fathers to guide and protect us in our efforts to perpetuate the principles which by his blessing they were able to vindicate, establish, and transmit to their posterity. With the continuance of his favor ever gratefully acknowledged, we may hopefully look forward to success, to peace, and to prosperity.

Inaugural Address of Jefferson Davis,
President of the Confederate States of America
Montgomery, Alabama
February 18th, 1861

Abraham Lincoln's First Inaugural Address

March 4, 1861

Fellow citizens of the United States: in compliance with a custom as old as the government itself, I appear before you to address you briefly and to take, in your presence, the oath prescribed by the Constitution of the United States, to be taken by the President "before he enters on the execution of his office."

I do not consider it necessary, at present, for me to discuss those matters of administration about which there is no special anxiety, or excitement.

Apprehension seems to exist among the people of the Southern States that by the accession of a Republican administration their property and their peace and personal security are to be endangered. There has never been any reasonable cause for such apprehension. Indeed, the most ample evidence to the contrary has all the while existed and been open to their inspection. It is found in nearly all the published speeches of him who now addresses you. I do but quote from one of those speeches when I declare that "I have no purpose, directly or indirectly, to interfere with the institution of slavery where it exists. I believe I have no lawful right to do so, and I have no inclination to do so." Those who nominated and elected me did so with full knowledge that I had made this and many similar declarations, and had never recanted them. And, more than this, they placed in the platform for my acceptance, and as a law to themselves and to me, the clear and emphatic resolution which I now read:

"Resolved: that the maintenance inviolate of the rights of the States, and especially the right of each State to order and control its own domestic institutions according to its own judgment exclusively, is essential to that balance of power on which the perfection and endurance of our political fabric depend, and we denounce the lawless invasion by armed force of the soil of any State or Territory, no matter under what pretext, as among the gravest of crimes."

I now reiterate these sentiments; and, in doing so, I only press upon the public attention the most conclusive evidence of which the case is susceptible, that the property, peace, and security of no section are to be in any wise endangered by the now incoming administration. I add, too, that all the protection which, consistently with the Constitution and the laws, can be given, will be cheerfully given to all the States when lawfully demanded, for whatever cause—as cheerfully to one section as to another.

There is much controversy about the delivering up of fugitives from service or labor. The clause I now read is as plainly written in the Constitution as any other of its provisions:

"No person held to service or labor in one State, under the laws thereof, escaping into another, shall in consequence of any law or regulation therein be discharged from such service or labor, but shall be delivered up on claim of the party to whom such service or labor may be due."

It is scarcely questioned that this provision was intended by those who made it for the reclaiming of what we call fugitive slaves; and the intention of the lawgiver is the law. All members of Congress swear their support to the whole Constitution—to this provision as much as to any other. To the proposition, then, that slaves whose cases come within the terms of this clause "shall be delivered up", their oaths are unanimous. Now, if they would make the effort in good temper, could they not with nearly equal unanimity frame and pass a law by means of which to keep good that unanimous oath?

There is some difference of opinion whether this clause should be enforced by national or by State authority; but surely that difference is not a very material one. If the slave is to be surrendered, it can be of but little consequence to him or to others by which authority it is done. And should any one in any case be content that his oath shall go unkept on a merely unsubstantial controversy as to HOW it shall be kept?

Again, in any law upon this subject, ought not all the safeguards of liberty known in civilized and humane jurisprudence to be introduced, so that a free man be not, in any case, surrendered as a slave? And might it not be well at the same time to provide by law for the enforcement of that clause in the Constitution which guarantees that "the citizen of each State shall be entitled to all privileges and immunities of citizens in the several States?"

I take the official oath today with no mental reservations, and with no purpose to construe the Constitution or laws by any hypercritical rules. And while I do not choose now to specify particular acts of Congress as proper to be enforced, I do suggest that it will be much safer for all, both in official and private stations, to conform to and abide by all those acts which stand unrepealed, than to violate any of them, trusting to find impunity in having them held to be unConstitutional.

It is seventy-two years since the first inauguration of a President under our national Constitution. During that period fifteen different and greatly distinguished citizens have, in succession, administered the executive branch of the government. They have conducted it through many perils, and generally with great success. Yet, with all this scope of precedent, I now enter upon the same task for the brief Constitutional term of four years under great and peculiar difficulty. A disruption of the Federal Union, heretofore only menaced, is now formidably attempted.

I hold that, in contemplation of universal law and of the Constitution, the Union of these States is perpetual. Perpetuity is implied, if not expressed, in the fundamental law of all national governments. It is safe to assert that no government proper ever had a provision in its organic law for its own termination. Continue to execute all the express provisions of our National Constitution, and the Union will endure forever—it being impossible to destroy it except by some action not provided for in the instrument itself.

Again, if the United States be not a government proper, but an association of States in the nature of contract merely, can it, as a contract, be peaceably unmade by less than all the parties who made it? One party to a contract may violate it—break it, so to speak; but does it not require all to lawfully rescind it?

Descending from these general principles, we find the proposition that in legal contemplation the Union is perpetual, confirmed by the history of the Union itself. The Union is much older than the Constitution. It was formed, in fact, by the Articles of Association in 1774. It was matured and continued by the Declaration of Independence in 1776. It was further matured, and the faith of all the then thirteen States expressly plighted and engaged that it should be perpetual, by the Articles of Confederation in 1778. And, finally, in 1787 one of the declared objects for ordaining and establishing the Constitution was "TO FORM A MORE PERFECT UNION."

But if the destruction of the Union by one or by a part only of the States be lawfully possible, the Union is LESS perfect than before the Constitution, having lost the vital element of perpetuity.

It follows from these views that no State upon its own mere motion can lawfully get out of the Union; that Resolves and Ordinances to that effect are legally void; and that acts of violence, within any State or States, against the authority of the United States, are insurrectionary or revolutionary, according to circumstances.

I therefore consider that, in view of the Constitution and the laws, the Union is unbroken; and to the extent of my ability I shall take care, as the Constitution itself expressly enjoins upon me, that the laws of the Union be faithfully executed in all the States. Doing this I deem to be only a simple duty on my part; and I shall perform it so far as practicable, unless my rightful masters, the American people, shall withhold the requisite means, or in some authoritative manner direct the contrary. I trust this will not be regarded as a menace, but only as the declared purpose of the Union that it WILL Constitutionally defend and maintain itself.

In doing this there needs to be no bloodshed or violence; and there shall be none, unless it be forced upon the national authority. The power confided to me will be used to hold, occupy, and possess the property and places belonging to the government, and to collect the duties and imposts; but beyond what may be necessary for these objects, there will be no invasion, no using of force against or among the people anywhere. Where hostility to the United States, in any interior locality, shall be so great and universal as to prevent competent resident citizens from holding the Federal offices, there will be no attempt to force obnoxious strangers among the people for that object. While the strict legal right may exist in the government to enforce the exercise of these offices, the attempt to do so would be so irritating, and so nearly impracticable withal, that I deem it better to forego for the time the uses of such offices.

The mails, unless repelled, will continue to be furnished in all parts of the Union. So far as possible, the people everywhere shall have that sense of perfect security which is most favorable to calm thought and reflection. The course here indicated will be followed unless current events and experience shall show a modification or change to be proper, and in every case and exigency my best discretion will be exercised according to circumstances actually existing, and with a view and a hope of a peaceful solution of the national troubles and the restoration of fraternal sympathies and affections.

That there are persons in one section or another who seek to destroy the Union at all events, and are glad of any pretext to do it, I will neither affirm nor deny; but if there be such, I need address no word to them. To those, however, who really love the Union may I not speak?

Before entering upon so grave a matter as the destruction of our national fabric, with all its benefits, its memories, and its hopes, would it not be wise to ascertain precisely why we do it? Will you hazard so desperate a step while there is any possibility that any portion of the ills you fly from have no real existence? Will you, while the certain ills you fly to are greater than all the real ones you fly from—will you risk the commission of so fearful a mistake?

All profess to be content in the Union if all Constitutional rights can be maintained. Is it true, then, that any right, plainly written in the Constitution, has been denied? I think not.

Happily the human mind is so constituted that no party can reach to the audacity of doing this. Think, if you can, of a single instance in which a plainly written provision of the Constitution has ever been denied. If by the mere force of numbers a majority should deprive a minority of any clearly written Constitutional right, it might, in a moral point of view, justify revolution— certainly would if such a right were a vital one. But such is not our case. All the vital rights of minorities and of individuals are so plainly assured to them by affirmations and negations, guaranties and prohibitions, in the Constitution, that controversies never arise concerning them. But no organic law can ever be framed with a provision specifically applicable to every question which may occur in practical administration. No foresight can anticipate, nor any document of reasonable length contain, express provisions for all possible questions. Shall fugitives from labor be surrendered by national or State authority? The Constitution does not expressly say. May Congress prohibit slavery in the Territories? The Constitution does not expressly say. MUST Congress protect slavery in the Territories? The Constitution does not expressly say.

From questions of this class spring all our constitutional controversies, and we divide upon them into majorities and minorities. If the minority will not acquiesce, the majority must, or the government must cease. There is no other alternative; for continuing the government is acquiescence on one side or the other.

If a minority in such case will secede rather than acquiesce, they make a precedent which in turn will divide and ruin them; for a minority of their own will secede from them whenever a majority refuses to be controlled by such minority. For instance, why may not any portion of a new confederacy a year or two hence arbitrarily secede again, precisely as portions of the present Union now claim to secede from it? All who cherish disunion sentiments are now being educated to the exact temper of doing this.

Is there such perfect identity of interests among the States to compose a new Union, as to produce harmony only, and prevent renewed secession?

Plainly, the central idea of secession is the essence of anarchy. A majority held in restraint by constitutional checks and limitations, and always changing easily with deliberate changes of popular opinions and sentiments, is the only true sovereign of a free people. Whoever rejects it does, of necessity, fly to anarchy or to despotism. Unanimity is impossible; the rule of a minority, as a permanent arrangement, is wholly inadmissible; so that, rejecting the majority principle, anarchy or despotism in some form is all that is left.

I do not forget the position, assumed by some, that Constitutional questions are to be decided by the Supreme Court; nor do I deny that such decisions must be binding, in any case, upon the parties to a suit, as to the object of that suit, while they are also entitled to very high respect and consideration in all parallel cases by all other departments of the government. And while it is obviously possible that such decision may be erroneous in any given case, still the evil effect following it, being limited to that particular case, with the chance that it may be overruled and never become a precedent for other cases, can better be borne than could the evils of a different practice. At the same time, the candid citizen must confess that if the policy of the government, upon vital questions affecting the whole people, is to be irrevocably fixed by decisions of the Supreme Court, the instant they are made, in ordinary litigation between parties in personal actions, the people will have ceased to be their own rulers, having to that extent practically resigned their government into the hands of that eminent tribunal. Nor is there in this view any assault upon the court or the judges. It is a duty from which they may not shrink to decide cases properly brought before them, and it is no fault of theirs if others seek to turn their decisions to political purposes.

One section of our country believes slavery is RIGHT, and ought to be extended, while the other believes it is WRONG, and ought not to be extended. This is the only substantial dispute. The fugitive-slave clause of the Constitution, and the law for the suppression of the foreign slave-trade, are each as well enforced, perhaps, as any law can ever be in a community where the moral sense of the people imperfectly supports the law itself. The great body of the people abide by the dry legal obligation in both cases, and a few break over in each. This, I think, cannot be perfectly cured; and it would be worse in both cases AFTER the separation of the sections than BEFORE. The foreign slave-trade, now imperfectly suppressed, would be ultimately revived, without restriction, in one section, while fugitive slaves, now only partially surrendered, would not be surrendered at all by the other.

Physically speaking, we cannot separate. We cannot remove our respective sections from each other, nor build an impassable wall between them. A husband and wife may be divorced, and go out of the presence and beyond the reach of each other; but the different parts of our country cannot do this. They cannot but remain face to face, and intercourse, either amicable or hostile, must continue between them. Is it possible, then, to make that intercourse more advantageous or more satisfactory after separation than before? Can aliens make treaties easier than friends can make laws? Can treaties be more faithfully enforced between aliens than laws can among friends? Suppose you go to war, you cannot fight always; and when, after much loss on both sides, and no gain on either, you cease fighting, the identical old questions as to terms of intercourse are again upon you.

This country, with its institutions, belongs to the people who inhabit it. Whenever they shall grow weary of the existing government, they can exercise their CONSTITUTIONAL right of amending it, or their REVOLUTIONARY right to dismember or overthrow it. I cannot be ignorant of the fact that many worthy and patriotic citizens are desirous of having the national Constitution amended. While I make no recommendation of amendments, I fully recognize the rightful authority of the people over the whole subject, to be exercised in either of the modes prescribed in the instrument itself; and I should, under existing circumstances, favor rather than oppose a fair opportunity being afforded the people to act upon it. I will venture to add that to me the convention mode seems preferable, in that it allows amendments to originate with the people themselves, instead of only permitting them to take or reject propositions originated by others not especially chosen for the purpose, and which might not be precisely such as they would wish to either accept or refuse. I understand a proposed amendment to the Constitution—which amendment, however, I have not seen—has passed Congress, to the effect that the Federal Government shall never interfere with the domestic institutions of the States, including that of persons held to service. To avoid misconstruction of what I have said, I depart from my purpose not to speak of particular amendments so far as to say that, holding such a provision to now be implied Constitutional law, I have no objection to its being made express and irrevocable.

The chief magistrate derives all his authority from the people, and they have conferred none upon him to fix terms for the separation of the states. The people themselves can do this also if they choose; but the executive, as such, has nothing to do with it. His duty is to administer the present government, as it came to his hands, and to transmit it, unimpaired by him, to his successor.

Why should there not be a patient confidence in the ultimate justice of the people? Is there any better or equal hope in the world? In our present differences is either party without faith of being in the right? If the Almighty Ruler of Nations, with his eternal truth and justice, be on your side of the North, or on yours of the South, that truth and that justice will surely prevail, by the judgment of this great tribunal, the American people.

By the frame of the government under which we live, this same people have wisely given their public servants but little power for mischief; and have, with equal wisdom, provided for the return of that little to their own hands at very short intervals. While the people retain their virtue and vigilance, no administration, by any extreme of wickedness or folly, can very seriously injure the government in the short space of four years.

My countrymen, one and all, think calmly and WELL upon this whole subject. Nothing valuable can be lost by taking time. If there be an object to HURRY any of you in hot haste to a step which you would never take DELIBERATELY, that object will be frustrated by taking time; but no good object can be frustrated by it. Such of you as are now dissatisfied, still have the old Constitution unimpaired, and, on the sensitive point, the laws of your own framing under it; while the new administration will have no immediate power, if it would, to change either. If it were admitted that you who are dissatisfied hold the right side in the dispute, there still is no single good reason for precipitate action. Intelligence, patriotism, Christianity, and a firm reliance on him who has never yet forsaken this favored land, are still competent to adjust in the best way all our present difficulty.

In YOUR hands, my dissatisfied fellow-countrymen, and not in MINE, is the momentous issue of civil war. The government will not assail YOU. You can have no conflict without being yourselves the aggressors. YOU have no oath registered in heaven to destroy the government, while *I* shall have the most solemn one to "preserve, protect, and defend it."

I am loathe to close. We are not enemies, but friends. We must not be enemies. Though passion may have strained, it must not break our bonds of affection. The mystic chords of memory, stretching from every battlefield and patriot grave to every living heart and hearthstone all over this broad land, will yet swell the chorus of the Union when again touched, as surely they will be, by the better angels of our nature.

Appendix J

The Kentucky Compact with Virginia, December 18, 1789

An Act concerning the erection of the District of Kentucky into an Independent State

Passed the 18th of December, 1789, by the Virginia General Assembly

WHEREAS it is represented to this present General Assembly, that the act of last session, entitled "an act concerning the erection of the District of Kentucky into an independent state," which contains terms materially different from those of the act of October session, one thousand seven hundred and eighty-five, are found incompatible with the real views of this commonwealth, as well as injurious to the good people of the said district:

SECTION 1. **Be it enacted by the General Assembly,** That in the month of May next, on the respective court days of the counties within the said district, and at the respective places of holding courts therein, Representatives, to continue in appointment for one year, and to compose a convention, with the powers, and for the purposes hereinafter mentioned, shall be elected by the free male inhabitants of each county, above the age of twenty-one years, in like manner as delegates to the general assembly have been elected within said district, in the proportions following: In the county of Jefferson, shall be elected five representatives; in the county of Nelson, five representatives; in the county of Mercer, five representatives; in the county of Lincoln, five representatives; in the county of Madison, five representatives; in the county of Fayette, five representatives; in the county of Woodford, five representatives; in the county of Bourbon, five representatives; and in the county of Mason, five representatives: *Provided,* that no free male inhabitant above the age of twenty-one years, shall vote in any other county except that in which he resides, and that no person shall be capable of being elected unless he has been a resident within the said district at least one year.

SECTION 2. That full opportunity may be given to the good people of exercising their right of suffrage on an occasion so interesting to them, each of the officers holding such elections, shall continue the same from day to day, passing over Sunday, for five days including the first day, and shall cause this act to be read on each day immediately preceding the opening of the election, at the door of the court house, or other convenient place; each of the said officers shall deliver to each person duly elected a representative, a certificate of his election, and shall transmit a general return to the clerk of the supreme court, to be by him laid before the convention.

SECTION 3. For every neglect of any of the duties hereby enjoined on such officer he shall forfeit one hundred pounds, to be recovered by action of debt, by any person suing for the same.

SECTION 4. The said convention shall be held at Danville on the twenty-sixth day of July next, and shall and may proceed, after choosing a president and other proper officers, and settling the proper rules of proceeding, to consider and determine whether it be expedient for, and the will of the good people of the said district that the same be erected into an independent state, on the terms and conditions following:

SECTION 5. **First,** that the boundary between the proposed state and Virginia shall remain the same as at present separates the district from the residue of this commonwealth.

SECTION 6. **Second,** that the proposed state shall take upon itself a just proportion of the debt of the United States, and the payment of all the certificates granted on account of the several expeditions carried on from the Kentucky District against the Indians, since the first day of January, one thousand seven hundred and eighty-five.

SECTION 7. **Third,** all private rights and interests of lands within the said District, derived from the laws of Virginia, prior to such separation, shall remain valid and secure under the laws of the proposed state, and shall be determined by the laws now existing in this state.

SECTION 8. **Fourth,** that the lands within the proposed state of non-resident proprietors, shall not in any case be taxed higher than the lands of residents, at any time prior to the admission of the proposed state to a vote by its delegates in Congress where such non-residents reside out of the United States; nor at any time, either before or after such admission, where such non-residents reside within this commonwealth within which this stipulation shall be reciprocal; or where such non-residents reside within any other of the United States, which shall declare the same to be reciprocal within its limits; nor shall a neglect of cultivation or improvement of any land within either the proposed state of this commonwealth, belonging to non-residents, citizens of the other, subject such non-residents to forfeiture or other penalty within the term of six years, after the admission of the said state into the Federal Union.

SECTION 9. **Fifth,** that no grant of land, or land warrant to be issued by the proposed state, shall interfere with any warrant heretofore issued from the land office of Virginia, which shall be located on land within the said district, now liable thereto, on or before the first day of September one thousand seven hundred and ninety-one.

SECTION 10. **Sixth,** that the unlocated lands within the said district, which stand appropriated to individuals or description of individuals, by the laws of this commonwealth, for military or other services, shall be exempted from the disposition of the proposed state, and shall remain subject to be disposed of by the commonwealth of Virginia, according to such appropriation, until the first day of May one thousand seven hundred and ninety two, and no longer: thereafter the residue of all lands remaining within the limits of the said district, shall be subject to the disposition of the proposed state.

SECTION 11. **Seventh,** that the use and navigation of the river Ohio, so far as the territory of the proposed state, or the territory which shall remain within the limits of this commonwealth lies thereon, shall be free and common to the citizens of the United States, and the respective jurisdictions of this commonwealth and of the proposed state on the river as aforesaid, shall be concurrent only with the states which may possess the opposite shores of the said river.

SECTION 12. **Eighth,** that in case any complaint or dispute, shall at any time arise between the commonwealth of Virginia and the said district, after it shall be an independent state, concerning the meaning or execution of the foregoing articles, the same shall be determined by six commissioners, of whom two shall be chosen by each of the parties, and the remainder by the commissioners so first appointed.

SECTION 13. *Provided, however,* that five members assembled, shall be a sufficient number to adjourn from day to day, and to issue writs for supplying vacancies which may happen from deaths, resignations or refusals to act; a majority of the whole shall be a sufficient number to choose a president, settle the proper rules of proceeding, authorize any number to summon a convention during a recess, and to act in all other instances where a greater number is not expressly required. Two-thirds of the whole shall be a sufficient number to determine on the expediency of forming the said district into an independent state on the aforesaid terms and conditions, provided that a majority of the whole number to be elected concur therein.

SECTION 14. **And be it further enacted,** that if the said convention shall approve of the erection of the said District into an independent state, on the foregoing terms and conditions, they shall and may proceed to fix a day posterior to the first day of November, one thousand seven hundred and ninety-one, on which the authority of this commonwealth, and of its laws under the exceptions aforesaid, shall cease and determine forever over the proposed state, and the said articles become a solemn compact mutually binding on the parties, and unalterable by either without the consent of the other.

SECTION 15. *Provided, however,* that prior to the first day of November, one thousand seven hundred and ninety-one, the general government of the United States shall assent to the erection of the said district into an independent state, shall release this commonwealth from all its federal obligations arising from the said district as being part thereof, and shall agree that the proposed state shall, immediately after the day to be fixed as aforesaid posterior to the first day of November, one thousand seven hundred and ninety-one, or at some convenient time future thereto, be admitted into the Federal Union.

SECTION 16. And to the end that no period of anarchy may happen to the good people of the proposed state, it is to be understood, that the said convention shall have authority to take the necessary provisional measures for the election and meeting of a convention, at some time prior to the day fixed for the determination of the authority of this commonwealth, and of its laws over said district, and posterior to the first day of November, one thousand seven hundred and ninety-one aforesaid, with full power and authority to frame and establish a fundamental constitution of government for the proposed state, and to declare what laws shall be in force therein, until the same shall be abrogated or altered by the legislative authority acting under the constitution so to be framed and established.

SECTION 17. **And be it further enacted,** that the electors in going to, continuing at, and returning from an election of members to the said convention, shall be entitled to the same privileges from arrest, as are by law allowed at an election of members to the general assembly;

and each person returned to serve as a member in said convention, shall be entitled to the same privileges from arrest in going to, during his attendance on, and returning from said convention, as are by law allowed to the members of the general assembly.

SECTION 18. This act shall be transmitted by the executive, to the representatives of this commonwealth in congress, who are hereby instructed to use their endeavors to obtain from Congress a speedy act to the effect above specified.

Source: William Littell, *The Statute Law of Kentucky*, vol. 1 (Frankfort: Kentucky Court of Appeals, 1809), 17–21.

The Kentucky Constitution

The Constitution of the Commonwealth of Kentucky (1891)

Preamble

We, the people of the Commonwealth of Kentucky, grateful to Almighty God for the civil, political and religious liberties we enjoy, and invoking the continuance of these blessings, do ordain and establish this Constitution.

Bill of Rights

Section 1: Rights of life, liberty, worship, pursuit of safety and happiness, free speech, acquiring and protecting property, peaceable assembly, redress of grievances, bearing arms.

All men are, by nature, free and equal, and have certain inherent and inalienable rights, among which may be reckoned:

First: The right of enjoying and defending their lives and liberties.

Second: The right of worshiping Almighty God according to the dictates of their consciences.

Third: The right of seeking and pursuing their safety and happiness.

Fourth: The right of freely communicating their thoughts and opinions.

Fifth: The right of acquiring and protecting property.

Sixth: The right of assembling together in a peaceable manner for their common good, and of applying to those invested with the power of government for redress of grievances or other proper purposes, by petition, address or remonstrance.

Seventh: The right to bear arms in defense of themselves and of the State, subject to the power of the General Assembly to enact laws to prevent persons from carrying concealed weapons.

Text as Ratified on: August 3, 1891, and revised September 28, 1891. History: Not yet amended.

Section 2: Absolute and arbitrary power denied.

Absolute and arbitrary power over the lives, liberty and property of freemen exists nowhere in a republic, not even in the largest majority.

Text as Ratified on: August 3, 1891, and revised September 28, 1891. History: Not yet amended.

Section 3: Men are equal—No exclusive grant except for public services—Property not to be exempted from taxation—Grants revocable.

All men, when they form a social compact, are equal; and no grant of exclusive, separate public emoluments or privileges shall be made to any man or set of men, except in consideration of public services; but no property shall be exempt from taxation except as provided in this Constitution, and every grant of a franchise, privilege or exemption, shall remain subject to revocation, alteration or amendment.

Text as Ratified on: August 3, 1891, and revised September 28, 1891. History: Not yet amended.

Section 4: Power inherent in the people—Right to alter, reform, or abolish government.

All power is inherent in the people, and all free governments are founded on their authority and instituted for their peace, safety, happiness and the protection of property. For the advancement of these ends, they have at all times an inalienable and indefeasible right to alter, reform or abolish their government in such manner as they may deem proper.

Text as Ratified on: August 3, 1891, and revised September 28, 1891. History: Not yet amended.

Section 5: Right of religious freedom.

No preference shall ever be given by law to any religious sect, society or denomination; nor to any particular creed, mode of worship or system of ecclesiastical polity; nor shall any person be compelled to attend any place of worship, to contribute to the erection or maintenance of any such place, or to the salary or support of any minister of religion; nor shall any man be compelled to send his child to any school to which he may be conscientiously opposed; and the civil rights, privileges or capacities of no person shall be taken away, or in anywise diminished or enlarged, on account of his belief or disbelief of any religious tenet, dogma or teaching. No human authority shall, in any case whatever, control or interfere with the rights of conscience.

Text as Ratified on: August 3, 1891, and revised September 28, 1891. History: Not yet amended.

Section 6: Elections to be free and equal.

All elections shall be free and equal.

Text as Ratified on: August 3, 1891, and revised September 28, 1891. History: Not yet amended.

Section 7: Right of trial by jury.

The ancient mode of trial by jury shall be held sacred, and the right thereof remain inviolate, subject to such modifications as may be authorized by this Constitution.

Text as Ratified on: August 3, 1891, and revised September 28, 1891. History: Not yet amended.

Section 8: Freedom of speech and of the press.

Printing presses shall be free to every person who undertakes to examine the proceedings of the General Assembly or any branch of government, and no law shall ever be made to restrain the right thereof. Every person may freely and fully speak, write and print on any subject, being responsible for the abuse of that liberty.

Text as Ratified on: August 3, 1891, and revised September 28, 1891. History: Not yet amended.

Section 9: Truth may be given in evidence in prosecution for publishing matters proper for public information—Jury to try law and facts in libel prosecutions.

In prosecutions for the publication of papers investigating the official conduct of officers or men in a public capacity, or where the matter published is proper for public information, the truth thereof may be given in evidence; and in all indictments for libel the jury shall have the right to determine the law and the facts, under the direction of the court, as in other cases.

Text as Ratified on: August 3, 1891, and revised September 28, 1891. History: Not yet amended.

Section 10: Security from search and seizure—Conditions of issuance of warrant.

The people shall be secure in their persons, houses, papers and possessions, from unreasonable search and seizure; and no warrant shall issue to search any place, or seize any person or thing, without describing them as nearly as may be, nor without probable cause supported by oath or affirmation.

Text as Ratified on: August 3, 1891, and revised September 28, 1891. History: Not yet amended.

Section 11: Rights of accused in criminal prosecution—Change of venue.

In all criminal prosecutions the accused has the right to be heard by himself and counsel; to demand the nature and cause of the accusation against him; to meet the witnesses face to face, and to have compulsory process for obtaining witnesses in his favor. He cannot be compelled to give evidence against himself, nor can he be deprived of his life, liberty or property, unless by the judgment of his peers or the law of the land; and in prosecutions by indictment or information, he shall have a speedy public trial by an impartial jury of the vicinage; but the General Assembly may provide by a general law for a change of venue in such prosecutions for both the defendant and the Commonwealth, the change to be made to the most convenient county in which a fair trial can be obtained.

Text as Ratified on: August 3, 1891, and revised September 28, 1891. History: Not yet amended.

Section 12: Indictable offense not to be prosecuted by information—Exceptions.

No person, for an indictable offense, shall be proceeded against criminally by information, except in cases arising in the land or naval forces, or in the militia, when in actual service, in time of war or public danger, or by leave of court for oppression or misdemeanor in office.

Text as Ratified on: August 3, 1891, and revised September 28, 1891. History: Not yet amended.

Section 13: Double jeopardy—Property not to be taken for public use without compensation.

No person shall, for the same offense, be twice put in jeopardy of his life or limb, nor shall any man's property be taken or applied to public use without the consent of his representatives, and without just compensation being previously made to him.

Text as Ratified on: August 3, 1891, and revised September 28, 1891. History: Not yet amended.

Section 14: Right of judicial remedy for injury—Speedy trial.

All courts shall be open, and every person for an injury done him in his lands, goods, person or reputation, shall have remedy by due course of law, and right and justice administered without sale, denial or delay.

Text as Ratified on: August 3, 1891, and revised September 28, 1891. History: Not yet amended.

Section 15: Laws to be suspended only by General Assembly.

No power to suspend laws shall be exercised unless by the General Assembly or its authority.

Text as Ratified on: August 3, 1891, and revised September 28, 1891. History: Not yet amended.

Section 16: Right to bail—Habeas corpus.

All prisoners shall be bailable by sufficient securities, unless for capital offenses when the proof is evident or the presumption great; and the privilege of the writ of habeas corpus shall not be suspended unless when, in case of rebellion or invasion, the public safety may require it.

Text as Ratified on: August 3, 1891, and revised September 28, 1891. History: Not yet amended.

Section 17: Excessive bail or fine, or cruel punishment, prohibited.

Excessive bail shall not be required, nor excessive fines imposed, nor cruel punishment inflicted.

Text as Ratified on: August 3, 1891, and revised September 28, 1891. History: Not yet amended.

Section 18: Imprisonment for debt restricted.

The person of a debtor, where there is not strong presumption of fraud, shall not be continued in prison after delivering up his estate for the benefit of his creditors in such manner as shall be prescribed by law.

Text as Ratified on: August 3, 1891, and revised September 28, 1891. History: Not yet amended.

Section 19: Ex post facto law or law impairing contract forbidden—Rules of construction for mineral deeds relating to coal extraction.

(1) No ex post facto law, nor any law impairing the obligation of contracts, shall be enacted. (2) In any instrument heretofore or hereafter executed purporting to sever the surface and mineral estates or to grant a mineral estate or to grant a right to extract minerals, which fails to state or describe in express and specific terms the method of coal extraction to be employed, or where said instrument contains language subordinating the surface estate to the mineral estate, it shall be held, in the absence of clear and convincing evidence to the contrary, that the intention of the parties to the instrument was that the coal be extracted only by the method or methods of commercial coal extraction commonly known to be in use in Kentucky in the area affected at the time the instrument was executed, and that the mineral estate be dominant to

the surface estate for the purposes of coal extraction by only the method or methods of commercial coal extraction commonly known to be in use in Kentucky in the area affected at the time the instrument was executed.

Text as Ratified on: November 8, 1988. History: 1988 amendment was proposed by 1988 Ky. Acts ch. 117, sec. 1; original version ratified August 3, 1891, and revised September 28, 1891.

Section 20: Attainder, operation of restricted.

No person shall be attainted of treason or felony by the General Assembly, and no attainder shall work corruption of blood, nor, except during the life of the offender, forfeiture of estate to the Commonwealth.

Text as Ratified on: August 3, 1891, and revised September 28, 1891. History: Not yet amended.

Section 21: Descent in case of suicide or casualty.

The estate of such persons as shall destroy their own lives shall descend or vest as in cases of natural death; and if any person shall be killed by casualty, there shall be no forfeiture by reason thereof.

Text as Ratified on: August 3, 1891, and revised September 28, 1891. History: Not yet amended.

Section 22: Standing armies restricted—Military subordinate to civil—Quartering soldiers restricted.

No standing army shall, in time of peace, be maintained without the consent of the General Assembly; and the military shall, in all cases and at all times, be in strict subordination to the civil power; nor shall any soldier, in time of peace, be quartered in any house without the consent of the owner, nor in time of war, except in a manner prescribed by law.

Text as Ratified on: August 3, 1891, and revised September 28, 1891. History: Not yet amended.

Section 23: No office of nobility or hereditary distinction, or for longer than a term of years.

The General Assembly shall not grant any title of nobility or hereditary distinction, nor create any office the appointment of which shall be for a longer time than a term of years.

Text as Ratified on: August 3, 1891, and revised September 28, 1891. History: Not yet amended.

Section 24: Emigration to be free.

Emigration from the State shall not be prohibited.

Text as Ratified on: August 3, 1891, and revised September 28, 1891. History: Not yet amended.

Section 25: Slavery and involuntary servitude forbidden.

Slavery and involuntary servitude in this State are forbidden, except as a punishment for crime, whereof the party shall have been duly convicted.

Text as Ratified on: August 3, 1891, and revised September 28, 1891. History: Not yet amended.

Section 26: General powers subordinate to Bill of Rights—Laws contrary thereto are void.

To guard against transgression of the high powers which we have delegated, We Declare that every thing in this Bill of Rights is excepted out of the general powers of government, and shall forever remain inviolate; and all laws contrary thereto, or contrary to this Constitution, shall be void.

Text as Ratified on: August 3, 1891, and revised September 28, 1891. History: Not yet amended.

Distribution of the Powers of Government
Section 27: Powers of government divided among legislative, executive, and judicial departments.

The powers of the government of the Commonwealth of Kentucky shall be divided into three distinct departments, and each of them be confined to a separate body of magistracy, to wit: Those which are legislative, to one; those which are executive, to another; and those which are judicial, to another.

Text as Ratified on: August 3, 1891, and revised September 28, 1891. History: Not yet amended.

Section 28: One department not to exercise power belonging to another.

No person or collection of persons, being of one of those departments, shall exercise any power properly belonging to either of the others, except in the instances hereinafter expressly directed or permitted.

Text as Ratified on: August 3, 1891, and revised September 28, 1891. History: Not yet amended.

The Legislative Department
Section 29: Legislative power vested in General Assembly.

The legislative power shall be vested in a House of Representatives and a Senate, which, together, shall be styled the "General Assembly of the Commonwealth of Kentucky."

Text as Ratified on: August 3, 1891, and revised September 28, 1891. History: Not yet amended.

Section 30: Term of office of Senators and Representatives.

Members of the House of Representatives and Senators shall be elected at the general election in even-numbered years for terms of four years for Senators and two years for members of the House of Representatives. The term of office of Representatives and Senators shall begin upon the first day of January of the year succeeding their election.

Text as Ratified on: November 6, 1979. History: 1979 amendment was proposed by 1978 Ky. Acts ch. 440, sec. 1; original version ratified August 3, 1891, and revised September 28, 1891.

Section 31: Time of election and term of office of Senators and Representatives.

At the general election to be held in November, 1984, and every two years thereafter, there shall be elected for four years one Senator in each Senatorial District in which the term of his predecessor in office will then expire and in every Representative District one Representative for two years.

Text as Ratified on: November 6, 1979. History: 1979 amendment was proposed by 1978 Ky. Acts ch. 440, sec. 1; original version ratified August 3, 1891, and revised September 28, 1891.

Section 32: Qualifications of Senators and Representatives.

No person shall be a Representative who, at the time of his election, is not a citizen of Kentucky, has not attained the age of twenty-four years, and who has not resided in this State two years next preceding his election, and the last year thereof in the county, town or city for which he may be chosen. No person shall be a Senator who, at the time of his election, is not a citizen of Kentucky, has not attained the age of thirty years, and has not resided in this State six years next preceding his election, and the last year thereof in the district for which he may be chosen.

Text as Ratified on: August 3, 1891, and revised September 28, 1891. History: Not yet amended.

Section 33: Senatorial and Representative districts.

The first General Assembly after the adoption of this Constitution shall divide the State into thirty-eight Senatorial Districts, and one hundred Representative Districts, as nearly equal in population as may be without dividing any county, except where a county may include more than one district, which districts shall constitute the Senatorial and Representative Districts for ten years. Not more than two counties shall be joined together to form a Representative District: Provided, In doing so the principle requiring every district to be as nearly equal in population as may be shall not be violated. At the expiration of that time, the General Assembly shall then, and every ten years thereafter, redistrict the State according to this rule, and for the purposes expressed in this section. If, in making said districts, inequality of population should be unavoidable, any advantage resulting therefrom shall be given to districts having the largest territory. No part of a county shall be added to another county to make a district, and the counties forming a district shall be contiguous.

Text as Ratified on: August 3, 1891, and revised September 28, 1891. History: Not yet amended.

Section 34: Officers of Houses of General Assembly.

The House of Representatives shall choose its Speaker and other officers, and the Senate shall have power to choose its officers biennially.

Text as Ratified on: August 3, 1891, and revised September 28, 1891. History: Not yet amended.

Section 35: Number of Senators and Representatives.

The number of Representatives shall be one hundred, and the number of Senators thirty-eight.

Text as Ratified on: August 3, 1891, and revised September 28, 1891. History: Not yet amended.

Section 36: Time and place of meetings of General Assembly.

(1) The General Assembly, in odd-numbered years, shall meet in regular session for a period not to exceed a total of thirty (30) legislative days divided as follows: The General Assembly shall convene for the first part of the session on the first Tuesday after the first Monday in January in odd-numbered years for the purposes of electing legislative leaders, adopting rules of procedure, organizing committees, and introducing and considering legislation. The General Assembly shall then adjourn. The General Assembly shall convene for the second part of the session on the first Tuesday in February of that year. Any legislation introduced but not enacted

in the first part of the session shall be carried over into the second part of the session. In any part of the session in an odd-numbered year, no bill raising revenue or appropriating funds shall become a law unless it shall be agreed to by three-fifths of all the members elected to each House.

(2) The General Assembly shall then adjourn until the first Tuesday after the first Monday in January of the following even-numbered years, at which time the General Assembly shall convene in regular session.

(3) All sessions shall be held at the seat of government, except in case of war, insurrection or pestilence, when it may, by proclamation of the Governor, assemble, for the time being, elsewhere.

Text as Ratified on: November 7, 2000. History: 2000 amendment was proposed by 2000 Ky. Acts ch. 407, sec. 1; 1979 amendment was proposed by 1978 Ky. Acts ch. 440, sec. 2, and ratified November 6, 1979; original version ratified August 3, 1891, and revised September 28, 1891.

Section 37: Majority constitutes quorum—Powers of less than a quorum.

Not less than a majority of the members of each House of the General Assembly shall constitute a quorum to do business, but a smaller number may adjourn from day to day, and shall be authorized by law to compel the attendance of absent members in such manner and under such penalties as may be prescribed by law.

Text as Ratified on: August 3, 1891, and revised September 28, 1891. History: Not yet amended.

Section 38: Each House to judge qualifications, elections, and returns of its members—Contests.

Each House of the General Assembly shall judge of the qualifications, elections and returns of its members, but a contested election shall be determined in such manner as shall be directed by law.

Text as Ratified on: August 3, 1891, and revised September 28, 1891. History: Not yet amended.

Section 39: Powers of each House as to rules and conduct of members—Contempt—Bribery.

Each House of the General Assembly may determine the rules of its proceedings, punish a member for disorderly behavior, and, with the concurrence of two-thirds, expel a member, but not a second time for the same cause, and may punish for contempt any person who refuses to attend as a witness, or to bring any paper proper to be used as evidence before the General Assembly, or either House thereof, or a Committee of either, or to testify concerning any matter which may be a proper subject of inquiry by the General Assembly, or offers or gives a bribe to a member of the General Assembly, or attempts by other corrupt means or device to control or influence a member to cast his vote or withhold the same. The punishment and mode of proceeding for contempt in such cases shall be prescribed by law, but the term of imprisonment in any such case shall not extend beyond the session of the General Assembly.

Text as Ratified on: August 3, 1891, and revised September 28, 1891. History: Not yet amended.

Section 40: Journals—When vote to be entered.

Each House of the General Assembly shall keep and publish daily a journal of its proceedings; and the yeas and nays of the members on any question shall, at the desire of any two of the members elected, be entered on the journal.

Text as Ratified on: August 3, 1891, and revised September 28, 1891. History: Not yet amended.

Section 41: Adjournment during session.

Neither House, during the session of the General Assembly, shall, without the consent of the other, adjourn for more than three days, nor to any other place than that in which it may be sitting.

Text as Ratified on: August 3, 1891, and revised September 28, 1891. History: Not yet amended.

Section 42: Compensation of members—Length of sessions—Legislative day.

The members of the General Assembly shall severally receive from the State Treasury compensation for their services: Provided, No change shall take effect during the session at which it is made; nor shall a session occurring in odd-numbered years extend beyond March 30; nor shall a session of the General Assembly continue beyond sixty legislative days nor shall it extend beyond April 15; these limitations as to length of session shall not apply to the Senate when sitting as a court of impeachment. A legislative day shall be construed to mean a calendar day, exclusive of Sundays, legal holidays, or any day on which neither House meets.

Text as Ratified on: November 7, 2000. History: 2000 amendment was proposed by 2000 Ky. Acts ch. 407, sec. 2; 1979 amendment was proposed by 1978 Ky. Acts ch. 440, sec. 3, and ratified on November 6, 1979; original version ratified August 3, 1891, and revised September 28, 1891.

Section 43: Privileges from arrest and from questioning as to speech or debate.

The members of the General Assembly shall, in all cases except treason, felony, breach or surety of the peace, be privileged from arrest during their attendance on the sessions of their respective Houses, and in going to and returning from the same; and for any speech or debate in either House they shall not be questioned in any other place.

Text as Ratified on: August 3, 1891, and revised September 28, 1891. History: Not yet amended.

Section 44: Ineligibility of members to civil office created or given increased compensation during term.

No Senator or Representative shall, during the term for which he was elected, nor for one year thereafter, be appointed or elected to any civil office of profit in this Commonwealth, which shall have been created, or the emoluments of which shall have been increased, during the said term, except to such offices as may be filled by the election of the people.

Text as Ratified on: August 3, 1891, and revised September 28, 1891. History: Not yet amended.

Section 45: Collector of public money ineligible unless he has quietus.

No person who may have been a collector of taxes or public moneys for the Commonwealth, or for any county, city, town or district, or the assistant or deputy of such collector, shall be eligible to the General Assembly, unless he shall have obtained a quietus six months before the election for the amount of such collection, and for all public moneys for which he may have been responsible.

Text as Ratified on: August 3, 1891, and revised September 28, 1891. History: Not yet amended.

Section 46: Bills must be reported by committee, printed, and read—How bill called from committee—Votes required for passage.

No bill shall be considered for final passage unless the same has been reported by a committee and printed for the use of the members. Every bill shall be read at length on three different days in each House, but the second and third readings may be dispensed with by a majority of all the members elected to the House in which the bill is pending. But whenever a committee refuses or fails to report a bill submitted to it in a reasonable time, the same may be called up by any member, and be considered in the same manner it would have been considered if it had been reported. No bill shall become a law unless, on its final passage, it receives the votes of at least two-fifths of the members elected to each House, and a majority of the members voting, the vote to be taken by yeas and nays and entered in the journal: Provided, Any act or resolution for the appropriation of money or the creation of debt shall, on its final passage, receive the votes of a majority of all the members elected to each House.

Text as Ratified on: August 3, 1891, and revised September 28, 1891. History: Not yet amended.

Section 47: Bills to raise revenue must originate in House of Representatives.

All bills for raising revenue shall originate in the House of Representatives, but the Senate may propose amendments thereto: Provided, No new matter shall be introduced, under color of amendment, which does not relate to raising revenue.

Text as Ratified on: August 3, 1891, and revised September 28, 1891. History: Not yet amended.

Section 48: Resources of Sinking Fund not to be diminished—Preservation of fund.

The General Assembly shall have no power to enact laws to diminish the resources of the Sinking Fund as now established by law until the debt of the Commonwealth be paid, but may enact laws to increase them; and the whole resources of said fund, from year to year, shall be sacredly set apart and applied to the payment of the interest and principal of the State debt, and to no other use or purpose, until the whole debt of the State is fully satisfied.

Text as Ratified on: August 3, 1891, and revised September 28, 1891. History: Not yet amended.

Section 49: Power to contract debts—Limit.

The General Assembly may contract debts to meet casual deficits or failures in the revenue; but such debts, direct or contingent, singly or in the aggregate, shall not at any time exceed five hundred thousand dollars, and the moneys arising from loans creating such debts shall be applied only to the purpose or purposes for which they were obtained, or to repay such debts: Provided, The General Assembly may contract debts to repel invasion, suppress insurrection, or, if hostilities are threatened, provide for the public defense.

Text as Ratified on: August 3, 1891, and revised September 28, 1891. History: Not yet amended.

Section 50: Purposes for which debt may be contracted—Tax to discharge—Public vote.

No act of the General Assembly shall authorize any debt to be contracted on behalf of the Commonwealth except for the purposes mentioned in Section 49, unless provision be made therein to levy and collect an annual tax sufficient to pay the interest stipulated, and to discharge the debt within thirty years; nor shall such act take effect until it shall have been submitted to the people at a general election, and shall have received a majority of all the votes cast for and against it: Provided, The General Assembly may contract debts by borrowing money to pay any part of the debt of the State, without submission to the people, and without making provision in the act authorizing the same for a tax to discharge the debt so contracted, or the interest thereon.

Text as Ratified on: August 3, 1891, and revised September 28, 1891. History: Not yet amended.

Section 51: Law may not relate to more than one subject, to be expressed in title—Amendments must be at length.

No law enacted by the General Assembly shall relate to more than one subject, and that shall be expressed in the title, and no law shall be revised, amended, or the provisions thereof extended or conferred by reference to its title only, but so much thereof as is revised, amended, extended or conferred, shall be reenacted and published at length.

Text as Ratified on: August 3, 1891, and revised September 28, 1891. History: Not yet amended.

Section 52: General Assembly may not release debt to State or to county or city.

The General Assembly shall have no power to release, extinguish or authorize the releasing or extinguishing, in whole or in part, the indebtedness or liability of any corporation or individual to this Commonwealth, or to any county or municipality thereof.

Text as Ratified on: August 3, 1891, and revised September 28, 1891. History: Not yet amended.

Section 53: Investigation of accounts of Treasurer and Auditor—Report, publication, submission to Governor and General Assembly.

The General Assembly shall provide by law for monthly investigations into the accounts of the Treasurer and Auditor of Public Accounts, and the result of these investigations shall be reported to the Governor, and these reports shall be semiannually published in two newspapers of general circulation in the State. The reports received by the Governor shall, at the beginning of each session, be transmitted by him to the General Assembly for scrutiny and appropriate action.

Text as Ratified on: August 3, 1891, and revised September 28, 1891. History: Not yet amended.

Section 54: No restriction on recovery for injury or death.

The General Assembly shall have no power to limit the amount to be recovered for injuries resulting in death, or for injuries to person or property.

Text as Ratified on: August 3, 1891, and revised September 28, 1891. History: Not yet amended.

Section 55: When laws to take effect—Emergency legislation.

No act, except general appropriation bills, shall become a law until ninety days after the adjournment of the session at which it was passed, except in cases of emergency, when, by the concurrence of a majority of the members elected to each House of the General Assembly, by a yea and nay vote entered upon their journals, an act may become a law when approved by the Governor; but the reasons for the emergency that justifies this action must be set out at length in the journal of each House.

Text as Ratified on: August 3, 1891, and revised September 28, 1891. History: Not yet amended.

Section 56: Signing of bills—Enrollment—Presentation to Governor.

No bill shall become a law until the same shall have been signed by the presiding officer of each of the two Houses in open session; and before such officer shall have affixed his signature to any bill, he shall suspend all other business, declare that such bill will now be read, and that he will sign the same to the end that it may become a law. The bill shall then be read at length and compared; and, if correctly enrolled, he shall, in the presence of the House in open session, and before any other business is entertained, affix his signature, which fact shall be noted in the journal, and the bill immediately sent to the other House. When it reaches the other House, the presiding officer thereof shall immediately suspend all other business, announce the reception of the bill, and the same proceeding shall thereupon be observed in every respect as in the House in which it was first signed. And thereupon the Clerk of the latter House shall immediately present the same to the Governor for his signature and approval.

Text as Ratified on: August 3, 1891, and revised September 28, 1891. History: Not yet amended.

Section 57: Member having personal interest to make disclosure and not vote.

A member who has a personal or private interest in any measure or bill proposed or pending before the General Assembly, shall disclose the fact to the House of which he is a member, and shall not vote thereon upon pain of expulsion.

Text as Ratified on: August 3, 1891, and revised September 28, 1891. History: Not yet amended.

Section 58: General Assembly not to audit nor allow private claim—Exception—Appropriations.

The General Assembly shall neither audit nor allow any private claim against the Commonwealth, except for expenses incurred during the session at which the same was allowed; but may appropriate money to pay such claim as shall have been audited and allowed according to law.

Text as Ratified on: August 3, 1891, and revised September 28, 1891. History: Not yet amended.

Section 59: Local and special legislation.

The General Assembly shall not pass local or special acts concerning any of the following subjects, or for any of the following purposes, namely:

First: To regulate the jurisdiction, or the practice, or the circuits of the courts of justice, or the rights, powers, duties or compensation of the officers thereof; but the practice in circuit courts in continuous session may, by a general law, be made different from the practice of circuit courts held in terms.

Second: To regulate the summoning, impaneling or compensation of grand or petit jurors.

Third: To provide for changes of venue in civil or criminal causes.

Fourth: To regulate the punishment of crimes and misdemeanors, or to remit fines, penalties or forfeitures.

Fifth: To regulate the limitation of civil or criminal causes.

Sixth: To affect the estate of cestuis que trust, decedents, infants or other persons under disabilities, or to authorize any such persons to sell, lease, encumber or dispose of their property.

Seventh: To declare any person of age, or to relieve an infant or feme covert of disability, or to enable him to do acts allowed only to adults not under disabilities.

Eighth: To change the law of descent, distribution or succession.

Ninth: To authorize the adoption or legitimation of children.

Tenth: To grant divorces.

Eleventh: To change the names of persons.

Twelfth: To give effect to invalid deeds, wills or other instruments.

Thirteenth: To legalize, except as against the Commonwealth, the unauthorized or invalid act of any officer or public agent of the Commonwealth, or of any city, county or municipality thereof.

Fourteenth: To refund money legally paid into the State Treasury.

Fifteenth: To authorize or to regulate the levy, the assessment or the collection of taxes, or to give any indulgence or discharge to any assessor or collector of taxes, or to his sureties.

Sixteenth: To authorize the opening, altering, maintaining or vacating of roads, highways, streets, alleys, town plats, cemeteries, graveyards, or public grounds not owned by the Commonwealth.

Seventeenth: To grant a charter to any corporation, or to amend the charter of any existing corporation; to license companies or persons to own or operate ferries, bridges, roads or turnpikes; to declare streams navigable, or to authorize the construction of booms or dams therein, or to remove obstructions therefrom; to affect toll gates or to regulate tolls; to regulate fencing or the running at large of stock.

Eighteenth: To create, increase or decrease fees, percentages or allowances to public officers, or to extend the time for the collection thereof, or to authorize officers to appoint deputies.

Nineteenth: To give any person or corporation the right to lay a railroad track or tramway, or to amend existing charters for such purposes.

Twentieth: To provide for conducting elections, or for designating the places of voting, or changing the boundaries of wards, precincts or districts, except when new counties may be created.

Twenty-first: To regulate the rate of interest.

Twenty-second: To authorize the creation, extension, enforcement, impairment or release of liens.

Twenty-third: To provide for the protection of game and fish.

Twenty-fourth: To regulate labor, trade, mining or manufacturing.

Twenty-fifth: To provide for the management of common schools.

Twenty-sixth: To locate or change a county seat.

Twenty-seventh: To provide a means of taking the sense of the people of any city, town, district, precinct or county, whether they wish to authorize, regulate or prohibit therein the sale of vinous, spirituous or malt liquors, or alter the liquor laws.

Twenty-eighth: Restoring to citizenship persons convicted of infamous crimes.

Twenty-ninth: In all other cases where a general law can be made applicable, no special law shall be enacted.

Text as Ratified on: August 3, 1891, and revised September 28, 1891. History: Not yet amended.

Section 60: General law not to be made special or local by amendment—No special powers or privileges—Law not to take effect on approval of other authority than General Assembly—Exceptions.

The General Assembly shall not indirectly enact any special or local act by the repeal in part of a general act, or by exempting from the operation of a general act any city, town, district or county; but laws repealing local or special acts may be enacted. No law shall be enacted granting powers or privileges in any case where the granting of such powers or privileges shall have been provided for by a general law, nor where the courts have jurisdiction to grant the same or to give the relief asked for. No law, except such as relates to the sale, loan or gift of vinous, spirituous or malt liquors, bridges, turnpikes or other public roads, public buildings or improvements, fencing, running at large of stock, matters pertaining to common schools, paupers, and the regulation by counties, cities, towns or other municipalities of their local affairs, shall be enacted to take effect upon the approval of any other authority than the General Assembly, unless otherwise expressly provided in this Constitution.

Text as Ratified on: August 3, 1891, and revised September 28, 1891. History: Not yet amended.

Section 61: Provision to be made for local option on sale of liquor—Time of elections.

The General Assembly shall, by general law, provide a means whereby the sense of the people of any county, city, town, district or precinct may be taken, as to whether or not spirituous, vinous or malt liquors shall be sold, bartered or loaned therein, or the sale thereof regulated. But nothing herein shall be construed to interfere with or to repeal any law in force relating to the sale or gift of such liquors. All elections on this question may be held on a day other than the regular election days.

Text as Ratified on: November 5, 1935. History: 1935 reenactment was proposed by 1934 Ky. Acts ch. 58, sec. 1; repeal (by implication) was proposed by 1918 Ky. Acts ch. 63, sec. 1, and ratified on November 4, 1919, effective July 1, 1920; original version ratified August 3, 1891, and revised September 28, 1891.

Section 62: Style of laws.

The style of the laws of this Commonwealth shall be as follows: "Be it enacted by the General Assembly of the Commonwealth of Kentucky."

Text as Ratified on: August 3, 1891, and revised September 28, 1891. History: Not yet amended.

Counties and County Seats
Section 63: Area of counties—Boundaries—Creation and abolishment of counties.

No new county shall be created by the General Assembly which will reduce the county or counties, or either of them, from which it shall be taken, to less area than four hundred square miles; nor shall any county be formed of less area; nor shall any boundary line thereof pass within less than ten miles of any county seat of the county or counties proposed to be divided. Nothing contained herein shall prevent the General Assembly from abolishing any county.

Text as Ratified on: August 3, 1891, and revised September 28, 1891. History: Not yet amended.

Section 64: Division of county or removal of county seat, election required—Minimum population of county.

No county shall be divided, or have any part stricken therefrom, except in the formation of new counties, without submitting the question to a vote of the people of the county, nor unless the majority of all the legal voters of the county voting on the question shall vote for the same. The county seat of no county as now located, or as may hereafter be located, shall be moved, except upon a vote of two-thirds of those voting; nor shall any new county be established which will reduce any county to less than twelve thousand inhabitants, nor shall any county be created containing a less population.

Text as Ratified on: August 3, 1891, and revised September 28, 1891. History: Not yet amended.

Section 65: Striking territory from county—Liability for indebtedness.

There shall be no territory stricken from any county unless a majority of the voters living in such territory shall petition for such division. But the portion so stricken off and added to another county, or formed in whole or in part into a new county, shall be bound for its proportion of the indebtedness of the county from which it has been taken.

Text as Ratified on: August 3, 1891, and revised September 28, 1891. History: Not yet amended.

Impeachments

Section 66: Power of impeachment vested in House.

The House of Representatives shall have the sole power of impeachment

Text as Ratified on: August 3, 1891, and revised September 28, 1891. History: Not yet amended.

Section 67: Trial of impeachments by Senate.

All impeachments shall be tried by the Senate. When sitting for that purpose, the Senators shall be upon oath or affirmation. No person shall be convicted without the concurrence of two-thirds of the Senators present.

Text as Ratified on: August 3, 1891, and revised September 28, 1891. History: Not yet amended.

Section 68: Civil officers liable to impeachment—Judgment—Criminal liability.

The Governor and all civil officers shall be liable to impeachment for any misdemeanors in office; but judgment in such cases shall not extend further than removal from office, and disqualification to hold any office of honor, trust or profit under this Commonwealth; but the party convicted shall, nevertheless, be subject and liable to indictment, trial and punishment by law.

Text as Ratified on: August 3, 1891, and revised September 28, 1891. History: Not yet amended.

The Executive Department

Officers for the State at Large

Section 69: Executive power vested in Governor.

The supreme executive power of the Commonwealth shall be vested in a Chief Magistrate, who shall be styled the "Governor of the Commonwealth of Kentucky."

Text as Ratified on: August 3, 1891, and revised September 28, 1891. History: Not yet amended.

Section 70: Election of Governor and Lieutenant Governor—Term—Tie vote.

The Governor and Lieutenant Governor shall be elected for the term of four years by the qualified voters of the State. They shall be elected jointly by the casting by each voter of a single vote applicable to both offices, as shall be provided by law. The slate of candidates having the highest number of votes cast jointly for them for Governor and Lieutenant Governor shall be elected; but if two or more slates of candidates shall be equal and highest in votes, the election shall be determined by lot in such manner as the General Assembly may direct.

Text as Ratified on: November 3, 1992. History: 1992 amendment was proposed by 1992 Ky. Acts ch. 168, sec. 1; original version ratified August 3, 1891, and revised September 28, 1891.

Section 71: Gubernatorial succession.

The Governor shall be ineligible for the succeeding four years after the expiration of any second consecutive term for which he shall have been elected.

Text as Ratified on: November 3, 1992. History: 1992 amendment was proposed by 1992 Ky. Acts ch. 168, sec. 2; original version ratified August 3, 1891, and revised September 28, 1891.

Section 72: Qualifications of Governor and Lieutenant Governor—Duties of Lieutenant Governor.

The Governor and the Lieutenant Governor shall be at least thirty years of age, and have been citizens and residents of Kentucky for at least six years next preceding their election. The duties of the Lieutenant Governor shall be prescribed by law, and he shall have such other duties as delegated by the Governor.

Text as Ratified on: November 3, 1992. History: 1992 amendment was proposed by 1992 Ky. Acts ch. 168, sec. 3; original version ratified August 3, 1891, and revised September 28, 1891.

Section 73: When terms of Governor and Lieutenant Governor begin.

The Governor and the Lieutenant Governor shall commence the execution of the duties of their offices on the fifth Tuesday succeeding their election, and shall continue in the execution thereof until a successor shall have qualified.

Text as Ratified on: November 3, 1992. History: 1992 amendment was proposed by 1992 Ky. Acts ch. 168, sec. 4; original version ratified August 3, 1891, and revised September 28, 1891.

Section 74: Compensation of Governor and Lieutenant Governor.

The Governor and Lieutenant Governor shall at stated times receive for the performance of the duties of their respective offices compensation to be fixed by law.

Text as Ratified on: November 3, 1992. History: 1992 amendment was proposed by 1992 Ky. Acts ch. 168, sec. 5; original version ratified August 3, 1891, and revised September 28, 1891.

Section 75: Governor is Commander-in-Chief of army, navy and militia.

He shall be Commander-in-Chief of the army and navy of this Commonwealth, and of the militia thereof, except when they shall be called into the service of the United States; but he shall not command personally in the field, unless advised so to do by a resolution of the General Assembly.

Text as Ratified on: August 3, 1891, and revised September 28, 1891. History: Not yet amended.

Section 76: Power of Governor to fill vacancies.

He shall have the power, except as otherwise provided in this Constitution, to fill vacancies by granting commissions, which shall expire when such vacancies shall have been filled according to the provisions of this Constitution.

Text as Ratified on: August 3, 1891, and revised September 28, 1891. History: Not yet amended.

Section 77: Power of Governor to remit fines and forfeitures, grant reprieves and pardons—No power to remit fees.

He shall have power to remit fines and forfeitures, commute sentences, grant reprieves and pardons, except in case of impeachment, and he shall file with each application therefor a statement of the reasons for his decision thereon, which application and statement shall always be open to public inspection. In cases of treason, he shall have power to grant reprieves until the end of the next session of the General Assembly, in which the power of pardoning shall be vested; but he shall have no power to remit the fees of the Clerk, Sheriff or Commonwealth's Attorney in penal or criminal cases.

Text as Ratified on: August 3, 1891, and revised September 28, 1891. History: Not yet amended.

Section 78: Governor may require information from state officers.

He may require information in writing from the officers of the Executive Department upon any subject relating to the duties of their respective offices.

Text as Ratified on: August 3, 1891, and revised September 28, 1891. History: Not yet amended.

Section 79: Reports and recommendations to General Assembly.

He shall, from time to time, give to the General Assembly information of the state of the Commonwealth, and recommend to their consideration such measures as he may deem expedient.

Text as Ratified on: August 3, 1891, and revised September 28, 1891. History: Not yet amended.

Section 80: Governor may call extraordinary session of General Assembly, adjourn General Assembly.

He may, on extraordinary occasions, convene the General Assembly at the seat of government, or at a different place, if that should have become dangerous from an enemy or from contagious diseases. In case of disagreement between the two Houses with respect to the time of adjournment, he may adjourn them to such time as he shall think proper, not exceeding four months. When he shall convene the General Assembly it shall be by proclamation, stating the subjects to be considered, and no other shall be considered.

Text as Ratified on: August 3, 1891, and revised September 28, 1891. History: Not yet amended.

Section 81: Governor to enforce laws.

He shall take care that the laws be faithfully executed.

Text as Ratified on: August 3, 1891, and revised September 28, 1891. History: Not yet amended.

Section 82: Succession of Lieutenant Governor.

The Lieutenant Governor shall be ineligible to the office of Lieutenant Governor for the succeeding four (4) years after the expiration of any second consecutive term for which he shall have been elected.

Text as Ratified on: November 3, 1992. History: 1992 amendment was proposed by 1992 Ky. Acts ch. 168, sec. 6; original version ratified August 3, 1891, and revised September 28, 1891.

Section 83: (Repealed 1992) Catchline at time of repeal: "Lieutenant Governor is President of Senate—Right to vote."

Repeal Ratified on: November 3, 1992. History: Repeal was proposed by 1992 Ky. Acts ch. 168, sec. 18; original version ratified August 3, 1891, and revised September 28, 1891.

Section 84: When Lieutenant Governor to act as Governor—President of the Senate not to preside at impeachment of Governor—Certification of disability of Governor.

Should the [Governor] be impeached and removed from office, die, refuse to qualify, resign, certify by entry on his Journal that he is unable to discharge the duties of his office, or be, from any cause, unable to discharge the duties of his office, the Lieutenant Governor shall exercise all the power and authority appertaining to the office of Governor until another be duly elected and qualified, or the Governor shall be able to discharge the duties of his office. On the trial of the Governor, the President of the Senate shall not preside over the proceedings, but the Chief Justice of the Supreme Court shall preside during the trial.

If the Governor, due to physical or mental incapacitation, is unable to discharge the duties of his office, the Attorney General may petition the Supreme Court to have the Governor declared disabled. If the Supreme Court determines in a unanimous decision that the Governor is unable to discharge the duties of his office, the Chief Justice shall certify such disability to the Secretary of State who shall enter same on the Journal of the Acts of the Governor, and the Lieutenant Governor shall assume the duties of the Governor, and shall act as Governor until the Supreme Court determines that the disability of the Governor has ceased to exist. Before the Governor resumes his duties, the finding of the Court that the disability has ceased shall be certified by the Chief Justice to the Secretary of State who shall enter such finding on the Journal of the Acts of the Governor.

Text as Ratified on: November 3, 1992. History: 1992 amendment was proposed by 1992 Ky. Acts ch. 168, sec. 7; original version ratified August 3, 1891, and revised September 28, 1891.

Section 85: President of Senate—Election—Powers.

A President of the Senate shall be elected by each Senate as soon after its organization as possible and as often as there is a vacancy in the office of President, another President of the Senate shall be elected by the Senate, if in session. And if, during the vacancy of the office of Governor, the Lieutenant Governor shall be impeached and removed from office, refuse to qualify, resign, or die, the President of the Senate shall in like manner administer the government.

Text as Ratified on: November 3, 1992. History: 1992 amendment was proposed by 1992 Ky. Acts ch. 168, sec. 8; original version ratified August 3, 1891, and revised September 28, 1891.

Section 86: Compensation of President of the Senate.

The President of the Senate shall receive for his services the same compensation which shall, for the same period, be allowed to the Speaker of the House of Representatives, and during the time he administers the government as Governor, he shall receive the same compensation which the Governor would have received had he been employed in the duties of his office.

Text as Ratified on: November 3, 1992. History: 1992 amendment was proposed by 1992 Ky. Acts ch. 168, sec. 9; original version ratified August 3, 1891, and revised September 28, 1891.

Section 87: Who to act as Governor in absence of Lieutenant Governor and President of the Senate.

If the Lieutenant Governor shall be called upon to administer the government in place of the Governor, and shall, while in such administration, resign, or die during the recess of the General Assembly, if there be no President of the Senate, it shall be the duty of the Attorney General, for the time being, to convene the Senate for the purpose of choosing a President; and until a President is chosen, the Attorney General shall administer the government. If there be no Attorney General to perform the duties devolved upon him by this section, then the Auditor, for the time being, shall convene the Senate for the purpose of choosing a President, and shall administer the government until a President is chosen.

Text as Ratified on: November 3, 1992. History: 1992 amendment was proposed by 1992 Ky. Acts ch. 168, sec. 10; original version ratified August 3, 1891, and revised September 28, 1891.

Section 88: Signature of bills by Governor—Veto—Passage over veto—Partial veto.

Every bill which shall have passed the two Houses shall be presented to the Governor. If he approve, he shall sign it; but if not, he shall return it, with his objections, to the House in which it originated, which shall enter the objections in full upon its journal, and proceed to reconsider it. If, after such reconsideration, a majority of all the members elected to that House shall agree to pass the bill, it shall be sent, with the objections, to the other House, by which it shall likewise be considered, and if approved by a majority of all the members elected to that House, it shall be a law; but in such case the votes of both Houses shall be determined by yeas and nays, and the names of the members voting for and against the bill shall be entered upon the journal of each House respectively. If any bill shall not be returned by the Governor within ten days (Sundays excepted) after it shall have been presented to him, it shall be a law in like manner as if he had signed it, unless the General Assembly, by their adjournment, prevent its return, in which case it shall be a law, unless disapproved by him within ten days after the adjournment, in which case his veto message shall be spread upon the register kept by the Secretary of State. The Governor shall have the power to disapprove any part or parts of appropriation bills embracing distinct items, and the part or parts disapproved shall not become a law unless reconsidered and passed, as in case of a bill.

Text as Ratified on: August 3, 1891, and revised September 28, 1891. History: Not yet amended.

Section 89: Concurrent orders and resolutions on same footing as bill.

Every order, resolution or vote, in which the concurrence of both Houses may be necessary, except on a question of adjournment, or as otherwise provided in this Constitution, shall be presented to the Governor, and, before it shall take effect, be approved by him; or, being disapproved, shall be repassed by a majority of the members elected to both Houses, according to the rules and limitations prescribed in case of a bill.

Text as Ratified on: August 3, 1891, and revised September 28, 1891. History: Not yet amended.

Section 90: Contest of election for Governor or Lieutenant Governor.

Contested elections for Governor and Lieutenant Governor shall be determined by both Houses of the General Assembly, according to such regulations as may be established by law.

Text as Ratified on: August 3, 1891, and revised September 28, 1891. History: Not yet amended.

Section 91: Constitutional State officers—Election—Qualifications—Term of office—Duties—Secretary of State to record acts of Governor and report them to General Assembly.

A Treasurer, Auditor of Public Accounts, Commissioner of Agriculture, Labor and Statistics, Secretary of State, and Attorney-General, shall be elected by the qualified voters of the State at the same time the Governor and Lieutenant Governor are elected, for the term of four years, each of whom shall be at least thirty years of age at the time of his election, and shall have been a resident citizen of the State at least two years next before his election. The duties of all these officers shall be such as may be prescribed by law, and the Secretary of State shall keep a fair register of and attest all the official acts of the Governor, and shall, when required, lay the same and all papers, minutes and vouchers relative thereto before either House of the General Assembly. The officers named in this section shall enter upon the discharge of their duties the first Monday in January after their election, and shall hold their offices until their successors are elected and qualified.

Text as Ratified on: November 3, 1992. History: 1992 amendment was proposed by 1992 Ky. Acts ch. 168, sec. 11; original version ratified August 3, 1891, and revised September 28, 1891.

Section 92: Qualifications of Attorney General.

The Attorney-General shall have been a practicing lawyer eight years before his election.

Text as Ratified on: August 3, 1891, and revised September 28, 1891. History: Not yet amended.

Section 93: Succession of elected Constitutional State Officers—Duties—Inferior officers and members of boards and commissions.

The Treasurer, Auditor of Public Accounts, Secretary of State, Commissioner of Agriculture, Labor and Statistics, and Attorney General shall be ineligible to reelection for the succeeding four years after the expiration of any second consecutive term for which they shall have been elected. The duties and responsibilities of these officers shall be prescribed by law, and all fees collected by any of said officers shall be covered into the treasury. Inferior State officers and members of boards and commissions, not specifically provided for in this Constitution, may be appointed or elected, in such manner as may be prescribed by law, which may include a requirement of consent by the Senate, for a term not exceeding four years, and until their successors are appointed or elected and qualified.

Text as Ratified on: November 3, 1992. History: 1992 amendment was proposed by 1992 Ky. Acts ch. 168, sec. 12; original version ratified August 3, 1891, and revised September 28, 1891.

Section 94: (Repealed 1992) Catchline at time of repeal: "Register of Land Office may be abolished."

Repeal Ratified on: November 3, 1992. History: Repeal was proposed by 1992 Ky. Acts ch. 168, sec. 18; original version ratified August 3, 1891, and revised September 28, 1891.

Section 95: Time of election of elected Constitutional State officers.

The election under this Constitution for Governor, Lieutenant Governor, Treasurer, Auditor of Public Accounts, Attorney General, Secretary of State, and Commissioner of Agriculture, Labor and Statistics, shall be held on the first Tuesday after the first Monday in November, eighteen hundred and ninety-five, and the same day every four years thereafter.

Text as Ratified on: November 3, 1992. History: 1992 amendment was proposed by 1992 Ky. Acts ch. 168, sec. 13; original version ratified August 3, 1891, and revised September 28, 1891.

Section 96: Compensation of Constitutional State officers.

All officers mentioned in Section 95 shall be paid for their services by salary, and not otherwise.

Text as Ratified on: August 3, 1891, and revised September 28, 1891. History: Not yet amended.

Officers for Districts and Counties
Section 97: Commonwealth's Attorney and Circuit Court Clerk—Election—Term.

In the year two thousand, and every six years thereafter, there shall be an election in each county for a Circuit Court Clerk, and for a Commonwealth's Attorney, in each circuit court district, unless that office be abolished, who shall hold their respective offices for six years from the first Monday in January after their election, and until the election and qualification of their successors.

Text as Ratified on: November 3, 1992. History: 1992 amendment was proposed by 1992 Ky. Acts ch. 168, sec. 14; original version ratified August 3, 1891, and revised September 28, 1891.

Section 98: Compensation of Commonwealth's Attorney.

The compensation of the Commonwealth's Attorney shall be by salary and such percentage of fines and forfeitures as may be fixed by law, and such salary shall be uniform in so far as the same shall be paid out of the State Treasury, and not to exceed the sum of five hundred dollars per annum; but any county may make additional compensation, to be paid by said county. Should any percentage of fines and forfeitures be allowed by law, it shall not be paid except upon such proportion of fines and forfeitures as have been collected and paid into the State Treasury, and not until so collected and paid.

Text as Ratified on: August 3, 1891, and revised September 28, 1891. History: Not yet amended.

Section 99: County officers, justices of the peace, and constables—Election—Term.

At the regular election in nineteen hundred and ninety-eight and every four years thereafter, there shall be elected in each county a Judge of the County Court, a County Court Clerk, a County Attorney, Sheriff, Jailer, Coroner, Surveyor and Assessor, and in each Justice's District one Justice of the Peace and one Constable, who shall enter upon the discharge of the duties of their offices on the first Monday in January after their election, and who shall hold their offices four years until the election and qualification of their successors.

Text as Ratified on: November 3, 1992. History: 1992 amendment was proposed by 1992 Ky. Acts ch. 168, sec. 15; 1984 amendment was proposed by 1984 Ky. Acts ch. 35, sec. 1, and ratified November 6, 1984; original version ratified August 3, 1891, and revised September 28, 1891.

Section 100: Qualifications of officers for counties and districts.

No person shall be eligible to the offices mentioned in Sections 97 and 99 who is not at the time of his election twenty-four years of age (except Clerks of County and Circuit Courts, who shall be twenty-one years of age), a citizen of Kentucky, and who has not resided in the State two years, and one year next preceding his election in the county and district in which he is a candidate. No person shall be eligible to the office of Commonwealth's Attorney unless he shall have been a licensed practicing lawyer four years. No person shall be eligible to the office of County Attorney unless he shall have been a licensed practicing lawyer two years. No person shall be eligible to the office of Clerk unless he shall have procured from a Judge of the Court of Appeals, or a Judge of a Circuit Court, a certificate that he has been examined by the Clerk of his Court under his supervision, and that he is qualified for the office for which he is a candidate.

Text as Ratified on: August 3, 1891, and revised September 28, 1891. History: Not yet amended.

Section 101: Qualifications and jurisdiction of constables.

Constables shall possess the same qualifications as Sheriffs, and their jurisdictions shall be coextensive with the counties in which they reside. Constables now in office shall continue in office until their successors are elected and qualified.

Text as Ratified on: August 3, 1891, and revised September 28, 1891. History: Not yet amended.

Section 102: Officers for new counties.

When a new county shall be created, officers for the same, to serve until the next regular election, shall be elected or appointed in such way and at such times as the General Assembly may prescribe.

Text as Ratified on: August 3, 1891, and revised September 28, 1891. History: Not yet amended.

Section 103: Bonds of county officers and other officers.

The Judges of County Courts, Clerks, Sheriffs, Surveyors, Coroners, Jailers, Constables, and such other officers as the General Assembly may, from time to time, require, shall before they enter upon the duties of their respective offices, and as often thereafter as may be deemed proper, give such bond and security as may be prescribed by law.

Text as Ratified on: August 3, 1891, and revised September 28, 1891. History: Not yet amended.

Section 104: Abolishment of office of assessor—Assessor may not succeed himself.

The General Assembly may abolish the office of Assessor and provide that the assessment of property shall be made by other officers; but it shall have power to reestablish the office of Assessor and prescribe his duties. No person shall be eligible to the office of Assessor two consecutive terms.

Text as Ratified on: August 3, 1891, and revised September 28, 1891. History: Not yet amended.

Section 105: Consolidation of offices of sheriff and jailer.

The General Assembly may, at any time, consolidate the offices of Jailer and Sheriff in any county or counties, as it shall deem most expedient; but in the event such consolidation be made, the office of Sheriff shall be retained, and the Sheriff shall be required to perform the duties of Jailer.

Text as Ratified on: August 3, 1891, and revised September 28, 1891. History: Not yet amended.

Section 106: Fees of county officers—Fees in counties having seventy-five thousand population or more.

The fees of county officers shall be regulated by law. In counties or cities having a population of seventy-five thousand or more, the Clerks of the respective Courts thereof (except the Clerk of the City Court), the Marshals, the Sheriffs and the Jailers, shall be paid out of the State Treasury, by salary to be fixed by law, the salaries of said officers and of their deputies and necessary office expenses not to exceed seventy-five per centum of the fees collected by said officers, respectively, and paid into the Treasury.

Text as Ratified on: August 3, 1891, and revised September 28, 1891. History: Not yet amended.

Section 107: Additional county or district offices may be created.

The General Assembly may provide for the election or appointment, for a term not exceeding four years, of such other county or district ministerial and executive officers as may, from time to time, be necessary.

Text as Ratified on: August 3, 1891, and revised September 28, 1891. History: Not yet amended.

Section 108: Abolishment of office of commonwealth's attorney.

The General Assembly may, at any time after the expiration of six years from the adoption of this Constitution, abolish the office of Commonwealth's Attorney, to take effect upon the expiration of the term of the incumbents, in which event the duties of said office shall be discharged by the County Attorneys.

Text as Ratified on: August 3, 1891, and revised September 28, 1891. History: Not yet amended.

The Judicial Department

Section 109: The judicial power—Unified system—Impeachment.

The judicial power of the Commonwealth shall be vested exclusively in one Court of Justice which shall be divided into a Supreme Court, a Court of Appeals, a trial court of general jurisdiction known as the Circuit Court and a trial court of limited jurisdiction known as the District Court. The court shall constitute a unified judicial system for operation and administration. The impeachment powers of the General Assembly shall remain inviolate.

Text as Ratified on: November 4, 1975, effective January 1, 1976. History: Repeal and re-enactment proposed by 1974 Ky. Acts ch. 84, sec. 1; original version ratified August 3, 1891, and revised September 28, 1891.

The Supreme Court

Section 110: Composition—Jurisdiction—Quorum—Special justices—Districts—Chief Justice.

(1) The Supreme Court shall consist of the Chief Justice of the Commonwealth and six associate Justices.

(2) (a) The Supreme Court shall have appellate jurisdiction only, except it shall have the power to issue all writs necessary in aid of its appellate jurisdiction, or the complete determination of any cause, or as may be required to exercise control of the Court of Justice.

(b) Appeals from a judgment of the Circuit Court imposing a sentence of death or life imprisonment or imprisonment for twenty years or more shall be taken directly to the Supreme Court. In all other cases, criminal and civil, the Supreme Court shall exercise appellate jurisdiction as provided by its rules.

(3) A majority of the Justices of the Supreme Court shall constitute a quorum for the transaction of business. If as many as two Justices decline or are unable to sit in the trial of any cause, the Chief Justice shall certify that fact to the Governor, who shall appoint to try the particular cause a sufficient number of Justices to constitute a full court for the trial of the cause.

(4) The Court of Appeals districts existing on the effective date of this amendment to the Constitution shall constitute the initial Supreme Court districts. The General Assembly thereafter may redistrict the Commonwealth, by counties, into seven Supreme Court districts as nearly equal in population and as compact in form as possible. There shall be one Justice from each Supreme Court district.

(5) (a) The Justices of the Supreme Court shall elect one of their number to serve as Chief Justice for a term of four years.

(b) The Chief Justice of the Commonwealth shall be the executive head of the Court of Justice and he shall appoint such administrative assistants as he deems necessary. He shall assign temporarily any justice or judge of the Commonwealth, active or retired, to sit in any court other than the Supreme Court when he deems such assignment necessary for the prompt disposition of causes. The Chief Justice shall submit the budget for the Court of Justice and perform all other necessary administrative functions relating to the court.

Text as Ratified on: November 4, 1975, effective January 1, 1976. History: Repeal and reenactment proposed by 1974 Ky. Acts ch. 84, sec. 1; original version ratified August 3, 1891, and revised September 28, 1891.

The Court of Appeals

Section 111: Composition—Jurisdiction—Administration—Panels.

(1) The Court of Appeals shall consist initially of fourteen judges, an equal number to be selected from each Supreme Court district. The number of judges thereafter shall be determined from time to time by the General Assembly upon certification of necessity by the Supreme Court.

(2) The Court of Appeals shall have appellate jurisdiction only, except that it may be authorized by rules of the Supreme Court to review directly decisions of administrative agencies of the Commonwealth, and it may issue all writs necessary in aid of its appellate jurisdiction, or the complete determination of any cause within its appellate jurisdiction. In all other cases, it shall exercise appellate jurisdiction as provided by law.

(3) The judges of the Court of Appeals shall elect one of their number to serve as Chief Judge for a term of four years. The Chief Judge shall exercise such authority and perform such duties in the administration of the Court of Appeals as are prescribed in this section or as may be prescribed by the Supreme Court.

(4) The Court of Appeals shall divide itself into panels of not less than three judges. A panel may decide a cause by the concurring vote of a majority of its judges. The Chief Judge shall make assignments of judges to panels. The Court of Appeals shall prescribe the times and places in the Commonwealth at which each panel shall sit.

Text as Ratified on: November 4, 1975, effective January 1, 1976. History: Repeal and reenactment proposed by 1974 Ky. Acts ch. 84, sec. 1; original version ratified August 3, 1891, and revised September 28, 1891.

The Circuit Court

Section 112: Location—Circuits—Composition—Administration—Jurisdiction.

(1) Circuit Court shall be held in each county.

(2) The Circuit Court districts existing on the effective date of this amendment to the Constitution shall continue under the name "Judicial Circuits," the General Assembly having power upon certification of the necessity therefor by the Supreme Court to reduce, increase or rearrange the judicial districts. A judicial circuit composed of more than one county shall be as compact in form as possible and of contiguous counties. No county shall be divided in creating a judicial circuit.

(3) The number of circuit judges in each district existing on the effective date of this amendment shall continue, the General Assembly having power upon certification of the necessity therefor by the Supreme Court, to change the number of circuit judges in any judicial circuit.

(4) In a judicial circuit having only one judge, he shall be the chief judge. In judicial circuits having two or more judges, they shall select biennially a chief judge, and if they fail to do so within a reasonable time, the Supreme Court shall designate the chief judge. The chief judge shall exercise such authority and perform such duties in the administration of his judicial circuit as may be prescribed by the Supreme Court. The Supreme Court may provide by rules for administration of judicial circuits by regions designated by it.

(5) The Circuit Court shall have original jurisdiction of all justiciable causes not vested in some other court. It shall have such appellate jurisdiction as may be provided by law.

(6) The Supreme Court may designate one or more divisions of Circuit Court within a judicial circuit as a family court division. A Circuit Court division so designated shall retain the general jurisdiction of the Circuit Court and shall have additional jurisdiction as may be provided by the General Assembly.

Text as Ratified on: November 5, 2002. History: 2002 amendment was proposed by 2001 Ky. Acts ch. 163, sec. 1; 1974 repeal and reenactment was proposed by 1974 Ky. Acts ch. 84, sec. 1, and ratified November 4, 1975, effective January 1, 1976; original version ratified August 3, 1891, and revised September 28, 1891.

Legislative Research Commission Note (11-15-02). 2001 Ky. Acts ch. 163, which contained the text of the amendment to this section that was ratified on November 5, 2002, also contained sec. 2, which reads as follows: "District judges elected for the term beginning on the first Monday in January of 2003, who possess the qualifications of a Circuit Judge and who are assigned by the Chief Justice to serve as family court judges on or before the commencement of the term, shall on that date become Circuit Judges with terms of office coinciding with the terms of Circuit Judges generally, and another numbered division or divisions of that judicial circuit shall be created. When a District Judge becomes a Circuit Judge pursuant to this provision, that District Judgeship shall be abolished and there shall be no vacancy to fill. The General Assembly, upon the ratification of this amendment, shall enact legislation to implement the provisions of this amendment in a manner consistent with the Supreme Court's adjustment of any Circuit Court division as a family court division."

The District Court

Section 113: Location—Districts—Composition—Administration—Trial commissioners—Jurisdiction.

(1) District Court shall be held in each county.

(2) The Circuit Court districts existing on the effective date of this amendment shall continue for District Court purposes under the name "Judicial Districts," the General Assembly having power upon certification of the necessity therefor by the Supreme Court to reduce, increase or rearrange the districts. A judicial district composed of more than one county shall be as compact in form as possible and of contiguous counties. No county shall be divided in creating a judicial district.

(3) Each judicial district created by this amendment initially shall have at least one district judge who shall serve as chief judge and there shall be such other district judges as the General Assembly shall determine. The number of district judges in each judicial district thereafter shall be determined by the General Assembly upon certification of necessity therefor by the Supreme Court.

(4) In a judicial district having only one judge he shall be the chief judge. In those districts having two or more judges they shall select biennially a chief judge and if they fail to do so within a reasonable time, the Supreme Court shall designate the chief judge. The chief judge shall exercise such authority and perform such duties in the administration of his district as may be prescribed by the Supreme Court.

(5) In any county in which no district judge resides the chief judge of the district shall appoint a trial commissioner who shall be a resident of such county and who shall be an attorney if one is qualified and available. Other trial commissioners with like qualifications may be appointed by the chief judge in any judicial district upon certification of the necessity therefor by the Supreme Court. All trial commissioners shall have power to perform such duties of the district court as may be prescribed by the Supreme Court.

(6) The district court shall be a court of limited jurisdiction and shall exercise original jurisdiction as may be provided by the General Assembly.

Text as Ratified on: November 4, 1975, effective January 1, 1976. History: Repeal and reenactment proposed by 1974 Ky. Acts ch. 84, sec. 1; original version ratified August 3, 1891, and revised September 28, 1891.

Clerks of Courts

Section 114: Selection—Removal.

(1) The Supreme Court shall appoint a clerk to serve as it shall determine.

(2) The Court of Appeals shall appoint a clerk to serve as it shall determine.

(3) The clerks of the Circuit Court shall be elected in the manner provided elsewhere in this Constitution. The clerks of the Circuit Court shall serve as the clerks of the District Court. The clerks of the Circuit Court shall be removable from office by the Supreme Court upon good cause shown.

Text as Ratified on: November 4, 1975, effective January 1, 1976. History: Repeal and reenactment proposed by 1974 Ky. Acts ch. 84, sec. 1; original version ratified August 3, 1891, and revised September 28, 1891.

Appellate Policy
Section 115: Right of appeal—Procedure.

In all cases, civil and criminal, there shall be allowed as a matter of right at least one appeal to another court, except that the Commonwealth may not appeal from a judgment of acquittal in a criminal case, other than for the purpose of securing a certification of law, and the General Assembly may prescribe that there shall be no appeal from that portion of a judgment dissolving a marriage. Procedural rules shall provide for expeditious and inexpensive appeals. Appeals shall be upon the record and not by trial de novo.

Text as Ratified on: November 4, 1975, effective January 1, 1976. History: Repeal and reenactment proposed by 1974 Ky. Acts ch. 84, sec. 1; original version ratified August 3, 1891, and revised September 28, 1891.

Section 116: Rules governing jurisdiction, personnel, procedure, bar membership.

The Supreme Court shall have the power to prescribe rules governing its appellate jurisdiction, rules for the appointment of commissioners and other court personnel, and rules of practice and procedure for the Court of Justice. The Supreme Court shall, by rule, govern admission to the bar and the discipline of members of the bar.

Text as Ratified on: November 4, 1975, effective January 1, 1976. History: Repeal and reenactment proposed by 1974 Ky. Acts ch. 84, sec. 1; original version ratified August 3, 1891, and revised September 28, 1891.

Offices of Justices and Judges
Section 117: Election.

Justices of the Supreme Court and judges of the Court of Appeals, Circuit and District Court shall be elected from their respective districts or circuits on a nonpartisan basis as provided by law.

Text as Ratified on: November 4, 1975, effective January 1, 1976. History: Repeal and reenactment proposed by 1974 Ky. Acts ch. 84, sec. 1; original version ratified August 3, 1891, and revised September 28, 1891.

Section 118: Vacancies.

(1) A vacancy in the office of a justice of the Supreme Court, or of a judge of the Court of Appeals, circuit or district court which under Section 152 of this Constitution is to be filled by appointment by the Governor shall be filled by the Governor from a list of three names presented to him by the appropriate judicial nominating commission. If the Governor fails to make an appointment from the list within sixty days from the date it is presented to him, the appointment shall be made from the same list by the chief justice of the Supreme Court.

(2) There shall be one judicial nominating commission for the Supreme Court and the Court of Appeals, one for each judicial circuit, and one for each judicial district, except that a circuit and district having the same boundary shall have but one judicial nominating commission. Each commission shall consist of seven members, one of whom shall be the chief justice of the Supreme Court, who shall be chairman. Two members of each commission shall be members of the bar, who shall be elected by their fellow members. The other four members shall be appointed by the Governor from among persons not members of the bar, and these four shall include at least two members of each of the two political parties of the Commonwealth having the largest number of voters. Members of a judicial circuit or judicial district nominating commission must be residents of the circuit or district, respectively, and the lawyer members of the

commission shall be elected by the members of the bar residing in the circuit or district, respectively. The terms of office of members of judicial nominating commissions shall be fixed by the General Assembly. No person shall be elected or appointed a member of a judicial nominating commission who holds any other public office or any office in a political party or organization.

Text as Ratified on: November 4, 1975, effective January 1, 1976. History: Repeal and reenactment proposed by 1974 Ky. Acts ch. 84, sec. 1; original version ratified August 3, 1891, and revised September 28, 1891.

Section 119: Terms of office.

Justices of the Supreme Court and judges of the Court of Appeals and Circuit Court shall severally hold their offices for terms of eight years, and judges of the District Court for terms of four years. All terms commence on the first Monday in January next succeeding the regular election for the office. No justice or judge may be deprived of his term of office by redistricting, or by a reduction in the number of justices or judges.

Text as Ratified on: November 4, 1975, effective January 1, 1976. History: Repeal and reenactment proposed by 1974 Ky. Acts ch. 84, sec. 1; original version ratified August 3, 1891, and revised September 28, 1891.

Section 120: Compensation—Expenses.

All justices and judges shall be paid adequate compensation which shall be fixed by the General Assembly. All compensation and necessary expenses of the Court of Justice shall be paid out of the State Treasury. The compensation of a justice or judge shall not be reduced during his term.

Text as Ratified on: November 4, 1975, effective January 1, 1976. History: Repeal and reenactment proposed by 1974 Ky. Acts ch. 84, sec. 1; original version ratified August 3, 1891, and revised September 28, 1891.

Section 121: Retirement and removal.

Subject to rules of procedure to be established by the Supreme Court, and after notice and hearing, any justice of the Supreme Court or judge of the Court of Appeals, Circuit Court or District Court may be retired for disability or suspended without pay or removed for good cause by a commission composed of one judge of the Court of Appeals, selected by that court, one circuit judge and one district judge selected by a majority vote of the circuit judges and district judges, respectively, one member of the bar appointed by its governing body, and two persons, not members of the bench or bar, appointed by the Governor. The commission shall be a state body whose members shall hold office for four-year terms. Its actions shall be subject to judicial review by the Supreme Court.

Text as Ratified on: November 4, 1975, effective January 1, 1976. History: Repeal and reenactment proposed by 1974 Ky. Acts ch. 84, sec. 1; original version ratified August 3, 1891, and revised September 28, 1891.

Section 122: Eligibility.

To be eligible to serve as a justice of the Supreme Court or a judge of the Court of Appeals, Circuit Court or District Court a person must be a citizen of the United States, licensed to practice law in the courts of this Commonwealth, and have been a resident of this Commonwealth and of the district from which he is elected for two years next preceding his taking office. In addition, to be eligible to serve as a justice of the Supreme Court or judge of the Court of Appeals or Circuit Court a person must have been a licensed attorney for at least eight years. No district judge shall serve who has not been a licensed attorney for at least two years.

Text as Ratified on: November 4, 1975, effective January 1, 1976. History: Repeal and reenactment proposed by 1974 Ky. Acts ch. 84, sec. 1; original version ratified August 3, 1891, and revised September 28, 1891.

Section 123: Prohibited activities.

During his term of office, no justice of the Supreme Court or judge of the Court of Appeals, Circuit Court or District Court shall engage in the practice of law, or run for elective office other than judicial office, or hold any office in a political party or organization.

Text as Ratified on: November 4, 1975, effective January 1, 1976. History: Repeal and reenactment proposed by 1974 Ky. Acts ch. 84, sec. 1; original version ratified August 3, 1891, and revised September 28, 1891.

Section 124: Conflicting provisions.

Any remaining sections of the Constitution of Kentucky as it existed prior to the effective date of this amendment which are in conflict with the provisions of amended Sections 110 through 125 are repealed to the extent of the conflict, but such amended sections are not intended to repeal those parts of Sections 140 and 142 conferring nonjudicial powers and duties upon county judges and justices of the peace. Nothing in such amended sections shall be construed to limit the powers otherwise granted by this Constitution to the county judge as the chief executive, administrative and fiscal officer of the county, or to limit the powers otherwise granted by the Constitution to the justices of the peace or county commissioners as executive, administrative and fiscal officers of a county, or of the fiscal court as a governing body of a county.

Text as Ratified on: November 4, 1975, effective January 1, 1976. History: Repeal and reenactment proposed by 1974 Ky. Acts ch. 84, sec. 1; original version ratified August 3, 1891, and revised September 28, 1891.

Sections 125–139 all repealed in 1975.

County Courts
Section 140: County Court for each county—Judge—Compensation—Commission—Removal.

There shall be established in each county now existing, or which may be hereafter created, in this State, a Court, to be styled the County Court, to consist of a Judge, who shall be a conservator of the peace, and shall receive such compensation for his services as may be prescribed by law. He shall be commissioned by the Governor, and shall vacate his office by removal from the county in which he may have been elected.

Text as Ratified on: August 3, 1891, and revised September 28, 1891. History: Not yet amended.

Section 141: (Repealed 1975) Catchline read at time of repeal: "Jurisdiction of County Courts."

Repeal Ratified on: November 4, 1975, effective January 1, 1976. History: Repeal was proposed by 1974 Ky. Acts ch. 84, sec. 1; original version ratified August 3, 1891, and revised September 28, 1891.

Justices of the Peace

Section 142: Justices' districts—One Justice for each district—Jurisdiction and powers of Justices—Commissions—Removal.

Each county now existing, or which may hereafter be created, in this State, shall be laid off into districts in such manner as the General Assembly may direct; but no county shall have less than three nor more than eight districts, in each of which districts one Justice of the Peace shall be elected as provided in Section 99. The General Assembly shall make provisions for regulating the number of said districts from time to time within the limits herein prescribed, and for fixing the boundaries thereof. The jurisdiction of Justices of the Peace shall be coextensive with the county, and shall be equal and uniform throughout the State. Justices of the Peace shall be conservators of the peace. They shall be commissioned by the Governor, and shall vacate their offices by removal from the districts, respectively, in which they may have been elected.

Text as Ratified on: August 3, 1891, and revised September 28, 1891. History: Not yet amended.

Section 143: (Repealed 1975) Catchline read at time of repeal: "Police Court may be established in each city—Jurisdiction."

Repeal Ratified on: November 4, 1975, effective January 1, 1976. History: Repeal was proposed by 1974 Ky. Acts ch. 84, sec. 1; original version ratified August 3, 1891, and revised September 28, 1891.

Fiscal Courts

Section 144: Fiscal Court for each county—To consist of Justices of the Peace or Commissioners, and County Judge—Quorum.

Counties shall have a Fiscal Court, which may consist of the Judge of the County Court and the Justices of the Peace, in which Court the Judge of the County Court shall preside, if present; or a county may have three Commissioners, to be elected from the county at large, who, together with the Judge of the County Court, shall constitute the Fiscal Court. A majority of the members of said Court shall constitute a Court for the transaction of business. But where, for county governmental purposes, a city is by law separated from the remainder of the county, such Commissioners may be elected from the part of the county outside of such city.

Text as Ratified on: August 3, 1891, and revised September 28, 1891. History: Not yet amended.

Suffrage and Elections

Section 145: Persons entitled to vote.

Every citizen of the United States of the age of eighteen years who has resided in the state one year, and in the county six months, and the precinct in which he offers to vote sixty days next preceding the election, shall be a voter in said precinct and not elsewhere but the following persons are excepted and shall not have the right to vote.

1. Persons convicted in any court of competent jurisdiction of treason, or felony, or bribery in an election, or of such high misdemeanor as the General Assembly may declare shall operate as an exclusion from the right of suffrage, but persons hereby excluded may be restored to their civil rights by executive pardon.

2. Persons who, at the time of the election, are in confinement under the judgment of a court for some penal offense.

3. Idiots and insane persons.

Text as Ratified on: November 8, 1955. History: 1955 amendment was proposed by 1954 Ky. Acts ch. 2, sec. 1; original version ratified August 3, 1891, and revised September 28, 1891.

Section 146: Soldiers or sailors stationed in State are not residents.

No person in the military, naval or marine service of the United States shall be deemed a resident of this State by reason of being stationed within the same.

Text as Ratified on: August 3, 1891, and revised September 28, 1891. History: Not yet amended.

Section 147: Registration of voters—Manner of voting—Absent voting—Voting machines—"Election" defined—Election laws—Illiterate and disabled voters.

The General Assembly shall provide by law for the registration of all persons entitled to vote in cities and towns having a population of five thousand or more; and may provide by general law for the registration of other voters in the state. Where registration is required, only persons registered shall have the right to vote. The mode of registration shall be prescribed by the General Assembly. In all elections by persons in a representative capacity, the voting shall be viva voce and made a matter of record; but all elections by the people shall be by secret official ballot, furnished by public authority to the voters at the polls, and marked by each voter in private at the polls, and then and there deposited, or any person absent from the county of his legal residence, or from the state, may be permitted to vote in a manner provided by law. Counties so desiring may use voting machines, these machines to be installed at the expense of such counties. The word "elections" in this section includes the decision of questions submitted to the voters, as well as the choice of officers by them. The General Assembly shall pass all necessary laws to enforce this section, and shall provide that persons illiterate, blind, or in any way disabled may have their ballots marked or voted as herein required.

Text as Ratified on: November 6, 1945. History: 1945 amendment was proposed by 1944 Ky. Acts ch. 5, sec. 1; 1941 amendment was proposed by 1940 Ky. Acts ch. 74, sec. 1, and ratified on November 4, 1941; original version ratified August 3, 1891, and revised September 28, 1891.

Section 148: Number of elections—Day and hours of election—Qualifications of officers—Employees to be given time to vote.

Not more than one election each year shall be held in this State or in any city, town, district, urban-county or county thereof, except as otherwise provided in this Constitution. All regular elections of State, county, city, town, urban-county, or district officers shall be held on the first Tuesday after the first Monday in November. All elections by the people shall be between the hours of six o'clock a.m. and seven o'clock p.m., but the General Assembly may change said hours, and all officers of any election shall be residents and voters in the precinct in which they act. The General Assembly shall provide by law that all employers shall allow employees, under reasonable regulations, at least four hours on election days, in which to cast their votes.

Text as Ratified on: November 3, 1992. History: 1992 amendment was proposed by 1992 Ky. Acts ch. 168, sec. 16; original version ratified August 3, 1891, and revised September 28, 1891.

Section 149: Privilege from arrest during voting.

Voters, in all cases except treason, felony, breach of surety of the peace, or violation of the election laws, shall be privileged from arrest during their attendance at elections, and while they are going to and returning therefrom.

Text as Ratified on: August 3, 1891, and revised September 28, 1891. History: Not yet amended.

Section 150: Disqualification from office for using money or property to secure or influence election—Corporation not to use money or other thing of value to influence election—Exclusion from office for conviction of felony or high misdemeanor—Laws to regulate elections.

Every person shall be disqualified from holding any office of trust or profit for the term for which he shall have been elected who shall be convicted of having given, or consented to the giving, offer or promise of any money or other thing of value, to procure his election, or to influence the vote of any voter at such election; and if any corporation shall, directly or indirectly, offer, promise or give, or shall authorize, directly or indirectly, any person to offer, promise or give any money or any thing of value to influence the result of any election in this State, or the vote of any voter authorized to vote therein, or who shall afterward reimburse or compensate, in any manner whatever, any person who shall have offered, promised or given any money or other thing of value to influence the result of any election or the vote of any such voter, such corporation, if organized under the laws of this Commonwealth, shall, on conviction thereof, forfeit its charter and all rights, privileges and immunities thereunder; and if chartered by another State and doing business in this State, whether by license, or upon mere sufferance, such corporation, upon conviction of either of the offenses aforesaid, shall forfeit all right to carry on any business in this State; and it shall be the duty of the General Assembly to provide for the enforcement of the provisions of this section. All persons shall be excluded from office who have been, or shall hereafter be, convicted of a felony, or of such high misdemeanor as may be prescribed by law, but such disability may be removed by pardon of the Governor. The privilege of free suffrage shall be supported by laws regulating elections, and prohibiting, under adequate penalties, all undue influence thereon, from power, bribery, tumult or other improper practices.

Text as Ratified on: August 3, 1891, and revised September 28, 1891. History: Not yet amended.

Section 151: Person guilty of fraud, intimidation, bribery, or corrupt practice to be deprived of office by suitable statutory means.

The General Assembly shall provide suitable means for depriving of office any person who, to procure his nomination or election, has, in his canvass or election, been guilty of any unlawful use of money, or other thing of value, or has been guilty of fraud, intimidation, bribery, or any other corrupt practice, and he shall be held responsible for acts done by others with his authority, or ratified by him.

Text as Ratified on: August 3, 1891, and revised September 28, 1891. History: Not yet amended.

Section 152: Vacancies—When filled by appointment, when by election—Who to fill.

Except as otherwise provided in this Constitution, vacancies in all elective offices shall be filled by election or appointment, as follows: If the unexpired term will end at the next succeeding annual election at which either city, town, county, district or State officers are to be elected, the office shall be filled by appointment for the remainder of the term. If the unexpired term will not end at the next succeeding annual election at which either city, town, county, district or State officers are to be elected, and if three months intervene before said succeeding annual election at which either city, town, county, district or State officers are to be elected, the office shall be filled by appointment until said election, and then said vacancy shall be filled by election for the remainder of the term. If three months do not intervene between the happening of said vacancy and the next succeeding election at which city, town, county, district or State officers are to be elected, the office shall be filled by appointment until the second succeeding annual election at which city, town, county, district or State officers are to be elected; and then, if any part of the term remains unexpired, the office shall be filled by election until the regular time for the election of officers to fill said offices. Vacancies in all offices for the State at large, or for districts larger than a county, shall be filled by appointment of the Governor; all other appointments shall be made as may be prescribed by law. No person shall ever be appointed a member of the General Assembly, but vacancies therein may be filled at a special election, in such manner as may be provided by law.

Text as Ratified on: August 3, 1891, and revised September 28, 1891. History: Not yet amended.

Section 153: Power of General Assembly as to elections.

Except as otherwise herein expressly provided, the General Assembly shall have power to provide by general law for the manner of voting, for ascertaining the result of elections and making due returns thereof, for issuing certificates or commissions to all persons entitled thereto, and for the trial of contested elections.

Text as Ratified on: August 3, 1891, and revised September 28, 1891. History: Not yet amended.

Section 154: Laws as to sale or gift of liquor on election days.

The General Assembly shall prescribe such laws as may be necessary for the restriction or prohibition of the sale or gift of spirituous, vinous or malt liquors on election days.

Text as Ratified on: August 3, 1891, and revised September 28, 1891. History: Not yet amended.

Section 155: School elections not governed by Constitution.

The provisions of Sections 145 to 154, inclusive, shall not apply to the election of school trustees and other common school district elections. Said elections shall be regulated by the General Assembly, except as otherwise provided in this Constitution.

Text as Ratified on: August 3, 1891, and revised September 28, 1891. History: Not yet amended.

Municipalities

Section 156: (Repealed 1994) Catchline at time of repeal: "Cities divided into six classes—General laws to be made for each class—Population limits for classes—Assignment to classes—Organization of cities."

Repeal Ratified on: November 8, 1994. History: Repeal was proposed by 1994 Ky. Acts ch. 168, secs. 1 and 6; original version ratified August 3, 1891, and revised September 28, 1891.

Section 156a: General Assembly authorized to provide for creation, governmental structure, and classification of cities.

The General Assembly may provide for the creation, alteration of boundaries, consolidation, merger, dissolution, government, functions, and officers of cities. The General Assembly shall create such classifications of cities as it deems necessary based on population, tax base, form of government, geography, or any other reasonable basis and enact legislation relating to the classifications. All legislation relating to cities of a certain classification shall apply equally to all cities within the same classification. The classification of all cities and the law pertaining to the classifications in effect at the time of adoption of this section shall remain in effect until otherwise provided by law.

Text as Ratified on: November 8, 1994. History: Creation proposed by 1994 Ky. Acts ch. 168, sec. 1.

Section 156b: General Assembly authorized to permit municipal home rule for cities.

The General Assembly may provide by general law that cities may exercise any power and perform any function within their boundaries that is in furtherance of a public purpose of a city and not in conflict with a constitutional provision or statute.

Text as Ratified on: November 8, 1994 History: Creation proposed by 1994 Ky. Acts ch. 168, sec. 1.

Section 157: Maximum tax rate for cities, counties, and taxing districts.

The tax rate of cities, counties, and taxing districts, for other than school purposes, shall not, at any time, exceed the following rates upon the value of the taxable property therein: For all cities having a population of fifteen thousand or more, one dollar and fifty cents on the hundred dollars; for all cities having less than fifteen thousand and not less than ten thousand, one dollar on the hundred dollars; for all cities having less than ten thousand, seventy-five cents on the hundred dollars; and for counties and taxing districts, fifty cents on the hundred dollars.

Text as Ratified on: November 8, 1994. History: 1994 amendment was proposed by 1994 Ky. Acts ch. 168, sec. 2; original version ratified August 3, 1891, and revised September 28, 1891.

Section 157a: Credit of Commonwealth may be loaned or given to county for roads—County may vote to incur indebtedness and levy additional tax for roads.

The credit of the Commonwealth may be given, pledged or loaned to any county of the Commonwealth for public road purposes, and any county may be permitted to incur an indebtedness in any amount fixed by the county, not in excess of five per centum of the value of the taxable property therein, for public road purposes in said county, provided said additional indebtedness is submitted to the voters of the county for their ratification or rejection at a special election held for said purpose, in such manner as may be provided by law and when any such indebtedness is incurred by any county said county may levy, in addition to the tax rate allowed under Section 157 of the Constitution of Kentucky, an amount not exceeding twenty cents on the one hundred dollars of the assessed valuation of said county for the purpose of paying the interest on said indebtedness and providing a sinking fund for the payment of said indebtedness.

Text as Ratified on: November 2, 1909. History: Creation proposed by 1908 Ky. Acts ch. 36, sec. 1.

Section 157b: Adoption of budget required for cities, counties, and taxing districts—Expenditures not to exceed revenues for fiscal year.

Prior to each fiscal year, the legislative body of each city, county, and taxing district shall adopt a budget showing total expected revenues and expenditures for the fiscal year. No city, county, or taxing district shall expend any funds in any fiscal year in excess of the revenues for that fiscal year. A city, county, or taxing district may amend its budget for a fiscal year, but the revised expenditures may not exceed the revised revenues. As used in this section, "revenues" shall mean all income from every source, including unencumbered reserves carried over from the previous fiscal year, and "expenditures" shall mean all funds to be paid out for expenses of the city, county, or taxing district during the fiscal year, including amounts necessary to pay the principal and interest due during the fiscal year on any debt.

Text as Ratified on: November 8, 1994. History: Creation proposed by 1994 Ky. Acts ch. 168, sec. 3.

Section 158: Maximum indebtedness of cities, counties, and taxing districts—General Assembly authorized to set additional limits and conditions.

Cities, towns, counties, and taxing districts shall not incur indebtedness to an amount exceeding the following maximum percentages on the value of the taxable property therein, to be estimated by the last assessment previous to the incurring of the indebtedness: Cities having a population of fifteen thousand or more, ten percent (10%); cities having a population of less than fifteen thousand but not less than three thousand, five percent (5%); cities having a population of less than three thousand, three percent (3%); and counties and taxing districts, two percent (2%), unless in case of emergency, the public health or safety should so require. Nothing shall prevent the issue of renewal bonds, or bonds to fund the floating indebtedness of any city, county, or taxing district. Subject to the limits and conditions set forth in this section and elsewhere in this Constitution, the General Assembly shall have the power to establish additional limits on indebtedness and conditions under which debt may be incurred by cities, counties, and taxing districts.

Text as Ratified on: November 8, 1994. History: 1994 amendment was proposed by 1994 Ky. Acts ch. 168, sec. 4; original version ratified August 3, 1891, and revised September 28, 1891.

Section 159: Tax to pay indebtedness in not more than forty years must be levied.

Whenever any city, town, county, taxing district or other municipality is authorized to contract an indebtedness, it shall be required, at the same time, to provide for the collection of an annual tax sufficient to pay the interest on said indebtedness, and to create a sinking fund for the payment of the principal thereof, within not more than forty years from the time of contracting the same.

Text as Ratified on: August 3, 1891, and revised September 28, 1891. History: Not yet amended.

Section 160: Municipal officers—Election and term of office—Officers ineligible—Fiscal officers.

The Mayor or Chief Executive, Police Judges, members of legislative boards or councils of towns and cities shall be elected by the qualified voters thereof: Provided, The Mayor or Chief Executive and Police Judges of the towns of the fourth, fifth and sixth classes may be appointed or elected as provided by law. The terms of office of Mayors or Chief Executives and Police Judges shall be four years, and until their successors shall be qualified, and of members of legislative boards, two years. When any city of the first or second class is divided into wards or districts, members of legislative boards shall be elected at large by the qualified voters of said city, but so selected that an equal proportion thereof shall reside in each of the said wards or districts; but when in any city of the first, second or third class, there are two legislative boards, the less numerous shall be selected from and elected by the voters at large of said city;

but other officers of towns or cities shall be elected by the qualified voters therein, or appointed by the local authorities thereof, as the General Assembly may, by a general law, provide; but when elected by the voters of a town or city, their terms of office shall be four years, and until their successors shall be qualified. No Mayor or Chief Executive of any city of the first or second class, after the expiration of three successive terms of office to which he has been elected under this Constitution shall be eligible for the succeeding term. No fiscal officer of any city of the first or second class, after the expiration of the term of office to which he has been elected under this Constitution, shall be eligible for the succeeding term. "Fiscal officer" shall not include an Auditor or Assessor, or any other officer whose chief duty is not the collection or holding of public moneys. The General Assembly shall prescribe the qualifications of all officers of towns and cities, the manner in and causes for which they may be removed from office, and how vacancies in such offices may be filled.

Text as Ratified on: November 6, 1986. History: 1986 amendment was proposed by 1986 Ky. Acts ch. 140, sec. 1; original version ratified August 3, 1891, and revised September 28, 1891.

Section 161: Compensation of city, county, or municipal officer not to be changed after election or appointment or during term, nor term extended.

The compensation of any city, county, town or municipal officer shall not be changed after his election or appointment, or during his term of office; nor shall the term of any such officer be extended beyond the period for which he may have been elected or appointed.

Text as Ratified on: August 3, 1891, and revised September 28, 1891. History: Not yet amended.

Section 162: Unauthorized contracts of cities, counties, and municipalities are void.

No county, city, town or other municipality shall ever be authorized or permitted to pay any claim created against it, under any agreement or contract made without express authority of law, and all such unauthorized agreements or contracts shall be null and void.

Text as Ratified on: August 3, 1891, and revised September 28, 1891. History: Not yet amended.

Section 163: Public utilities must obtain franchise to use streets.

No street railway, gas, water, steam heating, telephone, or electric light company, within a city or town, shall be permitted or authorized to construct its tracks, lay its pipes or mains, or erect its poles, posts or other apparatus along, over, under or across the streets, alleys or public grounds of a city or town, without the consent of the proper legislative bodies or boards of such city or town being first obtained; but when charters have been heretofore granted conferring such rights, and work has in good faith been begun thereunder, the provisions of this section shall not apply.

Text as Ratified on: August 3, 1891, and revised September 28, 1891. History: Not yet amended.

Section 164: Term of franchises limited—Advertisement and bids.

No county, city, town, taxing district or other municipality shall be authorized or permitted to grant any franchise or privilege, or make any contract in reference thereto, for a term exceeding twenty years. Before granting such franchise or privilege for a term of years, such municipality shall first, after due advertisement, receive bids therefor publicly, and award the same to the highest and best bidder; but it shall have the right to reject any or all bids. This section shall not apply to a trunk railway.

Text as Ratified on: August 3, 1891, and revised September 28, 1891. History: Not yet amended.

Section 165: Incompatible offices and employments.

No person shall, at the same time, be a State officer or a deputy officer or member of the General Assembly, and an officer of any county, city, town, or other municipality, or an employee thereof; and no person shall, at the same time, fill two municipal offices, either in the same or different municipalities, except as may be otherwise provided in this Constitution; but a Notary Public, or an officer of the militia, shall not be ineligible to hold any other office mentioned in this section.

Text as Ratified on: August 3, 1891, and revised September 28, 1891. History: Not yet amended.

Section 166: Expiration of city charters granted prior to Constitution.

All acts of incorporation of cities and towns heretofore granted, and all amendments thereto, except as provided in Section 167, shall continue in force under this Constitution, and all City and Police Courts established in any city or town shall remain, with their present powers and jurisdictions, until such time as the General Assembly shall provide by general laws for the government of towns and cities, and the officers and courts thereof; but not longer than four years from and after the first day of January, one thousand eight hundred and ninety-one, within which time the General Assembly shall provide by general laws for the government of towns and cities, and the officers and courts thereof, as provided in this Constitution.

Text as Ratified on: August 3, 1891, and revised September 28, 1891. History: Not yet amended.

Section 167: Time of election of city, urban-county, and town officers.

All officers required to be elected in cities, urban-counties, and towns by this Constitution, or by general laws enacted in conformity to its provisions, shall be elected at the general elections in November in even-numbered years.

Text as Ratified on: November 3, 1992. History: 1992 amendment was proposed by 1992 Ky. Acts ch. 168, sec. 17; original version ratified August 3, 1891, and revised September 28, 1891.

Section 168: Ordinance not to fix less penalty than statute for same offense—Prosecution under one a bar.

No municipal ordinance shall fix a penalty for a violation thereof at less than that imposed by statute for the same offense. A conviction or acquittal under either shall constitute a bar to another prosecution for the same offense.

Text as Ratified on: August 3, 1891, and revised September 28, 1891. History: Not yet amended.

Revenue and Taxation

Section 169: Fiscal year.

The fiscal year shall commence on the first day of July in each year, unless otherwise provided by law.

Text as Ratified on: August 3, 1891, and revised September 28, 1891. History: Not yet amended.

Section 170: Property exempt from taxation—Cities may exempt factories for five years.

There shall be exempt from taxation public property used for public purposes; places of burial not held for private or corporate profit; real property owned and occupied by, and personal property both tangible and intangible owned by, institutions of religion; institutions of purely public charity, and institutions of education not used or employed for gain by any person or corporation, and the income of which is devoted solely to the cause of education, public libraries, their endowments, and the income of such property as is used exclusively for their maintenance; household goods of a person used in his home; crops grown in the year in which the assessment is made, and in the hands of the producer; and real property maintained as the permanent residence of the owner, who is sixty-five years of age or older, or is classified as totally disabled under a program authorized or administered by an agency of the United States government or by any retirement system either within or without the Commonwealth of Kentucky, provided the property owner received disability payments pursuant to such disability classification, has maintained such disability classification for the entirety of the particular taxation period, and has filed with the appropriate local assessor by December 31 of the taxation period, on forms provided therefor, a signed statement indicating continuing disability as provided herein made under penalty of perjury, up to the assessed valuation of sixty-five hundred dollars on said residence and contiguous real property, except for assessment for special benefits. The real property may be held by legal or equitable title, by the entireties, jointly, in common, as a condominium, or indirectly by the stock ownership or membership representing the owner's or member's proprietary interest in a corporation owning a fee or a leasehold initially in excess of ninety-eight years. The exemptions shall apply only to the value of the real property assessable to the owner or, in case of ownership through stock or membership in a corporation, the value of the proportion which his interest in the corporation bears to the assessed value of the property. The General Assembly may authorize any incorporated city or town to exempt manufacturing establishments from municipal taxation, for a period not exceeding five years, as an inducement to their location. Notwithstanding the provisions of Sections 3, 172, and 174 of this Constitution to the contrary, the General Assembly may provide by law an exemption for all or any portion of the property tax for any class of personal property.

Text as Ratified on: November 3, 1998. History: 1998 amendment was proposed by 1998 Ky. Acts ch. 227, sec. 1; 1990 amendment was proposed by 1990 Ky. Acts ch. 151, sec. 1, and ratified on November 6, 1990; 1981 amendment was proposed by 1980 Ky. Acts ch. 113, sec. 1, and ratified on November 3, 1981; 1975 amendment was proposed by 1974 Ky. Acts ch. 105, sec. 1, and ratified on November 4, 1975; 1971 amendment was proposed by 1970 Ky. Acts ch. 186, sec. 1, and ratified on November 2, 1971; 1955 amendment was proposed by 1954 Ky. Acts ch. 111, sec. 1, and ratified on November 8, 1955; original version was ratified on August 3, 1891, and revised on September 28, 1891.

Section 171: State tax to be levied—Taxes to be levied and collected for public purposes only and by general laws, and to be uniform within classes—Classification of property for taxation—Bonds exempt—Referendum on act classifying property.

The General Assembly shall provide by law an annual tax, which, with other resources, shall be sufficient to defray the estimated expenses of the Commonwealth for each fiscal year. Taxes shall be levied and collected for public purposes only and shall be uniform upon all property of the same class subject to taxation within the territorial limits of the authority levying the tax; and all taxes shall be levied and collected by general laws.

The General Assembly shall have power to divide property into classes and to determine what class or classes of property shall be subject to local taxation. Bonds of the state and of counties, municipalities, taxing and school districts shall not be subject to taxation.

Any law passed or enacted by the General Assembly pursuant to the provisions of or under this amendment, or amended section of the Constitution, classifying property and providing a lower rate of taxation on personal property, tangible or intangible, than upon real estate shall be subject to the referendum power of the people, which is hereby declared to exist to apply only to this section, or amended section. The referendum may be demanded by the people against one or more items, sections, or parts of any act enacted pursuant to or under the power granted by this amendment, or amended section. The referendum petition shall be filed with the Secretary of State not more than four months after the final adjournment of the Legislative Assembly which passed the bill on which the referendum is demanded. The veto power of the Governor shall not extend to measures referred to the people under this section. All elections on measures referred to the people under this act shall be at the regular general election, except when the Legislative Assembly shall order a special election. Any measure referred to the people shall take effect and become a law when approved by the majority of the votes cast thereon, and not otherwise. The whole number of votes cast for the candidates for Governor at the regular election, last preceding the filing of any petition, shall be the basis upon which the legal voters necessary to sign such petition shall be counted. The power of the referendum shall be ordered by the Legislative Assembly at any time any acts or bills are enacted, pursuant to the power granted under this section or amended section, prior to the year of one thousand nine hundred and seventeen. After that time the power of the referendum may be ordered either by the petition signed by five percent of the legal voters or by the Legislative Assembly at the time said acts or bills are enacted. The General Assembly enacting the bill shall provide a way by which the act shall be submitted to the people. The filing of a referendum petition against one or more items, sections or parts of an act, shall not delay the remainder of that act from becoming operative.

Text as Ratified on: November 2, 1915. History: 1915 amendment was proposed by 1914 Ky. Acts ch. 94, sec. 1; original version ratified August 3, 1891, and revised September 28, 1891.

Section 172: Property to be assessed at fair cash value—Punishment of assessor for willful error.

All property, not exempted from taxation by this Constitution, shall be assessed for taxation at its fair cash value, estimated at the price it would bring at a fair voluntary sale; and any officer, or other person authorized to assess values for taxation, who shall commit any willful error in the performance of his duty, shall be deemed guilty of misfeasance, and upon conviction thereof shall forfeit his office, and be otherwise punished as may be provided by law.

Text as Ratified on: August 3, 1891, and revised September 28, 1891. History: Not yet amended.

Section 172a: Assessment for ad valorem tax purposes of agricultural and horticultural land.

Notwithstanding contrary provisions of Sections 171, 172, or 174 of this Constitution—

The General Assembly shall provide by general law for the assessment for ad valorem tax purposes of agricultural and horticultural land according to the land's value for agricultural or horticultural use. The General Assembly may provide that any change in land use from agricultural or horticultural to another use shall require the levy of an additional tax not to exceed the additional amount that would have been owing had the land been assessed under Section 172 of this Constitution for the current year and the two next preceding years.

The General Assembly may provide for reasonable differences in the rate of ad valorem taxation within different areas of the same taxing districts on that class of property which includes the surface of the land. Those differences shall relate directly to differences between nonrevenue-producing governmental services and benefits giving land urban character which are furnished in one or several areas in contrast to other areas of the taxing district.

Text as Ratified on: November 4, 1969. History: Creation proposed by 1968 Ky. Acts. ch. 103, sec. 1.

Section 172b: Property assessment or reassessment moratoriums.

Notwithstanding contrary provisions of Sections 170, 171, 172, or 174 of this Constitution, the General Assembly may provide by general law that the governing bodies of county, municipal, and urban-county governments may declare property assessment or reassessment moratoriums for qualifying units of real property for the purpose of encouraging the repair, rehabilitation, or restoration of existing improvements thereon. Prior to the enactment of any property assessment or reassessment moratorium program, the General Assembly shall provide or direct the local governing authority to provide property qualification standards for participation in the program and a limitation on the duration of any assessment or reassessment moratorium. In no instance shall any such moratorium extend beyond five years for any particular unit of real property and improvements thereon.

Text as Ratified on: November 3, 1981. History: Creation proposed by 1980 Ky. Acts ch. 113, sec. 2.

Section 173: Officer receiving profit on public funds guilty of felony.

The receiving, directly or indirectly, by any officer of the Commonwealth, or of any county, city or town, or member or officer of the General Assembly, of any interest, profit or perquisites arising from the use or loan of public funds in his hands, or moneys to be raised through his agency for State, city, town, district, or county purposes shall be deemed a felony. Said offense shall be punished as may be prescribed by law, a part of which punishment shall be disqualification to hold office.

Text as Ratified on: August 3, 1891, and revised September 28, 1891. History: Not yet amended.

Section 174: Property to be taxed according to value, whether corporate or individual— Income, license, and franchise taxes.

All property, whether owned by natural persons or corporations, shall be taxed in proportion to its value, unless exempted by this Constitution; and all corporate property shall pay the same rate of taxation paid by individual property. Nothing in this Constitution shall be construed to prevent the General Assembly from providing for taxation based on income, licenses or franchises.

Text as Ratified on: August 3, 1891, and revised September 28, 1891. History: Not yet amended.

Section 175: Power to tax property not to be surrendered.

The power to tax property shall not be surrendered or suspended by any contract or grant to which the Commonwealth shall be a party.

Text as Ratified on: August 3, 1891, and revised September 28, 1891. History: Not yet amended.

Section 176: Commonwealth not to assume debt of county or city—Exception.

The Commonwealth shall not assume the debt of any county, municipal corporation or political subdivision of the State, unless such debt shall have been contracted to defend itself in time of war, to repel invasion or to suppress insurrection.

Text as Ratified on: August 3, 1891, and revised September 28, 1891. History: Not yet amended.

Section 177: Commonwealth not to lend credit, nor become stockholder in corporation, nor build railroad or highway.

The credit of the Commonwealth shall not be given, pledged or loaned to any individual, company, corporation or association, municipality, or political subdivision of the State; nor shall the Commonwealth become an owner or stockholder in, nor make donation to, any company, association or corporation; nor shall the Commonwealth construct a railroad or other highway.

Text as Ratified on: August 3, 1891, and revised September 28, 1891. History: Not yet amended.

Section 178: Law for borrowing money to specify purpose, for which alone money may be used.

All laws authorizing the borrowing of money by and on behalf of the Commonwealth, county or other political subdivision of the State, shall specify the purpose for which the money is to be used, and the money so borrowed shall be used for no other purpose.

Text as Ratified on: August 3, 1891, and revised September 28, 1891. History: Not yet amended.

Section 179: Political subdivision not to become stockholder in corporation, or appropriate money or lend credit to any person, except for roads or State Capitol.

The General Assembly shall not authorize any county or subdivision thereof, city, town or incorporated district, to become a stockholder in any company, association or corporation, or to obtain or appropriate money for, or to loan its credit to, any corporation, association or individual, except for the purpose of constructing or maintaining bridges, turnpike roads, or gravel roads: Provided, If any municipal corporation shall offer to the Commonwealth any property or money for locating or building a Capitol, and the Commonwealth accepts such offer, the corporation may comply with the offer.

Text as Ratified on: August 3, 1891, and revised September 28, 1891. History: Not yet amended.

Section 180: Act or ordinance levying any tax must specify purpose, for which alone money may be used.

Every act enacted by the General Assembly, and every ordinance and resolution passed by any county, city, town or municipal board or local legislative body, levying a tax, shall specify distinctly the purpose for which said tax is levied, and no tax levied and collected for one purpose shall ever be devoted to another purpose.

Text as Ratified on: November 5, 1996. History: 1996 amendment was proposed by 1996 Ky. Acts ch. 98, sec. 1; original version ratified August 3, 1891, and revised September 28, 1891.

Section 181: General Assembly may not levy tax for political subdivision, but may confer power—License and excise taxes—City taxes in lieu of ad valorem taxes.

The General Assembly shall not impose taxes for the purposes of any county, city, town or other municipal corporation, but may, by general laws, confer on the proper authorities thereof, respectively, the power to assess and collect such taxes. The General Assembly may, by general laws only, provide for the payment of license fees on franchises, stock used for breeding purposes, the various trades, occupations and professions, or a special or excise tax; and may, by general laws, delegate the power to counties, towns, cities and other municipal corporations, to impose and collect license fees on stock used for breeding purposes, on franchises, trades, occupations and professions. And the General Assembly may, by general laws only, authorize cities or towns of any class to provide for taxation for municipal purposes on personal property, tangible and intangible, based on income, licenses or franchises, in lieu of an ad valorem tax thereon: Provided, Cities of the first class shall not be authorized to omit the imposition of an ad valorem tax on such property of any steam railroad, street railway, ferry, bridge, gas, water, heating, telephone, telegraph, electric light or electric power company.

Text as Ratified on: November 3, 1903. History: 1903 amendment was proposed by 1902 Ky. Acts ch. 50, sec. 1; original version ratified August 3, 1891, and revised September 28, 1891.

Section 182: Railroad taxes—How assessed and collected.

Nothing in this Constitution shall be construed to prevent the General Assembly from providing by law how railroads and railroad property shall be assessed and how taxes thereon shall be collected. And until otherwise provided, the present law on said subject shall remain in force.

Text as Ratified on: August 3, 1891, and revised September 28, 1891. History: Not yet amended.

Education

Section 183: General Assembly to provide for school system.

The General Assembly shall, by appropriate legislation, provide for an efficient system of common schools throughout the State.

Text as Ratified on: August 3, 1891, and revised September 28, 1891. History: Not yet amended.

Section 184: Common school fund—What constitutes—Use—Vote on tax for education other than in common schools.

The bond of the Commonwealth issued in favor of the Board of Education for the sum of one million three hundred and twenty-seven thousand dollars shall constitute one bond of the Commonwealth in favor of the Board of Education, and this bond and the seventy-three thousand five hundred dollars of the stock in the Bank of Kentucky, held by the Board of Education, and its proceeds, shall be held inviolate for the purpose of sustaining the system of common schools. The interest and dividends of said fund, together with any sum which may be produced by taxation or otherwise for purposes of common school education, shall be appropriated to the common schools, and to no other purpose. No sum shall be raised or collected for education other than in common schools until the question of taxation is submitted to the legal voters, and the majority of the votes cast at said election shall be in favor of such taxation:

Provided, The tax now imposed for educational purposes, and for the endowment and maintenance of the Agricultural and Mechanical College, shall remain until changed by law.

Text as Ratified on: August 3, 1891, and revised September 28, 1891. History: Not yet amended.

Section 185: Interest on school fund—Investment.

The General Assembly shall make provision, by law, for the payment of the interest of said school fund, and may provide for the sale of the stock in the Bank of Kentucky; and in case of a sale of all or any part of said stock, the proceeds of sale shall be invested by the Sinking Fund Commissioners in other good interest-bearing stocks or bonds, which shall be subject to sale and reinvestment, from time to time, in like manner, and with the same restrictions, as provided with reference to the sale of the said stock in the Bank of Kentucky.

Text as Ratified on: August 3, 1891, and revised September 28, 1891. History: Not yet amended.

Section 186: Distribution and use of school fund.

All funds accruing to the school fund shall be used for the maintenance of the public schools of the Commonwealth, and for no other purpose, and the General Assembly shall by general law prescribe the manner of the distribution of the public school fund among the school districts and its use for public school purposes.

Text as Ratified on: November 3, 1953. History: 1953 amendment was proposed by 1952 Ky. Acts ch. 89, sec. 1; 1949 amendment was proposed by 1948 Ky. Acts ch. 163, sec. 1, and ratified on November 8, 1949; 1941 amendment was proposed by 1940 Ky. Acts ch. 64, sec. 1, and ratified on November 4, 1941; original version ratified August 3, 1891, and revised September 28, 1891.

Section 187: Race or color not to affect distribution of school fund.

In distributing the school fund no distinction shall be made on account of race or color.

Text as Ratified on: November 5, 1996. History: 1996 amendment was proposed by 1996 Ky. Acts ch. 98, sec. 2; original version ratified August 3, 1891, and revised September 28, 1891.

Section 188: Refund of Federal direct tax part of school fund—Irredeemable bond.

So much of any moneys as may be received by the Commonwealth from the United States under the recent act of Congress refunding the direct tax shall become a part of the school fund, and be held as provided in Section 184; but the General Assembly may authorize the use, by the Commonwealth, of moneys so received or any part thereof, in which event a bond shall be executed to the Board of Education for the amount so used, which bond shall be held on the same terms and conditions, and subject to the provisions of Section 184, concerning the bond therein referred to.

Text as Ratified on: August 3, 1891, and revised September 28, 1891. History: Not yet amended.

Section 189: School money not to be used for church, sectarian, or denominational school.

No portion of any fund or tax now existing, or that may hereafter be raised or levied for educational purposes, shall be appropriated to, or used by, or in aid of, any church, sectarian or denominational school.

Text as Ratified on: August 3, 1891, and revised September 28, 1891. History: Not yet amended.

Corporations

Section 190: Regulation of corporations by General Assembly.

Except as otherwise provided by the Constitution of Kentucky, the General Assembly shall, by general laws only, provide for the formation, organization, and regulation of corporations. Except as otherwise provided by the Constitution of Kentucky, the General Assembly shall also, by general laws only, prescribe the powers, rights, duties, and liabilities of corporations and the powers, rights, duties, and liabilities of their officers and stockholders or members.

Text as Ratified on: November 5, 2002. History: 2002 amendment was proposed by 2002 Ky. Acts ch. 341, sec. 1; original version ratified August 3, 1891, and revised September 28, 1891.

Sections 191–194 repealed in 2002.

Section 195: Corporation property subject to eminent domain—Corporations not to infringe upon individuals.

The Commonwealth, in the exercise of the right of eminent domain, shall have and retain the same powers to take the property and franchises of incorporated companies for public use which it has and retains to take the property of individuals, and the exercise of the police powers of this Commonwealth shall never be abridged nor so construed as to permit corporations to conduct their business in such manner as to infringe upon the equal rights of individuals.

Text as Ratified on: August 3, 1891, and revised September 28, 1891. History: Not yet amended.

Section 196: Regulation of common carriers—No relief from common-law liability.

Transportation of freight and passengers by railroad, steamboat or other common carrier, shall be so regulated, by general law, as to prevent unjust discrimination. No common carrier shall be permitted to contract for relief from its common law liability.

Text as Ratified on: August 3, 1891, and revised September 28, 1891. History: Not yet amended.

Section 197: Free passes or reduced rates to officers forbidden.

No railroad, steamboat or other common carrier, under heavy penalty to be fixed by the General Assembly, shall give a free pass or passes, or shall, at reduced rates not common to the public, sell tickets for transportation to any State, district, city, town or county officer, or member of the General Assembly, or Judge; and any State, district, city, town or county officer, or member of the General Assembly, or Judge, who shall accept or use a free pass or passes, or shall receive or use tickets or transportation at reduced rates not common to the public, shall forfeit his office. It shall be the duty of the General Assembly to enact laws to enforce the provisions of this section.

Text as Ratified on: August 3, 1891, and revised September 28, 1891. History: Not yet amended.

Section 198: (Repealed 2002) Catchline at time of repeal: "Trusts and combinations in restraint of trade to be prevented."

Repeal Ratified on: November 5, 2002. History: Repeal was proposed by 2002 Ky. Acts ch. 341, sec. 2; original version ratified August 3, 1891, and revised September 28, 1891.

Section 199: Telegraph and telephone companies—Right to construct lines—Exchange of messages.

Any association or corporation, or the lessees or managers thereof, organized for the purpose, or any individual, shall have the right to construct and maintain lines of telegraph within this State, and to connect the same with other lines, and said companies shall receive and transmit each other's messages without unreasonable delay or discrimination, and all such companies are hereby declared to be common carriers and subject to legislative control. Telephone companies operating exchanges in different towns or cities, or other public stations, shall receive and transmit each other's messages without unreasonable delay or discrimination. The General Assembly shall, by general laws of uniform operation, provide reasonable regulations to give full effect to this section. Nothing herein shall be construed to interfere with the rights of cities or towns to arrange and control their streets and alleys, and to designate the places at which, and the manner in which, the wires of such companies shall be erected or laid within the limits of such city or town.

Text as Ratified on: August 3, 1891, and revised September 28, 1891. History: Not yet amended.

Section 200: (Repealed 2002) Catchline at time of repeal: "Domestic corporation consolidating with foreign does not become foreign."

Repeal Ratified on: November 5, 2002. History: Repeal was proposed by 2002 Ky. Acts ch. 341, sec. 2; original version ratified August 3, 1891, and revised September 28, 1891.

Section 201: Public utility company not to consolidate with, acquire or operate competing or parallel system—Common carriers not to share earnings with one not carrying—Telephone companies excepted under certain conditions.

No railroad, telegraph, telephone, bridge or common carrier company shall consolidate its capital stock, franchises or property, or pool its earnings, in whole or in part, with any other railroad, telegraph, telephone, bridge or common carrier company owning a parallel or competing line or structure, or acquire by purchase, lease or otherwise, any parallel or competing line or structure, or operate the same; nor shall any railroad company or other common carrier combine or make any contract with the owners of any vessel that leaves or makes port in this State, or with any common carrier, by which combination or contract the earnings of one doing the carrying are to be shared by the other not doing the carrying: Provided, however, That telephone companies may acquire by purchase or lease, or otherwise, and operate, parallel or competing exchanges, lines and structures, and the property of other telephone companies, if the state agency as may have jurisdiction over such matters shall first consent thereto, and if, further, each municipality wherein such property or any part thereof is located shall also first consent thereto as to the property within its limits, but under any such acquisition and operation toll line connections with the property so acquired shall be continued and maintained under an agreement between the purchasing company and the toll line companies then furnishing such service, and in the event they are unable to agree as to the terms of such an agreement the state agency as may have jurisdiction over such matters, shall fix the term of such agreement.

Text as Ratified on: November 7, 2000. History: 2000 amendment was proposed by 2000 Ky. Acts ch. 399, sec. 1; 1917 amendment was proposed by 1916 Ky. Acts ch. 125, sec. 1, and ratified on November 6, 1917; original version ratified August 3, 1891, and revised September 28, 1891.

Sections 202 and 203 repealed in 2002.

Section 204: Bank officer liable for receiving deposit for insolvent bank.

Any President, Director, Manager, Cashier or other officer of any banking institution or association for the deposit or loan of money, or any individual banker, who shall receive or assent to the receiving of deposits after he shall have knowledge of the fact that such banking institution or association or individual banker is insolvent, shall be individually responsible for such deposits so received, and shall be guilty of felony and subject to such punishment as shall be prescribed by law.

Text as Ratified on: August 3, 1891, and revised September 28, 1891. History: Not yet amended.

Section 205: Forfeiture of corporate charters in case of abuse or detrimental use.

The General Assembly shall, by general laws, provide for the revocation or forfeiture of the charters of all corporations guilty of abuse or misuse of their corporate powers, privileges or franchises, or whenever said corporations become detrimental to the interest and welfare of the Commonwealth or its citizens.

Text as Ratified on: August 3, 1891, and revised September 28, 1891. History: Not yet amended.

Section 206: Warehouses subject to legislative control—Inspection—Protection of patrons.

All elevators or storehouses, where grain or other property is stored for a compensation, whether the property stored be kept separate or not, are declared to be public warehouses, subject to legislative control, and the General Assembly shall enact laws for the inspection of grain, tobacco and other produce, and for the protection of producers, shippers and receivers of grain, tobacco and other produce.

Text as Ratified on: August 3, 1891, and revised September 28, 1891. History: Not yet amended.

Sections 207 and 208 repealed in 2002.

Railroads and Commerce

Section 209: (Repealed 2000) Catchline at time of repeal: "Railroad Commission—Election, term, and qualifications of Commissioners—Commissioners' districts—Powers and duties—Removal—Vacancies.

Repeal Ratified on: November 7, 2000. History: Repeal was proposed by 2000 Ky. Acts ch. 399, sec. 3; original version ratified August 3, 1891, and revised September 28, 1891.

Section 210: Common carrier corporation not to be interested in other business.

No corporation engaged in the business of common carrier shall, directly or indirectly, own, manage, operate, or engage in any other business than that of a common carrier, or hold, own, lease or acquire, directly or indirectly, mines, factories or timber, except such as shall be necessary to carry on its business, and the General Assembly shall enact laws to give effect to the provisions of this section.

Text as Ratified on: August 3, 1891, and revised September 28, 1891. History: Not yet amended.

Section 211: Foreign railroad corporation may not condemn or acquire real estate.

No railroad corporation organized under the laws of any other State, or of the United States, and doing business, or proposing to do business, in this State, shall be entitled to the benefit of the right of eminent domain or have power to acquire the right of way or real estate for depot or other uses, until it shall have become a body corporate pursuant to and in accordance with the laws of this Commonwealth.

Text as Ratified on: August 3, 1891, and revised September 28, 1891. History: Not yet amended.

Section 212: Rolling stock, earnings, and personal property of railroads subject to execution or attachment.

The rolling stock and other movable property belonging to any railroad corporation or company in this State shall be considered personal property, and shall be liable to execution and sale in the same manner as the personal property of individuals. The earnings of any railroad company or corporation, and choses in action, money and personal property of all kinds belonging to it, in the hands, or under the control, of any officer, agent or employee of such corporation or company, shall be subject to process of attachment to the same extent and in the same manner, as like property of individuals when in the hands or under the control of other persons. Any such earnings, choses in action, money or other personal property may be subjected to the payment of any judgment against such corporation or company, in the same manner and to the same extent as such property of individuals in the hands of third persons.

Text as Ratified on: August 3, 1891, and revised September 28, 1891. History: Not yet amended.

Section 213: Railroad companies to handle traffic with connecting carriers without discrimination.

All railroad, transfer, belt lines and railway bridge companies organized under the laws of Kentucky, or operating, maintaining or controlling any railroad, transfer, belt lines or bridges, or doing a railway business in this State, shall receive, transfer, deliver and switch empty or loaded cars, and shall move, transport, receive, load or unload all the freight in car loads or less quantities, coming to or going from any railroad, transfer, belt line, bridge or siding thereon, with equal promptness and dispatch, and without any discrimination as to charges, preference, drawback or rebate in favor of any person, corporation, consignee or consignor, in any matter as to payment, transportation, handling or delivery; and shall so receive, deliver, transfer and transport all freight as above set forth, from and to any point where there is a physical connection between the tracks of said companies. But this section shall not be construed as requiring any such common carrier to allow the use of its tracks for the trains of another engaged in like business.

Text as Ratified on: August 3, 1891, and revised September 28, 1891. History: Not yet amended.

Section 214: Railroad not to make exclusive or preferential contract.

No railway, transfer, belt line or railway bridge company shall make any exclusive or preferential contract or arrangement with any individual, association or corporation, for the receipt, transfer, delivery, transportation, handling, care or custody of any freight, or for the conduct of any business as a common carrier.

Text as Ratified on: August 3, 1891, and revised September 28, 1891. History: Not yet amended.

Section 215: Freight to be handled without discrimination.

All railway, transfer, belt lines or railway bridge companies shall receive, load, unload, transport, haul, deliver and handle freight of the same class for all persons, associations or corporations from and to the same points and upon the same conditions, in the same manner and for the same charges, and for the same method of payment.

Text as Ratified on: August 3, 1891, and revised September 28, 1891. History: Not yet amended.

Section 216: Railroad must allow tracks of others to cross or unite.

All railway, transfer, belt lines and railway bridge companies shall allow the tracks of each other to unite, intersect and cross at any point where such union, intersection and crossing is reasonable or feasible.

Text as Ratified on: August 3, 1891, and revised September 28, 1891. History: Not yet amended.

Section 217: Penalties for violating Sections 213, 214, 215, or 216—Attorney General to enforce.

Any person, association or corporation, willfully or knowingly violating any of the provisions of Sections 213, 214, 215, or 216, shall, upon conviction by a court of competent jurisdiction, for the first offense be fined two thousand dollars; for the second offense, five thousand dollars; and for the third offense, shall thereupon, ipso facto, forfeit its franchises, privileges or charter rights; and if such delinquent be a foreign corporation, it shall, ipso facto, forfeit its right to do business in this State; and the Attorney-General of the Commonwealth shall forthwith, upon notice of the violation of any of said provisions, institute proceedings to enforce the provisions of the aforesaid sections.

Text as Ratified on: August 3, 1891, and revised September 28, 1891. History: Not yet amended.

Section 218: Long and short hauls.

It shall be unlawful for any person or corporation, owning or operating a railroad in this State, or any common carrier, to charge or receive any greater compensation in the aggregate for the transportation of passengers, or of property of like kind, under substantially similar circumstances and conditions, for a shorter than for a longer distance over the same line, in the same direction, the shorter being included within the longer distance; but this shall not be construed as authorizing any common carrier, or person or corporation, owning or operating a railroad in this State, to receive as great compensation for a shorter as for a longer distance: Provided, That upon application to the state agency as may have jurisdiction over such matters, such common carrier, or person or corporation owning or operating a railroad in this State, may in special cases, after investigation by the appropriate state agency, be authorized to charge less for longer than for shorter distances for the transportation of passengers, or property; and the appropriate state agency may, from time to time, prescribe the extent to which such common carrier, or person or corporation, owning or operating a railroad in this State, may be relieved from the operation of this section.

Text as Ratified on: November 7, 2000. History: 2000 amendment proposed by 2000 Ky. Acts ch. 399, sec. 2; original version ratified August 3, 1891, and revised September 28, 1891.

The Militia

Section 219: Militia, what to consist of.

The militia of the Commonwealth of Kentucky shall consist of all able-bodied male residents of the State between the ages of eighteen and forty-five years, except such persons as may be exempted by the laws of the State or of the United States.

Text as Ratified on: August 3, 1891, and revised September 28, 1891. History: Not yet amended.

Section 220: General Assembly to provide for militia—Exemptions from service.

The General Assembly shall provide for maintaining an organized militia, and may exempt from military service persons having conscientious scruples against bearing arms; but such persons shall pay an equivalent for such exemption.

Text as Ratified on: August 3, 1891, and revised September 28, 1891. History: Not yet amended.

Section 221: Government of militia to conform to Army regulations.

The organization, equipment and discipline of the militia shall conform as nearly as practicable to the regulations for the government of the armies of the United States.

Text as Ratified on: August 3, 1891, and revised September 28, 1891. History: Not yet amended.

Section 222: Officers of militia—Adjutant General.

All militia officers whose appointment is not herein otherwise provided for, shall be elected by persons subject to military duty within their respective companies, battalions, regiments or other commands, under such rules and regulations and for such terms, not exceeding four years, as the General Assembly may, from time to time, direct and establish. The Governor shall appoint an Adjutant-General and his other staff officers; the generals and commandants of regiments and battalions shall respectively appoint their staff officers, and the commandants of companies shall, subject to the approval of their regimental or battalion commanders, appoint their noncommissioned officers. The Governor shall have power to fill vacancies that may occur in elective offices by granting commissions which shall expire when such vacancies have been filled according to the provisions of this Constitution.

Text as Ratified on: August 3, 1891, and revised September 28, 1891. History: Not yet amended.

Section 223: Safekeeping of public arms, military records, relics, and banners.

The General Assembly shall provide for the safekeeping of the public arms, military records, relics and banners of the Commonwealth of Kentucky.

Text as Ratified on: August 3, 1891, and revised September 28, 1891. History: Not yet amended.

General Provisions

Section 224: Bonds—What officers to give—Liability on.

The General Assembly shall provide by a general law what officers shall execute bond for the faithful discharge of their duties, and fix the liability therein.

Text as Ratified on: August 3, 1891, and revised September 28, 1891. History: Not yet amended.

Section 225: Armed men not to be brought into State—Exception.

No armed person or bodies of men shall be brought into this State for the preservation of the peace or the suppression of domestic violence, except upon the application of the General Assembly, or of the Governor when the General Assembly may not be in session.

Text as Ratified on: August 3, 1891, and revised September 28, 1891. History: Not yet amended.

Section 226: State lottery—Charitable lotteries and charitable gift enterprises—Other lotteries and gift enterprises forbidden.

(1) The General Assembly may establish a Kentucky state lottery and may establish a state lottery to be conducted in cooperation with other states. Any lottery so established shall be operated by or on behalf of the Commonwealth of Kentucky.

(2) The General Assembly may by general law permit charitable lotteries and charitable gift enterprises and, if it does so, it shall: (a) Define what constitutes a charity or charitable organization; (b) Define the types of charitable lotteries and charitable gift enterprises which may be engaged in; (c) Set standards for the conduct of charitable lotteries and charitable gift enterprises by charitable organizations; (d) Provide for means of accounting for the amount of money raised by lotteries and gift enterprises and for assuring its expenditure only for charitable purposes; (e) Provide suitable penalties for violation of statutes relating to charitable lotteries and charitable gift enterprises; and (f) Pass whatever other general laws the General Assembly deems necessary to assure the proper functioning, honesty, and integrity of charitable lotteries and charitable gift enterprises, and the charitable purposes for which the funds are expended.

(3) Except as provided in this section, lotteries and gift enterprises are forbidden, and no privileges shall be granted for such purposes, and none shall be exercised, and no schemes for similar purposes shall be allowed. The General Assembly shall enforce this section by proper penalties. All lottery privileges or charters heretofore granted are revoked.

Text as Ratified on: November 3, 1992. History: 1992 amendment was proposed by 1992 Ky. Acts ch. 113, sec. 1; 1988 amendment was proposed by 1988 Ky. Acts ch. 116, sec. 1, and ratified on November 8, 1988; original version ratified August 3, 1891, and revised September 28, 1891.

Section 226a: (Repealed 1935) Catchline read at time of repeal: "Manufacture, sale or transportation of intoxicating liquors prohibited—Exception—Legislature to enforce."

Repeal Ratified on: November 5, 1935. History: Repeal was proposed by 1934 Ky. Acts ch. 58, sec. 1; creation proposed by 1918 Ky. Acts ch. 63, sec. 1, and ratified on November 4, 1919.

Section 227: Prosecution and removal of local officers for misfeasance, malfeasance, or neglect.

Judges of the County Court, Justices of the Peace, Sheriffs, Coroners, Surveyors, Jailers, Assessors, County Attorneys and Constables shall be subject to indictment or prosecution for misfeasance or malfeasance in office, or willful neglect in discharge of official duties, in such mode as may be prescribed by law, and upon conviction his office shall become vacant, but such officer shall have the right to appeal to the Court of Appeals. Provided, also, that the General Assembly may, in addition to the indictment or prosecution above provided, by general law, provide other manner, method or mode for the vacation of office, or the removal from office of any sheriff, jailer, constable or peace officer for neglect of duty, and may provide the method, manner or mode of reinstatement of such officers.

Text as Ratified on: November 4, 1919. History: 1919 amendment was proposed by 1918 Ky. Acts ch. 62, sec. 1; original version ratified August 3, 1891, and revised September 28, 1891.

Section 228: Oath of officers and attorneys.

Members of the General Assembly and all officers, before they enter upon the execution of the duties of their respective offices, and all members of the bar, before they enter upon the practice of their profession, shall take the following oath or affirmation: I do solemnly swear (or affirm, as the case may be) that I will support the Constitution of the United States and the Constitution of this Commonwealth, and be faithful and true to the Commonwealth of Kentucky so long as I continue a citizen thereof, and that I will faithfully execute, to the best of my ability, the office of . . . according to law; and I do further solemnly swear (or affirm) that since the adoption of the present Constitution, I, being a citizen of this State, have not fought a duel with deadly weapons within this State nor out of it, nor have I sent or accepted a challenge to fight a duel with deadly weapons, nor have I acted as second in carrying a challenge, nor aided or assisted any person thus offending, so help me God.

Text as Ratified on: August 3, 1891, and revised September 28, 1891. History: Not yet amended.

Section 229: "Treason" defined—Evidence necessary to convict.

Treason against the Commonwealth shall consist only in levying war against it, or in adhering to its enemies, giving them aid and comfort. No person shall be convicted of treason except on the testimony of two witnesses to the same overt act, or his own confession in open court.

Text as Ratified on: August 3, 1891, and revised September 28, 1891. History: Not yet amended.

Section 230: Money not to be drawn from Treasury unless appropriated—Annual publication of accounts—Certain revenues usable only for highway purposes.

No money shall be drawn from the State Treasury, except in pursuance of appropriations made by law; and a regular statement and account of the receipts and expenditures of all public money shall be published annually. No money derived from excise or license taxation relating to gasoline and other motor fuels, and no moneys derived from fees, excise or license taxation relating to registration, operation, or use of vehicles on public highways shall be expended for other than the cost of administration, statutory refunds and adjustments, payment of highway obligations, costs for construction, reconstruction, rights-of-way, maintenance and repair of public highways and bridges, and expense of enforcing state traffic and motor vehicle laws.

Text as Ratified on: November 6, 1945. History: 1945 amendment was proposed by 1944 Ky. Acts ch. 9, sec. 1; original version ratified August 3, 1891, and revised September 28, 1891.

Section 231: Suits against the Commonwealth.

The General Assembly may, by law, direct in what manner and in what courts suits may be brought against the Commonwealth.

Text as Ratified on: August 3, 1891, and revised September 28, 1891. History: Not yet amended.

Section 232: Manner of administering oath.

The manner of administering an oath or affirmation shall be such as is most consistent with the conscience of the deponent, and shall be esteemed by the General Assembly the most solemn appeal to God.

Text as Ratified on: August 3, 1891, and revised September 28, 1891. History: Not yet amended.

Section 233: General laws of Virginia in force in this State until repealed.

All laws which, on the first day of June, one thousand seven hundred and ninety-two, were in force in the State of Virginia, and which are of a general nature and not local to that State, and not repugnant to this Constitution, nor to the laws which have been enacted by the General Assembly of this Commonwealth, shall be in force within this State until they shall be altered or repealed by the General Assembly.

Text as Ratified on: August 3, 1891, and revised September 28, 1891. History: Not yet amended.

Section 233A: Valid or recognized marriage—Legal status of unmarried individuals.

Only a marriage between one man and one woman shall be valid or recognized as a marriage in Kentucky. A legal status identical or substantially similar to that of marriage for unmarried individuals shall not be valid or recognized.

Text as Ratified on: November 2, 2004. History: Creation proposed by 2004 Ky. Acts ch. 128, sec. 1.

Section 234: Residence and place of office of public officers.

All civil officers for the State at large shall reside within the State, and all district, county, city or town officers shall reside within their respective districts, counties, cities or towns, and shall keep their offices at such places therein as may be required by law.

Text as Ratified on: August 3, 1891, and revised September 28, 1891. History: Not yet amended.

Section 235: Salaries of public officers not to be changed during term—Deductions for neglect.

The salaries of public officers shall not be changed during the terms for which they were elected; but it shall be the duty of the General Assembly to regulate, by a general law, in what cases and what deductions shall be made for neglect of official duties. This section shall apply to members of the General Assembly also.

Text as Ratified on: August 3, 1891, and revised September 28, 1891. History: Not yet amended.

Section 236: When officers to enter upon duties.

The General Assembly shall, by law, prescribe the time when the several officers authorized or directed by this Constitution to be elected or appointed, shall enter upon the duties of their respective offices, except where the time is fixed by this Constitution.

Text as Ratified on: August 3, 1891, and revised September 28, 1891. History: Not yet amended.

Section 237: Federal office incompatible with State office.

No member of Congress, or person holding or exercising an office of trust or profit under the United States, or any of them, or under any foreign power, shall be eligible to hold or exercise any office of trust or profit under this Constitution, or the laws made in pursuance thereof.

Text as Ratified on: August 3, 1891, and revised September 28, 1891. History: Not yet amended.

Section 238: Discharge of sureties on officers' bonds.

The General Assembly shall direct by law how persons who now are, or may hereafter become, sureties for public officers, may be relieved of or discharged from suretyship.

Text as Ratified on: August 3, 1891, and revised September 28, 1891. History: Not yet amended.

Section 239: Disqualification from office for presenting or accepting challenge to duel—Further punishment.

Any person who shall, after the adoption of this Constitution, either directly or indirectly, give, accept or knowingly carry a challenge to any person or persons to fight in single combat, with a citizen of this State, with a deadly weapon, either in or out of the State, shall be deprived of the right to hold any office of honor or profit in this Commonwealth; and if said acts, or any of them, be committed within this State, the person or persons so committing them shall be further punished in such manner as the General Assembly may prescribe by law.

Text as Ratified on: August 3, 1891, and revised September 28, 1891. History: Not yet amended.

Section 240: Pardon of person convicted of dueling.

The Governor shall have power, after five years from the time of the offense, to pardon any person who shall have participated in a duel as principal, second or otherwise, and to restore him to all the rights, privileges and immunities to which he was entitled before such participation. Upon presentation of such pardon the oath prescribed in Section 228 shall be varied to suit the case.

Text as Ratified on: August 3, 1891, and revised September 28, 1891. History: Not yet amended.

Section 241: Recovery for wrongful death.

Whenever the death of a person shall result from an injury inflicted by negligence or wrongful act, then, in every such case, damages may be recovered for such death, from the corporations and persons so causing the same. Until otherwise provided by law, the action to recover such damages shall in all cases be prosecuted by the personal representative of the deceased person. The General Assembly may provide how the recovery shall go and to whom belong; and until such provision is made, the same shall form part of the personal estate of the deceased person.

Text as Ratified on: August 3, 1891, and revised September 28, 1891. History: Not yet amended.

Section 242: Just compensation to be made in condemning private property—Right of appeal—Jury trial.

Municipal and other corporations, and individuals invested with the privilege of taking private property for public use, shall make just compensation for property taken, injured or destroyed by them; which compensation shall be paid before such taking, or paid or secured, at the election of such corporation or individual, before such injury or destruction. The General Assembly shall not deprive any person of an appeal from any preliminary assessment of damages against any such corporation or individual made by Commissioners or otherwise; and upon appeal from such preliminary assessment, the amount of such damages shall, in all cases, be determined by a jury, according to the course of the common law.

Text as Ratified on: August 3, 1891, and revised September 28, 1891. History: Not yet amended.

Section 243: Child labor.

The General Assembly shall, by law, fix the minimum ages at which children may be employed in places dangerous to life or health, or injurious to morals; and shall provide adequate penalties for violations of such law.

Text as Ratified on: August 3, 1891, and revised September 28, 1891. History: Not yet amended.

Section 244: Wage-earners in industry or of corporations to be paid in money.

All wage-earners in this State employed in factories, mines, workshops, or by corporations, shall be paid for their labor in lawful money. The General Assembly shall prescribe adequate penalties for violations of this section.

Text as Ratified on: August 3, 1891, and revised September 28, 1891. History: Not yet amended.

Section 244a: Old age assistance.

The General Assembly shall prescribe such laws as may be necessary for the granting and paying of old persons an annuity or pension.

Text as Ratified on: August 3, 1891, and revised September 28, 1891. History: Not yet amended.

Section 245: Revision of statutes to conform to Constitution.

Upon the promulgation of this Constitution, the Governor shall appoint three persons, learned in the law, who shall be Commissioners to revise the statute laws of this Commonwealth, and prepare amendments thereto, to the end that the statute laws shall conform to and effectuate this Constitution. Such revision and amendments shall be laid before the next General Assembly for adoption or rejection, in whole or in part. The said Commissioners shall be allowed ten dollars each per day for their services, and also necessary stationery for the time during which they are actually employed; and upon their certificate the Auditor shall draw his warrant upon the Treasurer. They shall have the power to employ clerical assistants, at a compensation not exceeding ten dollars per day in the aggregate. If the Commissioners, or any of them, shall refuse to act, or a vacancy shall occur, the Governor shall appoint another or others in his or their place.

Text as Ratified on: August 3, 1891, and revised September 28, 1891. History: Not yet amended.

Section 246: Maximum limit on compensation of public officers.

No public officer or employee except the Governor, shall receive as compensation per annum for official services, exclusive of the compensation of legally authorized deputies and assistants which shall be fixed and provided for by law, but inclusive of allowance for living expenses, if any, as may be fixed and provided for by law, any amount in excess of the following sums: Officers whose jurisdiction or duties are coextensive with the Commonwealth, the mayor of any city of the first class, and Judges and Commissioners of the Court of Appeals, Twelve Thousand Dollars ($12,000); Circuit Judges, Eight Thousand Four Hundred Dollars ($8,400); all other public officers, Seven Thousand Two Hundred Dollars ($7,200). Compensation within the limits of this amendment may be authorized by the General Assembly to be paid, but not retroactively, to public officers in office at the time of its adoption, or who are elected at the election at which this amendment is adopted. Nothing in this amendment shall permit any officer to receive, for the year 1949, any compensation in excess of the limit in force prior to the adoption of this amendment.

Text as Ratified on: November 8, 1949. History: 1949 amendment was proposed by 1948 Ky. Acts ch. 172, sec. 1; original version ratified August 3, 1891, and revised September 28, 1891.

Section 247: Public printing—Contract for—Officers not to have interest in—Governor to approve.

The printing and binding of the laws, journals, department reports, and all other public printing and binding, shall be performed under contract, to be given to the lowest responsible bidder, below such maximum and under such regulations as may be prescribed by law. No member of the General Assembly, or officer of the Commonwealth, shall be in any way interested in any such contract; and all such contracts shall be subject to the approval of the Governor.

Text as Ratified on: August 3, 1891, and revised September 28, 1891. History: Not yet amended.

Section 248: Juries—Number of jurors—Three-fourths may indict or give verdict.

A grand jury shall consist of twelve persons, nine of whom concurring, may find an indictment. In civil and misdemeanor cases, in courts inferior to the Circuit Courts, a jury shall consist of six persons. The General Assembly may provide that in any or all trials of civil actions in the Circuit Courts, three-fourths or more of the jurors concurring may return a verdict, which shall have the same force and effect as if rendered by the entire panel. But where a verdict is rendered by a less number than the whole jury, it shall be signed by all the jurors who agree to it.

Text as Ratified on: August 3, 1891, and revised September 28, 1891. History: Not yet amended.

Section 249: Employees of General Assembly—Number and compensation.

The House of Representatives of the General Assembly shall not elect, appoint, employ or pay for, exceeding one Chief Clerk, one Assistant Clerk, one Enrolling Clerk, one Sergeant at Arms, one Doorkeeper, one Janitor, two Cloakroom Keepers and four Pages; and the Senate shall not elect, appoint, employ or pay for, exceeding one Chief Clerk, one Assistant Clerk, one Enrolling Clerk, one Sergeant at Arms, one Doorkeeper, one Janitor, one Cloakroom Keeper and three Pages; and the General Assembly shall provide, by general law, for fixing the per diem or salary of all of said employees.

Text as Ratified on: August 3, 1891, and revised September 28, 1891. History: Not yet amended.

Section 250: Arbitration, method for to be provided.

It shall be the duty of the General Assembly to enact such laws as shall be necessary and proper to decide differences by arbitrators, the arbitrators to be appointed by the parties who may choose that summary mode of adjustment.

Text as Ratified on: August 3, 1891, and revised September 28, 1891. History: Not yet amended.

Section 251: Limitation of actions to recover possession of land based on early patents.

No action shall be maintained for possession of any lands lying within this State, where it is necessary for the claimant to rely for his recovery on any grant or patent issued by the Commonwealth of Virginia, or by the Commonwealth of Kentucky prior to the year one thousand eight hundred and twenty, against any person claiming such lands by possession to a well-defined boundary, under a title of record, unless such action shall be instituted within five years after this Constitution shall go into effect, or within five years after the occupant may take possession; but nothing herein shall be construed to affect any right, title or interest in lands acquired by virtue of adverse possession under the laws of this Commonwealth.

Text as Ratified on: August 3, 1891, and revised September 28, 1891. History: Not yet amended.

Section 252: Houses of reform to be established and maintained.

It shall be the duty of the General Assembly to provide by law, as soon as practicable, for the establishment and maintenance of an institution or institutions for the detention, correction, instruction and reformation of all persons under the age of eighteen years, convicted of such felonies and such misdemeanors as may be designated by law. Said institution shall be known as the "House of Reform."

Text as Ratified on: August 3, 1891, and revised September 28, 1891. History: Not yet amended.

Section 253: Working of penitentiary prisoners—When and where permitted.

Persons convicted of felony and sentenced to confinement in the penitentiary shall be confined at labor within the walls of the penitentiary; and the General Assembly shall not have the power to authorize employment of convicts elsewhere, except upon the public works of the Commonwealth of Kentucky, or when, during pestilence or in case of the destruction of the prison buildings, they cannot be confined in the penitentiary.

That Section 253 of the Constitution be amended so that the Commonwealth of Kentucky may use and employ outside of the walls of the penitentiaries in such manner and means as may be provided by law, persons convicted of felony and sentenced to confinement in the penitentiary for the purpose of constructing or reconstructing and maintaining public roads and public bridges or for the purpose of making and preparing material for public roads and bridges, and that the Commonwealth of Kentucky may, by the use and employment of convict labor outside of the walls of the penitentiary by other ways or means, as may be provided by law, aid the counties for road and bridge purposes, work on the State farm or farms.

Text as Ratified on: November 2, 1915. History: 1915 amendment was proposed by 1914 Ky. Acts ch. 93, sec. 1; original version ratified August 3, 1891, and revised September 28, 1891.

Section 254: Control and support of convicts—Leasing of labor.

The Commonwealth shall maintain control of the discipline, and provide for all supplies, and for the sanitary condition of the convicts, and the labor only of convicts may be leased.

Text as Ratified on: August 3, 1891, and revised September 28, 1891. History: Not yet amended.

Section 255: Frankfort is state capital.

The seat of government shall continue in the city of Frankfort, unless removed by a vote of two-thirds of each House of the first General Assembly which convenes after the adoption of this Constitution.

Text as Ratified on: August 3, 1891, and revised September 28, 1891. History: Not yet amended.

Mode of Revision

Section 256: Amendments to Constitution—How proposed and voted upon.

Amendments to this Constitution may be proposed in either House of the General Assembly at a regular session, and if such amendment or amendments shall be agreed to by three-fifths of all the members elected to each House, such proposed amendment or amendments, with the yeas and nays of the members of each House taken thereon, shall be entered in full in their respective journals. Then such proposed amendment or amendments shall be submitted to the voters of the State for their ratification or rejection at the next general election for members of the House of Representatives, the vote to be taken thereon in such manner as the General Assembly may provide, and to be certified by the officers of election to the Secretary of State in such manner as shall be provided by law, which vote shall be compared and certified by the same board authorized by law to compare the polls and give certificates of election to officers for the State at large. If it shall appear that a majority of the votes cast for and against an amendment at said election was for the amendment, then the same shall become a part of the Constitution of this Commonwealth, and shall be so proclaimed by the Governor, and published in such manner as the General Assembly may direct. Said amendments shall not be submitted at an election which occurs less than ninety days from the final passage of such proposed amendment or amendments. Not more than four amendments shall be voted upon at any one time. If two or more amendments shall be submitted at the same time, they shall be submitted in such manner that the electors shall vote for or against each of such amendments separately, but an amendment may relate to a single subject or to related subject matters and may amend or modify as many articles and as many sections of the Constitution as may be necessary and appropriate in order to accomplish the objectives of the amendment. The approval of the Governor shall not be necessary to any bill, order, resolution or vote of the General Assembly, proposing an amendment or amendments to this Constitution.

Text as Ratified on: November 6, 1979. History: 1979 amendment was proposed by 1978 Ky. Acts ch. 433, sec. 1; original version ratified August 3, 1891, and revised September 28, 1891.

Section 257: Publication of proposed amendments.

Before an amendment shall be submitted to a vote, the Secretary of State shall cause such proposed amendment, and the time that the same is to be voted upon, to be published at least ninety days before the vote is to be taken thereon in such manner as may be prescribed by law.

Text as Ratified on: August 3, 1891, and revised September 28, 1891. History: Not yet amended.

Section 258: Constitutional Convention—How proposed, voted upon, and called.

When a majority of all the members elected to each House of the General Assembly shall concur, by a yea and nay vote, to be entered upon their respective journals, in enacting a law to take the sense of the people of the State as to the necessity and expediency of calling a Convention for the purpose of revising or amending this Constitution, and such amendments as may have been made to the same, such law shall be spread upon their respective journals. If the next General Assembly shall, in like manner, concur in such law, it shall provide for having a poll opened in each voting precinct in this state by the officers provided by law for holding general elections at the next ensuing regular election to be held for State officers or members of the House of Representatives, which does not occur within ninety days from the final passage of such law, at which time and places the votes of the qualified voters shall be taken for and against calling the Convention, in the same manner provided by law for taking votes in other State elections. The vote for and against said proposition shall be certified to the Secretary of State by the same officers and in the same manner as in State elections. If it shall appear that a majority voting on the proposition was for calling a Convention, and if the total number of votes cast for the calling of the Convention is equal to one-fourth of the number of qualified voters who voted at the last preceding general election in this State, the Secretary of State shall certify the same to the General Assembly at its next regular session, at which session a law shall be enacted calling a Convention to readopt, revise or amend this Constitution, and such amendments as may have been made thereto.

Text as Ratified on: August 3, 1891, and revised September 28, 1891. History: Not yet amended.

Section 259: Number and qualifications of delegates.

The Convention shall consist of as many delegates as there are members of the House of Representatives; and the delegates shall have the same qualifications and be elected from the same districts as said Representatives.

Text as Ratified on: August 3, 1891, and revised September 28, 1891. History: Not yet amended.

Section 260: Election of delegates—meeting.

Delegates to such Convention shall be elected at the next general State election after the passage of the act calling the Convention, which does not occur within less than ninety days;

and they shall meet within ninety days after their election at the Capital of the State, and continue in session until their work is completed.

Text as Ratified on: August 3, 1891, and revised September 28, 1891. History: Not yet amended.

Section 261: Certification of election and compensation of delegates.

The General Assembly, in the act calling the Convention, shall provide for comparing the polls and giving certificates of election to the delegates elected, and provide for their compensation.

Text as Ratified on: August 3, 1891, and revised September 28, 1891. History: Not yet amended.

Section 262: Determination of election and qualifications of delegates—Contests.

The Convention, when assembled, shall be the judge of the election and qualification of its members, and shall determine contested elections. But the General Assembly shall, in the act calling the Convention, provide for taking testimony in such cases, and for issuing a writ of election in case of a tie.

Text as Ratified on: August 3, 1891, and revised September 28, 1891. History: Not yet amended.

Section 263: Notice of election on question of calling convention.

Before a vote is taken upon the question of calling a Convention, the Secretary of State shall cause notice of the election to be published in such manner as may be provided by the act directing said vote to be taken.

Text as Ratified on: August 3, 1891, and revised September 28, 1891. History: Not yet amended.

Schedule and Ordinance

Schedule

That no inconvenience may arise from the alterations and amendments made in this Constitution, and in order to carry the same into complete operation, it is hereby declared and ordained:

First: That all laws of this Commonwealth in force at the time of the adoption of this Constitution, not inconsistent therewith, shall remain in full force until altered or repealed by the General Assembly; and all rights, actions, prosecutions, claims and contracts of the State, counties, individuals or bodies corporate, not inconsistent therewith, shall continue as valid as if this Constitution had not been adopted. The provisions of all laws which are inconsistent with this Constitution shall cease upon its adoption, except that all laws which are inconsistent with such provisions as require legislation to enforce them shall remain in force until such legislation is had, but not longer than six years after the adoption of this Constitution, unless sooner amended or repealed by the General Assembly.

Second: That all recognizances, obligations and all other instruments entered into or executed before the adoption of this Constitution, to the State, or to any city, town, county or subdivision thereof, and all fines, taxes, penalties and forfeitures due or owing to this State, or to any city, town, county or subdivision thereof; and all writs, prosecutions, actions and causes of action, except as otherwise herein provided, shall continue and remain unaffected by the adoption of this Constitution. And all indictments which shall have been found, or may hereafter be found, for any crime or offense committed before this Constitution takes effect, may be prosecuted as if no change had taken place, except as otherwise provided in this Constitution.

Third: All Circuit, Chancery, Criminal, Law and Equity, Law, and Common Pleas Courts, as now constituted and organized by law, shall continue with their respective jurisdictions until the Judges of the Circuit Courts provided for in this Constitution shall have been elected and qualified, and shall then cease and determine; and the causes, actions and proceedings then pending in said first named courts, which are discontinued by this Constitution, shall be transferred to, and tried by, the Circuit Courts in the counties, respectively, in which said causes, actions and proceedings are pending.

Fourth: The Treasurer, Attorney-General, Auditor of Public Accounts, Superintendent of Public Instruction, and Register of the Land Office, elected in eighteen hundred and ninety-one, shall hold their offices until the first Monday in January, eighteen hundred and ninety-six, and until the election and qualification of their successors. The Governor and Lieutenant Governor elected in eighteen hundred and ninety-one shall hold their offices until the sixth Tuesday after the first Monday in November, eighteen hundred and ninety-five, and until their successors are elected and qualified. The Governor and Treasurer elected in eighteen hundred and ninety-one shall be ineligible to the succeeding term. The Governor elected in eighteen hundred and ninety-one may appoint a Secretary of State and a Commissioner of Agriculture, Labor and Statistics, as now provided, who shall hold their offices until their successors are elected and qualified, unless sooner removed by the Governor. The official bond of the present Treasurer shall be renewed at the expiration of two years from the time of his qualification.

Fifth: All officers who may be in office at the adoption of this Constitution, or who may be elected before the election of their successors, as provided in this Constitution, shall hold their respective offices until their successors are elected or appointed and qualified as provided in this Constitution.

Sixth: The Quarterly Courts created by this Constitution shall be the successors of the present statutory Quarterly Courts in the several counties of this State; and all suits, proceedings, prosecutions, records and judgments now pending or being in said last named courts shall, after the adoption of this Constitution, be transferred to the Quarterly Courts created by this Constitution, and shall proceed as though the same had been therein instituted.

Ordinance

We, the representatives of the people of Kentucky, in Convention assembled, in their name and by their authority and in virtue of the power vested in us as Delegates from the counties and districts respectively affixed to our names, do ordain and proclaim the foregoing to be the Constitution of the Commonwealth of Kentucky from and after this date.

Done at Frankfort this twenty-eighth day of September, in the year of our Lord one thousand eight hundred and ninety-one, and in the one hundredth year of the Commonwealth.

Cassius M. Clay, Jr., President of the convention and member from the county of Bourbon.

Thomas G. Poore, Secretary.

James B. Martin, Assistant Secretary.

James Edwards Stone, Reading Clerk.

From the county of Adair—James F. Montgomery.

From the county of Allen—William J. McElroy.

From the county of Anderson—Thomas Holman Hanks.

From the counties of Ballard and Carlisle—William J. Edrington.

From the county of Barren—S. H. Boles.
From the counties of Bath and Rowan—L. P. V. Williams.
From the county of Bracken—W. W. Field.
From the counties of Breathitt, Morgan and Magoffin—J. E. Quicksall.
From the county of Boone—L. W. Lassing.
From the county of Boyle—R. P. Jacobs.
From the counties of Boyd and Lawrence—Laban T. Moore.
From the counties of Bullitt and Spencer—Frank P. Straus.
From the counties of Butler and Edmonson—J. M. Forgy.
From the county of Breckinridge—William Miller.
From the county of Caldwell—Cornelius Tacitus Allen.
From the county of Calloway—W. W. Ayers.
From the county of Campbell—George Washington and George F. Truesdell.
From the county of Carroll—Hezekiah Cox.
From the counties of Carter and Elliott—R. T. Parsons.
From the county of Christian—John D. Clardy.
From the counties of Clay, Jackson and Owsley—S. P. Hogg.
From the county of Clark—W. M. Beckner.
From the counties of Crittenden and Livingston—Thomas J. Nunn.
From the counties of Clinton and Cumberland—J. A. Brents.
From the counties of Casey and Russell—John L. Phelps.
From the county of Daviess—Thomas S. Pettit and B. T. Birkhead.
From the counties of Estill and Lee—J. F. West.
From the county of Fayette—P. P. Johnston.
From the city of Lexington—C. J. Bronston.
From the county of Fleming—William Jackson Hendrick.
From the counties of Floyd, Knott and Letcher—F. A. Hopkins.
From the county of Franklin—Thomas H. Hines.
From the counties of Fulton and Hickman—Jno. M. Brummal.
From the county of Gallatin—James S. Brown.
From the county of Garrard—Wm. Berkele.
From the county of Grant—R. H. O'Hara.
From the county of Grayson—Chas. Durbin, Jr.
From the counties of Green and Taylor—J. M. Wood.
From the county of Greenup—Benj. F. Bennett.
From the county of Graves—T. J. Elmore.
From the county of Hardin—Harvey Harold Smith.
From the county of Harrison—W. H. Martin.
From the county of Hart—Simon Bolivar Buckner.
From the counties of Harlan, Bell, Perry and Leslie—J. G. Forrester.
From the county of Henderson—H. H. Farmer.
From the county of Hopkins—H. R. Bourland.
From the county of Henry—John D. Carroll.
From the county of Hancock—G. D. Chambers.
From the county of Jefferson—Sam E. English.
From the county of Jessamine—John W. Holloway.
From the county of Kenton—D. A. Glenn.

From the city of Covington—
First District—William Goebel.
Second District—William Hardia Mackoy.

From the counties of Knox and Whitly—Nathan Buchanan.
From the county of Larue—Iverson W. Twyman.
From the counties of Laurel and Rockcastle—William Randall Ramsey.
From the county of Lewis—Samuel J. Pugh.
From the county of Lincoln—W. H. Miller.
From the county of Logan—J. Guthrie Coke.

From the city of Louisville—
First District—Zack Phelps.
Second District—Meverell Knox Allen.
Third District—Morris A. Sachs.
Fourth District—Bennett H. Young.
Fifth District—Edward John McDermott.
Sixth District—Edward Emmett Kirwan.
Seventh District—John Thompson Funk.

From the county of Marion—J. Proctor Knott.
From the county of Madison—Curtis F. Burnam.
From the counties of Marshall and Lyon—Samuel Graham.
From the county of Mason—Emery Whitaker.
From the counties of Martin, Johnson and Pike—A. J. Auxier.
From the county of McCraken—W. G. Bullitt.
From the county of McLean—Jep. C. Jonson.
From the counties of Montgomery, Powell, Wolfe and Menefee—G. B. Swango.
From the county of Mercer—Jas. H. Moore.
From the county of Meade—Jas. F. Woolfolk.
From the county of Muhlenberg—Addison D. James.
From the counties of Metcalfe and Monroe—W. Scott Smith.
From the county of Nelson—J. W. Muir.
From the counties of Nicholas and Robertson—Hanson Kennedy.
From the counties of Oldham and Trimble—S. E. DeHaven.
From the county of Owen—Joseph Blackwell.
From the county of Ohio—John J. McHenry, successor to Henry D. McHenry.
From the county of Pendleton—Leslie Thomas Applegate.
From the county of Pulaski—John S. May.
From the county of Scott—Jas. F. Askew.
From the county of Shelby—J. C. Beckham.
From the county of Simpson—George C. Harris.
From the county of Todd—Hazel G. Petrie.
From the county of Trigg—W. W. Lewis.
From the county of Union—Ignatius A. Spalding.
From the county of Warren—Robert Rodes and Daniel C. Amos.
From the county of Wayne—J. S. Hines.

From the county of Washington—W. C. McChord.

From the county of Webster—W. F. Doris.

From the county of Woodford—James Blackburn.

Text as Ratified on: August 3, 1891, and revised September 28, 1891. Current through 2012 Regular Session of the Kentucky General Assembly.

Appendix L

Maps

Map L.1. Kentucky counties

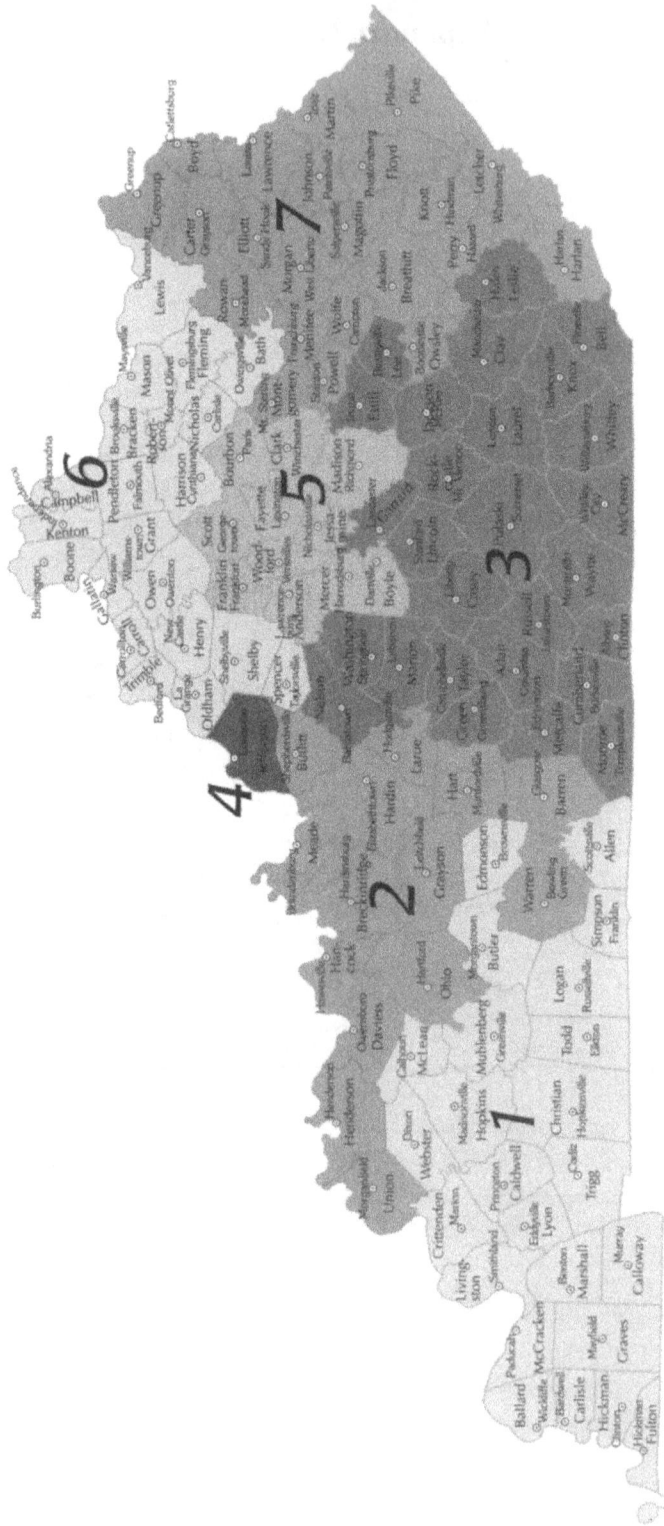

Map L.2. Kentucky Supreme Court and Court of Appeals districts

Other maps can be viewed at the Kentucky State Government GIS Center, http://kentucky.gov/government/Pages/gis.aspx.

Selected Bibliography

Apple, Lindsey. *The Family Legacy of Henry Clay: In the Shadow of a Kentucky Patriarch.* Lexington: University Press of Kentucky, 2011.

Aubrey, E. Lynn. *Kentucky Government.* Frankfort, Ky.: Legislative Research Commission, 2003.

Banks, Fontaine Jr. *Memoirs of a Political Legend: Half a Century in Kentucky Politics.* Lexington, Ky.: Clark Group, 2008.

Baylor, Orval W. *J. Dan Talbott, a Champion of Good Government: A Saga of Kentucky Politics from 1900–1942.* Louisville, Ky.: Kentucky Printing Corporation, 1942.

Brown, John M. *The Political Beginnings of Kentucky: A Narrative of Public Events Bearing on the History of That State Up to the Time of Its Admission into the American Union.* Louisville, Ky.: J.P. Morton and Co, 1889.

Colton, Calvin, ed. *The Works of Henry Clay, Comprising His Life, Correspondence and Speeches.* 10 vols. New York: G.P. Putnam's Sons, 1904.

Conn, Charles P. *Julian Carroll of Kentucky: The Inside Story of a Christian in Public Life.* Old Tappan, N.J.: Revell, 1977.

Cooper, John Sherman. *The Paradox of a Liberal Republican in Kentucky Politics.* Lexington: University of Kentucky Press, 1988.

County Government in Kentucky. Frankfort, Ky.: Legislative Research Commission, 1976.

Coward, Joan W. *The Kentucky Constitutions of 1792 and 1799: The Formation of a Political Tradition.* Evanston, Ill., 1971.

Fenton, John H. *Politics in the Border States: A Study of the Patterns of Political Organization, and Political Change, Common to the Border States: Maryland, West Virginia, Kentucky, and Missouri.* New Orleans: Hauser Press, 1957.

Freedman, Gregory A. *The Executive Branch of Kentucky State Government.* Frankfort, Ky.: Legislative Research Commission, 1992.

Galloway, Patton. *Bibliography on State and Local Government in Kentucky.* Lexington: University of Kentucky, Bureau of Government Research, 1955.

Goldstein, Joel. *Kentucky Government and Politics.* Bloomington, Ind.: College Town Press, 1984.

Hager, Greg. *Offshore Outsourcing of Kentucky State Government Services: Direct Contracting Is Limited but the Amount of Subcontracting Is Unknown.* Frankfort, Ky.: Legislative Research Commission, 2005.

Harmon, R. *Government and Politics in Kentucky: An Information Source Survey.* Monticello, Ill.: Vance Bibliographies, 1978.

Harmon, R. B. *Government and Politics in Kentucky: A Selected Guide to Information Sources.* Monticello, Ill.: Vance Bibliographies, 1990.

Harrison, Annie. *Women in Kentucky State Government, 1940–1980: A Chart of Commissioners and Other Appointees, Elected State Officials and Members of the General Assembly*. Frankfort: Kentucky Department of Library and Archives, 1981.

Harrison, Lowell H. *Kentucky's Governors*. Lexington, Ky.: University Press of Kentucky, 2004.

Hood, Fred J. *Kentucky, Its History and Heritage*. Saint Louis: Forum Press, 1978.

Ireland, Robert M. *Little Kingdoms: The Counties of Kentucky, 1850–1891*. Lexington: University Press of Kentucky, 1977.

———. "Capital Question: Efforts to Relocate Kentucky's Seat of Government." *Register of the Kentucky Historical Society* 104 (Spring 2006): 249–83.

———. *The Kentucky State Constitution*. New York: Oxford University Press, 2012.

Jewell, Malcolm E. *Kentucky Politics*. Lexington: University of Kentucky Press, 1968.

Jewell, Malcolm E, and Penny M. Miller. *The Kentucky Legislature: Two Decades of Change*. Lexington, Ky.: University Press of Kentucky, 1988.

Kell, Jeffrey J. *Salary Differentials between Men and Women in Kentucky State Government*. Frankfort, Ky.: Legislative Research Commission, 1983.

Kentucky Area Development Office. *Kentucky State Government Involvement in Selected New Federal Grant-in-Aid Programs*. Frankfort, Ky.: Area Development Office, 1965.

Kentucky Commission on Economy and Efficiency. *A Survey of Organization and Methods Operations in Kentucky State Government*. Frankfort, Ky.: The Commission, 1965.

Kentucky Historical Records Survey. *Duties and Functions of Kentucky County Government*. Louisville, Ky.: Historical Records Survey, 1938.

Kerr, Charles, William E. Connelley, and E. M. Coulter. *History of Kentucky*. Chicago: American Historical Society, 1922.

Lloyd, Arthur Y. *Kentucky Government*. Frankfort, Ky.: Legislative Research Commission, 1980.

Manning, John W. *Government in Kentucky Cities*. Local Government Study no. 3. Lexington: University of Kentucky Bureau of Government Research, 1937.

———. *The Government of Kentucky*. Lexington: Campus Bookstore, University of Kentucky, 1937.

Marshall, Humphrey. *The History of Kentucky: Including an Account of the Discovery, Settlement, Progressive Improvement, Political and Military Events, and Present State of the Country*. Frankfort, Ky.: Henry Gore, 1812.

Mathias, Frank F. *The Turbulent Years of Kentucky Politics, 1820–1850*. University of Kentucky PhD Thesis, 1966.

Miller, Penny M. *Kentucky Politics and Government: Do We Stand United?*. Lincoln: University of Nebraska Press, 1994.

Paine, C. *Kentucky Will Be the Last to Give Up the Union: Kentucky Politics, 1844–61*. Lexington: University of Kentucky PhD Thesis, 1998.

Pepper, Henry C. *County Government in Kentucky*. Fort Collins: Colorado Experiment Station, Colorado Agricultural College, 1934.

Powell, Robert A. *Kentucky Governors*. Frankfort: Kentucky Images, 1976.

———. *120 Kentucky Counties*. Lexington: Kentucky Images, 1989.

Rader, C. R. *The Legal and Constitutional Background of County Government in Kentucky*. 1946.

Ramage, James A. and Andrea S. Watkins. *Kentucky Rising: Democracy, Slavery, and Culture from the Early Republic to the Civil War*. Lexington: University Press of Kentucky, 2011.

Reeves, John Estill. *Kentucky Government.* Lexington: Lexington Bureau of Government Research, University of Kentucky, 1958.

Richardson, William C. *An Administrative History of Kentucky Courts to 1850.* Frankfort: Archives Branch, Public Records Division, Kentucky Department for Libraries and Archives, 1983.

Shannon, Jasper Berry. *A Decade of Change in Kentucky Government and Politics.* Lexington, Ky.: Bureau of Government Research, 1943.

———. *Presidential Politics in Kentucky, 1824–1948: A Compilation of Election Statistics and an Analysis of Political Behavior.* Lexington, Ky.: Bureau of Government Research, 1950.

———. *Presidential Politics in Kentucky, 1952: A Report on the Kentucky Delegations to the 1952 Republican and Democratic National Conventions.* Lexington, Ky.: Lexington, Bureau of Government Research, 1954.

Tuthill, E. *The Government of Kentucky.* New York: American Book Co., 1914.

Watlington, P. *The Partisan Spirit; Kentucky Politics.* New York: Atheneum, 1972.

Willis, George L. *Kentucky Democracy: A History of the Party and Its Representative Members—Past and Present.* Louisville, Ky.: Democratic Historical Society, 1935.

Wrobel, Sylvia, and George Grider. *Isaac Shelby: Kentucky's First Governor and Hero of Three Wars.* Danville, Ky.: Cumberland Press, 1974.

Contributors

Ann Beck is an Associate Professor at Murray State University. She has served as manager/director of human resources in local governments and as a manager in public medical facilities. She has served as the chair of the university's Health Insurance and Benefits Committee for five years and has published chapters on health benefits and compensation in *The Handbook of Employee Benefits and Administration*.

Murray S. Y. Bessette is Assistant Professor of Government IRAPP in the School of Public Affairs at Morehead State University. He received his PhD from Claremont Graduate University, and his doctoral dissertation, "Nietzsche in a Nutshell: An Interpretation of Twilight of the Idols," was under the supervision of Mark Blitz. His current research interests are modern political thought (from Machiavelli to Kojève), the nature of authority, the questions surrounding modern science and technology, the complexities of creating public policy for foreign and domestic security, and the character of the contemporary threat of terrorism. He recently completed an English translation of Kojève's "La notion de l'autorité" ("The Notion of Authority"). He is the editor of a 2013 published volume, *Liberty and Security in an Age of Terrorism*. His research specializations are homeland security and political theory.

Paul Blanchard taught political science at Eastern Kentucky University for nearly thirty years before he was named EKU's Executive Director of Government Relations in 2003. He retired from that position in 2008. During his academic career his research interest focused on Kentucky politics, and he was acknowledged as a leading authority in this field. He was widely quoted on political developments in Kentucky's leading newspapers and served as a frequent commentator on radio and television. Blanchard also received the two highest honors EKU gives to faculty members, the Foundation Professorship in 1996 and the National Alumni Association Excellence in Teaching Award in 1999.

Bradley C. Canon is Professor of Political Science Emeritus at the University of Kentucky. He is a past president of the Kentucky Political Science Association, the Southern Political Science Association, and the Law & Courts Section of the American Political Science Association. He has published articles in the *American Political Science Review*, the *Journal of Politics*, the *American Journal of Political Science*, and other journals and has served on the editorial boards of the *Journal of Politics* and the *American Journal of Political Science*. He has also written *Judicial Policies: Implementation and Impact* (CQ Press, 1998). He served two terms as chair of the political science department and also was Dean of the College of Arts & Sciences. His PhD is from the University of Wisconsin.

Lisa A. Cave is Assistant Professor of Economics in the School of Public Affairs at Morehead State University. She has published articles in the *Journal of Political Science and Politics, Ecological Economics,* and the *Annals of Public and Cooperative Economics.* She has authored a chapter in *Active Learning Exercises for Research Methods in Social Sciences* (Sage Publishing, 2012).

James C. Clinger is Associate Professor in the Department of Government, Law, and International Affairs and the Director of the Master of Public Administration program at Murray State University. He received his PhD from Washington University in St. Louis. He has published research in the *American Political Science Review,* the *Journal of Politics, Public Administration Review, Policy Studies Journal, Public Choice, Urban Studies, Criminal Justice Policy Review, Political Research Quarterly,* and a number of other journals. He is also the coauthor of *Institutional Constraint and Policy Choice: An Exploration of Local Governance.* He is a past president of the Kentucky Political Science Association. His research focuses on public policy, state and local government, and political economy.

Richard E. Day is an Associate Professor of Educational Foundations at Eastern Kentucky University. He has published articles in the *Register of the Kentucky Historical Society,* the *American Educational History Journal,* the *Journal of Negro Education,* and the *Researcher.* His 2003 dissertation, "Each Child, Every Child: The Story of the Council for Better Education, Equity and Adequacy in Kentucky Schools," received the Dissertation of the Year award from the Education Law Association.

Lucas Elliott is currently working with Metropolitan Nashville Public Schools as a middle school mathematics instructor after completing a year with the Nashville Teaching Fellows. He received his Master of Urban Planning from the University of Louisville in 2011 and his Bachelor of Science in Business Administration from University of Louisville in 2008.

Jo Ann G. Ewalt is a Professor and Director of the Master of Public Administration program at the College of Charleston in South Carolina. Before that, she taught public administration and political science at Eastern Kentucky University for twelve years. While on leave from the university, she served for two years as Director of Research for the Kentucky Office of Education Accountability. She serves on the editorial board of the *Journal for Public Affairs Education,* is a member of the Executive Council of the National Association of Schools of Public Affairs and Administration, and is a member of the Commission on Peer Review and Accreditation. Professor Ewalt has published articles in the journals *Public Administration Review, American Review of Public Administration,* and *State and Local Government Review,* as well as numerous chapters in edited volumes on public management.

Amie Goodin, MPP, is the Research Administrative Coordinator at the Institute for Pharmaceutical Outcomes and Policy at the University of Kentucky College of Pharmacy. She has recently published an article in *Pain Physician* and is completing a doctorate in public policy, specializing in health policy, at the Martin School of Public Policy and Administration.

Donald A. Gross is a Professor at the University of Kentucky. He serves on the editorial board of the *Ralph Bunche Journal of Public Affairs* and has published in numerous journals, including the *American Political Science Review* and the *American Journal of Political Science.* He has also authored *The States of Campaign Finance* (Ohio State University Press, 2003).

Michael W. Hail is Professor of Government in the School of Public Affairs at Morehead State University, where he also serves as Assistant Dean and Director of the MPA and Government Graduate Programs. Dr. Hail also serves as Director of the Somerset, Kentucky, IRAPP Office. He received his PhD from the University of Delaware. He has published in several journals, including *Publius: The Journal of Federalism, EURASIP: The Journal of Information Security, P.S.: Political Science and Politics*, and *The European Legacy: The Journal of the International Society for the Study of European Ideas*, and has contributed to numerous books, including *The Encyclopedia of the Constitution* and *Federalism in America*. He is the author of "Bush's New Nationalism: The Life and Death of New Federalism," in *Perspectives on the Legacy of George W. Bush*, edited by Michael O. Grossman and Ronald E. Matthews Jr. (Cambridge Scholars Press, 2009). He is the coeditor with John Kincaid of *The Federalism Report* and serves on the editorial board of *Publius: The Journal of Federalism* and the *Commonwealth Review of Political Science*. He is treasurer of the American Political Science Association, Organized Section One: Federalism and Intergovernmental Relations, and currently serves as treasurer of the Kentucky Political Science Association, of which he is a past president. His research interests include federalism and intergovernmental relations, state and local government, American political thought, and Western political philosophy.

Jeremy L. Hall is Associate Professor of Public Affairs at Rutgers, the State University of New Jersey. He serves on the editorial boards of *Public Administration Review* and *Public Performance and Management Review*. His research appears in the *Journal of Public Administration Research and Theory, Public Administration Review*, the *American Review of Public Administration, Publius: The Journal of Federalism, Policy Studies Journal, Public Performance and Management Review*, and *Economic Development Quarterly*, among others. His text *Grant Management: Funding Public and Nonprofit Programs* (Jones and Bartlett, 2009) is the first to explore grant management from the public administration perspective. Hall actively serves on American Society for Public Administration's Center for Accountability and Performance Board of Directors and that of ASPA's Section on Public Performance Management.

Robert M. Ireland is Professor of History Emeritus at the University of Kentucky. The second edition of his book, *The Kentucky State Constitution*, was recently published by Oxford University Press. Other publications include three books on the history of nineteenth-century Kentucky county governments by the University Press of Kentucky and numerous articles on crime and the criminal justice system of nineteenth-century Kentucky and the United States.

Edward T. Jennings Jr. is a Professor in the Martin School of Public Policy and Administration at the University of Kentucky. He is a fellow of the National Academy of Public Administration. He has published extensively on various aspects of public policy and administration. His most recent articles have appeared in the *Journal of Public Administration Research and Theory*, the *Public Administration Review*, the *Journal of Health Politics, Policy, and Law*, and the *Public Performance and Management Review*.

Steven G. Koven is Professor of Urban and Public Affairs at the University of Louisville. He serves on the editorial boards of the *International Journal of Public Administration* and *Public Organization Review*. He has authored or coauthored articles in many journals, including *American Politics Quarterly*, the *American Review of Public Administration, Administration & Society*, the *International Journal of Public Administration, Public Integrity, Economic Development Quarterly, Public Productivity and Management Review, Policy Studies Journal*, the *Journal of Urban Affairs*, and *Urban Affairs Quarterly*. He has authored *Economic Development for State and Local Government*, second edition, with T. Lyons (ICMA Press, 2010) and *American Immigration Policy: Confronting the Nation's Challenges* with F. Goetzke (Springer, 2010).

Scott Lasley is an Associate Professor at Western Kentucky University and serves as a fellow at the WKU Social Science Research Center. He has published articles in *Politics and Policy*, *Political Psychology*, the *Journal of Student Financial Aid*, and *Social Science Journal*. He also coauthored a chapter on the 2010 U.S. Senate race in Kentucky with Joel Turner that appeared in *Key States, High Stakes: Sarah Palin, the Tea Party, and the 2010 Elections* (Rowman and Littlefield, 2011).

Thomas M. Martin, PhD, is the Senior Associate for Research and Economic Initiatives at the Kentucky Council on Postsecondary Education. His research interests include executive power, higher education policy, and collective action. He is Vice President of the Eastern Kentucky University International Alumni Association, Chairman of the Board of Directors of At the Gap Communications, and has published in *Foreign Policy Analysis Journal*. Before coming to the council, Dr. Martin was a faculty member at Eastern Kentucky University.

Julie Cencula Olberding is an Associate Professor in the Department of Political Science and Criminal Justice and is currently serving as director of the Master of Public Administration (MPA) and Nonprofit Management graduate certificate programs at Northern Kentucky University. Before serving as MPA director, she was faculty director of the Mayerson Student Philanthropy Project at NKU. Her academic research has focused on student philanthropy, as well as collaboration in the public and nonprofit sectors and evaluation of various programs and policies. She has published articles in scholarly journals, including *Public Administration Review*, *Economic Development Quarterly*, the *International Journal of Public Administration*, *International Studies Perspectives*, *Innovative Higher Education*, *Academic Exchange Quarterly*, and the *Journal of Public Affairs Education*.

H. V. Savitch is the Brown and Williamson Distinguished Research Professor at the School of Urban and Public Affairs at the University of Louisville. He is a former coeditor of the *Journal of Urban Affairs* and former President of the Urban Politics Section of the American Political Science Association. He has published eleven books or monographs on various aspects of urban development, public policy, and regional governance. His coauthored volume *Cities in the International Marketplace* (Princeton University Press, 2004) received the award for the best book in the urban field by the American Political Science Association and has been translated into Spanish. His most recent work is a multiauthor volume, *Struggling Giants: City-Region Governance in London, New York, Paris, and Tokyo* (University of Minnesota Press, 2012). He has published more than eighty articles in leading journals, collected works, and research outlets.

Kendra B. Stewart is an Associate Professor and Director of the Joseph P. Riley, Jr., Center for Livable Communities at the College of Charleston. Her research interests include non-profit management, homeland security, state and local government, and women and politics. She is coeditor of a book titled *The Practice of Government Public Relations* (CRC Press, 2012). Articles she has authored have appeared in *Urban Affairs Review*, *Public Finance and Management*, *Perspectives in Politics*, the *Journal of Public Affairs Education*, and various scholarly books. Before her current position, she was a faculty member at Eastern Kentucky University and worked for the South Carolina Budget and Control Board.

Jeffery C. Talbert is Associate Professor and Associate Chair in the University of Kentucky College of Pharmacy, Department of Pharmacy Practice and Science, and the Director of the Institute for Pharmaceutical Outcomes and Policy. He has published articles in such journals as the *American Political Science Review*, the *American Journal of Political Science*, *Health*

Services Research, Inquiry, the *Journal of the American Medical Association,* and the *Journal of Politics.* Current projects include grants funded by the National Institutes of Health, the Kentucky Cabinet for Health and Family Services, and the Urban Institute. Professor Talbert has research interests in pharmaceutical policy, Medicaid policy, and public health informatics.

Joel Turner is an Associate Professor at Western Kentucky University and serves as a fellow at the WKU Social Science Research Center. He has published articles in *Political Behavior, Political Psychology,* the *American Journal of Media Psychology,* and *Social Science Journal.* He also coauthored a chapter with Scott Lasley that appeared in *Key States, High Stakes: Sarah Palin, the Tea Party, and the 2010 Elections* (Rowman and Littlefield, 2011).

Ronald K. Vogel is Professor of Politics and Public Administration at Ryerson University in Toronto, Canada. Previously he was Professor of Political Science and Urban and Public Affairs at the University of Louisville, where he served as Chair of the Department of Political Science (2008–2011) and Director of the PhD program in Urban and Public Affairs (2002–2007). He heads the Comparative Urban Politics group in the American Political Science Association. He was a Fulbright Scholar in Japan (1997–1998) and Hong Kong (2007–2008). He has published articles in the *Journal of Urban Affairs, Urban Affairs Review, Progress in Planning,* and the *American Review of Public Administration.* He heads the Comparative Urban Politics group in the American Political Science Association. Vogel is a member of the Governing Board of the Urban Affairs Association.

Index

All place names are in Kentucky unless otherwise indicated.

511